Praise for

BROKEN GREEK

'Oh, how I love Pete Paphides and this book. He can't write a paragraph that isn't funny or moving or insightful and often all three at once. For someone from a refugee family, like me, it just reads so true, but it's also a painting of another life so rich, so deep, that they should hang it in the National Gallery'   **Daniel Finkelstein**

'Brilliant. Sad, really funny and beautifully written . . . Just fantastic'   **Alexis Petridis**

'Heartwarming, sharp and beautifully observed'   **Roisin Ingle**

'An essential read for anyone who has 1) lived a life enlightened by pop music 2) is taken by heartbreakingly reflective honesty 3) neither of these things. I laughed out loud *many times*'
Felix White from the Maccabees

'A giddy delight. With its forensic levels of detail and immersive charm, it's Knausgaard meets Adrian Mole, and features some of the best Music Appreciation writing I've read'   **Nick Duerden**

BROKEN GREEK

PETE PAPHIDES

Quercus

First published in Great Britain in 2020 by

Quercus Editions Ltd
Carmelite House
50 Victoria Embankment
London EC4Y 0DZ

An Hachette UK company

HB ISBN 978 1 52940 443 2
TPB ISBN 978 1 52940 584 2
Ebook ISBN 978 1 52940 442 5

Some names and identifying details have been changed
to protect the privacy of indivuduals

Lyrics to all ABBA songs printed here with kind permission from
Björn Ulvaeus, Benny Andersson and Hal Leonard Europe Ltd.

10 9 8 7 6 5 4 3 2 1

Typeset by CC Book Production
Printed and bound in Great Britain by Clays Ltd, Elcograf S.p.A.

Papers used by Quercus are from well-managed forests and other responsible sources.

INTRODUCTION

My parents had never planned to stay in Birmingham too long. Like hundreds of thousands of young couples migrating to the UK from places as disparate as Bangladesh, Hong Kong, Italy, Punjab and the Caribbean, they had no reason to imagine that the children they would raise might feel more culturally connected to Britain than the place their parents considered home. Why would they? Our mothers and fathers were the first people in their families to try and get a foothold in adult life beyond the borders of their own countries. It wasn't unreasonable for them to believe that their influence would supersede that of their new surroundings.

But it didn't quite work out that way. If my parents had prioritised their desires above those of my brother Aki and me, they would have sold up and moved back to Cyprus decades ago. I would have done my two years of national service and, I guess, become a completely different person. But they stayed.

This book is dedicated to Chris and Victoria Paphides – and to Aki, who broke my silence and beat down a path to a version of adulthood that wouldn't suffocate him. In doing so, he saved me the bother.

CHAPTER 1

We had to be there at 11 a.m. on Monday. This left my parents with no alternative but to close the shop. There simply wouldn't be enough time to chip the potatoes, slice the fish and make the batter. This particular lunchtime, the policemen in the station across the road would have to go hungry. So would the local teenagers, who every weekday would shuffle in with a buttered roll from Elsie's two doors away, scrape together the money for a bag of chips, and proceed to make half a dozen chip butties. As I sat in the back of the car en route to the child psychologist, I worried about what Butch, Clive and Ranjo were going to put in their rolls.

For my parents to close the shop, it was a big deal.

I looked out of the car window as the red-brick two-up two-downs of Sparkhill and Moseley gave way to leafy, opulent Edgbaston. I assume that we were tuned to Radio 1 because the soothingly soporific sound of Leo Sayer's 'When I Need You' was billowing softly out of the speakers, and, this being 1977, there were hardly any other radio stations that played pop music. It was one of those weatherless days: no sun, no rain, no visible clouds, yet no clear sky. Those days reminded me of the 'Spot the Ball' contest in the sports section of the *Birmingham Evening Mail*. For what must have been the two years or more, I used to stare and stare at those pictures of action shots from recent football matches but with the actual football removed, imagining that if I looked long and hard enough into the white sky,

I might be able to make out the faint outline of a ball. It wasn't until much later that I realised it wasn't a sky. What happens is that they remove the sky and you have to put your 'X' on the spot where the ball had been.

This was just one of many things that adults weren't explaining to children at this time (see also: Fred Astaire, Freddie Starr – two different people; the *Mastermind* board game bearing no resemblance to the eponymous show; films called *The Pink Panther* that didn't feature a pink animated panther).

I didn't know what Leo Sayer looked like. Neither did I know that he was called Leo Sayer. At the beginning of 1977, that just wasn't the sort of information I was seeking out. 'When I Need You' existed independently of attendant facts. And without facts to anchor it, 'When I Need You' was a wholly metaphysical entity, allowed to soak thoroughly into the way I saw the world. Refracted through 'When I Need You' – which, of course, it was for quite a lot of that winter – the outside world looked like a place in which nothing much happened for very long periods of time, and when things did sometimes happen, they were frequently terrifying. Charged with the job of acting as an intermediary between myself and the outside world was my mother Victoria Paphides, who also happened to be the woman that Leo Sayer was singing about in 'When I Need You'. Except that, remember, there was no Leo Sayer in my mind. All that existed was the song, and given that the song was clearly about my mum, it must, in some way, follow that the song was by me. Confirmation that I was somehow Leo Sayer further came with the needy, weedy execution of its needy, weedy sentiments: 'I never knew there was so much love / Keeping me warm night and day.' Sounding as much like a plea for pity as a declaration of love, it didn't occur to me that anyone over the age of seven could have written such insightful lyrics.

My parents didn't utter a word to each other throughout the entire journey. This appointment must have felt to them like confirmation that they had, in some way, failed. Proof that not every problem thrown up by parenting could be solved under the roof of the Great Western Fish Bar. Even then, I remember feeling bad for them. I could make it all better at a stroke. I could make this all go away by opening my mouth and saying something, anything. But I chose not to. Two years previously, I had stopped speaking to everyone apart from my immediate family and – when the other children were out of range – my teachers. And I couldn't start now.

Instead, this is what we had to do and where we had to go. The place to which all parents in Birmingham had to go when there was a problem that couldn't be resolved with the mere action of a doctor tearing a prescription form off a jotter. I instinctively gauged the full gravity of the problem from the fact that this felt like neither a doctor's surgery or a hospital. This was the place they where they send the weird kids: the introverts who look for dead birds in the woods; the ones who press down the biro far too hard and draw black holes where eyes should be; the ones who spurn sunlight to read train timetables all day. And now me. I had joined their ranks.

My dad turned off the road, continued along a gravel driveway and parked the car next to the Victorian pile. We were beckoned up a wide, carpeted staircase to a brightly lit waiting room by the specialist who dealt with elective mutes. While she went back into her office, my parents sat together, leaving me to sit across the way from them. This was quite unusual for them. Normally in a situation like this, it would fall to my dad to sit apart while my mother and I sat next to each other. Looking back, I can see this would have been an unconscious attempt to present a united front in the face of whatever might happen next.

Quite what was about to happen next, though, was unclear to me. My mother pulled her skirt tightly over her knees. Her black hair, usually curly, was blow-dried as straight as it would ever be, brushed downwards against its will and held in that position by Elnett. Her unwavering loyalty to Elnett – always a fresh can waiting in reserve on the dressing table – would be acknowledged by me on Mother's Day for three consecutive years. Between 1976 and 1978, the same ritual would play out on her special day. While she took care of the Sunday roast, my dad drove me and my brother to Boots in Solihull – the only big shop open on a Sunday, on account of the fact that it had a pharmacy – and we clubbed together our pocket money to buy her an extra-large can of the stuff. As she brought out the roasting dish from the kitchen and scurried back to fetch the cutlery, we channelled our efforts into placing the Elnett on the table and waiting for her 'surprised' reaction. Happy Mother's Day.

Had my mum been able to drive, it's likely that my dad might not have even made it to that waiting room. He was five years older than her, just over a year shy of his fortieth birthday. The oldest picture we had of him in the house dated back to 1958. When he was twenty-one, Christakis Paphides took himself off to a photo studio in Kyrenia, Cyprus, about twenty miles from the village of Saint Ermolaos where he had grown up, and set aside a hefty proportion of that week's wages to have his portrait taken in colour and presented to him in a frame. Like most young Cypriot men in the late 1950s, his hair was carefully sculpted into an Elvis pompadour – not the duck's arse protuberance favoured by British Teds, but a tight, tonsorial bumper which gleamed with Brylcreem – a British brand and therefore exceedingly popular in Cyprus in 1958.

Some of the other Cypriot chip shop owners in Birmingham continued to look to Elvis for hair guidance in the seventies, abandoning their quiffs altogether and seeking to ape the raven hair helmet favoured by the King as he emitted his final belch, but not my dad. Albeit with taller pompadour, longer sideburns and shaggier nape, my dad maintained tonsorial fidelity to the Elvis of his youth. Decades later, it became clear that it was in his hair that he felt his magical powers lay: corralled by his grandchildren into playing that after-dinner cross-generational staple, the name game, my dad, now seventy-seven, picked out his own name from the hat when it got to the miming round, and – as if imparting his very essence – pretended to style his hair in an imaginary mirror.

We sat in silence in the waiting room. I carried on reading the book I had started earlier that day, *Mr Tickle*, which, even by Roger Hargreaves's blazingly high standards, was an absolute riot.

> He waited another minute, and then tickled the teacher again . . .
> All the children were laughing too at such a funny sight.
> There was a terrible pandemonium.

I'd never seen the word 'pandemonium' before. But I didn't need to. That was the genius of Roger Hargreaves. Along with his gift for separating the myriad tics and traits of humankind into different fictional protagonists, every one of them conveniently named after their defining quality, he was able to drop a word like 'pandemonium' into a situation that left you in no doubt as to what it meant.

It became clear that most of the conversation between my parents and the psychologist concerning my problem had taken place before today, because when she entered the room again, it was just me that she wanted to see. Following a quick exchange between her and my parents, my mum shot me a meaningful look which suggested that, whether any of us liked it or not, the next half hour simply had to happen, and nothing I could do was going to change that. I placed my book on her lap and allowed myself to be led upstairs by the psychologist. I wonder now if anyone seriously imagined that the intransigence of the previous thousand or so days would be magically eradicated in thirty minutes; that my parents would be beckoned in after the end of the session to see their youngest yakking away with the psychologist.

Certainly, in that short time, she tried everything. She asked me questions which required something other than a nod, the shake of a head or the raising of fingers. She told me that everyone was worried about me. And then, surely the clincher, she ostentatiously lifted a huge wooden lid atop a table next to her desk. Beneath it was a thrilling-looking farm. Did I want to play with it? Oh yes, I nodded. Well, I could only play with it if I answered the question by opening my mouth and uttering the word, 'Yes.' Could I do that? Could I just say 'Yes'? I shook my head. Just yes. I didn't need to say anything else. 'Yes' would constitute sufficient progress for today's session. I shook my head again.

Then something unexpected happened. She let me play with it anyway. Did I have a farm at home? I nodded. What I couldn't tell her though, was that my farm was totally crap compared to this one – one of those farms in a bag that hang from a newsagent's carousel: a few sheep, cows, pigs and stuck-together chickens interspersed among some desultory bits of fence. This was the sort of livestock that, decades later, I would see displayed on the shelves of north London toyshops, the sort of high-end swine that could concuss another child if hurled across a Montessori nursery at sufficient velocity.

Did I have a favourite animal? That's what she wanted to know. Of course I had a favourite animal. That had to be the goat. My shitty bag farm contained no goats. I could *really* use a goat like that. I held up the goat and smiled at her. It was far easier to like her now that I had decided there was no way I was going to talk to her. The pressure was off. My mind was made up; it felt like nothing could unmake it. How best to explain it? Quite simply, it was as though some unspecified terror would befall me if I let out a sound.

And so the entire morning was wasted. The nice lady with the farm led me back to my parents and somehow let it be known that no progress had been made. My mum gave me the sort of hug you give your kids in order to head off feelings of self-loathing. Never mind. *At least you tried.* But I hadn't really tried at all. Silence was safe. Why risk the alternative?

Silence also soundtracked the journey home, save for a few brief exchanges between my parents that obliquely attempted to address the problem in the back seat. My mother didn't need to be told that all matters concerning my brother and me came under her jurisdiction. It was made clear to her that my failure to speak to almost anyone outside of my immediate family was mine but also *her* failure – and I could see it was a sense of failure she felt acutely. My parents would have returned to the shop, stopping only to drop me off at school for the afternoon lessons. It's entirely possible that, in the car, they would have once again asked me to tell them why I had stopped speaking. And even though I had no problem talking to them or my brother Aki when no one else was around, this was the one question I couldn't answer. At least, not to them. All I knew was that something had changed. A trip switch had activated itself in my head, and it was best for me not to talk. I couldn't tell you why it happened, but I can tell you when.

In the summer of 1973, three and a half years previously, my parents closed the shop for two months, loaded up the boot of our Rover and drove all the way to Greece with Aki and me in the back. Onto the boat at Dover, off at Ostend and keep going. The journey took three days. Along the way, we did things that I realised, years later, were not at all typical of my parents. We pulled over at continental roadsides, lit Calor Gas camping stoves, onto which my mother would place tins of Heinz beans with the outer label removed, and when the beans were warm enough, she would attempt to toast some bread on the flame. My dad had been to the cash and carry the day before we left and had returned with a box of forty-eight Blue Riband bars and a box of Wrigley's Juicy Fruit gum, through which Aki and I munched and chewed all the way through Belgium, Austria and Yugoslavia.

In Yugoslavia, my dad drove all night and we listened over and over again to an eight-track cartridge which, inexplicably, featured George Harrison's 'My Sweet Lord' among a bunch of Greek songs. The otherness of 'My Sweet Lord' magnified its effect, telling me that while all the other songs belonged to my parents, this one was mine. George was singing about God – at four, even I could work that out – but the all-seeing, all-knowing object of his adoration seemed to elicit the same yearning devotion as the all-seeing, all-knowing object of my adoration, seated in the front passenger seat.

The somniferous loveliness of 'My Sweet Lord' didn't just extend to me. It also got the better of my dad, who drifted into a Yugoslavian verge after a long day of driving, only managing to correct himself when my mother's scream jolted him back into the waking world. We finally reached the pretty Athenian middle-class suburb of Nea Kifisia. Here was the house where my mother had grown up. While all the surrounding houses had either been rebuilt or modernised, the simple stone dwelling where she had grown up remained pretty much unchanged since her father had built it four decades previously. At the front, the house was overshadowed by a tall fir that made it impossible to walk anywhere for more than a few yards without kicking a pine cone. Her mother – my maternal grandmother, Panayioula Kalavas – still lived here, along with my mother's sister Rosa. My grandfather Kostas had died a few years previously. We spent a week here. We then got a taxi to the port of Piraeus and boarded a ship to Cyprus.

This wasn't so much a holiday as a recce, and all the talk was about the new life we would begin there. Ten years had elapsed since my parents embarked upon their big adventure. They must have been in love when they left behind everything and everyone they knew for England. Perhaps if they retraced their steps to the last place they felt that way, they might find that those feelings were still here.

This barely explains why my parents found themselves driving their off-white Rover off the ferry at Ostend in 1973. But it's a start.

This was to be a preview of our new life, a chance to work out where we would live, scope out likely locations for the garage my dad had dreamed of running. I don't recall any of us being anything other than excited about what lay ahead. When your children are four and eight, you're still in control of the narrative. It's still your story. You may have drifted from your original route, but there's still enough time to get back on course. In 1973, it wasn't too late to go back. My first language – the language we spoke in the house – was Greek. My internal voice was Greek. At nursery school the previous year, my teachers would speak to me in English and, if I forgot to translate my answer before opening my mouth, I'd answer in Greek. Registering their amusement when this happened, I'd sometimes do it deliberately. The implied approval that came with the laughter of adults was too easy to attain and too gratifying to resist. Everywhere we went, I was fussed over. Trays full of *baklava* and *loukoumia* were lowered before me with delightful regularity. It didn't feel like a holiday. It felt like we had finally come home.

We spent most of that summer with my dad's oldest sister Androulla and her husband Stratis, who owned a pottery workshop that he would ride to every day on his moped. Occasionally, he would let me go on the back and ring for our thirteen-year-old cousin Persephone to come and walk me back home. Persephone would buy me an ice cream and soon we were back at their house which sat slightly apart from the other buildings facing out onto the sea in Kyrenia.

More often than not, my dad's parents would be there too. My grandmother Persoulla was a tall, unsmiling woman with Arabian features. Her skin was the colour of tea and she would sit side-on from the dinner table with her legs apart, leaning forward on her walking stick. Her dress was always black, with a headscarf to match, and occasionally she'd break into some old folk song, before my dad or her other children told her to stop that awful racket. Her husband, Savvas – the source of Aki's full name, Savvakis – was a foot shorter

than her. He was the only person I saw wearing the *vraka* – the traditional Cypriot baggy breeches which ended just below the knees but
had an abundance of fabric between the legs – enough to carry an
injured goat back to safety. Occasionally, he'd find himself overcome
with joy at having his family around him and he'd plant an enormous
kiss on the cheek of the nearest available grandchild. After a while,
it became a thrilling game. Who could get away quickly enough to
escape one of his slobbery smackers?

But then, everything was a thrilling game. There was a road
between the garden and the beach, but we could get to the water
by climbing through a pipe that passed underneath it. We sliced
lizards in half and we poked snakes with sticks. When we weren't
tormenting reptiles in the afternoon sun, we would drive out to
Paphos, where my dad's brother Yiorgos had a farm. They had a
couple of ponies which we rode into the woods every morning. Then,
in the afternoon, we'd go into the kitchen and help his wife Vassoula
stir curds in a vast barrel which, once solidified, she would drop
into nets made from women's tights and take out into a hut where
she would hang the curds from a washing line. Two days later, the
contents of the tights had completed their transition from curds to
halloumi. She would take them back down again and place them
in buckets of brine which Yiorgos would load into his van and sell
locally, setting aside enough to provide us with breakfast for the
remainder of our stay there.

While we were in Paphos, we would also stop and visit my mum's
oldest sister Anna. In the mid-1950s, Anna had moved from Athens
to take up a post in Cyprus as a schoolteacher in the village where my
dad grew up. The first time I recall meeting her son Yioulis he was
standing on a chair at the kitchen sink, skinning the rabbit whose
throat he had just slit. He was five at the time, just a year older than
me. No one seemed to be doing much parenting, an arrangement
which suited everyone. In the daytime, the kids played outside.

Virtually the only time you saw someone's mum or dad, they were seated on a verandah sipping sweet black coffee from tiny cups.

And wherever you went that summer, you heard the same song, 'Ta Rialia', the newest release by Mihalis Violaris, a singer who had risen to fame as part of the *Neo Kyma* ('New Wave') movement, a vanguard of politicised songwriters who reclaimed the cultural heritage of traditional Greek music over American and British music, and in doing so gave Greece a musical agenda comparable to what songwriters like Woody Guthrie, Bob Dylan and Phil Ochs had brought to America. Unlike everything else played on the radio, 'Ta Rialia' was actually a Cypriot song by a Cypriot singer, defiantly using Cypriot vernacular (*ta rialia* is slang for money). Not only that, but it was a rousing everyman song which refuted the lie of social mobility and contended that the world was run by for the benefit of pimps (*pesevengides*). It was the song that blared out of the tannoy speakers of every Luna Park we went to with Persephone; the chorus that resounded from every dodgem into which our older cousins lowered us – dodgems that seemed so huge around me that surely only the tightness with which I gripped the steering wheel would stop me from being bumped clean out of the car.

For all that I remember, it might just be that I was bumped so hard from one of those dodgems that when I landed, it was in a small chair at a tiny desk 2,640 miles away, three weeks into the new term at Cottesbrooke Infant School, and I was refusing to talk. My first memory of that place was attempting to negotiate the quizzical glare of my new teacher, an austere Scotswoman called Miss Brechin, who asked me my name and couldn't understand why I wasn't able to tell her. Mrs Brechin's hair was short but back-combed on top in a manner that, thinking about it now, suggested the sixties had been good to her and she wasn't quite ready to let them go. She gave me a pencil, and when she saw that I held it with a bunched fist, she decided that this simply wouldn't do.

'Hold it like this,' she said brusquely.

I contorted my fingers around the pencil and attempted to copy what she was doing. None of the children was looking at Mrs Brechin. They were all staring at the new boy. The new boy was me.

'No. Not like this. Like *this*.'

Once again, I tried to hold the pencil exactly the way she was showing me, but no, that wouldn't do either. She had a lesson to teach. We would come back to this later.

I'd missed the morning register, but that afternoon she called every child's name in alphabetical order, assuming that at some point I had to start talking to her. To anyone at all, in fact. When it came to my turn in the register, I managed to say, 'Yekh, Mikh Brechin', suddenly self-conscious about my lisp. The day before, I had lost my front tooth, and every time I tried to pronounce the letter 's', my tongue pressing up against the new gap would produce a sharp whistling sound.

Once in the morning and once in the afternoon, 'Yekh Mikh Brechin' were the only three words I uttered at Cottesbrooke between the end of September 1973 and July 1974. It was the only ground I ceded. My parents were duly informed, but the fact that it had, to use a modern figure of speech, Become a Thing, only made it More of a Thing.

By November, I had sent everyone apart from my parents and brother to Coventry. No one understood it, but quite reasonably, they thought it constituted some sort of protest and that I, as the originator of this protest, might be able to explain it. I couldn't though. Not really. Still today, I'm not sure what was attributable to the lisp and what was down to the shock of my new surroundings. All I had in my head was: why were we even here? Why had we come back? How long would we be staying? What had happened to the sun? The tunnel to the beach? My uncle's moped? The endlessly patient Persephone, coming to fetch me in her denim hot pants? The lizards and the Luna Park? The donkey rides and the wide open spaces? What had happened to that feeling of being in the car together? Why were my parents suddenly always immersed in increasingly heated conversations about things I didn't understand?

CHAPTER 2

Suddenly all plans were off. Cyprus was a war zone. People were trying to escape the island, not move there. Archbishop Makarios had been deposed by a right-wing pincer movement comprised of the ruling Greek military junta and the Cypriot paramilitary organisation EOKA-B, whose ultimate goal was *enosis* – the union of Cyprus with Greece. Briefly installed in his place was pro-*enosis* Nikos Sampson, whose tenure would last eight days in July. My fifth birthday also fell within that time frame, but understandably my parents were somewhat distracted. Turkey used this (the right-wing coup, not my birthday) as a pretext upon which to forcibly take the northern half of Cyprus, and demarcate a safe area for the 50,000 Turkish Cypriots who already lived there. My dad's village was now under Turkish rule. He would never get to see it again. His parents were forced to flee to Limassol and stay with relatives while they waited for their new home to be built there, taking only the possessions they were able to carry.

I was spared the hard details, but the change in the emotional air pressure at home was tangible. My dad was regularly on the phone to Cyprus. In the mornings, my mother started to give me and my brother Greek lessons, presumably out of fear that the longer we stayed here, the less likely it was to become our first language.

In truth, it was already too late. Left alone with my toy cars and the TV constantly on in the background, the voice in my head had switched from something that articulated my thoughts in the same language that my parents used to English. This voice sounded like a continuity announcer. Sometimes it was my internal monologue; other times it was an invisible friend, to whom I'd whisper under my breath in case anyone heard.

On top of that, because of the unrest in Greece and Cyprus that summer, we stayed in Birmingham. My mum was too busy to continue with the lessons. I was left to make my own amusement while my parents spent the days meeting the fish and chip requirements of Acocks Green. Primarily, I'd do this in one of two ways. I would place my die-cast Matchbox toy cars front-to-tail in a line stretching away from my toy garage, occasionally picking them up and memorising the information on their undersides – perhaps a 1971 Citroën S.M., a 1970 Porsche 9.0 or a 1972 AMX Javelin – a cataloguing compulsion that would in time migrate to the labels of records. The garage had two levels, connected by a curvy ramp. It remains one of the quiet disappointments of adult life that, in the real world, multilevel garages with curvy ramps don't actually exist.

There were two rooms in which I could choose to do this: the upstairs sitting room and the downstairs sitting room. The upstairs room was for best and, as a result, rarely inhabited. But as far as I was concerned, downstairs was better because that's where the TV was, and from here I could look down the corridor that connected it to the shop. I had a side-on view of my parents as they faced the customers and rounded up the chips from the fryer in a single ostentatious S-shaped action. From their point of view, the location of my game was far from ideal. At any given teatime, when the shop was at its busiest, they would have to step over my cars maybe about forty times as they rushed through the sitting room, via the kitchen at the back and into the adjoining storeroom to fetch more chipped potatoes from the barrels where they were stored.

Inconvenient as it was for my parents, the downstairs option suited me way better. If you walked from the sitting room along to the corridor and stopped just before the threshold of the shop, where my parents were serving, you would see two things: a small side table with a phone on it and, just next to that, a door that would always be shut. Every evening, from around 6 p.m., if I stood next to that door, I could hear a sound that I would only know how to properly describe years later, when I finally read *Mr Tickle*. It was the sound of pandemonium. Broken down into its audible components, these were the constituent parts of that pandemonium:

the voices of older boys
flippers flipping
pinballs ricocheting off electrified chicanes
the radio.

It sounded like the most exciting thing in the world. The continuity announcer in my head occasionally floated the idea of turning the handle – 'Shall we open the door and see what's on the other side?' – but it was 1974 and I was five, and under the gaze of Sandy, the local teenager paid in pounds and chips to look after me for two hours every evening, there was no chance of that happening.

In the mornings when the shop was closed though, that was another matter. One by one, my dad would plug the pinball machines in and I'd stand in the middle of the room next to the pool table and watch the lights flash on, illuminating pop art scenes of high excitement: roller coasters full of people with mouths open and arms outstretched, coming at you from orange skies; Hawaiian women with hourglass figures dancing in front of silhouetted palm trees. Then he would crouch down so that he was eye level with the front panel of the pinball machine and use a key to open it. Next he would pull down a small wire lever at the rear of the panel, perhaps about twenty times, maybe more. Normally, the weight of a coin pushed through the slot would be enough to do this, and in doing so, make a credit register in the display at the front. All that remained was for me to pull up a chair and stand on it, so that I could reach the flippers and see where the ball was at any given time.

Over the summer holiday, this became my routine – a routine soundtracked by a series of number 1 singles which inadvertently accentuated the pensive atmosphere at home. By far the most alarming of these was the one which featured the couplet, 'Goodbye my friend it's hard to die / When all the birds are singing in the sky.' Terry Jacks's 'Seasons in the Sun' seemed to follow me around. I remember hearing it in the car as we went to church and feeling like I had stumbled into a conversation that hadn't been meant for my ears. I didn't need to ask my parents what he was singing about. Everything about 'Seasons in the Sun' – a Jacques Brel song translated years previously by Rod McKuen and modified by Jacks – was understandable to a small child. It was a song whose protagonist contemplated his imminent death, written in words a five-year-old could understand. 'Goodbye to you my trusted friend / We've known each other since we were nine or ten / Together we've climbed hills and trees / Learned of love and ABCs . . .' If you had been tasked to write a secular instructional song to teach children what it meant to die, you couldn't have written a more effective one than the song which sat at the top of the British charts for the whole of April and carried on being played throughout the summer.

In fact, thanks to the song that preceded 'Seasons in the Sun' in the top spot, the pop narrative that year boasted an unusually high body count. Paper Lace's 'Billy Don't Be a Hero' told the story of a young man who succumbs to the overtures of the army recruiters who happen to be passing through his town – much to the consternation of his fiancée. The tale clearly touched a nerve with my brother because Paper Lace's sole number 1 was, by a margin of at least four years, the first record he ever bought. In order to hear it, he would have to go upstairs to the posh room, remove the record from its sleeve, lift the lid of the radiogram, place it on the spindle, where it lay suspended halfway up, then using his thumb, slide the plastic lever which made the turntable rotate: to the middle for 'MANUAL' and all the way to the right for 'AUTO'. 'AUTO' would lift up the needle and release the record so that it fell onto the turntable in time for the needle to drop onto the run-in groove. At this point, the military drums of the intro to 'Billy Don't Be a Hero' would usher in the song. I didn't need to pay too much attention to the verses. Really, you knew Billy was coming back in a body bag the moment that female voice urged Billy to *keep his pretty head low*.

Aki repeated the action over and over again – and, as was frequently my wont, I just sat and watched, attempting to understand the complicated emotions being instilled in me by the harrowing narrative found in a chart-topping single by a mainstream pop band. The sense of pop music being a place where the big issues were addressed was further accentuated by two more records that scaled the charts during the same period. In April, ABBA won the Eurovision Song Contest with 'Waterloo' and the Rubettes put out 'Sugar Baby Love'. Over the decades, I'd come to a fuller appreciation of ABBA's Eurotriumph. The grammatical precision of the line about meeting your destiny in quite a similar way would raise a smile every time I heard it. But in 1974 it elicited a response in me that I can only liken to hearing a recording of fireworks or war. In other words, it might be the former but it could just as easily be the latter.

Oddly, 'Sugar Baby Love' had also started life as an intended Eurovision entry before its writers Wayne Bickerton and Tony Waddington offered it to Showaddywaddy and Carl Wayne, both of whom turned it down. The version that made it to record shops featured all of the session musicians who played on the demo except for singer Paul Da Vinci who signed a solo deal instead. None of this was information in which I was remotely interested at any point during

1974. For the time being, all I knew about the Rubettes I learned when I chanced upon Aki standing in the hallway by the games room with the telephone receiver pressed against his ear. After that, I don't know what happened. I don't know if he put down the phone and redialled it for me. Or maybe he just handed the receiver to me. What ensued was, in its way, an experience as unsettling as hearing 'Seasons in the Sun' for the first time.

> *Sugar baby love*
> *I didn't mean to make you blue*
> *Sugar baby love, sugar baby love*
> *I didn't mean to hurt you*

It was perfect then and it's perfect now: the ascending vocals of the intro that, at some subconscious level, I must have been expecting to reach some sort of plateau; the doubling up of the tempo on the snare drum signalling that, actually, the very opposite was about to happen and then – just fifteen seconds in – the emotional bottle rocket of Da Vinci's falsetto, shattering the canopy of restraint and taste and propelling you with it into a world far more exciting than the back of a fish and chip shop in Birmingham.

This was my introduction to British Telecom's Dial-a-Disc service. And, now that I think about it, it was also my introduction to the howling anguish of irreversible regret and guilty self-recrimination. I might not have picked up *all* of that in a single listen, but enough hit home to leave me feeling like something deep and important had happened. The remainder of my fascination with 'Sugar Baby Love' merely stretched out over the summer, barely contained by the transistor speaker that struggled to be heard over the pinball machines in the Great Western back room.

Do you sometimes feel like the music you're hearing is explaining your life to you? Do you sometimes feel like your emotional reaction to a set of circumstances is interwoven into the words and notes and chords of a song, so that the circumstances and the emotions can never be disentangled from each other? I felt like my elective silence had ruined everything. I could sense the embarrassment it was causing my parents: my dad who just wanted to have normal, boyish boys who played with cars until the age when the relative size of cars and boys would be reversed and they could actually fix and drive them; and my mum who desperately wanted her kids to be happy. I didn't know who sang 'Sugar Baby Love' or what they looked like. I didn't know if their motives were craven or sincere. Of course I didn't. I was five. But what they were singing about seemed to mirror what was happening in my family.

The embarrassment was real, however, both mine and my parents', and at key moments it was almost impossible to bear. That December was hard. We would receive a trickle of visitors in the run-up to Christmas, all of whom would be received with varying degrees of fuss. Other Cypriot chip shop owners weren't such a big deal, because they wouldn't pay me much attention. There were loads of those – they smoked endless cigarettes and poured themselves frequent shots of cognac without waiting to be asked. They gossiped about other chip shop proprietors with the hangdog air of travellers in a departure lounge whose flight home had been indefinitely delayed. Most of them were older than my dad. They'd seen their children start school, make English friends and gradually default to English as a first language.

But on such special occasions, another sort of visitor presented all kinds of challenges to me. Irene Gibson was one such visitor. Shortly after moving from Greece to Birmingham in the 1950s, Irene got a job at the MEM factory in Tyseley, quainter and homelier than anyone in the twenty-first century could imagine an electrical fittings factory to be. Waitresses dressed in black and white would push trolleys that rattled with bone china crockery to the senior members of staff (the ordinary workers had separate urn trolleys with everyday crockery) and the toilets had full-time attendants. One of those senior members of staff was her future husband Jack. Shortly after they embarked on their courtship, Jack joined the Birmingham freemasons – in the process propelling Irene into the British middle-class respectability she had craved since the moment she walked off the boat. It was hard to believe that Irene had ever worked on a factory floor. Her deportment transformed her into something akin to a minor member of the royal family.

One day in 1964, Irene embarked on her usual walk from the factory on Reddings Lane, past Yardleys School, to the bus stop opposite Fat Frank's grocery where my art teacher Mr Hawker would later regularly send me to fetch a buttered cob containing a piece of ham, sliced while I waited, wrapped in waxy paper. She boarded the bus and, as she looked for somewhere to sit, chanced a glance at my mum who was on her way home from the Le Rose clothes factory where she worked. There was an empty seat next to her. Irene smiled at her as she sat down and then, after a minute or two, said, 'Excuse me, are you Greek?'

And that was my mum's first friend. She would have been delighted to hear Irene's Athenian accent mirror her own as she slipped into Greek. Over the years, the lines on Irene's face had arranged themselves around her smile like ripples around the point at which a rock plunges into a pond, which meant that she always looked happy. By the end of the bus ride, they had exchanged details and Irene made my mum promise to come with her to MEM the following day, where Jack would give her a job there for more money than she was getting at Le Rose.

That half-hour was enough to establish a dynamic that stayed in place for the ensuing fifty years of their friendship. Irene and Jack looked out for us. They were by far the poshest people we knew. They had a coffee table on which were placed copies of the latest

Radio Times and *The Lady*. They celebrated royal jubilees more than any other British couple, and at any given point Irene had the same hairstyle as Queen Elizabeth II. Whenever they visited our house, they always left in time to make it home for *Sunday Night at the London Palladium*. Decades later, after Jack died, Irene gave me their complete run of Elvis Presley singles up to and including 'Return to Sender'. I was pleased but not surprised to see that they were in pristine condition and that their record collection stopped at the Beatles. Irene and Jack hadn't needed the Beatles or any other band after them. By 1962, they had found each other.

In 2015, I thanked her for the Elvis records. But back in Christmas 1974 I wasn't able to do anything of the sort when she and Jack arrived at our house with presents in arms. In my mind, it was all so clear: I couldn't possibly accept mine. How can you receive a gift if you can't say thank you? If you can't bring yourself to utter those two words, or indeed any two words, how can you accept kindness? Surely they would understand this? But, of course, Irene and Jack didn't understand any of this. I pushed my beautifully wrapped present back into their hands; they told me not to be so silly. Then they unwrapped it to show me what it was, in case that persuaded me to accept it. Contained in the box was an aquamarine *Joe 90* Dinky car with push-button retractable wings, which I pushed back into her hands. In the ensuing silence, Irene looked across at Jack, who at all times, looked like a reliable gentleman toad who considered himself happy as long as all the other amphibians in the pond were happy.

'Take the present,' my mother said, brightly but anxiously. 'It's all right.'

As I shook my head, the incipient panic rose up and started to press on my windpipe.

'Take it,' my mother repeated, as Irene once again pushed it my way. 'Are you going to thank her?' she added.

I smiled beseechingly at Irene. 'It's OK,' said my mother, almost broken by the exchange. 'I'll say it for you. He says "Thank you very much, Auntie Irene."'

Talking to outsiders was just one of many new aversions that had ossified into a phobia, but there were others which would manifest themselves one by one over the next few years. Two of them were brought to me via our first colour television, a free-standing Philips TV with two rows of three silver-coloured plastic buttons which, rather than being flat-fronted, protruded towards the bottom like a light switch does. The top three had BBC1, BBC2 and ITV written on them. And while, in most regards, the television brought boundless joy to the sitting room, it also allowed *The Osmonds* immediate access to our home.

The centrepiece of Denim's 1992's album *Back in Denim* is 'The Osmonds', an eight-minute free-associative epic which ebbs and flows around a single recurring line, delivered by singer Lawrence Hayward in a Brummie accent pitched equidistantly between exasperation and panic: 'In the 70s there were . . . lots of little Osmonds everywhere.' That was exactly how it seemed to me too. I couldn't understand where they were all coming from, these emissaries of honest-to-goodness Mormon fun. Not only did they have their own television show, but they seemed to perpetually turn up on other people's shows too. And the worst Osmond of all the Osmonds was the youngest one. Little Jimmy Osmond.

I saw him as a threat. I was convinced that my parents wanted to swap me for him. After all, why wouldn't they? He sang and he told jokes and all the adults seemed enraptured by him. He was also the youngest in his family. I imagined him as a version of me that functioned properly. Every time he appeared, I would hide behind the sofa and start crying, which, of course – in my mind – merely widened the gulf between his accomplishments and my handicaps.

The other well-known figure who lived in the television and sent me cowering behind the sofa was Emu, the feathered expedient by which its operator Rod Hull would attempt to maul whoever he happened to be sharing a sofa with. The way my mother dealt with this was inspired. Noticing that the petrol station near our shop was selling vaguely emu-like soft toys with long legs and long necks through which you placed your hand to operate the beak, she handed one over to me and told me that I could make this one do whatever I liked. Unaware of the reasons for my terror of Jimmy Osmond, my mother could only gaze on in bewilderment when she saw the reaction he triggered. But at least I now had someone to keep me company behind the sofa whenever the tiny twinkle-eyed Satan of kid-pop burst into 'Long Haired Lover from Liverpool'.

Over the next twelve months I racked up phobias, intolerances and panic triggers at an impressive velocity. Insects. Worms. Standing next to tall buildings. Biting into mushrooms. Getting my hair cut. The woman two doors away with a skin-coloured plastic mask obscuring the bit of her face that was missing after her car caught fire. People with other bits of their bodies missing. People such as Yvette Morris, who sat at the table next to me when I joined Miss Haylor's class in the second year of infant school. Yvette had a perfectly good left hand and a shapeless stump where her right hand should be. She had been born like that. No one needed to explain to me that it was wrong to be squeamish about physical disabilities, so I did my best to avoid any reaction that anyone – especially Yvette – might pick up on. Any idle observer of life in Miss Haylor's class would have struggled to notice anything that might have come close to instilling even a hint of discomfort in the children there. But Yvette's hand was a perpetual source of anxiety.

After a year of stern, censorious Miss Brechin, I had totally fallen on my feet with Miss Haylor. When you're five, there's no greater accolade you can bestow on anyone than Kind Lady – and Miss Haylor was the paradigmatic Kind Lady. She allowed me to hold the pencil however I liked, and placed no pressure on me to talk in class. When I finally confided my dilemma concerning Yvette and her hand, she refrained from judgement. Not only did she acknowledge my phobias, but she understood that hurrying them away would only serve to magnify them. The same applied for my continuing silence. I remember her keeping an eye on me a little more than the other children, just in case my inability to speak got me into trouble.

She must have been around on the day that the photographer came to Cottesbrooke. My recall of that episode is so, well, photographic, that I have come to assume that I must have embellished some details along the way. But decades later, when our paths crossed again, Miss Haylor confirmed all of them: the single-file line of pupils snaking out of the classroom and into the corridor which ran alongside the school hall; the waist-high bookshelves with large windows above them which allowed you to see the photographer summoning the next child in the queue to have their picture taken; the position you were expected to assume, which was right at the front of the stage with your little legs dangling off the side. Just a couple of shutter clicks and that was it. Off you go.

You had to smile. That was the problem. But my front tooth was still missing and there was no way I was going to oblige. Convinced that any refusal to smile was going to land me in deep trouble, the anxiety became overwhelming. The walk from the front of the line, past the photographer, to the stage seemed to go on forever.

'Hello sunshine!'

Nothing.

'What's your name, then?'

Nothing. Maybe a conciliatory shrug.

'All right. Are you going to give me a smile, then?'

Nothing.

'Come on, you silly sausage!'

That was it. The laughter came twice: first from the line of children queuing in the hall, and then from the line of children snaking out into the corridor, who were told about it by the line of children in the hall. Silly sausage! The photographer knew his audience all right. In 1975, the one accusation an adult could level at a child, secure in the knowledge that it would be considered the funniest thing ever, was 'silly sausage'.

Knowing that I had to give him something, I grimaced a smile which nonetheless just about managed to hide what felt like a canyon where once there was a tooth, and sensing that this was about as good as it was going to get, he sent me on my way, back to a classroom in which I would be called 'silly sausage' by everyone for what seemed like an eternity. Far from being a subconscious cry for attention, it was actually the opposite. I didn't want anyone to notice that there was anything different about me. In the playground, I had to go to bizarre lengths to try and ensure that was the case.

Because I was late to start at Cottesbrooke, most friendships had already been made. It wasn't that I didn't have any friends, but all my friends were in existing gangs. If I could open my mouth and inveigle my way into those friendship groups, I could have tried to do just that. But that was a barrier that simply couldn't be crossed. So instead, I embarked on a course of damage limitation. If I was going to be unpopular, it seemed crucial that I minimise the embarrassment of a teacher noticing the fact. And so, each playtime became a simple routine. Wherever Miss Haylor was at any given time, I need to inhabit the furthermost point of the playground to her. But, of course, Miss Haylor wasn't stationary. She patrolled the concrete expanse in slow motion, sipping her tea while ponytailed girls followed her around and competed to tell her about their lives. Every time they moved in my direction, I'd move further away.

But these weren't problems that were exacerbated by the school. I laid the blame squarely on my own shoulders and expected no pity. I was as happy as I could possibly be there. Miss Brechin notwithstanding, kindness and gentility were dyed into the fabric of school life. Next to our classroom was Miss Zimnovodski's class. She was thin in a way that only people in the seventies were. Her torso was flat and bendy like one of those fruit bars that middle-class parents give to their children instead of Kit Kats. She wore tight roll-necked jumpers and, after Christmas, she got a perm which transformed her super-straight hair into a sensational Afro. After that, very little of her face was visible except for her enormous round glasses. She always wore trousers which went high up over her waist and her flares covered her shoes entirely. Taken as a whole, all these attributes conspired to make it look like she'd just stepped out of a forgotten Hanna-Barbera cartoon. Every Friday, when the lunch-time bell rang, Miss Zimnovodski would discharge her children, cross the few steps past the communal clothes pegs and peer into our classroom to collect Miss Haylor. The two would then proceed to the pub a few doors away from our chippy, where they would drink half a pint of beer each and eat a cheese roll. Years later I learned that Miss Zimnovodski would usually put the two class gerbils in her pocket and bring them with her too, often letting them out for a run in the pub.

Acocks Green was one of many stops on the North Warwickshire line of a network that was operated by the Great Western Railway between 1833 and 1948. Also known as God's Wonderful Railway, on account of the fact that these lines would take Midlands holiday-makers to holiday resorts such as Minehead, Newquay and St Ives, the Great Western Railway also gave its name to the pub where Miss Haylor, Miss Zimnovodski and Miss Zimnovodski's gerbils would have their lunch – and, of course, to our chip shop.

My class was a microcosm of the way British cities were changing. Perhaps a quarter of it comprised children of immigrants who had come here in the sixties: Reginald Harrison, Delroy Bell and Natalie Johnson from Jamaica; Taro Suzuki, whose parents ran Kwong Ming, the Chinese takeaway down the road; Eamonn Wright from Ireland; and Vijay Singh whose parents ran the corner shop a stone's throw away from the school, and in whose house I had my first ever chapati.

Cottesbrooke rode those changes with a benign elegance that seemed to beam outwards from the smile of its headmistress, the regal Mrs Walker. The differences between our backgrounds were explored and celebrated. There was a day on which everyone was encouraged to come to school in their national costume. Everything I remember about Cottesbrooke accorded with my parents' memories of their first years in Birmingham. Of course there was prejudice, but it tended to happen in inaudible mutters and behind closed doors, in the company of other xenophobes. Most of my parents' lowest moments in their first years here invariably featured a British stranger showing them extraordinary generosity, for example the kindly foreman at MEM who gave my mum the rest of the day off when the lunchtime bell sounded and she burst into tears after she ran out of the factory thinking it was a fire alarm.

The gentle and loving atmosphere at Cottesbrooke could have been summed up by Mrs Walker's reassuring catchphrase, which she uttered at the end of every assembly: 'Just remember, children, your best friend is someone who knows all about you, but loves you just the same.' At the beginning of each day, we would file into the hall, class by class, to the sound of this morning's selected music diffusing upwards from the single speaker of the school record player, which was placed on its own table next to a vase of fresh flowers. Behind the record player was an easel where a large sheet of paper was held in place by two clips. On that paper was written the name of the piece of music you were hearing. Over the course of a year, you would get to hear the same one several times. Schubert's Symphony no. 5 was a favourite, to the extent that it has banished almost every other piece of music in those assemblies from memory. But there was also Mozart's *Eine kleine Nachtmusik*, which though pretty and sweet and memorable had the effect of making me stand a little stiffer and feel like I had to be just that bit better-behaved in its presence.

It wasn't the only piece of music by Mozart that left a lasting impression that year. Seeking to extend the Wombles' chart dominance throughout 1974, Mike Batt – the man responsible for turning Elizabeth Beresford's children's books' creations into pop stars – took a phrase from the third movement of Symphony no. 41 in C, wrote some words over it and created 'Minuetto Allegretto'. Just as the 1960s compelled you to side with the Beatles or the Stones and the 1990s made you commit either to Blur or Oasis, it was no less clear to my developing brain in the 1970s that only the Wombles could save me from the cult of the Osmonds. They were all over Miss Haylor's wall friezes until the summer of 1975 – and, of course, they were in our house too, in the bittersweet 5.40 p.m. slot – the last five minutes of fun before TV went back to the grown-ups.

Prior to my late twenties, I was simply unable to place *The Wombles* theme in any sort of context. I needed to hear eccentric British jazzers like Acker Bilk, Chris Barber and Tubby Hayes in order to place it as a downbeat offspring of something they might have toyed around with. 'Underground overground / Wombling free', sang Mike Batt. I thought he was singing, 'The Wombles of Wimbledon / Common are we'. Why would I know there was a Wimbledon Common? Why would I even know what a common was? In Birmingham, we only had parks. And so, on the Sundays my dad took us to Cannon Hill Park, I'd keep an eye out for Wombles, common as they were.

Around the same time – possibly via my brother – a Wombles album arrived in the house. *Wombling Songs* remains, to the best of my knowledge, like no children's album before or since. Every turntable mile accrued by the Wombles on the radiogram was like a mile added to the distance between Cyprus and England. In years to come, I'd fall hard for the Kinks' *Village Green Preservation Society* and Kate Bush's *Lionheart* and, in doing so, understand what people meant when they spoke about the ineffable Englishness of those records. But actually, the first music I heard in which the notes and chords seemed to correspond to the 'magic hour' morning light of wet parks in October, empty playgrounds through rain-flecked classroom windows and the overgrown verges which concealed the towpath at the bottom of Malvern Road – it was all on this oddly melancholy collection of songs. On 'Wombles Everywhere', frontwomble Orinoco – voiced by Mike Batt himself – hymned the global ubiquity of womblekind, but the execution was anything but declamatory. Proceeding with all the velocity of an elderly shire horse, it saw him dolorously singing, 'We've got Wombles everywhere / North south east and west / Though personally we're from Wimbledon / Cos Wimbledon is best' over an ornate chamber pop arrangement. I couldn't stop playing it.

'The Wombles' Warning' further served to accentuate a sense that seemed prevalent, through 1970s public information films, that even the most seemingly innocuous bit of untended land was fraught with danger. Save for a bucolic instrumental coda, the arrangement mostly comprised of piano and the radioactive squelch of an ARP Odyssey, over which Orinoco urged, 'Don't you be tempted to the nettlebeds, my friends / By bits of ironmongery / If there are mushrooms in the nettlebeds my friends / It's better to go hungry'. I must have had access to happier music than this, surely, but I couldn't tell you for sure what it was at this point because I don't remember it. I was, however, word perfect on the episode of *Bagpuss* which featured the ballad of Uncle Feedle – this being on account of the fact that, in order to persuade me to go to school one day, my mother positioned a cassette recorder in front of the television and recorded the episode which told the story of Feedle and the inside-out house he sewed for himself.

When I say they don't write children's television music like they used to, I mean that they literally don't. The songs we were exposed to were a marriage of convenience between, on the one hand, avant-garde library musicians, left-leaning folk enthusiasts and experimentally-minded classical musicians, and on the other, the commissioning editors who enlisted their services. *Fingerbobs* presenter Yoffi was really Rick Jones, a bearded Canadian hippy who, with the help of coloured surgical gloves, could transform his hands into a mouse, a tortoise and a dove. His theme song for *Fingerbobs* had a dark soporific quality about it which fed into his enigmatic persona – this roll-necked, soft-spoken loner broadcasting to children in an era where 'Let me show you my tortoise' had yet to acquire dark connotations. Classical guitar composer Freddie Philips was the man responsible for giving the sedate stop-motion storytelling of *Camberwick Green* and *Trumpton* its musical character. He made narrator Brian Cant sit in a cupboard lined with egg boxes to sing Peter the Postman's song, and then – seeking to do 'something special' for the main *Camberwick Green* theme – he experimented with tape speeds and backwards clockwork noise to create a two-minute welcome, comprised of three mesmerising mini-suites.

Even if Freddie Philips – who believed that children should be raised on a diet of Boulez and Stravinsky – reined in his avant-garde instincts for his *Trumpton* and *Camberwick Green* music, others didn't feel the need to try. Vernon Elliott's music for *The Clangers* catapulted me to worlds which depicted outer space as a place where tiny curiosities happened against a backdrop of vast emptiness. Come to think of it, that wasn't so different to the brief Elliott set himself in evoking rural Wales for his music in *Ivor the Engine*. In 1975, I'd never spent a rainy Wednesday in a small Welsh market town, just after half-day closing, but Elliott's *Ivor the Engine* music captured the experience.

However, none of these musicians managed to create anything quite as unearthly as the piece of music chosen to open a programme called *Picture Box* which would be shown on ITV in the section of the schedule set aside for pre-lunchtime schools programmes. What this meant was that there were two situations in which you would wind up watching *Picture Box*. Occasionally, you could convene in the school hall where a teacher would push a tall trolley with a TV on it and then show you an episode which might be relevant to something you were studying. But the more common scenario would be that you were off sick and, with your parents working, find yourself farmed out to the front room staring listlessly at whatever happened to be on TV. And on weekdays at around 10 a.m., whatever happened to be on was usually *Picture Box*, in which a short film from around the world was topped and tailed by a hello and goodbye from presenter Alan Rothwell.

Typical *Picture Box* fare was a film called *Tumbleweed*. There were no words in this film, which showed us a day in the life of a piece of tumbleweed as the wind impassively blew it to a number of different places before, finally, it met its ultimate fate, blowing into a crackling bonfire. Unsettling wordless narratives about tumbleweed ending in the protagonist's incineration couldn't fail to leave a mark if you were watching from the altered state of a raging fever. Alan Rothwell's friendly greeting was counterbalanced by his mannequin-like stillness. He looked like he'd been sitting in that chair for days, waiting for us to arrive. And for some reason it wasn't such a stretch to imagine that you might open your bedroom door and see him waiting for you there too. This was probably less to do with what Alan was deliberately putting out and everything to do with the title sequence that faded into Alan: an out-of-focus film of a revolving *Picture Box* title soundtracked by a piece of music for which even a crack team of musicologists would struggle to find a suitable category.

In time, I would find out that the febrile waltz-time fantasia that opened *Picture Box* was called 'Manège' and was one of a series of recordings made by a team of three maverick French artists who sought to blur the distinctions between sculpture and sound. They were a composer called Jacques Lasry and two brothers, Bernard and François Baschet, who built an array of unique and beautiful musical sculptures. The actual sound of the *Picture Box* theme was that of Lasry stroking a row of glass rods, but it might as well have been a ghost choir of stillborn Victorian babies scratching at the underside of your unconscious mind.

Alone in my front room, I thought I was the only child who remembered this music and the way it made me feel. But it percolated into the records that several artists roughly my age made when they started to create their own music. Stereolab, Broadcast, Belle and Sebastian, Pram, Saint Etienne, Belbury Poly – while none of these groups sounds too much like each other, there's an invisible cord that links them all to the otherworldliness of the music they heard on early 1970s children's programmes. In 2003, when Radiohead set about making a video for the single 'There There', they first approached Oliver Postgate and Peter Firmin – creators of *Bagpuss* – to direct it. In fact, the single was subtitled 'The Bony King of Nowhere', a title of one of the songs and stories in *Bagpuss*. In 2016, their film for 'Burn the Witch' recreated *The Wicker Man* with puppets made to resemble those in *Trumpton* and *Camberwick Green*. In a pre-video age, we might have watched each episode of these programmes once, maybe twice, certainly no more than three times, but they became indelibly dyed into our mental fabric. Not just the storylines and the music, but the vast empty spaces either side of them.

Sometimes those empty spaces might be taken up by the test card and the music written to soundtrack the test card by music library composers. The fascination of the test card was heightened by the fact that no one ever explained it to you. As an adult, I can extrapolate what the test card is from its name. It's a piece of card, positioned in front of a camera which features a geometric patchwork of monochrome patterns and stripes bordered by colours, with a photograph in the middle of it featuring a small girl next to a small blackboard and her toy clown. You would infer with your adult brain that this is a card used to test whether the transmitter is beaming an active signal into people's television sets. But at the age of five or six, it was inconceivable to me that an image so unchanging and perfect in its way could exist in the corporeal world. That it could actually just be *a piece of card*. In the same way, it seemed beyond the realm of my imagination that the sight of closing credits moving from the bottom to the top of the screen and disappearing one by one, was an effect achieved by winding a transparent plastic roll with the words printed on it until, finally, you got to the BBC logo and the year in roman numerals. I thought it was TV magic. We all did.

CHAPTER 3

One day, Sandy, my teenage childminder, didn't turn up. Years later, I learned it was because she had raided my piggy bank and, on being confronted, burst into tears and begged my mum not to tell her mum. In the aftermath, there was no one to keep an eye on me and my brother while my parents dealt with the teatime rush. Because this was the seventies, and it was fine to let ten-year-olds stay out as long as they wanted to stay out, Aki was a fleeting presence. He had made friends with a local boy called Edward whose dad worked in a furniture showroom and was obsessed with a singer called Scott Walker.

Pending the appointment of another childminder, one of my mother's interim ideas was contingent on my intensifying obsession with coin-operated machines. While the back room of the shop – a hubbub of flippers, chicanes, silver balls and bells – was still out of bounds, my parents relaxed the rules when it came to the front. Here, just beside the counter where they could keep an eye on me, resided two machines. Of lesser interest to me was the one-armed bandit, on account of the fact that: (a) there appeared to be no skill involved in playing it; and (b) you couldn't get near it anyway. As long as the policemen in the station across the road turned a blind eye to the fact that it paid out a jackpot of £5 – five times the maximum jackpot legally permitted – the fruit machine was constantly in use. My dad couldn't say for sure why they hadn't called him out about it, but he suspected it might be something to do with the fact that he'd never charged the chief inspector there for his haddock and chips. However, one day when another officer was sent to get five portions of cod, plus a haddock for the chief inspector, my dad charged for the lot. An hour later, the same officer was sent over with instructions to turn the machine to face the wall.

The day it happened, I barely registered it. For me, the far more exciting machine at the front of the shop was the wall-mounted coin-operated penny arcade game which rewarded you with the return of your own 2p coin if you managed to stop the coin going down four out of five chutes. In order to do this, you had to push open a trapdoor at the split second the coin travelled across it. Anything less than a hundred per cent accuracy meant that you didn't get your money back. My mum would open the till and give me ten 2p coins to put in the machine. When I used them all up, she would unlock the front panel, return them to me along with another 10p and give me special dispensation to use two more machines.

The first of these machines was the vending one outside Elsie's grocery, two doors away from our shop. There were only two things you could get at this vending machine: a one-pint carton of milk and a half-pint carton of milk. My 10p got me half a pint, refrigerated, which landed at the bottom with a pleasing metallic thwack. It wasn't like we didn't have milk in the house, but it wasn't robot milk. Nothing tasted as good as robot milk.

The second machine was the red telephone box directly outside the shop. Having been instructed not to call Dial-a-Disc from the house phone after listening to 'Sugar Baby Love' two years before, this became the place I went to instead. You didn't know what you were going to get when you called Dial-a-Disc. It was always a record in the top 10, but I was a few months off discovering *Top of the Pops*, so I didn't know what was in the top 10. The first time I did it, Aki was on hand to show me. We squeezed into the phone box and dialled the number. The moment the beeping noise sounded, I got the first of my 2p coins and pushed it into the slot. And from my low vantage point, it really did require some pushing. You had to force the coin down so that it pushed a metal bar back, and only when the coin dropped did the beeping stop.

It must have been 1976 by this point because of the songs I remember being piped out of the receiver. Tina Charles's 'I Love to Love (But My Baby Loves to Dance)' and Candi Staton's 'Young Hearts (Run Free)' introduced me to disco – not that I knew this was the genre I was listening to. Neither did I know that Tina's song (British, white, poppy, provincial) was far less cool than Candi's (American, black, soulful, tinged with autobiographical sadness). In fact, it was only years later that I would even find out the names of the singers. Dial-a-Disc didn't tell you who they were or even what the songs were called. In the space between fascination and information, I imagined personalities and stories and ascribed them to the people singing the songs. Tina and Candi merged into the same person: a bounteously benign mum/sister/cousin/teacher/childminder hybrid who had somehow selected me as the sole recipient of her kindness.

Inside the phone box, I don't remember moving. I just held the receiver and succumbed to what felt like an intravenous ingestion of melody. Decades later, I told my children about Dial-a-Disc, increasingly conscious that the scene I was describing sounded like something that people might have done a hundred years previously: standing in a phone box and paying to hear a song that you didn't even get to choose. Listening to Dial-a-Disc in a phone box effectively converted it into something akin to an Edwardian iPod.

Other songs made fewer demands of my imagination on account of the fact that I knew them already. I'd seen ABBA do 'Mamma Mia' on *Crackerjack* at the end of the previous year and, well . . . you didn't forget a song like that in a hurry. Performing 'Save Your Kisses for Me' in *A Song for Europe* – the show which saw various singers going head to head for the chance to represent Britain in the Eurovision Song Contest – Brotherhood of Man placed their thumbs in their belt loops, did their funny little foot-flick shuffle, outstretched their arms and reeled me in. In that moment, it was as though 3D television had been invented just for me, trialling exclusively in the back room of the Great Western Fish Bar in Acocks Green, on existing technology.

'Save Your Kisses for Me' was my prepubescent 'Starman' moment. But this was no alien gang leader exhorting me to help him over-throw the hidebound post-war torpor of my parents' generation and invert this monochrome dystopia to reveal an iridescent post-apoca-lyptic ambisexual utopia. No, this was serious. I felt like Brotherhood of Man – the dark-haired bloke with the moustache; the sleepy-eyed, super-affable guy with brown shoulder-length hair, just the way I secretly wanted my hair to be; the kind-faced blonde woman; the only slightly less kind-faced looking dark-haired woman – under-stood me.

Over time, 'Save Your Kisses for Me' would go on to mean different things to me. There would be the years in which I would have felt I'd outgrown it. Then there would have been the arch, twenty-something years which had me mischievously ascribing some darker motive to the song's pay-off line, 'Even though you're only three.' Finally, there would have been the years in which I became a parent and realised that the love you feel for your kids is easily intense and all-consuming enough to bear the weight of a song about the pain of leaving them. In that moment, I understood the song in exactly the way I under-stood it as a six-year-old. The circle was complete.

It might be that a lot of six-year-olds felt a comparably intense bond with Brotherhood of Man. My love for them, however, fed into an existing neurosis that felt specific to my circumstances. I was becoming increasingly convinced that my parents were secretly planning to leave me. In my mind, the reasons were clear and entirely understandable. My inability to talk to anyone other than my par-

ents, my brother and – on rare occasions – my teachers had ruined
the family. Their embarrassment was palpable every time another
visitor entered the house and my mum – it was almost always my
mum – apologised to them on my behalf or leaned her ear into my
mouth so I could whisper what I wanted her to relay to them. It must
have looked like I was possessed by Sooty.

My dad rarely confronted me directly, but I overheard conversations in which he blamed my mother for what had happened. She
was struggling to moderate my neurotic eccentricities. My hair had
now grown into a pretty groovy mop, a state which earned me the
nickname *Mallouras* from my dad – a Greek word which has no
precise translation, although 'hairy' repurposed as a noun comes
closest. When my mother attempted to frogmarch me to Nick's
Continental Hairdresser, a five-minute walk from our shop, she
spent ten minutes chasing me around Nick's car which was parked
outside. The embarrassment was compounded by the fact that Nick,
who could see all of this happening from the floor of his salon, was
from Cyprus. There was no reason to think that he wouldn't take
some delight in telling the other Greeks about Victoria Paphides and
her weird son. I ran all the way home with hair intact, my demoral-
ised mum trailing behind me, almost certainly anticipating a tense
exchange with my dad in which he would once again bemoan her
inability to impose her will over me.

I sometimes wonder why he didn't step in and force me to snap
into line. He could certainly be intimidating enough to do that, but
I think the one thing that held him back was the fact that my mum
and I were closer to each other than I was to him. I don't think he
wanted to risk losing me altogether, and even at that age, I realised
that gave me power. Three years previously, my earliest memory
of any intimate exchange with him involved him picking me up
and attempting to kiss me. Instantly recoiling at the roughness of
his stubble, I ran away – and when he tried to get closer, I picked

up a carved wooden antelope from the mantelpiece and threw it at him. This archetypal embodiment of Mediterranean manhood rose up from the table in the sitting room, turned to face my mum, absolutely heartbroken, and walked down the corridor to the shop. I burst into tears. No one ever asked me to explain why I'd done what I'd done. It was almost too grave an incident to warrant further discussion.

In my interior world, these were all details in an overall picture confirming to me that I was now a liability. Most visitors setting eyes on me for the first time assumed I was a girl. This was especially true of Greek Cypriots, who simply couldn't understand why I – unlike all the other Cypriot boys – wasn't dressed and coiffed like a miniature version of their dad. Every time such a case of mistaken gender happened, my dad referred them to the ruinous leniency of my mother. I felt something approaching anguish about the impossible position in which I had put my mother. My dad might have put the blame on her, but I placed the blame squarely on myself. If I returned home from school one day and they were both gone, it would be my fault.

Not only had I accepted this outcome, but I had already started making contingency plans. My mother couldn't possibly have known what those plans were on 3 April 1976, when my dad gave her the evening off work to watch the Eurovision Song Contest with me. We had watched *A Song for Europe* together, but Eurovision was the biggie. This annual televisual spectacular mattered to Greeks in a way that was hard for British people to conceive at the time. Mainland Europeans had little cultural representation outside of their own countries, but in the 1970s, Eurovision offered them a chance to send their musical emissaries out to an audience spanning the entire continent and show them that they could do music too.

As if to affirm the importance of this evening, chip paper was repurposed for scorecards and crisps and peanuts were emptied out into bowls. It had somehow been made clear to me that the song we were backing was the Greek entry, a woman called Mariza Koch, who looked and sounded like Mary Hopkin trying desperately to remember where she'd hidden the tune to the song she was supposed to be singing. But, of course, in the weeks between *A Song for Europe* and the Eurovision Song Contest, I had decided that if my parents really did leave me, then I wanted Brotherhood of Man, who were also performing that night, to adopt me. I hadn't worked out the logistics. It didn't occur to me that bands toured or undertook promotional schedules. I just imagined that Lee, Nicky, Martin and Sandra all lived together in their Brotherhood of Mansion and beamed themselves magically to TV studios as and when they were needed. The rest of the time, they could look after me. Even if they won, how hard could that be? There were four of them, after all, and as long as I had enough 2p coins to ring Dial-a-Disc and get milk from the robot milk machine, I was really no trouble. In the event, of course, they won it with a performance of understated insouciance, making nervelessly light work of the plaintive harmonies on 'Bye bye baby / Bye bye'. I gave Greece a full ten out of duty, but I gave Britain a full ten out of love.

Out of my obsession with Brotherhood of Man an aesthetic of sorts was forged. All the music I liked was performed by people who might feasibly step in and take care of me if something happened to my parents. Thankfully, 1976 and 1977 constituted a golden age for acts who fitted these stringent criteria. Sometimes you didn't even have to see the singers to confer those qualities upon them. One evening in the payphone outside the shop, I shoved in my 2p coin and found myself parachuted into the scenic undulations of Elton John and Kiki Dee's 'Don't Go Breaking My Heart'. Like so much mainstream pop at the time, there was nothing sharp to catch your fingers on. It was entirely devoid of edges. Like a beach ball or an egg. It was impossible not to be soothed by the reassurances dispensed by this unidentified lady in response to the man's worried entreaties

– not least because of the way it slipped into the past tense on the chorus, where she recalled being his 'clown' when he was 'down'. There wasn't a single element of jeopardy in 'Don't Go Breaking My Heart' that wasn't washed away by a warm malty sip of resolution. Within the space of about four 2p coins, 'Don't Go Breaking My Heart' had become my new favourite song – this in spite of the fact that I didn't know who sang it or what it was called. But this was only the beginning.

A few weeks later, my first actual memory of watching *Top of the Pops*, I got to see what the man and the lady looked like and what they were called. It turns out that I had already seen Elton John some months before, in a *John Craven's Newsround* story about the unveiling of Elton's waxwork at Madame Tussauds. Like almost any six-year-old would, I plugged the gap that might be actually filled with an explanation of who the hell Madame Tussaud was by conflating her with Madame Cholet from *The Wombles*. It seemed entirely sensible to me that one pop star – Madame Cholet played violin in *The Wombles* – should induct another pop star into her waxwork museum. But even factoring that into consideration, for me, Elton was very much the makeweight in this arrangement. I was Team Kiki. Dressed in pink dungarees, she looked like she'd wandered in off the set of *Play School* singing the song, and simply carried on as she approached a waiting Elton. In the ongoing attempt to line up replacements in the event of my parents' disappearance, Kiki soared into serious contention alongside Brotherhood of Man. You could tell she was a nice person, not least because of her immense generosity in letting Elton join in her song.

My final year at Cottesbrooke Infant School had been a good one. Miss Haylor couldn't teach me for a second consecutive year, but I got the next best thing. She made sure I got to be in the class of Mrs Waters, the woman who had just become her mother-in-law. Mrs Waters was in her fifties and, as a consequence, seemed less lively than Miss Haylor. But she used it to her advantage. What seemed like entire afternoons were spent reading us Enid Blyton's *Faraway Tree* trilogy. The only pressure Mrs Waters applied on me to break my silence was an assembly she planned which involved every child in her class standing in front of the school and reciting their part in a presentation concerning all the different jobs that grown-ups did. My part in all of this was to say that I was a fireman and that my favourite bit of being a fireman was sliding down the pole. Mrs Waters presented me with this fait accompli as if it were something that, come the day, I would simply do and that was that. And because of the casual way in which this contract was struck, I assumed that come the Friday, I probably *would* be able to get the words out.

Throughout the week, we rehearsed our parts, and every time we did so, I stalled on my line. In the days leading up to the moment, my fireman line was consuming me with anxiety. There was no one to whom I felt I could confess this rising sense of mortification. I had already caused my parents enough embarrassment without piling on more. Mrs Waters was behaving as though my contribution would be a mere formality. Yet getting through that Friday's assembly felt as onerous a prospect as getting across the Grand Canyon on a bicycle. Sure, it was better than not having a bicycle and I was going to pedal like crazy, but it was pointless to plan beyond that moment.

At last, Friday arrived. We only got to file into the school hall once every class was inside: the youngest and second-youngest year sitting cross-legged in rows, while the third-year children stood upright at the back of the hall. Mrs Walker rose from her seat at the side of the stage to lift the needle from the record player. The silence was awful. The inescapability of my situation was akin to those nightmares where maybe twenty per cent of you knows that this is a nightmare, but that isn't enough to overcome the sleep paralysis and climb through into the waking world.

My cue to speak was the end of Simon Tuohy's bit, in which he told the throng the best thing about being a mountaineer or a racing driver. Anyone in the audience seeing Simon confidently impart his bit would have then been alerted to a strangulated croak on the far left-hand side of the stage. My breathing accelerated to a shallow pant and I tried again, but I wasn't even making words. My memory tells me this went on for about half a minute. In reality, I don't suppose more than ten seconds elapsed before Mrs Waters intervened. 'Takis is a fireman, and he says that the best thing about his job is that, instead of stairs, he gets to slide down a fireman's pole.' The moment she stepped in to take care of my line, it was like having an oxygen mask drop down from a hitherto invisible overheard compartment. A sweet, sweet reprieve.

The school year ended uneventfully except for one thing. Until that moment I had been Takis. That was the name called out on the register every morning and every afternoon: the name my parents called me, albeit with the 's' dropped when addressing me directly. It was short for Panayiotakis, which in turn was long for Panayiotis. When their children are young, it's common for Greeks to drop the final syllable and replace it with '-akis', as a term of endearment. All this had happened while I was still a baby. Hence, when I started school, I was Takis. However, as my time at infant school ended, I decided that I was going to have an English name. I let Mrs Waters know that when the time came for me to start at the junior school across the road, I would be Peter and not Takis. If my parents were informed, I don't understand why they went along with it. Whoever heard of a seven-year-old boy suddenly deciding to change his name and that being in any way acceptable? But no one kicked up a fuss. It was as if they were preoccupied with weightier matters. Or maybe they thought that they might still return to Cyprus imminently, and that if they did, this would cease to be an issue. As the summer holidays began, I'm not sure I really expected people to suddenly start addressing me as Peter. But I was now clearly desperate to assimilate.

I didn't feel like a Takis. I'm not sure I felt like a Peter either, but if people started to call me that, then maybe I might.

For the second year in a row, we didn't leave Birmingham. Seemingly undeterred by the total absence of two-way conversation that came with the post, Vijay Singh signed up to become my best friend. His family had a corner shop a few buildings away from the school. His dad was rarely around, on account of his job, which involved working long shifts at the Sunblest bread factory in West Bromwich. His absence meant that it was left to Vijay's mum to run the shop, but I don't know how she managed through the mythically hot summer of 1976 because she had just given birth to a baby girl – who, inconveniently for Vijay, had arrived just before his birthday. It was a situation that Vijay politely explained to my mum, by way of asking her if she would mind making him a birthday cake – a task she undertook with delight.

Vijay was pretty handy in the kitchen himself. Before leaving for hospital, his mum taught him how to make chapatis. Once in a while he'd disappear into the kitchen and return with a chapati on a plate for each of us, served with some chutney on the side. I couldn't handle the chutney, but the chapatis were wonderful. When we weren't eating Vijay's chapatis, we looked for discarded Player's cigarette packets. Vijay had a cousin called Ashok who lived in Aston and had told him that if you found a Player's cigarette packet, you had to cut out the picture and keep it on you for good luck – but only if you said this rhyme out loud: 'Sailor, sailor, bring me luck / If you don't I'll rip you up.' Of course, my problem was that I couldn't say the rhyme out loud, but Vijay was nothing if not a loyal friend. We would find two sailors and he'd recite the rhyme both times, once on my behalf, before handing my sailor back to me.

As it happens, the summer of 1976 got off to a lucky start for me. One Friday evening, with no permanent childminder in place, I wandered along the corridor from the front room and, as I had done so many times, hovered at the far end listening to the sound of the pinball machines on the other side of the door to the games room. This time, however, the continuity announcer in my head went off-script and encouraged me to open the door. I was now facing the door itself: over my left shoulder, through the other door, my parents were dealing with the teatime rush. They were oblivious to my presence. I turned the handle and pushed.

The smoke was briefly overwhelming, but adjusting my gaze beyond it, I could see maybe a dozen men, scattered around the place in separate clusters, all of them around pinball machines, with the exception of one cluster whose attention was fixed on the pool table. Some of them were eating chips, which they would pick out from a hole they'd torn in the chip paper. They'd been coming here since the early seventies as schoolkids every lunchtime, during which they'd forgo their lunch and spend the money on the machines. When my mum realised we were effectively depriving these kids of food, her conscience got the better of her and she'd beckon them over one by one and give them the chips for free. Decades later, she still occasionally gets stopped in the street by men in their late fifties and early sixties, unrecognisable from their younger selves, thanking her for the chips.

It took ages for any of the customers to notice me, so I just carried on watching, paying particular attention to their pinball techniques and their average scores, comparing their ability to mine. Finally, one of them – a lantern-jawed guy with well-tended shoulder-length hair and matching denim jacket and trousers – spotted me.

'A'roight, nipper!' he smiled. I smiled back. 'What's your name?'

I shrugged at him.

'Don't you know your own name?!'

I shrugged again.

'Oi, Ranjo! This kid's forgotten his own name,' he said, calling over to a shorter West Indian kid who had just voided his game by tilting the machine too hard.

'That's Chris's boy,' said Ranjo – and from there, it became apparent that, at least until my parents turfed me out, I wouldn't be unwelcome here. In the games room, I quickly realised that my silence wasn't an inconvenience. In fact, it somehow made these people like me more. Within half an hour, it had ceased to be an issue. I timorously walked over to a machine, standing on tiptoe to monitor the progress of the pinball. Noticing that I was struggling to see properly from up close, someone went into the front section of the shop and grabbed one of the chairs that was next to the sole dining table and brought it back so I could stand on it. From there it was just a matter of time before someone's interest was piqued further and they paid for me to have a game.

It must have been 7.30 p.m., maybe 8 o'clock, before my parents finally discovered my whereabouts. I turned around and saw my dad standing beneath the arch where, at some point, the wall separating the two rooms had been knocked down. I don't know how long he had been standing there. But instead of intervening, he just carried on smoking his cigarette and watching. Eventually, I climbed down and walked into the sitting room where my mum was waiting with my pyjamas and my bedtime drink: warm, sweetened milk, poured into a small empty Coca-Cola bottle. Then we watched David Wilkie win gold in the men's 200-metre breaststroke at the Montreal Olympics. I finally went to sleep not really understanding why I wasn't in trouble.

The following evening I waited until the shop got busy, and once again slipped into the games room. This time, they greeted me straight away. I walked through the smoke towards my favourite machine and, once again, someone pulled up a chair for me. What I really wanted was for someone to challenge me to a game, but obviously I couldn't ask anyone, and there was no reason why someone would offer. Then again, I figured that if I stood there long enough, it might just happen. Finally, on my next sortie to the toilet upstairs,

I ran into my bedroom and grabbed my piggy bank, shaking it until a 5p coin dropped out. Re-entering the games room, I waited until one of the machines finally became free and pushed the chair in front so that I could stand on it and see what I was doing. One coin meant one chance to show the room what I could do. I pulled back the ball shooter and got to work. Each 'go' consisted of three balls. Maybe I reached quadruple figures with my first ball. I can't remember for sure, but quadruple figures on most pinball machines is no big deal.

By my second ball though, I was fully immersed. I knew just how much to push the machine without the word 'TILT' appearing in its little display window and the power shutting out. I had long since realised that only mugs flip the two flippers at exactly the same moment. The trick was to release one fractionally after the other. This created too narrow a space for the ball to pass through. I also knew the exact point on the right flipper on which the ball had to roll before flipping it up into a tunnel on the other side of which three balls would emerge. When I finally used up all my goes, I turned around and found myself almost hoisted aloft on a dozen denim shoulders. It was perhaps around 9 o'clock before my mum came to get me. Again, no one was cross with me. Saturday night was the night she always washed my hair. The smell of Vosene supplanted the smell of cigarette smoke – not that the smell of cigarette smoke on my hair would have been especially remarkable then. In 1976 everything smelled of cigarette smoke.

As the summer rolled on, my evening routine solidified. It gradually became apparent to me that my parents saw my pinballing proclivities as a form of free childcare. Although I was unaware of its existence, I was almost certainly the beneficiary of Ken Russell's film adaptation of the Who's *Tommy*, which had been released the previous year. I wasn't deaf or blind, but I was dumb, and I looked like the young Tommy with the hair of Roger Daltrey's grown-up Tommy. And, of course, like Tommy, I was unbeatable at pinball, better than anyone else in that shop, including the apprentice plasterers who came here straight after work, stopping only out front to buy a scallop (a slice of potato, dipped in batter and deep-fried; in some shops these were called fritters) and a can of Lockwoods cola: the boy with the Afro comb sticking out of his back pocket; and Butch the square-faced outsider with the perpetually knotted brow and coffee-coloured bell bottoms.

In the wake of Evel Knievel's heroic but ill-fated attempt to ride his motorcycle over thirteen single-decker buses at Wembley Stadium, my dad traded in one of the generic beach-scene machines for a branded Evel Knievel machine. Butch swiftly made it his own and got visibly shirty on the occasions he came into the shop and saw someone else on it. This, in turn, made him even more of a figure of ridicule to the other regulars – and, as children always are, I was quick to clock the power dynamic. Within a week of the machine's arrival, someone had taken a knife and etched the words 'BUTCH IS A WANKER' on the side of his favourite machine. It was the first thing you saw as you walked towards the far end of the games room. I didn't know what a wanker was, but I now knew that Butch was one.

Amused by this latest development, I went off into the downstairs sitting room, picked up a pen and paper, and wrote a poem which I proudly headed, 'BUTCH IS A WANKER'. Over the course of four or five verses, I detailed all the ways in which Butch was a wanker. When it was finished, I made my way from the sitting room into the games room, past the pool table to the Evel Knievel machine, and silently handed it up to Butch. Some of the others stopped what they were doing and walked over to see what it was that Butch was reading. They seemed to think it was hilarious – more so than Butch, who took my poem to the shop counter and calmly handed it to my horrified dad.

Once again, I waited to see what my punishment would be, and this time, I didn't have to wait long. It was the only time I remember being scared of my dad. He found me upstairs in the posh room. I was already in tears, but that didn't moderate his response. Years previously, he had jettisoned his Cypriot accent in order to snap into line with my mum's Greek accent. But his fury brought it all back. He sounded like he was speaking in tongues. I couldn't have been more terrified if he ended his tirade by coughing up a live snake. As it was, he ripped up my poem and, while the pieces were still landing on me, turned to leave, pausing only to let me know that I was banned from the games room. To be fair, I'd pretty much worked that out for myself.

CHAPTER 4

All the records in the house could be found in the alcoves built into either side of the turntable on the radiogram. There were about thirty in total, of which nine were not Greek. Two of them were 7-inch singles: Paper Lace's 'Billy Don't Be A Hero' and Chuck Berry's 'My Ding-a-Ling'. Five of them were Jim Reeves albums, lent to my dad by a customer who died before my dad was able to return them. Another was the Wombles album that had so obsessed me the year before. And the final one was a 1971 compilation called *Pick of the Pops*, a budget-price alternative to the *Top of the Pops* albums, which themselves were conceived as a budget alternative to TV-advertised compilations of current hits by original artists.

The *Top of the Pops* and *Pick of the Pops* albums were, if nothing else, a huge feat of ingenuity – comprised as they were of a dozen songs, every one the work of session musicians who had to replicate as closely as possible the recordings by the original artists under punitive time constraints. Years later, I would learn that the voice on my parents' *Pick of the Pops* album telling me what a lovely precious dream it was to be young, gifted and black was that of a pre-fame Elton John. But in the summer of 1976, this wasn't the message that resonated with me. No, the sound that transfixed me as I served my exile from the games room was that of an unnamed session musician pretending to be Mary Hopkin singing her 1970 Eurovision Song Contest entry 'Knock, Knock, Who's There?' By the second Saturday of my exile from the games room, I had fallen into a pitiful routine: reading and rereading this week's issues of *Whoopee!* and *Whizzer and Chips* while playing 'Knock, Knock, Who's There?' over and over again. There was no singer credited on the record, but unconsciously I imagined that it was the woman on the sleeve – a sad-eyed blonde in a plain red blouse with big round shades pulled up over her forehead. Another one for the list of possible childminders.

There's no way of knowing how long my obsession with 'Knock, Knock, Who's There?' would have lasted if left to run its course, because one evening my reverie was broken by the arrival of my mother, who wanted to know how I was doing. In general terms, I was fine. I was planning my future with the *Pick of the Pops* lady, and if she was even a quarter as friendly as she sounded on 'Knock, Knock, Who's There?', we were going to be very happy together. I adored my mum too much to hurt her by relaying this news to her. Besides, I understood why she might be secretly planning to run away and accepted that I was partly to blame – there were no hard feelings. No, this wasn't the time to go into detail. Besides, she had news for me that comfortably eclipsed any of that. Apparently, the regulars downstairs had been asking after me. Even Butch was ready to forgive me, not least because he had done pretty well out of the indignity: chicken and chips with a bottle of Corona lemonade, all on the house. His fondness for the Evel Knievel machine seemed undiminished by the words etched on its side. My mum, who I suspect had never wanted to ban me in the first place, pressed a few 5p coins into my hand and sent me downstairs to a chorus of affectionate greetings.

It wasn't just the pinball machines I loved about that room. It was also the fact that no one in there regarded it as a problem that I didn't talk. In every other room of the house, of course, it was absolutely a problem. No one knew how long this was going to continue, least of all me – and certainly not the psychologist in the big house in Edgbaston, who had declared there was nothing more she could do.

A move to the new school across the road from the infant school yielded no progress. Arriving for my first day at Cottesbrooke Junior School, we were introduced to our new teacher Miss Spibey and, as she called out the names on the register, I was shocked to find that my request had been accepted. I was suddenly Peter and it felt a little weird, as though my bluff had been called. The discomfort was made worse at playtime when my classmates clustered around me in the playground and asked me about my new name. I addressed any questions that could be answered with a shake of the head, a nod or a shrug. Kids, of course, are pretty good at accepting things at face value – and to them, from that moment on, I was Peter. I thought that by being called Peter, I'd suddenly feel like a Peter. But what did a Peter feel like? Well, Peter felt proper. Peter felt like he was going places. Peter fitted in. Peter was British. And that almost certainly explains the ballooning sense of guilt that I somehow couldn't find the words to caption. The world of British things – pinball, pop, comics – felt increasingly like home.

Perhaps sensing that my brother and I were pulling towards a place from which ultimately she might never be able to retrieve us, my mother decided to step up the Greek lessons. Our grammar had started to deteriorate and, in conversation with each other and with our parents, Aki and I were starting to replace Greek words with the occasional English one. My dad was still fixed upon moving back to Cyprus and, of course, if that happened we needed to remain fluent in the language. Formal sessions – in the posh room every Sunday morning, straight after breakfast – were the only thing for it. My mum procured some text books from somewhere. Each page depicted wholesome scenes of Greek life – a little girl helping her mother bake a cake; children in a classroom singing the national anthem – with sentences that corresponded to the illustrations. Aki and I had both learned Greek before we picked up English, but the confusion of alien squiggles that formed the corresponding alphabet was another matter entirely.

Almost at their instigation, Greek lessons became another aspect of my parents' culture at which I seemed fated to disappoint. In spite of it all, my mum gamely struggled on with the lessons, fighting against the apathy of her children and their attempts to make each other laugh, either by attempting to fart at will and blame it on the other, or quite simply by giving the other a dead leg under the table while simultaneously exclaiming 'ow!' to make it sound as though we were the one who had been hit. The lessons would have no fixed end; they would finish, finally, when my mum lost control of our tiny attention spans.

Sundays were the only day on which the centre of activity migrated up from the shop and into the posh room directly above it. After six days spent tolerating the sound of the transistor in the games room permanently pumping out chart hits, Sundays presented my dad with the chance to redress the cultural balance. The first thing he did after our lesson was to walk over to the mantelpiece above the fireplace which had been modernised with the installation of a three-bar heater. There were two things on the mantelpiece, one of which was, by a mile, the most futuristic-looking thing in the house: a metallic upright stem from which maybe seventy or eighty coloured balls emerged, placed equidistantly on a 'spray' of wires. If you blurred your eyes, the balls looked like they were floating unaided.

Great as that was, the focus of my dad's attention was the thing next to it: a giant Philips radio which he bought in 1968 for £160. That's a lot to pay for a radio now. But five decades ago, it was an unthinkable amount. An unjustifiable outlay, really. He had just taken out a loan to buy a fish and chip shop. With such a huge debt to surmount, why would he have spent what, in modern money, would be something like £2,000 on a radio? I think this was the point at which he realised he wouldn't be going back any time soon. He was stuck here for the foreseeable future. If he couldn't teleport himself to Kyrenia every Sunday, the least he could do was create a little bit of Kyrenia in Acocks Green. His radio allowed him to do just that. Its importance was reflected in the fact that it had two aerials and a panel that lifted up to reveal an inscribed world map and lines pointing to parts of the world in order to help you determine what time it was in whatever country the tuning dial had alighted on.

When the radio was turned on, the backlit window revealed eight or nine wavebands on which the names of countries were written. But most of these were countries I had never heard of. This was because they weren't countries, but the towns and cities that hosted the transmitters. Hilversum. Helvetia. Athlone. In 1990, Van Morrison would zone in on the romance of these faraway place names to write 'In the Days Before Rock 'n' Roll': a memorial to the formative early years he would spend 'down on my knees . . . at those wireless knobs', divining for the voices of Ray Charles, John Lee Hooker and Fats Domino. But my dad wasn't looking for American blues singers. He was looking for the Greek stations Radio Athens and RIK which, on Sundays, would both broadcast live eucharists. The solemn sound of Greek Orthodox liturgies resounded loudly around the house. You had to leave to escape it – which, in sunny weather I did. But on a rainy Sunday in November it was harder to do.

Once the service was over, my mum would carefully carry the radio to the tiny spare bedroom that abutted the posh room and place it on an occasional table next to her knitting machine. She would slide the waveband switch to long wave in order to hear the sound of Greek sailors out at sea communicating with their families back home. For maybe an hour at a time, all you could hear from that room was the rhythmic sound of the knitting machine carriage moving across the row of needles from left to right and back again, punctuated by poignant snippets of conversation between loved ones.

Back in the posh room, my dad would now be some way along the process of placing a record onto the radiogram turntable. He would always start with the same song. Always. Over the crackle of scratched vinyl, an opening shot of plaintive bouzoukis would chime forlornly into a room in a street in a city that, to the record's owner, merely accentuated how far away home really was. The voice was exotic, tarry and slightly foreboding – all qualities that conferred a pall of solemnity onto the posh room which seemed to find its physical manifestation in the fug of my dad's cigarette smoke.

> *You are a day like that day*
> *in which I lost my joy.*
> *Cloudy Sunday,*
> *you make my heart bleed.*

The song – 'Cloudy Sunday' (*Sinefiasmeni Kiriaki*) – written by Vassilis Tsitsanis and sung by Stelios Kazantzidis, came from a compilation whose title translated as 'The Calendar'. The record was comprised of a song for each month, encased in a sleeve which somehow further compounded the sense of imminent peril that 'Cloudy Sunday' instilled in me: a metallic pagan sun suspended on an intense pink backdrop. Wherever I went in the room, it seemed to be staring at me.

> *When I see you in the rain,*
> *I can't rest even for a moment.*
> *You make my life black*
> *and I deeply sigh.*

Sometimes I'd gaze at the windows of the police station across the road in the hope that some activity might be discernible. I was seven now and – confusing reality with a dream I had maybe two years previously – I still believed that the banister visible in the upstairs window of the station was a balcony overhanging a pool with sharks inside it. As the music played, I sat and patiently waited to catch sight of freshly apprehended murderers being thrown over the balcony of Acocks Green police station by fully suited coppers, two for every miscreant. I knew it went on in there, because I had a memory of it being so. But why did my parents deny the existence of the shark room every time I challenged them about it? Surely one of them was with me when I visited the police station and caught sight of what was going on there?

On the self-titled third album released by Chicago singer-song-writer Daniel Knox in 2015, there's a song that mirrors the mystery of the Acocks Green police station shark room. The track is called 'Blue Car', and over a pretty music-box motif, 'Blue Car' returns, dreamlike, to a simple childhood scene that the author's logical adult mind has yet to resolve: a memory of seeing a driverless car pull up to the family home before driving away, unseen by another soul. Knox later explained that this is what he remembered having seen. 'I assumed . . . the future me [had] come to pay me a visit. But, as we know, when you time-travel you can't see your future self or your past self.' In the second verse of 'Blue Car', Knox evokes the crushing scepticism of grown-ups when you have just confided experiences that feel far too real to be a mere product of your imagination:

> *You can't win*
> *The beast will appear*
> *But only to you and no one*
> *Believes you*
> *No one.*

The proximity of sharks in the police station didn't do much to leaven the atmosphere of Sunday mornings in the posh room above the Great Western. Even with the privilege of access to the pinball machines, the homesick melancholia that dispersed throughout the building on a weekly basis would somehow find me there. I didn't think I was paying attention, but decades later I realised I had memorised every song on every record that my dad played up there: the illicit love described on Markos Vamvakaris's 'Francosyrian Girl'; the heavy-hearted singalong of Mikis Theodorakis's 'O Kaimos' ('The Sadness') which, by decades, seemed to presage the lugubrious lamentations of Blur's 'Tender' or Nick Cave and the Bad Seeds' 'Foi Na Cruz'; and a rare, uncompromisingly female perspective from Haris Alexiou on 'When a Woman Drinks': 'You tell me not to get drunk / Because it's not allowed / But you have no idea of the pain in my heart.'

I was listening to the blues without even realising it. Greek blues. Sadness is soaked into the fibre of every Greek song that isn't trying to sound like an American or British song. Four centuries of Ottoman rule prior to the twentieth century would be enough to see to that, although we Greeks hardly needed any encouragement. Even at the peak of Greek civilisation 2,500 years ago, when things were going pretty well for us, we still made time to invent Greek tragedy.

Years later, I'd discover the Greek blues even had a name of its own. *Rebetika*. Its roots dated back to the hash dens or *tekedhes* that lined the port of Piraeus – much of it created by Greeks and Turks forced to flee Smyrna (now Izmir) after the catastrophic Greek assault on the city ended in capitulation in 1922. Many of the songs by names such as Anestis Delias and Markos Vamvakaris – written to the rhythm of the *zeibekiko*, the heavily sedated dervish dance of the Piraeus *teke* – explicitly alluded to the substances that inspired them.

But this wasn't the stuff that middle-aged Greeks in the 1970s were playing in their down time. The version of *rebetika* that made it onto our turntable had been cleansed of explicit drug references. It wasn't the drugs per se that bothered Greeks of a certain generation, rather the ethnic associations that came with it. For those keen to keep their cultural bloodline separate from that of the Turks, *rebetika* was a thorny issue. In 1936, for Greece's incoming fascist prime minister Ioannis Metaxas, it was a huge embarrassment. If Metaxas had his way, everyone would be listening to Mozart rather than a corpus of songs whose roots could be traced to Asia Minor. Many of *rebetika*'s foremost practitioners may have been refugees, but their survivalist instincts and camaraderie created a subculture of sharply-dressed, streetwise men known as *manges*. 'Hey Mangas,' began 'Poser', written in 1935 by Anestis Delias, 'If you're going to carry a knife, You'd better have the guts, poser, to pull it out.' Though Metaxas's instinct was to outlaw the people who made this music, what he actually did was far cleverer. He co-opted them. Tsitsanis removed cadences from his music that might be deemed 'Asian' in character – although listening to the harmonies on 'Cloudy Sunday', it was clear that he didn't try that hard. Also, the words could be changed, but it revealed its hand in other ways. The best Greek music of the post-*rebetika* era has a rhythm absolutely unique to it. Every other bar is extended by an extra beat. The effect of that is tantamount to feeling the ground beneath your feet constantly shifting; like attempting to get up and losing your centre of gravity every time. A feeling of constantly being thwarted. It's an ingenious device, and you'll only find it in Greek music.

It was only when I left home as a young adult that I had any inclination to hear it again. One afternoon in 1991, I walked into a second-hand record shop in rural Wales and found a copy of my dad's record, 'The Calendar', sitting on a stack of old rock albums, the only one of its kind. I paid £1.95 for it, more out of curiosity than anything else. The following morning I opened the window to a view mostly comprising grass, trees and sheep, and waited for 'Cloudy Sunday' to start. Its beauty almost floored me. All I remember about hearing it in the room above the Great Western was a sense that it was sucking all the air out of the room, and me with it.

CHAPTER 5

There were two coexisting worlds which sometimes intersected: the Hellenocentric world of my parents, a domain whose terms and conditions extended to the four walls of our house; and the world beyond the counter of the Great Western fish and chip shop. But even at seven, I realised that just because something was huge in one, it didn't necessarily mean it existed in the other. Music was a case in point. Until 1977, neither of my parents had expressed an opinion on any record whose sleeve didn't have Greek writing on it. Perhaps that's why I was wholly unprepared when I walked into the storeroom where my parents were preparing that day's fish and my dad turned to ask me which of the girls in ABBA I thought was the prettiest. I didn't know their names and neither, I think, did he. But I could answer his question. I knew who ABBA were. Not because of 'Waterloo' – that hadn't counted, because I hadn't known I was watching ABBA at the time and, to be honest, it was the song I remembered more than the singers or their wonky Nordic glam get-up. When they re-entered my life over a year later, performing 'Mamma Mia' on the BBC's Friday teatime kids' variety show *Crackerjack*, I was mesmerised. 'Mamma Mia' was a great thing to call a song. I'd never heard the Italian phrase before, but it seemed as novel and joyful to me as it must have done to Björn when he earmarked it for a song.

For my dad, it was the release of 'Money, Money, Money', almost a year later, that made him take notice – and it doesn't take a psychologist to work out the reason. 'Money, Money, Money' was an immigrant lament. It was 'If I Were a Rich Man' repurposed for a post fairy-tale world. Money had flung my dad to the other end of Europe and kept him there for far longer than he had anticipated. I didn't share his adoration of that song. It sounded tense and threatening to me. There was no mistaking the tormenting quality of Benny's piano part, and in particular of the song's introduction, which acts as a reset when it returns after each chorus, underscoring the Sisyphean futility of the protagonist's situation: she'll never break free of the forces conspiring to thwart her. No wonder my dad loved it. It was pretty apparent that the one thing which made standing behind the fryer for seven hours at a time more bearable was thinking about all the things he could do if he had a little money.

ABBA were the first non-Greek pop stars he deemed worthy of discussion. And here he was discussing them with me. Not only did this ratify their importance, it multiplied it. So who *did* I think was the prettiest girl in ABBA?

'The one with yellow hair,' I said.

My dad proudly turned to face my mum, who seemed unhappy with this entire conversation. I couldn't tell if her disapproval was rooted in envy or in the fact that my dad deemed this a suitable conversation to be having with his seven-year-old son.

'She's sexy, isn't she?'

'She looks kind,' I said. At this point, there was still no higher accolade than kind. I didn't know what to do with sexy. It would be a long time before that happened.

In truth, my obsession with ABBA had taken root some months previously with the launch of a new Saturday morning children's show fronted by Radio 1's tittering tiger of the airwaves, Noel Edmonds. It's perhaps hard to convey to subsequent generations just how much of an evolutionary leap, in children's TV terms, *Multi-Coloured Swap*

Shop seemed. Before you even saw it, there were four key promises embedded in its name that meant being elsewhere on a Saturday morning simply wasn't an option.

It was some sort of shop.

It was multicoloured.

It wasn't a normal shop – it involved swapping in some way,
   and swapping things was quite exciting in the 1970s.

The proprietor of this shop was Noel Edmonds.

Multi-Coloured Swap Shop was three hours long, which, taken as a fraction of the life of a small child, is a luxurious serving of time. It's an expanse in which you can truly lose yourself. *Multi-Coloured Swap Shop* was so long that it swallowed up other programmes, like a snake swallows other animals, so you can still see their outlines. Entire episodes of *Scooby-Doo* and *The Hair Bear Bunch* were contained within *Multi-Coloured Swap Shop*. Further enhancing the sense that it was a channel within an already-existing channel, it had its own dedicated news person, John Craven, from *John Craven's Newsround* – who managed to retain a slightly detached, 'newsy' air about him throughout the show, as if he might suddenly be needed to tell us about some urgent new changes to the way maths was taught in schools. Statistically, this was likelier than you might think, as roughly once a fortnight, the lead item on *Newsround* was about new changes to the way maths was taught in schools.

Then there was the swapping. The ostensive *raison d'être* of *Swap Shop* was that it would act in a non-profit capacity as a broker between a child (let's call them Child A) who had an item – usually a toy – that they no longer needed and sought to exchange with another child's (Child B) unwanted item, preferably a child who wanted the very thing that Child A no longer required. Once the necessary information was collated, the climax of *Swap Shop* would be a *Top of the Pops*-style countdown, detailing that week's top ten swaps and the names of the people who initiated them. A typical transaction might involve, say, ten-year-old Sarah McMahon from Carlisle seeking to trade a Spirograph for KerPlunk. Of the thousands of thoughts that no doubt occurred to me in the five or six years that *Swap Shop* was a regular feature in my life, none of them got close to dwelling on the fact that a three-hour live television show was a costly and cumbersome expedient by which to run a weekly juvenile toy swap meet.

A key component of *Swap Shop* show was music. Thanks to his ongoing tenure at *The Radio 1 Breakfast Show*, Noel knew many of the bands who would pop in and patiently press the receiver to their ear as Lucy on line 1 or Oliver on line 2 asked them where they got their ideas from. But the group with whom Noel had the strongest connection was ABBA. Not for ABBA the health-and-safety-flouting, feral free-for-all that was ITV's *Swap Shop* rival *Tiswas*. ABBA's reductive, rationalist approach to the business of record promotion meant that any show involving the random upturning of buckets of water on guests, and the incarceration of children in a pur-pose-built cage, was an absolute no-no. It pleases me to think that, at some point, someone from their record company would have run through the comparative merits of both programmes and, in doing so, would have had to explain to ABBA the concept of the Phantom Flan Flinger – a caped assailant whose sole purpose on *Tiswas* was to fling flans (typically a paper plate full of shaving foam) at partici-pants and presenters.

No, ABBA were perfect for what felt like just the right amount of state-approved fun for a Saturday morning. Björn had already put serious distance between his 'Waterloo' attire – knee-high silver platform boots, star-shaped guitar and the sort of make-up that only a man with minimal experience of cosmetics would apply on himself – and his 1977 dress code. In repose, he favoured double denim and, along with Benny, would field Noel Edmonds's entreaties with the careful consideration one might expect from the head of a Scandinavian delegation attending a plastics expo in order to try and choose between bulk orders of two different office chair mouldings.

Somehow, the underwhelming nature of ABBA's appearances on *Multi-Coloured Swap Shop* heightened my fascination with them. How could such sensible, sober people make such emotionally charged music? I watched the video for 'Knowing Me, Knowing You' – aired for the first time on *Swap Shop* – and felt . . . well, what did I feel? Concern. Profound concern. Directed by Lasse Hallström in a manner that invited you to infer that you were watching something rather more (or less) than acting, the film showed the two couples moving between each other, shot amid snowy wastes and grey interiors, describing the end of a relationship in terms that corresponded far more closely to the way a child understands the end of their parents' relationship. They made it sound like the end of the world.

In the music papers I was too young to read, punk was the big news. ABBA were mums and dads making music about mum and dad stuff for mums and dads. But, of course, that was what I liked about them. While Björn and Benny sat in the *Swap Shop* studio earnestly telling Noel Edmonds about the way they worked in the studio, Agnetha and Anni-Frid would zone out and gaze lovingly at the children sitting obediently around the periphery of the studio. If I were in that studio, they would be staring lovingly at me. Unlike Brotherhood of Man, with ABBA, it wasn't a matter of wanting them to be my parents. In a child's mind, where the contents of the corporeal world and the imagined world frequently seep from their designated spaces, it sometimes felt like they *were* my parents. Agnetha's eyes were a well of sadness whose depths seemed impossible to plumb. That was something she had in common with my mum. If my dad thought Agnetha was sexy, why didn't he seem to find my mum sexy? And why on earth did my dad think I should find Agnetha sexy? I was seven. I wanted to express my affection for her in the purest way I knew – which, at this point in my life, amounted to holding her hand on the way to the supermarket.

Increasingly, it became apparent that I was a source of increasing consternation to both of my parents. We were due to go away that summer – our first holiday since I had stopped talking to anyone who wasn't a teacher or a member of my immediate family – and there was a certain amount of pressure to 'fix' the problem by then. In extended Cypriot families, competitiveness masquerades as concern; empathy comes freighted with *Schadenfreude*. The Greek word for eccentric is almost the same as the English one, but in the latter culture, there are no pejorative connotations. In Greek, if you describe someone as eccentric, the pronouncement comes with a whiff of disapproval. The unspoken implication was that eccentricity is never sought out; it's something that befalls people, like a stammer or a rash. Through closed doors, I could hear my dad telling my mum that the mop-headed mute pushing presents back into the arms of confused visitors was the result of her laxity – and although she tried not to transfer the resulting anxiety to me, sometimes it was too much for her to handle.

One April evening that year, something snapped in her usually yielding nature. In the small sitting room behind the shop, Aki, then eleven, and I sat on the sofa watching television. Directly above our heads were three wooden rails suspended from the ceiling, on which she would hang the washing out to dry. Something would have almost certainly happened. Perhaps an errand unrun because it involved me having to say something to someone. Maybe a phone left ringing too long because I was too scared to lift the receiver. Or maybe a shrug offered in response to a question from a customer which came across as rudeness. On any given day, it could have been any of these.

Today, maybe it was all of them. 'Why are you doing this?' she asked me. I didn't really know any more. Gentle exhortations turned into shouting and shouting turned into tears – both hers and mine – and all I could think was, 'Why does this even matter?' She left the room, presumably to compose herself. Aki turned to face me. He stared at me, more in pity than exasperation. Venturing out in pursuit of a result that my parents, my teachers, my friends and child psychologists had all failed to achieve, Aki sensed that maybe he could find a way in. It was just the two of us in the room now.

'I've had an idea,' he said.

'I'm not going to do it,' I replied.

'You don't have to do it,' he continued. 'Listen. You know Marcus, who lives around the corner on the Avenue?'

Marcus was just a boy, perhaps a year older than me, who we played with from time to time. His mother had recently died, which is probably why we hadn't seen him for a while. Aki suggested it would be nice to knock on his door.

'And then what do I do?' I said.

'And then, if his dad answers, you just say, "Excuse me. Is Marcus there?"'

Just those five words, Aki assured me. I didn't have to think beyond those five words. And if it felt weird or scary or wrong, I never had to utter another word.

And if it felt fine?

'Then I want you to promise that you'll go to school tomorrow and start talking.'

He made it seem reasonable. He made it seem like I didn't have to do anything I didn't want to. No one else had ever made it seem like that. Everyone else had made it sound like I needed to commit to something huge. Something akin to pulling a lever that would open a hatch that would release thousands of birds into the sky, never to be seen again. It was a terrifying prospect. But Aki was asking me to do something different. Just this one thing. And if it felt weird or scary, we never needed to speak of it again.

I had a good long think.

'OK, then.'

'Promise?'

'Promise.'

'Swear on your life?'

'Swear.'

I commenced the short walk to Marcus's house, muttering 'Is Marcus there?' over and over again. If I just kept saying it until his dad opened the door, I could just say it one more time and that would be fine. And even if I didn't want to speak when he called Marcus, I could decide not to, and Marcus would never know. And because Marcus didn't know anyone at my school, I could go to school in the morning and resume my silence and no one would be any the wiser.

Marcus's dad didn't even seem to notice anything unusual. And beyond that, I don't even remember if Marcus came to the door. I don't remember anything until the bit where I came home and told Aki that I'd done it. But none of that mattered. I had opened my mouth, words had come out and the world hadn't tumbled off its axis.

The following morning, I embarked on the walk to school and wondered when someone would say something to me that required something other than a nod or a shake of the head. It didn't happen until we shuffled into class and sat at our desks. Keith Smith, who sat opposite me, leaned over to borrow my pencil; I placed my hand over his and asked him what he was doing. Within a few seconds, half the class had left their desks and gathered around me – and, startled, I attempted to play it down with a series of shrugs and so-whats.

In truth, the next hour assumed an otherworldly quality. I was watching my classmates as intently as they were watching me, scrutinising their fascination behind a mask of diffidence. This wasn't a tactic. It was an instinct, born of the need to merge into the background. The sooner everyone stopped looking at me, the better. In the far corner, my teacher Miss Spibey pretended not to notice what was going on. After seven months of gently trying to coax conversation out of me, she realised that making a fuss about it might undo the breakthrough of that morning and seal my mouth shut again. She took the register and then produced a tin which contained fifteen bread rolls sliced in half to make thirty pieces, each one of them spread with butter and a layer of honey. 'Today,' she began, as she moved from desk to desk, handing out the rolls, 'we're going to learn about bees.' I wonder if she had originally intended to do the bee lesson later in the day, but brought it forward in order to create a distraction.

It was decided, possibly as a result of recent developments, that for my eighth birthday in July I could have a party, and that my friends and I would get exclusive use of the chip shop: fish and chips for everyone and unlimited use of the pinball machines. It was the birthday party of the year, hands down. How could it not be?

At 2 p.m. on the day of my birthday, instead of turning off the fryer and closing for the afternoon, which is what they did on a weekday, my parents kept it on. It was only after all my friends finally arrived that my mother put the 'C L O S E D' sign up. My dad opened up the front panels of all the pinball machines and, pressing down the wire lever on the inside of the machines – once for each credit – he racked up enough games to keep us all amused for an hour. Then, when we were done, we were beckoned out from the back room of the shop and to the table beside the window, where everyone was given their bag of fish and chips, and their own choice of pop: Tango, Corona lemonade or Lockwoods cola.

After that, we spilled out into the back garden and crossed over a collapsed section of the wall which separated our garden from next door. No one lived in the neighbouring house. The old woman who had lived there had vacated it either towards the end of her life or shortly after it. On this basis, my friends and I decided then and there that it was haunted, and when we found the back door unlocked, we terrified ourselves and each other by playing hide and seek in it. Most of the furnishings were intact. The curtains were the colour of old blancmange and if you crouched down in the corner of her bedroom, your lungs felt as dirty and dusty as the carpet beneath you. In her kitchen was a rabbit hutch which smelled so awful none of us could bring ourselves to look inside it for fear of what we might find.

A single blurred black-and-white photograph places that afternoon in time. Without even a discussion, we did what any group of eight-year-old children did when posing for a picture in 1977: we assumed a Bruce Forsyth 'thinker' pose – forehead resting on raised left fist, back leg up. Didn't we do well? Conspicuous by his absence in that line-up is poor Paul Blunn – victim of his own terrible timing. Days before the invites were issued, Blunn had decided to taunt me on the basis that: (a) I was Greek; (b) Greece sounds a bit like grease; (c) I lived above a chip shop; and therefore, (d) this made me 'a greasy chip'. 'Greasy chip! Greasy chip!' he had repeated, until I had waited outside the school gates and – excuse the pun – battered him. Our friendship never recovered. He didn't know what he missed, but it was all explained to him in detail the following Monday. There had never been a better party. No one else had fish and chips, a room full of pinball machines and a haunted house at their disposal. For the first time, I sensed that, far from being something to be embarrassed about, living above a chip shop might actually be better than living in a plain old house.

CHAPTER 6

Thanks to *Top of the Pops*, I finally got to see what the 'When I Need You' man looked like. He was called Leo Sayer. He wore a canary-yellow V-neck jumper and his hair was a dense halo of tight curls. He looked utterly incapable of managing his day-to-day situation without the pity of grown-ups and, because of that, I totally identified with him. No less steeped in self-pity was David Soul's 'Silver Lady', a song whose protagonist bemoans the fact that his appalling behaviour has left him alternately homeless and reliant on 'seedy motels and no star hotels' and, faced with the inclement weather of Indiana, wants to be given another chance. Without a stellar chorus and an FM-friendly string arrangement that gleamed like chrome hubcaps at high noon, this loser wouldn't have stood a chance. But, of course, this loser shared an entire face with Hutch out of *Starsky & Hutch*; 1977 was David's *annus brilliant* and we were powerless to resist the overtures of a man who was too cool to open the door before getting into his car and driving off to solve some crime. That I would have taken him back like a shot reveals the flaws in my method of gauging the kindness of adults. It seemed perfectly clear to me that men in their late twenties with blond hair and blue jeans were smashing people whose presence in your life couldn't be anything other than benign.

I felt similarly well disposed towards the singer in a group called Wings. Not even the Beatles are immune to the law that the stock of any pop cultural phenomenon is at its lowest in the decade following the one in which it existed. And so, in the 1970s, it was entirely possible to go for weeks on end without hearing a Beatles song. The ten-year anniversary of *Sgt. Pepper's Lonely Hearts Club Band* went unnoticed. All of which meant that 'Mull of Kintyre' was the first Paul McCartney song I knowingly heard. Indeed, upon its release, it was a difficult song to avoid. Racing ahead of his own modest expectations, this sweet waltz-time campfire love letter to Paul's beloved Kintyre peninsula in the south-west of Scotland, lodged itself at number 1 for nine weeks.

Somehow, I sensed that its ubiquity was a source of annoyance for some people, but these were grievances I most definitely did not share. Paul's trusting eyes gazed outwards from the TV screen as he leaned on the fence outside (presumably) his farmhouse and invited me into his country idyll. By the time 'Mull of Kintyre' completed its tenancy at the top of the charts, it had surpassed 'She Loves You' to become Britain's bestselling record of all time. I took this as confirmation that 'Mull of Kintyre' actually was the best record of all time, a fact I would earnestly relay to anyone who wanted to question its demonstrable excellence. Furthermore, if anyone wanted to tell me that the Beatles were generally held to be the better group than Wings, I would have told them that this simply could not be the case, as Wings had just released the best song of all time. Then I would have asked them to tell me who the Beatles were.

Wings declined to appear on *Top of the Pops*. This meant that, over nine weeks, I was able to get to know the 'Mull of Kintyre' video in meticulous detail. The more I watched it the more Paul assumed the air of groovy sect leader: joined on the second verse by phlegmatically compliant sideman Denny Laine and then a passing parade of bagpipers. The bagpipes – perhaps the thing that most people find upsetting about 'Mull of Kintyre' – was and remains my second favourite thing about the song. I never had a problem with bagpipes. It didn't even strike me as a particularly outré sound to have on a record. After all, I was a regular viewer of *Blue Peter* and, as any regular viewer of *Blue Peter* in the late seventies will tell you, it was impossible to watch that programme for a fortnight without some fully attired Black Watch guardsman or Highland Fusilier emerging into shot with pipes at full pelt.

The stirring uplift of the pipes in 'Mull of Kintyre' was surpassed only by the bit where Paul emphasised the line 'nights when we sang like a heavenly choir' by singing it accompanied only by a 'heavenly choir' of harmonies. By this point, the video saw Paul and Denny, now with Linda McCartney and aforesaid pipers, leading a dusk procession of villagers towards a vast campfire. As holidays go, it couldn't have been more different than our trip to Greece that summer, which was spent mostly telling my parents that I really missed not being able to read my usual comics, being told to go to the nearby kiosk and seeing what comics they had there, shuffling home to try and read a Greek comic book about Donald Duck, failing miserably, rereading my *Sparky* annual for the umpteenth time and then being sent to buy an ice cream by my poor parents whose own holiday I was no doubt ruining by making no attempt to hide my boredom. Why couldn't we go on holidays that were exactly like the video to 'Mull of Kintyre' in every way?

As far as I was concerned *Top of the Pops* was a news programme. The news is where you go to learn about all the new important things that have happened, a criterion totally met by the content and format of *Top of the Pops*. The genius of it was quite simply that it showed you what was popular. Any record in the top 40 that had: (a) climbed up the chart; and (b) hadn't been on the show the week before, stood a chance of being featured. Children need certainties to help them make sense of an unfathomably complicated world, and the top 40 rundown offered some of that. Someone had gone to the trouble of counting who was buying which records over a seven-day period and reported back with a list of this week's winners.

The sense that *Top of the Pops* was really all the news you needed was underscored by the fact that the chart was able to reflect events in the wider world. In August, I learned of Elvis Presley's death by virtue of the fact that his single 'Way Down' had leapt from the lower reaches of the top 40 to the top spot. On the basis that I hadn't heard the subject discussed at home, I was immediately sure that: (a) my dad hadn't heard this piece of information; and (b) upon being told about it, he would be absolutely distraught by the news. After all, it was 1977 and he had kept his Elvis hairstyle intact. As the closing credits rolled, I decided that the best way to break it to him was to write it down for him. This being breaking news of the most cataclysmic sort, it seemed appropriate to put the piece of paper in an envelope and write the word 'IMPORTANT' on it. The only paper I knew I could get my hands on in that moment was chip paper, so I ran into the shop, removed a sheet from the pile at the counter, ran back to the sitting room and wrote down my message. Once the chip paper was folded over enough times to fit in the envelope, I solemnly walked along the corridor back to the shop and waited until the shop was empty. As he rounded up the latest batch of chips from the fryer, I advanced gingerly and handed the envelope to him.

'This is for you,' I said.

He looked down at the envelope. I think he registered from my face that this wasn't part of a game, and a look of mild trepidation spread across his own features. He removed the letter. 'ELVIS PRESLEY DIED', it said. Having felt like I should use up the whole of the chip paper, I had written the statement out in colossal letters which gave it an unintended celebratory tone. He looked at my grave expression again, and then handed over the piece of paper to my mother.

'Yes, I heard about it on the news. It's sad.'

I nodded sympathetically, although I could increasingly see that my sympathy wasn't necessarily needed. In fact, he looked like he was trying not to laugh.

Further confirmation that *Top of the Pops* could be relied upon to keep abreast of momentous events taking place in the wider world came with Neil Innes, who performed his single 'Silver Jubilee' on the show. A few years later, I would have erroneously assumed that the former Bonzo Dog Band singer's reggae paean to our reigning monarch was a gesture of ironic whimsy. But in 1977 I took it as confirmation – along with the special Duckhams Motor Oil Jubilee coin given to me by my dad and the BP commemorative stamp album Aki and I were trying to fill – that the Queen's Jubilee was indeed something to get excited about. It was an excitement I could measure merely by walking along the high street and clocking the shop displays, promotions and commemorative magazines that sat a shelf or two above *Whizzer and Chips* and *Whoopee!* in the newsagent's.

Two streets away on the Avenue, where weeks previously I had knocked on Marcus's door and broken my silence, there was a big party, which slightly blew my mind as it seemed to contravene all sorts of rules about public life that I had hitherto deemed uncontravenable. People removed tables from their houses and joined them together with the tables other people had removed from their houses. My parents took no part in the celebrations. It might have been because they didn't feel sufficiently integrated as British subjects to toast our reigning monarch's twenty-fifth year on the throne. But then again, it might also have been the fact that 7 June was a Tuesday and they literally had other fish to fry. I felt no such restraint. What was once a plain red-brick residential thoroughfare had been transformed into a kaleidoscope of plastic plates, watery squash, party hats, fairy cakes, jelly, balloons and hundreds of tiny triangular sandwiches. Buzzing from squash, jelly and the thrill of participating in my first ever conga – to Showaddywaddy's 'Under the Moon of Love' – I sprinted all the way back to the Great Western with a Union Jack flag which I thoughtfully handed over to my dad without breaking stride.

About 120 miles away on the Thames, Malcolm McLaren and Virgin Records had chartered a private boat on which the Sex Pistols were due to maximise the intended controversy around their new single 'God Save the Queen' by playing the song as they floated past Westminster Pier and the Houses of Parliament. In the event, the police closed in on the boat and sealed off the gangplanks. But because my primary news source was *Top of the Pops*, the Sex Pistols were nothing more to me than a fuzzy photograph on the chart rundown. Though widely believed to have outsold every other record in the chart that week, 'God Save the Queen' was denied the top spot by Rod Stewart's 'I Don't Want to Talk About It'.

Other punk bands were allowed onto *Top of the Pops*, but if you didn't read the music press you wouldn't have known which ones they were. The Jam came on to do 'In the City', but they all wore suits so that surely couldn't be punk. The Saints and Eddie and the Hot Rods looked like they had just walked out of the games room in our chip shop, so surely they couldn't be punk either.

I was still operating the same strict criteria of acceptability, still auditioning putative carers that might step in if the unthinkable happened. Kiki Dee returned on the back of 'Don't Go Breaking My Heart' with 'Night Hours', a song she delivered with the benign gaze of a skilled childminder. Mike Moran and Lynsey de Paul sang sat either side of opposing baby grands to sing their Eurovision runner-up 'Rock Bottom'. He was hard to read in his aviator shades, but Lynsey de Paul was a dream.

Occasionally, I would accompany my mum to a place containing dozens of women who looked just like Lynsey de Paul: cascading golden locks, confident blue eyes, perfectly applied lipstick. They could all be found in the cosmetics section at Rackhams department store, beaming their pearlescent smiles at me, every one of them poised in readiness to squirt Charlie, Tatiana or Rive Gauche at a second's notice. And though my mum would occasionally stop and extend her wrist outwards, this wasn't the purpose of her visit. Her eventual destination was the treatment rooms where she went to get her legs waxed. In order to get there, we had to walk across the ground-floor cosmetics section which was lit like the inside of a spaceship and, by a laughable distance, was the most futuristic-looking place in the entire city. These brief afternoon excursions were among the few times I saw my mother happily doing something that benefited no one other than herself. And while there was ostensibly nothing in these excursions for me, there wasn't a single aspect of them that I didn't enjoy.

Unbeknownst to me at the time, the blinding modernity of Rackhams cosmetics section had also caught the attention of a bunch of older boys. Having had their heads turned by punk, founding members of Duran Duran, Stephen Duffy and Nick Rhodes, accompanied by another local musician Dave Kusworth, would spend long afternoons in the very same Rackhams, living out their Warholian fantasies among the neon-lit displays bearing the logos of Max Factor, Chanel and Dior. With freshly applied eyeliner, rouge and lipstick, they would then ascend to the fifth floor and decant tea into tiny cups while the coutured ladies on the surrounding tables, many of them born in the Edwardian era, gazed on in bewilderment. These afternoons were immortalised in an early unreleased Duran Duran song, 'Big Store', which went, 'Woah-oh-oh / It's the biggest store in town!' Maybe their excitement at being in the Rackhams cosmetics department wasn't so different to mine.

When Lynsey de Paul appeared on *Top of the Pops*, I convinced myself that she was one of the women in Rackhams. Or maybe all of them. It didn't matter that 'Rock Bottom', a lugubrious show tune about abject failure, was more Shaftesbury Avenue than Broadway –

it still held me transfixed. Decades later, shortly after the invention of YouTube, I looked for 'Rock Bottom' and, as with so much music from that period, I felt unequipped to appraise it critically. I loved it just as much as I did in 1977. But I couldn't help noticing that the *Top of the Pops* audience didn't feel the same way. Their look of incomprehension was more akin to the reception that might have first greeted Stravinsky as he unveiled *The Rite of Spring*. And yet, in spite of all the available evidence, they seemed fine with Elkie Brooks. How could this be?

In little more than the time it took for my eyes to alight upon Elkie Brooks, my thoughts turned to the fate that might await me if she ever ended up being my mum. She was rising up the charts with a song called 'Pearl's a Singer'. I'd never heard a woman with a voice as horrible as Elkie Brooks's. I thought there was something wrong with her, a conclusion compounded by her miserable song about a woman who stands up when she plays the piano in a nightclub. In my mind, Elkie Brooks and Pearl became one and the same: women who disappeared at night, leaving me hastily scrawled instructions concerning the Findus Crispy Pancake in the otherwise empty freezer and tomorrow's breakfast – which would, in all likelihood, be another Crispy Pancake. Of course, in one sense, I was right. There was enough overlap between Pearl and Elkie Brooks to pack an emotional punch. Here she was enjoying her first top 10 hit with arguably the last truly great song ever written by Lieber and Stoller, the American songwriting pioneers – thirteen years after her debut single, a cover of Etta James's 'Something's Got a Hold on Me', and three years after the dissolution of Vinegar Joe, the band she co-fronted with Robert Palmer. There aren't many songs which contrast the evanescence of fame against the drudgery incurred in its pursuit with greater acuity. But in 1977, I couldn't understand why anyone would want to make or buy a record like that.

Neither did I have any use for the Stranglers, who landed in the sitting room while I was totally unsupervised and, in doing so, scared the shit out of me. By now I would have seen images of punk rockers (in Britain at this time, they were rarely called punks; punk was more often a pejorative term directed at young upstarts in American films) but they looked like circus entertainers compared to the group charging into 'Go Buddy Go' with a sinister brio that, in hindsight, might be partly attributable to the preceding hours spent at the BBC bar. They looked too old to be punk. They looked like the sort of people you pass in the street and your mother puts her arm around you, stares down at the pavement and doubles her walking speed. Jean-Jacques Burnel, slightly too tall for the mic, utilised his reptile neck to its full capability, leaned forward and bellowed the words to what was really just a straight-up rock 'n' roll number with a demonic intent. I could deal with that. The point at which it all got too much was when the camera cut to Dave Greenfield, jabbing at his keyboard while looking straight ahead with what seemed, beyond doubt, to be the eyes of a murderer – an effect somehow compounded by the army surplus boiler suit he had decided to wear for the occasion and, of course – bloody great clue – the fact that his band were called the *Stranglers*. Just like that, my list of phobias had got a little longer: Rod Hull and Emu; Little Jimmy Osmond; worms; biting into mushrooms; getting my hair cut; physical disfigurements; the fibreglass King Kong that stood next to a ring road in Birmingham city centre for most of the 1970s; insects; tall buildings; and now, Dave Greenfield from the Stranglers.

Sometimes it was just better to not know what people looked like. Continuing to act as a wellspring of context-free contemporary tunes, devoid of any extraneous information, Dial-a-Disc would dispense a song a day and frequently left me excited at what I had heard. Heatwave's 'Boogie Nights' was a song whose title places it at a point in the pop timeline when boogie was still a quaint byword for disco. I didn't know what nightclub 'Boogie Nights' was describing, but I dearly wanted to go there, preferably with the gang I could hear rattling out an irresistible locomotive groove on this song. It seemed like the happiest place in the world. Further emphasising a sense that the ability to boogie was as important in 1977 as the proximity of a decent Wi-Fi signal would be forty years later, along came Baccara's ravishing chart-topping Eurohit 'Yes, Sir I Can Boogie', in which the group's two singers seemed to be applying for a new joint post at the newly created Spanish High Commission of Boogie.

And, in a startlingly different way, 'Black Betty' by Ram Jam was also unlike anything I ever heard: a driving, percussive slice of blues rock that, actually, was pretty light on information save for the fact that its protagonist: (a) had a child; (b) which went wild; and (c) was based in Birmingham (only decades later did I discern that they weren't referring to the birthplace of Jeff Lynne and Jasper Carrott).

But what the song did manage to vividly impart was a sense that you could, through no fault of your own, have a child who brought embarrassment upon the family. Or, at the very least, be very different to the one you had planned to raise. Even though I was no longer mute, an awareness was growing both in me and my brother that all the things that we found exciting were culturally alien to our parents. Rightly or wrongly, it increasingly felt as though it was our destiny to disappoint them.

CHAPTER 7

I couldn't stop looking at Kenny Dalglish. He was just beautiful. His face, captured in profile, was pink and smooth. His eyes, oblivious to the cameraman's lens, were narrowed in concentration, but not so much that you couldn't see the August sun twinkling in them. Behind him, out of focus, was the crowd that had turned out to watch Liverpool's latest signing. I guess this must have been near the beginning of the game because his straight golden hair looked cleaner than any man's hair had ever looked. He looked serious and clever, more so than any other footballer in Panini's Football 78 album. The rest of them had been photographed face on, usually smiling obligingly for the Panini photographer. Birmingham City's Trevor Francis looked like David Essex's excitable younger brother; Arsenal's David O' Leary bore an expression reminiscent of Gunner Nigel 'Parky' Parkin in *It Ain't Half Hot Mum*, which suggested he was the blinking beneficiary of preferential treatment from team manager Terry Neill; Queens Park Rangers' Phil Parkes bore the faithful grin of a beloved Afghan hound. In fact, compared to Kenny Dalglish – who projected the purposeful acuity of an Icelandic sheepdog – all the other footballers looked like pets on parade.

Not all of this disparity could be put down to the thoroughbred superiority of Kenny Dalglish. Between the end of the '76–'77 season and the beginning of the '77–'78 season, Liverpool sold their star striker Kevin Keegan to FC Hamburg and urgently needed to find a replacement. Celtic's Kenny Dalglish made the move so late that he missed the usual photo calls. The picture in the Panini album must have been taken perilously close to the print deadline, hence the image of Kenny in the field of action.

It should have followed that I became a Liverpool fan. At least half the boys in my class had pledged their allegiance to Liverpool. Who you supported generally depended on your father (because in the late seventies, any interest in football came from fathers). Those whose fathers were either not present or weren't into football simply elected to support the best team. This, in turn, meant that the reigning champions (Liverpool) attracted disproportionate support from children with disrupted backgrounds or from Indian or Pakistani families where football was usually superseded by cricket.

In families where the father regularly turned out to support a particular team, my contemporaries merely inherited pre-existing allegiances. Given that I'd never had a conversation about football with my dad, I might have been expected to do as Vijay Singh had done and support Liverpool. Three years earlier, when Aki got into football, he decided to throw his weight behind Derby County – then enjoying a dominant spell of mayfly-like brevity. Now in his fifties, Aki continues to honour a commitment made when he was still in single figures. Derby County is still the first result he seeks out in the sport section.

However, to support Liverpool as a direct consequence of the nameless exhilaration I felt when I looked at my Kenny Dalglish sticker was to encourage something I didn't necessarily want to encourage. Boys in my class were openly accusing each other of being 'homos', although the lack of Kenny Dalglish swaps doing the rounds suggested that I wasn't the only eight-year-old boy in Birmingham with this strange fascination. At the end of one lesson at school, as we filed out towards the playground, I dared to engage in what I thought was some clever wordplay. We had recently been learning about the evolution of human beings, from Australopithecines to our present incarnation as *Homo sapiens.*

'Guess what!' I said to a bunch of boys who happened to be within earshot. 'I'm a homo!!'

I left a pause just long enough to allow the surprise to sink in, but not long enough to prompt the inevitable horror and ridicule. The only problem was that, when the time came to deliver the punchline, a momentary neural misfire resulted in the wrong word coming out.

'A homoSEXUAL!'

No amount of frantic back-pedalling could save me. In fact, it made it worse.

'HOMO SAPIENS! I MEANT HOMO SAPIENS!' I protested, as the chorus of jeers reverberated out of the cloakroom and back into the classroom. Slowly, the realisation was beginning to dawn upon me that it had been easier to evade unwanted attention in the years when I hadn't been speaking to anyone.

The benefits of having a fully operational fish and chip shop stuck onto the front of your house were more apparent to me than my parents. It didn't matter where you were in the house, there was a smell from which you couldn't quite get away. No amount of wiping down or disinfecting could erase the damp stink of soily potatoes coming from the storeroom, the lingering scent of vinegar on chips, even on a Sunday, or the faint aroma of the huge cubes of palm oil that my dad would lower into the fryer and wait as they shrunk into a rising pool of hot, translucent, golden liquid.

The relentless demands of running a shop while raising a young family were compounded by my dad's unwillingness to cede control of any aspect of his daily work routine. Rival chip shop owners were getting their fish delivered every other day. My dad would wake up at 5 a.m. and drive to the wholesale market in Digbeth and choose his own fish – cod, haddock and plaice that had been caught the previous day and freighted from Scotland overnight. While he was there, he would also buy fresh chickens, which were larger and tastier than the quartered, frozen pieces of chicken used by other shops. He noted with satisfaction that we were selling four times more chicken than our friends and rivals at the nearby Dolphin chip shop across the other side of Acocks Green. When it came to potatoes, we used floury, flavoursome Maris Pipers, while our competitors settled for cheaper varieties.

The shop was now turning a steady profit, but my dad was exhausted and irascible. On market days, he'd go back to bed for an hour or two and take a second nap midway through the afternoon when the shop was closed. In the autumn of 1977, he received an offer from a high-rolling Cypriot friend who had speculated and accumulated his way to four fish and chip shops across the Midlands. My dad felt it was too good an opportunity to refuse. In what felt like the blink of an eye, the shop was to be sold and we immediately had to find somewhere else to live. On a late November Monday, I left our house in the morning, knowing that I wouldn't be going back. My mother told me I'd be collected from school at the usual time, but nagging doubts remained. The speed of the move, coupled with the vagueness of her instructions, inflamed my persistent, irrational worry that my parents were trying to lose me.

I tried to put this thought to the back of my mind, but at 3 p.m., as the sun went down and the fluorescent strip lighting flickered on in the classroom, my fears started to intensify. Where did I live now? I had no idea. Who would I tell if no one turned up to collect me? And how would they get in touch with my parents? In the fifteen minutes before the bell rang, my teacher Mrs Leach – a grey-haired woman who never wore make-up and radiated a quiet, unsoppy warmth that Birmingham women born in the first half of the twentieth century did especially well – conducted the daily general knowledge quiz to see which children could have that day's leftover milk bottles from the crate delivered to every infant and junior school classroom across the country. If your hand shot up fast enough and you knew the correct answer, then the milk was yours. Afternoon milk was deemed a greater treat than morning milk on account of the fact that you had to win it, and also because having slowly come to room temperature it tasted creamier.

Usually, I would manage to secure myself a bottle two or three days in any given week. But on this day, I was preoccupied by weightier matters. The bell rang and I walked across the playground to the gate that led to the alleyway where all the parents waited. It was now dark and my worst fears were materialising before me. Every child paired off with their mother and disappeared along the narrow thoroughfare towards the glowing shop fronts of Yardley Road, the sort of bustling twilight street scene that Judith Kerr depicted in *The Tiger That Came to Tea*. With no one left by the school gate, I followed the last stragglers down to Yardley Road and, feeling the anxiety ossify into nausea, ran past the front of the school, past Mr Lovett's sports shop, past the Chocolate Box sweet shop whose signage had remained unchanged since the 1930s and past the Washland launderette, whose name was rendered in jolly-looking, different-coloured perspex letters.

Finally, I stopped and stared across the road at our shop. The same shop, with the same fittings. The same pinball machines. The same name. But standing behind the fryer were a middle-aged couple I'd never seen before. At the sole dining table, opposite the counter, clearly visible in the window were two children, eating chips. One was playing with a toy car.

What would have been the sensible course of action at this point? I could have approached the new incumbents of the Great Western Fish Bar; they would have made a couple of calls and told me to wait until someone had contacted my parents. Or I could have simply walked into the police station and told them what was up. But in my eight-year-old mind, both options were terrifying. I was staring

across the road at the sort of situation you dream about: you go home
and your house belongs to strangers who have no idea who you are.
Behind me was a police station which I was convinced contained a
pool of live sharks.

With no other acceptable option available to me, I ran back to the
alleyway next to my school with no greater plan than just to stand
there and hope for the best.

The previous year, William Osborne and I were pretty much told
that we would be friends and that was all there was to it. His brother
Edward had become Aki's best friend, and so, given that William
and I were in the same school year, this seemed like a sensible way to
proceed. I was standing at the bottom of the stairs by the door that
led to the chip shop. He was waiting there with Edward and Aki. We
were introduced. It was a fait accompli. I hadn't started talking yet,
so I wandered off with him as he told me all about a TV programme
called *Doctor Who* in which a man who wasn't really a man or a
doctor travelled through time in a phone box that didn't look like a
phone box and had 'POLICE' written on it for reasons no one ever
explained. The man who wasn't a man or a doctor was nonetheless
referred to as 'the Doctor', but never 'Doctor Who' because that
wasn't actually his name. No one knew what his name was, but that
didn't matter. Neither did it matter that the Doctor had been played
by four different actors because, actually, that was the other thing
about the Doctor: once every few years, he would inhabit a different
body. He had lots of enemies all over the universe and the most
frightening of these by far were the Daleks (although the excitement
in William's voice as he talked about the Daleks suggested that he
wasn't that scared of the Daleks).

At once envious of the way *Doctor Who* had become the immov-
able centre of William's life, I attempted to watch it too, but there
seemed to be an awful lot of running through corridors, either from

or towards monsters – corridors which abruptly ended to reveal bleak, rocky landscapes where the Doctor, played at the time by curly thespian Tom Baker, would strategise quizzically. Few close friendships are truly equal. There's almost always a dominant character. And William assumed dominance from the outset, an arrangement formalised by the fact that he was ten months older than me and for the first few months of our friendship, I hadn't said a word to him. Even when I started to speak, it was clear that he would talk and talk and talk about *Doctor Who* and I would listen. I never minded. His enthusiasm was infectious and his tone authoritative. I just hoped that one day, I could find a way in too.

When I finally arrived back from the stretch of pavement outside Acocks Green police station that day we moved house, William was waiting for me at the gate by the school. He had been sent there by his mum, who had been called by my mum, who had been delayed waiting for a removal van. We sat on the low soft sofa in his front room and watched *Graham's Gang* – a BBC children's comedy about five boys whose main motivation in life was to find ever more elaborate ways to avoid a posh girl called Mildred. An hour or so later, the Osbornes' doorbell finally rang and there, making small talk on their doorstep with William's mum, Pat Osborne, was my dad.

'Are you ready to see the new house?' he asked me.

He made no reference to what had happened at the school gates – but then why would he? At my age, he had been teasing snakes out of holes, bashing their brains out with rocks and hanging rabid dogs for cash from the local police. Nothing, really, had happened. Not by his reckoning.

'Where's our new house?' I asked him.

'It's in South Yardley,' he said.

'What's our road called?'

'Willard Road. Number 9.'

I murmured our new address to myself – '9 Willard Road, South

Yardley' – over and over again as we drove past the nearby cemetery
and reached a huge roundabout with tower blocks either side of it.
The light from the subways which fed in and out of the roundabout
gave off a soft glow. To the right, above the small covered shopping
centre was a square block of flats, perhaps about thirteen storeys
high. On the left was a remarkable rectangular curved office tower.
Horizontal stripes of smoked black windows alternated with the grey
concrete. I gripped onto the car door handle, pushed myself down
into my seat and willed my dad to keep on driving. The feeling of
disorientation, terror and panic that I felt whenever I found myself
near a tall building, especially one in a wide open space had a name
– batophobia – although I didn't know that at the time. I had recurring nightmares about being deposited in uninhabited spaces next
to metallic skyscrapers, hazarding a glance at them and feeling the
sensation that the ground was dissolving beneath me.

We took the final exit at the roundabout, turned into a small
cul-de-sac and pulled into the driveway of a small semi-detached
two-up two-down. For the first time, we had a proper front door.
The wardrobes in the upstairs bedroom smelled of lacquer and pine.
For the first time, our posh room and our sitting room were both
downstairs. It had been a long day. I had my tea and fell asleep to
the sound of a strange squeaking noise coming from the house next
door – a sound I'd go on to hear every evening during our time there.
It was our elderly next-door neighbour Bert, unscrewing his false leg.

The following morning I pulled open the curtains and, before I
could even register what my eyes had seen, my knees gave way. On
the other side of the wall at the end of our back garden, like an ogre
trying to hide behind a bollard, was the massive curved office block.
I turned away from the source of anxiety and knew I had to keep
this to myself. It seemed pointless to tell anyone, given that we had
just moved in. After all, it wasn't like we could move back out again.
For the most part, I would never enter the back garden or indeed

look out of the back windows as long as we lived there. I would also just steer clear of the roundabout or, if I was with my mum, hold her hand and stare at the pavement until we had left the area. But my Football 78 album needed filling up and soon I was going to have to confront the very thing I had been elaborately trying to avoid.

Aki returned from one of his occasional autograph-hunting sorties to Elmdon Heath. Birmingham City's training sessions there had been given an unexpected shot of glamour, thanks to the arrival of quixotic Argentinian full back Alberto Tarantini. On his way back, Aki had discovered a rogue newsagent's that traded individual Panini stickers: three of your swaps for one of their stickers. The only problem was that, in order to get there, I had to leave the house, turn left at the bottom of our road and left again alongside the length of the silver-and-black tower block and down into the subway under the busy roundabout. From here I needed to negotiate a walkway precariously suspended over the straight stretch of expressway which bypassed the roundabout. Directly below me, cars exiting and entering the Coventry Road whizzed by at 50mph, and every time they did so, a shearing noise would resound around the centre of the roundabout as you tried to make it to the second underpass, the one that would finally get you to the other side, directly underneath the second tower block. I would then have to walk another five minutes, past the Comet showroom and Key supermarket, until finally I'd reach a swap shop far more useful to me than the one staffed by Noel Edmonds.

In desperation to get my empty Panini spaces down to the final fifty (once you needed fewer than fifty stickers, you could send off for the rest and complete your collection), I would undertake this journey alone twice a week, fixing my eyes on the pavement until I saw the first subway, then crab-walking across the vertiginous suspended walkway inside the roundabout – all the time gripping the handrail. Once I had cleared that, I'd sprint to the newsagent's, making sure that I could only see exactly what I needed to see in order to avoid colliding with anyone or anything.

For a few brief months, my team had been Aston Villa. They were the better of the two Birmingham teams, but my reasons for supporting them were more to do with their strip. Almost all the other top-flight teams wore red, white or blue. The yellow and green of Norwich City was a pleasing exception – and, of course, West Ham also wore claret and blue, but it would have been perverse to support them instead of their Midlands doppelgängers.

Because this was an era when football managers still had names like Ron Saunders, Aston Villa's manager was called Ron Saunders. He was a taciturn man who patrolled the touchline with the unsmiling countenance of a parent whose approval was almost impossible to earn yet all the more tantalising a prize because of it. His captain, a hardworking midfielder called Dennis Mortimer, had a beard – unusual for the time – and was known for his penetrating runs into the heart of the opposition's defence. With his tiny head, long hair and a fringe that was maintained by no one with any formal hairdressing qualifications, Villa centre forward Brian Little looked like a cross between a mole rat and Dave Hill from Slade. He was the first footballer I ever saw launch a snot rocket – or, as they're known in rural America, a 'farmer's Kleenex'. This involved sticking a finger up one nostril, closing your mouth and blowing really hard out of the other, in the process ejecting whatever was blocking that nasal passage.

By February 1978, four months after we'd moved, my sticker album was almost complete. I had memorised the potted résumés of every player. I could tell you that Villa midfielder Ken McNaught was born in Kirkcaldy in Fife and that Alex Cropley – nicknamed Alex Crippley by fans because of his inability to play more than a few games without incurring an injury – had earned two Scottish caps.

But February 1978 was also the twentieth anniversary of the

Munich air disaster and, on *John Craven's Newsround* and even *Multi-Coloured Swap Shop*, all the talk was of the catastrophe, in which British European Airways flight 609 crashed on the third attempt to take off from the snowy runway at Munich-Riem Airport, taking the lives of seven Manchester United players in the process. The news was so shocking to me that I couldn't understand why it had taken an anniversary for me to hear about it. I processed it as though it had happened yesterday, parroting key details polished over the years by hundreds of reports and retellings, earnestly explaining the injustice of it all to anyone who cared to listen. This young team lovingly assembled by Matt Busby – the Busby Babes – hadn't even peaked, and yet they were set to win the European Cup and become English League Champions. Cornering my dad in the kitchen while he was trying to eat his breakfast, I told him about poor Duncan Edwards, who I decided had been the greatest central defender Manchester United had ever seen, cruelly taken from us on that icy runway, aged just twenty-one. It didn't matter that I had never actually seen any footage of Duncan Edwards.

Along with Matt Busby's subsequent rebuilding of the Manchester United team, leading them to the English league title in 1967 and, finally, to the European Cup in 1968, ten years after tragedy struck, this became the founding myth of my switch of allegiance to Manchester United. I spent weeks agonising over the decision, searching deep within myself to ascertain which of the two sides – Villa or United – were more deserving of my support. Like a mini Rupert Murdoch pondering which of the main two parties *The Sun* would be backing in the next general election, I treated the matter with a gravitas that stopped just short of announcing a press conference.

In the event, the lure of the Manchester United spread in my Panini album was too great to resist. Their manager, Dave Sexton, beamed benignly at me from the page, a picture of avuncular equanimity. He looked more like a caretaker than a top-flight manager. I liked that

about him. Increasingly, I seemed to warm to also-rans. First-teamers
such as Alex Forsyth, Stewart Houston, David McCreery – names
long mislaid by posterity – all looked like photo-shoot placeholders
for more famous footballers. This Manchester United were a pale
shadow of their world-beating predecessors. Their combined tally of
caps was woeful. But none of that mattered to me. In fact, it amplified
my sympathy for them. In 1978, I might have been the only person
in Britain that started supporting Manchester United out of pity.

The first people to hear my news were Aki and Edward Osborne.

'I've stopped supporting Aston Villa,' I told them. 'I love Manchester United now.'

'You can't choose to support a different team,' Aki said. 'No one
does that.'

'It's final. I've decided,' I told him, 'And, for my birthday, I'm going
to get a full Manchester United strip. And a tracksuit, if Mum lets
me.'

'What's wrong with supporting a Birmingham team?' inquired
Edward. 'When have you ever been to Manchester?'

'You don't have to be from a place to support their team,' I
informed him. 'Half the people in my class support Liverpool. And
that's just because they're winning everything. I'm supporting Man
United because of Munich.'

I self-righteously emphasised the word 'Munich' and duly regurgitated John Craven's dramatic report for the benefit of Edward, who
hadn't previously been apprised of the events of that fateful evening.
Unlike his brother William, Edward could be won around to almost
any point of view – or, at the very least, come to an accommodation
with it. Upon hearing my explanation, he shrugged, turned to Aki
and, in his lugubrious Brummie drawl, mumbled, 'Well, that's fair
enough, then, isn't it?'

Edward's arrival at our house that day was memorable for the fact
that he had dramatically changed his hairstyle. In the wake of punk,

the longest acceptable style for any teenage boy was a sort of layered feathery helmet such as that favoured by Larry Mullen Jr in the early days of U2. Throughout 1977 and the first months of 1978, this was Edward's favoured hairstyle. But on this particular day, he turned up at our house with a lovingly sculpted quiff. Through the marbled front-door windows, I hadn't recognised him at first, dressed as he was in blue jeans, white T-shirt and leather jacket. When he turned around, I saw that the word 'T-Birds' had been carefully painted onto the back. Only his ever-present thick prescription glasses prevented Edward from going full Travolta. Under his arm was a record. It was, of course, the soundtrack to *Grease*.

As I opened the door, my mum breezed past from the kitchen, commending Edward on his transformation. 'You look very fresh,' added my mother. 'Fresh' was one of her most sparingly used compliments.

Edward couldn't possibly have been more ahead of the curve. The *Grease* soundtrack had only been released that week. It would be two months before the movie landed in British cinemas, but in the meantime, 'You're the One That I Want' was racing up the charts like a roadrunner, whipping up a dust cloud of hysteria as it did so. Not that this occurred to any of us in the lead-up to or the aftermath of the film, but the video for 'You're the One That I Want' – which was actually just the bit of the movie that featured the song – acted as an enormous spoiler, depicting as it did Sandra Dee's shocking transition from virginal schoolgirl to sexy, cigarette-smoking tease in skin-tight leather trousers.

Edward had come straight from the record shop to play the record at our house. It wasn't that he didn't have a record player, more that this was frequently what you did when you bought a new record. You'd go to a friend's house and you'd listen to it together. Aki, Edward and I filed into the room at the front of the house where the window jutted slightly out from the wall, just enough for the radiogram to snugly fit there. Rather than listen to it in sequence, they dropped the needle straight onto the middle of side two where 'Greased Lightnin'' was located.

We had all heard about 'Greased Lightnin'', its infamy sealed by the presence of rude words. Only weeks previously, Aki had conducted a speculative trawl through the dictionary in our house and, to our incalculable amusement, not only discovered the word 'fart' in it, but that the definition of the word 'fart' also contained the word 'anus' – which, if anything, was even better than 'fart'. Aware of the fact that no one had really invited me to join in on this session, I placed myself at a slight remove from Aki and Edward. But we all shared the same anticipation as John Travolta explained, 'Well, this car could be systematic / Hy-y-y-dromatic / Ultramatic . . . WHY IT COULD BE GREASED LIGHTNIN'!'

We sat there, the three of us, listening to a song about customising an old car with the express purpose of attracting girls who might confer the car's qualities upon the person driving it and might furthermore deduce that these qualities make the prospect of a relationship with them seem appealing. Almost every line in 'Greased Lightnin'' contained a reference that we didn't understand. None of us knew what an overhead lifter or a four-barrel quad was. Neither did we know what a fuel injection cut-off or chrome-plated rod was. Ditto pistons, plugs, shocks. And even though we knew what a dashboard was, no one in the room on that particular Saturday could have picked out a Palomino one from an identity parade of them. However, none of that mattered, because really, the *raison d'être* of 'Greased Lightnin'' was contained in the line that contained the rude words we'd wanted to hear: 'You know that ain't no shit, we'll be getting lots of tit.'

Inevitably, my presence in the room dampened the impact of that line. With a younger child present, it was important for Aki and Edward to at least affect some seen-it-all-before worldliness while I

emitted a scandalised squeal. 'He said "shit!" And then he said "tit"!
'Shit *and* tit!' Aki and Edward rolled their eyes wearily at my crass
reaction – although their maturity didn't extend to the realisation
that there was a third rude word in the song that we had all missed.
'You know that ain't no braggin', she's a real pussy wagon', sang John
Travolta in the final verse. Clearly this was a car so brilliant even
pets would want to ride in it.

By the time the actual film started to screen in British cinemas,
'You're the One That I Want' had spent a month at number 1. There
was no question of just turning up to see it. For a fortnight, our
nearest cinema – the Warwick Bowl in Acocks Green, so called
because it also contained a bowling alley – showed morning-to-
evening screenings, every one a packed house. Finally, we got tickets
to see it on the final Sunday evening of September, during which
we would be seated apart. As we left the house, my mum pushed a
bag of Galaxy counters and a Kia-Ora orange squash drink into my
hands – the drink came in a long plastic container with square sides
and a raised area on the top, the centre of which you had to pierce
with your straw – and told me and my brother to wait outside the
Barclays Bank after the film. She and my dad, having gone on ahead
to get the car, would come and fetch us.

Between that moment and our next encounter, everything
changed. Yet to be released as a single, 'Summer Nights' opened the
film and, with its ingenious split-screen conceit, covered the entire
backstory. He saved her life – she'd nearly drowned. He showed up
splashing around. Then they made their 'true love' vows. Aged nine,
I didn't realise what a clever device that was. Instead, sitting among
strangers, I fell into the narrative that opened up in front of me and
beamed approvingly at the version of Olivia Newton-John revealed
before me. She looked so much nicer in her skirt and pastel-pink
sweater, with her straight blond hair, clutching her folder to her chest
and reminiscing about her perfect summer with Danny Zuko. By

the end of 'Summer Nights', Olivia or pre-makeover Sandra Dee – I hadn't really paused to disentangle the two from each other – had zoomed straight to number 1 in another chart: right to the top of my list of fantasy childminders. There was another list too, for poor Rizzo, the same list that featured Elkie Brooks and the Stranglers. Such was the brutal polarity of my lists.

So much more than I could truly understand happened in the space of those 110 minutes. Sung by Frankie Valli, Barry Gibb's imperious theme song intimated the excitement of a night-time world for which I might one day be brave enough to swap the cast-iron certainties on which I was so dependent. Together with the music, the cinema screen supersized emotions of which I had no first-hand experience. I had yet to experience unrequited love but, thanks to 'Hopelessly Devoted to You', the sight of Sandra Dee lamenting the humiliation meted out to her by Danny Zuko in front of their Rydell High gangs, and then the subsequent rejection, parachuted me abruptly into the sidecar of whatever emotional journey she was set to undertake from this moment on. The transition from verse to chorus might not have seemed like much on the page, but with Olivia Newton-John's vocal mainlining the all-or-nothing totality of teen love, it was a transition from incredulous shock to bawling devastation.

The credits rolled to the end and I sat in the middle of my row until the house lights went up. I didn't have a choice anyway. Everyone in my row stayed immobile in their seats, defying the impatient glare of the house lights to savour every note of Frankie Valli's theme tune. When I finally rose and advanced towards the exit, I noticed, to my consternation, that I had completely forgotten how to walk like myself. I looked down at my legs, each knee involuntarily bending down a little more than usual to create a bounce which then pushed back up into my pelvis to launch the other leg into an identical move-ment. I was walking like Danny Zuko. I attempted to correct myself, knowing that if my legs were still doing this by the time I got to the designated meeting place, my brother was going to absolutely rip the piss out of me. I needn't have worried. Looking out to my right at the furthest-away door of the Warwick Bowl, I could see that Aki was experiencing the same problem.

CHAPTER 8

My dad had been in the cinema watching *Grease* with us. This was the only time I ever went to see a film with him, and that was because he was out of work at that point. He had sold the shop for a quick profit without thinking his next step through. Suddenly, the evenings came and there he was, his incongruity of his presence in our new front room evoking those photographs of fully grown lions in the Knightsbridge penthouses of groovy young 1960s aristocrats. Happily for him, his sudden sabbatical coincided with the launch of a new ITV sitcom that would have totally passed him by had he been still frying fish at the Great Western.

Aired at 7 p.m. every Friday, *Mind Your Language* followed the exploits of an evening class attended by ten foreigners, each one from a different country. Faced with the job of teaching them English was Jeremy Brown (Barry Evans), who frequently found himself overwhelmed by the cultural differences between his students. In a half-hour sitcom there was no time for complex characterisation. Neither, in truth, would it have been expected by most of the audience who tuned in on a weekly basis to laugh at the exploits of flirtatious French au pair Danielle Favre, Pakistani Muslim Ali Nadim who says 'Squeeze me please' instead of 'Excuse me please' and Chinese embassy employee Chung Su-Lee who frequently quotes from the copy of Mao Zedong's *Little Red Book* she always carries with her. In our house, *Mind Your Language* was a game changer. And far from being upset by its depiction of shipping agency employee Max, my parents were thrilled to see a Greek character on a prime-time sitcom. They could have scarcely been more excited if it had been them on the telly.

In the opening episode, we saw Jeremy Brown begin his first class by going around the room and taking down the names of his students. The first person he approaches, pen and notebook in hand, is the Greek, who stands up and gives his full name: 'Maximilian Andrea Archimedes Papandreou.'

JEREMY: 'I'll just put you down as Max. I take it you're Greek?'
MAX: 'Is right! From Athens!'
JEREMY: 'And what is your job?'
MAX: 'I wolk with sheeps.'
JEREMY: 'You walk with sheeps?'
[MAX nods enthusiastically]
JEREMY: 'You're a shepherd? You work on a farm?'
MAX: 'Ah, no no. Not farm.'
JEREMY: 'But you just said you work with sheep.'
MAX: 'No no no no! Ships! Big ships!'
    [Max pulls down an imaginary cord and makes a sound like
    a foghorn]
JEREMY: 'Ships!'
MAX: 'Yess! Ships! Tonkers!'
JEREMY: 'Tonkers?! *Tankers!*'

Jeremy then moves over to the Italian student and Max's arch rival in the affections for the French au pair Danielle.

JEREMY: 'And what's your name?'
GIOVANNI: 'Giovanni Cupello. Italian!'
JEREMY: 'Where do you work?'

GIOVANNI: 'I work in *ristoranti de populi*!'

JEREMY: 'A waiter?'

GIOVANNI: 'No! Not a waiter! A cookatter!'

JEREMY: 'A cookatter?'

GIOVANNI: 'Si! I cookatter ravioli! I cookatter spaghetti! I cookatter lasagna! I cookatter *everything*!'

A few minutes later, we see Max and Giovanni squabbling over who gets to sit next to Danielle. All the time, Danielle is staring straight ahead into a compact mirror as she fixes her hair.

GIOVANNI: 'Look! I'm a gonna sit here!'

MAX: 'No! Issa me who's gonna be sitting here!'

GIOVANNI: 'But before, you sit over there!'

MAX: 'And before you were sit-a-over there!'

GIOVANNI: 'You take-a-da mickey!'

MAX: 'Who, me?'

GIOVANNI: 'You go back sit where you were before!'

MAX: 'No, I sit-a-here!'

[Giovanni forcefully places his hand on the back of the chair]

GIOVANNI: 'You NOT sit here!'

[Max squares up to Giovanni]

MAX: 'Who is gonna be stopping me?'

GIOVANNI [pointing a finger at his own puffed-out chest]: 'Me! Yourself? You think-a-you're tough? [removes his jacket] Come out-a-side!'

MAX [opportunistically eyeing up Danielle as he does so]: 'Hokay!'

[Jeremy walks back into the room]

JEREMY: 'Where are you going?'

GIOVANNI: 'We go outside to 'av-a-da punch-down!'

JEREMY: 'You mean a punch-up?'

MAX: 'I'm going to, ah, how you say . . . knock his bloody block off!'

GIOVANNI [jabbing his finger at Max]: 'We see whose bloody blocker is a knockered off!'

Mind Your Language had my parents at the mere utterance of Max's full name. With the delivery of the line, 'We see whose bloody blocker is a knockered off!' my dad was actually crying with laughter. It was the only time I ever saw him cry during my entire childhood. If you had sat my parents down and tried to explain to them that this crude stereotyping – a Mr Men-style approach of reducing each nationality to a single trait – did their heritage and culture a disservice, they would have taken far more offence at your insinuation than anything on *Mind Your Language*. If you'd suggested to them that the show's creator Vince Powell – whose previous successes included *Love Thy Neighbour*, a sitcom about what happens when a black family moves in next door to a white family – was a racist, their response would have been one of tetchy bafflement. Powell was at least acknowledging the existence of other nationalities in the UK. For my parents, it was enough to see a version of themselves on a British prime-time TV show, and to know that up to eighteen million viewers a week were also seeing a version of them on a British prime-time TV show.

As it happens, the sort of suspicion with which *Love Thy Neighbour*'s Eddie Booth regards his new West Indian neighbours Bill and Barbie wasn't at all dissimilar to that which greeted us in our new house. On the day he learned that his new neighbours at Willard Road were foreign, Bert Chance responded with a brief explanation of his position, in which he informed us that he didn't want to live next door to people like us. In the meantime, he continued, the best thing we could do was to stay out of his way. But not before he received answers to a couple of pressing questions. Pointing to my dad's Chrysler Sunbeam, Bert wanted to know why English people who had been living here for years and years were driving around in old cars, and yet here was my dad parking his brand-new Sunbeam outside our brand-new house. How did you answer a question like that?

'I work hard,' my dad told Bert. 'How else do you think I can afford it?'

Bert shook his head and limped back indoors. My mum, who kept none of this from us, told us to be respectful around him. He had fought in both wars and lost his wife some years previously, and sometimes old people can get a bit angry about the way the world has treated them.

About a month later, on Christmas Day, we sat down to eat. As usual, my mother's knack of having the turkey ready just as the Christmas edition of *Top of the Pops* was about to start meant that, far from being grateful, Aki and I reacted to the news that dinner was ready as though we had just been asked to cook it ourselves.

In the normal course of events, we would have inhaled the entire thing in the time it took for Showaddywaddy to finish their lacklustre number 2 hit 'You Got What It Takes', racing into the front room in time for Deniece Williams to sing the far superior 'Free'. On this occasion, however, my mum had other plans for us. She prepared a fifth plate, ensuring that it contained a bit of everything: turkey, mash, roast potatoes, sprouts, carrots and, of course, stuffing. Not your classic pork and sage stuffing, but the sort favoured by Greeks: small pieces of turkey liver fried together with chopped onions and pine nuts, mixed together and fried with rice. She placed it onto a tray, along with a jug of gravy (Bisto granules – in 1978, the idea that anyone actually made gravy from scratch was as outlandish as the notion that one day, three-metre stretches of supermarket aisle might be devoted to olive oil).

'I want you to knock on Bert's door and give this to him,' she said.

Aki and I did as we were told.

We could hear Bert advancing nearer every time the metal bracket of his prosthetic lower leg – which jutted out from the heel of his shoe and into the back of his knee – hit the floor.

'Merry Christmas,' I said nervously, after he undid various chains and locks, and finally opened the door. 'This is from my mum.'

We followed him into his small lean-to kitchen as he removed from the hob a small pan which we could see contained some tinned stew. He then turned to receive the plate, weeping as he did so. Not just a few tears, but pendulous drops that ran off his cheekbones and into the saucepan he was still holding.

Frozen in shock at his response, Aki and I awaited further instruction. Neither of us had a clue what we were supposed to say to the sobbing pensioner standing in front of us. We made it back to the house in time to catch the end of 'Free', still startled by what had just happened. Of course, we still wanted to watch the rest of *Top of the Pops*, but when our mother told us to sit down we didn't have the heart to complain. Perspective abruptly restored, we reverentially slowed down to half our usual eating speed.

In the next room, I could hear 'The Floral Dance' by the Brighouse and Rastrick Brass Band – a noise made entirely by humans briefly stepping outside of their own interior worlds in order to be part of something far greater than their constituent parts. A collective rapture powered by the spirit and sinew of people simply trying their best. It sounded then, as it does now, like Christmas itself.

My dad's enforced sabbatical throughout the first half of 1978 gave my parents options that seemed to increase rather than reduce the tension between them. He had optimistically imagined that, for a while, the interest accrued from the sale of the Great Western might be enough to support us. But it didn't even come close. Other chip shop owners were driving around in Mercedes and BMWs, living in huge houses. They could barely afford these things, but they had them.

By contrast, my dad was set on a course of delayed gratification. The Chrysler Sunbeam was a hatchback, which meant that once he was up and running with a new shop, he'd have enough space for all the fish and chickens from the market. The Mercedes and the swimming pool were the proverbial pot of gold. And the rainbow, of course, ended somewhere just south of the United Nations 'Green Line' which separated the Turkish-occupied northern half of his native island from the Greek Cypriot part. If it all seemed like a bit of a struggle at times, he assured my mum that things would be different when we finally left Acocks Green behind. Instead of cleaning the house, she could employ a cleaner. She could learn to drive, have a car of her own, drive it to the most upscale boutiques and buy whatever took her fancy.

The thing about rainbows, of course, is that they're gone almost as soon as they arrive. Every month a new venture failed to materialise was another month that saw us eating into our savings. The faster they eroded, the more distant the dream of moving back to Cyprus became. My dad would go and see friends who ran other chip shops, to see if anyone had heard of any potential business opportunities. The best way to add value to a shop was to find a place that had been closed for years – preferably one whose owner was desperate to sell – and build it up from scratch. But such places were hard to come by.

Occasionally, he would drop into a social club in Erdington, five miles away, where all the membership you needed was possession of a Cypriot accent. Along with traditional Sunday sorties to the Greek church in the city centre, this was the best place to scope out possible new business opportunities. There was a pool table and a kitchen in which a black-clad Cypriot *yiayia* (a grandmother-type figure) would prepare traditional culinary staples such as *kleftiko*, *afelia* and *fasolakia*. The older sections of the clientele – the Cypriots who had moved here in the early fifties – would wear a pinstripe suit and white shirt, *mangas*-style – and drink cognac while playing backgammon or cards. Some played with *komboloia* (worry beads). Others sat on their own reading one of the Greek newspapers that lay scattered around the place. My dad would take me on occasion, introducing me to some of his friends before allowing me to slope off into a corner and read a comic. He never joined in with the card games or the backgammon, but he drank cognac and smoked with impunity. After my patience was exhausted and I'd asked, 'When are we going home?' one too many times, he'd accept defeat, say his goodbyes and we'd get back into the car. I don't know which bit of his brain the alcohol reached, but it didn't seem to be one that affected his driving.

Then again, I wasn't paying that much attention. In April, keen to stop me from fiddling with his prized Uher reel-to-reel tape recorder, my dad handed me a bright-red BASF C90 cassette and directed me to the radio cassette recorder that usually sat next to my mum's knitting machine. He pointed to the tuning dial and asked me to find a song I liked. We arrived at 'With a Little Luck' by Wings, a sweet, simple song about counting your blessings in an uncertain world, a song which, in the eyes of his critics, confirmed Paul McCartney's transformation from sonic innovator to purveyor of middling, middle-aged, middle-of-the-road dreck. But I had never met any of Paul McCartney's critics, less still heard what they had to say about him.

As instructed, I pressed 'play' and 'record' at the same time and then waited until the end of the song. My dad pushed down on the 'rewind' button and – lo! – there was my first recording. 'The willow turns its back on inclement weather,' sang Paul, 'And if he can do it / We can do it / Just you and me.' I pictured Paul dispensing his Zen reassurances through the single speaker of the Binatone machine, imagining what it would be like to have him as a dad instead of the one in front of me. Whatever my dad's shortcomings, he didn't deserve to be pitted against Paul McCartney, lead singer of Wings and owner of a Scottish promontory – certainly not in such a moment of generosity.

Presented with a magical recording machine, the scale and urgency of the job that awaited me was more than I could take in. I wrote down a list of the best songs of all time. Brotherhood of Man, ABBA and Kiki Dee jostled for supremacy at the top, with Olivia Newton-John and Wings snapping at their heels. Then I resolved to stay near the radio like a Labrador waiting for its owner to return from work. Halfway through my first encounter with the Motors' 'Airport', I was already ruing my decision not to press 'play' and 'record'. By the next time, a couple of hours later, I had already used up the entire tape. With the song's plaintive synthesiser hook scorched into my brain, I wandered into the empty posh room, increasingly aware that I was about to do something that might get me into trouble. Stopping at my dad's teak-effect cassette carousel, I pulled each tape out individually and attempted to work out which one he was least likely to miss. There was an Agfa one without an insert and, on the label, something written in Greek in sun-faded ink.

It's a lyrical device so perfect that I suspect not even the Motors stopped to think about how clever they had been on the day they came up with 'Airport'. I bet the entire thing poured forth in one sad splurge of inspiration. It's almost certain that no one in the Motors exclaimed, 'I'll write a song about how much unhappiness airports cause, and in this song, my departing lover will be referred to in the third person, making her seem like an unwitting accessory to the machinations of the accused – the accused, in this case, being not a person but a vast complex of runways and buildings for the take-off, landing, and maintenance of civil aircraft, with facilities for passengers.' The story was sad enough anyway, but with such an anxious, accelerating turnover of minor chords hastening to such a distressing denouement – 'I help her with her baggage for her baggage is so heavy / I hear the plane is ready by the gateway / To take my love away' – 'Airport' was as close as I had come to finding a song emotionally unprocessable. After recording the entire song, I played the tape throughout all of June, conflating its lyrical content with my existing separation anxieties.

To my immense relief, my dad's discovery that I had recorded over a 1970 radio broadcast of a concert by Mikis Theodorakis resulted in absolutely no punishment. Instead, he bought me a pack of ten TDK cassettes. The reasons for this gift were twofold. A friend of his had alerted him to a vacant chip shop that required a quick sale. Within a week of hearing about it, my dad's offer had been accepted. His magnanimity was an expression of: (a) relief; and (b) concern that his absence from the house would imperil the rest of the tapes on his carousel.

In fact, his high spirits were an attempt to put a brave face on what was a risk that might undo all the work my parents had put into the first shop. They had no sure way of knowing that they had what it would take to turn the new one into a profitable business. This element of chance was reflected in the amount my parents paid for it – a knockdown £5,000. It was also rather unusual. It stood on its own at the end of a small post-war parade of shops and had no signage on it anywhere. However, its curious shape – almost the same as that of the old twelve-sided three-pence coin – meant that the locals referred to it as the Threepennybit. From across the road at night, this geometrically perfect construction radiated a golden glow. Standing there on its own, it looked like the friendliest UFO in the universe had chosen to make an overnight stop in West Bromwich.

For all my mother's youthful dreams of becoming an architect, the aesthetic qualities of the Threepennybit offered scant mitigation when set against all the other challenges it presented. For a start, it was fourteen miles away from our new house, which meant that she would have to travel with my dad in the mornings and prepare everything for lunchtime before embarking on a three-bus, one-and-a-half-hour journey across the West Midlands in time to collect me from school, make dinner for me and Aki and do all the other things that mums had to do in 1978. Then there was the frantic three-week period of preparation which involved scrubbing down all the surfaces, replacing tiles, sealing cracks, repainting walls, replacing faulty fryers and reconnecting the gas and electricity. Every week that the shop wasn't open was a week of wasted income, which was why I hardly saw her during that time.

The one day I would get her all to myself was Saturday. While I immersed myself in the sensory overload of that day's comics, *Multi-Coloured Swap Shop* and *Football Focus*, she'd blitz through the housework in time for 1 p.m. After that, Saturday television descended into a torpor of interminable horse racing and black-and-white films. So I'd put my shoes on and accompany her to Key supermarket, gripping her hand extra-tightly as we walked past the wavy tower and into the subway.

It was on one of these shopping trips that the nature of our relationship entered a new phase. She took her purse out of her handbag and showed me the contents. Every Friday evening, my dad would hand over her weekly shopping allowance – a total of £70, which had to cover shopping for food, clothes and utility bills. Immediately she would set aside £30 for the bills. In her purse was the remaining £40, which had to cover the cost of everything else.

I was no longer just her son. I was now her confidant. As she pushed the trolley up and down each aisle, she told me what she was buying and what she would be using it for. A chicken for today's *avgolemoni* soup, a traditional Greek broth made with chicken, rice, lemon juice and eggs, the latter to be added gradually and gently so that they don't solidify and break off into small bits. A lamb shoulder for Sunday. Minced beef for her Greek version of a Bolognese which, although perfectly nice, featured pureed peppers and wasn't very much like anything you'd find on the menu of an Italian restaurant.

I think making Greek food fed into some sense of pride that she was trying to partition off – something that predated what must have increasingly felt to her like a denouement of her own making. If she couldn't go back to Athens, at least she could try and serve it up on a plate. Apart from the occasional deep-fried chicken breast, we rarely ate food from the shop. *Moussaka*, *dolmades* and *keftedes* always took precedence over pies, saveloys and cod. Even when I had chips, my mum would prepare them *spitiko* (home) style, which meant parboiling them, then finishing them off in a mixture of vegetable and olive oil.

Supplementing this roll call of 'proper' meals were tins of beans and hoops which would naturally be served on toast. We sometimes looked forward to those meals more than the Greek dishes that took longer to prepare. The one we dreaded most was *louvi*, a Cypriot dish comprised of black-eyed beans and chard in olive oil, with flat parsley and onions chopped into it; the resulting onion fumes billowing off my dad proved an insurmountable deterrent. *Louvi* was one of several dishes cooked for my dad by his mother, that my mum then learned to make for him.

Every time she served it, the same ritual would ensue. He'd eat a couple of forkfuls and then he would tell her how today's effort compared to the way his mother or sister used to make it. In those moments, she hated him and he knew it. In later years as she got more combative, she would tell him he was welcome to go back to Cyprus and move in with his sister so he could eat her *louvi* every day. Other times, she would turn to me and make sure I had witnessed the exchange, occasionally adding something along the lines of, 'See how your father appreciates my cooking?' The casual, almost playful disingenuity of his replies merely served to entrench her animosity. These would range from, 'Well, you must surely understand no one could ever make it like my mother!' to specific criticisms centred around certain ingredients, be it not enough onions in the *stifado* or that the lamb had been left in the oven too long. His ability to push her buttons just slightly short of outright violence was something he finessed to a fine, sometimes dark art over the years.

Sometimes, however, he would miscalculate. And when that happened, it didn't matter where you were in the house, you knew about it. One May afternoon that year, I was in the posh room at the front, crouched down in front of the Binatone radio-cassette player when all hell broke loose in the kitchen. I'm not sure how long they had been shouting at each other. After a three-week reign, the Motors had now been supplanted in my affections by Raffaella Carrà's 'Do It, Do It Again', a frantic Latin celebration of sensual rapacity which she performed on *Top of the Pops* wearing a gold body stocking. Only as it reached its crescendo did I hear my distressed mum hurling a plate onto the kitchen floor right at my dad's feet. The crying mother; the impassive patriarch; the shards of crockery in an otherwise spotless kitchen; the incongruously euphoric Latin soundtrack. It was the full Pedro Almodóvar bingo card. A few days later, my dad exchanged contracts on the Threepennybit. It couldn't come soon enough. Another week of his unbidden reviews and we would have been eating off napkins.

CHAPTER 9

We were more of a family during the summer holidays than we had been for a long time. Almost every morning, we'd all leave the house at around 8 a.m., my brother and I sitting in the back as our car crawled through the outskirts of Birmingham city centre towards the shop in West Bromwich. Here we'd be given some pocket money and would head off to the vast green expanse of Sandwell Valley with a football and pass it between us until someone absorbed us into their game. If we got hungry, we'd head back for chips, sometimes with two or three new friends we'd made during that morning's football match, then return to while away a couple of hours on the pitch and putt course. On those morning drives to West Bromwich, the tuning dial was fixed on Radio 1, my dad listening out for traffic updates and us absorbing whatever Dave Lee Travis – whose brief tenure on the *Breakfast Show* earned him the nickname the Hairy Cornflake – chose to play that morning. That whole summer, he seemed hell-bent on a solo mission to make Billy Joel's 'Movin' Out (Anthony's Song)' a hit. In the end, his persistence may have had the opposite effect. The song stalled at number 35, but that didn't stop DLT from persisting with it throughout the summer.

Twenty-eight years later, I found myself in another part of Birmingham – Billy Joel's dressing room at the NEC, to be precise – telling my idol all about the effect his song had on me that summer. We were both significantly different people to our 1978 selves. He

was a bald, portly fifty-seven-year-old multimillionaire whose love
of yachts had long since supplanted any desire to record new music,
and I was no longer nine. Having maintained professional decorum
throughout the interview I was there to conduct, something snapped.
I told him all about the parallels between the characters in the song
and my own family: similarities that were by no means obvious,
yet impossible to miss. It's a song about immigrants working long,
soul-sapping hours in a shop so that they can get on in life and
provide a surer future for their children than the one they had. In
Joel's lyrics, Anthony is Italian and he works in his parents' grocery
store in New York. We were Greek and we had a fish and chip shop
in the Black Country. But every morning, the story of Anthony and
the other characters in the song dyed itself a little more indelibly into
my psyche: the tension between the verses, which detail the travails
of its protagonists, and the chorus, in which Anthony decides that
he doesn't want to play that game. For years, I thought the final verse
about Sergeant O'Leary who works a second job for Mr Cacciatore
said that 'he can't fry with a broken back / And he used to demolish
the Fenders'. I imagined that Sergeant O'Leary was once in a rock
'n' roll band, occasionally smashing up a guitar, and now he was
reduced to standing in front of a fryer, just like my dad. A few years
later, I found out what the real lyrics were:

He's tradin' in his Chevy for a Cadillac
You oughta know by now
And if he can't drive
With a broken back
At least he can polish the fenders.

The real verse is even better – a perfectly poignant sketch of what
remains once work has taken away your best years. But it was too late.
The image of Sergeant O'Leary, rounding up chips from a hot fryer

while placing his right hand on his failing spine became inextricably intertwined with my dad.

Fast-forward to 2006 and there I was backstage with the man who wrote 'Movin' Out', telling him all of this. I thought he might be touched to learn that his song had such a profound effect on such a young listener so many thousands of miles away. However, I realised halfway through, by his polite but slightly absent smile, that this was a story that a thousand Billy Joel fans had told him over the years. Well, of course it was. That's why the song resonated. It was about all those people.

'Movin' Out' also touched on my parents' diverging views about their situation. My mother saw Aki and me assimilating into our respective schools and gradually came to accept that the optimal moment of escape had come and gone. Other émigrés had reached the same conclusion. Some Sundays, we'd visit their houses and feel a frisson of excitement as a pimped-up, cigar-chewing bizarro-world version of my dad came to the door wearing identical tinted steel-rimmed glasses to those of cockney comic, *Runaround* host and future Frank Butcher, Mike Reid. For Aki and me, the sequence of events was reassuringly predictable. The adults would ruffle our hair and ask us if we liked ice cream. We'd nod excitably and be directed to a fridge-freezer with a special button that dispensed cold water. In the freezer would be Cornettos in all three flavours, although it would be several years before I felt brave enough to try the mint.

We didn't just feel poor when we went to these houses. We felt physically small. They had forecourts for driveways and lawnmowers with steering wheels. The ceilings were high, the three-piece suites were vast, and the distance between them and the TV necessitated a short walk. The TV would be less like a TV than a small cinema attached to wall-mounted speakers which, on one visit, made Nelson Riddle's opening theme to *El Dorado* sound like the most stirring piece of music ever recorded. I hated westerns, but on these televisions, everything was gripping. Peter Fenn's organ playing on teatime quiz show *Sale of the Century* was transformed into something Bach might have knocked up for people who found Toccata and Fugue in D minor a little too vanilla. *Songs of Praise* appeared to be transmitting live from heaven itself. And the stand-alone broadcast in which Derek Nimmo issued an appeal on behalf of Sherborne Abbey which needed £200,000 to repair its roofs and protect its fan vaults sounded like a desolate supplication issued from the precipice of irreversible devastation.

Everyone who lived in these houses seemed happy. There were no visible signs of struggle here: certainly not in the showboating patriarch or in their slick, mini-me sons seated at the edge of their bunk beds, playing *Pong* on consoles attached to televisions in their actual bedrooms. And crucially, not in those children's mothers – women of leisure with walk-in wardrobes who had never emptied a sack of potatoes into a peeler in all their lives, and furthermore would file for divorce if you dared suggest such a thing. Was my mother envious of them? She gazed at women who lacked the education and ambition that she had left home to fulfil. Here they were, enjoying a level of comfort that had been denied to her. Yes, I imagine she was envious.

Her entire life had been a thirty-eight-year exercise in delayed gratification. She was a war baby, born in 1942, four days before the Axis powers of Germany, Italy and Bulgaria officially took Athens. The name with which she was born, Victoria Kalavas, tells you something about what her mother, Panayioula Kolletis, wanted and what she had to settle for. With its connotations of empire and antiquity, you didn't call your daughter Victoria with any expectation that they might not get on in life. By contrast, the surname Panayioula took when she married Kostas Kalavas belonged far more to the dry dirt tracks of rural nineteenth-century Cyprus than twentieth-century Athens. No one knows whether Panayioula ever loved Kostas, because in all likelihood no one ever asked her. Fairy tales were lovely, but that's all they were. Marriage was about fulfilling your biological destiny – and if you were lucky, you might get to do so with someone you actually liked. But by 1930, Panayioula was in her mid-thirties and still living at the family home in Davleia, approximately 150 kilometres north-west of Athens. The stigma of encroaching spinsterhood and the continuing burden on her parents meant that when a painter and decorator called Kostas cycled into view with his buckets and brushes, it wasn't just work he attracted.

There were virtually no cars and few train stations in rural early twentieth-century Greece. A new face was headline news. And Kostas had a better story than most. He had grown up on the streets of rural Nicosia after, aged six, he had lost both of his parents in quick succession. He survived for eight years on the kindness of nearby villagers, until aged fourteen, he signed up to fight in the First World War. After four years of active service, he was still a teenager. Freshly demobbed, he took his few belongings with him and lived a peripatetic existence, until the search for casual work brought him to the house of the Kolletis family. Within a year, he and my maternal grandmother had married and moved to Nea Kifisia in Athens because he had passed through there once and liked the look of it. They found a small patch of land and Kostas built a small dwelling on it, to which rooms were added as and when they were needed. They had three girls, and the youngest of them was my mum.

By the time the Second World War began, the house had expanded to take in a *kafenio* at the front, which served Greek coffee (the same sweet, tarry drink, served in small cups, that Turks call Turkish coffee) and wine. Kostas also had a cellar built for the wine. None of the other houses in Nea Kifisia had cellars. This meant that every time the air raid sirens sounded to warn against incoming German bombers, everyone would descend upon the Kalavas house and squeeze into whatever windowless space was available between the wine barrels. Though it was possible to hide from air strikes, there was no means of protection from the Germans when they finally advanced on foot through Nea Kifisia, which – in terrifying numbers – they did less than a month after my mum was born.

Embedded in several acres of generously irrigated terraces, the house across the road from my grandparents' stone dwelling was owned by the Christodolous – a fiercely religious family of property tycoons who also owned several other houses across Nea Kifisia. When the Germans arrived, they took one look at the Christodolous' house, with its whitewashed verandahs, gleaming colonnades, lovingly tended vines and lush meadows and decided that this would make a nice base for them. Faced with no survivable alternative, the Christodolous fled to one of their other residences.

Panayioula and Kostas would peer through the slats in their blinds wondering what plans their new German neighbours had in store for them. All over Europe, people must have been having the same nightmare: what would you do if there was a knock on the door and there was a Nazi waiting for you? After three days of uncertainty and fear, the reality, when it happened, was only slightly mitigated by the fact that this Nazi was holding a pile of dirty washing. Neither he nor my grandmother spoke the other's language, but it wasn't difficult to discern what they wanted her to do with it – or, indeed, what they would do to her if she refused. If a German soldier wanted you to wash their clothes that at least meant you were useful enough to live. In relative terms, she was doing well from this arrangement. Besides, it wasn't as if they all lacked compassion. On the collection days, which alternated with the drop-off days, one of the German soldiers would bring a loaf of bread with him and hand it over. Decades later, she would still talk about him as though he were an angel in disguise. It turns out that you never forget the kindness of a Nazi.

By the time Axis forces were finally sent into retreat, Athens was mad with hunger. British Army vehicles drove through the streets of Nea Kifisia, each manned by two officers: one to drive and the other to throw loaves of bread at waiting children – 'both brown and white bread,' my mum recalled, 'The brown you had because it was good for you, and the white you ate as though it were the most delicious cake you had ever tasted.' There was no money. Kostas had a job painting and decorating for the British Army, but in 1946, they stopped employing locals so that British soldiers could do the same work instead. Panayioula sold her jewellery and best hand-crocheted blankets and bought a goat with the proceeds.

Were it not for that goat, the eggs from the few chickens they had and the cod liver oil vouchers provided by the British government, my mother might not have survived. For the first four or five years of her life, she was unable to stand unsupported. Many of her earliest memories centre around foraging, something she was encouraged to do on account of the fact that her tiny frame allowed her to sneak under the fences of bigger, wealthier houses and come back with whatever was edible. By thirteen, my mother was foraging to order. From the house across the road, she would run around the perimeter, shielded by pine trees, to a field at the back where she found artichokes, grapes and wood for the hearth. Further along, near the foot of a mountain, there were asparagus shoots, and in the woods she found blackberries. There was also a river, where freshwater crabs could be found.

She made it sound so idyllic when she described it, especially the secret sorties to spots that no one else knew about: an oregano bush near someone's garden, underneath which you would always find freshly laid eggs. There were also mushrooms. The ones she liked the best were white with spots of beige, looked like hares' ears, and always grew near rocks. I think these years left her believing that she was capable of anything. But I never really got to see that side of her.

The more spoils she returned with, the more favour she found with her father who instilled terror throughout the rest of the house. Both of my mother's sisters dealt with his mood swings in different ways. The oldest, Anna, sought sanctuary in books, and the middle sister Rosa kept herself to herself. Any self-belief that might have been there was filleted out of her. In every family photograph that features her, she looks like a startled woodland creature, paralysed by the light – so detached from her own sense of agency that she would never move away from home.

Kostas made no attempt to conceal the preferential treatment he meted out to my mother, and from an early age she understood her crucial role in the family dynamic. In helping bring food back to the house, she was relieving pressure from her mother. In keeping Kostas sweet, she could act as an intermediary between him and her sisters. 'I wasn't scared of him,' she told me, 'But the others were. So whatever they wanted from him, they would make me go and get it.'

And when she wasn't pulling up buckets from wells or foraging for supper, she drew houses. She drew the house that she thought she might live in one day, and then when she thought of a better house, she would draw that one too. She learned the basics of draughtsmanship at school and started looking to see if she might get a job in an architect's office. She was eighteen when she received a letter from her bookworm sister Anna, who had moved to Cyprus and got a job as a schoolteacher in the tiny village of Saint Ermolaos. Having failed to make any friends there, lonely Anna offered to send my mum a free ticket to join her.

My mother arrived a fortnight later and could see straight away why Anna felt so isolated. 'Xero' was how she described Saint Ermolaos – a word whose meaning in this context sits somewhere between 'dry' and 'stale'. It was an archetypical sleepy town, powered almost entirely by the turbine of human chatter. In a place where the need to gossip was perpetually frustrated by the lack of day-to-day action, tension needed to be built into the infrastructure. And my mother's arrival in Saint Ermolaos satisfied that need. No one told her that all the coffee shops in the village were divided along political lines.

One day, she arranged to meet a distant relative in one of the left-wing cafés, and that was all it took for word to spread everywhere: the teacher's sister was a communist!

A couple of days later, she was invited to another coffee shop by a friend. Within hours, she had strangers in the street asking her why she had sat in the right-wing 'traitor café'. Her accidentally acquired reputation as a troublemaker was made worse when she attempted to deal with an infestation of flies at her sister's house. While Anna was teaching at school, my mum traced the problem to a crack in the wall over which Anna had placed a framed picture of then-leader Archbishop Makarios – who, just a year previously, had been swept to power as the first ever president of the Republic of Cyprus. She carefully removed the picture from the wall and, proceeding to fumigate the place, left it outside along with several more of her sister's belongings. The picture was placed against the chicken coop, which attracted the attention of a passer-by. Within hours, she had cemented her infamy. Victoria Paphides was The Woman Who Put Makarios Out With The Chickens. You just didn't do that to Archbishop Makarios.

Another person who had noticed her was my dad, who had been sitting in the *syllogos* on that very first occasion she walked through the door. He wanted to know her better, and his car gave him the perfect pretext. She sometimes visited friends in Kyrenia. Oh really? Well, *he* sometimes visited friends in Kyrenia too. Did she want a lift? He could drop her off in the morning, then visit his own friends, and drive her back at night. Landing a new job in an architect's office twice as far away in Nicosia, she quickly made herself indispensable. Her boss's elderly parents lived in an apartment that adjoined the studio and she regularly went in to see them, bearing cakes.

She was enjoying her work, and was certainly not looking for a partner just yet. But my dad was persistent. Sometimes she would hear the engine of his swish Austin A40 Somerset running as she was packing up to go home. Leaning against the chassis with flowers picked from a nearby field and *that* hair, there were only so many times she could turn down the offer of a lift. He took her home to visit his mother, a tall, unsmiling woman with distinctly Indo-European features, who dismissed my mother on the basis of her 'work-shy' hands. Her disapproval merely entrenched my dad's conviction that Victoria was the woman for him.

He was a contrarian. He had always been that way. Argumentative as a child, rebellious by nature. His mother wanted him to marry someone with at least some money in the bank (as well as the visibly hardworking hands that surely ran contrary to that requirement); my mum was barely getting by. Her opposition appealed to the principled, fiery self-image my dad was hell-bent on cultivating – and to which his brilliant hair was integral. Even my mother, who spent over five decades ruing her decision to leave Athens for Cyprus, freely admitted that my father was the most eligible bachelor in the village. 'Girls were desperate to be introduced to him. Girls with money, girls with houses.' And, no doubt, my dad's defiance in the face of his mother's disapproval helped to finish what the flowers, the car and the hair had already started. Eighteen months into their courtship, they decided to marry and move away together.

She didn't want to live in my father's village and my dad didn't fancy Athens. They were making decisions that would determine the entire course of their lives on the flimsiest of pretexts. But then, I don't think that was too unusual in those days. I've spent more hours in total standing in front of the chiller cabinet in Marks & Spencer choosing my dinner than my parents did deciding where to emigrate.

This is how they went about their decision:

Post McCarthyism, America was problematic for a young communist in 1963.

A British major at the offices of the Ministry of the Interior where my dad was employed as a civil servant befriended him and said, 'If you ever decide to go to England, I can give you the address of my brother-in-law, who works as a manager at the Rover plant in Longbridge. You go there and he'll help you.'

And that was that. The address was in Birmingham, so that's where they decided to head. My mum gave up her job, briefly returned to Athens to break the news to her parents and then left for Piraeus, where she had arranged to meet my dad as he alighted the ferry from Cyprus. Once reunited, they boarded the ship to Venice. From there, they got a train to Calais, where my dad recalls seeing John F. Kennedy's face on all the newspapers in a French kiosk and having another waiting passenger explain to him that the American president had been assassinated the day before.

They moved their six suitcases onto the waiting ferry and then back onto the Golden Arrow boat train to Victoria station in London, and from there they headed to Paddington, where they spent one night in a cheap hotel. In London they saw fog for the first time. The next day in Birmingham, Snow Hill lived up to the promise of its name. A line of black cabs outside the station bisected the pristine snowfall. Leaning into the window of the front taxi, my dad told the waiting driver that he needed to get Sparkhill – a working-class area about two miles outside the city centre, mostly red-brick terraces inhabited by factory workers and students. 'Whereabouts in Sparkhill?' asked the driver, but my dad didn't really know. He explained that he had been told, back in Cyprus, that Sparkhill was the area with the most accommodation, and whatever happened, he and my mother needed a bed that night.

'I can see you need help,' said the cab driver, who stopped the clock, turned off his engine and waited while my parents walked up the steps of a house – one of many that had 'FLAT TO LET' signs on the door. They knocked, only to be told by one of the tenants that the landlord was away until the next morning. 'I'm sure it'll be fine if I let you in for the night,' said the tenant, 'but there's no gas or electric.' It was night time now. Tired and cold, with no real alternatives, they moved their cases into their room and, to their relief, were offered the chance to stay there for £3.50 a week – about £68 in today's money.

The contact they were given by my dad's army major colleague – the reason they chose Birmingham over any other city – never materialised. But they were here now. The plan was that my father would go to college and qualify as a mechanic. A few years later, he and my mother would return to Cyprus. He'd fix cars and she'd run the business. They were still in love, and of course, they needed to be, because what on earth else would have persuaded my mother to embark on a plan – moving far away from her family to a place where the only person she knew was her Cypriot lover – that had generated such hardship for her mother thirty years previously?

Even in a country where you know the language, to be faced with the prospect of finding somewhere to live and somewhere to work with little more than the change in your pocket to sustain you must be overwhelming. Having gone to school in colonial Cyprus, my dad spoke English, but my mother had no words. Accompanied by my dad, she turned up at Le Rose, a clothes factory near their new bedsit. When they gave her a jacket with a collar that needed a little finishing work, she handed it back to them, completed, in the space of a few minutes.

The beginning of her time at Le Rose coincided with a week of thick fog, which reduced visibility to just a few feet. It just arrived one morning and failed to lift. When the bell sounded to signal the end of the working day, my mother left and attempted to make her way home, but within ten minutes, she was lost. With nowhere to go, she started to cry. A much older woman walking past her in the other direction stopped to ask her what was the matter. My mother showed her a piece of paper with the name of her road, Showell Green Lane, written on it. The woman took my distraught mum by the hand and walked with her until the two reached her doorstep.

It bothered both my father and my mother that they were living together but unmarried, but to get married you needed a best man. One day, my dad spotted a fish and chip shop opposite the nearby Sparkhill Park. On a section of road which is now almost entirely populated by balti houses and sari shops, the sign on the shop said, 's. PHILIPPAKIS' – a Cypriot surname. My dad walked in and introduced himself. Socrates Philappakis had a taciturn countenance. He was twenty-five years older than my dad, and he'd just seen his son disappear to Leeds with an English woman, seemingly never to return.

'If your fiancée is one of ours, I'll help you,' he told my dad, 'But if she's British, you can leave now and don't bother coming back again.'

A date was set for the other side of Christmas – a January wedding. In the meantime, my parents spent their first Christmas together. They bought a small turkey and my mum cooked it in the tiny kitchenette adjoining the room where they slept. On the morning of her wedding, she baked her own cake, of which all those present – five including the officiating bishop – had a slice.

Afterwards, Socrates and his wife returned to my parents' flat and enjoyed a dinner that my mum cooked for them. There was no honeymoon; the next day my mum returned to work and my father to the job he briefly held down at the Jensen plant in West Bromwich – loading carburettors into sports cars – before being offered an engineering apprenticeship with motoring giants Rootes. On evenings they might go for a walk in the park, or for a spin in the used estate car that my dad had bought for £40.

Though the language barrier presented my mother with more problems, she thought she could eventually envisage a time when she might be happy here. My dad, by contrast, firmly held on to the idea that Birmingham was a means to an end that involved returning to Cyprus at the earliest opportunity. Neither expected it to be quite so hard – but to admit as much to the families they had left behind was problematic. My mum had already felt guilty about leaving her mother alone to deal with her father, and to add to her misery with letters detailing her own loneliness was something she couldn't bring herself to do.

For my dad, it was more of a face-saving exercise. That was something I'd come to realise repeatedly through decades of overhearing phone conversations between my father and his relatives in Cyprus. This is what Greek Cypriots do when they call their families: they present their successes as major news and endlessly dissect the adversities that befall other parts of the family with barely disguised relish. And so, having left the security of small-town Cyprus to seek his fortune in Britain, it was necessary to keep up appearances. But, of course, the more successful a picture he painted in his letters home, the more his family wanted a piece of that success and, before long, envelopes from Cyprus started to land on the doorstep – inside them, requests to send money.

In reality though, my parents didn't know what had hit them. Still unable to speak English, my mum had to be realistic about the sort of work she could get that would be more rewarding than the tough manual labour of Le Rose. It had to be monotonous, conveyor-belt work for her. She was walking the snowy streets to Le Rose in shoes that were held together with Sellotape, setting aside any savings in order to put down a deposit on a house. It isn't hard to imagine how she felt when she was told that some of that money would have to be allocated to pay for her sister-in-law's wedding dress. Her own wedding dress had been hired from a shop in Small Heath. Even her coat ended up in a parcel which had her mother-in-law's address written on it. It seemed like nothing was more important than saving face. In the meantime, the only way to reach a better future was by surviving the present.

By the spring of 1965, my parents had finally scraped together almost £500, which was just enough money to get a mortgage on a £3,500 house in Sparkhill. On the day they turned up to collect the key, the previous owner – a teacher in her forties, Mrs Monaghan – took a good long look at my mother who, by now, was heavily pregnant, and fired off a few questions at my dad. Did they have furniture? Not yet, he told her, but they would gradually buy some. Did they have curtains? No, but don't worry. That could all be sorted out in time. Without pausing to consult her husband, who was at work in his nearby butcher's shop, she told my dad to explain to my mum that she would be leaving them the curtains, their double bed and an armchair. Years later, the first thing my mum did when I attempted to explain the worldwide web to her, was get me to try and track down Mrs Monaghan, so she could find a way of repaying her.

And then in May, my brother Aki arrived. Metaphorically, my parents were now shovelling coal into the fireplace of a building that didn't have a roof. My dad's apprenticeship had yet to end, and with no extended family nearby, my mother had nowhere to leave my brother, so returning to work was impossible. The world contracted to the four walls of their flat and the surrounding streets. She was trying to get to grips with the language, but it would be several years before she could hazard a magazine or a newspaper. For similar reasons, television was difficult. In other circumstances, she almost certainly wouldn't have given more than a cursory glance to the newspaper that landed on their doormat every Thursday. But there was nothing else to read.

To Bema was a free paper subsidised by pages of adverts for mostly London-based companies and services and sent to Cypriot expats in the UK. One week, my mother opened it up and saw details of a competition to come up with a series of advertising slogans, three

in all, for a Greek food brand called Doriti. One had to be for macaroni, one for olive oil and the other for wine. The winning prize was
a case of each. In 1965, when the only olive oil you could buy came
in tiny bottles at the chemist, the prospect of winning a case of the
stuff consumed all her thoughts. She sat there with my brother on
her lap, writing down ideas, crossing them out, and writing more
down, until finally she alighted on the combination of words that
she thought might put her in with a chance. She once told me what
she wrote down. To tell the truth, it didn't seem much in English
– 'Housewives: you'll be proud of your macaroni if you use Doriti
macaroni' – but she sent her entry and, three weeks later, the paper
arrived with the news that Victoria Paphides from Birmingham had
won the Doriti competition. She hadn't even told my dad that she
had entered for fear that he'd deride her for having the temerity to
think she stood a chance.

By the time he came home that evening, she had called the offices
of the paper to find out how she could go about collecting her prize.
They told her they would need her to come to the offices, where a
photographer would be present to immortalise her with her spoils.
When the day came, she dressed Aki in his best clothes and bought
a special outfit for herself, but the journey to London saw him evac-
uating the contents of his stomach all over her new top. They quickly
had to rush off to a nearby clothes shop where my dad explained
to the female shopkeeper what had happened and why we urgently
needed a replacement top. Another act of exceptional kindness from
a stranger towards my mother, who somehow had a way of drawing it
out of people just as it was most needed: the woman in the shop took
one look at her and led her into a back room, where she handed her a
dress and told her it suited her far better. It didn't, but her generosity
underscored my mother's sense that this – the day that a Cypriot
freesheet photographed her with a case of olive oil – was her special
day. And so, decades later, this was still how she talked about it.

Beyond this point though, fond reminiscences of the sixties dry up almost completely. There are no memories of epochal events to impart. No films that they enjoyed together. My parents effectively absented themselves from the most exciting pop-cultural decade of the century. If they found a television that showed England beating West Germany in the 1966 World Cup final, it wasn't a recollection they passed on. If they heard Beatles songs on the radio, they never told me about it. My dad remembers Englebert Humperdinck's 'Release Me' but has no memory of 'Strawberry Fields Forever' or 'Penny Lane' – the double A-side single that it kept from the number 1 spot. Their memories predominantly concern getting by. I suspect that would be true of most immigrants who landed in big British cities in the 1950s and 1960s. In the summer of 1966, my dad was waiting for the exam results that would allow him to finally get work as an engineer. As much as she desperately wanted to have a family of her own, my mother also knew she had to get back to work to ensure that there was some money coming into the house. A plan to leave Aki with a neighbour who was bringing up three children of her own unravelled in less than a week. Aki just kept shouting, 'Mum! Mum! Mum!' at her until she couldn't stand it any longer.

Just as my mum's sister had sent her a ticket to join her in Cyprus, my mum now took it upon herself to contact her other sister Rosa and see if she could help her escape her predicament. Could Aki stay with her in Athens until my mum figured out what to do next? On arriving, Aki was scooped up by his grandparents who loved him straight away, as did their dog Fidel. Minutes later, he found himself mesmerised by a line of ants which extended all the way from the gate to the doorstep where twenty-six years previously German soldiers had stood and handed over their dirty washing. He was eighteen months old. The ants blew his mind. He lay obstacles in their way and poked them with sticks, enthralled at the way they returned to the line at the first opportunity. Apparently he was still poking ants

by the time my mum, in tears, climbed the steps to get on the plane
and return back to England and – partly in order to punish herself
for the terrible thing she had done and partly to save as much money
in as short a space of time as possible – she took all the overtime that
was available to her. The harder she worked and the more money she
saved, the sooner she might be able to fly back to Greece and retrieve
Aki. They just needed to get through this sticky patch.

On Sundays, my mum and dad would go to the social epicentre
of Greek life in the West Midlands and, of course, the place where
they had married. The imposing Greek Orthodox Cathedral of the
Domition of Theotokos and St Andreas sat on a hill on the outskirts
of Birmingham city centre, a stone's throw from Snow Hill where
they had alighted the train on their second day in Britain. You had
to access the church via a slip road that rose up to meet the church;
in the hour or two before the sweet, heavy aroma of incense served
notice that the service was about to begin, the road would be lined
with parked Mercedes cars. Every time my dad got chatting with one
of their owners and asked them what they did for a living, the answer
was always the same: fish and chips. If they could trade their flat for
a shop with living quarters attached to it, that might be the solution
to all of their problems. My mother could then pick up where she
left off with Aki and have him nearby when she was helping with
the shop. How difficult could it all be?

Once again, with few other friends to ask, my parents enlisted
the help of Socrates, the chip shop proprietor who had stepped in to
be my dad's best man four years previously. My father took a week
off and spent it in Socrates's shop, getting the hang of portioning
fish, mixing up the batter, commandeering the potato peeler and
wrapping up the chips. When a shop came up for sale, Socrates went
in as a sleeping partner, stumping up fifty per cent of the cash in
exchange for half the profits.

Aki was three years old when my mum's sister flew back with

him from Athens. With no male role model in Greece to supplant, Aki gelled immediately with the father he hadn't seen for eighteen months, but my mother had to start anew with a son who had no real idea who she was. He hated Birmingham and, for a time, he resented her for bringing him back there. At a bus stop he kicked her so hard that, within a minute or two, she could feel her shoe filling up with blood. She remembered passers-by looking down at her feet and then looking back up at her before deciding that they didn't want to get involved. When my mother describes her memories around this time, she sounds like she's describing a non-custodial sentence imposed by herself upon herself – as if she were doing her time in order to silence the voices that had tormented her during the period she gave Aki up.

Even after I was born, she never stopped. Once she had finished cleaning up at the end of each day, she would get to work hand-washing our clothes (there wasn't a washing machine) and then she would iron them. Even the socks. It was unbearable to her that someone might judge her on the basis that she worked in a fish and chip shop. But she had no control over that. Instead, she made sure we turned up to school in spotless starched shirts and Clarks leather shoes. At the shop in West Bromwich, she let it be known that she could make jumpers to order and soon she had a waiting list of customers. During the months when she and my dad didn't know if the Threepennybit was going to turn a profit, it was another way of earning money. But it wasn't just that. It was a way of broadcasting the fact she hadn't come here to ask people if they wanted salt and vinegar on their chips. Every day, she had to rebuild her self-image from the ground up. This was how she did it.

CHAPTER 10

A fortnight's holiday in Cyprus ended dramatically when my mum received news that her mother, now in her late seventies, had slipped in the bathroom and broken her hip. The phone call came through just as we were leaving for the airport. My mother desperately wanted to detour to Athens – and, tantalisingly, the plane was landing there to pick up the remainder of its passengers – but the shop was due to reopen in a couple of days, with Aki and I going back to school at the same time. Perhaps she could fly out again at a later point, but right now, she was coming home with us.

In fact, no one who boarded in Cyprus got to go home that night. As the plane attempted to take off again from Athens, one of the engines cut out. We taxied back to the terminal and were told that hotel accommodation would be arranged for us that night. We declined the hotel offer, choosing instead to catch a late night bus to Nea Kifisia. With Aki and I doing the last leg alone, my parents alighted outside the huge Metera hospital in Marousi, a couple of miles away from the house where my mum had grown up.

Aki had all sorts of reasons to be resentful towards me. His eighteen months away from my mum had frayed the bond between them. If he had stopped to compare the way she was with me, he would have had every reason to resent me for it, but it never seemed to occur to him. One Friday teatime, when I was two and Aki was six, I fell and tore open the skin just above my right eye. Aki rushed me into the shop where my parents were managing the teatime rush. My mum took one look at the blood pouring around and into my eye, scooped me up and ran to the nearest doctor's surgery. The doctor on duty took one look at the gash and decided it was too close to my eye to risk stitches. He applied a butterfly plaster which might succeed in patching up the wound, but that was wholly dependent on me being distracted enough to not touch the wounded area.

By the time my mum returned, the queue for fish and chips was stretching out into the street. She looked at my brother and asked him if he thought he could watch me for the next couple of hours and make sure my hands didn't go anywhere near the plaster. Every few minutes, she'd pop in to see how he was doing, and every time, there he was setting up games with my toy cars and singing at me to distract me until, finally, I fell asleep. Two hours after the accident had happened, my dad was finally able to manage being in the shop alone, and my mother removed her overall and returned to the front room to see Aki, still staring at me as though he had been given the most important job in all the world. She returned to the shop, asked my dad to remove a pound note from the till and presented it to him with a hug.

And now, at thirteen, here he was again, the only person who had succeeded in getting me to talk to strangers, holding my hand with his nose pressed against the bus window, gazing at unfamiliar suburban boulevards, until finally he recognised the news kiosk fifty yards away from my mother's childhood abode. 'This is it!' he said, pulling the cord which stretched from the front to the back of the bus and ringing the bell. We ran the short distance to the house, into the garden and past the old well where my mother used to pull up water before heading to school. We fell asleep in the same bed, long before my parents returned from the hospital, and then in the morning, we all got back on the bus to the airport, defaulting to the dumb optimism that all children deploy when events too emotionally complex to understand suddenly happen around them. My mum didn't mention the hospital visit at all. Imagining that our grandmother would gradually recover we reverted to the main focus of our excitement, which was the beginning of the school year.

The World Cup final had reached its conclusion just before the beginning of the summer holidays, with Argentina beating Holland by three goals to one. Between that evening and the beginning of the next school year, it became a matter of absolute urgency that I get better at football. If you were good at football, your popularity never sank below a certain level. You were privy to conversations and in-jokes that would otherwise be closed off to you. Silky skills were the Amex Centurion of the playground.

For my birthday in July, I had asked for a full Manchester United home strip. My mother had started to set some money aside, having received an order for four hand-knitted pullovers from the enormous landlord of the pub near our chippy, which meant that she could buy me an official tracksuit to go with my new strip. After school, she and I went to the Co-op department store in town where, inexplicably, the entirety of Kate Bush's debut album *The Kick Inside* had been chosen to soundtrack the final hour of business. As I held up Manchester United's red home shirt in one hand and their white away shirt in the other, Kate was singing 'The Man with the Child in His Eyes' and a holy shiver of strings swirled around the sports section, conferring a sense of otherworldly portent upon the entire process, making the selection of a football strip feel like a decision of momentous importance. Which, of course, it was.

The next song on the record was 'Wuthering Heights'. As Kate channelled Catherine Earnshaw's tormented pleas for Heathcliff's forgiveness, I finally chose my desired combination of strip and tracksuit. However, there remained one final decision before we walked over to the counter. As part of a special offer, you were allowed to have a number ironed onto the back of your shirt. It was a standard procedure. Your chosen number corresponded to that of your favourite player in the team, my hero *du jour* being centre forward Jimmy Greenhoff.

'Number 8, please!' I trumpeted excitably.

The assistant rummaged through the shallow wooden drawer where the iron-on numbers were kept.

'Sorry. We're out of number 8,' she told me.

Oh dear. Who else did I like? I mentally scanned the Man United spread in my sticker album and decided it would be almost as cool to brandish the same number as the team's hotly tipped winger Steve Coppell.

'Number 7, please!' I said.

She looked through the drawer one more time. There were no number 7s either. Finally she told me what numbers she did actually have left. Amid a limited range and under pressure to decide, I accepted the same number as that worn by Scottish hollow-eyed, square-jawed, brick shithouse, Gordon McQueen. Number 5. Whichever way you looked at it, this was a rubbish number, and it would have ramifications. At school, every time we played football in PE, my ownership of the same shirt as Gordon McQueen consigned me to defence – a position almost always reserved, at this age, for the special substrain of beta boys whose congenital unsportiness compelled them to recoil or run away when the ball came towards them.

When it came to the playground matches though, there was still everything to play for. I spent the summer immersed in techniques and tactics that, once learned and deployed, were sure to surprise and impress everyone when we reconvened in September. For my ninth birthday, Aki had bought me a football skills book authored by legendary Spurs footballer Danny Blanchflower and set out in comic strip form. It showed you all about how you use different parts of your feet to control the ball in multiple ways. And even though I was struggling to get into double figures with keepie-ups, I felt that with Danny as my virtual co-pilot, I might make up some ground on the alpha boys in my year.

My internal continuity announcer, the one who had been there since I was four, would hand over to a football commentator the moment we spilled out into the playground, and for the duration of those games, I was no longer Peter Paphides, I was Jimmy Green-hoff, making penetrating runs into the opposition's penalty area, perpetually sniffing out half-opportunities that I could convert into a winning goal. The only problem with this was that, actually, it's hard to implement the teachings of Danny Blanchflower when the ball has landed at your feet and twenty children are closing in on you like wasps to a bin at the seaside. To make matters worse, we never played with a normal size football, because they weren't allowed at Cottesbrooke. Our football was in fact a tennis ball. For the skilful boys, this wasn't a problem. Pelé had developed his close ball control as a child by practising on tennis balls and rolled-up socks.

Whatever the ball, your first priority was to look up, stay calm, quickly assess your options and keep moving. You might dribble past a couple of players first, but when the time came to release the ball, you had a pretty good idea where it was going to go. However, the moment the ball landed at my feet, I didn't dare look up for fear I might lose it, which meant that I was forced to run with the ball in the opposite direction to the oncoming throng. If they didn't manage to dispossess me in time, I would pass the ball to whoever was nearest, often the person who had passed it to me in the first place. Every day, I would put myself through this daily ignominy in the hope that I might fluke a moment of glory that would make the cool kids re-evaluate their view of me. The more I tried, however, the less attainable that goal became – until eventually I was placed on the transfer list.

The transfer list in this case was a simple switch of sides. At Cottes-brooke, there were only ever two sides. In increasingly multiracial

Acocks Green, we played Blacks vs Whites – this was literally how we referred to it. Every day, it was like this. It didn't occur to any of us that, to an outside observer, this might have uncomfortable connotations. With a roughly equal ratio of white to non-white kids, this seemed the logical way to do it. You knew instantly who was on which team. The only problem was that, by and large, the non-white kids were much better than the white kids. Weeks went by without the Whites winning. So, finally, it was decided that the Blacks should have some of the rubbish Whites. From October onwards, I lined up alongside Delroy Bell, Amar Ali, Reginald Harrison, Martin Graham, Roger Morgan and Vijay Singh as a Black. If they were put out by the prospect of having me on their team, they were good enough to keep it from me. Maybe they'd been getting bored with winning all the time and relished the handicap.

Jimmy Greenhoff had chosen me as much as I had chosen him. I think that's the case with all children and their favourite footballers. You gaze at the pictures in your sticker album, watch them on TV and see something of yourself reflected in them. In the Football 78 album, Jimmy Greenhoff looks just a touch confused, like he accidentally walked into the first-team photo shoot and, by virtue of some admin error, ended up being chosen to play against South-ampton the following Tuesday, electing not to say anything for fear that the resulting inconvenience would spoil things for everyone. While most centre forwards could be assured a centre spread in *Shoot!* weekly, Jimmy Greenhoff was strictly single-page fare. Unlike his brother Brian, who played in midfield, he never won an England cap. Speaking to *Shoot!* in an article which I, naturally, kept and stuck to my wall, he said, 'Brian tells me it's the greatest thrill you can imagine to learn you've been chosen to play for England,' before adding, 'Well, I wouldn't know.'

A year previously, I had started voraciously gobbling up *Peanuts* comic strips, collecting each new book as it had come out. Charlie

Brown's obsession with journeyman baseball player Joe Shlabotnik mirrored that of my love of Jimmy Greenhoff. In a series of beautifully observed storylines, Charles Schulz chronicled Charlie Brown's unfailing faith in Shlabotnik's abilities, a faith which merely became stronger as Shlabotnik found himself demoted to the minor leagues.

Just as Charlie Brown sought out Shlabotnik memorabilia (rare, by its very nature), I sent a stamped addressed envelope to Man United, asking if they could use it to send me a photo of Jimmy. Incredibly, they obliged. I tore open the Man United-postmarked envelope and there was Jimmy in action, looking just as surprised by the ball as I was whenever it landed at my feet. In *Peanuts*, when Linus arranged a testimonial dinner for Charlie Brown – a belated acknowledgement of his consistently unsuccessful role as coach of his own side – he invited Joe Shlabotnik to appear in person. The final frame in one of the daily instalments showed Charlie Brown dressed in a suit, sitting beside the empty space that should have been occupied by his favourite player. Joe Shlabotnik had got lost en route from his day job at a car wash. In another series of strips, we learned that Shlabotnik had been invited to appear at a sports banquet in which fans could pay to sit at the same table as their favourite athletes. Charlie Brown seized the opportunity to finally meet his hero, only for Shlabotnik to fail to appear again. It turned out that Shlabotnik had marked the wrong event, city and date on his calendar.

While I was attempting to arrest my plummeting stock in the playground, my mum's thoughts were further afield. After three weeks in hospital, my grandmother had taken a turn for the worse – not that Aki and I were made aware of the fact. For the main part, Mum just got on with the enervating business of each passing day: the daily twenty-eight-mile round trip to and from West Bromwich; keeping Aki and me clean, dressed and fed; and sating the growing demand for pullovers from Threepennybit customers.

But one October evening, about forty minutes into the first series of ITV's new flagship Saturday night show *Bruce Forsyth's Big Night*, she left the room to take a phone call and returned ten minutes later, shoulders shaking, weeping uncontrollably. On the TV, Bruce was reaching the punchline of a gag that had taken a minute to set up. Unable to navigate the requisite emotional gear change in such a short space of time, I laughed at the punchline, a reaction followed instantly by a burning sense of shame.

'Your grandmother,' she said. 'My mother.'

I'd never heard her referred to as 'my mother' before, and it had the effect of making my mum seem as much of a child as I was.

Her sister, Rosa, had called from the hospital and suggested to my mum that she ought to fly over without delay. Panayioula was passing in and out of consciousness and had, earlier that day, issued one precisely worded wish: 'I want Victoria to close my eyes.'

Arrangements were swiftly made. She boarded the flight to Athens the next day. Aki and I were to stay with the Osbornes, making the chip shop my dad's only responsibility. She landed in Athens that evening and took a taxi straight to the hospital. Unaware if she had made it in time, she ran to the third floor and, as per the directions she had been given, found the ward. My grandmother turned to face my mum as she held her hand. She then exhaled, expelling a low sigh as she did so, and that was that. My mum leaned forward, and, as requested, closed her mother's eyelids.

My mum and her two sisters stayed up talking late into the evening. If Panayioula's request that her youngest daughter be the one to close her eyes afforded my mum some sort of comfort, it turned out to be short-lived. Rosa – Rosa who stayed; Rosa who mothered my brother for eighteen months – decided this was the right time to finally let my mum know what had happened back in 1961 when my mum left Athens for Cyprus and then went to England, never to return. For months, possibly even years, Panayioula carried a handkerchief which she would use several times a day to dab her eyes. My mum's presence in the family home had been the one thing that had made her mother's marriage tolerable. She had backed Panayioula up in the face of her father's worst tirades, knowing that her father craved her approval and feared her censure. She had been her mother's closest confidante. And the reason I understood all of this, of course, was because I was my mother's closest confidant. And because my dad was becoming increasingly aware of the fact, he began to solicit my approval and fear my censure. I knew this dynamic well.

The guilt that surged upwards with Rosa's revelation instantly floored her.

'I would have come back,' she told her. 'If I had known, I would have come back.'

But my mum hadn't known. No one in her family had told her. Her sister had reasoned that it was far too cruel an act to reel my mother all the way back to Athens from Birmingham where, surely, she and my dad would make a small fortune in no time. *Then*, at least they would return to Cyprus – and Cyprus really isn't so far from Greece.

My mum's grief came in waves – not just grief for her mother's death, but for the life that preceded it: the marriage to a man she never loved, and the ensuing years of hardship. On top of that came her own grief: the guilt of having run away to a life that bore no resemblance to the one she had planned. The guilt of not coming back in time. And for what? Factory work and fish and chips? The final blow, however, happened on the day of the funeral. As the casket lay there in the chapel, my mum approached and, in doing so, noticed that the dress worn by her mother was one that she had sewn and sent to her from Birmingham three Christmases previously. It was a three-quarter length, long-sleeved cotton dress in the traditional Greek style. The day she removed it from the parcel, Panayioula Kalavas placed it in her wardrobe and told Rosa that this was the dress in which she wanted to be buried.

CHAPTER 11

I walked downstairs after my first night's sleep at the Osbornes' to see William standing on the doorstep. In his arms were two bottles of milk and a bottle of lemonade. The bottle of pop was enormous. If he had turned it upside down and strapped it to his back, it could have passed for a jetpack. He placed the three bottles on the dining table where the Osbornes ate all their meals. Emanating pensively from the Osbornes' radio was the lead single from Jeff Wayne's musical adaptation of H.G. Wells's dystopian sci-fi novel *The War of the Worlds*. With lyrics that seemed to speak just as easily to the collective mood of Cold War-era anxiety, 'Forever Autumn' depicted its singer Justin Hayward as a dazed refugee of the apocalypse surveying the desolation around him like a man left with nothing to show for his time on this godforsaken rock, save perhaps for the size 28 Wranglers around his waist and a proto-Diana shell of golden hair, rendered disaster-proof by half a can of Gillette Dry Look. I had clocked Justin on *Top of the Pops* several weeks previously. Even when issuing devastated dispatches from a hellish futurescape, I still wouldn't have said no if he had turned up at the Great Western, cherry-red Gibson 335 in hand, and offered to sing me a bedtime lullaby.

Given that heart-tugging pay-off at the end of each verse – 'Now you're not here!' – 'Forever Autumn' ought to have rendered me inconsolable as I contemplated my longest ever separation from my mother. But no one was more surprised than me to discover that I was already quite enjoying being part of a British family – not just thinking in English but talking in it too, immersed in an ambience I knew from sitcoms and soap operas. The small talk was subdued and conspicuously unfreighted with emotional charge or submerged resentments.

I was fascinated by those minor details that vary from one house to another – everything was the same, yet different in small, barely consequential ways, like in dreams. The Osbornes' milk of choice was sterilised, which came in taller bottles with metal caps like the ones you get on beer bottles. 'This is the best milk,' William informed me, because even among friends, everything at that age is a competition. I asked him what 'sterilised' was. He didn't know, but seconds later he returned from the kitchen with an answer. 'It lasts longer,' he said. Looking at the bigger bottle, I had to agree. That would indeed last longer.

We seemed to drink lemonade constantly, thanks to the fact that every morning, yet another colossal bottle of the stuff would appear. In fact, I don't think I drank any water that week. The cheese on toast that William's mum made him was only toasted on the side that also had the cheese on, so you had to support it with your entire hand. I wore pants under my pyjamas; William didn't. 'Takis doesn't take off his pants when he goes to bed!' he called to his mum downstairs. With our lives outside of school so intertwined, William had long declared himself exempt from suddenly having to call me Peter. 'Be quiet, William,' she replied. 'We don't talk about those sorts of things!' They always had pudding, and pudding was nearly always ice cream. In my family, pudding had never really been a given. Maybe an hour after supper, my mum would make us *krema*, a creamy dessert with cocoa, milk and cornflour. But we didn't think of it as pudding so much as an occasional treat. 'You don't have pudding?!' exclaimed William, a mixture of incredulity and pity. I shook my head. 'MUM! Takis doesn't have pudding!' 'Be quiet, William!' she replied again. 'We don't talk about those sorts of things!'

As any nine-year-old would, William took my temporary residence at his house as an opportunity to show me around his world. We'd come home from school, hang our coats at the bottom of the stairs and sit on his bed while he pulled out *Doctor Who* books from his shelf. He had some records in his room, which he would have to go downstairs to play. Almost all of them were by his favourite band, which wasn't really a band in the conventional sense, but the *Doctor Who* house band, the BBC Radiophonic Workshop. Most of William's Radiophonic Workshop records were soundtracks to specific *Doctor Who* stories, but there were others too. The 1968 album *BBC Radiophonic Music* had been something of a calling card for them – their *What's Going On* or *Sgt. Pepper*, and this seemed to be the most frequent return visitor to the Osborne family turntable. If there was no one else in his front room, he'd put it on and you'd look out of the single-glazed window to an instantly transformed world. The wobbulator-assisted opening chords of Delia Derbyshire's 'Ziwzih Ziwzih OO-OO-OO' turned the hitherto unremarkable intersection of Bramley Road and Lime Tree Road into what could become, at any minute, a scene of unspeakable horrors: an army of Cybermen dispersing into the neighbouring front gardens of Acocks Green; a predatory pack of Shrivenzales freshly descended from the catacombs of Shur.

For our final full day after a week with the Osbornes, a Sunday, my dad came over for lunch. Watching him assimilate into such a quintessentially English scenario was weirder than I had any reason to expect. Just as every culture has its own indigenous music forms, every language both reflects and accentuates the temperament of its users. If our Sunday lunches were measured in the halting tempo and discordant harmonies of Greek folk songs, lunch with the Osbornes was something akin to Edward White's *Puffin' Billy*, later used to great effect in the Comic Strip's Enid Blyton parody, *Five Go Mad in Dorset* – its buoyant forward motion not so much suggesting that everything was OK, but that three-quarters of everything being OK was pretending that everything was OK. Seeing my dad instinctively snap into line with the social protocol at the Osbornes was like watching one of those episodes of *Laverne & Shirley* where Mr Cunningham from *Happy Days* pops up. I found myself quietly willing him to relax in their company, but he didn't even get close. I saw him attempting to eat a leg of chicken with a knife and fork for the first time and figured that I'd probably better do the same.

It had hardly been a holiday, and yet, on her return, my mum was expected to hit the ground running. Aki and I assumed that eight days was easily enough time to get over the death of your mother, and my dad – who had been running the chip shop single-handedly – was keen for her to rejoin him in the shop, a shift which would end with the daily, three-bus, cross-county journey to my school, where somehow she would always manage to arrive on time. As she did on the day of her return, a rainy Monday afternoon. We hugged at the school gates and I asked her nothing whatsoever about how it had been for her to see her mother die and help organise and attend her funeral.

Instead, I told her about a new kind of food I'd seen advertised while watching TV at the Osbornes' house. It was called Pot Noodle and it looked delicious and exciting. The adverts showed an all-singing, all-dancing ensemble in some sort of cabaret nightspot hymning the joys of this new snack innovation. It came in a plastic tub and all you needed to do was add hot water to it. In 1978, it wasn't easy to explain the concept of Pot Noodle to a bereaved and probably depressed Greek woman who has almost certainly never touched a noodle in her life, let alone cooked with one, and whose first language doesn't even have a word for 'noodle'. She nodded absently as she waited for me to finish – nods that I almost certainly took to be signs of interest.

I was far from done though. Every Sunday, tasked with the job of getting us out of the house for a couple of hours while my mum made lunch, my dad's reluctance to complicate what was already a chore by actually having to lay down some rules meant that petrol station and newsagent stops always provided opportunities for free stuff we weren't usually allowed. Returning from the park that Sunday, we stopped off at a newsagent's which – joy of joys! – had an entire display of Pot Noodles. I seized my chance. I knew that the best way to get free stuff from him was to place any desired item on the counter at the exact point at which he was paying for his newspaper. Worried that he might give the shopkeeper the impression that he was tight with money, my dad would always capitulate. Sure enough, I was soon clutching a plastic tub in which was contained the must-have dehydrated comestible of 1978.

Aki was no less excited about the Pot Noodle than I was and the entire conversation in the car on the way back was centred around how exactly we would divide it so that we had exactly the same amount as each other. We burst into the house at 2 p.m., as promised, just as my mum was bringing out a slowly roasted, marbled shoulder of lamb, studded with garlic and finished off with salt and pepper. The roast potatoes and vegetables were already on the table. Aki and I made straight for the kitchen to put the kettle on, which we just about managed to do before we were summoned to the table by my increasingly agitated mum.

The rules of Pot Noodle haven't changed in the four decades since they were launched in this country. You pour the boiling water to the 'FILL LEVEL' arrow indicated on the outside of the pot, then you let it stand for two minutes. After that, you give it a thorough stir, making sure you've agitated it enough to not leave any powder bombs at the bottom. Then you let it stand for two more minutes before adding whatever sachet came with the pot. With the beef and cheese flavour varieties of Pot Noodle, you got ketchup. With the curry one, you got mango chutney. For millions of people, myself included, this would be the closest we had got to tasting a mango.

Keen to make sure that I had left exactly two minutes before the first stir, I sat at the table, counting, 'One elephant, two elephant, three elephant . . .' and so on, until there were 120 elephants in the room alongside my increasingly dejected-looking mum, and my dad, who had fully disengaged from what was happening. It's not like I wasn't picking up the social cues, merely that I was choosing to pretend they weren't there, in anticipation of the Pot Noodle. I ran into the kitchen to give it a stir. I had to be quick because my mother's sadness was now mutating into the straight-up anger of someone clearly wondering why they'd even bothered boarding the flight back from Greece. It was Aki who ran into the kitchen when it got to four minutes. He removed half of his noodles and placed them onto the plate. The beefy sauce from the Pot Noodle ran into the juices from the lamb. Credit where it's due. In exactly four minutes, I had managed to turn a beautiful Sunday lunch into a gag-inducing metaphor. The noodle and the damage done.

I had developed an unhelpful habit of seeing the fun and merriment enjoyed by British families on television, then attempting to inject some of it into our house. As Christmas approached, I chose my presents carefully, with a view to maximising the amount of Family Fun we could have during the only two consecutive days in the year that my parents didn't have to work. Two of the most heavily advertised games that year were Twister and Perfection. The ads for Twister centred around a dad and his kids getting their limbs tangled up while their mum – falling into line with traditional sitcom characterisation – did the joyless work, spinning the spinner which determined the coloured spots on which the next player would have to place their limbs. Perfection looked no less exciting. You had to put approximately twenty different shapes into their correct holes before the integrated timer completed a full rotation and made all the shapes pop out of their holes. As was de rigueur with boxed games at the time, the photograph on the lid served to emphasise exactly how much collective joy the contents of this box could bring to your home.

When Christmas morning finally came around though, I ripped off the wrapping paper on the first box only to see that my poor mum, misreading my list, had gone to the games department at WH Smith and picked up a cerebral card game called Perception which bore a greater resemblance to bridge than anything involving putting shapes in holes against the clock. Registering my crestfallen expression, she said, 'Is that OK? That was the game you wanted, wasn't it?' I nodded brightly, knowing at least that the main event was still to come. I opened the package containing Twister and immediately looked around to see who was going to play. I turned to Aki and was met with a look of mild distaste. 'Don't look at *me!*' he scoffed. 'You're not going to catch me playing that!' The more I beseeched him, the more adamant he became. With his four extra years on this planet, he'd long come to the realisation that we simply weren't that sort of family. As he rose to leave the room, I addressed my dad. His back was turned to me as he leaned over his expensive radio, quickly attempting to plumb in some of the ambience of his own childhood Christmases by finding a live broadcast of a Greek Christmas liturgy. 'I've got this really great game!' I began. As with the Pot Noodle incident, I made light work of ignoring the subtle social signals being transmitted in my direction. 'It's called Twister and . . . look!' He turned around, registered the box, and with a limp nod, carried on rotating the dial and switching between tuning frequencies. 'You have to spin the wheel and put your hands and feet on these different-coloured . . . well, it's hard to explain if you're not looking.' As I spoke, I laid out the plastic Twister mat with the spots.

'Perhaps later,' he said. 'After dinner.' The pool of Paphides family members who hadn't eliminated themselves from contention for a Christmas game of Twister now numbered just two.

It's impossible to play Twister on your own. You would have to remember which limbs were on which spots and the exact way they crossed over and around each other, before leaving the mat and spinning the dial to see what you have to do next. Even if that were just about possible, who would you be playing against? What would be the point? Still, even Twister for one wouldn't be quite as sad a game as when two people attempt to play it. Because when two people play it – one operating the dial, and the other on the mat – it means that someone is watching. It means that someone is a witness to the poignant spectacle being played out on a plastic mat feet away. On Christmas Day 1978, that witness was my mum, gamely spinning the Twister dial as I persisted in my determination to create levels of Christmas cheer comparable to the one enjoyed by the family on the box. I would be surprised if the whole spectacle lasted as long as five minutes. Even as I packed the box away, I did so in the dementedly cheerful belief that, perhaps later that evening, I'd finally lure everyone onto the spotty mat of Family Fun.

But, of course, as Aki already knew, it just wasn't us. We weren't a games family. Apart from the card games my dad used to sometimes play with his Cypriot friends, Monopoly was the only game that didn't seem childish to him. That's because, to him, it was scarcely a recreational pursuit. It was a miniaturisation of the immigrant experience. A game set in an unfamiliar place, in which the only sure route to success and status was the shrewd procurement of bricks and mortar. In the real-life Monopoly of their shared existence, my parents were some way short of Mayfair. Sixteen years after alighting the ferry at Dover, a fish and chip shop in West Bromwich and a two-up-two-down in South Yardley were the extent of their acquisitions. And in the posh room of that two-up two-down – a space for guests that rarely came and parties that never happened – was an area that perhaps I could start to commandeer. Standing stiffly to attention at the bay window, the radiogram didn't seem to get too much love these days. My parents hadn't brought a new record home in all the time I could remember. It was much easier to bring tapes back from Cyprus. Were it not for Edward Osborne's decision to premiere the *Grease* soundtrack a few months previously, I'm not sure the turntable would have made a single revolution in almost the entire time we'd lived here. But that was all starting to change.

CHAPTER 12

It was Friday, the day before pocket money day. My mum collected me from school and we boarded the number 11 bus to the big scary roundabout, only this time we stayed on and overshot the roundabout, alighting at a row of shops, each of which existed to service a different essential everyday requirement. A greengrocer. A butcher. A baker. A hardware store. And also – because this was 1978, the year in which physical record sales reached an unsurpassable 2,750 million worldwide – a record shop. This being early December, it was already dark. From across the road, I saw the low-lit browsers behind the window display of new releases and a wall on which were stuck posters and artfully stapled, overlapping record sleeves, some of which curved outwards. The shop was called Discus. I must have stared at it a bit longer than usual because my mum clocked me and asked me if I'd like to go in and have a look.

The door to the shop was on the left, the same side as three wall-mounted listening stations, at least one of which no longer appeared to be in use. I'm guessing they would have been there since the 1960s, when it was customary to ask for a few records at a time and listen to them on the record players in each booth before deciding which one you were going to take home. The price of a new album in 1966 was 12s 6d – which, in 2019, in real terms, would be the equivalent of just over £17. If you wanted to hear the Beatles' *Revolver* all the way through, your only choices would be to: (a) add your name to the list of people waiting to borrow it from the local library; (b) go to the house of a friend who owned it; or (c) buy it yourself. But with so much money at stake, (c) wasn't a decision undertaken lightly. Hence the need for listening booths – sonic changing rooms that enabled you to 'try on' your putative purchase and see if it suited you.

Although I could have probably asked for my pocket money a day in advance, I wasn't in the habit of asking for things. I knew how tight my mum's weekly budget was, and I also knew that if I asked her for a record, she wouldn't have the heart to refuse. In the event, my mere longing was all it took for her to capitulate. She pointed to a smoked Perspex shelf of 7-inch singles which were divided by tabs indicating chart positions going up to 40. 'You can have two of those,' she said. Two! From zero to two was more than it would have occurred to me to hope for. One is just one. You take your first record home by itself, and it's just a record. But two! Two is hitting the ground running! Two, if you include the B-sides, is four songs. Two is the beginning of a collection!

I didn't need to think too hard about my first choice. The previous evening, I had seen self-styled pop jesters the Barron Knights on *Top of the Pops* for the first time and my mind had been blown. They had just leapt up the charts with their single 'A Taste of Aggro', which repeated a formula that had briefly given them success in the mid-1960s: a medley of three recent hits, all of which had their original lyrics replaced with funny ones. At the age of nine, it didn't even occur to me that a recording artist might be allowed to do this. Such naughtiness on an organised scale, sanctioned in part by a record label and the TV station airing it, was hitherto unimaginable to me. Hence, as I sat in my front room to watch *Top of the Pops* and heard the familiar hummed intro of Boney M's 'Rivers of Babylon' give way to the lines, 'There's a dentist in Birmingham / He fixed my crown / And while I slept / He filled my mouth with iron', it seemed to me an act of such arrant, insolent silliness that, in that moment, I adored its perpetrators. If you had told me at this point that whimsical rewrites of recent pop hits might be a less than noble way to make your mark on the hit parade, I would have glared at you in total incomprehension. Other people may have seen in the Barron Knights the desperate opportunism of a fading cabaret turn. For me though, they were the class clowns in the school assembly of pop, inverting its affectations and mystique for the sake of a cheap laugh. Watching them sing about the Smurfs breaking out of prison to the tune of 'The Smurf Song' was, to this nine-year-old viewer, as thrilling as the Sex Pistols being goaded into swearing by Bill Grundy on the *Today* show two years previously.

From this moment on, the Barron Knights could do no wrong. I walked up to the counter in Discus and confidently asked the assistant for 'A Taste of Aggro' by the Barron Knights. She reached up, pulled out the record in question and handed it over to me. The Barron Knights were on Epic Records. I'd never seen the word 'epic' before. I didn't know that epic could be used to describe something that was dramatic or vast in scale. Had I known, I might have used that very word to describe what happened to me in that record shop.

The second record I chose had already been out for a few months, but I hadn't tired of hearing it. 'Summer Nights' by John Travolta and Olivia Newton John was released on RSO, the label founded by Bee Gees manager Robert Stigwood which – by virtue of having also released the *Saturday Night Fever* soundtrack – was untouchably successful by the end of 1978. Unlike the Barron Knights single, the information in the centre of 'Summer Nights' wasn't on a paper label. It was embossed into the record: black letters stamped onto a coffee-coloured background. If you placed a sheet of chip paper on it and shaded over it with a pencil, just like you might do with a coin, you could recreate it. My two records were placed into a small plastic bag and although, of course, there were other records in the house, these were mine. I felt the sense of their ownership more keenly than with anything else in my possession. Before we even arrived at the house, I knew that tomorrow, when I received my pocket money for the next week, I'd go and get two more.

My first play of 'A Taste of Aggro' was only the second time I heard it. But between the memory of last night's *Top of the Pops* appearance and the moment the needle landed on the record, my excitement about hearing it again rose to the brink of mania. Comedy records rarely get any funnier with repeated plays, but by dint of my unshakeable fidelity to the moment the Barron Knights' star crossed with mine, I laughed harder and more dementedly at the exploits of that dentist in Birmingham than I did the first time.

By Saturday lunchtime, I had four records. The naughtiness of the Barron Knights had now been superseded by the significantly more transgressive language of John Travolta's 'Greased Lightnin''. Sounding to me almost as grown-up as 'Greased Lightnin'' was ABBA's recent single, 'Summer Night City'. This wasn't ABBA's first foray into disco, of course. 'Dancing Queen' had set a high bar, even by ABBA's standards. On the night they finished recording 'Dancing Queen', Björn was so excited by what they had managed to achieve on the track that he drove around Stockholm with a tape of the song, looking for friends to whom he could play it. When Frida heard the song, she famously burst into tears, so overwhelmed was she by its euphoric beauty.

In 1997, when the Sex Pistols marked the twentieth anniversary of *Never Mind the Bollocks* with a reunion show in Finsbury Park, they decided to walk on stage to 'Dancing Queen', the idea being that the song would come to an abrupt halt when the Pistols appeared, as if to remind people about the bland MOR dreck they blew away on their arrival. The problem was that, twenty years on, all the battle lines had long been erased. A park full of ex-punks spontaneously started dancing to the ABBA song.

Whatever the Pistols had in their armoury, nothing could compete with the intertwined euphoria and sadness of the line, 'You can dance / You can jive / Having the time of your life', a line which tells you that such moments of transcendence are over as soon as you realise they were ever there in the first place. It's no accident that, of all the songs in ABBA's canon, 'Dancing Queen' is the song to which traditionally, children and, in particular, young girls have most easily related. It's a song with the words 'Dancing' and 'Queen' in the title, for God's sake. It's a coronation song. It's a fairy tale, a moment that doesn't exist outside of the song written to provide it.

And as if to prove the transience of the moment described in 'Dancing Queen', here was 'Summer Night City', a song that, actually, could be set in the same evening, but four hours later. 'Summer Night City' is a messy track. Indeed, as if not quite understanding the power of their own creation, its messiness – its not-quite-rightness – was what caused Benny and Björn to agonise over it in the studio, tweaking and finessing it, jettisoning an extended intro for the song, until, with time running out, they reluctantly submitted it for release. When it stalled at number 5, they all but disowned it, citing its relatively lowly chart position as proof of its inferiority. But, of course, 'Summer Night City' was never going to get to number 1, any more than *Return to Oz* – with a destroyed yellow brick road, a witch with thirty-one interchangeable heads and Auntie Em forcing Dorothy to receive shock therapy – was going to leave people feeling as good as *The Wizard of Oz* did. 'Summer Night City' was the sound of an evening veering at speed along the thin line which separates memories from regrets: 'In the pale light of the morning / Nothing's worth remembering / It's a dream, it's out of reach / Scattered driftwood on a beach'. Even with its allusions to al fresco sex, I was too young to *really* understand the abandon at which the song was grasping, purely by playing the record.

Thankfully though, I had seen the video some weeks previously. Once again, Noel Edmonds bagged the premiere. And, as with

'Knowing Me, Knowing You' a year previously, the tone of the film that accompanied the song seemed out of step with anything else you might have expected to find on *Swap Shop*: Agnetha and Frida throwing off the chains of decorum on a packed dance floor while the floating heads of Benny and Björn mimed their bits into the camera, as if somehow controlling the girls' antics with the power of their music; an unsteady-looking Frida and Benny engaged in animated conversation in the early hours of the day, in an otherwise deserted Stockholm. Watching Benny lose his balance trying to walk along a kerb was only slightly less odd than the thought of seeing my parents totter unsteadily back from the pub. 'Summer Night City' resounded from the radiogram for most of Saturday morning, and when finally even I didn't want to hear it any more, I flipped the record and attempted to get my head around the experiment that was ABBA's stab at a folk medley. Even at the age of nine, the sound of Agnetha shrieking her way through an American slave song – 'Oh Lordy! / Pick a bale of cotton' – sounded a clang of ineluctable wrongness.

If my conception of naughtiness in pop was confined to John Travolta rhyming 'shit' with 'tit' and the Barron Knights changing the words of recent hits, Aki and Edward had graduated to heavier stuff. There was no gradual shift, but then there rarely is with children. Edward just turned up at the house one day, in March 1979, the John Travolta quiff from his last metamorphosis dramatically supplanted by an arrangement of spikes held upright by raw eggs. On his T-shirt was Sid Vicious, who had died of a heroin overdose just a month before under suspicion of having murdered his girlfriend Nancy Spungen. On his legs was a pair of black bondage trousers and under his arm was a record, the newly released soundtrack of the Sex Pistols film of the same name, *The Great Rock 'n' Roll Swindle*. All that remained of the old Edward Osborne was his thick steel-rimmed spectacles and his unfailingly polite manner when engaged in conversation with my mum.

'That's lots of pockets,' exclaimed my mum, who had almost never seen a pair of bondage trousers before.

'They're bondage trousers, Mrs Paphides,' said Edward respectfully. 'I'm a punk now.'

My mum stared at them for a couple more seconds, as if to do so might make what Edward had just said any more comprehensible to her. But it was no good. Nothing was going in. And, to be fair, I wasn't much further ahead. It would be several years before I realised that the word 'bondage' didn't come from the Latin for 'many zips'.

Malcolm McLaren had been funnelling what his art school background had taught him about situationism since 1974 when he changed the name of his King's Road store from Let It Rock to SEX, in the process co-opting fetish wear into the shop's aesthetic. Now that the Sex Pistols were reduced to two members and a revolving-door cast of guest singers, the extent to which this project was just another McLaren exercise in monetising notoriety was clearer than ever. With Glen Matlock, Johnny Rotten and Sid Vicious all out of the picture, *The Great Rock 'n' Roll Swindle* line-up comprised Steve Jones on guitar and Paul Cook on drums, variously abetted or replaced by a freakish assortment of hired hands. A posh eccentric associate of the group called Eddie Tenpole – later to briefly enjoy pop stardom as Tenpole Tudor – fronted a piece of orchestral whimsy called 'Who Killed Bambi?' McLaren himself stepped forward to do one vocal, on 'You Need Hands', but actually his fingerprints were all over the record: the African funk medley of early Pistols hits credited to 'Black Arabs'; a song which recounted the group's controversial departure from EMI in the wake of 'Anarchy in the UK' and, most jarringly, a couple of vocal turns from infamous train robber Ronnie Biggs on 'No One Is Innocent' and 'Belsen Was a Gas', an old song which both Sid Vicious and Johnny Rotten claimed to have had a part in writing.

For two thirteen-year-olds and a nine-year-old listening to it all, this amounted a lot of a new information. We didn't know who Ronnie Biggs was or, for that matter, what happened in the Great Train Robbery. We didn't know what Belsen was, and even when we found out, we didn't know how to process that song. At school, history lessons told us about crop rotation, the internal combustion engine and made it abundantly clear that the Romans did quite a lot for us, but once our O levels were done, we would leave with absolutely no idea why either world war had happened or exactly what the Nazis orchestrated at Belsen. Consequently, our unsatisfactory entry into this entire subject was a Sex Pistols song fronted by an exiled criminal. In this corner of Birmingham, we had no awareness that critical consensus barely deemed this line-up of the Sex Pistols worthy of the name.

In London, 'proper' punk was all but spent after the release of *Never Mind the Bollocks*, the Clash's first album two years previously, and the first few singles by the Damned. In the provinces beyond the M25 though, it was a different story. Not only did punk make more sense, but for bored teenagers like Aki and Edward, so did the ersatz nihilism of late adopters like Cockney Rejects and Sham 69. Aki brought home the second single by Camberley four-piece the Members, entitled 'The Sound of the Suburbs', which somehow simulated the hot oil and cold water mix of ennui and pent-up energy that passed for teenage life in a place where any sort of escape beyond the expectations of your family and teachers was scarcely a more plausible possibility than flying to the moon. These were the musical bat signals reaching out to Aki and Edward from the radio and TV screen.

Before they even made it to secondary school, their academic prospects were deemed virtually nonexistent by their teachers at Cottesbrooke whose appraisal of their potential saw them start their secondary school education in the fifth stream out of a possible six. Far from acting as a spur to try and claw their way up, this had the effect of making them lose their faith in school altogether. Aki excelled at football and table tennis, representing the school at regional level – achievements which served to legitimise his indifference to what happened in the classroom. Edward was similarly phlegmatic in his outlook. He had already decided that he would get a job as soon as he had failed his O levels, just as most of the faces on his bedroom wall had done.

The attitude of punk had also percolated into the music of countless other musicians, who recognised that, if they narrowed their trousers and ties and incorporated jerky, spasmodic body movements into their *Top of the Pops* performances, then they too could mark out some territory on musical terrain being hastily divvied up and rebuilt after the dust clouds from the great tremor of punk had dispersed. Over the past twelve months, some of the primary beneficiaries of that change had been Elvis Costello, Ian Dury and the Blockheads and Squeeze. As if some secret motion had been unanimously passed at an AGM attended by British musicians trying to crack the charts in the wake of punk, the jerky body actions were like a secret sign that not only did you approve of the changes ushered in by punk, but that you in some way aligned yourself to them. Writing in the liner notes of the 2002 reissue of his album *Armed Forces*, Costello recalled that he wrote 'Oliver's Army' on his way back from a trip to Belfast in which he saw 'mere boys walking around in battle dress with automatic weapons' – but once again, this all sailed right over my head. The reason I marched down to Discus in February 1979 and handed over some of my pocket money in exchange for 'Oliver's Army' was more to do with the sweet piano adornments laid on by Steve Nieve, every one of them inspired by his admiration for Benny Andersson's work in 'Dancing Queen'. Nieve's work on the record was what elevated a putative B-side into the biggest hit of Costello's career.

Vying alongside 'Oliver's Army' for the top spot was another single by a band seeking to smuggle traditional songcraft into a Trojan horse freshly made over in new wave colours. Squeeze's arrival in the chart at number 33 with 'Cool for Cats' instantly opened the doors of the *Top of the Pops* studio to them, an eventuality for which they had clearly prepared. Relieved of the burden of having to stand in front of a microphone, Glenn Tilbrook affected an eye-rolling picture of strung-out collapsey-limbed diffidence while Chris Difford itemised the disappointing details of an average day in his life. Either side of Difford, two over-caffeinated female backing vocalists in leather jackets, shades and skin-tight red disco trousers danced around him while echoing the title of the song. For Aki to go down the same route as Edward – that is to say, as near a facsimile of a fully paid-up King's Road punk as the combined stock of all the stalls in Birming-ham's Oasis market could allow – would have registered so hugely on the family seismograph that my dad might have driven straight to the Greek church and looked into the feasibility of having him exorcised. Opting to tag along to the new wave end of punk meant that Aki didn't need to make any drastic changes to his wardrobe. He just needed to get my mum to tighten his Wranglers and add a leather jacket to his birthday wish list. For the time being, he decided to give the caterpillar on his top lip a stay of execution – it would take the prospect of an actual relationship with a girl to get rid of that – and Aki started to plough his pocket money into music papers and records.

Not that he had to set aside any cash for his copy of 'Cool for Cats'. Accompanying our mum on trips into town always opened the door of possibility to a new record. Every department store had a music section. Aki knew that if he promised to keep an eye on me, that would afford my mum the chance to look at some clothes without having to worry about me getting bored. 'One record each!' she said, as Aki and I headed for the escalator towards the music basement of Debenhams on Bull Street.

Every record department had its own way of presenting the records in the chart. Unlike Discus, where the singles were kept beyond the reach of mucky young fingertips, Debenhams had a deep counter which housed five rows, each of which measured fifteen records long – one place for every single in the Top 75. Each single sat inside its own recessed space – one side about three inches lower than the other, so that the right-hand side of each pile pointed up upwards. If I bent down slightly so that I was eye level with the counter, the horizontal display would have made a wonky zigzag pattern. Aki followed the pattern of chart positions until his eyes alighted on 'Cool for Cats'. It came on pink vinyl with a picture sleeve that depicted a matching pink tiled surface on which were placed a plastic saxophone and guitar, a cat figurine, a dice, some coloured pills and an illustration depicting a dance move. Coloured plastic letters spelled out the song and the name of the group.

But new wave was *his* thing. It wasn't *my* thing. It was important to both of us that clear blue water separated our respective allegiances and that this separation would form the basis of our sibling rivalry. We were scouting the hit parade for versions of ourselves. Just as Aki saw something of his own outlook in Chris Difford's lackadaisical delivery, the moment I first heard Racey's debut hit 'Lay Your Love on Me', it was like looking into a magical mirror that reflected a pop star version of yourself back at you. With their matching suits and elementary stabs at choreography, they were one last hurrah by RAK's in-house songwriting magicians, Nicky Chinn and Mike Chapman. A dud Mud. A Showaddywaddy lacking a waddy. At least, that's how they're fated to be remembered. But that's not what I was seeing and hearing. In the diminutive Richard Gower they had a singer who would struggle to be eligible for most of the good rides at Alton Towers. His perpetually needy expression was somehow discernible merely by listening to his pleading delivery of the vocals. 'Lay Your Love on Me' was a song delivered from the perspective of someone who realises they're attempting to punch way above their weight, but who nonetheless entreats the girl of his dreams to go out with him anyway. If I were to try and ask someone out in 1979, this was absolutely how I would have gone about it, possibly pausing only to offer them half of my Lord Toffingham by way of a deal-breaker.

In the spring of 1979, the requisite qualities of the dream girl were clear in my mind:

A kind face.

A pretty smile.

Not too much make-up. If you're pretty, you don't need too much make-up.

They needed to be clean. You can tell if someone's clean because they smell of perfume and soap.

With her first and only top 20 hit, 'Mirrors', Sally Oldfield aloha'd her way barefoot onto *Top of the Pops*, effortlessly meeting all four criteria as she did so. Wearing a cotton nightie and an expression of transcendent bliss, she danced around the stage and trilled her Pacific faerie-folk mission statement with brazen indifference to the ridicule that might ensue. No one else who appeared on *Top of the Pops* in 1979 appeared to give less of a fuck than Sally Oldfield. Not the Stranglers or the Damned; not the UK Subs or the Boomtown Rats (whose pianist Johnnie Fingers also favoured nightwear when appearing on TV). For a brief period, Sally cruised to an altitude in my affections hitherto scaled only by a select few: the ABBA and Brotherhood of Man ladies, Kiki Dee, Kate Bush and, of course, Olivia Newton-John.

However, with the exception of the 'Summer Nights' scene on *Top of the Pops*, my most recent memory of Olivia had been the final scene in *Grease*, in which she had permed her hair, worn skin-tight trousers and TAKEN UP SMOKING in order to make herself attractive to John Travolta. As happy endings go, this one felt unsatisfactory to me. It was the only bit of *Grease* I didn't want to believe was real. The rest of the time, I was happy to consider that Sandra Dee and Olivia Newton-John were pretty much interchangeable. Now, with the release of her first post-*Grease* single, came the hope of resurrecting some of that fantasy. 'A Little More Love' was premiered on Michael Parkinson's Saturday night chat show. I would have been staying up for *Match of the Day* when Olivia stepped onto the stage and emphatically met criteria 1–3, while leaving me in no doubt that 4 was also probably a shoo-in.

After the turbulent teen drama of *Grease*, 'A Little More Love' – written by John Farrar, who had also penned 'You're the One That I Want' and 'Hopelessly Devoted to You' – opened a portal into a deeper, darker dynamic, involving people that had long since stopped seeking out fairground amusements as a suitable backdrop for their developing relationship. The opening few seconds drew you into a sonic establishing shot of instant jeopardy. Farrar landed a succession of sharp, serrated D7 downstrokes on the off-beat and, in doing so, left you in no doubt that this landscape was no place for a girl to be navigating alone. And yet, here was Olivia Newton-John – not just a girl, but Sandy from *Grease*! – setting out her protagonist's insoluble torment: 'Because it gets me nowhere / To tell you no / And it gets me nowhere to make you go'. While I adored the two John Farrar songs in *Grease*, this seemed to come from a more complicated and fascinating place. In the face of her lover's emotional coldness, Olivia Newton-John's character asks herself: if he won't show me any more warmth, is it down to me to turn up the heat even more?

The real genius of the song, however, is that, seconds after she asks the questions, 'Will a little more love make you start depending? / Will a little more love bring a happy ending?', the music is already answering it. Beneath the next line – 'Will a little more love make it right?' – the circular motif of the intro snaps back into place, supplanting the fleeting hope of the previous two. We're back where we started.

'A Little More Love' is a song about forsaking innocence in order to feed your emotional dependence on the partner you're desperate to keep. It's a song about how women blame themselves for the shortcomings of their men. I'm not sure to what degree I explicitly understood that in 1979, or how I squared that to the aforesaid list of desirable qualities. 'A Little More Love' had helped push the outermost point of my understanding of the female condition ever so slightly further out. It also was the last record I bought in Discus. Soon, we'd be on the move again.

CHAPTER 13

I saw Bert Chance cry for the second time when we told him we were moving. 'But you only just arrived,' he exclaimed. In just over a year, Bert had grown to love us. Every week, my mum would fill one or two old ice cream tubs with whatever was left over from weekend mealtimes and leave them outside his front door. If, for whatever reason, we didn't hear him screwing his leg on in the morning, we would knock and make sure he was OK. But although we had apparently cured him of his xenophobia, his continuing welfare wasn't enough to make us stay in a house we hated. The noises of lorries whizzing past in the rain never seemed to let up, the kitchen was tiny and – the deal-breaker – my dad wanted a garage. As with the Willard Road house, our parents didn't see any need to give us much advance notice of the move. We spent our final weekend there in April 1979, and this time, I was given an address to find all by myself.

I must have matured over the previous year or so, because the no-show drama of our previous move caused me nothing more than mild embarrassment when I looked back upon it. After school, I boarded the number 11 bus, rode past our old shop opposite the police station and alighted outside the Warwick Bowl – the cinema-cum-bowling alley where I had seen *Grease*, failed to follow the plot of *Star Wars* and, despite being underage, had been allowed inside to sit and wonder why Danny Zuko was so much less likeable in this new film where he stays out all night in New York nightclubs, swears at his parents and tries to rape his dance partner.

Once I was off the bus, the first thing I did was walk past the random remonstrations of the raccoon woman – so called because of the periorbital ecchymosis which had given her permanent black eyes and seemingly contributed to the mental breakdown which made her a permanent fixture on the Acocks Green roundabout. From here, it was a short walk up the road until I saw a hotel called the Westley Arms, and right across from there was Overlea Avenue, the little paddle-shaped cul-de-sac which contained our new house. We were at the far end. Number 14.

I quickly registered a succession of firsts. Our first house with an inside and outside toilet. First house with a side gate. First house with a little cloakroom. First house to have mixer taps. First house with a kitchen big enough to have a table in it. And, of course, our first garage. I spent five minutes going from room to room before my mum – eager to get me out of the way while she unpacked boxes – gave me a pound note and told me to go back into Acocks Green and amuse myself until it was time for tea.

Our new home felt like a step up, not just in terms of its size, but also its proximity to exciting shops. I don't think I seriously considered spending my pound anywhere other than Woolworths. After all, they sold everything. Why would I need to go anywhere else? I walked into Woolworths on my own for the first time and wondered what I was going to buy with my pound. I could just about afford a chart single or maybe I could get some sweets. Back in the late seventies, Woolworths also used to have a cold meat counter. This was where I first saw the word 'haslet'. If I wanted, I could buy myself some of that. But I didn't. Instead, my eyes were drawn to a brightly coloured display a little beyond the far end of the cold meats counter.

A few months previously, some TV ads for a new drink called Just Juice had just appeared. 'No pips, no peel, no pith, no powder, JUST

JUICE! / No oils, no acids, no preservatives, JUST JUICE!' went the catchy funk tune in the ad. In 1979, I could conceive of no more luxurious food item than the juice of a freshly squeezed orange. As far as I was concerned, the idea that you might discard perfectly good oranges once you had squeezed all the juice out of them was the absolute height of decadence. And yet, once every five or six months, perhaps if I had been unwell, or if oranges were cheap at the market, my mum would present me with a glass of juice, lovingly extracted from seven or eight specially sliced sun-kissed hemispheres of orange. The ingenuity of humans had sent other humans into space and built airplanes that crossed the Atlantic at supersonic speed, so I hadn't entirely understood why there had been such a hold-up with the invention of juice that you could buy in shops – juice which tasted just like the juice my mum made for me. It's not that I hadn't been looking out for it either. I had been burned once or twice before with products that purported to contain the same drink occasionally served up to me by my mum – but this always turned out to be bitter, saliva-thickening Britvic gak in tiny bottles. Surely though, Just Juice had to taste exactly like the stuff my mum made for me, didn't it? By virtue of their own claim – 'No pips, no peel, no pith, no powder' – this had to be the real thing?

Stacked in a massive pyramid in Woolworths, my dream had surely come true, and an entire litre of it could be mine for 79p. I paid my money and left the shop with 21p still left in my pocket. I took the short walk back to the new house with my carton of Just Juice clutched in both hands like a prize. This time, the front door was closed. I pressed the doorbell and noted with some satisfaction that it made a proper bing-bong noise and, once in my kitchen, poured myself a long glass of Just Juice, waiting for that tingly sweetness to touch my tongue. And then ... PTCHYUH! FYUCGK! BLEH! I'd been sold a syrupy, claggy, TV-advertised LIE.

I barely had time to process the injustice before the doorbell rang again. 'Welcome to Overlea Avenue!' chirped a woman holding a teal plate on which was a cake that she had decorated herself. 'I'm Joyce. I live at number 12!' Joyce wore comfortable trousers that matched the plate and she had let her hair go grey. She had no idea what sort of people might answer the door when she rang our bell. She wouldn't have had any time to form an impression of us before baking a cake. She didn't seem worried that we might be mad or hostile. But none of that mattered.

Because, in that moment, Joyce Hughes was honouring one of her core values. Neighbourliness was stitched into every fibre of her outlook. When she found out we were Greek, she was all the more intrigued. She wanted to know all about it. She wanted us to teach her Greek words and to tell her about Greek islands whose names we barely knew how to pronounce. She thought it was wonderful that she was living next to some Greeks, and she assured us that her husband Frank, who had yet to cycle home from the GPO depot where he worked as an engineer, would also think it was wonderful.

Even in these first impressions, there were clues as to what sort of family the Hugheses were, but I would have been too young to pick up on them: the cycling, the relaxed dress code, the undyed hair. They weren't exactly bohemians. They were too working class to fit into the modern-day associations we have with that word. They weren't trying to be unconventional. Joyce and Frank were churchgoing Catholics. And yet, to my mum, they seemed wildly unconventional. They had wooden floors – which in Acocks Green in 1979, was almost unprecedented – and an upright piano in the front room. They hadn't felt the need to upgrade from the modest black-and-white television which they would frequently eschew in favour of the piano. There were books everywhere. Their kitchen had shelves with pots of herbs scattered about the place. They had a pan on the hob that was as heavy as a carburettor and they never washed it, because, apparently, that would ruin it. In marked contrast to our bing-bonging doorbell, theirs went bink-bonk. The respective sounds reflected what we were aspiring to be and what the Hugheses were happy to be.

It would be a few days before we would meet the Hugheses' youngest daughter, Geraldine – or, as she insisted on being called, Ged. She was fourteen and went to the local Catholic comprehensive school, Archbishop Ilsley. Her hair was dark brown and, for the time being, cut into a style that was seventy per cent page boy and thirty per cent Purdey from *The New Avengers*. Aki was in our back garden and Ged, accompanied by one or two of her schoolfriends, got reckless with the hose in her own garden. Before hellos were even exchanged, they had drenched each other over the fence. He never seemed entirely comfortable around her – but still only nine, I was thrilled by any attention she paid me. And oddly enough, she seemed endlessly patient around me. As the summer holidays began and my boredom increased, I'd bink-bonk on her door three or four times a day. Did she want to play tennis? Did she want to play hide and seek? Did she want to go to the library? I don't remember her telling me to get lost once. She even turned up to my tenth birthday party. One solitary fourteen-year-old girl among a pack of screeching ten-year-old boys. My parents got me a brown leather football, or a 'caser', as you called them then. We all ran to the park with it. When we came back, Hani Tahur accidentally kicked it into the road and a lorry ran over it.

So the ball didn't make it to the end of the day, but I still have the record that Ged gave me. I must have mentioned that I liked Gerry Rafferty's 'Night Owl', because that's what she handed over to me as she arrived at my party. Its sleeve image was identical to that on the eponymous album: an illustration of Gerry in aviator shades and stripy pyjamas, louchely resting on a giant owl in a fantastical night-time scene. I played it over and over again, but it would be years until I realised what he was singing about. Gerry's blessing and his curse was that he was only able to score hit singles with songs which vented his bitterness at the exploitative machinations of the music industry. He'd managed it once when he was in Stealers Wheel, with 'Stuck in the Middle With You', and five years after that, he managed it with 'Baker Street': a world-weary paean to the solitary, soul-sapping grind that amounts to the life of a travelling musician.

If you wanted to buy a record that was currently in the charts, the shops orbiting the roundabout that gave Acocks its Green presented you with two options. Preedy's was the first. It was our local equivalent to WH Smith. The bit at the front sold magazines, and further back there were some bookshelves, a range of stationery and a dedicated record department. Here I eased into a reassuring routine: stepping up to the raised area where the 7-inch singles were kept, picking out sleeves of records that had never been hits and wondering what they sounded like. There was also a section devoted to reissues of singles by the Beatles and the Rolling Stones. Those by the former were presented in uniform green-bordered picture sleeves – probably the first time the Beatles' existence registered in my mind. In the Stones section, I approvingly noted the presence of hilariously titled singles '19th Nervous Breakdown' and 'Get Off My Cloud' – and wondered if their creators were a comedy band in the vein of the Barron Knights. .

If I stood outside Preedy's with my back turned to it, I would be staring across the road directly at Woolworths, the second option. With my orange juice dream now in bits, the main attraction in Woolworths was its singles display, a vertically ordered variation on what Debenhams had done with their layout. Here you were greeted with a floor-to-ceiling gallery of seventy-five small wall-mounted racks housing seventy-five different records – every one of them corresponding to a position in that week's chart. A wall of sound. A pop share index – a rock exchange, if you like – charting the differing fortunes of the artists seeking to establish a surer foothold in the affections of the nation. Oasis had their Wonderwall; this quickly became mine. It felt like all the news I needed to sustain my connection to the wider world was contained on the picture sleeves and label centres positioned opposite me.

Woolworths' chart wall allowed me to see what records were likely to remain unsold as they dropped out of the chart. If, say, Blondie's 'Sunday Girl' was at number 70, and there were still copies in stock, I soon came to realise that the following Wednesday – the day after the new chart was announced – the display would be updated and any remaining copies would be moved to the 49p rack. On Wednesdays, I'd return home from school about half an hour later than usual and head straight for the record player. In the middle of June, the Police's first chart run ended when 'Roxanne' dropped from 51 right off the bottom of the 75. That same week, I also bagged 'Sultans of Swing' by Dire Straits. As was customary at the time, both records had the right-hand corner snipped off their sleeves to denote that they had been reduced.

The two songs complemented each other well. Both groups were formed around songwriters from Tyneside who grew up fourteen miles apart from each other. Despite emerging in the wake of punk, neither group made any attempt to hide their virtuosity. Indeed, Dire Straits seemed indifferent bordering upon scornful of the punk combos with whom they suddenly found themselves sharing chart space. 'Sultans of Swing' told the story of what could have been any of a thousand bar bands playing jazz or rhythm and blues sets up and down the country: a paean to the part-timer with no drive for acclaim beyond the applause of the regulars who come to watch them play. 'Sultans of Swing' easily felt like my most grown-up purchase up to this point. I sat in front of the record player and imagined Guitar George who 'knows all the chords', but never deviates beyond rhythm guitar because 'he doesn't want to make it cry or sing' and Harry who 'doesn't mind if he doesn't make the scene'. In my mind, every time the song's insistent guitar motif appended these lyrical thumbnail sketches, it would freeze the picture on each character, as if I was watching the closing credits on a film about them.

The irony of 'Sultans of Swing' was that its success turned Dire Straits into the very thing that the group depicted in the song had no interest in becoming. Mark Knopfler didn't look too interested in the paraphernalia of pop stardom either. By contrast, the Police's frontman Sting had gone to great lengths to ingratiate himself with the zeitgeist. All three of his band bleached their hair, with Sting favouring a short spiky do similar to that of Generation X's Billy Idol and the Damned's Captain Sensible. He also, lest we forget, called himself Sting – which carried far more punk muster than his previous name Gordon Sumner. All these concessions meant, seemingly, that they didn't have to dumb down their actual music for punk. Though it took me decades to notice it, 'Roxanne' was compositionally closer to something that might have tumbled from the mouth of Billie Holiday or even Janis Joplin in previous decades – something, perhaps, to do with the hoarse, yearning delivery of Sting's vocal, its unshowy assimilation of jazz and blues tropes and the song's empathy for its protagonist. I strained to make out the words so that I might better decode them, but the relationship between Sting and the song's subject seemed to beg more questions than answers. Why did Roxanne have a red light? Why didn't Sting want her to turn it on? Why didn't he want her to wear that dress tonight? Why was she walking the streets for money? These were all questions I eventually directed at Aki one June evening as we got into our beds and prepared to fall asleep.

Aki: 'She's a prostitute. It's about a prostitute.'

I had heard the word prostitute almost a year earlier, when I overheard some boys in my class singing, 'I'll be your prostitute / Whenever you want me' to the tune of 'Substitute' by Clout. I didn't know what a prostitute was, and neither, I suppose, did they, or else they probably wouldn't have chosen to sing about being one while walking from the classroom to assembly.

'What does a prostitute do?' I asked Aki.

'You pay to have sex with her,' he said, sounding as worldly as a fourteen-year-old boy wearing a sky-blue Adidas V-neck top and only slightly flared Wranglers had ever sounded. 'If you go past a house and it's got a red light on, that means there's a prostitute there. That's how you can tell.'

Given that I wasn't actually sure – mechanically speaking – what you did in sex, I'm not sure why I was so shocked at the news that there were women who did it for a living. A few days later, directly after the Sunday evening chart rundown, my parents drove me to the big Wimpy restaurant on Corporation Street – an infrequent treat – for a Kingsize with chips and a chocolate milkshake. I sat in the back of the car in silence, looking through the window for red lights.

In the brief period since Aki's helpful deconstruction of 'Roxanne', I'd undergone what felt like something of a crash course in the hard realities of being a sex worker. The search for the Yorkshire Ripper had rumbled on for some time – enough for most children of my age to know that he existed and was still at large – but if it didn't make it to the front page of the *Evening Mail*, it didn't interest us greatly. That all changed on 20 June, when every news broadcast was dominated by the announcement that Assistant Chief Constable George Oldfield, the police officer heading the investigation, had received a cassette from someone purporting to be the killer. 'I'm Jack. I see you are still having no luck catching me. I have the greatest respect for you George, but Lord! You are no nearer catching me now than four years ago when I started.' Despite happening 200 miles north of Birmingham, this was splashed all over the front of the *Evening Mail*. I opened up the paper and stared at the gallery of women whose lives had been taken by 'Jack'. It said that most of them were prostitutes.

I was struggling to join up the disparate things I had so far learned about prostitutes. If it was illegal to do what they did, did that mean it was bad? And did this enrage someone so much that he decided to kill them? I read the reports and watched the news. The idea that I was 'listening' to the voice of a killer was as fascinating as it was terrifying. I had no real understanding of the circumstances that compelled women to become sex workers, less still of the potential dangers they faced on a daily basis. Part of me didn't want to read on, or tune in. But this was also a real-life thriller whose ending had yet to be written. I was gripped.

Almost at the end of our journey, we took the Digbeth flyover. This was a single-lane low-sided structure that was barely wider than a bus, appeared to be made of Meccano and, because you couldn't see the sides, felt utterly terrifying when experienced from the top deck of a number 44 bus. As we made our descent and rejoined the carriageway, there it was – a third-storey window illuminated in red, just a few doors away from the famous 'Lesbians are everywhere' graffiti which somehow managed to stay intact well into the mid-eighties. My parents didn't ask me why my nose was pressed against the car window and even if they had, I reasoned that 'I'm trying to spot prostitutes' probably wasn't the answer they'd want to hear. Besides, the prospect of catching a glimpse of one was something about which I felt anxious and ambivalent – like the sharks in the police station. I worried that I wouldn't be able to unsee what I might see. And yet, armed with the new knowledge given to me by Aki and Sting, I couldn't stop looking.

My dad parked the car near the newly built brutalist edifice of the Central Library and we walked along the deserted streets towards our destination. With McDonald's and Burger King yet to reach the British provinces, Wimpy was the go-to burger experience for anyone who didn't want to subject their insides to the Westlers burger stands dotted around town. The Wimpy menu offered a quantum upgrade from these soft grey meaty rusks whose short time between tin and bun was spent in a holding pen of warm water. But the brief Wimpy had set itself didn't just stop at not poisoning its customer base. Wimpy's bold mission was to take the quintessential modern American fast food item and somehow try to make it seem as British as a round of croquet with Frankie Howerd.

Instead of a clown whose gaze called to mind the pecked-out eyes of a dead marmoset, the Wimpy mascot was Mr Wimpy, a cartoon version of the Yeomen Warders of Her Majesty's Royal Palace and Fortress of the Tower of London, more commonly known as Beefeaters (although the punning assimilation of these two separate entities was lost on me as I'd never seen a Beefeater). There wasn't a single establishment in Birmingham that sold 'fries', and Wimpy was no exception. Their parent company Lyons owned dozens of Corner Houses in the early part of the century: beautifully ornamented yet affordable gathering places that remained popular well into the fifties. By turning them into Wimpy restaurants, Lyons were striking a pre-emptive blow against an inevitable American invasion of burger restaurants. We all know how well that turned out. In 1995 I interviewed Cher, and she recalled visiting London as Sonny & Cher's 'I Got You Babe' was racing up the British chart. Tired and overwhelmed by homesickness in her hotel room, she asked someone if they could go and fetch her a McDonald's. When they returned with a Wimpy, she burst into tears.

It turned out that there was a reason for this particular Sunday night trip into town. My dad was now pressing quite hard for a move to Cyprus. He also wanted a holiday, and he wanted to take me and Aki out there while my mum ran the shop. I looked at my mum, who in turn was trying to avoid eye contact with me. This was simply what was going to happen.

'You'll enjoy yourself,' she said limply. 'Your father can take you to the beach every day.'

I asked her how long we had to go for. I'm not sure why I was addressing her directly, when my dad was sitting right opposite me and this was all clearly his decision. Actually, I think I do know. Even now, I can trace a line of causality that goes all the way back to the way he looked at my mum when I threw the wooden antelope at him. A look that said, 'Are you pleased with what you've done?' Every time I displayed any sort of preference for her over him, it seemed clear to me that she would hear about it at some later point. He was convinced that she was using me as a confidant. Often when he had to leave the house, he would tartly joke that we could start talking about him now. Back at the Wimpy, I knew the drill. Show no emotion. Accept and move on. I didn't want to be the possible cause of any later repercussions. I had finished my burger, but I had barely started my milkshake. Sensing that I might be about to cry, I redeployed all my facial muscles into the act of drawing up the sweet, chocolatey contents of the cup through the straw as we commenced the walk back to the car.

Once we made it back home, the first thing I did was head over to the record player and place 'Roxanne' on the turntable, marvelling at the compassionate entreaties of Roxanne's kindly friend Sting, trying to show poor old Roxanne a better way to live. In my head, this was as much what Sting did as sing for the Police. He visited prostitutes, telling them to do something else instead. I imagined the prostitute next to the Digbeth flyover getting a knock on the door and thinking it was another person after some sex, but instead it was Sting, persuading her to do a different job. I could see why he called his band the Police. He was like a special sort of policeman who, instead of arresting prostitutes, gently tried to take them by the hand and make them change into a different dress, preferably one not worn by a prostitute. And the more I played 'Roxanne', the more I loved sensible, selfless Sting. If he could spare a moment from rescuing prostitutes and rescue me from what looked set to be the worst summer holiday of all time, I'd be really *really* grateful.

CHAPTER 14

We never went on holiday, the four of us, again. From now on, someone would always stay behind. The morning of our departure, we dropped off my mum at the Threepennybit. Like us, she had packed a suitcase, but she wasn't going anywhere. Faced with the prospect of working in the shop for fourteen hours a day, six days a week, she arranged to lodge with Flo, an elderly lady who lived across the road from the shop. I was inconsolable for two overlapping reasons. The prospect of a month spent apart from her was unimaginable. Secondly, the prospect of a month being looked after by my dad was equally unimaginable. He had never even had to look after us for a day. I'd never seen him cook a meal that didn't involve a fish fryer. What was he going to do when we ran out of clean clothes? What was he going to do if we fell ill? What was his plan beyond lunchtime?

He jabbed a forefinger at his watch and beckoned us out of the chip shop and back into the car. Through tears, my mum addressed her parting words as much at my brother as me. 'You'll make sure he's OK, won't you?' Aki didn't look too happy about what was going to happen either, but his method was to emotionally disengage. He stared at me in mild bafflement as I cried all the way to the M6/M1 intersection and finally fell asleep. When I awoke, we were negotiating one of the service roads going towards Heathrow, a roundabout on which stood a miniature replica of Concorde. I read my all comics on the outbound flight: *Buster, Whoopee!, Whizzer and Chips* and *Roy of the Rovers*. So much for my plans to stagger them throughout the holiday.

Our first stop-off was my aunt's house in Nicosia. To mark his return, my dad's youngest sister Irinoula moved all the tables from inside the house out into the front garden and an assortment of relatives descended upon the place, each of them bringing one or two dishes that they had prepared. She brought out an enormous pan of sheep's brains boiled in their own juices and proceeded to ladle them out into bowls which were passed along the line. I leaned over to my dad and, keen not to cause offence, told him that I didn't think I'd be able to eat them. In truth, I couldn't even look at them. In the afternoon sun, the smell of the brains merged with the steam from a pan of trotters in the kitchen. My dad had a word with his sister, who turned to me and asked me if I just wanted a bowl of spaghetti instead. I responded with a relieved nod. She took the pan in which she had boiled the sheep's brains and emptied the pasta into it. No one else was eating pasta. This was just for me. I knew that, whatever happened, in ten minutes' time, I would have to eat it. She placed the bowl in front of me. Trying to keep the gelatinous stink out of my nostrils, I consciously stopped breathing through my nose and ate as much as I could as quickly as possible. I managed about half before excusing myself.

I went for a walk to the nearest *manaviko* (grocery) and attempted to take the taste away with an ice cream. I kept walking alongside the baking-hot playing fields, making sure not to turn left or right in case I got lost, until I realised I was going to be sick. I turned and ran back to my aunt's house and gazed at the long table with maybe a dozen or so aunts, uncles and cousins all immersed in conversation. If I got any nearer, the lingering smell would only cause me to throw up right in front of them. I crossed the road and, leaning forward onto a tree, projected a mound of molten ice cream and unchewed spaghetti onto the patch of ground beside it. My stomach went into near constant spasm from that point onwards. My route over the next few hours could be traced by coordinates of vomit, all within a half-mile radius of my aunt's house. I managed to be sick five times in total – the precise number scorched on my brain because, of course, in all areas of human endeavour, children are perpetually aware of their previous best tally.

Over the next few days, it slowly dawned on me that my dad's main childcare strategy while he was on holiday involved delegating most of the parenting to his sisters and sisters-in-law. The only exception was the mornings, which involved him driving us to a beach outside Limassol which couldn't quite decide what it was called. The first sign read, 'Ladies' Mile', while a sign further along read 'Lady's Smile'. Occasionally, a cousin or two would join us. In Limassol, I was told that Persephone would be dropping by to say hi. I hadn't seen her since that magical summer in 1973 when she decided to partner with me in the bumper cars because she was a teenage girl and I was four, and teenage girls will always choose to partner with a four-year-old in a bumper car situation. But Persephone was about to go to medical school to become a doctor and I was no longer a cute four-year-old.

With further invitations to Luna Parks unforthcoming, Persephone's older brother Notis, on leave from national service, offered to take Aki and me into Limassol town for a milkshake. I was shocked to see Notis. The last time I had seen him, he was wearing flared denims and his shirt was unbuttoned almost down to his navel. His thick, lustrous hair had curved out like a pair of furry headphones, over his ears and back in again, resting elegantly on his shoulders. The softness of his face was accentuated by his heavy-lidded gaze and beatific smile. It was a look that ticked all the teen idol boxes. But the Notis who walked through the door of his parents' house in 1979 and crouched down to plant a manly smacker on my cheek was unrecognisable. He was dressed in army regulation jacket, and trousers and boots that laced all the way up his calves. His hair was short and he wore a green beret that complemented his khaki uniform. He had also grown a moustache. He was still handsome, but he now looked like a man. Which in turn made me acutely aware of what I was. A ten-year-old boy who missed my mother more than I ever thought imaginable.

Notis changed out of his army gear and re-emerged in a crisp white shirt and jeans with the flares ironed into them.

'What's it like being a soldier?' I asked him as he walked me and Aki into town.

'It's a huge shock to start with. But you can't show that you're weak, or else all the others will pick on you. Of course, it's a shock for them as well, but you have to fit in and act like a man. I hated it at first. I didn't want to talk to anyone about it when I got the letter. It upset me to even talk about it.'

'But you have to do it?' I said. 'You can't do something else instead?'

'No. If you're a boy, you have to do two years of national service.'

'I would hate that,' I said. 'I can't think of anything I would hate more.'

'Well, if you move back to Cyprus like your dad's planning, then you'll have to. But don't worry. I've made lots of friends there. It's hard, but we also have a great time together.'

Notis reached into his pocket and pulled out a packet of cigarettes.

'You've started smoking,' I said, unable to hide my surprise.

'I know. I'm going to give up when I'm out. But everyone smokes in the army.'

'You look so different,' I said.

He laughed at that. 'I had to cut all my hair off. They'll do that to you, when you join the army!'

'All of it? Can't they just leave a bit of it?'

'It's the first thing they do when you get there. You join a line and they shave your heads one by one. But actually, if you're smart, you'll

go to a barber the day before you start and get it done there. That's
what I did. It's best not to let anyone see what you were like before.
Arrive a soldier. Don't let them see the person.'

Arrive a soldier. I looked over at Aki, who had said almost nothing
the whole time we'd been in Cyprus. I knew he'd make a much better
soldier than me. I had asthma, eczema, a perpetually runny nose and
I was still being mistaken for a girl. The fear was real. I'd be flayed
alive within a day of arriving.

I was now starting to worry that this was a ruse. That my dad had
no intention of bringing us back to Birmingham. I kept reminding
myself about our new house. Surely we wouldn't have just moved
house if my parents were secretly planning to move back to Cyprus?
But what if my mum wasn't privy to that plan? *What if he just called
her and told her we were staying?* Without any outlet in the daytime,
the anxiety fed into my dreams. In one nightmare, I returned to
Birmingham only to find that national service had been introduced
there. All my friends had joined the army the previous week. I was
driven straight to my barracks and everyone sat and watched while
my clothes were removed and my head was shaved. I woke up to
my own panicked gasps and the impact of Aki's copy of *The Hobbit*,
whose journey across the room was broken by the side of my head.

The only thing that might have put my self-pity into perspective
was a phone call from my mum telling me how she was managing.
Her working days would finish at 11.30 p.m. She would lock up the
shop and walk across the road to Flo's terraced two-up two-down
and let herself in. Knowing that Flo always waited up for her, my
mum always brought something back from the shop and they'd
enjoy a late supper together, before my mum headed up to bed.
Sometimes my mum would hear a voice, but there was nothing so
unusual about the idea of someone in their mid-eighties talking to
themselves. Sometime into the third week of her stay though, my
mum was awoken by the clink of cutlery on crockery and animated

laughter. She crept downstairs in her nightgown and saw an entire table laid out with cups, saucers and cake. In the middle of the table were three lit candles. A 3 a.m. tea party.

'Victoria!' exclaimed Flo. 'Why don't you join us? We have company!' Flo addressed the unoccupied chair adjacent to her. 'Carol, have you met Victoria before? She works at the Threepennybit.'

On hearing the name, my mother twigged. Carol was the name of her only daughter, who had been killed in a car accident in 1976. A few nights previously, Flo had tried to give my mum Carol's mink coat by way of a thank you for all the free meals. She'd refused the coat, but she thought better of refusing this invitation to tea with a ghost. She took her seat as Flo poured her a cup of tea and handed her a slice of Bakewell tart. As the morning sun began to rise, my mum helped Flo clear away the crockery, gently reuniting Carol's uneaten slice with the remainder of the cake, and went back up to bed. It was never mentioned again.

Next to my mum, the other thing I longed for was music. I had taken to writing down the top 40 every week. On the day we left, the Boomtown Rats had sprung from number 15 to the top spot with 'I Don't Like Mondays'. Although I'd kept punk at a distance, I had my eye on the Boomtown Rats ever since seeing them do 'She's So Modern' on *Top of the Pops* the year before. You couldn't resist a song like 'She's So Modern', with its catchy, knockabout execution and the line, 'She's so 1970s', which had a full two years to go before it sounded the opposite of modern. Aki and Edward seemed to find them ridiculous, which cleared the path for them to be My Punk Band. And, really, they were the perfect punk band for a ten-year-old. For a start, they were called the Boomtown Rats, which is pretty much what any ten-year-old boy would call a punk band if the idea occurred to them. I liked Bob Geldof too. Even before seeing Johnny Rotten on *Juke Box Jury* with his teeth painted green, I had an immediate and profound sense that the Sex Pistols' frontman would not want people like me to buy his records. I disdained the Damned and the Stranglers for similar reasons. But Bob Geldof was different. Whenever he was on *Top of the Pops*, he would lean down and beckon the camera closer. It was as though he was leaning down to address me, and me only.

Bob further finessed his stagecraft with the Boomtown Rats' first number 1 single in October 1978. To the outrage of the Musicians Union, he blew into a lit candelabrum for the saxophone intro of 'Rat Trap', and when the song ousted 'Summer Nights' from the top spot, he tore a picture of John Travolta and Olivia Newton-John in half! 'Rat Trap' wasn't what you'd call obvious hit material. Bereft of a chorus or a single hook, the tale of Billy's dead-end provincial existence clocked in at five minutes. Save for that one sax motif, no element of the song is repeated more than once. If the Boomtown Rats were bothered about punk authenticity, this new wave operetta was a funny way of showing it. But 'Rat Trap' clearly struck a chord. Everyone who had heard Bruce Springsteen assumed that 'Rat Trap' was Bob Geldof's attempt to write a 'Born to Run' set on the streets of Dublin, although twenty-five years later, Geldof would tell me, '[it] was meant to be a take on Van Morrison, or maybe even a Phil Lynott take on Van Morrison, creating something mythical out of the people and the suburbs where I'd grown up.'

I was untroubled by any such authenticity-related caveats. I didn't know who Bruce Springsteen, Van Morrison or Phil Lynott were. As far as I was concerned, Bob was just the sort of energised team leader punk needed. This was one army I was happy to join. I was convinced that, were Bob to visit the suburbs on some sort of recruitment drive for his nation of Boomtown, he'd take one look at me, address me by some sort of nickname which he would have thought up on the spot – something like Curly or Chips – and know that I would be forever loyal to the cause.

To my mind, the Boomtown Rats' superiority to their punk peers was evidenced by the fact that none of the other lot had managed to scale the top of the charts. Now here they were again with 'I Don't Like Mondays', a baroque pop melodrama that wasted no time in letting you know how important it was. Johnny Fingers's piano intro was dispatched with a grandiosity that corresponded with what followed. 'I don't like Mondays' was the explanation given by San Diego schoolgirl Brenda Spencer when asked why she decided to lean out of her bedroom window and randomly start shooting people at her school across the road. Should we ever make it back to Birmingham, I wasn't going to be borrowing Aki's air rifle any time soon, but Bob's vivid evocation of soured childhood innocence and the bewilderment of the story's unwitting accessories stirred something uncomfortable in me. Thousands of miles away from home, surrounded by cousins who looked and spoke like the children our parents expected us to turn into, the silicon chip in my head also had a bit of work to do.

It was almost enough to stand next to the newspaper carousel at the seafront kiosk in Limassol and merely breathe in the comforting fumes of newsprint gently baking in the hot summer sun. On any other day, that would have sufficed. But the arrival of Wednesday's *Daily Mirror* on Thursday morning brought with it urgent information: the brand-new top 30. I pinched open the clip which attached the *Daily Mirror* to the carousel and turned the first pages to check that the chart was in there. Because I had no idea what had happened the previous week, the numbers in brackets which indicated last week's chart positions were just as important as this week's numbers. We went back to the house where we were staying, but I didn't go inside. I stayed on the front porch, opened out the newspaper on the low table in front of me and slowly absorbed the following information:

1 (1) THE BOOMTOWN RATS 'I Don't Like Mondays'

2 (2) CLIFF RICHARD 'We Don't Talk Anymore'

3 (6) IAN DURY AND THE BLOCKHEADS 'Reasons to Be Cheerful, Part 3'

4 (14) EARTH WIND & FIRE 'After the Love Has Gone'

5 (3) ABBA 'Angel Eyes'/'Voulez-Vous'

6 (7) SHAM 69 'Hersham Boys'

7 (4) THE POLICE 'Can't Stand Losing You'

8 (5) THE DOOLEYS 'Wanted'

9 (17) DARTS 'Duke of Earl'

10 (8) ELECTRIC LIGHT ORCHESTRA 'The Diary of Horace Wimp'

11 (27) B.A. ROBERTSON 'Bang Bang'

12 (11) SPARKS 'Beat the Clock'

13 (32) ROXY MUSIC 'Angel Eyes'

14 (24) THE SPECIAL AKA 'Gangsters'

15 (9) DAVE EDMUNDS 'Girls Talk'

16 (18) JUDY TZUKE 'Stay with Me till Dawn'

17 (29) SHOWADDYWADDY 'Sweet Little Rock 'n' Roller'

18 (10) PATRICK HERNANDEZ 'Born to Be Alive'

19 (25) GIBSON BROTHERS 'Ooh! What a Life'

20 (23) SPYRO GYRA 'Morning Dance'

21 (16) THE KORGIS 'If I Had You'

22 (39) BONEY M 'Gotta Go Home'/'El Lute'

23 (30) JOE JACKSON 'Is She Really Going Out with Him?'

24 (13) SUPERTRAMP 'Breakfast in America'

25 (12) THE KNACK 'My Sharona'

26 (15) CHIC 'Good Times'

27 (31) RANDY VANWARMER 'Just When I Needed You Most'

28 (21) DONNA SUMMER 'Bad Girls'

29 (44) ANGELIC UPSTARTS 'Teenage Warning'

30 (47) FLYING LIZARDS 'Money'

As far as I was concerned there was more news squeezed into this corner of a single page of the *Daily Mirror* than there was in the rest of the paper. After the complexities of 'Roxanne', the simultaneous release of two singles – 'If I Had You' and 'Duke of Earl' – by different British artists, both with almost identical sentiments, peddled a version of love that, more than anything in the world, I wanted to be true. And, in fact, I think that upon hearing them, I decided it *was* true. The Korgis were a group formed from the ashes of a proggy Bristol combo called Stackridge whose main claim to fame was that they were the first band to play at the inaugural Glastonbury Festival. There was nothing remotely prog about 'If I Had You', though. For this record, they appeared to be using the multitracked yearning of John Lennon's '#9 Dream' as a vessel in which to launch the perfect defences-down, this-is-what-it's-like love song. 'I could change the world / If I had you', sang James Warren on a chorus of sweet hymnal allure and unshakeable sincerity. OK, so that's how it feels to be in love. This is what you look out for.

If the Korgis song posed a question: *What would happen if you went out with me?*, the Darts song, a cover of Gene Chandler's 1962 doo-wop rhapsody 'Duke of Earl', represented one of two possible answers. You're the Duke of Earl, walking through your dukedom, hand in hand with your Duchess of Earl. *This will be how it feels.* This will be what I need to look out for. Thank you, Darts. When it happens, I'll know, and it will have been all because of your song.

In the week we left for Cyprus, both singles were climbing the chart. The Korgis had leapt up to 13 from 20, while Darts had jumped ten places to 22. By the time we returned, I fully expected both to be sitting in the top three. In fact, 'Duke of Earl' was still climbing, but 'If I Had You' had begun its descent. While the injustice of the Korgis' relatively modest showing rankled, it was good to see Sting – conscientious supply teacher of the punk borstal – improve on his previous chart position with a song that, as chance would have it, represented the other possible answer to the Korgis' question. While 'Duke of Earl' offered a three-minute balloon ride into the thrilling thermal current of new love with the person who completes you, the Police's 'Can't Stand Losing You' was a stark pencil sketch of an alternative so unbearable that it appears to end in suicide.

Not here the intravenous Valium whoosh of the Korgis' song or Darts' giddy sense of dominion over a world which loves lovers and none more so than the lovers in 'Duke of Earl'. Both musically and lyrically, 'Can't Stand Losing You' was a stark inversion of those records. Admittedly, there was some black humour in the line about her 6-foot 10-inch brother killing our protagonist and, later, the bit about her returning all his records scratched, but the most startling thing about the Police song is just how sparse it was. With Sting and Andy Summers keeping their bass and guitar parts to a bare minimum, the qualities that made it memorable were also the qualities that made it slightly disturbing, the repetition of the single line in the chorus sounding to me like transmissions from a place beyond security or sanity. I'd heard two Police songs now, and neither of them painted a picture of adulthood that I wanted any part of.

All I wanted to talk about now was music and, to a decreasing extent, football. Unlike Birmingham though, Limassol had just one record shop, Studio 67, and I didn't have the means to find it on my own. Notis told me that Studio 67 provided a bespoke taping service. You paid them something like £3, supplied them with a list of songs and they filled an entire cassette with them. This was the stuff of dreams! Notis explained that Studio 67 had a huge music library and, famously, no one had ever requested a song that they didn't have. I wrote out my list and badgered my dad to drive us there. Studio 67's brazen illegal taping racket was clearly a hit with the locals. I handed my piece of paper up to a Cypriot woman standing on the other side of a very high counter. She scrutinised the track list and handed it over to a colleague who took it through to a brightly lit back room full of hi-fi equipment. The far wall was filled floor-to-ceiling with shelving full of records. I could have happily spent the rest of my holiday in that room, but disappointingly, no one offered. Two hours later, I had a cassette full of new music in my hand – none of which would have prompted Studio 67 to search too hard: Dave Edmunds's 'Girls Talk', Patrick Hernandez's 'Born to Be Alive', the Gibson Brothers' 'Que Sera Mi Vida' and, of course, Darts, the Korgis, the Police and the Boomtown Rats. Also on there was a song by Eruption called 'One Way Ticket', whose protagonist mourned her insoluble sadness at having a 'one-way ticket to the blues'. Unsure whether we'd come here on a return ticket, I saw far more of myself in her plight than was comfortable.

By the time we finally returned to the long-stay car park at Heathrow, my dad, while not exactly feeling that he'd had the holiday he needed, unlocked the car doors with a renewed appreciation for his job that only four weeks abroad in sole care of your children can bring. There was a lot more to solo parenting than driving your kids to the beach for a couple of hours. After a brief sleep, I awoke to the sight of red buses and the sound of my dad swearing in Greek. We'd missed our turn for the motorway.

'Where are we?' I asked.

He told me we were on the North Circular Road, and that seemed to me like a much cooler name for a road than any of the roads in Birmingham. I told him I was hungry and he handed me half a bag of pistachio nuts. I had a few. Now I was thirsty as well as hungry. Surely by now contemplating the thanklessness of being a sole carer, he saw a food shop and pulled over. Five minutes later, he was back with a large bottle of Corona lemonade – in 1979, the idea of buying bottled water was as bizarre as buying tinned sunlight – and a pizza. The pizza was uncooked: a thick doughy disc topped with red sauce, wet grated cheese and a few pieces of soggy green peppers, stabilised by a polystyrene wheel and wrapped in plastic. I'm not sure if I'd ever even had a pizza at this point, but I was fairly certain that, on the occasions that people did have pizzas, they were always cooked. I looked at it and momentarily thought of pointing out that perhaps we weren't supposed to eat it like this. But then again, it wasn't as if: (a) he didn't know that; and (b) there was anything he could do about it. I ate a few mouthfuls and went straight back to sleep.

CHAPTER 15

'Go on! Punch me! Punch me there! I swear I won't feel a thing!'

Standing at Mr Butcher's desk waiting for him to finish inspecting another pupil's handwriting, Nicholas Shough addressed me directly. He was leaning against his desk facing out towards the rest of the class. I was seated at mine, just a couple of feet away from where Nicholas was standing. He was wearing high-waisted trousers with a brass belt buckle positioned directly over his tummy, and he wanted me to punch him on the area protected by the buckle. I shook my head, but Nicholas insisted. Finally, I released my fist as instructed. At that moment, Mr Butcher looked up. He didn't want to hear my protestations. I was sent to a single desk facing the wall, at the far corner of the classroom. I had to spend the rest of the day there.

It was the first day of the final year before secondary school. Mr Butcher was new at Cottesbrooke Junior School, straight out of teacher-training college. Perms were still the height of fashion among footballers throughout Europe. Kevin Keegan marked his arrival at FC Hamburg from Liverpool by spending an afternoon in the hairdresser's chair. Upon seeing a picture of his ex-teammate in the newspaper, seasoned Liverpool midfielder Tommy Smith dared Phil Thompson to follow suit. Thompson rose to the challenge and paid a visit to Charlie Wynn's Chopping Block hair salon in Kirkby. Within a few months, dozens of top-flight footballers had the 'bubble cut'. Once the new fashion spread among the ranks of footballers, it was inevitable that twenty-something PE teachers would be next to succumb to the curlers. Strictly speaking, Mr Butcher wasn't a PE teacher – he was our form teacher – but sports science was what he had studied prior to arriving here. There had been a vacancy at Cottesbrooke for a teacher who would be able to take charge of the football and netball teams. Mr Butcher was one of two male members of staff newly appointed to the school, in the process tripling the number of male teachers. He would intermittently tend to his perm with a special comb which he kept in the back pocket of his pastel-blue polyester-cotton trousers which he wore tight around his backside but which maintained a sharp flare around his ankles. In the mornings, he would enter the classroom wearing a shiny blue zip-up jacket, elasticated around the waist.

In less time than it took for my fist to make contact with Nicholas Shough's belt buckle, Mr Butcher decided that he didn't like me, and that was that. Not only was he my first male teacher, he was also the first teacher who I didn't feel any great desire to please. It might be that these two facts are connected. Whatever the reason, just when I needed it the most, I had backup. For the first time, William Osborne and I had been put in the same class. Not just the same class, but neighbouring desks. Even in the minutes before Beltgate, William had already made up his mind about Mr Butcher. With his militant unsportiness and his love of *Doctor Who* – an obsession which had now expanded to take in *Blake's 7*, a new series by Daleks creator Terry Nation – William knew that the only thing that would get him through this year would be his own superiority to all the values represented by the bubble-headed goon standing before him.

By the time Nicholas Shough was finished at Mr Butcher's desk and I was reinstalled at the desk of shame, Nicholas was the proud owner of a red Berol handwriting pen. Mr Butcher's first job on his first day had been to get pupils to line up in groups of four at his desk and write a sentence for him on a sheet of paper. The neatest writers were rewarded with a pen; the rest of us were fated to keep writing in pencil until Mr Butcher deemed us eligible for the next handwriting test. By December, roughly two-thirds of Class 10 were using pens. The divide between the pen people and the pencil people was felt acutely by the latter, who longed for the soft scratch of a nylon pen tip on lined paper.

In the playground, another division persisted. The lunchtime football game continued to dominate about a quarter of the available outside space. Nothing had changed between the previous year and this. We were still not allowed anything larger than a tennis ball. The Whites continued playing against the Blacks, with just a couple of white anti-ringers like me on the Blacks' team to give the Whites a chance of winning.

That all came screeching to a halt one morning when the other new male member of staff, Mr Welbeck, stepped forward to take one of his rare assemblies. Freshly installed as the headmaster, Mr Welbeck had a thrusting managerial air that must have seemed quite modern in a primary school in the late 1970s. He was in his mid-to-late thirties and wore a black suit, which accentuated the luminescence of his carrot-coloured hair. In a lecture which predated Paul McCartney and Stevie Wonder's 'Ebony and Ivory' by almost three years, Mr Welbeck embarked on a long homily about the white notes and the black notes on a piano and how, if you attempt to play a melody using only the white notes or the black notes, the results will be pretty rubbish. We didn't see what was coming until the very end. Because we literally thought we were learning about pianos, we didn't understand why Mr Welbeck was getting so worked up. Even when Mr Welbeck's speech took a hard left into South Africa and apartheid, we *still* didn't know what was coming. Why would we? What could an oppressive political regime 8,000 miles away possibly have to do with anything taking place at Cottesbrooke Junior School? We were about to find out.

'Until yesterday,' continued Mr Welbeck, 'I thought that apartheid was something that existed far, far away from our playground here at Cottesbrooke.' He paused for a moment, just long enough to inadvertently reveal that he had rehearsed the next bit and he was pretty proud of it. 'I'm talking about the *small ball marvels* who play football in the playground every school dinner time, and think it's acceptable to choose their teams according to the colour of their skin. Well, let me tell you: here at Cottesbrooke, we have no place for that sort of racial segregation. If I hear of any further games like this being played, you will be banned from the playground until further notice. Do I make myself clear?'

We were aghast. For us, Blacks vs Whites wasn't a race issue. It was purely an admin matter. The atmosphere in the playground later that day was muted. New teams were carefully selected, but the resulting game was a shambles, with players continually passing to boys on the opposing side. After a few days, someone hit upon an inspired idea. 'Why don't we play "England vs Brazil?"' they said. Within a few days, it was business as usual. Did Mr Welbeck really not notice what we had done? Or had he been merely waiting for a pretext upon which to launch his piano keys riff?

In fact, the only part of our schooldays that involved any racial segregation was football. The world – or at least the bits of the world that interested us – was multiracial. Pop, or at least the bits of pop that interested us, was multiracial. Following on swiftly from the success of their debut single 'Gangsters', the Specials cracked the top 10 with their second single 'A Message to You, Rudy'. They weren't the first mixed-race British group to catch our attention. Darts and Hot Chocolate had got there first, but the Specials were different. Terry Hall awkwardly shifted his body weight from one foot to the other, reluctantly holding the mic like he was looking after it while its owner found a parking space.

Far from acting as a deterrent, his manner was key to the band's appeal with boys of my age. Any kid from round here, if asked to sing in a band, would have carried themselves in the same way – or perhaps they would have chosen to move like Neville Staples, who – standing beside Hall – performed some choreography of his own devising, moving with a robotic motion from left to right. A month previously, we'd seen Madness land in the *Top of the Pops* studios, wearing similar clothes – straight-legged suits and pork-pie hats – and open their debut appearance on the show with the lines, 'An earthquake is erupting / But not on Orange Street'. Orange Street was the birthplace of Jamaican music giant Prince Buster, whose song 'Madness' was covered on the flipside of 'The Prince' and gave the erstwhile North London Invaders a snappier name to call themselves. Of course, none of us knew what Orange Street was at the time or, indeed, that the Prince was Prince Buster, but the perspicacity of those two lines registered on impact. The Selecter also made their *Top of the Pops* debut in the same month, shortly to be followed by the Beat.

With the exception of Madness, all these groups were from the West Midlands – Coventry or Birmingham – and all released their first singles on 2 Tone, the label founded by the Specials' keyboard player and primary songwriter, Jerry Dammers. Just as importantly, all of them were unified by an aesthetic that felt like a logical third act in the wake of the nihilism of punk and the crafted ennui of new wave. The dress code was clear not only from *Top of the Pops* and pictures in a new pop magazine called *Smash Hits*, but also on the 2 Tone sleeve and label design: a monochrome graphic of a man in a two-piece narrow-trousered suit, white shirt, narrow black tie, low-ankled black shoes and pork-pie hat.

One revivalist trend merged with another in November when the Jam stepped up a level and trailed the release of their new album *Setting Sons* with their first top 10 hit. 'Sup up your beer and collect your fags / There's a row going on down near Slough' remains one of the all-time great opening lyrical salvos, although it wouldn't have meant too much to me in 1979. Aki explained to me that 'The Eton Rifles' was about a posh private school and the children who went there. Everything we knew about private schools took place in the playground of Eastbourne House, on the other side of the diagonally criss-crossed fence which separated our playground from theirs. Their playtimes coincided with ours. They wore grey uniforms and hats. We were allowed to wear whatever we wanted. Halfway through my time at Cottesbrooke, a girl called Caroline Sweet – (almost) like in the Neil Diamond song – moved across to the other side. Occasionally, we'd catch sight of her. Her new uniform and identical-looking friends gave her an air of regal detachment. Glimpsing her seemed as strange as waving goodbye to a friend and seeing them pop up in the pages of *The Beano*.

By Christmas, the changing musical landscape claimed its first sartorial convert in Cottesbrooke. Ant McKenzie's parents were separated. His mum was younger than most of the other mums and this almost certainly had a bearing on his early adoption of mod/rude boy fashions. One day, he turned up to school with short hair and trousers narrowed. His coat completed the makeover: a green oversized mod parka with the 2 Tone man drawn on the back. The accuracy of its replication strongly suggested that Ant's mum had acted as a proud accessory to his transformation. Within a few months, at least a dozen boys had followed suit. Most called themselves mods, but it was the glut of records released by 2 Tone artists and their affiliates that were making the running. Madness in particular were firing new singles into the chart with alarming frequency. Just as one commenced its descent, another one would appear. 'The Prince' and 'One Step Beyond' – and then 'My Girl', the one that displayed sufficient songwriting chops for Terry Wogan to play it on his Radio 2 show.

Even if I waited for these songs to drop out of the charts and into Woolworths' bargain basket, my pocket money simply couldn't extend to every single hit record that was consuming my world. I was now dividing much of my spare time between three shops. At the far end of Acocks Green, beyond Woolworths and Preedy's, was a new dedicated record shop. I'd seen the carrier bags before I found the actual shop. They were Caramac brown and featured an illustration of an old wind-up gramophone. Across the top in groovy capital letters, not dissimilar to those of the Mystery Machine in *Scooby-Doo*, was the name of the shop: 'EASY LISTENING'. The same logo featured on the shop itself, rendered in orange on a green perspex background.

When I went there for the first time, I felt a profound sense of well-being. You had to walk to the far end of the shop to get to the counter. On the counter itself was the current Top 75, pulled out from the centre pages of industry trade paper *Music Week*. To the right of the Top 75 was a wooden browser which featured two rows of 7-inch singles and had 'New Releases' written on it. This would remain unchanged for the next decade. Positioned at a right angle to the main counter were several more browsers. One featured ex-chart releases and oldies, while the other one was set aside for cut-price ex-jukebox records. These were typically records that had been in the chart about six months previously and had run their course at whatever pub jukebox they happened to have served in.

I'd like to be able to say I was there to buy the Madness record or the Specials record or the Jam record. But much as I loved them all, none of those records was at the top of my list. The artists with whom I was emotionally connecting were still either groovy parent/sibling/childminder types or adult personifications of my most grating traits. A couple of weeks previously Sad Café – occupants of the former category – made their *Top of the Pops* debut with 'Every Day Hurts'. It was a lot to take in. Their singer Paul Young (not the same Paul Young who would inundate charity shop LP sections with his 1983 album *No Parlez*) bore a powerful resemblance to Manchester United captain Martin Buchan. Only Aki's firm assurances that Buchan and Young were two separate entities allowed me to focus on the song – a first-person lament for the dissolution of a relationship he'd thought would last forever. This wasn't 'Hopelessly Devoted to You' or 'Can't Stand Losing You'. This came from a place beyond teenage idealism, closer to the emotional terrain of ABBA songs such as 'Knowing Me, Knowing You' or 'SOS'. Songs that held the secret that no adult will ever look you in the eye and willingly impart: sometimes, it's not going to be OK.

It was Sad Café's best song by a mile, and when it came to maximising its potential, they didn't fuck about. You could strip 'Every Day Hurts' down to its two core components – Paul Young's vocal and Vic Emerson's piano part – and it would still stop you in your tracks. Young's falsetto sigh just after the chorus is a case in point, sung in a manner which suggests he didn't know he was going to make that sound before it came out of his mouth, while Emerson's playing is a masterclass of dewy desolation. For the recording of 'Every Day Hurts' though, Sad Café enlisted the services of 10cc's Eric Stewart, who, having written and produced 'I'm Not in Love', knew a thing or two about constructing sub-zero sonic landscapes vast enough to convey the scale of the universe's indifference to human heartbreak. He certainly didn't disappoint. Under his supervision, multitracked harmonies and string arrangements swooped into the heart of the action in time to lift every successive chorus to new heights. In doing so, Eric Stewart and Sad Café created a song which reversed the Commercial Union insurance ads' famous claim. It absolutely made a drama out of a crisis.

I spent at least half an hour in Easy Listening before handing over my pound note. Two people worked there. One was the owner, a well-spoken man in his fifties – dark hair, bald on top and a penicillin-pink round-necked jumper under which you could nonetheless see a shirt and tie. The other guy was his marginally groovier son, Richard. The absence of a Birmingham accent suggested he had been sent to a school a bit like the one in the Jam song. His well-tended beard told you that punk had made absolutely no impact on his world. Indeed, had you asked me a decade later, I still couldn't have told you what music he liked (although now I'm thinking James Taylor and Clifford T. Ward were probably safe bets). The younger guy took my money before walking out to pull the shutters down over the windows either side of the door, a hint that would be directed at me hundreds of times throughout the ensuing decade.

It was impossible to buy everything, but the existence of TV-advertised albums of current hits went some of the way towards stretching my budget over as many songs as possible. The big compilation album that year was *Hot Tracks*: twenty songs, ten on each side, housed in a sleeve depicting some railway tracks through a blue filter, two of them coloured bright red – as literal a representation of the album title as you could wish. Three of my big summer obsessions – Darts, the Korgis and the Boomtown Rats – were present. The 2 Tone acts were conspicuous by their absence, but British reggae was represented by two songs that stood comparison to the very best that 1979 had to offer in any genre.

Eddy Grant's Guyanese parents had already been working in the UK for several years before they attained the necessary financial security to pay for Eddy, then aged twelve, to come and join them. He was still in his teens when he formed the Equals, the first interracial rock group to enjoy major success in Britain. 'Living on the Frontline' was clearly a show of solidarity with the roots consciousness of Bob Marley and Steel Pulse: 'To all my brothers in Africa / Stop shooting your brother'. But I hadn't heard either of those artists. Neither did I know who was shooting who in Africa or why they were doing it. But the assured austerity of the song's arrangement – most notably the audacious squelch of a keyboard that prefigured both the beginnings of acid house and reggae's transformation into dancehall – conferred an air of importance upon the song and the singer.

Like Eddy, Dennis Bovell was also twelve when he arrived in Britain, not from Guyana but from nearby Barbados. Nine years after steering Britain's first reggae band Matumbi to wider prominence, Bovell decided he had amassed enough knowledge to write a reggae song so irresistible that it couldn't fail to be a colossal hit in the actual pop chart. 'Silly Games' was, he said, 'a song constructed with a verse and a chorus and a bridge and a "tickling piece" at the end, and an intro to catch you so you would have to sit up and listen to what was coming next.' For Bovell though, writing 'Silly Games' was only half of the challenge. Finding a singer to do it justice was key to the entire undertaking. Two years previously, Janet Kay topped the reggae charts with her version of Minnie Riperton's 'Loving You'. If she could scale the heights of 'Loving You', that meant she was one of only a handful of singers who would be able to handle 'Silly Games'.

It was the first reggae music I'd heard, knowing that what I was listening to was reggae music, and while that was new terrain, the thematic content was strangely familiar to me: a first verse in which the singer's emotions are laid on the line; the sense of the ground moving beneath your feet, achieved in this instance by an unexpected key change on 'You're as much to blame / Cos I know you feel the same'; and then a chorus which basically says *enough is enough, I'm moving on now* – only for the protagonist to go over the same ground on the next verse ('Yet in my mind I say / If he makes his move today . . .'). In 'Silly Games', Kay's vulnerability echoed the uncertainty of Olivia Newton-John's 'A Little More Love'. The other obvious point of comparison was ABBA's 'The Name of the Game', whose love-struck narrator edges by tiny increments towards emotional disclosure, ever wary that her feelings might not be recip-rocated: 'If I trust in you, would you let me down? / Would you laugh at me, if I said I care for you? / Could you feel the same way too?'

Given that my parents had little that corresponded to my somewhat idealised definition of a relationship, it probably wasn't surprising that I was searching ABBA records for clues. Waiting for me on Christmas morning alongside *Hot Tracks* was their most recent studio album *Voulez-Vous*. This was clearly the work of a group seeking to consolidate their position in a post-*Saturday Night Fever*, post-*Rumours* world. Setting trends had never been ABBA's forte. They were never innovators. They were master assimilators, sniffing the prevailing pop wind, breaking down its constituent elements and surpassing the best of what their peers had to offer. ABBA were sculptors of the *zeitgeist*, borrowing the techniques and tools of their peers and using them to create increasingly devastating self-portraits.

The key detail about *Voulez-Vous* that seemed to elude critics at the time was the wildly contrasting state of the relationships of the two couples in ABBA. The photograph on the gatefold sleeve of ABBA's first *Greatest Hits* album in 1976 was nothing if not prescient: the two couples on a park bench, Benny and Frida kissing passionately, while a denim-clad Björn reads the paper beside a fed-up looking Agnetha. By the time *Voulez-Vous* came out, Benny and Frida were still very much in love. They had married during the recording of the album and, with no small children to care for, the evenings were theirs to do as they wished. It seemed like no accident that the dishevelled hedonists in the 'Summer Night City' video were Benny and Frida. By contrast, Agnetha and Björn, parents to two small children, decided to separate three months after Benny and Frida's wedding. Rarely did an interview go by without Agnetha confiding that it made her sad to leave home without her kids. Indeed, she often chose not to. While Frida and Benny got to unwind at the after-show, Agnetha was being a mum and divorcee, pondering her options while Björn eased into a new relationship with the woman who became his second wife. These were the two worlds that coexisted and sometimes collided on *Voulez-Vous*.

For the record's title track, they abandoned the home comforts of Polar Studios and headed for Criteria Studios in Miami, where the Bee Gees had reinvented themselves with 'Jive Talkin'" and recorded some of 'Stayin' Alive'. 'Voulez-Vous' is a lasting monument to ABBA's audacity. When Robert Stigwood asked the Bee Gees to supply him with songs for *Saturday Night Fever*, he explained to them that the inspiration for the film was Nik Cohn's 1976 *New York* magazine cover story, 'Tribal Rites of the New Saturday Night'. Cohn's piece described the nocturnal rituals of young clubbers in Brooklyn, most notably a character called Vincent (who Cohn later admitted existed only in his imagination). The Bee Gees gave Stigwood some songs they had already written and added 'Stayin' Alive' to the tally, building the song up from a sampled loop. 'Voulez-Vous' is a glimpse into a parallel world in which Stigwood had asked ABBA and not the Bee Gees to do the same job. Lyrically and musically, it perfectly fits the brief – 'A sense of expectation hanging in the air / Giving out a spark / Across the room your eyes are glowing in the dark' – and, as such, is hard to think of as anything other than a blinding show of arrogance. When ABBA returned from Miami, they had a house band service them with a string of world-class funk and disco backing tracks.

I was too young to know what it was like to fall in love, but I'd found plenty of songs that trailed that feeling. The final two songs on *Voulez-Vous* hinted at something I was also too young to experience. On 'Kisses of Fire', we heard Agnetha exhorting her lover to 'touch my lips, close your eyes and see with your fingertips' before the song launches its supersonic vertical ascent to something that: (a) sounded unutterably thrilling; and (b) I was pretty sure my parents couldn't possibly have done with each other. Whatever sort of sex resulted in me and my brother, it must have been a very different sort to the one being described here. Just as there are two entirely different tube stations called Edgware Road, I figured there must be two completely different procedures called sex. At the risk of seeming disloyal to my parents, ABBA's one sounded better.

Further confirmation was afforded by Frida's vocal turn on 'Lovers (Live a Little Longer)', a song predicated on a news report which may have been no more real than Cohn's piece about Brooklyn nightclubbers. In today's newspaper, she sang, there was a study which showed that people who regularly have sex enjoy a longer life than those who don't. I can't be sure what orders Benny and Björn gave their bassist and drummer, but I suspect they fully availed them of the song's subject matter. Even before the first line, the steamy, pneumatic interplay of the drummer Ola Brunkert's bass drum, hi-hat and snare combined with a bassline that drops in and out as if playfully holding back. As filthy rhythm tracks go, 'Lovers (Live a Little Longer)' is up there with Serge Gainsbourg's 'Melody' and Donna Summer's 'Love to Love You Baby'. As lyrics go, it's also pretty close, albeit with intimations of the Beatles' 'Why Don't We Do It in the Road?': 'I just don't care if they're watching 'cause listen / We've got a reason for each time we're kissin'.'

But the amorous songs on *Voulez-Vous* were only half the story. There was another emotional storyline which somehow you couldn't help associate more closely with Agnetha. 'If It Wasn't for the Nights' was a song about the depression that takes hold when the mundane distractions of daytime give way to the long shadows of night. The only marriage in ABBA that ultimately lasted was the one between Benny and Björn, whose working relationship took precedence during the band's time together and continued in the decades that followed. Their perfectionism was all over *Voulez-Vous*, and yet it was their first album in four years not to yield a UK number 1 single.

They almost managed it with 'Chiquitita' and 'I Have a Dream', two number 2 singles about enduring hard times in the belief that better days will prevail. Both songs also had components built into them that seemed to serve as distractions from their underlying melancholia. On 'Chiquitita' it was a rump-tiddly-ump-pump bar-relhouse outro that seemed to go on forever. On 'I Have a Dream', it was a children's choir, sweetening the sentiments of a song that, without it, sounded like far more of an SOS than the 1975 single of that title. ABBA's exhortations to cheer up never came with a guar-antee. That wasn't their style. They always stopped short of promising that things would get better. It was more that to imagine better days might just about make the present more bearable. Hence, 'If you see the wonder of a fairy tale / You can face the future / Even if you fail'.

The song that stopped 'I Have a Dream' from reaching the top spot at Christmas also featured children singing. ABBA and Roger Waters probably had more in common with each other than Waters was prepared to admit when I interviewed him in 2007. 'From the first bar I ever heard by them,' he told me, 'I was an ex-listener.' But some unlikely similarities persisted. The Australian tour footage in *ABBA: The Movie* captured a group wholly unprepared for the clamour that greeted them. ABBA's collective discomfiture in public was that of a band keen to impress upon their fans that their songs were the most fascinating thing about them, a message that only seemed to make them even more fascinating to those same fans. Had Roger Waters not been so swift to declare himself an ex-listener, he would no doubt have empathised. While ABBA were barricading themselves in their Australian hotel rooms, Pink Floyd were on a tour that would culmi-nate at the Montreal Olympic Stadium with Roger Waters spitting on one fan who attempted to scale the stage. The episode inspired him to write *The Wall*, an album about building a wall between himself and his audience, and spawned 'Another Brick in the Wall (Part II)', the song I heard in the West Bromwich shop on the first day of the Christmas holidays, blaring out of the radio that sat between bottles of Daddies ketchup and the huge jar of pickled eggs.

Remember, I had never heard Pink Floyd before. I didn't know what they looked like. I didn't know if they were posh or poor or young or old. The sum of what I knew about Pink Floyd was increasing one line at a time, one guitar solo at a time, over the course of four minutes. 'We don't need no education,' intoned a voice pitched just this side of threatening. 'We don't need no thought control / No dark sarcasm in the classroom / Teacher! Leave those kids alone!'

I imagined that Pink Floyd were mean-looking, denim-clad and probably a bit smelly, like a fatter version of the Stranglers. In real life, they all had cockney accents, like the Smurf jailbirds from Catford on the Barron Knights record. And because Mr Butcher had all but announced his hostility towards me and because Pink Floyd had declared war on the entire teaching profession, they were one of a growing number of pop allies who, in my imaginings, might storm the school gates at any minute and come to my defence. Perhaps Pink Floyd had heard about the infamous Cottesbrooke spelling test incident a couple of weeks previously in which Mr Butcher had invited suggestions that included 'er' in them. Spelling being something of a forte for me, I had put my hand up and proffered the word 'perambulator'. To say Mr Butcher seemed displeased at my suggestion was putting it mildly. His expression was the sort you might deploy on discovering that a house guest had taken a dump in your wardrobe. 'What was that word, Peter? *Perambulator*? And would you like to tell the class what a *perambulator* is?' I didn't know what a perambulator was. I'd just heard the word somewhere and remembered it. 'Not so clever now, are we? If you don't know what a word means, Peter, don't waste our time by nominating it.'

In my fantastical league table of rock rescuers who might, at any minute, burst through the door of Class 10 with the express aim of delivering us from the daily torpor of Mr Butcher, there was one singer who ranked even higher that Pink Floyd. As Mr Butcher ended each day with one of his tedious storytelling sessions, I would set about polishing the disused copper inkwell on my desk, cleaning all the gunk out of it so that I might once again be able to slide the cover

across its rails from left to right. Week by week, I restored it to its
former glory, in the process burnishing my sense of superiority to Mr
Butcher. And as I did so, the pop saviour I most regularly imagined
bursting through the door of Class 10 with a guitar dangling in front
of his muscular torso was none other than kind, compassionate Sting.

In my reverie, Mr Butcher would be momentarily dumbstruck at
the blond pop god standing before him. Sting would announce that
Mr Welbeck had said he was to come straight here and relieve Mr
Butcher of his duties for the day. A stammering Mr Butcher would
hastily gather the photocopied worksheets on his desk and ask Sting
if he could stay and watch. But Sting would calmly inform him
that he preferred to work alone. As Mr Butcher reached for the peg
and donned his shiny blue jacket, Sting would turn to us and ask if
anyone who knew who he was. Naturally, my hand would be first up.

'You're . . . St— Mr Sting!'

'That's ri—'

'But your real name is Gordon Sumner! I read it in *Smash Hits*!
And before you were in the Police, you were a teacher!'

'Hey, you *really* know your stuff, kid! But you can just call me
Sting. No "Mr" here.' Addressing the whole class, Sting would continue, 'Apparently, they don't have music lessons at Cottesbrooke, so
I thought I'd drop in and give you one myself. I've got a new record
out at the minute. It's called "Message in a Bottle". Can anyone here
tell me what a message in a bottle is?'

Of course, my hand would be the first up again. After all, this was
my fantasy. 'Wow! You again! What's your name, kid?'

'Peter Paphides!'

'Cool name, Peter Paphides! Go on, then!'

'It's when you're stuck on a desert island and you find a bottle and
you write an SOS and put it inside the bottle and then the bottle
gets washed up in a place with lots of people and they send a boat
out to rescue you.'

'Spot on, Peter Paphides! That's exactly what a message in a bottle is. Who wants to hear my song? It went straight into the charts at number 8. Pretty cool, huh?'

The thing about each of the Police's first three hit singles was that each of them made Sting seem like a totally fantastic person in a different way to the others. In 'Roxanne' he was both tormented Romeo, compassionate case worker and furrow-browed Prince Charming to the song's titular sex worker. In 'Can't Stand Losing You', his only crime had been to love someone who didn't love him back. 'Message in a Bottle' was also written in the first person from the perspective of someone who had lost everything. Perhaps because of the goodwill accrued on the previous two singles, I felt totally invested in Sting's authorial voice and clearly I wasn't the only one. The song leapt to the top spot in its second week. Setting aside Stewart Copeland's irrepressible syncopations, the song's almost dirge-like verses seemed closer to plainsong or folk music. And that in turn accentuated the jolt into the chorus.

> *I'll send an SOS to the world*
> *I'll send an SOS to the world*
> *I hope that someone gets my*
> *I hope that someone gets my . . .*

In 'Message in a Bottle', the firm resolve at the beginning of the chorus – like a balloon being inflated in one final burst of demented energy – pops to reveal his one final feeble hope of salvation.

> *. . . message in a bottle.*

In these lines, I saw something that resonated with my own situation and the looming identity crisis I was trying to will out of existence. If I wrote an SOS to the world, what would it have said, exactly? It would have probably said that I didn't feel very Greek at all. That all the things I seemed to love, give or take *dolmades*, *pastitsio* and *souvlakia* – were British. And that I lived in fear that my parents would one day announce we were moving back to Cyprus. It would have said that I couldn't see myself ever turning into the adult my parents expected me to become. If I ever married, I didn't see myself marrying a Greek woman and taking to the floor at my own wedding reception, dancing in time to the bouzoukis while my parents' friends pinned bank notes to my suit.

I was like the round-headed boy born to pointy-headed parents in Harry Nilsson's animated film *The Point*. Of course, they loved me. And I loved them. It's just that I didn't quite seem to be one of them. My English was now way better than my Greek. When I conversed with relatives and my parents' Greek friends, I occasionally had to replace Greek words I didn't know with their English equivalents. Looking slightly embarrassed, my mum would sometimes step in and have to explain that my Greek was *spasta* (broken) as a result of having been born here.

However, in the company of my parents' friend Angelos, there was no need to feel any such awkwardness. Since buying his first shop in the late sixties, Angelos had speculated to accumulate at velocity – five chippies in a twenty-mile radius, each with his name on them. Perhaps because Britain had been so good to him, he was happy to cede some of his identity to his host country. Angelos also sometimes spoke in a sort of broken Greek – a 'silly cow' here or a 'Bob's your uncle' there – but his wasn't born of necessity. It felt like a natural extension of his fun, flashy demeanour. And so, when Aki and I were informed we would be spending the final night of the year at the swish Solihull pile belonging to Angelos and his family, we greeted the news enthusiastically. After all, we were waving goodbye to an entire decade, and it felt like a relief to be doing something other than being at home. To be able to spend those hours in Angelos's mock Tudor mini-palace made me feel like a competition winner.

At 11 p.m., Aki and I decamped to the spare room with the bunk beds and lay on the top bunk watching a seasonal version of *The Kenny Everett Video Show*, retitled *Will Kenny Everett Make It to the 1980s?* TV Hogmanays prior to 1979 had been a jumble of televised bagpipers, the chimes of Big Ben and footage of people my parents' age joining hands and singing a dirge that seemed ill suited to their jubilant expressions. So *Will Kenny Everett Make It to the 1980s?* amounted to a radical departure. As far back as his Radio 1 days, Everett had established himself as a one-man, pop-literate, state-educated Monty Python. He spent two days a week in a BBC base-ment studio using sound effects records, bits of old news footage and self-created alter egos to create sketches and surreal sound collages he interspersed with the music selections on his show. His TV shows were an extension of those early radio programmes.

It was a mark of the Boomtown Rats' lofty stock at this point that they were the only guests performing their new single ('Someone's Looking at You'). Everyone else did a turn from their back catalogue. Cliff Richard did his signature late seventies/early eighties 'dance' – that of a man carefully emerging through a foggy clearing at night in a glade where a puma has been reportedly sighted – and performed his 1976 hit 'Devil Woman'. He also participated in a recurring gag which involved him quickly running onto the set with a guitar and playing 'Living Doll', before Kenny caught up with him and bundled him out of the studio. Kenny blacked up and put on a preposterous Jamaican accent to introduce Bryan Ferry and Roxy Music doing 'In the Midnight Hour', while complaining that 'dis man's a HONKY!' And it was also the second time I saw David Bowie in action. The first had been the high camp of the 'Boys Keep Swinging' video two years earlier, whose depiction of three cadaverous ladyBowies prompted his American label to withhold from releasing it as a single. But this was something else entirely. Looking mesmerisingly handsome, Bowie was shot from the shoulders up, his disparately sized pupils impossible to miss as he sang 'Space Oddity' with an intensity that silenced both me and my brother. Halfway through, the camera panned back and he walked across to another set. It was the padded cell that he also used for another song which mentions Major Tom, 'Ashes to Ashes'. But, of course, we weren't to know that at the time. 'Ashes to Ashes' was six months off being released.

The whole thing ended with a supergroup featuring the two remaining Sex Pistols and Phil Lynott and Scott Gorham of Thin Lizzy marking the tail end of the holiday season with a medley of 'Jingle Bells' and 'We Wish You a Merry Christmas', as pretend snow fell on them. Aki thought it was great. I just remember the low-level confusion of seeing punks and heavy rockers playing in the same group and being genuinely surprised that this was allowed. It was the first time I had knowingly experienced the end of one decade and the beginning of a new one. Kenny Everett had turned out the lights on the 1970s, and all that remained was a long wait for our parents to decide it was time to go home.

If that seems a little anticlimactic, well it was and it wasn't. That depended on who I compared myself to. Being Greek, we didn't do 'Auld Lang Syne', and if there was a Hellenic equivalent, we didn't do that either. In fact, neither of my parents sang. And because Aki and I never once heard either of our parents burst into song – whether singing along with whatever was playing on the radio or unaccompanied just because sometimes you feel like singing – it was something that we never did either. Furthermore, because it was something we had never heard anyone doing in the house, it would have seemed as random as if one of us had simply started mooing. So, on New Year's Eve, it seemed perfectly natural for the ten-year-old me to find myself idly wondering what the British families were up to right now.

Somewhere out there, the family on the Twister advert were having a New Year's Eve of organised fun with, of course, plenty of limb-tangling zaniness and a steady supply of Mars and Marathons in their 'fun-size' denominations. I didn't know exactly where Brotherhood of Man lived, but it seemed as clear to me as it did on the day I first set eyes on them that they and all their three-year-old children (it wouldn't have occurred to me that their children had aged since 'Save Your Kisses for Me') were presiding over a lovely sing-song by the glow of a crackling fire. However, even these cockle-warming idylls paled in comparison to the merry bonhomie I imagined enveloping the Mull of Kintyre home of Paul and Linda McCartney, as Wings joined hands and sang in the New Year with the help of all their bagpiping neighbours.

Despite all that though, I was far from sad. This was a significant upgrade on all our previous New Years. I'd got to spend it a house with an ice-making fridge, a one-armed bandit and remote-control curtains. Furthermore, I had yet to learn that a pessimist is never disappointed. Just because *this* wasn't the year we all joined hands and burst into song like a normal family, that didn't mean it wasn't going to happen next year.

CHAPTER 16

Gary Numan had no plans to record an album. His punk band Tubeway Army had released two singles but their record company, a new indie label called Beggars Banquet, were keen for the band to keep building momentum with a more substantial release. After acceding to Beggars' request in 1979, Tubeway Army turned up at Spaceward Studios in Cambridge. Left behind in their studio by the previous occupants was a Minimoog synthesiser. Curious to see what sort of a noise it made, Numan flicked the switch and waited for the valves to heat up. He pressed on one of the keys. The resulting sound, vast and otherworldly, virtually floored him. 'In that moment,' he later said, 'I knew exactly what I wanted to do.'

Influenced by Philip K. Dick and J.G. Ballard, Numan wrote his own short stories. Perhaps the most prescient one described a version of London thirty years into the future, in which machines – 'friends' – are programmed to supply various services to your door. The 'friends' in Numan's story looked exactly like human beings, but were actually robot prostitutes. That spring, when Numan turned the story into a song and called it 'Are "Friends" Electric?', it climbed to the top of the charts, brushing past the Police's marginally more conventional paean to prostitution as it did so.

The epiphany Gary Numan underwent on hearing that synthesiser was passed on wholesale to William Osborne the first time he heard 'Are "Friends" Electric?' Just as Numan's life would never be the same again on hearing that alien *whoosshh*, William knew upon seeing that first *Top of the Pops* performance that he had a new favourite singer. Not only did Gary Numan complete William's interior world; he perfectly described the exterior world in a way that merged with William's perception of it – a reality long augmented by years of *Doctor Who* programmes and books in which the stillness of an empty park at night could, at any minute, be obliterated by the blinding lights of an alien spacecraft.

William's relationships with other people could sometimes leave him exasperated. Compromise didn't come naturally to him, and on reflection, I think it was no accident that our friendship was founded during a period where I didn't utter a single word to him. The age gap between us – he, the oldest in the year; me, the youngest – also helped establish an order of rank.

We briefly fell out when, in advance of a school talent contest, William somehow persuaded me to sing 'UFO Shanty', a song that we'd seen Neil Innes do in the guise of Tom Baker's Doctor, but in a Lancashire accent, and blacked up like a Black and White Minstrel, on his Monday night BBC2 show *The Innes Book of Records*. What we didn't remember of the lyrics we made up from scratch. But between the Monday of the broadcast and the Friday of the talent contest, I had decided that there was no way I could go through with any sort of public singing. In all likelihood, I almost certainly knew I couldn't do it within minutes of him asking me to, but I had never once stood up to William and I didn't know how to start now. Rather than summon the nerve to tell him, I feigned illness and got the day off school. 'I knew you'd chicken out,' he said when he saw me the following Monday. We didn't speak to each other for the remainder of the week.

But it was perhaps 'Cars', the follow-up to 'Are "Friends" Electric?' and the first Gary Numan single to dispense with the Tubeway Army name, that would accord Numan a forever unassailable place

in William's affections. Prior to 1979, thousands of songs had been
written about cars. A year had passed since I had watched Aki and
William's brother Edward listening to 'Greased Lightnin'' for the first
time. The pursuit of girls seemed a more typical way cars were used
in pop songs. But in Gary Numan's song, the car was a protective
membrane, an escape pod.

William's adoration of Gary Numan further hardened with the
release of Numan's fourth album *Telekon* and, in particular, the
track 'This Wreckage': 'And what if God's dead? / We must have done
something wrong / This dark facade ends / We're independent from
someone'. All my other friends still believed in ghosts, and some of
us were still not entirely sure about Santa Claus and Victorian fairies.
For my part, I was far too invested in God's existence to goad Him
into punishing me. Being the last person in my house to still be
awake was another one of my irrational fears, so every night before
going to sleep, I'd stick my head under the sheets so that Aki couldn't
hear me asking God to make sure I was unconscious before my dad
came home from work on the other side of midnight.

You might have been into synth-pop but not into the mod revival.
You might have been into 2 Tone yet not so crazy about new wave
or punk. But 1980 was the year that a mist of dystopian unease
seemed to seep into all pop's disparate tribes and confer a sort of
kinship upon all them. The upshot of this was that a bunch of very
different songs in different genres by bands that were very different
to each other all raced into the chart at roughly the same time and
yet somehow they all felt connected. While William was in his
room still making sense of Gary Numan's seismic impact on his
world, Edward – now shorn of his punk spikes – was listening to
the Specials' 'Too Much Too Young' on Roy Osborne's downstairs
music centre. In Overlea Avenue, I could hear Aki in our bedroom
repeatedly playing his first ever 12-inch single. The Clash's refusal to
appear on *Top of the Pops* worked in their favour on 'London Calling'.

A studio performance would have been no match for a grainy night-time video which depicted the band performing in torrential rain from a floating platform in the Thames, a setting which mirrored Joe Strummer's apocalyptic pronouncements: 'The ice age is coming, the sun is zooming in / Meltdown expected, the wheat is growin' thin / Engines stop running, but I have no fear / 'Cause London is drowning and I, I live by the river'.

A weekend-long school trip to Atherstone Youth Hostel, seventeen miles away, began after school on a Friday in January – up to twenty of us in a minibus, seated on wooden benches facing each other, the floor between us taken up by a pile of rucksacks and holdalls. I don't think we even had seatbelts on. From the front, UB40's 'Food for Thought' came on and through the rain beating down on the wind-screen, it seemed to rise up and disperse like a vapour that enveloped the world outside: the Chrysler factory glistening in the rain on Coventry Road; the sulphurous light of the subways underneath the Bull Ring. So this was what happened to reggae when you deprived it of sunshine. It sounded damp and subterranean. It shivered. We were all fascinated by this song with food in its title but not in its lyrics, written by Robin Campbell to address 'the fact that there are starving people in Africa and here we are all sat around eating our Christmas dinner and praising the Lord'.

Just as, in 1970, the pages of *Disc* and *Music Echo* were scattered with ads for loon pants, *Smash Hits* was now thick with ads for the Jam T-shirts and mod gear: boating blazers, union jack transfers and target patches. Though Aki never committed to a wholesale change of uniform and the tedious parental scrutiny it would have brought with it, his immersion in certain records was total. His obsession with the Jam's fourth album *Setting Sons* opened up his interior world to me in a way that wouldn't have otherwise been possible, and it happened so naturally that I didn't even register it at the time.

This was the album on which Paul Weller began to fancy himself as a writer comparable to his hero Ray Davies. And as with Ray Davies on the Kinks' *Arthur (Or the Decline and Fall of the British Empire)*, it allowed us to see the young adult pulling back his gaze to see life's arc as it lies ahead, its curve defined by key coordinates, each represented by a different song. 'Private Hell' told the story of a family who gradually become strangers to each other. It wasn't the story of us in 1980, but I could see lines start to appear that might in time become cracks, which if not treated soon enough, could turn into ravines. Aki was beginning to turn into something my parents didn't understand. If they couldn't persuade us to move to Cyprus with them, then at the very least they could one day leave him in charge of the chip shop. *It might not seem glamorous now,* they'd tell him, *but when the time comes, you'll be glad it's there. You'll never have to worry about setting up a business of your own. Do you know how many years we had to work to get to this point?*

Similar processes were already under way at chip shops across Birmingham. My parents' Cypriot friends Nick and Maria had a chippy three hundred yards down the road from our house. Their oldest son, also called Nick, was already working there most evenings. I would sometimes walk past their shop on the way back from school and see father and son next to each other behind the fryer. They had the same face, but Nick Snr was fat, fifty-something and bald – while Nick Jr was thin, nineteen and had hair like Andy Gibb. The very last time I'd ever see Nick Jr, in 1982, he let me rifle through his record collection. It was mainly 12-inches. I picked out Frantique's 'Strut Your Funky Stuff' and Lipps Inc.'s 'Funkytown' and he let me keep them. 'I don't have time to listen to that stuff any more,' he said. I should have been thrilled – and, of course, I *was* thrilled. But it also underscored what I risked losing if I ended up like Nick. A life in which 'Funkytown' by Lipps Inc. was something you simply outgrew seemed like no sort of life at all.

Other songs on *Setting Sons* had a similar impact on Aki also because of the sheer recognisability of its world: the intimacies exchanged 'among the shit – the dirty linen / The holy Coca-Cola tins – the punctured footballs / The ragged dolls – the rusting bicycles' ('Wasteland'); and memorials to the inhabitants of a world to which their author could never truly return. 'Thick as Thieves' was a forewarning that even the most intense friendships can burn out once they outlive the circumstances that created them. Weller wrote the song about Steve Brookes and Dave Waller, the friends with whom he started the Jam. These were his first reflections on his pre-fame life, and the affection for those irretrievable days was palpable even to me as I sat on the end of Aki's bed, reading the inner sleeve.

We stole the love from young girls in ivory towers
We stole autumn leaves and summer showers
We stole the silent wind that says you are free
We stole everything that we could see

On 'Saturday's Kids', Weller sang about 'girls [who] work in Tesco's and Woolworths / Wear cheap perfume 'cause it's all they can afford'. We didn't have a Tesco near us, so I supplanted that mental image with one of my own: the two teenage new wave twins who worked in Preedy's on a Saturday – one on records and the other on magazines, both in their regulation uniform, but with eye shadow and hair styled to the same specifications favoured by the yet-to-be-famous Bananarama.

The intense exposure to *Setting Sons* merged with the release of the Jam's first single of 1980. Because the reception to 'The Eton Rifles' had propelled Paul Weller to a place far beyond the mod and punk scenes with which his band were associated, the expectations that piled onto 'Going Underground' were massive. It was one of those beautiful moments that happens from time to time when an artist sees their opportunity for greatness approaching and delivers a song that not only meets the brief, but surpasses it. How much of this did I really clock? I heard the references to choosing your leaders and placing your trust and the bit about kidney machines being replaced by rockets and guns, but more than this, it was Weller's perpetual frown and the performance itself – lean, agile, direct, purposeful – that told me this was an important and serious record.

Such was the clamour to hear what the Jam had done this time around that even Ged came over from next door for Aki's inaugural play of the record. As it came to an end, we watched the needle automatically lift up and return to its cradle. When the automatic switch on the turntable moved to the 'STOP' position, Aki slid it across to the right, and in doing so triggered the automatic function again. The needle dropped onto the dry staccato opening chords played on Weller's guitar once more. The uptight rigidity of Bruce Foxton's bass playing perfectly accentuated his front man's puritanical disdain for the political classes.

Everyone visibly relaxed on the second play. With the realisation that Weller had pulled it off, fidgety air drumming and light chit-chat could commence. Then, remembering that this was actually billed as a double A-side, Aki flipped the record and our introduction to psychedelic pop began. Weller plundered two inspirations to write 'The Dreams of Children'. Prompted by the Beatles' use of backwards recordings on *Revolver*, he asked Alan Douglas, the engineer on *Setting Sons*, to give him a cassette of the entire album played in reverse. Listening to the tape, Weller alighted on a section of harmonies in 'Thick as Thieves' (you can hear them at the beginning of 'The Dreams of Children'), and from there, he wrote down some words which he said were initially inspired by a recent reading of 'The Forbidden', a Clive Barker story which centres around a serial killer of children called the Candyman.

'The Dreams of Children' and 'Going Underground' were both, in different ways, repudiations of the rational world.

I caught a glimpse from the dreams of children
I got a feeling of optimism
But woke up to a grey and lonely picture
The streets below left me feeling dirty, and . . .

. . . and into a chorus that sounded unlike anything we'd heard before at that point.

I was alone, no one was there
I was alone, no one was there

The same line repeated twice. And then a third time, but with a sudden spike into pleading urgency . . .

I was alone no one was there.

. . . and then the return of those backwards harmonies, sounding unreachable and indifferent to the singer's remonstrations.

'He left school with one CSE, you know!' said Ged in the short silence after the record finished, a fact that instantly blew my mind. In a pre-GCSE world, CSEs were the exams you took when you weren't bright enough to be entered for O levels, so the notion that Paul Weller could only get it together to pass one of them was utterly bewildering to me. I was young enough to want to believe that O levels and CSEs were objective metrics of intelligence. Like most children, I needed to believe that the world could be understood by a network of observable, interconnected rules that, once mastered, made adult life a less terrifying prospect. Isn't that why young minds are so vulnerable to cults and belief systems? Why be the CEO of your own failing company when you could just accept the rules and regulations set down by someone else and venture forward in blind, blithe acceptance?

Copies of *Smash Hits* magazine started to appear in our house, usually produced from Aki's school bag, but sometimes Ged would bring them over. 'Going Underground' made it onto the singles page on the same week as 'Geno' by Dexys Midnight Runners. The female reviewer praised the former's 'relentless attack' and 'uncomfortably sobering lyrics' but poured scorn on the latter, singling out Kevin Rowland's singing – 'the vocalist has a bad attack of hiccoughs' – for special attention. To invert the old blues lyrics, the women didn't know but the little boys understood.

There was a lot to take in when Dexys appeared on *Top of the Pops*. A lot to inspire prepubescent devotion. The 'Geno! Geno! Geno!' chanting at the beginning. The fact that we were clearly watching a gang as much as we were watching a band. And, perhaps most importantly, but also easiest to overlook, just as Terry Hall had perfected his awkward mic-management method, Kevin had his. With his microphone at eye level, he had to raise his chin when singing into it, which had the possibly unintended but welcome effect of making him seem a bit more like the boys in my class – like he was squaring up to an invisible assailant twice his size. 'Geno' leapt from number 12 to 2 before ousting Blondie's 'Call Me', after just a week in the top spot. UB40 and the Jam were also still in the top 20. Madness were up there too with 'Night Boat to Cairo'.

In Acocks Green there was a clothes shop called Nelson House, one of a few identically named shops owned by a flashy local entrepreneur, Mr Addleman, who was easy to spot on account of the ever-present Homburg on his head. When it came to fashion developments, Nelson House's response times were second only to those of the *Sports Argus* – the bright-pink Saturday afternoon paper which somehow managed to hit local newsstands with full match reports of that afternoon's action, often within an hour of the final whistle. Nelson House's reaction to the changes in the pop-cultural air pressure ushered in at the very end of the seventies was typically

decisive. A rainbow of Fred Perry shirts in the window and a prominently displayed cut-out of two boys, one in his mid-teens, the other
maybe old enough to drive a car, both slightly skinheady, modelling
Sta-Prest trousers. Three kinds of jacket and coat: Crombies, donkey
jackets, Harringtons – all of which conspired to consign Budgie
jackets to the back of the shop and, ultimately, oblivion.

From the relatively protected vantage point of Easy Listening
across the road, I could see boys from my year and, sometimes,
their older brothers, queuing to get into the shop. As I saw it, Dexys,
UB40 and the Specials all belonged to them. Instead, I focused my
enthusiasm on a series of releases by artists who seemed to disappear
as quickly as they appeared. Bereft of build-up or context, all there
was for me to get a handle on them was their song and the way they
looked in the video or on *Top of the Pops*. Several months after it
left the chart, I finally managed to get my hands on an ex-jukebox
copy of the Buggles' 'Video Killed the Radio Star', a song easily good
enough to justify the cloud of self-importance on which it sailed into
our lives. In the accompanying clip for the song, the Buggles – Trevor
Horn and Geoff Downes – looked like two moonlighting dentists
who use their day job to deter the wider world from discovering that
they're cloning a race of tinsel-headed replicants in giant test tubes,
presumably with a view to creating a new super-strain of pop stars
for the video era. Like all the best morally complex geniuses, these
pop Robert Oppenheimers seemed to entertain fleeting moments of
ambivalence concerning the march of progress.

'Video Killed the Radio Star' was a requiem to the very era it was
helping to kill. That, at any rate, was how MTV saw it when they
decided to launch their new channel with the Buggles' single. Had
I known what had inspired the song in the first place, I would no
doubt have felt an even greater kinship with it. Horn got the idea
for it after reading a short story called 'The Sound Sweep', which
centred around a mute boy who vacuums up stray music in a world

where new technology has rendered it obsolete. You can measure the brilliance of 'Video Killed the Radio Star' by drawing up a list of the disparate artists who would have envied the Buggles for coming up with it. David Bowie would have recognised something of his own worldview in the song's underlying message – that much of what we love will inevitably be trampled beneath the march of progress. As their respective songwriters pondered the challenges of staying relevant in the new decade, both ABBA and ELO would have marvelled at the song's marriage of state-of-the-art production with symphonic intricacy. Kraftwerk, too, would surely have had occasion to look at the themes it addressed and thought to themselves that this would have been appropriate subject matter around which to build an album. Neither was its impact lost on Queen, who simply repurposed the song's sentiments for their own equivalent of the song, which they entitled 'Radio Ga Ga'.

Around that time, Martha and the Muffins catapulted themselves into contention from nowhere with 'Echo Beach'. Martha and the Muffins were Canadian, but they didn't sound like they were from anywhere, and furthermore this beach they sang about didn't conform to any pre-existing notion in my mind concerning why you went to the beach or what you did when you got there. The protagonist of 'Echo Beach' isn't there with their friends. They haven't gone there to swim or to lie in the sun. Indeed, the thing about 'Echo Beach' is that you never see anyone there ('there's not a soul around') and they've gone there to 'watch the sun go down'. The intro alone featured the best use of tension and release I'd heard since the Rubettes' 'Sugar Baby Love'. Each note of Mark Gane's pensive guitar intro sounded like a single raindrop bouncing onto cold corrugated iron – a phrase he repeated seven times, each building anticipation of the real action, a full-throttle ninety-degree acceleration into the main instrumental hook. Before singer Martha Johnson even uttered a word, any suggestion that this was a song anyone would put on a

C90 of feel-good summer anthems was nixed by the twin attack of Gane's guitar and Johnson's Acetone organ. This was much closer to the graphite vistas of beaches used to represent alien landscapes in *Doctor Who* than anything celebrated on, say, a Beach Boys record.

'Echo Beach' was a consolation song. Its message was impossible to miss. Adulthood had failed its office clerk protagonist. Adulthood was disappointing. There was a lot of this sort of thing around in the wake of punk. Sixties pop stars hadn't entertained the notion that their moment in the spotlight was much more than just that. Even the Beatles in 1964 believed that if they had any long-term future in the music industry, it would be more as songwriters than performers. When the Zombies split up at the end of the sixties, their singer Colin Blunstone got a job in an insurance company. It had been good while it lasted, but no one in the sixties imagined that pop stardom was something you could do as your thirties beckoned. The outcome that sixties pop stars hadn't dared expect – that with a bit of luck, you might never have to get a 'proper' job in an office or a factory – was one that, in the wake of punk, was seen as a basic human right. Echoing the sentiments of Bruce Foxton's 'Smithers-Jones' on the Jam's *Setting Sons*, the Members released 'Solitary Confinement', which suggested that having 'a good job' and 'working in the city' left its protagonist unsure if he was 'dead or alive'.

As we sat at our neighbouring desks polishing our inkwells, I remember William Osborne telling me about XTC's recent hit 'Making Plans for Nigel' with an earnestness that left me in no doubt what a daring and impressive gesture XTC had made. The song was written by XTC's co-frontman Colin Moulding from the perspective of proud parents whose son Nigel was about to get a job working for British Steel with whom, presumably, he would stay until he was old enough to retire. Once the song became a hit, British Steel arranged for four Nigels from its Sheffield plant to appear in *Steel News*, enthusing about their career prospects. Having poured scorn on the idea of getting married young on 'Too Much Too Young', the Specials' next single, released in the spring of 1980 also dismissed the notion of putting in the effort to get to university. The subject of 'Rat Race' had stayed on to secure himself a Ph.D., but to Specials' guitarist Roddy Radiation, who wrote the song, he was still wasting his time.

Of course, other records came out at the beginning of the eighties. But the most exciting singles released by new British artists at the beginning of the new decade seemed to usher you inexorably to one conclusion. Our future was as unavoidable as it was terrifying.

CHAPTER 17

Twelve months spent shuttling between Acocks Green and West Bromwich was starting to take its toll on my mum, more than I could have begun to realise at the time. Having done just enough to turn the fortunes of the Threepennybit around, my parents placed it on the market and began to search in earnest for a shop closer to home. On their final day as owners of the Threepennybit, I made a point of going with them, not so much out of loyalty, but in the hope that I might get a few signatures for my autograph book. A few weeks previously, my dad had mentioned in passing that, on match days, several West Bromwich Albion first-teamers, in varying states of inebriation, would visit the shop after last orders and get themselves fish and chips to eat on the way home. This was big news. West Bromwich Albion were enjoying their most successful spell in decades. Several years later, their brash, cigar-chewing manager Ron Atkinson would lose his job as a TV pundit when he was recorded questioning the work rate of Chelsea's Marcel Desailly by calling him a 'fucking lazy thick n****r'. For someone like Ron Atkinson to sabotage his standing in such a manner was baffling and ironic. Back in the late seventies, he did more than any other top-flight manager to field a team that reflected the changing racial demographic of his team's locale. Brendon Batson, Cyrille Regis, Laurie Cunningham and Remi Moses all became first-team regulars in his time at the club – unprecedented for black players at that point. More than that, they played with a continental flair that routinely humiliated many of Albion's more prestigious rivals.

Sitting in the back of our latest car – a sandy Talbot Alpine – beside a box of jumpers and scarves that my mum had promised to complete for customers, I approached that Saturday much as you would a stake-out. Swapping Noel Edmonds's *Multi-Coloured Swap Shop* for my parents' multisided chip shop, I brought enough comics and activities to try and see me into the evening. And I also had my autograph book, which was in dire need of signatures. The only one in it so far dated back to a Friday teatime in 1976 when a man, wielding a guitar case and dressed entirely in denim, joined the queue at the Great Western and proceeded to entertain everyone around him with Tony Christie's 'Is This the Way to Amarillo?' and Tony Orlando and Dawn's 'Tie a Yellow Ribbon'. I was left in absolutely no doubt that this guy was famous because, as far as I was concerned, if you were dressed entirely in denim and you could confidently play two well-known songs to a spellbound chip shop queue, then you had to be famous. As 'Amarillo' galloped to its resounding conclusion, I sprinted up to my bedroom, eager to get back down to the shop before he left, and located an autograph book that had come as a free gift with an otherwise forgotten comic.

I silently handed it to him at the end of 'Tie a Yellow Ribbon'. Had he signed it 'Tony Orlando' or 'Tony Christie', I would have been none the wiser. Even though I recognised the songs, I had no idea who had sung them originally. In the event, it transpired that this was a different Tony. A third Tony. Tony *Telfer*.

'What's your name, kid?' he said, crouching down to make direct eye contact with me. This being towards the tail end of the mute years, I shrugged apologetically and looked across at my parents who were too busy serving customers to notice my quandary. Nevertheless, Tony Telfer didn't miss a beat. 'Is that your little boy?' he asked my mum. Unlike a lot of adults who met me for the first time,

Tony Telfer didn't mistake me for a girl just because I had long hair. That's because Tony Telfer was a pop star and he knew that boys could have long hair too. Indeed, his hair was almost as long as that of Chris Norman from Smokie, with whom he also shared the same tender countenance. 'His name is Taki!' replied my mum, writing it down on a piece of greaseproof paper and handing it over to Tony Telfer as she did so. I wasn't altogether happy about this – at school, I'd been Peter for a full six months, but this wasn't the right time to raise the matter with her. 'Taki! That's an unusual name,' said Tony Telfer, as he wrote down his own name on the first page of my autograph book. 'But . . . I like it. See you around, *Taki!*' He handed the book back to me and I stared at it, certain that this was the most extraordinary thing that had ever happened in the Great Western Fish Bar. Perhaps an hour later, Aki returned from Edward's house and I pounced on him with the news of what he'd missed. 'Guess what!' I squealed. 'TONY TELFER was here!!'

'Who's Tony Telfer?' replied Aki.

'The singer, Tony Telfer!! He came into the shop and did two songs! And look!' I showed Aki the autograph book. 'I got this!'

Aki inspected Tony Telfer's signature and nodded in a manner that suggested he was authenticating it. Exactly four years later, as I waited for the West Bromwich Albion first team to enter the shop, I anticipated showing Aki the same book. What with his frequent visits to the Birmingham City training ground, I knew this would really impress him. By 10 p.m., only the steady consumption of chips was preventing me from getting overexcited. 'Are you sure they're going to come?' I asked my dad.

Yes, he was sure. With the shop empty at this point, he told me about what had happened the previous week, when Albion stars Peter Barnes, Len Cantello, Cyrille Regis and midfield star Bryan Robson arrived in high spirits after a thrilling 4–4 draw at home to Bolton, in which Barnes had scored a hat-trick. As was customary, the hat-trick hero got to take the match ball home with him and, indeed, still had it with him when he and his teammates entered the Threepennybit. While the four footballers were waiting for their orders, an impromptu kickabout ended when one of them put the ball through one of the shop windows. Profuse apologies ensued, with Bryan Robson promising to come back later in the week to reimburse my dad. By the time of my own vigil, four days later, the window had been repaired. Robson personally popped by with a payment that generously exceeded the cost of the replacement glass. Every few years, usually to relatives or friends of mine, my dad would revisit the legend of Bryan Robson and the smashed window. It was a story whose cachet rose in the wake of Robson's record-breaking £1.5 million move to Manchester United.

I would usually be the one prompting him to tell my friends the story because, in the event, that was as close as I would ever get to meeting Bryan Robson. The one thing I had forgotten to do that day was check to see if West Bromwich Albion had played at home that day. And sure enough, if any post-match lads' night out followed that day's away draw against Norwich City, it never reached the Three-pennybit. Not only had I not managed to add to the sole name in my autograph book – that evening I realised that even the autograph I *did* have wasn't what it seemed. On the way home in the car, I leaned forward into the gap between the driver's seat and the front passenger seat and showed it to my dad.

'Do you remember this?' I asked him. After further prompting, a dim memory of Tony Telfer's impromptu performance seemed to form in his mind.

'Do you know what happened to him?' I continued.

'Nothing happened to him,' said my dad. 'We gave him some free fish and chips. He came back the following week and we realised he was trying it on again. When we charged him, he asked us to put the fish back. He could only afford the chips.'

In the intervening years, I had imagined all sorts of lives for Tony Telfer, but for some reason, the one thing that had never occurred to me was that he was a busker who literally sang for his supper. Far from taking off in spectacular fashion, my collection of star signatures on 25 March 1980 had shrunk from one to zero. Such disappointment required a fitting soundtrack. I looked into the bag I had packed to sustain me through that day. The latest issues of *Shoot!*, *Smash Hits* and a couple of cassettes. I pulled out the first one – a red BASF C60 onto which I'd recorded *Star Special*, a Radio 1 show broadcast on Sunday nights which saw celebrities of the day choosing the music. My cassette contained the selections of Trevor Francis, former Birmingham City hero and the first footballer to change hands for £1m when Brian Clough bought him for Nottingham Forest.

Our route home through West Bromwich took us directly past the football stadium which had the letters 'A L B I O N' displayed on the side of the stand that faced onto the Birmingham Road. My dad silently took his left hand off the steering wheel and bent his forearm back over his shoulder to take the cassette off me. He shoved it into the machine, and with a comforting clunk, the spools started to turn. I gazed up at those chunky equidistantly spaced letters for the last time. The heater started to purr warm air into our faces and Chicago's 1976 hit 'If You Leave Me Now' turned the car into a comforting cocoon of melancholia. Years later when I read about the way Prozac starts to work on people with depression, I was reminded of 'If You Leave Me Now'. It wasn't uncommon for people on Prozac to consider walking off the edges of buildings and sticking their heads into nooses in the same way they might ponder whether to spread jam or marmalade on their toast. Prozac didn't alleviate the negative feelings, it just levelled out the good and the bad. There was something of that in the way that 'If You Leave Me Now' was produced. It was devastation with the emotional Dolby pressed on.

An exhaust pipe fed into a womb. At least that's what I loved about it. What Britain's most expensive footballer loved about it is forever lost to the 'pause' button. A crude edit took us to ELO's 'Livin' Thing', as perfect a song as I'd ever heard until that point. A sharp succession of holy shivers: among them the gliding euphoria of the acoustic guitar which found a route through the ominous weather front of strings on the verses; and the 'higher and higher' shift from F minor to E minor – the chord change that told Jeff Lynne 'the song was gonna work' when he was still trying to write it.

Realising that none of Trevor Francis's remaining selections were likely to improve on that, I got my dad to press 'eject' and shove in my other cassette, a compilation of recent hits also taped from the radio. In moments like this, I really wanted either of my parents to show some interest in the song that was playing, be it to voice their approval or ask me a question about it. The fact that – with the exception of my dad's love of ABBA and, latterly Boney M – they had never done so didn't seem to lower my expectations that this might be the day they started. I wanted them to see what I saw in pop music. At the very least, I wanted them to not see my love of records as something that put distance between what I was and what they wanted me to be. I could see how hard they were working. And even though I didn't really understand why they couldn't just ease off a little and get the sort of jobs that involved both of them being home at night, I felt they'd be doing themselves a favour if they saw pop as less of a threat and more as a third parent, taking the heat off them a little. Something that explained the world to me so that they didn't have to. Besides, it wasn't even as if the music I was listening to was incubating thoughts of insurrection and nihilism in me.

In recent months, Cliff Richard's stock had shot up to heights unscaled since his early sixties run of wet lullabies for sappy newly-weds. 'Carrie' was his eagerly anticipated follow-up to 'We Don't Talk Anymore' – a song which, with months to spare, allowed him to claim that he had topped the charts in three consecutive decades. Cliff's new song cast him as the fearful friend of the song's subject, pacing the pavements for clues concerning her whereabouts. As vocal performances went, he never quite topped this one. He sang it like an actor, seasoning lines such as the one about young people 'wear[ing] their freedom like cheap perfume' with a taut, anguished urgency. Through the car window, rows of orange street lights beamed down onto the grass verges of Edgbaston's deserted wet boulevards. Cliff may have been part of the old pop order, but to these ears, the message of 'Carrie' wasn't so different to that of 'Echo Beach', 'Another Brick in the Wall', 'Making Plans for Nigel' or 'Roxanne'. It's grim out there. The only grown-ups who seemed to be having a great time whenever you saw them seemed to be Madness and the Barron Knights. Maybe that was something I could do. Maybe I could be a Barron Knight too.

I'd started recording Barbara Dickson's 'Caravan Song' towards the end of the first verse, when it became apparent that this was a chord progression constructed to funnel anyone who heard it into a chorus of devastating desolation. Of course I was going to love 'Caravan Song'. This was, albeit in a once-removed sort of way, the saddest Wombles song of all time. The man behind those Wombles records and 'Caravan Song' was Mike Batt. A year earlier, Batt had launched Art Garfunkel to the top of the British charts for six weeks with 'Bright Eyes' – and actually, both this and 'Caravan Song' dealt with the idea of moving on, albeit in different ways. Batt wrote 'Bright Eyes' when *Watership Down* director Martin Rosen asked him to come up with a song about death; 'Caravan Song' was written for a 1978 film about gun-running nomads. However, as with his Wombles and *Watership Down* work, the liberal use of cor anglais ensured that nothing in 'Caravan Song' evoked any scene more exotic than the lights that trailed beyond motorway slip roads and into the rape fields that bordered the outlying conurbations of south Birmingham.

Years later, Mike Batt revealed that the song was actually written about the realisation that he wasn't going to be able to salvage his first marriage. He barely had to say it really.

> *I wish I had the wisdom*
> *To find some simple words to make you see*
> *The things that mean a lot to you*
> *Don't always seem to mean a lot to me*
> *I need to breathe, I need to leave*
> *When the sands of time go drifting by*
> *I may be on my own*
> *But I'll be free.*

Next up was Rupert Holmes's 'Escape (The Piña Colada Song)', a piece of work that seemed to exist so far outside the narrative of contemporary pop that I barely knew what it was. First and foremost it was a story with a beginning, a middle and an end – about a couple whose marriage has long lost its spark. He reads a lonely hearts ad placed by a woman in search of a man who likes piña coladas, getting caught in the rain and making love at midnight in the dunes of the cape. The twist, of course, is that he replies to the ad, they arrange a date and he discovers that it was his wife who placed the ad.

I didn't know what a dune was or, indeed, a cape. And, if you'd pushed me to tell you, I might have struggled to tell you exactly what making love was. But nevertheless, there was valuable information in Rupert Holmes's parable of midlife marital *ennui*. I was interested by the way people's parents spoke to each other, rather than their children. I noticed the way certain other couples in our lives were around each other. If Joyce and Frank at number 12 argued, we never heard it. Then there was Irene and Jack. Though they'd been together several years longer than my parents, Jack's body language around Irene was nurturing and supportive. Whenever they got up to leave, he'd hold up her coat so she could put her arms through the holes. I'd never seen my dad do that for my mum. He didn't notice when other people did it, so there was nothing to embarrass him into doing it himself. He quite simply didn't function at that level.

I'd never seen my parents kiss each other or engage in any sort of tender exchange. They never held hands in public or, indeed, in private. My mum's birthday always proceeded along the same lines. Aki and I would hand over her present and then my dad, who had clearly forgotten it was her birthday, would reach into his pocket and hand her some cash in front of us. It was better than nothing, but it didn't exactly look like love.

Coming less than a month after Mother's Day, my mum's birthday always presented me with certain challenges. In the years preceding 1980, I had realised that given that there was only so much Elnett she could get through in a year, I really had to think about what gift she might find useful. Thus far I had presented her with a set of three plastic tubs with 'TEA', 'COFFEE' and 'SUGAR' written on them (1977), a can of air freshener (1978) and some cornflake-topped fairy cakes (1979). Twelve months later, by the time her thirty-eighth birthday came around, the memory of the cornflake-topped fairy cakes was already a source of embarrassment to me. My main contribution to the creation of the cakes had mostly centred around the idea of them. When it came to procuring the ingredients and turning the oven on, I needed some help and, needless to say, the only person in a position to assist was my mum, which, obviously wasn't ideal, given that she was: (a) also the intended recipient of the present; and (b) working in the chippy until 2 p.m. Without realising it, her birthday surprise would be waiting for her at the end of the that three-bus, fourteen mile journey back from West Bromwich to our new house in Acocks Green. All she needed to do to receive it was help me find the ingredients, get me to mix them together, tell me when it was time to spoon the mixture into the pleated paper cupcake holders and, once they were baked, make sure I was wearing oven gloves as I removed the golden cakes so I could then ceremonially present them to her.

Naturally, the first thing she did, once the cakes were transferred onto a fancy plate, was hand one over to me. As she wiped down the surfaces and washed and dried the mixing bowl, tray and spatulas, she would have no doubt considered the care and consideration I had put into her present. Sadly, I have no way of confirming this, as by this point, I was in the front room watching M perform a strange but catchy new record called 'Pop Muzik' on *Cheggers Plays Pop*. But, like I said, that was 1979. Now I was ten. I'd had time to reflect. And now, in 1980, I realised that for my mum's present to really feel like a present, she had to have no part in making it.

With four days to go before her birthday, I still had no idea what that present was going to be, but seventeen songs into the live broadcast of the Eurovision Song Contest, that all changed, thanks to a glum-faced Irishman whose cherubic features called to mind the expanding array of ornamental porcelain farmhands, shepherds and altar boys that peered out from our mantelpiece. Johnny Logan was more smartly turned out than any of those little guys. His hair was neatly brushed forward and the top three buttons of the black shirt beneath his white two-piece suit were all undone. Perched on a stool before the audience in The Hague, Johnny balefully gazed side-on into the middle distance as he set out his existential stall: 'What's another year / To someone who's lost everything that he owns? / What's another year / To someone who's getting used to being alone?'

'Did you like that?' I asked her.

'What a nice boy,' she said. 'What a pretty song. What a *sad* song.'

There were two more songs to follow after 'What's Another Year', but she barely paid any attention to them. Her desire to hear Johnny Logan again was matched only by what appeared to be considerable concern for his welfare. Johnny soared to an unassailable lead and we saw him and his entourage looking ever more animated, but crucially, his sad spaniel eyes remained unchanged. As is customary, he was called to the stage to collect his trophy and sing his song one more time. He couldn't have come along at a better time. 'What's Another Year' hit the shops two days later, on 20 April, three days before my mum's birthday.

Prior to this, not a single song had been released that had moved my mother enough to want to own it. On these criteria, every piece of music that had inhabited the same airspace as her had been a failure. But it was different with Johnny. If you had tried to construct a song with the specific purpose of locating my mother's emotional defences and launching itself in their direction with the pinpoint accuracy of a heat-seeking missile, you couldn't have done a better job than 'What's Another Year'. If not quite the perfect storm, it was certainly a timely drizzle. Stuck behind a chip shop counter in Birmingham as she headed along the final straight of her fourth decade, far from the place of her upbringing, married to my dad more in deference to the sanctity of marriage than to the man she married – this wasn't quite how she'd planned the transition into middle age.

On the day of her birthday, I didn't see her until the late afternoon. My parents had exchanged contracts on their third and final fish and chip shop and every day they weren't able to open it was a day of lost revenue. There were fryers and peelers and chipping machines. There was an enormous round, free-standing, dome-topped steamer which bore a dramatic resemblance to the robot star of Saturday teatime ITV sitcom *Metal Mickey*. This would be used to soften the marrowfat peas and steam the rice for the chicken curry (a new addition to my parents' repertoire). Beneath the dome were four steel containers which formed a circle, two for mushy peas and two for curry sauce. And all of it needed to be cleaned and tested.

Situated about a mile away from our house, the Kingfisher looked cute from the outside. Located on the border of Acocks Green and

its more well-appointed suburb Olton, it was the sole shop in a long
row of identical two-up two-downs. Its window curved outwards
and divided into several small panels of glass, like the window in
which Bagpuss slept. The surrounding streets were heavily residential
and, across the road was the enormous Lincoln Poacher pub. The
previous owner of the Kingfisher had moved to South Africa a year
earlier, leaving locals to look elsewhere for their fish suppers. But
if my parents could lure even a fraction of the people who lived in
all these houses back to the Kingfisher, then it might be our most
successful shop yet. Leaving nothing to chance, my dad hit on the
exciting idea of getting 2,000 leaflets printed, announcing the grand
reopening of the Kingfisher.

The evening of my mum's birthday arrived, but I had already left
the house and her present back there. The reason? Something more
exciting had come up. I had answered a ring on the doorbell to find
Ged standing there with a clipboard.

'Hi Takis!' she said brightly. 'Do you want to sign this petition to
save Moseley Bog?'

I had no idea what Moseley Bog was, but that didn't matter. When
the fifteen-year-old girl next door thinks your signature on a petition
is worth the trouble of ringing your doorbell, the rush of flattery
exceeds all other considerations.

I screwed my face up. 'Moseley bog?! Why do you want to save a
TOILET?!'

Ged brightly explained that the word bog had another meaning
and that she wasn't trying to save a toilet. A bog could also be an
untouched area of wetland which supports a diverse range of wildlife.
The one in Moseley had been known as the Dell in previous decades,
but urban conservation campaigner Joy Fifer, the woman responsible
for 1980's 'Save Our Bog' campaign, single-handedly popularised
the appellation that gave me so much amusement on the doorstep
of 14 Overlea Avenue. The bog was part of a wider expanse where

J.R.R. Tolkien had played as a child. 'It was kind of a lost paradise,' he told the *Guardian* in 1966. 'There was an old mill that really did grind corn with two millers, a great big pond with swans on it, a sandpit, a wonderful dell with flowers, a few old-fashioned village houses and, further away, a stream with another mill.' He added, 'I always knew it would go – and it did.' Between the 1930s and the 1960s, Birmingham City Council used some of the area as a landfill site before levelling it off and turning it into a playing field for the nearby Moseley Grammar School – a purpose entirely unsuitable for an expanse of mud that not even the mythical summer of 1976 could solidify.

If Moseley Bog was to be saved, Ged was going to need a lot more signatures than those of her neighbours. She wanted to know if I was up for standing with her by the bus stop where Westley Road met the end of Overlea Avenue and gather signatures from people getting off the number 11 bus. Sure. Why not? My ability to picture this bog was, in spite of Ged's patient explanations, sketchy. Was there really not much more to it than a piece of muddy ground? I didn't understand why you might feel so strongly about some mud that you'd be prepared to stop strangers in the street and ask them to help you save it.

In Greece, my mum had grown up surrounded by nature, picking wild mushrooms and artichokes in order to survive. She used to pick flowers too because, in the absence of pencils, you could use the pigment in the petals to do colouring in. Though she never lost that connection with nature, it rarely seemed to find an adequate space in which to express itself. She would sometimes pick the camomile flowers that grew between the paving stones outside our front garden and use them to make tea. She enjoyed nature but I couldn't imagine her, say, going for a walk in the woods as an end in itself rather than a means to one. In another life, of course, this was absolutely what she would have been doing. Her parallel-life job, probably in an architect's office or maybe a school, would have seen her finish work in time for tea, with weekends entirely free for walks in the woods or cycle rides. The nearest that we, as a family, got to enjoying the surrounding countryside was a Sunday afternoon drive to a pick-your-own strawberry farm. Aki and I would eat as many strawberries as we picked, imagining that we had exploited a fatal loophole in the farm's business idea. It wouldn't occur to me until decades later that the money saved in not having to pay farm workers to pick the berries was more than the total value of berries that even the fattest of overexcitable ten-year-old ABBA fans could have packed away in one hour.

On the other side of the wall, however, at 12 Overlea Avenue, it was a different story. Sometimes, on a Sunday afternoon, I'd look out of the window and see the entire Hughes family – a peloton of them – pedalling out of their driveway, off in the direction of Warwick or Henley. Ged's brother Tim was the high achiever of the family. He was blond, bright and perpetually interested in what you had to say. His infant Beatles obsession propelled him to the guitar at a young age and, even though he'd just become a teacher, he still managed to make time to sing and write songs for his band the Jackets, with whom you would sometimes see him rehearse in the Hugheses' front room. Occasionally, they'd be joined by Ged's oldest sister Christine and her sons Joshua and Nell, all of whom lived in the historic market town of Berkhamsted in Hertfordshire – a geographical detail worth noting for the fact that Berkhamsted was also home to a man whose mere name, if uttered within earshot, was enough to make all the Hughes women drift off into a distant reverie: Richard Mabey.

'Haven't you heard of Richard Mabey, Takis?' asked an incredulous Ged as we waited for the next number 11 to decant some more 'Save Our Bog' signatories onto Westley Road. 'He's written all these books about nature. He knows which plants and mushrooms are safe to eat.

He's really into conservation and wildlife. And he lives just around the corner from Christine! Whenever we visit, we're always looking out for him. We know where he lives now, so when we go past his house, we look and see if we can make him out. He's *dreamy*, Takis.'

There was very little I could say at times like this. I'd never been around a family like Ged's family. Every minute was a portal into a world hitherto unknown to me. Within five minutes of attempting my most grown-up looking signature on Ged's petition, I had crossed over into this world, morphed from someone who found the word 'bog' hilarious to Ged's conservationist wing-boy – still not entirely clear about what it was I was trying to save, but happy enough to abandon my mum's birthday and stand beside Ged as she did the hard work. After about forty minutes, we'd filled two A4 sheets. My parents drove past us, turning right onto Overlea Avenue and into the driveway we shared with Ged's family. I explained to Ged that it was my mum's birthday and I needed to go back, but as we turned to leave, my dad had parked the car and was walking back in our direction.

'What are you doing now?' he asked.

'I was just going back to—'

'Your mum doesn't feel very well, so she's going to have a rest at home.' My dad then turned to Ged, who he always addressed as Geraldine. 'If you can spare an hour or two, I need you and Taki to help me put these through the letterboxes in all the streets around the shop. Then I'm going to test the fryer for the first time. Would you like some chips to take home to your family, Ged?' Perhaps feeling obliged to reciprocate my assistance in the preservation of Moseley Bog, Ged followed me into my dad's car. We pounded the pavements of Olton until the sun went down and my dad was as good as his promise. We adjudged the first chips to leave the fryer of the Kingfisher a great success. Ged and I finally got home at around half eight. I handed my mum her card and her present. She unwrapped it, taking a few seconds to register that the record she was holding in her hands was the Johnny Logan song. She looked wiped out.

'Do you want to hear it?' I said.

'Yes. Put it on,' she replied as she handed it over.

I turned on the music centre, removed the record from its die-cut blue sleeve and lowered the needle onto the record.

I've been praying such a long time,
It's the only way to hide the fear,
What's another year?

Happy birthday, Mum.

CHAPTER 18

By the final day of our final year at Cottesbrooke, William and I knew that, when we started the next academic year in September, we'd do so at the same secondary school. We had even contrived a pact to sabotage our eleven-plus exams to ensure this outcome, the anticipation of which had made us almost inseparable in the ensuing weeks. As July ended, I had some money left over from my birthday and, stopping via William's house where he persuaded his mum to advance him some pocket money, we headed into Acocks Green to buy ourselves a record each.

For William, the usually straightforward choice of buying whatever Gary Numan record happened to be in the chart was complicated by the emergence of a new group called Orchestral Manoeuvres in the Dark (to whom I'll henceforth refer as OMD even though it would be at least another year before the initialism caught on). For almost any young boy looking to pop music for emotional instruction, soppiness was something to be avoided at all costs. OMD went about their business like human emissaries who had been commissioned to prepare a variety of short modules concerning human behaviour to a colony of newly arrived Vulcans. It wasn't as if 'Messages' wasn't vulnerable. It's a song about the distance opening up between estranged lovers, written from the perspective of a protagonist who doesn't want the relationship to end.

It worries me this kind of thing
How you hope to live alone
And occupy your waking hours

But with the exception of the rhythm section, everything was
played on synthesisers – and when synthesisers were used to frame
songs about love and loss, something incredible happened. The
medium seemed to rein in the sentimental excesses of the message.
Songs about distress acquired a diagnostic sheen. A thematic area
which had hitherto seemed like the domain of girls now appealed
to boys. Originally written as a riposte to a journalist from a science
fiction magazine who suggested that Gary Numan was an incog-
nito alien sent to Earth on some sort of mission, 'We Are Glass'
presented itself like a robot reboot of Simon & Garfunkel's 'I Am
a Rock'. And like that song, if you were young enough to take its
lyrics at face value – if you were a rock too – there was nothing
to stop you.

We are glass, we are glass
We are cold
We're not supposed to cry

William's loyalties to Numan were so firmly entrenched now that
the OMD song never stood a chance. He briefly attempted to get me
to buy 'Messages', but Aki had already bought the 10-inch single a
few days previously. Another one of his new acquisitions, 'Love Will
Tear Us Apart' by Joy Division, served as a reminder that there was
another way for white boys to sing about failing relationships in a
way that inspired the unending respect of other white boys. Unfortunately for them, it involved not surviving to reap the benefits.
William's brother Edward had taken to taping as many of John Peel's
nightly Radio 1 shows as he could afford to, so he knew Joy Division's

music well enough to feel the shock of Ian Curtis's death when Peel announced it on his 19 May show.

For Aki, seeing the singer of one of Edward's favourite bands nudged into the hereafter was enough to light the touchpaper of his fascination. The issue of *NME* dated 14 June 1980 featured an Anton Corbijn photo of Joy Division beneath the weak light of the stairwell at Lancaster Gate tube station. All the band have their backs to the camera, with the exception of Ian Curtis who gazes back at the lens. The unromantic adult eye sees the singer in a band obeying the photographer's instructions. Aki's teenage eye would have no doubt seen something different in Curtis's gaze, an invitation into the interior world of the tortured soul now posthumously racing up the top 40. Aki and Edward would have needed no encouragement to imbue Curtis with mythical qualities. The manner of his demise, in combination with Joy Division's ectoplasmic squall of anguish, would have been enough to ensure that. But the design of the record's sleeve – the artist and title inscribed on stone, in the manner of an epitaph – sealed it.

It wasn't the only song in the charts that was synonymous with suicide. In a move that seemed irresponsible on the face of it, Robert Altman, director of *M*A*S*H*, asked his fourteen-year-old son Mike to write the words to the film's theme tune. Altman Snr's delight on seeing what his son came up with must have been tempered by his sheer alarm at, well . . . seeing what his son came up with.

> *The sword of time will pierce our skin*
> *It doesn't hurt when it begins*
> *But as it works its way on in*
> *The pain grows stronger, watch it grin*

In the wake of the final episode of the spin-off TV show, 'Theme From M*A*S*H (Suicide Is Painless)' fended off Hot Chocolate's

'No Doubt About It' and Lipps Inc.'s 'Funkytown' to occupy the number 1 spot, ensuring that Mike Altman would go on to earn more royalties for his contribution than his father ever saw from the film. It sat right in the middle of what might be the most depressing trio of consecutive chart toppers of all time. Either side of it were Johnny Logan's 'What's Another Year' and Don McLean's version of Roy Orbison's 'Crying'. So, when Olivia Newton-John and ELO supplanted Don McLean with 'Xanadu', it felt like an intervention, and a thrilling one at that – an unprecedented coalition between two entirely separate pop entities. At that age, such deviations from standard practice were almost gasp-inducing to me. It was more than Olivia and ELO making a record together. They had 'joined forces' (this being the phrase used when one of your favourite comics merged with another beloved title). On 'Xanadu', Jeff Lynne traded lines with Olivia on the chorus, both of them riding the song's synth percolations into a neon sunset. Along with the standard single release, 'Xanadu' was also released on a pink 10-inch single, with its sleeve die-cut to reveal a record label with nothing but Olivia's face on it. On a separate solo visit to Easy Listening, I stood over the small browser that they had set aside for 12-inch singles and counted out the remainder of my pocket money. If I contented myself with the 7-inch of 'Xanadu', then I could afford to buy a second record from the discounted browsers. Among my possible options was 'Modern Girl', the debut single by a new singer called Sheena Easton. *Sheena Easton*. With a name like that, I figured she was probably American and already had some success there. The record had started life in the new releases box and then, when it failed to enter the top 40, found itself pushed further and further towards the back of the box until finally it was retired to the 50p browser. So when Sheena Easton's name was featured in the *Radio Times* entry for a documentary called *The Big Time*, I was able to place it straight away. It turned out that Sheena wasn't American at all, but – as the *Radio*

Times listing explained – 'a 19-year-old student from Glasgow, who has always dreamed of becoming a pop star'.

Every week, *The Big Time* would chart the progress of someone trying to catch a break in some prestigious field or other, be it as a footballer, magician or haute cuisine chef. The prospect of seeing an ordinary person transformed into a recording artist was sufficiently thrilling for me to remember the anticipation almost four decades later; the memory of actually watching the process take place was so deflating that I didn't forget that either.

I expected something life-affirming and aspirational. In the event, it turned out that to be a singer with dreams of becoming a recording artist wasn't really all that different to being a pig who dreams of getting into sausages. It started with Sheena singing 'I Can See Clearly Now' at a dinner dance for dentists – her final engagement before heading south to audition for EMI's 'boss of A & R' Brian Shepherd. From this point onwards, we got to see Sheena's route to pop stardom masterminded by shadowy men smoking endless fags in poorly lit rooms. Never feeling the need to mention Sheena by name, Shepherd explained what he was after. 'The girl has to please the eye. She has to have a voice, but it can be done with the record.'

Much of what followed reminded me of that conversation in Cyprus with our cousin Notis, where he explained what you have to do to become a soldier. His description of arriving in a strange place and being catapulted clear of your comfort zone, of having your identity stripped away and having to replace it with something that could withstand the rigours to come – all of that came back as I watched Sheena undergo the process of commodification. Even being handed her first ever glass of champagne to celebrate passing her audition, she looked out of her depth. With the ink barely dry on her contract, Sheena was given new hair and new clothes and sent off to be inspected by a selection of singers who had all been through versions of the same process. Still only thirty-two in 1980,

Lulu brought her manager Marion London with her and stayed quiet for long enough to let Marion systematically dismantle her. Looking like Davros in drag, Marion explained, 'I wouldn't see her as a pop star', citing her lack of 'rugged individuality' and adding that the hair was all wrong too.

I didn't know who Lulu was, but I knew she was important because, like Sting, Odysseus and Kojak, she only had one name. Neither did I know who 1950s singing sensation Dorothy Squires was, but she must have been important too because, as narrator John Pitman pointed out, she lived in the house that Edward VII had built for his mistress. She also appeared to be utterly bananas, wildly declaiming that 'if [Easton] gets a hit record, she'll never become a star. NEVER. Because the sharks won't allow her to! They'll bleed her dry!'

The Big Time was one prolonged humiliation ritual. As if to confirm the futility of the entire experiment, 'Modern Girl' limped to number 60 in the chart. And that would have been the end of that, were it not for EMI's decision to release '9 to 5', a second single, off the back of the documentary. Public sympathy for indignities endured during the making of the programme was what ultimately made a household name of Sheena Easton. But actually, the job of pretty much everyone else here – the producer, the plugger, the marketing manager, oleaginous Radio 1 DJ Simon Bates – looked more fun than the job of being Sheena Easton. And the only truly magical bit of *The Big Time* had nothing to do with its subject. It was the footage of sheets of EMI labels being printed, cut into shape and stuck onto the records as they came out of the machine.

On the pre-teatime and Saturday morning TV schedules – *Cheggers Plays Pop, Razzmatazz* – the beginnings of a chart war were being played out that, unlike Blur vs Oasis fifteen years later, would yield no winners. The third series of American soap opera *Dallas* had ended with a cliffhanger that, as per the CBS network's objective, made it the main topic of conversation throughout that month. Amoral oil baron J.R. Ewing had fallen victim to a mystery would-be assassin. As betting shops started to offer odds on the identity of the killer, Jimmy Carter – seeking to become president for a second term – jested that he'd have no trouble financing his campaign if he knew who had pulled the trigger.

When Larry Hagman, who played J.R., arrived at Ascot in June 1980, the crowd repeatedly yelled his character's name at him. If you traced this tornado of quotidian hysteria all the way down to its grubby underside, you would find the Wurzels and the Barron Knights slugging it out on the children's TV schedules in craven pursuit of the hit that had now eluded both of them for well over a year. The Wurzels' single, 'I Hate J.R.', was a self-released shocker which betrayed very little knowledge of *Dallas* or the character it purported to hate. Given my existing loyalties, I was pleased to observe that it didn't come close to the Barron Knights' single. With over fifteen years' experience of fast-response *zeitgeist* exploitation behind them, 'We Know Who Did It' was nothing if not thorough. At the beginning of the record, a mock-Texan accent rattled through the internecine betrayals and resentments that had brought us to this point in the show's storyline. Over the tune of Gary Numan's 'Cars', the group then outlined all the possible motives that might have prompted various characters to shoot J.R., teasing us throughout that, actually, they knew who did it.

Back at Easy Listening, having already chosen the 'Xanadu' 7-inch, I removed 'We Know Who Did It' from the new releases box on the countertop, paid for both records and hastened to William's house, knowing how thrilled he'd be that the Barron Knights had deemed Gary Numan worthy of one of their parodies. 'Listen to this!' I said, going straight to the record player so I could play it without him knowing what it was. I could feel my face overselling what was about to happen, and yet I was powerless to stop it. It might have been more artfully executed than the Wurzels song, but in truth there was nothing beyond my militant belief in the union of music and comedy to commend the Barron Knights' Dallas cash-in to the wider world. I can see now that singer Pete Langford's approximation of Numan's detached nasal style was instantly going to make William suspicious that Gary Numan wasn't being accorded his due respect.

'That's not funny,' William said flatly as the record ended. Sometimes it was all too easy to remember that William had been alive for ten months longer than me.

'I thought it was funny,' I said. The brightness of my response didn't even come close to disguising my embarrassment – not least because, at some level, I also knew it wasn't funny. Really, I should have cut my losses with the Barron Knights there and then. But I had spent too much money on those records. Travelled too many turntable miles with those gags to feel that it had all been a mistake. I needed to spend more money and receive a far greater setback than the disdain of my best friend. For that to happen, it would take nothing less than a heartbreaking denouement to an evening with the band twelve months later, in full view of my appalled parents. Yes, that would finally do it.

Right now though, things were pretty good for me. My most difficult year at Cottesbrooke was behind me. Buoyed by the confirmation that we wouldn't be going to Greece or Cyprus this year, I decided that this was going to be the best summer of my life. Tennis fever had gripped Britain. Björn Borg had won half of the Wimbledons for which I'd been alive, although this one – a five-set slog against John McEnroe, decided on a tiebreak – felt to everyone like it would be his last.

Tennis fever had also extended to the children of Overlea Avenue. If you imagined our road as a paddle, Ged, Aki and I would play in the circular bit, using the kerb that encircled most of that area as the boundary of our 'court'. There was no net, but that didn't concern us.

Sometimes we'd be joined by another girl who lived two doors away from us at number 18. I'd remembered Emily May from infant school assemblies, standing at the very back with the other children in her year. I was two years younger than her and, with her waist-length, neatly brushed hair, thought she was one of the prettiest girls I'd ever seen. Now that I was ten and she was twelve, I didn't really think of girls in that way any more. But I was flattered by the friendliness she showed towards us. Over a year had elapsed since we'd moved into Overlea Avenue and her parents, who were probably in their forties but dressed older, had still refused to speak to us or make eye contact. It took me years to work out why.

Free of obligations and responsibilities, I was faced with no greater challenge than that of making it from breakfast to bedtime in order to do it all over again the following day. This was slightly less true of Aki and Ged, whose holidays marked the halfway point in the two-year ascent to their O level exams. But I don't remember it weighing heavily on either of their minds. Ged's music taste – mostly canonical pre-punk songwriters, augmented by a scattering of emerging new wave artisans, in particular, Joe Jackson – was different to that of Aki, who was still far from done with punk and new wave. That summer he bought records by the Ruts, Skids, UK Subs, the Clash, Siouxsie and the Banshees and also the unspeakably bad yob-rock debut by Sex Pistols offshoot the Professionals.

The advent of punk had clearly affected the generation of musicians who predated it. Some just pretended it hadn't happened, while others who, in some way, saw themselves as inspirations to the Sex Pistols, the Clash and the Damned, were happy to invite comparisons. Having had their early single 'Substitute' covered by the Sex Pistols, the Who had more reason than most to align themselves to the new vanguard of three-chord nihilists. And in August, when the Who's singer Roger Daltrey appeared as a guest presenter alongside Tommy Vance on *Top of the Pops*, it was immediately apparent which side of the line he had decided to place himself. Using all the acting skills in evidence on *McVicar*, the film he was ostensibly there to promote, the opening shot of the show saw Daltrey affect a grumpy, disengaged air, while beside him, Vance attempted to ascertain why. 'You're looking a bit miserable,' he ventured.

'For good reason, mate. For good reason,' huffed Daltrey. 'I come all the way here to see the Clash and I find that they're not on.'

With new short hair and a leather jacket, Daltrey's resolute surliness persisted into other areas of conversation. Vance asked him about the Who's recent US tour which had seen him venture as far south as Texas.

'I was wondering where you got that suntan,' said Vance.

'Yeah,' said Daltrey, still transmitting from his own private cloud of chippy diffidence, 'They got all that sun down there, mate.'

When it came to the job of introducing *Top of the Pops*' in-house dance troupe Legs & Co., who that week were dancing to ELO's 'All Over the World', Daltrey addressed the camera without the aid of Vance. 'There's an awful lot I'd like to say about Legs & Co.,' he said, struggling to hide the nervous smirk of a schoolboy who has told all his friends that he'll shout out a swear word in tomorrow's assembly, 'but I'm afraid they'd probably bleep me out if I do.'

Did I notice any of this at the time? Yes and no. I took everything at face value. I was just watching a man in a bad mood. Were it not for Aki's increasingly animated response, I would have almost instantly erased it from my memory. But there was worse to come. Having rehearsed an entire exchange in order to let us know that he loved the Clash, Daltrey set out to finish the job by telling us what he thought about disco. 'Urrgh! Can't stand it! It's terrible', he exclaimed.

'It's a terrible shame, Rog,' replied Vance, 'because here come *the Village People.*'

This was the moment that has since passed into infamy. As we cut from the studio to the video of Village People's 'Can't Stop the

Music', Daltrey could be heard cheerfully calling out, 'Watch your backs!' Aki was aghast. 'Did you hear that?!' he squealed, pointing at the screen. 'Did you hear it?'

'Hear what?'

'He said, "Watch your backs!"'

'So? What does that mean?'

'Well you know they're homosexuals, don't you? He's telling you to watch your back because they're homos. Do you get it?'

There was a lot for me to get in a short space of time. First of all, I didn't know that Village People were gay – or 'homos', as my brother and, indeed, most people called them. How could I have possibly known this? For a start, look at the way Village People were dressed. A cowboy, a Native American, a soldier, a policeman and a biker. These were arguably the five manliest professions imaginable. How on earth could I be expected to gauge from their appearance that they might be homosexuals? It was almost as though they were deliberately throwing us off the scent by dressing like that. I mean, if they were all dressed as fairies, it would be a different story. If gay men wanted everyone to know that they were gay, that would surely have been a better way to go about it. And anyway, how did Aki know it? It wasn't in *Smash Hits*. It wasn't in the *Evening Mail*. It wasn't on *John Craven's Newsround*. Where was he getting his news from?

Then there was also the matter of Roger's actual remark. Why did you need to watch your back if there was a homosexual nearby?

'I don't get it,' I said to him. 'Why is it funny?'

I always knew when Aki got exasperated, because his voice leapt up two octaves. 'How do you not get it?'

'I just don't. Why have you got to watch your backs when Village People are there?'

'Because . . . because . . . oh, it doesn't matter.'

Thankfully, Ged was more patient with me. Knowing that I could rely on her for difficult explanations of sensitive topics, I asked her to explain both Village People's dress code and Roger Daltrey's remarks when I next saw her. She went to great lengths to explain everything, and yet at the end of it all, I understood basically nothing. I was some way off enlightenment, but even as an eleven-year-old about to start secondary school, it didn't seem plausible to me that homosexuals might try and anally penetrate unsuspecting straight men.

'They're not,' explained Ged. 'He's just being a wally.'

I was increasingly relying on Ged for any stray nuggets of worldly and musical knowledge that might help me deal with whatever lay ahead in life. She would generously call in on me whenever she ventured out to Easy Listening, and I would always willingly tag along, knowing that being with someone who was about to buy a record was the next best thing to getting one myself. On the afternoon of 26 August, Ged decided it was time to induct me into the genius of Paul Simon. She had ordered his new single 'Late in the Evening' from Easy Listening, which was something you sometimes had to do if the record in question didn't look likely to chart. Ged had grown up with Paul Simon's music. Her siblings constantly had it playing around the house but, between the release of his last album, *Still Crazy After All These Years*, and this one, five years had passed and all her siblings had moved out. Now Ged had to buy her own Paul Simon records.

'Have you never heard Paul Simon, Takis?' she asked me. In the ensuing years, I wondered why she had the remotest inclination to get an eleven-year-old boy into Paul Simon. Most fifteen-year-olds would have surely thought it beneath them. It was only when I became a parent and found myself doing the same thing that I realised why you do it. Watching someone else discover one of your favourite artists for the first time is the nearest you'll get to reliving that moment yourself.

I told her that I didn't have the faintest idea who Paul Simon was. She told me about the duo he used to sing in, alongside the guy who did 'Bright Eyes'. The previous summer holidays had seen Art Garfunkel sitting at the top of the charts with his song. Knowing that Ged had gone to the trouble of ordering the Paul Simon single especially, this confirmed to me that Simon had plummeted from the lofty perch he once enjoyed in Simon & Garfunkel to his present ignominy. If Simon didn't want to be left permanently in the shade by Garfunkel, then Simon had better hurry up and write a song as good as 'Bright Eyes'.

Not that Ged seemed to see it this way. 'He's too good to get to number 1, Takis. He's better than that.' She may as well have uttered that last sentence in Flemish for all I really understood of it. The idea that anything could be 'too good' to get to number 1 was utterly alien to me, although from here on I was willing to adopt it in defence of the Barron Knights' and Racey's disastrous recent chart showings.

'Paul Simon does whatever he wants,' continued Ged as we made our way down the hill, past the Warwick Bowl. 'He doesn't care if it gets in the charts. Do you know his song "50 Ways to Leave Your Lover"?'

Of course I didn't. I was eleven.

Ged burst into song: '"Just slip out the back, Jack, make a new plan, Stan / Don't need to be coy, Roy, just listen to me / Hop on the bus, Gus, don't need to discuss much / Just drop off the key, Lee . . ." He lists all the ways you can leave your lover! It's really funny!'

In that moment, I didn't understand what was supposed to be clever or funny about the Paul Simon song Ged had just sung to me, but with William's reaction to my Barron Knights record fresh in my memory, I worked hard to conceal my disappointment at her impromptu demonstration of this man's lyrical genius. '50 Ways to Leave Your Lover' sounded a bit simple to me. Perhaps the sort of thing I might have liked at nursery. Still, I had to be careful what I said – I liked Ged's attention far too much to want to jeopardise my future supply of it.

Twenty minutes later, back in Ged's house, she placed the Paul Simon record on the turntable and handed me the sleeve so I could properly examine Paul's dreaminess with my own eyes. The corduroy peaked cap. The side-eye gaze which depicted him as a thoughtful loner. The clay-hued contours of his face. It was a still from *One-Trick Pony* – a film for which Simon had not only written the soundtrack but also played the lead role, that of a journeyman troubadour struggling to maintain his integrity and his relationship in the decade after scoring his last hit. Had I seen it, I would have no doubt suggested he take a leaf from his old mate's book and get himself a song like 'Bright Eyes'.

Ged played 'Late in the Evening' twice, all the better for me to anticipate the mini-Mardi Gras horn breakdown which walked the song home to an emphatic climax. 'Don't you think it's great, Takis? The way he uses all this extra percussion? And everything he's saying sounds like something he overheard in a conversation. Paul Simon doesn't like to repeat himself. His records are always different. He's not interested in reliving past glories. It's great, isn't it, Takis?'

I didn't notice it at the time, because you never do notice this when older children are doing it, but Ged was repeating observations she'd heard her brother Tim make about Paul Simon. A month later, I'd be asked to do my first ever piece of homework, an English assignment in which we had to write a few lines about a favourite poem. I chose 'Late in the Evening', making specific reference to the fact that Paul Simon doesn't like to repeat himself and the way everything he's saying sounds like something he overheard in a conversation. If I'd been a pupil at the school where Tim was now teaching, I would be handing his own deconstruction right back to him.

Had Ged not invited me back to her house, I would have gone straight to my house and noticed that the door was ajar. Pushing it open, I would have noticed my mum's handbag left in the hallway along with maybe one or two shopping bags, but no other immediate

sign of recent activity. I would have looked at my watch and seen
that the time was 1.30 p.m., indicating that my dad would be at the
shop for at least forty more minutes. A few minutes behind, Ged's
mum Joyce was also making her way back to Overlea Avenue. While
Ged and I were listening to Paul Simon, Joyce noticed our front door
and peered around it to see if everything was OK. She called out a
few times and, hearing no answer, began to advance up the stairs,
looking for signs of life. Still nothing. Having checked every room
in the house, she finally checked the toilet. And that was where she
found my mother lying unconscious.

CHAPTER 19

Everyone agreed that ABBA had pushed into new territory with 'The Winner Takes It All'. The language that DJs and critics used to talk about them underwent a subtle change. *The Sun* and the *Daily Mirror* had both reported on the break-up of Björn and Agnetha's marriage, gossip that percolated upwards into the music press, subtly bringing ABBA more into line with the criteria by which serious critics evaluated the artistic merit of a band's new record: you got extra points for honesty and authenticity; and if you were singing about something that happened in your life – sculpting art out of pain – then what could be more honest and authentic than that? 'The Winner Takes It All' helped ratify this shift, inviting you to believe that you were privy to a confessional. A dispatch from the darkest moment of any marriage – the moment it's over.

The speed with which ABBA released 'The Winner Takes It All' was telling – just seven weeks between conception and release – suggesting that everything to do with the song had been part of a single sustained act of catharsis. And nowhere was that more apparent than in the lyrics themselves. The opening line is the giveaway.

I don't wanna talk

When a song begins with those four words, you know the protagonist is going to do quite a lot of talking.

About things we've gone through

And now we know what she's going to talk about. Even at the age of eleven, listening to the song for the first time in the car with my dad, I can dimly recall a sense that things were about to get messy. You could all too easily imagine the protagonist reaching up, sliding open the glass door of the drinks cabinet and opening a bottle of something red and ballsy. Several years later, when I interviewed Björn and Benny in Stockholm, I voiced a hunch that the lyrics were perhaps written under the influence of alcohol. Once you get that idea in your head, it seems almost unimaginable that 'The Winner Takes It All' could have been written while sober. Spillage on this scale almost never happens without the aid of a corkscrew. Another telltale sign was the dogged devotion shown by Björn to the titular metaphor. Surely emboldened by Dutch courage to run with the 'game' imagery far longer than most people would bother, Björn was still at it three-quarters of the way into the song, summoning images of gods with 'minds as cold as ice' casually rolling dice to determine the fate of mortals in love.

And yet, I was still taken aback when Björn confirmed my theory: 'As a matter of fact, I was quite drunk. And that's unusual, too, because it never works. Whenever you write drunk, whether it's music or lyrics, you look at it the next day and it's bullshit. But that was a good one. I remember presenting it to the girls, and there were tears, you know?'

We knew. How could we not know? You don't write a middle eight like the one in 'The Winner Takes It All' and not expect tears.

> *But tell me does she kiss*
> *Like I used to kiss you?*
> *Does it feel the same*
> *When she calls your name?*

Imagine writing those lines and getting your ex-wife to sing them. Was that an act of empathy or an act of sadism? I'm not sure that even Björn knew. And certainly, in the summer of 1980, it's debatable how much I could have truly intuited. By this point in my life, I had amassed only slightly more emotional intelligence than the Action Man in the garden that Aki had nailed to a tree for his occasional bouts of air rifle practice. In the first half of August 1980, the only woman whose welfare seriously concerned me was the one seated at the table of a waterside restaurant on the Swedish island of Marstrand. Agnetha's desolate expression in the video for 'The Winner Takes It All' told its own story, as did her solitary presence in the restaurant, addressing the camera while, outside, her three bandmates appeared to be sharing a joke, either oblivious or indifferent to her distress.

That discombobulated me in a way that no music clip had previously done. This, of course, was no accident. The band's regular video director Lasse Hallström had repeatedly storyboarded videos which drew upon the interpersonal dynamic of the two couples in the band. But this was different. This was a world away from the sub-zero melodrama of 'Knowing Me, Knowing You' or the simple, sad-faced pleas of 'SOS'. Art blurred into life as messily as Agnetha's tear-stained eye shadow blurred into her mascara. She looked exhausted. Hollowed out. Spent. It was a look I recognised straight away. It was the same look as the one on my mum's face whenever she'd had a row with my dad. Not just one of their standard rows, but the thermonuclear quarterly display of mutual acrimony which would see my mum retreat to bed for a day (usually after he had started taking potshots at her relatives) and my dad serve out his subsequent penance by not coming back from the shop in the afternoons.

These rows would only start to subside on the second or third morning, when I'd catch my dad on the upstairs landing bringing up a cup of tea for my mum to drink in bed. My instinct at these moments was always to say, 'That's not how she likes her tea – it's far too milky', but I knew that would further entrench his conviction that I was batting for her side. And besides, it wasn't about the tea anyway. I knew that and he knew that. The tea always lay there undrunk until a terracotta-coloured film formed on top of it. The tea was his way of telling her he was sorry and that he really needed her to get out of bed and help him run the shop.

It turns out that my mother had quietly been bleeding through the spring and summer. Smallish quantities at first. The last few journeys from West Bromwich had been touch and go. If she didn't make her bus connections, the sanitary towel would no longer be able to absorb any more. She'd get home, run straight upstairs, get changed and hope for the best. Some days were better than others, but no days were great, and besides, there was just too much to do. If it turned out to be nothing serious, then whatever had broken or split would gradually repair itself, wouldn't it? And if it *was* serious, well . . . it had just better not be, because we had a shop to run and, even if my dad agreed to do the unthinkable and delegate the management of the shop to someone else, what was he going to do with us? The only meal he knew how to cook at home was a sort of hash of eggs and potatoes all mixed together. He had never been in a supermarket, operated the washing machine, ironed a shirt, made a bed or run a vacuum cleaner across a carpet. If he had, it would have made him unique among Cypriot men of his age. No one expected him to start now, not even my mum. It would have been like expecting a guide dog to round up sheep. That's not what they're trained to do.

Years later, I asked her a long overdue question. Why didn't she see a doctor? Just for peace of mind? She figured that she must be generating enough new blood cells to replace the ones she was losing. And besides, now that she no longer had to schlep back from West Bromwich, she convinced herself that the bleeding wasn't as bad. In reality, not having to make those ninety-minute journeys made it easier to manage her symptoms. But that didn't mean that her symptoms were getting better. Was she worried? Of course she was. But her worry would have turned into terror if she discovered that her condition might be life-threatening. For the time being, her best idea was to get through today, sleep at night and do the same thing again tomorrow.

She was in the toilet at British Home Stores when she realised she might not make it back. I can picture it perfectly. Until I was six or seven, it had always been the ladies toilet at British Home Stores she took me to if we were in town and needed to go. We'd then go through the lighting section and into the canteen where I had always asked for sausage, beans and chips. The women had never minded that I was there. I looked more like a girl than a boy anyway. Mercifully alone on this occasion, she had gone to town to buy my new school uniform. She was planning on buying me shirts from British Home Stores, then walking across the road to the Co-op department store – where Kate Bush had soundtracked the purchase of my first Manchester United strip – for my blazer and tie. Feeling increasingly faint, she sat in the cubicle and realised that, if she made it to the ground floor and outside the shop, she could probably hail a taxi home and forgo the Co-op for now. Arriving home twenty minutes later and bleeding more heavily than ever, she dropped the bag with the shirts and climbed the stairs to the toilet. And that's where Joyce found her, flat out at first, then gradually coming to her senses. Joyce helped prop her up and told her to wait there while she called 999. Not 999, insisted my mum. Even now, she was trying to defer the undeferrable, as if a more convenient time to address her haemorrhaging might present itself.

Finally, a compromise of sorts was reached. Joyce made two phone calls in close succession: the first to our GP; the second to Ged next door telling her to keep me there for at least the next hour, long enough to hear the entire debut album by an artist she adored even more than Paul Simon. Joe Jackson's *I'm Your Man* album drowned out the sound of Dr Hilary Lowe's claret wooden-framed Morris Minor as it pulled into the driveway we shared with the Hughes family.

Dr Lowe was a rangy, gentle man with curly carrot-coloured hair and glasses, who wore knitted V-neck tank tops over a shirt and bow tie. Nothing about him suggested that rock 'n' roll or the Beatles had impacted on his life in any significant way. His clothes and countenance quietly imparted telltale signs that, while this was a man who would do almost anything for his family and his patients, Sunday afternoons were set aside exclusively for the enjoyment of Chris Barber and Acker Bilk records in his favourite chair. He had strong views about immigration, enthusing at length about all the wonderful ways in which immigrants had enriched the fabric of British life. On seeing my mum propped up by Mrs Hughes as she knelt to support her head, Dr Lowe gave my mum some sort of restorative drink and told her that she most probably had uterine fibroids. He called for an ambulance and, on arriving at Solihull hospital, she was given two pints of blood. Following a formal diagnosis from the specialist gynaecologist, she was told that the following morning she would undergo a hysterectomy. What, she asked, was a hysterectomy? Upon being told that her womb would be removed, she began to cry uncontrollably. 'Why are you crying?' asked the gynaecologist. 'Do you want your boys to lose you for a few days or lose you forever?'

By the time I arrived home, my dad had come and gone. While he was getting the shop ready for teatime, Joyce stayed with me and Aki and told us the least upsetting version possible of what had happened. She promised to find out if we would be allowed to visit her tomorrow. 'When you get hungry, your dad says you're to go to the shop,' she added. 'But you're very welcome to eat with us if you like.'

Aki and I thanked her. She hugged us and left. I turned on the TV and felt something that was almost like excitement, but not quite.

It was the sense of being in a new place. Of being caught between cliffhanger and resolution, and not quite knowing what, in real life, happens between the two. After a couple of hours or so, Aki and I commenced the twenty-minute walk to the Kingfisher. My dad gave us our tea, which we ate as we walked home. We only opened the front door to grab a football from the lean-to veranda by the kitchen. Then we walked through the gap in the hedge, which ran all the way down the far side of Overlea Avenue, and played penalties against the gate of the yard of the radiator installation company that lay on the other side. We stayed out until we could no longer see the ball in the fading light.

The following morning, my dad came into the room where Aki and I were sleeping and told Aki that he'd need him to help him open the shop. My mum's surgery was the first scheduled operation of the day. The procedure would take about ninety minutes in total. Assuming she was in any state to see us, I was to arrive at the shop by 2 p.m. and my dad would drive Aki and me to Solihull hospital about ten minutes away. We took fruit, which my dad had brought with him to the shop that morning. I was given the job of holding the flowers, which we bought from a kiosk on the ground floor. The newness of the hospital made the sight of elderly, half-dressed patients attached to tubes and colostomy sacks wheeling themselves into designated areas for a cigarette more startling. The lift doors opened to reveal a woman in a wheelchair with one and a half legs, at which I flinched involuntarily. At the ward a nurse told us we would be allowed to see my mum, but if she became upset or overwhelmed we would be asked to leave. There were four beds in the ward. Hers was on the near side, to the right of the door as we entered. The ward sister walked ahead of us, put her head through the curtains that were drawn around her bed and told my mum that her family were here to see her.

Her eyelids were heavy. I'd never seen her like this before. Aki was standing on one side of the bed, while my dad and I stood to her right, on the other. Beyond 'Hello' and 'How are you feeling?' I simply didn't know what to say to her. And, for the first time, she wasn't in a position to step in and fill the silence. I held up the flowers.

'*Orea*,' she croaked. Nice.

Could we get her anything else?

'*Ligo nero*, Taki.' Some water, Taki.

My dad leaned over to reach the jug, but perhaps because the request for water had been made in reply to my question, I grabbed the handle before him and, with my right hand, steadied the plastic cup into which I poured the water. My mum tried to raise her head sufficiently to drink from the cup, but she couldn't muster the strength. I gently pressed it to her dry lips, and repeated the action maybe three or four times until she raised her hand to indicate 'enough'.

Over the years, I've gone back and replayed what happened next. I think about the options that presented themselves to my dad at this point. Seemingly denied by his background the ability to draw on the instinctive tenderness you would normally display to a loved one at such a time, he asked her how she was. She responded with something like a shrug. With nothing else to fill the silence, he began to list all the things he had to do in the shop now that she wouldn't be around to help. The potatoes that needed to be prepared. As the sole driver, he'd always be the one to get the fish from the market, but it was my mum who sliced it into portions and made the batter. Now that all fell to him. When did they tell her she might be out?

I don't know if Aki noticed at the same time as me, but it took my dad a few seconds longer to notice that my mum was crying.

'*Christaki, stamata. Se parakalo. Christaki . . .*' Christaki, stop. Please. Christaki.

Nearby a nurse, quick to notice something of what was happening, stepped into view. Directly addressing my mother she asked, 'Is everything all right? Would you like to be alone for a while?'

Chastened into silence, my dad stepped back. I could feel my face burning. A surge of hatred I had never felt before. Hatred that had nowhere to go. To display it here would further upset my mother. But then, neither could I display it later. For the time being, the object of my fury was my sole carer. I had questions that I couldn't ask and he was in no position to answer.

What was he thinking? Where was his compassion? Why couldn't he look at my mum, captive in a hospital bed after major surgery, and see what most other people would see?

I didn't imagine that I would ever forgive my dad for that exchange. Now, almost forty years later, I'm surprised to find that I struggle to even apply the concept of forgiveness to that scene. Like so much of what happened between them, I've come to feel that it's not my place to retrospectively referee the key scenes of their relationship. My life has been so different to theirs. I've never had to start a new life in a new country without the support network of a nearby extended family. My marriage has never had to withstand those sorts of rigours. It doesn't feel useful or fair to stand in judgement. What feels more useful is to accept that things happen and that you can try to understand them in the hope that the mistakes of the past aren't repeated.

It does you no good to weight memories with the knowledge of what ought to have happened. That doesn't teach you anything. It merely reinforces what you felt at the time. What helps is to go back to the scene and try and ask yourself why everyone assumed the roles that they did. What was it about my dad that meant he could look at my mother in her condition and park any visible concern in order to tell her what her operation meant for *him* over the next fortnight or so? Was it that he didn't care? Was he trying to guilt-trip her? At the age of eleven, that was exactly how it seemed to me. And now?

And now . . . I think he was scared. Relative to other Cypriot men of his generation, there was nothing unusual about my father. If, at this precise moment, I wanted him to disappear, I still wouldn't have swapped him for any of the other Cypriot dads. If anything, he was more lenient with us than most of them. Other Cypriot dads forced their children to come to church with them every Sunday. Other Cypriot dads used to spend their nights off in Cypriot gambling dens. Other Cypriot dads made it clear to their sons from the outset that, if they were to stay in Britain, they would be taking over the family business. Although ours saw the latter as the only desirable alternative to a move back to Cyprus, he stopped short of telling us this was what we *had to do*. I was grateful for that.

For all of that though, he was still a fairly typical Cypriot man of his generation. These men had never felt the need to analyse their own emotions, or break them down into their constituent parts. In their early twenties, these men pursued women, who became their wives, who then became the mothers of their children. The distinct roles set out for mothers and fathers released men from any expectation that they should provide their children with emotional nourishment. Irrespective of whether you think this system obsolete, unfair, stifling, patriarchal or all of these things, it's a system that would have probably worked for my parents had they put down roots in the place where my father had grown up.

And now, in 1980, if my parents had been in a place where they were surrounded by extended family, my dad wouldn't have panicked at the prospect of having to run everything while my mum was recovering from major surgery. Aunts and uncles would have swooped in to look after us and, perhaps, help in the shop. This might have allowed my dad to arrive at the hospital, look at my ailing mum in front of him and respond to her in a way most people would recognise as empathetic. In this century, even relatively unreconstructed men are expected to know the difference between need and love. In this century, 'I can't manage alone' became a poor substitute for 'I love you'.

In this century, 'I can't manage alone', – or its dashing twin, 'I need you' – sounds nice enough, but if you're the person being addressed, 'I can't manage alone' isn't quite enough to elevate you from the status of mere staff. And in the world that brought my parents together, those lines were still blurred. Think of Golde in *Fiddler on the Roof* itemising her love for Tevye, duty by duty: milking his cow, sharing his bed, cooking his meals, cleaning their house and so on and so on. 'If that's not love,' she concludes, 'what is?' Surely a marriage needs to have more than that going on? It seems obvious now. But for men like my dad, it wasn't at all obvious. And in 1980, nearly all Cypriot men were like my dad. It didn't occur to them that, increasingly, their wives wanted to feel something more than needed. To understand that is to understand how my dad was able to stand in front of my mother after her operation and only see what it meant for *him*. This was a pattern of behaviour I didn't dare repeat in my own marriage. And in a strange way, I have my parents to thank for that.

The next few days followed a similar pattern. I'd go downstairs, pour myself a bowl of Frosties, watch TV, mooch down the road to Acocks Green and stare at the records in Easy Listening, Preedy's and Woolworths, keeping a running total of what I could afford and what I might buy next. With each new single, Roxy Music were starting to seem more and more important. I'd picked up somewhere along the line that they had been around in the early seventies and recently returned after a period of inactivity. People who remembered them from before seemed more enthused about the old stuff than their current run of singles. They talked about innovation and originality, as though these qualities were determinants of listenability. About a year later, I'd finally get to see and hear what it was about early Roxy Music that got people excited. As the closing credits of Mike Read's *Pop Quiz* rolled, Roxy Music's *Top of the Pops* performance of 'Virginia Plain' revealed a confusion of androgynous aliens marauding into uncharted territory on their sequinned sonic steamroller. Bryan Ferry's hair was longer and his eyelids were brushed with something shiny. He wore the collar of his black top up and his pointy shoulders gave him a camp, vampiric air – a hypercaffeinated younger brother to the casually coutured ghost who fronted Roxy Mk 2: Heathcliff dressed by Antony Price. In time, I'd come to appreciate the former, but from the moment I set eyes on Bryan Ferry, I was a little bit enraptured by the latter.

Had I been a little older, I could have seen how Roxy Mk 1, coming along at the right time, might save your life. Those songs would be like a club filled with outsiders you've yet to meet, the outsiders you didn't know existed – outsiders just like you. But what would you listen to six months later when one of those outsiders broke your heart and left you feeling like the world and your place in it had forever been changed? What would be your lifeline at the lowest moment? I'd never had my heart broken. But Roxy Music's run of singles from 1979 to 1981 were a periscope into that world. They were the first band I heard that depicted sadness as a space you could lovingly furnish and luxuriate in. The genius of 'Oh Yeah (On the Radio)' was that it explained this to me in almost literal terms. 'Oh Yeah' is not just the name of the song – it's the name of the song that the song is about. It was the very thing it was describing.

'One day,' Bryan Ferry seemed to be saying, 'you might be driving somewhere and this song might come on the radio, and it will be *your* "Oh Yeah".' Five years later, music journalists would be falling over themselves to heap praise on Scritti Politti and Prefab Sprout for releasing singles that tried to forge new ground by being the very thing to which they were simultaneously paying tribute. But with 'Oh Yeah (On the Radio)', Roxy Music comfortably beat them to the punch.

As Chic's Nile Rodgers would make clear in his autobiography *Le Freak*, without Roxy Music there would almost have certainly been no Chic. And without Nile Rodgers and Bernard Edwards to write and produce it for her, Diana Ross wouldn't have been enjoying her biggest hit in almost a decade with 'Upside Down', which had just been released. Chic were enjoying a run of imperial dominance which didn't just stop at their own records. They had turbocharged the hitherto modest fortunes of Sister Sledge by writing and producing 1979's *We Are Family* album for them. The method they used for Sister Sledge and Diana Ross was identical to the one which had made Chic such a huge success. The Sister Sledge album was a testing ground of sorts – proof that the Chic formula could be wholly transplanted to another artist. By the time Rodgers and Edwards were introduced to Diana Ross, they had earned the right to face their heroine and effectively hire her as Chic's star vocalist for an album. 'Upside Down' was Chic through and through – opulent melancholy from the heart to the hip and back again. Diana Ross might have hated the song – at least she voiced grave doubts about it until it raced up the charts on both sides of the Atlantic – but she still managed to deliver a vocal turn which was freighted with all the embattled nobility that the song required. For a song about being hostage to the emotions you feel for an unworthy recipient, nothing less was needed.

As a Chic single in all but name, 'Upside Down' felt familiar from the off. By contrast, the outergalactic otherness of David Bowie's return to action ensured that there was nothing stylistically familiar about it – a fact that prompted *Smash Hits* reviewer Deanne Pearson to confidently declare that it was 'not a hit'. Its total ubiquity in this of all weeks was uncanny. I don't know what the grown-ups were getting out of it. But I can tell you this. If you tune into *Top of the Pops*, aged eleven, while your father is at work and your mother is lying in a hospital bed and unable to move for fear of aggravating the incision across the middle of her body, 'Ashes to Ashes' sounds overwhelming. Not upsetting, you understand. 'Ashes to Ashes' didn't make what was happening to my mum any sadder. It was more that my mum's situation somehow authenticated the sentiments of the song. Furthermore, Bowie's vocal seemed to come from a place near the edge of life itself. Either awakening from a period of unconsciousness or about to enter one. Over time, I would come to realise that his ability to refract unspeakable, unknowable peril through the prism of melody was unsurpassable. It was there in 'Five Years', 'The Man Who Sold the World' and 'Life on Mars?'. By the time he released *Blackstar*, knowing that he had weeks to live, it didn't occur to anyone that Bowie might, this time, actually be writing about his own death. In the right hands, the chasm between knowing exactly what awaits us and not knowing at all what awaits us can be turned into a gallery space. Bowie had created such extraordinary work in that space, we didn't imagine that, this time, he was facing that abyss for real. With 'Ashes to Ashes', Bowie explained that he was trying to write a nursery-rhyme requiem to the 1970s and, indeed, to childhood itself – a song that made children and adults in 1980 feel the way he had done when he first heard 'Inchworm', performed by Danny Kaye in the 1952 film *Hans Christian Andersen*. 'There's a child's nursery rhyme element in it,' he told *Performing Songwriter* magazine in 2003, 'and there's something so sad and mournful and poignant about it. It kept bringing me back to the feelings of those pure thoughts of sadness that you have as a child, and how they're so identifiable even when you're an adult. There's a connection that can be made between being a somewhat lost five-year-old and feeling a little abandoned and having the same feeling when you're in your twenties.'

With Aki roped into helping in the shop most mornings, I'd stand on his bed, reach up for the shoe box where he kept his records – every one orphaned from its sleeve – and pull out a few favourites, among them the new single by the Clash, 'Bankrobber'. Thanks to the group's continuing refusal to do *Top of the Pops*, the previous week's show had seen resident dance troupe Legs & Co. get to grips with the job of interpreting this sweet, soporific dub lullaby about seizing back the spoils of the system that conspires to keep you down. Playing seven not-entirely-convincing felons, they spent the entirety of the song exercising behind their cell doors in standard-issue stripy convict leotards.

Then, at around 1.30 p.m., I'd head to the shop and my dad would ask me what I wanted for lunch. If there were no other customers, he'd come round to the front, unlock the front panel of the new Asteroids machine and notch up a few free games for me. Keen to ensure we got away as close to closing time as possible, thus maximising the minutes spent in hospital with my mum, I'd walk to the door at 2 p.m. and pull the little tab on the sign hanging at the door which changed the word written on it from 'O P E N' to 'C L O S E D' – always a pleasing action. For the remainder of my mum's stay in hospital, Aki was given some money to help make sure that our food requirements were met. Most nights, one of us would get the bus from the house to the chip shop, but one evening we decided we'd get a 'proper' takeaway. In 2018, takeaway or delivered food accounted for six per cent of all meals eaten in the UK. But in 1980, even pizza delivery had yet to arrive in Acocks Green; hence takeaways – when offered to us – were rare enough to be greeted with the sort of simple joy more commonly found when you show a dog a sausage. Of course, now that I think about it, food from our shop technically counted as a takeaway, but it never ever occurred to us to think of it as such. For the first eight years of my life, 'taking away' a portion of chips would have involved taking it from the front of the building and carrying it to another room. And even though our current shop was a mile away from the house, I simply never updated that thought.

No, for us, takeaways were synonymous with one meal from one place. Kwong Ming was the Chinese 300 yards from our first chip shop on Yardley Road. Once in a while, my dad would ask if anyone fancied a beef curry from Kwong Ming – always with egg fried rice, of course. For some reason, no alternative was ever offered – and none was needed. I couldn't imagine there could be anything tastier on Kwong Ming's extensive menu than their beef curry. And furthermore, I couldn't imagine there could be any curry anywhere in Birmingham than the comforting spicy gravy in which those pleasingly uniform strips of beef and a few luminescent peas were suspended. It would be years before I'd finally dare to deviate from our regular family order – and when I finally mustered the temerity to ask for noodles instead of rice, my dad shot me a look as if to say, 'So you're too good for rice now, are you?' But that was all way down the line. Having decided to get a takeaway, Aki and I decided that Kwong Ming was too far to go. Perhaps we'd get a curry from Noor Jahan, the Indian takeaway that had just opened down the road. We didn't know anything about the difference between Indian and Chinese curries. After all, how different could two similarly coloured, sauce-based dishes with the same name be?

'They didn't do beef,' said Aki, holding our dinner. 'I got lamb instead.' He placed the brown paper bag on the low table in the sitting room. Some of its contents had spilled out onto the side of the bag, leaving a dark orange mark. The smell of curry filled the room. It was oddly comforting.

'It doesn't smell like curry, does it?' I said.

'What does it smell of, then?' he replied.

I suddenly realised what it reminded me of. Vijay's house. I made a mental note to tell Vijay that I'd eaten curry when we started at our new school. Aki handed me my food and I peeled back the lid. It was a variation of a dish I've had hundreds of times since. But at that moment, clocking the oily top layer and the unfamiliar consistency of what was underneath it, I was taken aback. I took the second foil container. 'They didn't have egg fried rice,' said Aki, 'so I got boiled rice instead.' I managed about a third. I didn't have any frame of reference for what I was eating. I thought the Indians had tried to copy the Chinese and got it badly wrong. Furthermore, I concluded, if they were serious about overtaking the Chinese in the curry stakes, they were going to have to raise their game.

The days before the start of the new school term were now well into single figures. I had to somehow sort out my school uniform. There was no question of my dad being able to provide anything other than the money with which to pay for it. Maybe Aki could come to town with me and show me which shops I needed to go to. As he got ready to join my dad in the shop one morning, I mentioned it to him.

'Do you know what you really need to get?' he replied.

I shrugged back at him.

'You need to get your hair cut, otherwise everyone's going to pick on you. And if you're starting in a new school, that's the last thing you want to happen.'

The thought of it filled me with terror, but I knew he was right. Usually it was my mum's job to tell me that the hair situation could no longer continue as it was. The idea that I would have to go there and put my hair into the hands of Continental Nick was bordering on unthinkable to me. And yet, this was what had to happen. After two hours of anxious procrastination, I left the house at midday, all the time rehearsing what I was going to say in order to avoid an all-out tonsorial atrocity.

I alighted the bus outside the barber shop and walked past once, casually glancing through the window to gather intelligence that might help me avoid receiving a nightmare haircut at the time it mattered the most. How many barbers were cutting hair? How many people were waiting to be seen? If I timed my arrival correctly, I might get one of Nick's assistants and not Nick himself, whose hairstyling repertoire continued to function on a binary basis: James Bolam in 1964 or Rodney Bewes in 1974. His assistants tended to be younger and, as a result, happier to give you something marginally more tolerable. My hair goals were, in the general scheme of things, modest, and entirely covered by the styles sported by a range of Radio 1 DJs: Noel Edmonds, Steve Wright, David 'Kid' Jensen. Any of them, really, apart from Andy Peebles (bald) or Jimmy Savile (everything about it and him). I must have walked back and forth about twenty times before pushing the door open and joining the queue at the optimal point of Nick-avoidance. It worked a little too well. Sensing my jumpiness, the woman who beckoned me over to the chair erred so far on the side of caution that no one believed I'd been for a haircut in the first place. The other problem was that I dithered outside Nick's shop for so long that I was late getting back to the Kingfisher in time for the lift to the hospital. Waiting for me outside the locked shop was Aki.

'You're too late. He left without us,' he said. 'Where did you go?'

'I was getting my hair cut,' I said.

'Which hair did you get cut?'

'What are you on about?'

'Have you really had it cut?'

'Yes. That's where I just came from.'

'Anyway, he's gone without us. What do you want to do?'

I knew my mum would be expecting us. I didn't have the heart to simply not go. 'We can still go, can't we?' I said to Aki.

'Have you got the bus fare?' he asked.

I checked my pockets. All I'd had was money for the haircut.

We started to walk. The hospital was just under an hour away. We figured that might leave us just enough time to see my mum for ten minutes before getting a lift back with my dad. Sensing that time was against us, we even ran for the final few minutes. We were still out of breath when the lift doors opened on the second floor. I thought she'd be happy to see us once we arrived. It wasn't quite like that. My dad had already been and gone and, with him, so had our lift home. Clocking our slightly fraught state, she defaulted to mum mode, asking us if we had eaten. Aki had eaten at the shop. 'It's OK, I'm not hungry,' I told her, mortified at the idea that, even when convalescing in her hospital bed, the job of feeding us might still fall on her shoulders.

'They keep giving me sandwiches,' she said, leaning across to the tray on her bedside table. 'I've already had my lunch. Here, have these.' She pushed an egg, cress and tomato sandwich in my direction. The bread was soft, white and thinly sliced. The sandwich was heavenly. I didn't want to bring up the subject of my school uniform, not with my mum, but I was really beginning to worry now.

'I start at my new school on Monday,' I told her. 'When you went to British Home Stores, did you . . .?'

'Your shirts. They're in the bag in the spare room. Don't worry. I'll think of something.'

Visiting time was over. I leaned over so she could kiss me. Aki did the same. As we left, a nearby nurse who had somehow worked out what had happened silently left and returned with some fresh sandwiches for my mum to eat. Together, Aki and I walked back along the busy stretch of the Warwick Road that connects Solihull to Acocks Green. I don't know what we talked about, but all I could think about was my school uniform or rather, the lack of it.

In the event, some neighbours turned out to be more neighbourly than we could have possibly expected. To our right, at number 12, the Hughes family represented one version of Englishness: self-improving, tolerant, community-minded, resourceful. Had they not gone away for the weekend, they would have no doubt helped me buy my uniform. And our other neighbours? To our left, at 16, the Hunts represented an altogether different sort of Englishness. They were the longest-standing occupants of Overlea Avenue. The nine houses on our little road had originally been paid for by the local car parts manufacturer Lucas for their employees to live in. Dennis

Hunt had spent all his working life training up the apprentices at Lucas. Perhaps, one day, he might have occasion to train me.

Everything you needed to know about the Hunts could be extrapolated from their tulips, which stood equidistantly along the length of the garden, like soldiers awaiting inspection. The only variety in the Hunts' life was of the carefully planned sort, and that was just how they liked it. Every afternoon at 5.05 p.m., Dennis's wife Iris – a slight, unsmiling woman with a pigeon-like gait – would emerge into the front garden and sweep the front path so that it was perfect at 5.15 p.m., which was exactly the time Dennis turned the corner onto our road from Westley Road and negotiated the final straight home for dinner.

His walk seemed designed to broadcast his status: chest out; vertebrae locked into a rod of permanent propriety; chin slightly raised to accentuate the impressive curvature of his nose, the tip of which overshot his nostrils and had to gather itself back in to meet them. As late as 1980, there were still hundreds of thousands of people like Dennis and Iris Hunt up and down the country. Raised in the aftermath of one war, survivors of a second, they equated happiness with systems – systems and structures that existed to offer stability and security in the wake of a prolonged period that lacked either. They were the people Ray Davies described in the Kinks' 'Shangri-La', with little 'kingdom[s]' to command: 'You can go outside and polish your car / Or sit by the fire in your Shangri-la.'

For my dad, the Hunts were a source of mystification. From the very beginning, he mistook their austere bearing for standoffishness. What didn't help matters was the fact that, if he had occasion to knock on their door, they would step forward and conduct the conversation on the doorstep, resolutely never inviting him in. Greeks tend to swing to the other extreme. Beckoning callers in from the doorstep and offering them tea and *baklava* – even if they were trying to deliver a letter or sell you cosmetics – was an irreducible imperative for my parents. By contrast, the Hunts' house was the subject of animated speculation, not just among us, but the Hugheses, who had also never looked inside. So, in 1984, it was quite a coup for my dad when Dennis had to prevail upon him to help carry a huge framed picture into their kitchen. My dad returned looking as triumphant as I'd ever seen him. 'They've got a noticeboard hanging up in their kitchen!' he reported. 'All their meals for the week are written on it. If you ask them what they're going to eat next Thursday evening, *they'll be able to tell you!*' He couldn't have looked more astonished if he'd gone in and found a cat smoking a pipe, reading *Punch*. Not that the Hunts had a cat, of course. Not only did the Hunts disapprove of pets; they also disapproved of the animal kingdom in general, or at least the bits of it that wandered into their garden. The 2-foot metal plate curved around the trunk of the large fir tree in their garden bore testament to that uneasy relationship. Personally installed by Dennis, its purpose was to stop the squirrels climbing up the tree and dropping pine cone cores onto their lawn. The squirrels barely registered its presence.

But people aren't always what they seem. Perhaps about an hour after Aki and I made it back home from the hospital, Dennis and Iris Hunt broke their hitherto unbreakable routine and drove to Solihull hospital to see my mum. I can't imagine what she would have talked about with those two, or how Dennis would have softened his shoehorn spine into anything approaching a bedside manner. But a visit took place and words must have been exchanged. Words of friendliness sufficient to embolden my mum into asking Iris if she had any plans to go into town the following day.

And Iris, somehow sensing the fix that my mother was in, replied, 'Yes, I can go into town, Victoria. Is there anything you need?'

The following day, with a piece of paper containing my waist and leg measurements and some cash which my mum had kept in the cabinet next to her hospital bed, Iris Hunt went into town and picked up two pairs of trousers, two jumpers, one green blazer with my new school crest on the breast pocket and a tie to match. I looked out of the window and saw her walk all the way to the end of her driveway with Co-op and Marks & Spencer bags in her hands, and then into ours, all the way to our front door.

The fence separating our front drives was no more than two feet tall. Most people would have just stepped over it. Not Iris though. She stood on our doorstep and curtly told me what she had come to give me. She then handed over the bags and, without establishing eye contact, smiled to signify the completion of this transaction. Relieved of the weight of the bags, she fluttered back down our drive looking as vulnerable to a sudden gust as Woodstock when he launches himself off Snoopy's kennel. I can't recall a single word she uttered to me after that.

CHAPTER 20

No one sat me down and explained what secondary school would be like, but it was OK because Madness had just released a song about it. 'Baggy Trousers' had the strange effect of making me nostalgic about something I was about to experience for the first time. The accompanying video first had them performing the song in a school hall and then in the adjoining park surrounded by a swarm of schoolkids roughly my age. Looking at it now, it seems that the director told the kids to just run around having fun and pretend the band weren't there. That lack of direct interaction has the effect of making Madness look like a figment of the kids' collective imagination, faithfully reporting what children see but forget to tell you by the time they drop their bags in the hallway and open the fridge door.

A few days previously, Madness turned in an appearance on *Tiswas* that, even by their standards, was exuberant. They sprayed the programme's presenter Sally James with silly string, dislodging her false eyelashes in the process. If Chas Smash and Suggs seemed especially wired, that would have had something to do with the fact that they hadn't gone to bed before *Tiswas*, choosing instead to take acid in Coventry with the Specials. No band seemed to be having as much fun as Madness but, with 'Baggy Trousers', even they seemed to be suggesting that their time at secondary school constituted an unsurpassable golden age. I guessed it was time to find out.

With my mum due to be discharged on the first day of term, I needed to enlist Aki's help once again. I ventured down to the posh room at the front of the house where I could hear him playing his latest acquisition. Skids' new single 'Circus Games' was their most unsettling release to date. For a song about people in power making mistakes that it's left to the next generation to correct, the band had the inspired idea of having schoolchildren sing the hook, 'Come and play circus games / Come and play at circus games'. The record came in a fold-out poster sleeve, which Aki had laid out on the dining table that, although fully set, hadn't been used once in the eighteen months we'd lived there. The wardrobe of Skids frontman Richard Jobson had now left punk fully behind. He was wearing a V-neck tank top with starched white shirt done up to the top and what appeared to be a school tie. Richard clearly knew how to tie his own tie and now it was my turn. Dressed for the first time in my new uniform, I presented Aki with my green, black and yellow striped tie and asked him if he could teach me how to put it on. Four years earlier, the night before I'd started junior school, it was also Aki who taught me how to tie my shoelaces. Not the proper way, but the single-loop 'lazy' way that I still use now. It didn't take long to master the tie, maybe one and a half plays of 'Circus Games'. 'Take the fat end, pass it up and over the back and down through this little hole you've made here. Got that? Now you do it.'

Knowing that my mum had yet to leave hospital, William Osborne called me on the evening before our first day at secondary school. His dad would be driving him there. If I wanted, he could detour via our house and we could go together? We followed the murmuration of green blazers through the main gates and into the school hall where, four years previously, our brothers had stood on their first day. The fumes of newly applied floor polish dispersed up towards the skylight whose individual panes of glass I would try and count in their entirety during the most boring assemblies. This was a two-step process. The first bit would involve grouping them into individual colours, then – trying to memorise the quantities of each colour – the objective was to add together the numbers for each colour before coming up with a final tally. It took me over two years to finally get to all 632.

Yardleys School was a secondary modern but, confusingly, it wasn't located anywhere near Yardley and neither was it modern. Aki's year had been Yardleys' first intake after it lost its grammar school status. By the time my year arrived, academic excellence had been almost entirely flushed out of this once-proud institution.

If you went to a school that used the streaming system, it meant that everyone in your class was supposed to be roughly as bright as you were. No one knew what information each primary school submitted to ensure that children ended up in the appropriate class. Our involvement in the process began in that school hall on that first morning. Our elderly headmaster Mr Wilford tottered on stage and welcomed us. Like most of the teachers at Yardleys, he had pre-dated the move to secondary modern. We were told – by whom I'm not sure – that Mr Wilford kept a cane in his office and that he was the only teacher allowed to use it. However, if you made it as far as his office, you could see the marks left on the back of a leather-uphol-stered wingback chair. And if you had been sent there to be caned, the secret you were ordered to keep was that it was the chair that took a beating on your behalf.

Mr Wilford didn't spend very long on stage. It was left to his deputy, Mr Mellor, to oversee the process by which we were grouped into our classes. In any given year there were six classes. When it came to the naming of these classes, no great attempt was made to conceal how they ranked. Each class corresponded to a letter in the name of the school, with Y being the top stream, then A, and then R, D, L and E. Even the children banished to the lower streams weren't quite slow-witted enough to look around and not realise what it meant to be in their allotted class. William and I stood there next to each other, waiting for our names to be announced. At no point did it occur to us that we would end up in different classes. After all, Edward and Aki had been within compass-throwing distance of each other since day one. Surely the same would apply to us? First to be called out were the children who were to be in 1Y. With their names announced in alphabetical order, Mr Mellor cruised past the M's and on towards the next letters. 'Norris, Malcolm! O'Donnell, Rebecca! Osborne, William! . . .' With O coming before P in the alphabet, surely my name would be next? 'Pooley, Mark! Rea, Karen! . . .'

William looked at me apologetically and walked off to join his new classmates in the toppermost form. The fate of every other child was to wait in the hall until their name was called out. Imagine seeing the last of the L's called out, casting your gaze around a near-empty hall and, perhaps for the first time in your life, having to narrow your life expectations accordingly. Thankfully, I didn't have too much longer to wait. If your name was among those called to join 1A, you had to walk over to Miss Friday – a short, red-haired woman in a cotton sports top and tracksuit bottoms who, for the remainder of my time at Yardleys, I would never see without a clipboard pressed to her chest and a whistle hanging around her neck.

We were led out of the hall and through to the playground at the back, where three prefabricated classrooms stood side by side. In our classroom were three rows of five desks, each with room for two pupils – one boy, one girl. Miss Friday called out the names of every child in alphabetical order. If you heard your name, you had to come to the front and take an exercise book from the pile on her desk. These, she explained, were rough books and they were to be used to note anything down that shouldn't go in a proper exercise book. More than anything else that happened that day, this was the one thing that conferred upon us a sense that we were significantly more grown up than our primary school incarnations. A year previously,

I couldn't even be trusted with a pen. Now I had an entire book in which to indulge my downtime obsession for practising record label logos. If I couldn't master a decent Epic Records imprimatur by Christmas, then what good was I to anyone?

'I want you all to say hello to the person next to you,' said Miss Friday. 'Unless I say so, you will be sharing your desk with them all the way through your first year at Yardleys.'

I turned to the girl on my left. She had dark skin and her hair had been cut into a crude bob. In keeping with the strictures of her religion, she wore trousers under her school skirt.

'Hello,' I said. 'I'm Peter Paphides.'

'I'm Shabana,' she said. 'Shabana Quereshi.'

Shabana had a sweet smile. I think she must have been the oldest sibling of maybe three or four. From this day on, her relaxed disposition would always suggest that school made fewer demands on her attention than her home life.

'Shabana Cabana!' I chirped – an utterance so asinine that she could do nothing other than smile politely at me.

'Like the chocolate!' I added. 'Shabana Cabana!' Rowntree's had recently launched an exotic new chocolate bar with cherries and coconut called Cabana. Unsurprisingly, this was not the first Shabana had heard about it.

'Yes!' she nodded. 'Have you had one?'

I hadn't. The idea of something cherry-flavoured oozing out of a chocolate bar didn't appeal to me. 'Have you had one?' I asked her.

'No,' she shrugged, almost apologetically. And that was the end of that.

Shabana wasn't the only girl in 1A with an exotic name. Two rows to the left, sharing a desk with Henry Bannatyne, was Sultana Bolia. Oddly, beyond a few muffled sniggers, the novelty of having a Sultana in our class dissipated almost immediately. If she had a name that sounded like 'Sultana', we could have derived mild hilarity by

calling her Sultana. But *actually* being called Sultana? You couldn't
go anywhere from there.

There were no such limitations on the potential for amusement
in our very first lesson. Clutching our new timetables, we hurried
back towards the main block and up the stairs, past the cigarette
fumes dissipating outside the staff room. A few yards further on
was the classroom where our German teacher Mr Thoms had
already laid a single textbook and exercise book on each desk. Mr
Thoms was a tall man in a tweed jacket with thick short hair that
really didn't look happy about being kept in a side parting. He had
a moustache which I suspect had once been attached to a beard,
possibly discarded at around the same time as the Henry Cow and
Hatfield and the North albums that had sustained him throughout
teacher-training college. He asked us to turn to page six of our
books so we could acquaint ourselves with Hans and Lieselotte,
the dead-eyed line-drawing children through whose exploits we
would expand our German vocabulary. This was the spread where
Hans and Lieselotte told us about their family. Clearly the reason
Mr Thoms decided to start us here was so that we could, without
further delay, get beyond the fact that some German words had
the word 'fart' in them. It was a clever move. We had spent less
than an hour in the same room as each other. Most of us were too
abashed to make the most of the news that the German word for
father (*Vater*) was pronounced 'farter'.

Not Terry Violett though. Terry had quickly emerged as One to
Watch. When, earlier on, Miss Friday had asked him to remove his
black Harrington jacket so she could see his blazer, he had replied,
'Yes, Miss Thursday' – a response so magnificent that we'd be reminiscing about it for months to come. Terry looked around to see if
anyone else found the word *Vater* as funny as he did. Sitting directly
behind him, I certainly did, but he couldn't see me. Ten minutes later,
it transpired that the third-person singular application of the word

meaning 'to travel' was '*fahrt*'. I couldn't imagine a time could come
when I wouldn't find this bowel-judderingly hilarious.

Within a couple of hours, everyone seemed to know what part
they were here to play. The class clowns – as Terry Violett had
already done – moved quickly to establish themselves in their roles.
By the morning break they had an entourage of willing lieutenants
around them. Then you had smaller clusters of children who had
been friends in their previous schools and, as a result, didn't need to
put themselves out to get to know kids like me. Our first PE lesson,
immediately before lunchtime, acted as an ad hoc showcase for the
sporty kids and, in doing so, assigned all the remaining covetable
roles that were up for grabs. Jeremy Maher had come to Yardleys
from the same school as me but his family were new to the area. He
had only been at Cottesbrooke for the final few weeks of the previous
year. All I really knew about him was that he had the orangest hair
I'd ever seen and that he was called Jeremy. And, in 1980, the only
children who had it worse than Jeremys were Gaylords and the only
Gaylords left were in America (over 6,000 according to the most
recent figures).

But on the first day of the first term of a new school, with the
second half of our first PE lesson set aside for a football match, it
was, in every sense, a level playing field. One moment of brilliance
could launch you to hitherto unscaled heights of popularity. Jeremy
Maher would have known this. I knew it too. So when, at 4–4 with
five minutes to go, I found myself in the other team's eighteen-yard
box with their defence behind me, just the keeper to beat and the
John Motson in my head about to burst a synapse, I knew exactly
what was at stake. All I needed to do was strike the ball cleanly in the
direction of the net but not straight at the goalkeeper. In the event, I
did neither. Like a seagull to a burger bun, Jeremy Maher swooped
in from nowhere, dispossessed me, and single-handedly commenced
a scorching counter-attack, beating perhaps four of my teammates

along the way before releasing the ball to Terry Violett for a simple tap-in. The fact that Jeremy made no attempt to finish it off himself merely made his messianic aura glow that little bit brighter. In that moment, Jeremy rose up the leader board like a country that gets their first *douze points* from the third Eurovision jury of the evening. Henceforth, he became Jez and I became Paphides. You could pretty much deduce from that moment how the next five years were going to be.

We trudged through the mud across the road and back towards the school changing rooms. Our PE teacher Mr Nash turned on his best drill sergeant impersonation, told us that it was compulsory to shower and that he would be watching us to make sure we had properly washed ourselves. Most of us had never been seen naked by anyone other than our mothers. Quite how you dealt with this situation further established the pecking order. The more streetwise kids were fine with it. The rest of us scurried through the line of showers like startled lambs hoping we wouldn't be the ones singled out by Mr Nash to go through again.

Even if they hadn't been made to form a separate queue, it wasn't hard to spot the children whose parents couldn't afford the school lunches. Their future at Yardleys could be measured out in a long line of salty mash domes dispensed in daily squeezes of a scoop lever by the Irish dinner ladies who worked the free hatch. To the left of them, the paying hatch had colours you simply never saw in the free hatch: the bright orange of the baked beans and the golden glow of the chips. You'd think that growing up surrounded by chips might have inclined me towards the free hatch. But it turns out that humans have no upper tolerance level for chips. Besides, these pre-sliced, fast-frozen floury digits of nugatory nutritional value were a totally different foodstuff to the ones my parents had in the shop or, for that matter, the ones that my mum made on the kitchen stove. These ones had beans ladled over them. The sauce from the beans made its way through the pile, leaving almost no chip untouched and, in doing so, created a composite entity that was greater than chips, beans or the sum total of those constituents. It created a sweet-savoury symbiosis of sensory comfort which would ensure that, as long as I opted into school dinners, I would be fifty per cent less receptive to any form of education that took place in the afternoon at Yardleys. Now that I think about it, it's no accident that almost every straight-As high achiever in my class at Yardleys queued at the free hatch.

It was exciting to think that, by the time I got home, I'd be able to tell my mum about the day I'd had. Unbeknownst to me, that she was going home at all was a source of consternation for the doctors taking care of her. The hospital's concerns for her post-operative recuperation suggested Dr Lowe had confided his misgivings about the extent to which she would be allowed to fully recover at home. They wanted to send her to a residential recovery unit outside Birmingham for another fortnight, but she felt she had left us alone long enough. In the end, they made her sign a waiver, indemnifying them from any liability if she left earlier than they had recommended.

I was too young to really understand what she had undergone or what the recovery time would be. My dad arranged for a woman to come to the house and do the ironing. A few days after her return, he also bought my mum a present of sorts. Like most of his big-ticket purchases, it had been procured from a customer who knew someone who worked in the factory. The item in question was still in the hallway when I returned home from school one day – a bright orange Vax vacuum cleaner with a special water compartment for washing carpets. Compared to our old upright branded Hoover, this was a behemoth. It didn't even resemble a vacuum cleaner. It was orange and cylindrical and it moved around on large castors, like R2-D2, if R2-D2 had just fallen asleep on a sunbed. For twenty-four hours, the Vax machine sat motionless in the hallway, as if waiting to acquire the power of autonomous motion. In the end, my mum had to get my brother to carry it up the stairs. She couldn't lift it without bursting her stitches. As post-hysterectomy get-well-soon presents go, a bunch of flowers might have sent a more welcome message, but presumably my dad didn't know anyone who worked in a flower factory.

In Manchester United, I found an unlikely Greek chorus to the ensuing weeks. For most football-loving non-alpha children, the hopes and dreams of a new year can disintegrate in parallel to those of your team. This time, you tell yourself, things really will be better. Over the summer, you assess your prospects for the upcoming school year in much the same way as a manager does for his team. You make changes that, similarly, you hope will see you off to a flying start. It could be a branded holdall. A bomber jacket. New Doc Martens. In your first year at secondary school, you see yourself as a team from the old second division that has just been promoted to the top flight. If you hit the ground running and don't look back, who knows what might happen? Baseless optimism is rampant. It's still summer. You're Wile E. Coyote and if you just keep running without looking down, you might never need to stop. That's the September experienced by almost every child and every football team. Baseless optimism followed by an almighty thump.

For some though, this was the year that, against all odds, really did deliver. I was just one class down from William and I could see him racing ahead of me. At primary school, I had been his only close friend – a friendship which, most of the time, both of us were happy to conduct on his terms. And even if I was no longer silent all the time, I was happy to keep playing a supporting role. But now, looking across the playground, I could see that his eccentricities played out well in a wider group. Every morning he walked through the school gates wearing the scarf that my mum had knitted for him a couple of years previously – a creditable attempt to simulate the one worn by Tom Baker in *Doctor Who* – and minutes later, two or three high-achieving alpha boys would snatch it off him. I could see that William's indifference to their goading and his ability to unleash a volley of obscene insults was endearing them to him. Every group of high-achieving, alpha boys needs a token nerd, and William filled that hole.

And me? The incident with Jeremy, sorry, *Jez* Maher on the playing field was a cast-iron indicator of things to come. Just like Manchester United, who limped through to Christmas with just four victories from sixteen games, I lowered my expectations accordingly. I attached myself to the outer fringes of two or three pre-existing friendship groups, and did what any eleven-year-old boy desperate for popularity did as Christmas appeared on the horizon. I accepted that my personality alone wasn't going to pull me through; I begged my parents to get me an Atari 2600 for Christmas and resolved to try and keep my head down for the preceding three months. In the event, I got the Atari – my best present to date – but its desired effect was neutralised by the fact that most of the boys in my class also got one that Christmas.

Most afternoons were a slow countdown to the school bell. If the final lesson happened to be in a classroom near the front gate, then my chances of getting a decent position at the nearby bus stop increased. On a good day, I could be in Woolworths or Easy Listening within fifteen minutes of leaving school. Dinner was rarely ready before 7 p.m. If I wanted to stay in those shops right until closing time, only the annoyance of the people who worked there could deter me. In Woolworths, that never seemed to be a problem. On weekday afternoons, the record and tape department was staffed by one of the new wave twins who had previously worked across the road in Preedy's. If you worked at Woolworths, they gave you a badge with your name on it. She was called Bridget and, over successive afternoons, it became apparent that Bridget was obsessed, to the exclusion of all others, with just one band.

UB40's *Signing Off* had been released at the end of August. Throughout September and much of October, anyone who filled their pick 'n' mix bag or stood at the deli counter waiting for their ham to be sliced did so to the strains of an album of heavy, politicised British reggae songs which variously addressed the misdeeds committed in the name of colonialism ('Burden of Shame'), the suspicious grounds upon which teenage African American Gary Tyler was convicted of murder by a white Louisiana jury ('Tyler') and a thirteen-minute dub reggae excoriation of Margaret Thatcher entitled 'Madame Medusa'. A few weeks later, UB40 followed it up with a double A-side which, if anything, turned the dimmer switch even further down. 'Dream a Lie' locked into the sort of blissful dub groove that presaged the later work of sonic explorers like Mad Professor and Massive Attack. Tapping into the collective cold war anxiety of the age, 'The Earth Dies Screaming' featured one of Ali Campbell's most soulful vocals. Once again, this sort of fearlessness paid off, securing UB40 their third top 10 single in a row.

There was one trait common to the post-punk vanguard of British artists – not just UB40, but the Specials, the Beat, Gary Numan, XTC and Joe Jackson – and that was their apparent indifference to the commercial expectations generated by their early successes. The more they had to lose, the less bothered they were by the prospect of losing it. In the autumn of 1980, Paul Weller had more to squander than any of those artists. The Jam's previous two singles had both topped the chart. They'd followed 'Going Underground' with the most unsentimental song ever written about the life-changing power of pop. At key times in his life, Weller would refer to his mod knowledge like a Christian having a crisis of faith might refer to his Bible, thus reminding both himself and the world around him who he was. 'Start!' was as potent in its simplicity as an arrow emerging from a target. *Impact*! was what that exclamation mark is all about, because *impact*! was what 'Start!' was about. It was the apogee of Weller's fascination with pop art, an attempt to achieve in 150 seconds the same effect as a Lichtenstein or a Warhol. Thanks in part to its use of Paul McCartney's 'Taxman' bassline, it was knowing yet utterly sincere. 'Start!' was a song which both embodied and described itself. It sounded nothing like any other Jam song. You wanted to earn the approval of anyone who followed their biggest hit with something like that. This, as much as anything, explains why it reached number 1. When someone keeps a cool head in the face of such scrutiny and pressure, you'll follow them into a burning building.

Weller's pop art preoccupation revealed itself more fully between the announcement and release of the Jam's fifth album. A fortnight before the release of *Sound Affects*, the window display of Easy Listening was given over to posters exclaiming 'WHAAM!', 'BANG!' and 'POW!', comic-strip style, with the Jam's logo in the top left-hand corner and 'SOUND AFFECTS' splashed across the bottom. Stapled onto the wall were myriad sleeves. This being the first time any of us had got to see what the new Jam album looked like, we stood outside the shop for a minute or two trying to absorb what we saw. This wouldn't normally have detained me too long, but Ged seemed impressed by what they'd done with the window display. There were twenty-two separate photographs: on the top section, two blue-tinted rows of five; on the bottom, two pink-tinted rows of five. Then in the middle row, two in violet, and to their right a rectangular box with the title and logo on it. The design was a pastiche of the first eight releases in the BBC's series of *Sound Effects* albums which had appeared between 1969 and 1972. Among the photos that made up the sleeve there was an aerial view of rows of terraced houses, a '£' symbol, a Hackney carriage with its 'TAXI' light on, a red telephone box at night and, yes, an exclamation mark. In interviews at the time, Weller explained that each of these images related to some aspect of the record.

It wasn't unreasonable to assume that, were he able to, Aki would have been in Easy Listening handing over his pocket money in exchange for *Sound Affects*, but on the day of its release he was being decanted out of a minibus on a mountainous Powys slip road, along with eight or nine of his classmates. On this particular morning, the protestations of Helen Riley, a skilled orienteer who had represented Yardleys at regional level, failed to dissuade Mr Nash from embarking on the scheduled morning hike to the craggy peaks of Waun Fach in the Black Mountains. It wasn't that Mr Nash chose to ignore her fog warnings completely – more that his precautionary measures, once told about the fog, left something to be desired. Not having been there, I like to imagine Mr Nash dressed for the 2,661-metre ascent in the same clothes he wore during my entire time at Yardleys: sky-blue cotton tracksuit with a slight flare on the trousers and dark-blue stripe along the side seams, with top zipped right up to the collar. Given what happened next, it's not an implausible assumption. With the mountain wreathed in thick fog, Mr Nash instructed his pupils to complete the walk around Waun Fach in conga formation. It was the best way to keep everyone together. Aki held on to Edward Osborne who, in turn, held on to the tail of the parka belonging to Simon White. From his hospital bed a few days later, Aki relived for me the moment he called out to Simon and asked him who he was holding on to. 'I'm not following anyone,' replied Simon. Which, of course, is the most mod answer you could possibly give.

With the rest of the expedition out of earshot, it was down to Aki, Edward and Simon to find their way back to the minibus. Fancying his chances, Aki headed out to lead the depleted party and almost immediately stepped off a ledge, only to have his fall broken by another ledge about eight feet below. It could have been a lot worse. He said he could feel his left arm swelling up beneath his jacket, but it was only when the fog lifted and they saw the minibus in the distance that Aki began to wonder if he had fractured it. 'Can you move it?' asked Mr Nash. He could. 'You'll be fine, then,' said the teacher.

Back home four days later, it transpired that the diagnosis of a Birmingham PE teacher might not have been absolutely watertight. That night, pushing himself up with his right arm to turn off his nightlight, Aki lifted up his left arm and saw his forearm just sort of detach itself from its socket, as though the hinge connecting them had finally broken off. His involuntary gasp attracted my attention. I turned around and instantly wished I hadn't. My mum rang for a taxi and took him to A&E straight away. With his arm in a makeshift sling, Aki sloped off reluctantly. 'It really doesn't hurt that much! Can't we just go tomorrow?' he protested. My mother must have had some idea that he wouldn't be returning that night. She'd packed an overnight bag for him and, sure enough, when I later heard the key turning the front door lock, it was just her on her own.

The next morning, while Aki was in the operating theatre having his arm reassembled with pins and brackets, I got a bit of extra money from my parents on the pretext that I knew exactly what would cheer him up when we visited him that evening. *Sound Affects* had been out for almost a week. Despite the impressive window display, I eschewed Easy Listening in favour of Woolworths, whose week-of-release discounts were hard for independent shops to beat. The difference in price left me with enough change to buy a cassette and tape the album on my dad's new Fidelity music centre so that Aki could listen to it in hospital. Virtue was its own reward. As the needle hit the plastic and skated into the run-in groove, I plunged my forefinger and middle finger onto the play and record buttons.

Sound Affects was, in its way, as psychedelic a record as the Beatles' *Sgt. Pepper* or the Moody Blues' *The Days of Future Passed*. As with those records, it ensured the surrounding streets would never be the same once you'd seen them as these songs saw them. In contemporaneous interviews, Weller hymned the beauty of electricity pylons (there was one of those on the sleeve too). Caught somewhere between William Blake and Colin MacInnes, he set about making the suburbs sparkle. It was a record which sought to reassure you that, even though life could be tough, you controlled the magic. It was right there in the very first song 'Pretty Green', a tune which oscillated at a perfect point of tension between the innocent release of spending your wages and the shit you have to go through in order to earn them. It also had a hook so catchy I remembered Ged singing it a few days previously, before telling me what the song was about.

'He's singing about pound notes, Takis! "I've got a pocket full of pretty green." I've never heard them called that before. It's clever, isn't it, Takis? Don't you think it's clever?'

It was clever, but it wasn't cleverness that forged that afternoon into my memory. Aki and I frequently fought in the way that brothers do, but in the simple act of taping this record for him, I missed him terribly. With the exception of two hours the previous evening, I hadn't seen him for nearly a week – the longest we'd ever been separated. I liked having him around. There was a space between the world as I saw it and the world as Aki saw it. Paul Weller's songs, caught between childhood innocence and the looming obligations of adulthood, occupied that space. For 'Monday', he set himself the challenge of 'writing a love song about the least romantic day of the week . . . the weekend's over, this character is having to go back to work but is so in love that they can't wait to see the other person again.' In my head, one ideal of love – the fairy-tale 'Duke of Earl' one – was swiftly supplanted by a new one. 'Monday' ached like no other Paul Weller song had ached. It ached like your first 7 a.m. starts in a strange workplace when all you want to do is be with your sweetheart. And perhaps most incredibly, 'Monday' took all of this and made it aspirational. The character in the song was anything but a victim. His hardship was fuel for the promise of what the weekend had in store.

. . . a sunshine girl like you
It's worth going through
I will never be embarrassed about love again.

Writing to John Peel in the late sixties, David Bowie said that out in the suburbs of Kent, he could be found 'dancing a furious boredom'. The same could be said about *Sound Affects'* most universally adored track. 'That's Entertainment' took Weller 'maybe fifteen, twenty minutes' to write. Its muted arrangement – barely four chords on an acoustic guitar, bass, drums just about audible – glistened like a wet Cortina under a street lamp, a precise sonic simulation of eventless days in unloved conurbations. He knew because this was where he came from. Almost any other writer would have removed a line as mundane as 'watching the telly and thinking about your holidays', but these were the details that authenticated the entire thing, setting everything up for a final verse whose bittersweet intimacies would emotionally blindside me for decades to come.

Two lovers kissing amongst the scream of midnight
Two lovers missing the tranquillity of solitude
Getting a cab and travelling on buses
Reading the graffiti about slashed seat affairs –
that's entertainment

Lest anyone doubt Weller's genius at this time, the clincher is right there, in 'slashed seat affairs', a perfect three-word encapsulation of the top-deck trysts forged by fumbling teens on every night bus between town and terminus. Every moment of joy described on *Sound Affects* was a sweet steal from a world in which romance and wonder were busted currencies. What a record to make when you're twenty-two and you know a hefty chunk of your generation is waiting to hear it.

I wrote the track listing on the tape insert, put the tape back in its box and placed it into the rucksack that Aki had taken to Wales, alongside my chunky headphones and battery-operated cassette player. On the way back from Woolworths, I had also dug into my own pocket money to get the second issue of a new music magazine called *Flexipop* – its unique selling point being that each monthly issue came with a flexi disc attached to the cover. This one was fluorescent yellow and featured two Jam songs, an alternative version of a *Sound Affects* song called 'Boy About Town' and a previously unreleased song called 'Pop Art Poem'. Aki's expression on receiving the cassette was the vindication of my lobbying to get him the record. His arm was in a freshly applied plaster cast. He was clearly pleased to see me, which had the effect of suddenly making me feel shy. Sincere expressions of affection were simply not part of our shared emotional vocabulary.

'Cool,' he said, examining the contents of the cassette. 'Have you heard it? Is it better than *Setting Sons*?'

The Jam being more one of his bands than mine, I didn't trust my judgement enough to provide Aki with a definitive answer to that question. Instead, I told him about Ged, her best friend Siobhan and a girl in their year, Gemma McAuley, who everyone knew as Kleppy on account of the kleptomania she'd put to good use by stealing things to order for a small 'handling' charge. Kleppy had managed to procure Ged a cassette of *Sound Affects* which Ged and Siobhan had spent the previous two evenings getting to know. 'According to Ged, Paul Weller is now a poet,' I reported back to Aki.

As 1980 wound to a close, the art of making carefree pop seemed to be deserting even its most reliable practitioners. Suddenly, with the release of Madness's 'Embarrassment', eleven-year-old children were reading *Smash Hits* and memorising the words of a song about the vilification of the immediate family of saxophonist Lee Thompson when his sister discovered she was expecting a mixed-race child. Two years previously, Ram Jam's 'Black Betty' had dealt with the idea of children bringing shame to a family, but 'Embarrassment' wasn't set in the American south. Thompson's sister hadn't even given birth by the time the song was released. Next door, Ged had now entered a full-on obsession with Joe Jackson, brought on by the release of his new single. 'Beat Crazy' somehow fashioned something coherent and compelling from a hyperventilating intro riff, a misfiring ska rhythm, a bassline borrowed from Augustus Pablo's 'King Tubby Meets Rockers Uptown' and an anguished vocal which seemed to posit teenage nihilism as the only sensible course of action under the Cold War threat of instant annihilation.

But then, *everyone* sounded worried. Even Barbra Streisand seemed to be staring at the business end of a 4 a.m. re-evaluation. 'Life is a moment in space / When the dream is gone, it's a lonelier place', began her new, soon-to-be chart-topping single. 'Woman in Love' was one of the first singles I bought that I remember being too self-conscious to openly discuss with my friends. There was no getting around the fact that someone like me really shouldn't be listening to music made by someone who looked like that. On the sleeve, a tanned, soft-focus Streisand, sporting the mum perm *du jour*, gazed longingly into the camera. In for a penny, in for a pound. If I was spending my pocket money on Barbra Streisand records, I may as well continue beyond the pale and bag myself the sole copy of the Bee Gees' 1979 album *Spirits Having Flown*, on sale for £1.99 at Preedy's on account of the fact that it was missing its outer sleeve. The ensuing decades have left me with a plausible but entirely false memory of Streisand's song featuring on the Bee Gees' record. Plausible because the song was written by Barry and Robin Gibb, and that's also Barry you can hear harmonising prominently on the chorus. Plausible, also, because both 'Woman in Love' and most of *Spirits Having Flown* were distinguished by the Bee Gees' peculiar, poetic genius for writing about love as though it were an existential affliction. It was a trick they'd established over a decade previously with sky-high creations such as 'To Love Somebody', 'Words' and 'I Can't See Nobody'.

When sessions began for the Bee Gees' first post-*Saturday Night Fever* album, four songs in the *Billboard* top five were Gibb compositions. Listening to the resulting record, it doesn't seem unreasonable to surmise that all they could see from that pinnacle was the way down. Certainly, the mood was one of anxiety. 'Love You Inside Out' and 'Too Much Heaven' appeared to be obsessing about the transience of perfect love, but it might be that these were proxy concerns for what was actually about to happen to their career – the backlash against disco and, with it, the commercial freefall of the Bee Gees, no matter that they had never seen themselves as a disco group, and no matter that they hadn't even got to put out a full studio album during the moment when their stock was at its highest. All these years later, *Spirits Having Flown* sounds like the work of artists who know the world is waiting and listening, but might not be waiting and listening much longer. On the extraordinary title track, Barry depicted himself as a tormented free spirit, a hurricane or a fire, looking for someone to turn his longing into belonging. The ascent into falsetto on the chorus – 'How long must I live in the air?' – turned the song into an actual cry for help. On 'Tragedy', Barry took this elemental fixation to literal extremes. When stuck for a convincing thunderclap sound, he merely made one with his mouth.

Even in 1980, I couldn't listen to these songs and not feel some concern for the people who had made them. Perhaps I might not have felt this way if I'd bought *Spirits Having Flown* when it was released eighteen months previously. It might have made a difference if my copy of the album had a sleeve. But to listen to a sleeveless *Spirits Having Flown* in 1980 was like watching footage of astronauts nervously embarking on the final mission of a decommissioned space programme. The crew are at the absolute peak of their capabilities.

The vessel is a state-of-the-art wonder of human engineering. And although the mission is successful, the astronauts will be all but forgotten on their return. From their lunar vantage point, they can see the world revolving without them, and when they return they realise that the world will, to all intents and purposes, continue to revolve without them.

Encoded into our notion of pop is a set of values we rarely stop to question. But when we hear a record that decides not to observe those values, it registers with us at some level. In pop, teen angst is the most important sort of angst – and it's the most important sort of angst because: (a) teenagers have traditionally been the primary consumers of pop; and (b) in the early days of rock 'n' roll, most of the people who made pop were only a few years older than the people who bought the records. If the Bee Gees, pushing towards middle age, found themselves struggling to work within those parameters, it soon became clear that ABBA weren't even going through the pretence of trying. *Super Trouper* was as emotionally complicated an album as middle age itself can be. 'I was sick and tired of everything / when I called you last night from Glasgow', began the eponymous opener. A super trouper is the name given to a powerful free-standing spotlight found in TV studios and theatres – although, as Björn helpfully pointed out when I interviewed him in 2002, the words can also refer to 'someone who is a super trouper' – someone like the protagonist of the song, who decides to go ahead with her schedule, despite 'wishing every show was the last show'.

In ABBA's tapestry of mid-life turbulence though, this was just one scene. Alongside this and 'The Winner Takes It All', there were also youthful affairs idealised through the heavy haze of hindsight ('Our Last Summer'), bittersweet folk hymns to hard-won detente ('The Way Old Friends Do') and queasy disco dispatches from single people looking for love in a dystopian world ('On and On and On'). Nestled amongst all this was the song which – more than any of their previous releases – formalised the special relationship between ABBA and their gay fans. There was enough in 'Lay All Your Love on Me' to have even the most unresponsive gaydar spinning like a helicopter blade. To start with, it was an Agnetha lead vocal. Almost all ABBA songs in which the protagonist has been abandoned or mistreated in some way tended to go to Agnetha, and this was no exception. In addition to that, you had a hook which seemed to belong to a requiem mass as much as a nightclub. A single Andersson finger on an Oberheim OB-X picking out a pensive hi-de-hi over a choir of multitracked Agnethas, all of them beseeching her lover to extinguish thoughts of other women and reciprocate her feelings for him. With the entire drama played out at 133 beats per minute, listening to 'Lay All Your Love on Me' as loudly as my parents would allow me was – more than, say, any of Aki's punk records – as close to the feeling of reckless exhilaration as I could get without following the example of the older boys at the far end of the playing field tipping out tins of Evo-Stik into polythene bags.

It didn't hurt ABBA's standing among their gay constituency that, in the Venn diagram of life and art, the overlapping space seemed to be growing with every record. Although I didn't know it at the time, I was living refutation of the argument espoused by so many homophobes that homosexuality can be nurtured into you. More than at any other point in my life, the preconditions were perfectly lined up. I was exceptionally close to my mother. She was as protective towards me as I was towards her. My parents' volatile marriage merely entrenched in me a demented belief that, with the right partner, you could fall in love and live that fairy tale in perpetuity. I watched *The Wizard of Oz* and the Eurovision Song Contest every year without fail. Two doors away, Emily May had just given me a complete run of *Misty*, a comic for girls which specialised in stories involving young girls in terrifying situations. I devoured them all over a weekend.

Among the stories featured in *Misty* were 'The Dummy', in which 'lonely, neglected Rhoda' longed for her father to care for her like he cared for his collection of ventriloquists' dolls. Then there was 'Four Faces of Eve', which concerned a girl who, in spite of her outward normality, was a female Frankenstein's monster comprised of four girls. In 'The Purple Emperor', the horrible butterfly-collecting Betty was turned into a butterfly herself and met her demise by suffocating in a killing jar along with all her other specimens.

One song on the ABBA album that could have been directly lifted from a *Misty* comic was 'The Piper'. With a chorus that invited you to imagine an army of Nazi Oompa-Loompas banging their tin drums into a sulphurous sunset, the song turned the Pied Piper tale into a parable about the insidious proximity of fascism, even in an ostensibly liberal world. Both on a personal and political level, ABBA's unwillingness or inability to lift the veil of their own pessimism was dismantling their Eurovision-winning, steady-does-it, middle-of-the-road persona before our eyes. And nowhere was this more apparent than on lyrics that Björn had completed almost a year previously. Caught between trying to make sense of the dying decade – a decade which would freeze him in the minds of the millions of people who had bought his records – and the one about to begin, he started writing. Our dreams, he ventured, were as dead as used confetti. Furthermore, who in their right mind could confidently predict we would be here to see the end of the next decade?

And what to call this sombre sermon? This musical confirmation of Søren Kierkegaard's contention that we are doomed to live life forwards yet only able to understand it backwards? What name might best sum up this sad screed placed square at the centre of an album that many of their fans would be hearing for the first time shortly after removing it from its festive wrapping? They called it 'Happy New Year'. Oh ABBA.

More than any other song of the preceding months however, there was one single that took this non-specific consternation enveloping the collective pop mind and created a brutalist sonic edifice in which to house it. Cometh the hour, cometh the . . . um, drummer out of Genesis. On the basis of previous activity, Phil Collins made an unlikely Mother Shipton, but in the first days of 1981, that all changed, and 'In the Air Tonight' was the record that changed it. No one knew for certain what the 'it' was that Phil could feel coming. An urban legend circulated which suggested that the lyrics concerned someone who witnessed a man drowning in a nearby lake but chose not jump in and save him, while Phil – standing much further away – couldn't get there in time. Over the years, Phil himself intimated that anger over his recent divorce probably paid a part, but by no means formed the whole story. The original lyrics had been written on the back of a piece of wallpaper, which was symbolic in view of the fact that Phil's wife had gone off with the painter and decorator. It also explained his decision to perform the song on *Top of the Pops* with a pot of paint and a brush on top of the piano.

Both at home and on the radio, the message being transmitted from the lonely, lofty crag of middle age was one and the same: look what the relentless weather of life does to your teenage dreams. Only one record elected to stand up and say it doesn't have to be like this. Hearing John Lennon's '(Just Like) Starting Over' on the radio for the first time was a moment of sweet, simple joy. As with Paul McCartney and 'Mull of Kintyre' three years previously, I didn't know anything about the history of the person who had made it. Everything I knew about John Lennon between the release of '(Just Like) Starting Over' in late October and the beginning of December was information imparted by DJs and music journalists in relation to this song, his first new music in five years.

It was the first time I sensed a clear disparity between a mainstream take on an artist and the music press critical consensus which echoed what Aki and his friends would have thought about it. 'It sounds like a great life, but it makes for a lousy record,' said *NME*'s Charles Shaar Murray. 'I wish Lennon had kept his big happy trap shut until he had something to say that was even vaguely relevant to those of us not married to Yoko.' *Melody Maker*'s review of Lennon's new album said that it 'reeks with self-indulgent sterility'. The subtext of all these reviews – that this Lennon was a poor substitute for the radical firebrand of his early solo albums or the Beatles who gave us 'Strawberry Fields Forever' – was lost on me. Neither did I care that '(Just Like) Starting Over' was as derivative as hell. The deliberate nods to sixties girl groups, and to Elvis Presley and Roy Orbison; the steal from the Beach Boys' 'Don't Worry Baby' ('but when I saw you darling . . .') – that was of no interest to me either. I was hearing all these things for the first time, albeit fast-fossilised into a single source of melodic fuel. I didn't just disagree with anyone who disliked '(Just Like) Starting Over'. I didn't believe them.

I thought John Lennon would top the charts by Christmas and, of course, I was right. But not in the way I'd imagined. Having peaked at 8, he had slipped down from 10 to 21. The bedside clock-radio, which was tuned to Radio 1, woke me up with a sound collage of confusion and ballooning devastation. If sadness and shock at Lennon's death were being divvied out in proportion to the amount of hours spent listening to his music, I would have been near the bottom of a very long list. But that's not how sadness and shock work. All I knew about John Lennon was this one song that I adored. Because I didn't know any others, my entire picture of him was shaped by that song. And because that song made him sound like the nicest husband in the world and therefore probably a totally brilliant dad too, I struggled to square that with the way his life was taken.

Other people's reactions seeped into my own. I didn't cry. I don't think I even spoke about it too much. But what I do remember was thinking and thinking and thinking about it. Just over thirty-five years later, I'd see my children reacting to the world's reaction to

David Bowie's death, and watch something similar taking root in their thoughts. But the world's reaction to John Lennon's death – at least, the world as heard through my clock-radio – wasn't one echoed by my parents. They were already in the kitchen when I came down to breakfast. It was like Elvis's death all over again, except that this time, my dad didn't have to feign unawareness and I didn't feel the need to write it out on an enormous piece of chip paper. I told them everything I knew, which wasn't very much at all.

'Did you know that John Lennon's been killed?'

'John Lennon from the Beatles?' asked my dad.

'Someone shot him dead.'

My dad addressed my mum, who was making his breakfast, 'Did you hear that, Victoria? John Lennon from the Beatles died.'

She tutted and shook her head. Why would someone do such a thing? It kept coming back to that question. But, of course, there was no answer, and more to the point, no sense that this had really changed anything in their world. It was the saddest, weirdest event in a day on which potatoes still had to be chipped, fish still needed to be battered and household chores still needed to be undertaken.

But what gave my sadness the right to be greater than theirs? *I'd only heard one of his songs!* And it wasn't even a Beatles song! Even from their position of relative indifference, my parents' knowledge of John Lennon's oeuvre was way greater than mine. They'd arrived in the UK just as Beatlemania was kicking off. They were here for the whole thing and yet, of course, they weren't able to join in with any of it. They had been working on production lines and in car factories. They'd been making a family and learning how to run a business. The Beatles were a peripheral presence in their 1960s. For them, music didn't exist to enhance the present. It was a means of temporarily obliterating it. They didn't need to tell me that. A decade of Sundays had taught me. In this moment, it didn't matter that I had only heard one John Lennon song. I'd already chosen the cultural universe in which I wanted to live and it was this one – the one of the Beatles and *Top of the Pops* and *Smash Hits* – not the one to which my parents kept returning.

Sad as this moment was, it didn't really represent anything to my mum and dad. Their 'John Lennon moment' had happened ten months previously when they learned that their favourite Greek singer had finally succumbed, aged forty-four, to a long battle with cancer. The death of Cretan singer Nikos Xylouris on Friday, 8 February plunged Greece into mourning. But without any British newspapers or news bulletins covering it, the news only reached them on Sunday morning when my dad turned on his radio and heard a succession of Xylouris's songs interspersed with grieving testimonies from people who knew him either in person or through his music.

If Lennon's folk hero status was hotly disputed by many, Xylouris's standing in the eyes of the million or so Greeks who trailed his funeral cortege was unassailable. His music had risen to prominence during the reign of the fascist junta between 1967 and 1974. During the Athens Polytechnic uprising of 1973 – a protest which both foreshadowed and hastened the subsequent demise of the ruling Colonels – Xylouris appeared with his lyre and addressed the crowd with a rendition of '*Pote Tha Kanei Xasteria*', a Cretan song dating back to the 1821 revolution for independence from Turkey that had been repurposed as a symbol of the country's present struggle.

If Xylouris's presence at the uprising rubber-stamped his credentials in the eyes of his followers, his subsequent arrest inadvertently anointed him as the voice of the new resistance. Xylouris's wasn't the only voice, but listening to him even now, it isn't hard to fathom why the ruling regime attempted to silence him. He even recorded a song full of words that – a rain of alleluias notwithstanding – had no meaning in any language, but whose intent couldn't be misunderstood. And, on the day my parents learned about his death, this was the record my dad pulled out first. I could hear the hellfire exhortations of 'Zabarakatranemia' through the floor of my bedroom. It sounded both transcendent and terrifying. It sounded like nothing else I'd hear until over twenty-years later when I first heard the rapt Sufi invocations of Nusrat Fateh Ali Khan.

Xylouris's songs stirred the Greek folk memory deeper than those of his contemporaries. Part of that was deliberate – he adapted poems by Nikos Gatsos, Yannis Ritsos, Giorgos Seferis, all of whom had aligned themselves to the left-wing resistance forces that defied the Axis occupation during the Second World War. But it was also down to the sound he made when he opened his mouth. In full flight, nothing sounded like Xylouris's elemental evangelising. It wasn't hard to see what my dad saw in him. They shared the same politics and they were also the same age. Xylouris personified his favourite aspect of his younger self – his disdain for authority and his romantic connection to the traditions of his native country. Xylouris's proud parochialism was a cracked mirror to the nostalgia my dad felt for Cyprus. I understand it totally now, but in 1980 I'm not sure I could have done, even if my parents had patiently attempted to deconstruct it for me. However I needed no assistance when it came to measuring the effect of John Lennon's death on the house next door.

Ged's brother Tim hadn't taken his Beatles records with him when he moved out, so she kept them in a biscuit tin inside the leather pouffe beside their record player. When I returned from school that day, I didn't even bother dumping my bag in our house before pressing the doorbell of number 12.

Bink-bonk.

'Takis! Hello! Are you looking for Ged?'

'Yes please, Mrs Hughes.'

'GED! Takis for you . . . Isn't it just awful about John Lennon? I just can't take it in. Can you? It's all we've been talking about all day. Oh, Ged. Takis is here. Do you want a cup of tea, Takis?'

'I'm all right, thank you, Mrs Hughes.'

Ged beckoned me into the front room. Somehow knowing exactly what I was there for, she lifted the seat of the pouffe beside the record player and removed the biscuit tin containing Tim's Beatles records.

'I was crying this morning, Takis. What about *you*? Were you crying?'

I hadn't been crying, but even if I had, I was now at an age where I wouldn't have admitted it. Currently, I had no plans to ever cry again.

Ged explained how John hadn't been her favourite Beatle. That would always be Paul.

'Paul who?' I said.

My reply caught Ged too off guard to prevent her emitting something between a snort and a laugh. 'Paul who? Paul McCartney!'

The news that Paul McCartney from Wings had been in the Beatles with John Lennon was instantly mind-blowing to me. And because my passage into the Beatles was a reverse journey from the solo work of John and Paul, this effectively: (a) turned them into a supergroup; and (b) made listening to them a burning imperative. I didn't have long to wait. She emptied the biscuit tin onto her lap and briefly inspected its contents before deciding which of these she would place on the turntable.

If only Søren Kierkegaard could have seen what was happening to me right now. Ged dropped the needle onto the queasy violin intro of 'I Am the Walrus' and suddenly I was travelling backwards through life in order to understand it forwards. I was looking through a microscope right into the petri dish from which Jeff Lynne would grow ELO. This alleviated some of the pressure to instantly like what I was hearing. If only for the fact that it had invented ELO, 'I Am the Walrus' was important. And being important was almost as important as being good. What also helped, of course, was Ged's willingness to try and explain what I was hearing.

'I bet you're wondering why he's singing "I am the egg man", aren't you, Takis? It's psychedelic. When it's psychedelic, it can mean anything you want it to mean. That's the great thing about it. What do *you* think it means, Takis?'

The year before, I remembered Ged raving about Wings' new album *Back to the Egg*, in particular its lead single 'Old Siam Sir'. 'Has this song got anything to do with *Back to the Egg*?' I asked, in mild desperation.

'Oh, I hadn't thought of that!' she replied brightly. 'What is it about the Beatles and eggs?' Ged turned off the record player, a cue for me to leave too. 'I'm afraid I've got to go now, Takis. But I tell you what. If you want to get into the Beatles, you can tape this and give it me back tomorrow.' She reached up above her head to a shelf and pulled out the record that would formally introduce me to the Beatles. With the LP and my shoes in one hand and my school bag in the other, I padded back home in much the same way as a dog will bring a bone or a valued item of food back to the designated place – maybe a basket or a rug – where all important new acquisitions have to be kept.

Almost fourteen years had elapsed since the release of *A Collection of Beatles Oldies*, but I was looking at a sleeve that bore so little correlation to any aesthetic template established in my own memory that it might just as easily have been beamed in from the future. Suspended before green hills rolling into a rainbow horizon beneath a purple sky was a Byronic beat dandy – perhaps a stylised composite of all four Beatles – in a lilac jacket, reclining in an armchair upholstered in orange and apricot stripes to match the ones on his trousers. Everything about the 1960s that embarrassed the 1970s was abundant on the sleeve of *A Collection of Beatles Oldies*. But, of course, I didn't know or care about that. Neither did I stop to take in the fact that this sleeve, which anticipated the iridescent overload of the Beatles' *Sgt. Pepper* threads, was out of sync with the time period covered by these songs. None of that mattered to me.

Great art doesn't happen in a void. Sometimes it's a reaction to its immediate environment. Sometimes it can only make sense if the immediate environment is able to receive it – be that the space or the people in it. Great art doesn't have to meet both these criteria, but it almost always meets at least one. Great art means you didn't have to be there at the time. Once that synergy of creation and reaction has happened, it can't unhappen. And so, when you're experiencing great art, you're also stepping into the space where it happened.

There are two songs on *A Collection of Beatles Oldies* that bear this out more forcefully than almost any piece of music of that era. Two songs on which you can absolutely hear the magnesium of excess energy burning in the pop-cultural void created by post-war affluence and the end of conscription. It doesn't matter if you're five or fifty. It doesn't matter whether you know the context or not. That's why the 'loaf-haired secretaries' described in Philip Larkin's 'Toads Revisited' suddenly felt like screaming their heads off. Built into those songs are spaces where, nearly five decades on, you're almost moved to do the same thing. That was what these songs were built to do. And thanks to the indestructible self-belief of the people who wrote them, they didn't just do it by bringing you onside with a strong verse and a catchy chorus.

Listening to 'She Loves You' and 'I Want to Hold Your Hand' was like being parachuted into battle. The first seven seconds of 'I Want to Hold Your Hand' existed to make you *lose your fucking mind*. That's what they were for. The first few seconds of 'She Loves You' existed to make you forget whatever the hell you were doing immediately beforehand. That's how shock works too. People who experience sudden traumas usually struggle to recall what happened in the preceding seconds. I figured that must have been the effect the Beatles had on everyone who was ready to receive them in 1963. Because that was certainly what happened to me several times over on 9 December 1980. 'From Me to You' into 'We Can Work It Out' into 'Help!', each song contriving to obliterate the previous one from my thoughts. Only the relative lull of 'Michelle' going into 'Yesterday' allowed me to catch my breath and remember that the reason I had finally found these songs was that one of the people who had written them had just been murdered.

While John's death didn't change the music, it absolutely changed the popular perception of the music and the band that had made it. It took the death of a Beatle to solidify their canon in our collective perception. And it didn't happen gradually. It happened so quickly that the drummer famously replaced by Ringo, Pete Best – all but forgotten prior to that point – found himself able to hand in his notice at the Liverpool job centre where he was employed and start getting work as a musician. Four months later, a bunch of Dutch studio musicians calling themselves Starsound recorded snippets of Beatles songs set to a disco beat and the resulting track, 'Stars on 45' reached numbers one and two in America and Britain respectively. Only John Lennon's death created an appetite for this sort of opportunism.

All that remained once I returned Ged's Beatles album to her was to casually try and ascertain why my parents had been keeping this music from me. Why on earth would you have heard these songs and not consider it a matter of the utmost importance to steep your offspring's infant brains in them? I didn't fancy my chances of getting an answer from my mum, so I waited until Sunday, the only day I might get my dad's undivided attention for more than five minutes. And when my mum told him not to be too long at the dump because she'd be serving dinner in an hour, I seized the opportunity.

The Sunday trip to the municipal tip in Tyseley, about a mile away, was a fortnightly ritual. It involved filling up the car with waste from the shop and driving home with it on Saturday night, so that it was ready for its final journey the following morning.

'Are you going to the tip?' I asked him, as he was about to get in the car.

As indeed anyone would do, when standing in heavy rain next to a Talbot Sunbeam full of fish and chip shop waste, he shot me a quizzical gaze. Then he nodded.

'I'll come too!' I announced. 'I'll help.'

Reluctant to draw attention to any inconvenience my company might incur, my dad silently removed the flattened cardboard boxes from the front passenger seat and pressed down the rubbish in the back to make room for me. As he finished doing that, I got in, removed the tape from the cassette box in my hand and ejected the tape of Greek music that was already in the machine. If he was annoyed, he hid it well. I let him know that this cassette was full of songs by the Beatles, and waited for him to say something, anything about it.

'Ah, Beatles!' he finally exclaimed, a few seconds into 'Help!'

'Do you like this one?' I asked.

One of the reasons I remember his exact reply is that it was a sentence he would fall back on from time to time. '*Afisan epohi*' literally translates as 'They bequeathed an era.' I think it was a sentence that allowed him to endorse the importance of something without necessarily having to pretend he was invested in it. After 'Help!' came the somewhat damp 'Michelle', a song I felt both of us could do without hearing at that moment in time. I flipped the tape and, within a couple of minutes, 'Ticket to Ride' gave way to 'Eleanor Rigby', by which time we had turned off the busy Warwick Road and found ourselves turning off beyond Tyseley train station and along the access road to the municipal tip.

The rain started to come down in sheets. We reached a manned barrier where my dad was required to wind his window down and explain what he had in the back of the car. As soon as he did so, an overwhelming stink of putrefaction flooded the interior of the car. Preoccupied as he was by the imminent disposal of several flattened empty boxes that had once contained blocks of palm oil and fresh chickens, my dad's indifference to Eleanor's plight, brought to life by Paul's masterful storytelling and George Martin's hair-raising arrangement, formed a parallel narrative of sorts. While Eleanor was sizing up her own existential abyss, I alighted the car and peered over the precipice of the concrete ravine into which all the rubbish had to be slung. Once the car had been emptied of waste, my dad removed one last thing. The Beatles. He pushed the 'eject' button, placed it in the recess next to the gearstick and put his cassette back in. Poor old Eleanor Rigby. Even in death, it was just one indignity after another.

CHAPTER 21

Over eighteen months had elapsed since our move to Overlea Avenue. My neighbour Emily May had been generous enough to give me her entire set of *Misty* comics, but her parents had yet to offer more than an uneasy nod in our direction. I had assumed they were just shy – and, being shy myself, elected to keep my distance until a more suitable time. At some point, they would surely realise that the nearest I'd ever come to spoiling the tone of the neighbourhood was the rhythmic *clunh-tchft* noise of my new pogo stick. Throughout January, the sight of the youngest Paphides child on his new pogo stick, trying to beat his previous record – sometimes bouncing up to 200 times beyond the dying rays of daylight – became a daily occurrence. Clunh-tchft! Clunh-tchft! Clunh-tchft! Clunh-tchft! Clunh-tchft! Clunh-tchft! Surely the only thing that stopped any of the neighbours complaining about the noise was the pitiful sight of the person making it. This being December going into January, there was never anyone else out there. If you looked out of your window any time between the ITV news at 5.45 and the beginning of *Nationwide*, you'd have seen it: me dancing a solitary pogo beneath the greenish glow of Overlea Avenue's only street light.

It was years before I realised the real reason for the Mays' 'shyness': they didn't want Greeks moving into Overlea Avenue. Ged and her family knew from the outset, but they decided to spare us the hurt. And, of course, my parents had long since worked it out. Which was why, shortly after Christmas 1980, they decided to host a small New Year's Eve soirée. Invitations were issued, not just to the Mays, but also to the Hughes family, and to Dennis and Iris – who, while not hostile, would have hardly chosen to live next door to Greek fish and chip people who shoved their Greekness, well, if not down their throat, then up their noses by frequently cooking the Sunday roast in the back garden. This occasional al fresco ritual would see my dad emptying a bag of charcoal into the low 'village-style' Cypriot *souvla* barbecue and setting fire to it. While we waited for the flames to subside, my mum would impale maybe a dozen fist-sized chunks of pork or lamb on two skewers, which my dad would then fix onto the battery-operated motors which rotated them. If it was warm enough, Greek music would disperse through the open windows, merging with the aroma of the meat and smoking bay leaves.

Some of my parents' friends might pop by, usually a couple of other chip shop owners, but on occasion our house would also be graced by a more illustrious presence. The newly ordained Greek Orthodox Bishop of Birmingham, Irineos of Pataras, had been friendly with my parents for as long as they had lived in the city. Every Sunday, once the congregation received their communion and dispersed, Bishop Irineos's post-church Sunday routine involved deciding which of the dozens of weekly lunch invitations offered to him he would accept. There were bigger, posher houses competing for the kudos of being able to say that the bishop had joined them for Sunday lunch, but none of those families had anyone who could cook as well as my mum. Sometimes, if my parents hadn't made it to church, Irineos would call ahead and ask if we would be receiving visitors that afternoon. The purpose of the call was twofold. It wasn't just a matter of checking that we would be there. Irineos had no teeth, so if my mum knew he was coming, she would prepare something soft like a *moussaka* or *fava*. If it had rained, my mum would take a bucket and, oblivious to the neighbours' surveillance, head towards the grass verge on Overlea Avenue and fill it with snails, which she would fry in garlic butter and also present to the bishop.

Despite the lack of teeth, he had a starry aura that couldn't be explained with mere reference to his robes and chains. Both in face and physique, Irineos bore an uncanny resemblance to Orson Welles in his final years. We looked forward to his visits. He never once asked us why he hardly ever saw us in church. He'd tell my mum that her soup, which she would pack into a Tupperware container and send to him at church via my dad, was the only thing that ensured he survived Lent. The best thing about his visits, though, was the moment of his arrival. As he emerged from his car with his walking stick and his Alsatian, Amor, you could see the Hunts and the Mays peering out at him from their upstairs windows. In my memory, he is wreathed perpetually in a cloud of incense, but of course, it was cigarette smoke – the same cigarette smoke that ultimately left Amor with emphysema and meant that the bishop had to replace him with another Alsatian which he also called Amor.

As if the prospect of spending the evening of 31 December with Greeks wasn't daunting enough for the neighbours, my parents also arranged for Irineos to join us. Although it had rained all day, even my mother sensed that including snails in the buffet might be too much for the Mays and the Hunts. The bishop arrived early and was led into the kitchen, where he and my dad sucked the meat out of all the shells. I could hear the slurping from the front room as I attempted to watch the final ever episode of *Citizen Smith*, which had Robert Lindsay riding his Lambretta into the Italian sunset over a song which would take me years to realise was the Beatles' 'Here Comes the Sun'.

By the time Mr and Mrs May arrived, the other neighbours were already here. I opened the door to see them looking as nervous as I did on the day Aki sent me off to Marcus's house to break my three-year silence. Mr May handed my dad a bottle of red wine, which he placed in the fridge next to the claret that Joyce and Frank Hughes had brought us. Perhaps because he had been briefed, the bishop rose to his feet and almost immediately launched into an impassioned testimonial to my parents.

'I have known Chris and Victoria all the time they have been living in Britain! They came here with NOTHING! And now they have this beautiful house!' He ostentatiously gestured towards the nest of tables, which for the first time since we moved here was being fully utilised to display a range of *dolmades*, *keftedes*, dips, pitta bread and slices of *spanakopita*. Sole occupant of the smallest table was a *vassilopita* – a traditional Greek cake made to greet the New Year, in which a lucky coin is concealed and said to ensure a year's worth of good luck for whoever ends up receiving it. 'No one works harder than these two,' continued the bishop. 'And this woman here!' He grabbed my mother's hand and clasped it in between his. 'Her moussaka is the best in the world!'

My mum gently attempted to free her hand, but the bishop hadn't finished with it. Still holding it, he turned to face my dad. 'And this man! Chris is one of the most talented men I have ever met. He fixes my car! He is a world expert on politics! And, you know Eftihia from the Dolphin Fish Bar on Warwick Road? He saved her finger!'

If you were standing behind the bishop, as Aki and I were, you could clearly see the startled, smiling faces of Mr and Mrs May.

'Did he?' replied Mr May.

'She pushed her hand too far into the chipping machine,' explained the bishop. 'Chris was there! He took her finger out of the bucket, put it in a bag of frozen scampi and drove her to the hospital. Didn't you, Chris?'

'That's right,' confirmed my dad. 'It's as good as new now. She can bend it.'

An hour later, my mum cut the *vassilopita* in half. For reasons that, even now, I don't quite understand, I half expected to find a finger in that too. By now, Ged and Emily had joined us. Leaving the adults in the front room, we wandered upstairs to the bedroom I shared with Aki. In 1981, it was entirely normal for thirteen-year-old girls in Birmingham to bring records to other people's houses just as a thirteen-year-old girl in the twenty-first century might automatically pack lip balm and her iPhone. Emily was no exception.

'Can we listen to this?' she asked, as she pulled down the seams of the bag to reveal the record in question.

'I really want to hear that too!' exclaimed Ged, before turning to address Aki and me. 'What do *you* think of Adam and the Ants?'

She handed me the album. As I removed it from its sleeve, dozens of newspaper and magazine cuttings about the band came out with it and fell onto the carpet – a collection that Emily had begun on 17 October, the day after Adam and the Ants, then at number 37 in the chart, made their *Top of the Pops* debut with 'Dog Eat Dog'. Emily must have kept them in a separate folder or maybe her desk drawer for seventeen days until the release of *Kings of the Wild Frontier*, the record I was about to place on the turntable. And make no mistake, it would have been exactly seventeen days, because eighteen days prior to the release of *Kings of the Wild Frontier*, no one other than a narrow band of punk diehards, scornful music journalists and John Peel show listeners knew who Adam and the Ants were.

Not only that, but even the people who *thought* they knew who Adam and the Ants were didn't really. That was because the Adam and the Ants in the collective memory of all those people – the group who had enjoyed a modicum of cult acclaim with indie releases such as 'Zerox' and 'Young Parisians' – no longer existed. After a desperate Adam Ant enlisted the services of former Sex Pistols manager Malcolm McLaren to boost their profile, McLaren's first move in February 1980 was to ditch Adam, replace him with a thirteen-year-old launderette Saturday girl called Annabella Lwin and call this new line-up Bow Wow Wow. Prior to sacking him, however, McLaren had lent Adam a compilation tape which featured French musician Michel Bernholc playing over a recording of drummers from Burundi in Africa and, in the process, bequeathed him the seed of a new idea which, it has to be said, looked as commercially unpromising on paper as everything else he'd released up to this point.

For his new Ants, Adam recruited guitarist and songwriting foil Marco Pirroni and told him that he wanted to do something involving tribal drums with songs about outlaw archetypes: pirates ('Jolly Roger'), cowboys and Indians ('Los Rancheros', 'Kings of the Wild Frontier') and, a year later, the dandy highwayman of 'Stand and Deliver'. Quite why they thought this might present a way out of their current slough is a total mystery. The two most exciting new developments in British music had been the emergence of the 2 Tone vanguard and the groundswell of synth-prodding futurists – OMD, Ultravox, Visage, the Human League – looking to follow Gary Numan into the upper reaches of the charts. A few weeks into 1981, Duran Duran's debut single, 'Planet Earth', introduced the term 'new romantic' into the pop cultural vernacular and gave the music press a name which encompassed both what the futurists were doing and what Adam and the Ants were doing. But really, only one other band sounded remotely like Adam and the Ants – and that was Bow Wow Wow, who were also trying to take their version of McLaren's Burundi pop blueprint up the charts.

When I think about Adam and the Ants' prime-time TV debut now, I have a split-screen scenario in my head. On the left is Emily in her front room with her parents. She is, by far, the youngest of three sisters, the other two having long left home. Her chestnut hair is worn loose and parted at the side, with a single hair grip, usually with a small flower on it just above her left temple. On that week's *Top of the Pops*, there's an extended intro in which presenter Tommy

Vance asks Michael Palin to tell him about the new Monty Python album. Michael's forced attempts at surreal jollity drag on for what feels like a tiny eternity, which merely compounds the impact of what happens once we cut to a close-up of a drum kit – the nearer of two, somehow managing to simulate the sound of hot hooves advancing across a dusty plain. The camera swings around to reveal a stage partly obscured by dry ice. Adam knows that this is the camera into which he'll be looking. It's forty-five degrees to his left – his head isn't turned totally but his gaze is fixed to the side, revealing more of the whites of his eyes in the process. This is important because it accentuates his eyeliner beautifully. And these are the first words that ten million viewers hear him sing.

> *You may not like*
> *The things we do*
> *Only idiots*
> *Ignore the truth*

There's a white stripe painted across his nose, and he's wearing a replica of the gold Hussars military jacket made famous by Jimi Hendrix. His trousers are leather, and every time he moves his arm in time with Pirroni's Wild Western power chords, the printed neckerchief on his wrist flies up with it. Adam's eyes follow the camera constantly. His hips are the sixth member of the band, gyrating and thrusting to the rhythmic stampede behind him. Adam and the Ants had barely scraped onto the show that night. 'Dog Eat Dog' was at number 37 in the chart, not usually enough to secure a *Top of the Pops* slot, but someone else had dropped out at the last minute. This was a contingency for which the band had clearly prepared, because everything about this performance was deliberate and meticulously realised. Decades later, Pirroni recalled, 'I'd seen Bowie doing "Starman" . . . on *Top of the Pops* and in the back of my mind that's exactly what I wanted to achieve. You wanted to cause that argument in the playground the next day.'

For anyone who knew Adam Ant but had lost track of his movements in the previous eight months, his *Top of the Pops* debut will have been as startling as turning on the news, seeing live footage of a hijack and realising that you knew the gunman. It was that unlikely.

Which brings us to the other side of the split-screen scenario. On the evening of that *Top of the Pops* appearance, McLaren's Bow Wow Wow had already released two singles, both of which failed to chart. Eight months previously, McLaren had just given Adam Ant his marching orders. Adam didn't have a band, and not a single song on *Kings of the Wild Frontier* had been written. Watching Adam and the Ants on *Top of the Pops* that night, McLaren would have been enough of a pop scholar to understand immediately that this was the most important British music television performance since the Bowie one that Pirroni had longed to emulate. Not only had McLaren failed to spot what Adam Ant was capable of, but he'd also let him steal his last great idea. In the words of one of his previous discoveries: ever got the feeling you've been cheated?

The change in Emily was instant. Because we were at the same school, I would see her walk out of her house in the morning, looking exactly as she had done on any school morning in the previous two years. By the time she had arrived at the school gates though, the extent of her devotion to Adam stopped just short of a white stripe across her nose. Her tie had been loosened and the top button of her shirt undone, obscured in part by a frayed red cotton scarf. Bead necklaces and chains magically materialised around her neck. Small patterned fragments of ribbon were tied around bits of hair. Two lines of rouge followed the line of her cheekbones. By Christmas, she could sit on the top deck of the 44 bus and apply eyeliner with the steady hand of a pro – a process she would just as skilfully reverse on the way home.

Emily was by no means the only one. While there had been nothing happening in pop to suggest that the idea of Adam and the Ants had any commercial potential, what happened in playgrounds up and down Britain in the ensuing weeks made it apparent that – with *that* frontman and *those* songs – it couldn't have been anything other than massive. While Adam Ant spoke to the inner pirate and Wild West hero of every other boy in our playground, the girls got on with the business of fantasising about him – and of course, so did several of the boys.

I saw the effect that Antmania was having on other children and somehow felt – as I had done with 2 Tone and the mod revival – that this wasn't going to be my epiphany. For a start, I was too scared to commit to any pop-cultural trend that would require me to change, lest I fuck it up. I wanted everything to stay exactly as it was. If there could be a way of making the transition from childhood to adulthood without attracting any attention or having anyone pass judgement or scrutinising your progress, that's the route I would have taken.

And this, in turn, was why I was so fascinated by Emily and her increasingly fractious relationship with her parents. Ged would occasionally relay tantalising details to me: her increasing tendency to stay out late; the angry face-off prompted by her purchase of a leather miniskirt; her radical new spiky hairdo. I wondered where it would all end. Would she get into drugs? Would she fail her exams and have to work in a factory? And, more to the point, if a record is all it takes to set off a chain reaction that might ultimately derail your life prospects, how could I be sure that it wouldn't happen to me?

It wasn't even that I didn't want it to happen. It was more that I knew I couldn't shoulder the guilt of disappointing my mum, who clearly had enough to contend with. Her expectations for Aki had taken a sizeable dent when she learned that he'd been placed in the second-from-bottom stream at Yardleys School. She even arranged an appointment to see his form teacher about it, and frequently recounted the humiliation she felt on being told that Aki should probably set his sights on factory work rather than university, because to go for the latter would almost certainly result in failure.

For his part, Aki merely brushed aside the low expectations of his teachers and replenished his self-esteem in the arena of teenage endeavour that conferred most peer group approbation – football. He had somehow developed a way of honing his ball skills in a way that was quintessentially Aki. His close control was unbelievable. He never seemed to run. Instead, thanks to a repertoire of deft pull-backs, dummies and nutmegs, he just walked the ball around the opposing players before delivering the pass or the shot on goal. Outward displays of urgency were the last thing you expected from Aki. Shortly into the new year, however, that had changed.

Just as Emily received her epiphany at the optimal moment, now it was Aki's turn. He was ready to receive the Thing. There had been a few almost-Things prior to this point. The Sex Pistols. Skids. The Ruts. But not quite. Neither had the Thing been Paul Weller, although it certainly came close. The new Thing couldn't just offer him a version of who he was (although maybe it had to be a bit that too), it had to signpost a way ahead. Because the way ahead was also a way out. The Thing wasn't something he could design himself, because that wouldn't add anything to the total of what Aki knew about Aki. I can now see that by the end of January 1981, Aki had found the Thing. And his way of announcing it to me happened one or two weeks later – via *Top of the Pops* once again – when the video for The Teardrop Explodes' 'Reward' began and Aki, who these days preferred it when I *didn't* like his music, ordered me to shut up and watch what was about to happen.

I'd heard the song already. Between listening to it for the first time in the record shop and that night's *Top of the Pops*, Aki had bought the 7-inch single with its zebra-patterned sleeve and, on returning home from school every evening, had played it four or five times without interruption. January had only just ended but it was clear that no one was going to come up with a better opening line in 1981 than 'Bless my cotton socks I'm in the news'. It was a line that validated the formative narcissism of every teenager who bought into it. But, in the event, it was the video that cannoned Aki's adoration of what he was hearing into a new dimension. For the first half a minute so, we were shown an open-topped military jeep with about ten passengers crammed into it, mostly men, but a couple of women too, some playing trumpets. They stopped abruptly and suddenly there beside them we got to see The Teardrop Explodes' leader Julian Cope for the first time. His hair was a shaggy blond mop and he was wrapped in an orange rug which he removed to reveal a brown fur-lined flying jacket.

'When we recorded it as a single,' recalled Cope decades later, 'I urged the producer to make it sound hectic and frenetic, like we were playing in an ice rink.' The single speaker of our Philips colour television honoured his directive. The song's relentless four-to-the-floor clatter combined with Cope's exotic get-up instantly gave Aki a cause. It was as though he had been recruited by the art school wing of Hezbollah.

Within a couple of days, it wasn't just 'Reward' charging out of Aki's room. There was an entire album where that came from. With nowhere else in the house to direct his enthusings, Aki kept forgetting that he wanted The Teardrop Explodes all to himself. On the sleeve of *Kilimanjaro*, you could see all four members of the group partly obscured in shadowy orange light. The other three are holding something back, probably out of shyness rather than any attempt to project mystique. But leaning forward as if trying to climb out of the photograph and into your room is an impish-looking Julian Cope. A few months later, the band's label Mercury would reissue the album with a library shot of some zebras at the foot of Kilimanjaro. But this, the original sleeve, was crucial to the relationship that Aki had with the record. And it was all because of Julian. Julian Cope looking you in the eye and saying, 'Come on. Are you with me? Are we gonna do it or what? ALL RIGHT!!!'

No record in Aki's life would ever have such a catalysing effect. The folder of course work he was amassing for his art O level suddenly bulged with character studies of lost-looking teenagers and destitute pensioners (oddly never anyone in between), their gazes unreachable behind a membrane of blurred watercolours. His teacher, a wiry beatnik called Mr James, was a stranger to the other staff on account of the fact that he never left his classroom, preferring to remain there and play Jamaican ska and bebop on a paint-splattered cassette player. The presence of a sink in the classroom also enabled him to keep a kettle in there. Mr James provided the tea bags on the understanding that the pupils brought the biscuits. He told Aki that, at this rate, he was cruising towards an A – a forecast which emboldened Aki to head into more abstract territory, handing in macabre pencil-drawn, post-apocalyptic landscapes that Mr James adored and had my mum worrying that Aki was committing an act of self-sabotage. In reality, it was the opposite. He was making a break for freedom.

And, in my memory, the driver of this deviation from any narrative that had been expected of Aki was this record. There was nothing else quite like *Kilimanjaro*, and a huge part of the reason for that was that there was no one else quite like Julian Cope. One fact that emerged early on about him was that he had once played Oliver in his secondary school's production of the eponymous musical. Another was that, despite emerging from Liverpool's fiercely competitive post-punk scene, Cope was originally from the Staffordshire market town of Tamworth. He was tall, blond and photogenic and made no attempt to hide his middle-class accent, either in person or on the records. When handsome young men like Julian Cope end up fronting bands like The Teardrop Explodes, something needs to have gone wrong. It's what becomes of prefects who have their drinks spiked. Or children who realise they can't be a vessel for their parents' unrealised ambitions.

In the songs that comprised *Kilimanjaro*, beneath the brushed aluminium production of a record designed to turn Julian Cope into a bona fide pop star, were intimations of all this disturbance. There was no single song that laid it all bare (that would come with the next album). Rather, it revealed itself in phrases and lines which lay scattered across the entirety of the album, like the very debris of childhood itself. These were songs which depicted their protagonist beyond the reach or comprehension of concerned onlookers. 'I see a change in you,' he sang on a fidgety lysergic interrogation called 'Poppies', 'Can you see a change in me / But I can't explain at all / I can't explain what I feel'. On 'Brave Boys Keep Their Promises', Cope issued a list of what sounded like Methodist edicts for children, before suggesting in the final verse that the ultimate test of character is the one where you get to pit every member of your family against you. He was, of course, one in a long tradition of frontmen who invited you to believe that their existential struggle was a lot like yours. On 'Thief of Baghdad', he'd been climbing a hill all day with the sun on his back only to have his efforts derided by his subject. On 'Bouncing Babies', he cast himself as a prodigal agitator, destined to disrupt from day one: 'I was a bouncing baby / I fell down / I looked around / I didn't stay too long'.

But the most intriguing thing about *Kilimanjaro* – with its keyboards half-inched from Doors albums that we'd yet to hear, and its brass interjections inspired by Love records of whose existence we were unaware – was the harder it tried to be a mainstream pop album, the stranger it sounded. There was no straighter love song on the record than its closing song 'When I Dream', but with every passing minute, it wasn't the lyrical sentiments that grabbed your attention. It was the increasingly ominous washes of synth noise rising underneath Cope's vocal until, like every other component in the song, it was all but submerged in alien noise.

The Teardrop Explodes may have presented Aki with a version of his own future, but they didn't sound like *the* future any more than Adam and the Ants did. The emerging wave of groups whose music was built around what Saint Etienne, in their 2012 song 'Over the Border', would call 'the strange and important sound of the synthesiser' moved the world outside William Osborne's head a little closer to the one inside it. I remember William pointing out to me with some pride that, in the space of a few weeks, two groups featuring occasional Gary Numan collaborator Billy Currie were in the top 10. Currie's main group had been Ultravox!, a group who lost their exclamation mark at the same time as their lead singer John Foxx.

Together with new Ultravox frontman Midge Ure, Currie helped write and record songs for a studio-based project fronted by Steve Strange. Prior to the success of Visage's debut hit 'Fade to Grey', Strange had achieved a measure of renown for two things: (i) his cameo in the video for 'Ashes to Ashes'; and (ii) Blitz, the London club night hosted by him, where he operated a legendarily strict door policy, restricting access to only 'the weird and wonderful'. His alliterative handle imprinted itself on our brains immediately. He sounded as much like a character from the pages of *Whizzer and Chips* as he did a pop star. And because Steve Strange was his name, that somehow legitimised his androgyny to boys who might have otherwise been reluctant to profess affection for music made by men in dresses and make-up.

In this regard, it probably also helped that 'Fade to Grey' was made using machines that couldn't adequately process the emotions of the people playing them. Every synth-pop hit of the early eighties was made on instruments that made the same sound, no matter how hard or soft you pressed the keys. For a lot of people who were raised on guitars, this left synth-pop open to accusations that it was less 'real' than its predecessors. But this music made up the shortfall in other ways. The potency of 'Fade to Grey' lay in the disparity between the emotion of the song and the indifference of the hardware.

One man on a lonely platform
One case sitting by his side
Two eyes staring cold and silent
Show fear as he turns to hide

And while the lyrics were almost certainly written in less time than it took to stop and work out what it was actually about, it was somehow consistent with the darkening tonal shift that seemed to grip so much pop over the previous year and would continue to do so. For some musicians, the process of reflecting that shift was undertaken in a conscious, deliberate way. Gary Numan and OMD could take you line by line through their songs and tell you exactly what they were trying to do with each release. If you had the musical equivalent of an air pollution sensor – a device you could use to identify the particulate composition of whatever song happens to be playing at that time – every futurist/ new romantic hit in the eighteen months that followed the release of 'Fade to Grey' contained one or more of these components:

(a) ambivalence concerning our place in an increasingly depersonalised world
(b) themes that had appeared in the work of J.G. Ballard
(c) Cold War paranoia and/or the attendant threat of nuclear annihilation
(d) exposure to the *fin de siècle* glam-dram of Ziggy Stardust
(e) total musical and lyrical (and sartorial) Eurocentricity: Teutonic disco noir in preference to anything that might be mistaken for the work of American musicians
(f) the synthesiser as the predominant instrument, preferably aided by synthetic drums.

Singles featuring various combinations of the above included Spandau Ballet's 'To Cut a Long Story Short', Duran Duran's 'Planet

Earth', Soft Cell's 'Tainted Love', the Human League's 'The Sound of the Crowd', Depeche Mode's 'New Life', Japan's 'Quiet Life', Kraftwerk's 'Computer Love'/'The Model', Landscape's 'Einstein a Go-Go', OMD's 'Souvenir', Gary Numan's 'This Wreckage' and, of course, the second top 10 hit in the space of a few weeks featuring Midge Ure and Billy Currie, Ultravox's 'Vienna'. These artists spent 1981 moving around the top 40 like ghosts around a *Pac-Man* screen. And yet, true to form, out of all of them, the ones I connected with were the ones by musicians who wouldn't have stood a chance of getting into Steve Strange's club. I'd bought all three top 40 singles by New Musik, the group fronted by producer Tony Mansfield, whose discomfort at the visual side of being in a band was impossible to miss. For New Musik's *Top of the Pops* performance of their single 'Living by Numbers', Tony discharged his promotional obligations with the air of a six-year-old child who had been frog-marched to the studio at gunpoint. To watch him go through it was like reliving that nightmare infant school assembly in which I had been expected to break my silence. And, needless to say, this only served to strengthen the bond between me and New Musik.

Susan Fassbender was another case in point. The pre-fame arc of a pop star tends to feature periods of teenage alienation, playground bullying and the search for a brave new identity, possibly with a group of like-minded outsiders who have had to go through the same sort of experience. Performing the elastic robo-funk of her only hit 'Twilight Café' on *Top of the Pops*, Susan Fassbender appeared to have skipped the finding-a-new-identity bit. It seemed to me that what I was looking at when I was looking at Susan Fassbender was manifestly the same person who had spent much of her formative years fishing her spectacles out of the girls' toilet. On 'Twilight Café', Susan made the transition from keyboard nerd to pop star without any visible concession to the demands of show business. Whether I liked it or not, these were my people.

It was too dangerous to allow myself to get fully invested in the cooler pop stars. I bought their records and taped their songs off the radio, but the fate of Michael Mycroft in the class below me was a salutary reminder of what happens when beta boys momentarily forget their status and attempt to raise their stock. With the pages of *Smash Hits* gradually being invaded by Spandau Ballet, Duran Duran, Adam Ant, Haysi Fantayzee and other new romantic pace setters, often photographed with drinks in hand at the Blitz club, Billy's and the Beat Route, Michael persuaded his mother to book him in for an appointment at the Birmingham branch of Vidal Sassoon for a professionally executed new romantic hairdo. When he finally alighted on the style he wanted, on a page ripped out from a fashion spread in a new magazine called *The Face*, he brought it in to show to everyone in the playground. His current hairstyle was a sort of longish mousey helmet, but he was going to dye it cherry red and cut it short at the sides, but permed on top. No one voiced anything other than encouraging words prior to Michael's potentially life-changing trip to Vidal Sassoon. The girls called it brave. The boys voiced only admiration.

But four days later, when hitherto plain, unremarkable Michael Mycroft paraded into the playground fully expecting that his new hair would instantly elevate his standing, he received a brutal awakening.

I was standing next to Terry Violett when he saw Michael Mycroft. As one of the most popular boys in the year, Terry would have been one of the boys Mycroft would have been keenest to impress. On seeing him, Terry's eyeballs momentarily left his skull.

'FANNYHEAD!'

In that mortifying moment, the scale of Michael Mycroft's delusion became apparent to him. He stood rooted to the spot. The very thing that he hoped would turn his fortunes around would – for every remaining minute of a schoolday that hadn't even started yet

– be the subject of unrelenting derision. And worst of all, he couldn't even hide it. There it was, on top of his head. On top of his *fannyhead*.

'LOOK, EVERYONE! MYCROFT'S GOT A *FANNY* ON HIS HEAD!'

By midday, alerted to a massed-ranks chorus of 'FANNYHEAD!', even the teachers on playground duty were going out of their way to smirk at it. It had been all very well for Steve Strange to reflect upon his South Wales schooldays from the security of the *Swap Shop* phone-in and reminisce about the days when dressing like Ziggy Stardust meant you ran the very real risk of getting your head kicked in. But Steve Strange was no longer at school in South Wales. By waiting until he left school, Steve Strange got to choose what he wanted to be called. By attempting to ape Steve Strange when he was still only eleven, Michael Mycroft also ended up with a different name. But Fannyhead hadn't been the name that Mycroft had chosen for himself. By the end of the week, Mycroft was faced with no choice but to cut his cranial bush and his losses with it.

Contrary to what Adam Ant would later have us believe, out here in the West Midlands suburbs, ridicule was everything to be scared of. But it was by no means the only thing on the list. Some children could measure their developing maturity by looking back to the things that had caused them consternation and observing that their occult power had long since dissipated. Not me though. I just augmented my old fears with a bunch of new, bigger ones. Left to my own devices, I would have almost certainly avoided a new ITV series called *Hammer House of Horror*, which comprised ten stand-alone, hour-long tales of macabre goings-on in the British suburbs. As long as I was friends with William Osborne though, that wasn't an option. Having religiously watched *Doctor Who* for half his life, the move into British horror was a mere sidestep for him. The qualities that thrilled him in the former were also abundant in the latter: the sense of imminent threat from forces that didn't adhere to the observable laws of nature; the sense that even the anonymous English settlements that surrounded us, with their parks and their corner shops and impromptu cups of tea with the neighbours were vulnerable to unknowable forces; and, of course, the discombobulating incidental music.

William was keen that, every Saturday night, we both watch *Hammer House of Horror* so we could talk about it at school the following week. Far from being put out by his suggestion, I felt something approaching gratitude for it. Having hit the ground running at Yardleys, William had been pulling away from me. As a consequence, I was grateful that he was establishing some terms on which our friendship could continue. And so, dutifully, every Saturday, at around 9.15 p.m., I commandeered the TV and affected the enthusiasm to convince Aki and my mum that I was really looking forward to watching stories with titles such as 'Visitor from the Grave' or 'The Mark of Satan'. In 'The House That Bled to Death', a couple and their young daughter moved into a house whose previous owner had hacked his wife to death. Weird things started to happen almost as soon as they moved in. Two rusty ceremonial knives on the wall seemed to take on a life of their own. A severed hand appeared in the fridge. We were shown the bloody, dismembered corpse of Timmy the family cat on the ledge of the front-room window. And, most dramatically, their daughter's birthday party came to a traumatic end when a dislodged water pipe spurted vast amounts of blood directly over the table where all the children were gathered.

My upbringing in the suburbs of Birmingham was far removed from the wartime poverty of my mum's early childhood and my dad's tough self-sufficient teenage years. There was nothing much to fear, not really. At least, that's how it seems to me now. But that wasn't how it seemed then. With the Yorkshire Ripper freshly apprehended and details of his reign of terror splashed all over the papers, the events depicted in *Hammer House of Horror* didn't feel far removed from those of the real world. Every tabloid published a gallery of Peter Sutcliffe's victims with brief details underneath: their names, their ages and the date and location of their death. I looked at photographs of Sutcliffe with his beard and curly hair and attempted to reconcile my first impressions of him with what he'd done. Possibly as a result of all the ads which featured lorry drivers manfully staring down at their Yorkie chocolate bars, I'd got it into my head that lorry drivers were nice people. Or, at the very least, people who liked chocolate, which was almost the same thing. Had I seen a photo of Peter Sutcliffe in any other context, with his curly hair and his beard, I might have thought he was a nice guy too.

One photograph in the victims' gallery kept drawing me back to look at it. She was called Helen Rytka. Sutcliffe had picked her up and driven her to a timber yard in Huddersfield, attempting to have sex with her before taking a hammer to her head and then stabbing her in the chest. She was just eighteen. In the photo her hair was brushed away from her face and stood upright. Her eyes were huge and her expression a little startled – and it was because of that startled gaze that I fixated on her, by turns trying to imagine her final moments, and then, when I imagined them a little too vividly, trying to do anything but imagine them.

I wasn't the only one. Unusually for a music paper, *Record Mirror* had an agony aunt. The compassionate gaze of Susanne Garrett in her byline picture inspired a sense that this was a woman who could furnish you with sober, sympathetic counsel. One week, in the wake of the Ripper trial, a letter from Fran in Bolton was headlined, 'Cold sweats, Ripper fear. Am I going mad?' It began, 'Sometimes I think I'm going mad as I keep breaking out in a cold sweat when I think of things like the Yorkshire Ripper trial . . . Even when I'm in my room alone at night, I'm scared of the dark, and listen to the radio or read about my favourite pop stars to get over the fear. I've been frightened of the dark ever since I was a small child.' It was oddly comforting that eighteen-year-old Fran in Bolton was as spooked by the Yorkshire Ripper murders as I was – and that, like me, she also needed to fall asleep with the light on. Susanne's reply was similarly reassuring. 'Facts which have been released as a result of the Ripper trial at the Old Bailey have prompted a similar reaction of disgust in a large proportion of the population. Your reaction isn't unusual.'

Terror felt like one of the elements, something you ought to be able to measure with a meter. Not only that, but it seemed the most ubiquitous of all the elements, on account of its ability to travel across the lines that demarcate fact from fiction and whatever lies in between. And in the early months of 1981, there seemed to be so much in between. I hit the paranormal section of Acocks Green library hard. The librarians let slip only the faintest hint of a smirk as I solemnly handed over my blue library card and they stamped the same gazetteers of ghost sightings for the third month in a row. Upstairs at home, I could sometimes hear the wheezing keys of the Bontempi organ bought for me a few Christmases previously playing by themselves, even when it wasn't plugged in. It's the same sound I hear now, from time to time, when a strong gust blows through the back door. Back then, far from revealing itself to be the real cause of the noise, the sound of the wind merely fuelled the fear.

I read quasi-scientific studies of poltergeists and saw that the phenomenon seemed far more prevalent in houses containing teenagers. Could it be that, as you approached puberty, you were especially receptive to communications from the spirit world? Perhaps some children even liked the idea that they might be 'chosen' in this way, but I definitely wasn't one of them. What if I were able to move objects with my mind even when I didn't want to? I lay in bed staring at the pencil case which was partly propped up by my clock radio and became convinced that it was about to move. And if that, indeed, had happened, I'd have absolutely lost my mind with fear. I found myself gathering evidence even when it wasn't in the interests of my mental well-being to do so.

I quickly became acquainted with the work of leading ghost hunters such as Peter Underwood and Harry Price. I read everything I could find about their investigations into the hauntings of Borley Rectory, generally regarded as Britain's most haunted building. Usborne's series of books for children about paranormal phenomena was another staple. Featuring illustrations that were far more chilling than they needed to be, given their intended audience, the volume on ghosts exerted a particular hold on me. The more it terrified me, the more I read it. I memorised locations such as Glamis Castle in Scotland, which was said to be haunted by Lady Janet Douglas, who was burned at the stake after plotting to kill James V, and people like the female servant of an earl who witnessed a crime and had her tongue cut out to ensure that she didn't incriminate the culprit.

From the spooky shelf at Acocks Green library, it was a short leap to the real crackpot stuff. In the books section at Preedy's, I found *The Prophecies of Nostradamus: The Man Who Saw Tomorrow* by Erika Cheetham, a *Daily Mail* journalist to whom I instinctively entrusted the job of interpreting the elliptical four-line forebodings of a Frenchman who'd died 415 years previously, and whose findings I elected to use as an aid in decisions regarding my own possibly very brief future on this planet.

If Cheetham was to be believed, the prognosis for me was bleak. We were due one more pope before the end of the world. This was set to happen sometime in 1999 when the third antichrist (following Napoleon and Hitler) set about wreaking unholy terror upon the world. Perhaps surprisingly, he would be called Roy – which even the most devout of Nostradamus's followers would have to concede was not a terribly frightening name. His surname would be d'Angolmois, which Cheetham took to be a cryptic and not entirely accurate anagram for Mongols. Cheetham might have thought to mention that

Angolmois was *also* a variant spelling of Angoumois, which was a province of western France. But, of course, no one's going to make too much of a fuss about the prospect of a man called Roy from Angolmois embarking on a reign of terror.

Besides, there was much circumstantial evidence to suggest that we ought to be taking Nostradamus's quatrains very seriously indeed. He had, after all, predicted a mighty skirmish in Germany against Hister. Cheetham suggested that, give or take a minor typo on Nostradamus's part, this was clearly a reference to the rise of Hitler. Yes, 'Hister' *might* also refer to Hister, the Latin name for the lower course of the Danube, a name explicitly used by Nostradamus when writing about the Danube in his 1554 almanac. But I would only discover this years later – Erika hadn't thought to clear up that ambiguity at the time.

With hindsight, I can see pretty clearly what was going on here. But, in 1981, I wasn't the only child struggling to understand why the grown-ups were calmly going about their everyday business when it quite clearly said in this widely available paperback that the world would be reduced to rubble sometime around my birthday in 1999. Aki said it was all bullshit and that these 'prophesies' could be taken to mean just about anything. But Nostradamus's quatrains were no harder to decode than Ted Rogers's impenetrably cryptic clues on prime-time ITV quiz show *3-2-1* – and *they* clearly meant something. So surely it followed that Nostradamus must also mean something. And now, thanks to the heroic work of Erika Cheetham, we had a pretty good idea what it was.

In some ways, the annihilation predicted by Nostradamus got me off the hook. Our parents had all sorts of expectations for Aki and me – all of which involved taking over the family business and settling down with Greek wives, most likely from families who were known to them. This was traditionally how courtship and marriage had been conducted in Greece and Cyprus. Marriage wasn't simply regarded as a union of two individuals. The exchange of vows between bride and groom was the expedient by which two families became joined together. Of course, there were exceptions. Exceptions such as my mum and dad, who had met by chance in St Ermolaos. But if anything, the fact that their relationship had long since changed from romance into mere arrangement strengthened their belief in the old ways. Another factor in retrenching their belief in marrying 'in', preferably at the end of a supervised courtship, was the fact that they were far from home. Had they never come to England, they wouldn't have had to worry about us not marrying Greek girls. But here in Birmingham, beyond the four walls of our house, we couldn't be *passively* Greek. Almost all of the culture we were receiving was English. There were Greek books on our shelves, but we didn't go near them. And while, in years to come, I'd grow to love them, the Greek records in my dad's collection remained synonymous with Sunday ennui.

Somehow, those negative associations coloured my feelings about the record that raced up the charts in the first weeks of 1981 and, in doing so, famously managed to keep Ultravox's 'Vienna' from reaching number 1. Interviewed about 'Shaddap You Face' in the years following its success, its Italian American creator Joe Dolce claimed that the song had become 'important' to immigrants because, in its own way, it alighted on the tension between the values retained by people who lay down roots far away from their native country and those of their children, whose outlook is inevitably more aligned to that of the country where they have had to grow up. You might think that's a pretty lofty view to take of a record whose chorus, sung in a comedy Italian accent, involves someone's mum telling them to cheer up and lose the attitude – but then again, it was his record to analyse. Certainly I could see in my parents' response to it something similar to their response to *Mind Your Language* three years earlier. And even if they weren't Italian, the resonances weren't lost on them. Having spent my money on far worse comedy records, I should have loved it too, but every time it came on the radio, my immediate instinct was to recoil. 'Shaddap You Face' was a song about remembering where you came from and honouring that debt. But in 1981, my guilty secret was that I didn't feel it was my debt to honour.

Nearly a decade went by before I heard a song that nailed the realisation that – through no fault of your own – you had turned into something that your parents didn't quite recognise. Perhaps it was no surprise that when it happened, it was a record made by a second-generation Greek Cypriot whose parents had accidentally devolved a significant part of his upbringing to pop music: 'I think there's something you should know / I think it's time I told you so / There's something deep inside of me / There's someone else I've got to be'. If George Michael's 'Freedom! '90' had come out nine years earlier, I think it would have instantly become my favourite record of all time.

CHAPTER 22

Like the words in the George Michael song, there was someone else Aki had to be too. But he couldn't decide if that was Julian Cope or Echo & the Bunnymen frontman Ian McCulloch. For his sixteenth birthday in May, he lobbied hard for a fur-lined leather flying jacket just like the one worn by Julian in the 'Reward' video. Within days of receiving it, he finished off the job and presented his barber with a photograph of McCulloch. Short at the sides and long on the top and the front were his strict instructions. The fringe had to be able to cover his eyes. Aki wore it flat for a few days, and then, gradually, it started to get taller and spikier. My dad would send him upstairs to brush it, and Aki would simply go up to his room, do nothing at all, and only return once my dad had gone to work. Having seen the music papers that Aki had left lying around the house, I knew what he was doing. But I kept his secret.

Instead of reworking his image, he should have been studying hard for his O levels and CSEs. One afternoon during the Easter holidays, I came home from William's house to find the garage door wide open and, further in, Aki brushing up on his darts skills. 'Shouldn't you be revising?' I said. He laughed, handed me three darts and drew a line in chalk on the ground to indicate the oche – a word we knew but had no idea how to spell, because the only time we heard it was when it was uttered by *Bullseye* host Jim Bowen. On the bit of floor next to me, he drew a vertical line with his initial and mine either side of it and '501' at the top of each column. As I aimed my darts at the board, he walked over to the cassette player which he had brought into the garage and pressed 'play'. Inside the machine was a pre-recorded four-song cassette which, rather than a conventional plastic case, came in a box which flipped open at the top like a cigarette packet. It had been sitting in the half-price basket at Woolworths – a solitary cassette among a hundred or so ex-chart singles, every one with the top right-hand corner snipped off. Thankfully, it's hard to cut the top corner off a cassette, so Echo & the Bunnymen's 'Shine So Hard' EP was spared the humiliation.

'Listen to this. Just listen.'

A brand-new obsession is like a new tattoo. It will stay with you forever, but for this brief period it glistens and it hurts and you want to show it to everyone. You want to show it to all the people you want to impress and perhaps one or two people who appal you. And if none of those people are available, then you set up a game of darts in the garage and you wait for your little brother to come home. Because maybe, just maybe, he'll hear what you're hearing.

And, on this occasion, I heard everything. All four songs on the cassette had been recorded live in concert. The Bunnymen had already made one incredible album and they would go on to make more, but they never quite equalled the pugilistic brio of these performances. If there had been a period of easing in or warming up at the concert, it didn't make the selections here. The first song, 'Crocodiles', hit the ground at a full-pelt amphetamine charge. Four kicks to the bass drum on each bar from drummer Pete de Freitas before, just thirteen seconds in, a snare drum artillery fire. The genius of de Freitas's drumming, especially on those early Bunnymen records, was that he made everything sound like an emergency. While bassist Les Pattinson locked into whatever his drummer was playing, guitarist Will Sergeant created a slightly separate role for himself in the band. Like a seabird among mammals, he'd take off skywards on his own trajectory, only to swoop suddenly back down into the centre of things with a quick-fire succession of astringent downstrokes. Not that I consciously noticed this stuff. I just felt its effect – and if the eleven-year-old felt it, then it must have shaken the fifteen-year-old like a snow globe.

What was impossible not to notice, of course, was the demonic heat of Ian McCulloch. Some frontmen are driven by a desire to impart a message to the world. But actually the very best ones – the ones for whom you'll jettison your entire identity – just want you to look at them. It's the thing that makes them brilliant in their young manhood but it's the thing that can make them look silly as they approach middle age. That's why, from the lofty perch of early stardom, their best chance at longevity is to successfully make the crossing from exhibit to artist; from pin-up to person. One exists to be stared at, and the other wants to impart something of what they've learned. We seem pre-programmed to have that expectation of musicians. As we gradually work out who *we* really are and what *our* story is, the artists in whom we stay invested are the ones who appear to be moving along the same arc.

But that all comes much later. Right now, at the beginning of 1981, the key detail about Ian McCulloch was that he wanted more people to look at him than his nearest rivals. The songs on the 'Shine So Hard' EP were performed at Buxton Pavilion on 17 January – two weeks before the release of The Teardrop Explodes' *Reward*. The clamour to be the first from Liverpool's fiercely competitive post-punk scene had been intensifying for over a year. Along with Pete Wylie from Wah!, McCulloch and Cope had briefly been in a group called the Crucial Three. Depending on who you believed, the group wrote something between 'one crap song' (McCulloch) and four (Wylie). They barely rehearsed and never played live, but the notion that these three megalomaniacs should have countenanced the idea of being in the same group confirmed the Crucial Three's mythical status.

For McCulloch, the idea that Cope might be the first to crack the top 40 was intolerable. Cope was a relative outsider in the Liverpool scene. He had arrived from Tamworth in September 1976, a month before the opening of Eric's – the club where outlandishly dressed scenesters such as Holly Johnson, Jayne Casey and Pete Burns would go to check out the competition. Cope arrived with a posh accent, long hair and an uncool excess of enthusiasm. The Bunnymen got their album out first, in the summer of 1980. In his memoir *Head On*, Cope recalled the mortification he felt on hearing it for the first time. 'It was brilliant. Just brilliant. It was like Television and it chimed like crazy.' Within three months though, The Teardrops had their album out. At some point, one of these groups was going to be the first to have a hit. *Reward* had just made it onto the Radio 1 playlist. And that's why the timing of the Buxton Pavilion performance is so revealing. Because it's the sound of a man in second place in a race that isn't over yet.

I read it in a magazine
I don't want to see it again
I threw away the magazine
And looked for someone to explain . . .

I pulled out three darts from the dartboard and handed them to Aki. Not for the first time, I felt flattered that he thought I might be capable of understanding the importance of what was happening. But really, these songs made it easy for me. The extended breakdown section in 'Crocodiles' saw Will's guitar pared right back. Most of what you were hearing was Pete de Freitas's seismic backbeat and McCulloch's off-piste pronouncements.

Work all day
Live on hay
With your pie in the sky when you die
With your pie in the sky when you DIE DIE DIE

From there it was back to Sergeant, who had somehow managed to locate a point of intersection between ethereality and nastiness, riding a raga-psych coda into the space vacated by McCulloch's nihilistic outpourings. I don't recall more than a handful of words being exchanged throughout the three remaining songs. With the funereal lamentations of 'Zimbo', the Bunnymen rustled up an emotional heft of which they might have hitherto thought themselves incapable. Certainly, it wasn't what I was expecting after the previous song, but it also created a welcome moment of reflection before two songs which – in spite of the fact that their studio versions reside on different albums – still feel like two expressions of the same burning impatience. 'Where the hell have you been?' began 'All That Jazz', 'We've been waiting with our best suits on'. McCulloch's lyrics rarely withstood close scrutiny, but it didn't matter. The last song, 'Over the Wall' offered up more inarticulate longing executed with combustible zeal. Neither of us said anything for a few seconds after the Bunnymen rode it home to a raging climax.

In its own way, this darts match was as fraught with drama as Adrian Lewis and Phil Taylor's legendary 2013 Grand Slam of Darts clash. 'It's ace, isn't it?' said Aki, and not for the first or last time, I would feel a strange pang of sympathy for him over the fact that there was no one more suitable on hand to bear witness to his epiphany.

Until now, we had shared the same bedroom. It was an arrangement which hadn't always been ideal. As per the popular advert of the time, he took great delight in farting in bed, then sticking his head beneath the sheets and exclaiming, 'Ah, Condor!' The greater my disgust, the more he did it. I never thought he'd voluntarily move to the 'guest' bedroom, which was really just a box room, but he got my dad to pick up a second-hand music centre that was advertised in the small ads of the *Evening Mail* and, from then on, he had everything he needed. He bought the Bunnymen's second album *Heaven Up Here* on the day it came out, just a week after getting the first one. Barely a day passed without either record or both surging out from his room. I got to know every song, but for years I didn't know which one appeared on which album. The ones that stuck with me were the prettier tunes from *Crocodiles*, in particular a brace of songs about hallucinogens – 'Villiers Terrace' and 'Pictures on My Wall' – which appeared to be respectively narrated from the perspective of outsider and participant. Did I need to have this explained to me? Well, there wasn't much to explain. There didn't even need to be a drug aspect to 'Villiers Terrace' because what really stuck with you was the sense of walking into a room in which you immediately feel like the outsider. Even the piano intro, later repeated in between verses, vibrated with a thrilling air of portent. 'People rolling round on the carpet / Passing round the medicine . . . You said people rolled on carpet, boys / But I never thought they'd do those things'. If 'Villiers Terrace' was the 'before' shot, then 'Pictures on My Wall' was the 'after', the answer to the question as to why the protagonist was going to 'Villiers Terrace' in the first place. It wasn't hard to see why Julian Cope, Liverpool's self-styled emissary of psych, was so envious. Ten years later, when I took mushrooms for the first time, 'Pictures on My Wall' corresponded almost exactly to that experience – both the nerve-jangling anticipation and the concomitant realisation that, for the next eight hours, floors and ceilings can no longer be trusted to go about their usual business.

Only one song surpassed those two songs in my affections. 'Stars Are Stars' was the song that made me enter Aki's room when he was out and borrow his copy of *Crocodiles*. It wasn't as if he wouldn't have lent it to me, had I asked him – in fact, I took better care of my records than he did – but as with his previous obsessions, it didn't feel like I needed to have a view about Echo & the Bunnymen. It was music for older boys, and I would no sooner start writing their name on my rough book than start supporting his beloved Derby County.

So why did I keep coming back to this song?

> *The sky seems full*
> *When you're in the cradle*
> *The rain will fall*
> *And wash your dreams*
> *Stars are stars*
> *And they shine so hard*

Perhaps the more salient question is, 'Why wouldn't I?' I was obsessed with the future, terrified by its unknowability. Some people like to scroll through 'Where Are They Now?' clickbait listicles. In 1981, I was drifting off into anxious reveries wondering where we'll all be later. 'Stars Are Stars' offered a sad new twist on songs like XTC's 'Making Plans for Nigel', Martha and the Muffins' 'Echo Beach' and Talking Heads' 'Once in a Lifetime'. They were songs about settling for the life that's available rather than the life you longed for. But I'd never heard a song that asked, 'What happens if you get the thing you dream about? *What then?*'

> *I caught that falling star*
> *It cut my hands to pieces*

'Stars Are Stars' must have got Aki the same way because it was one of two Bunnymen songs that accrued more turntable miles than all their other songs. The other was their July single 'A Promise', an audacious bid for panoramic grandeur blown into the blue by a superhuman guitar display from Will Sergeant. It was good but I had limited use for it. 'Stars Are Stars', on the other hand, was very useful to me. At school I was unexceptional at every subject save for one: my ability to memorise words and their spellings and meanings allowed me to punch above my weight at English. One day, in lieu of a test, we were given free rein to write a story about whatever took our fancy. Basing my story on the lyrics of 'Stars Are Stars', I made up a parable about Ricky Talent, a rock star who succumbed to all the temptations that come with fame and wealth. I thought my *coup de grâce* would be the conclusion in which, having exhausted the goodwill of his record label and his friends, Ricky wrote and recorded one last song and left it on a cassette before hanging himself. The words of the suicide note were also the lyrics of 'Stars Are Stars' – or, at least, as much of them as I could discern.

I'd thought long and hard before passing off the Bunnymen song as my own. By no means a wholly ungroovy man, the default outfit of my English teacher Mr Garbett was an autumnal ensemble of dark chocolate-brown corduroy jacket (with elbow patches), royal-green cords and a knitted tie. I spent an entire lesson sizing him up. I couldn't imagine him having bought any more recent record than Frankie Miller's 1978 hit 'Darling' – and, with this in mind, decided there was no way he could know that I wasn't really the author of Ricky Talent's dramatic swan song.

I was right. In a pre-Google world, there was no easy way for Mr Garbett to verify my outrageous deception. But he knew. *Of course he knew.* The cover of my exercise book had a giant drawing of Snoopy on its inside cover, next to another one of Nookie Bear, recalcitrant furry foil to TV ventriloquist Roger De Courcey. Elsewhere were other key indications that I wouldn't be accelerating towards any state of poetic precocity any time soon. On my pencil case, I had written my address which, instead of stopping at my postcode, went on to say, 'UNITED KINGDOM, EUROPE, THE WORLD, THE SOLAR SYSTEM, THE UNIVERSE, INFINITY', yet another giveaway sign that we weren't in the presence of a young Coleridge. Were further confirmation required, Mr Garbett would have only needed to unzip the pencil case and examine the two halves of what was once a Helix Shatterproof ruler – bent into two in a bid to 'prove' its inventor wrong. On one half of the ruler, you could make out the letters, 'O O O O O O' drawn on in a metallic marker, while on the other, you could see the letters, 'K A A A A A Y ! ! !' – a reference to Lenny Henry's affable Rastafarian alter ego Algernon Razzamatazz, whose single 'The (Algernon Wants You to Say) Okay Song', I'd recently picked up from the 15p last-chance saloon box at Easy Listening.

And while Mr Garbett was unable to complete a successful investigation of the disjuncture between Ricky Talent's poignant adieu to the world on the final page of my English book and the satanic cockeyed glare of Roger De Courcey's potty-mouthed bear on the adjacent flap, he stopped short of giving me the benefit of the doubt. 'Disappointed,' he wrote in the margin, '5/10'. I didn't dare contest it.

As soon as Aki had finished his O levels, an altogether different sound could be heard emerging from his room. For a few weeks, he suddenly had no need of The Teardrop Explodes or the Bunnymen. Save for the occasional airing of a UK Subs or Ruts single, punk was all but a dot in the rear-view mirror of his early adolescence. Something else was needed for the summer, and on the day of his final paper, I was called upon to expedite it.

We had both sat up and taken notice of north London Brit-funk duo Linx with the release of their second single 'Intuition' in March 1980, and although the song was great, the part that the video had to play couldn't be underestimated. In it, we saw a child constantly being thwarted in various acts of minor naughtiness by his mother who perpetually knows what he's about to get up to. Aki and I saw something in the disparity between the mannerisms of the voluptuous West Indian mother and those of the boy who – had he been wearing a different uniform – could have stepped out of the school gates at Yardleys. She was clearly from far away; he clearly wasn't. And that difference was accentuated by the song which was steeped in influences from far away, yet sounded absolutely like the work of musicians who had grown up right here. Back then, I wouldn't have been able to put my finger on the reason why and I'm not entirely sure what it is now. It might have been something to do with the pay-off line of the chorus – 'Intuition!' – which briefly made the song sound like the theme to an eponymously named children's TV sitcom, possibly a *Rentaghost* spin-off centred around a psychic mum who always knows when her kids are about to get into scrapes.

So when it transpired that, on 15 June 1981, the two main guys in Linx, singer David Grant and bassist Peter 'Sketch' Martin, were in Birmingham to sign copies of their new album *Go Ahead*, Aki immediately declared his interest. He *really* wanted a signed copy of *Go Ahead* but he also *really* needed to be physically present for his biology CSE paper. Could I perhaps find a reason to bunk off school and get it for him? He handed me that week's *Record Mirror*. On the back cover was a full-page ad for the record with the times and locations of the shops where Linx would be signing records. They'd be in the Birmingham New Street branch of HMV at 2 p.m. To get there, I'd have to find a reason to skip school in the afternoon, and then finagle a means of getting to HMV without my parents knowing – or, the more likely option, contrive a situation which necessitated an immediate journey into town. Of course, I didn't *have* to do any of this, but by the same token, it was the most important job with which Aki had entrusted me since 1977 – ever since I agreed to walk around the corner to Marcus's house and break my three-year silence.

In most respects, we were like any two brothers. We competed with each other and we fought over the tiniest things. But when he asked me to do something that mattered to him, it felt good to oblige. So I formulated a plan, the efficacy of which rested on the gullibility of the teacher responsible for us in the period prior to dinner. Thankfully, the biology department's newest recruit – perpetually pink-faced pushover Miss Ross – offered no real resistance. As she handed out our exercise books with just-marked homework, I pulled out my handkerchief and clamped it over my mouth.

'Miss! I feel sick!'

I was released immediately into the empty corridors of the school. I didn't actually need to use the toilet, but I got so caught up in my own lie that I just ended up there, staring at the wall which was lined on one side with about fifteen urinals and, on the other, about the same number of sinks. That said, the toilets had a crucial part to play in the fib that would hopefully enable me to get Aki's record. In the story I would tell my mum, this would be where, bent double in a toilet where the lock had broken, dealing with chronic diarrhoea, I leaned forward to fashion a makeshift lock with my school tie. Then, flustered by the dramatic evacuation of my insides, I ran away before anyone could come in and see where the smell came from – unfortunately leaving the tie there as I did so.

Thirty minutes later I was at home, relaying the entire fabrication over the phone to my mum who was in the shop trying to slice the last of the fresh fish before opening time. My relief at her understanding response to the loss of the tie (which I just threw in a bin on the way home) was tempered by guilt over my slightly cunty behaviour, which in turn was offset by the giddy frisson of telling a lie which might result in me being in a record shop while the rest of 1A were sitting in Geography learning about the irrigation of paddy fields. At the same time, it was important not to get too ahead of myself.

'Is your tummy still bad?' my mum asked.

'I think it's all out now. I could *try* and go back to school, but . . .'

'No. It's OK. Once the shop's open, I can come back. Monday lunchtimes are quiet. Your father will be fine.'

I turned on the TV and destroyed asteroids on the Atari while I waited for her. The moment I heard her key in the lock, I turned off the TV and moved to the sofa onto which I'd artfully scattered exercise books and pens to give the impression that it would take more than a dicky tummy to throw me off course in my scholarly pursuits. My mum did what she always did when I had an upset stomach. She unscrewed a jar of dried camomile flowers and strained them in hot water, adding a teaspoon of honey. I drank it all and told her I was definitely feeling better.

'Well, I'm home now. What do you want to do?'

'I guess we could get the bus into town and see if we could get a replacement tie. I won't be allowed back in school without one.'

Inwardly, I punched the air when she agreed. But I needed to make sure I didn't get too complacent about my prospects of success. The shop that sold the ties was directly across the road from the bus stop. Once we were in town, I needed to contrive a reason to detour past HMV which was about 300 metres around the corner. By the time we sorted out the tie situation, there were ten minutes remaining before Linx were due to sign their first record. I couldn't work out what was making me more nervous: the possibility of falling at the final hurdle or the prospect of meeting someone famous.

'Do we have to go back straight away?' I asked my mum.

'Well, your father will probably be having his afternoon nap if we go back now, so we should stay out for another half an hour if you're well enough.'

'I've just remembered. I need some pencils!' I said. 'From the art shop. Art pencils!' I said this knowing that we wouldn't get as far as the art shop because HMV was en route to the art shop. The moment we turned the corner onto New Street and saw the queue stretching forty yards along the road towards the Odeon cinema, a new confidence surged through me. With one more lie, I might finally have two more autographs to add to that of the mysterious Tony Telfer.

'Look at that!' I said.

'What is it?' replied my mum.

'I don't know. Shall we go in?'

We advanced fifty more yards before I allowed sheer excitement to overcome me. It wasn't difficult. I was merely expressing what I was now feeling, and she could see that. 'They're actually here! That's Linx! They're *really* famous. Can we see?'

If my mum possessed the same powers of cognition as the mum in the video for 'Intuition', she was doing a good job of hiding them. She didn't seem to suspect a thing. Instead, she pulled out her purse and counted out what money she had remaining for the rest of the week. Of course, Aki had given me the money for the record, but I couldn't tell her that.

'It's OK. I've still got some of my pocket money left,' I told her. 'I can pay for half of it.'

But swept up as she was by this cosmic confluence of improbables, she insisted that she pay for the whole thing. We had about twenty minutes before it was time to head back. Over the speakers, HMV were playing *Go Ahead*, the album I was about to buy. Linx's sonic default was right between funk and soul. As with 'Intuition' a few months before, all of it and none of it sounded American. A closer point of reference was 'Searching', the 1980 single by Italian disco-soul group Change which, by virtue of featuring him on lead vocal, launched the solo career of Luther Vandross. As with that song, everything on *Go Ahead* radiated funk heat, and yet there was no avoiding the light melancholy breeze that swept through almost every song. It sounded like a hurriedly recorded follow-up to a surprise success. And, in this instance, that was something that worked in its favour. A strange ambivalence characterised 'I Won't Play the Game', 'All My Yesterdays' and 'Tinsel Town (You Don't Fool Me)', songs that respectively addressed their protagonist's struggle to meet the expectations of people who purport to understand him, the realisation that fame replaces one sort of self-doubt with another, and the realisation that the place of the artist in the entertainment industry is closer to serf than lord.

At the age of eleven you no longer want people to think you're cute, but once in a while, when it works to your advantage, you'll relax the rules. It was clear to me, pushed up against the counter of HMV, record in hand, with about 150 adults behind me, that I probably did look quite cute at that precise moment. David Grant peered down his large, thick-rimmed glasses and, clocking me, gave me a smile that was somehow different to the one he'd given to everyone else. 'Sketch!' he said, turning to his bassist, who was adding his signature to the previous customer's album. 'Look at this guy!'

Sketch gazed over at me and flashed me a smile. Sketch didn't smile much in the videos and on *Top of the Pops*, so that felt especially good.

'Are you here on your own?' asked David. I nodded and smiled. 'Haven't you got school today?' he added.

'Kind of,' I said. 'But my mum knows I'm here.'

I'm not sure if David Grant believed me, but I didn't care. 'Well, thank you so much for buying our album. It means a lot to us. How old are you?'

'I'm twelve next month,' I told him.

'What's your name?'

I suddenly realised that I couldn't give a different name to Aki, because it was Aki's album I was here to get signed.

'It's Aki!' I said. In my right hand was the autograph book with Tony Telfer's name in it. In that moment, I realised I couldn't hand it over because they'd sign it to Aki as well – and besides, if my mum caught sight of the book, she'd know that coming here had been my plan all along. I quickly shoved it in my pocket as David Grant extended a friendly right hand in my direction. With his left hand, he gave the record to Sketch. 'He's called Aki,' said David Grant.

'How do you spell that?' said Sketch.

'Oh, it's just Aki. A-K-I.'

'Well . . . *Aki*. I hope you like our record. Come and see us in concert!'

Back home, Aki wanted to know everything they had said and done, especially Sketch. Aki liked bassists, or at the very least, he liked the nonchalant ones. Over the next three years, before finally buying his first bass guitar, I'd see him fanboying over Washington from Wah!, Adam Clayton from U2 and Peter Hook from New Order. Beyond emulating their hairstyles, he couldn't imagine himself being any of the singers standing next to them – Pete Wylie, Bono and Bernard Sumner – but the statuesque diffidence of a certain sort of bassist, well, that was really just how Aki was anyway. All he needed to complete the look was a bass guitar. The only bassist that didn't impress him was Bruce Foxton, uptight Goose to Paul Weller's gum-chewing Maverick; Potsy to his Fonz. Other bassists looked like they were secretly running the whole show. Bruce never quite shook off the breathless gratitude of an earnest competition winner.

On the weeks when I appeared to be getting somewhere in the playground hierarchy, I felt quite a lot like Bruce. The transition from primary school to senior school was tougher for some than for others. If you had a clear sense of who you were, it helped immeasurably. There was a cluster of boys in my class who had all attended the same primary school and, as such, didn't need to expand their peer group.

I remember the emotion I felt when I gazed over at them. It was envy, but I couldn't admit that to myself at the time. So I had to think of other reasons I didn't like them. I decided they thought they were superior to everyone else and that I didn't want to be friends with them anyway. Terry Violett, bomber-jacket clad cock of the walk, liked me sometimes, but if, for whatever reason, you did something to attract ridicule – being seen to suck up to teachers; being too embarrassed to run through the shower without your underpants;

grassing someone up; being collected at the school gates by your mum; having your hair cut so that it looked like a vagina – then even the most basic freedoms and privileges were withdrawn. Sometime towards the end of the school year, during a swimming lesson, it was finally my turn. In order to determine who got to advance onto the big pool, we were all asked to swim a length. If you made it to the end without your feet touching the ground, then you were free to move up. I only knew one stroke, but I figured it didn't matter. With the rest of my class watching, I lowered myself in and doggy-paddled all the way to the other side.

The first day of relentless barking and yapping whenever I walked into the playground or classroom was tolerable; the second, third and fourth, less so. In physics, I was asked a question in front of the rest of the class, and when I got it right, Terry piped up, 'Give him a Scooby Snack!' The entire class erupted with laughter and, even now, as I recall it, I'm smiling too. Even with the hindsight of four decades, it's hard to tell if the days of sitting alone in the dinner hall while neighbouring tables barked at me were character-building. But after a while it was almost impossible to affect the requisite indifference to that sort of unrelenting derision. To let slip the merest hint of impatience with the taunts would be to succumb to a rain of dead legs or have your tormenter suddenly square up to you and ask you if you wanted to settle the issue with fists. By Wednesday, most of the teachers seemed to know. And finally, when I saw William Osborne gaze across from the entrance leading to the adjacent classroom and silently clock what was happening, it merely underlined the disparity in our experiences of that year. I didn't expect him to leap to my defence, and he knew that. I didn't want to risk him being ostracised for my sake, and he knew that too.

These periods of isolation were typically over within a week. Usually the arrival of the weekend would wipe the slate clean in time for Monday. A few days of normality would ensue before it was some other poor sod's turn. I can't remember what transgression had led Henry Bannatyne to receive his week of persecution. Within a day or two, it had stopped being specific and descended into general abuse and ridicule. No one deserved this sort of treatment, especially not him. He was slight and cheeky, a comfortable beta, happier to goof around on the periphery than jockey for seniority. His mother was Trinidadian and very beautiful; his dad was British with red hair and a beard. Henry had inherited his mum's colouring and his dad's freckles. One Saturday morning in May, he and I had caught the bus into town to spend some of our pocket money on records. It was the first time I'd been allowed to venture into the city centre without an adult. We found a record stall in the Bull Ring indoor market which sold ex-chart singles for 40p. I bought '(Somebody) Help Me Out', a massed-ranks hard luck *cri de coeur* from London jazz-funk collective Beggar & Co, 'Rapture' by Blondie and 'Good Thing Going', the sole UK hit by reggae star Sugar Minott. Henry bought 'I Missed Again' by Phil Collins and 'Skateaway' by Dire Straits. Sophisticated purchases for a twelve-year-old.

I wonder if I would even remember that morning were it not for what happened in the final week of the school year, when Henry found himself attempting to withstand the harassment of his classmates.

This is what I do remember though.

We're all sitting on the long wooden benches in the gym. We're waiting to be summoned by Mr Nash, the PE teacher, to vault the hobby horse. Terry Violett is asking Henry Bannatyne where his parents are from. Henry is pretending not to hear him. Someone else asks him, that bit louder and more forcefully. Henry tells them.

Someone shouts 'Half-caste'. Someone else, trying to outdo them, shouts 'Mongrel'. Then Terry, amused that he's created this one all by himself, calls out 'Half-breed!'

Henry looks at me. I make no attempt to stick out from the pack.

'Half-breed!' I call out too. Terry and I lead the chorus. Soon, everyone's doing it. Not just that day, but the following day and the day after that.

Half-breed.

The third day, I look at Henry Bannatyne, momentarily hoping that this moment will pass and that further down the line, we can be good again. He momentarily catches my eye and turns away. It's the last day of term. The bell rings and we go off to our respective houses. How guilty do I feel? I simply choose to tell myself that everything will be OK. He knows I'm not a racist. How could I be a racist? He was with me when I bought the Sugar Minott and Beggar & Co records.

But. But . . . *Half-breed.*

A few weeks earlier, in physics, we learned about mercury. Our teacher, Mr Tuft, brought out a bowl of the stuff. A liquid metal! Who knew such a thing existed! He told us about the uses of mercury and about how, if it was ingested, it was impossible to expel from the human body. It slowly drives you nuts.

Half-breed.

For a week or so, I didn't think about that moment when Henry Bannatyne and I exchanged glances. But, like mercury, that word – with its hideous, subhuman connotations, travelled through my system, lodging itself in my brain. In a flash, I had sold out my friendship with him in order to gain favour with a group of kids who could and would turn on me in an instant, just like they had done weeks before.

Half-breed.

Maybe, he'd forgotten about the whole thing. Maybe it was fine. After all, when the new term began and the hard kids had also put it behind them, Henry Bannatyne was hardly going to freeze them out, was he? So why would he commit to the double standard of freezing me out?

Half-breed.

Because, of course, he knew exactly what the game was with those boys. We all did. We knew they would say anything to you, no matter how hurtful, if it stood a chance of getting the desired reaction. You didn't look to the hard kids for moral consistency. But I wasn't one of those kids.

Half-breed.

In the final fortnight of July, I wondered if I could contrive a reason to see him. I looked for his address in the phone directory and somehow, among all the other Bannatynes, found it. Even though it was a Wednesday, everyone had a day off because Lady Diana Spencer and Prince Charles were getting married today. In Overlea Avenue, preparations were being made for a street party. It had been Mr and Mrs Hughes's idea. If we all cooked one thing and provided a drink, Tim's band could do a gig. We'd play some games. And when the ceremony actually took place, we could run inside someone's house to watch it.

After breakfast, I made the twenty-minute walk to Henry Bannatyne's house. His mother opened the door.

'Hello Mrs Bannatyne. We're having a party in my road for the royal wedding and I was wondering if Henry would like to come.'

'Sorry,' she said, 'Henry's busy today.'

We never spoke again. I decided that if I were him, I wouldn't want to talk to me either. So I simply didn't approach him. Even on weeks when our classmates turned on us once again, we didn't join in. I wanted him to rip me to shreds. Instead, he pretended I didn't exist. And somehow, that was the worst thing of all.

CHAPTER 23

Since Ged's brother Tim had qualified to become a teacher, it had been harder to set aside rehearsal time for the Jackets. He and his best friend, John, had formed the band while still learning to play as schoolchildren. While Tim went through the education system and on to teacher-training college, John had taken a little longer to work out what he wanted to do. Sometimes, walking through the centre of Acocks Green, I'd see John busking outside Don Miller's Hot Bread Kitchen. I never quite knew what to do when I saw him. The only other busker I'd spoken to was Tony Telfer and, well, actually, I hadn't even spoken to him. I had just nodded while he told me I had a cool name and signed my book. But that was different because Tony Telfer was famous – or, at least, I believed he was. And besides, I didn't know him outside of his impromptu performance at the Great Western Fish Bar – a show which, in my mind, had become as mythical as Johnny Cash's visit to Folsom Prison.

But with John, it was different. I'd sometimes see him rehearsing in the front room of 12 Overlea Avenue with the other Jackets. That seemed cool and glamorous to me. By contrast, sitting outside Don Miller's Hot Bread Kitchen in a Budgie jacket, with your guitar case open for people to throw in loose change – that looked a lot like begging to me. And so, as a consequence, I thought I was probably sparing him a modicum of embarrassment by walking straight past him.

On the day of the royal wedding though, he looked like a rock star again. He and Tim moved their amps from the back seat of Tim's Ford Escort and into the turning circle of Overlea Avenue. Microphone stands had been procured from somewhere and a drum kit was already set up. Tim's new responsibilities at school may have robbed the Jackets of rehearsal time, but in other ways, they provided fresh inspiration. After a brief period being called Canoe and then Kayak, a minor incident involving one of his pupils and a box of Tic Tacs prompted one final name change. It was Ged who relayed the news to me.

'When are Kayak on?' I asked her.

'Oh, they're not called Kayak any more, Takis. They've changed their name again.'

'What are they called now?'

'Well, there's a boy in one of the classes that Tim teaches. He's called Jon Zaib.' Ged pronounced it so that it rhymed with 'tribe', but she made a point of spelling it out for me. 'Z-A-I-B. Zaib! Isn't that a cool name?'

I nodded. It *was* a cool name. Anyone could see that.

'Anyway, one day, Jon Zaib brought some Tic Tacs into class and Tim caught him eating them. So he confiscated them. Then it occurred to him that Jon Zaib's Tic Tacs would be a good name for a band, but on the way home, he realised that it would be even better if it was Jon Zaib's *Tactics*! Then he made Jon Zaib all one word. So now it's *Jonzaib's* Tactics! What do you think, Takis? Jonzaib's Tactics! I think it's great. Don't you? I can picture it on a poster. Can *you* picture it on a poster, Takis?'

I *could* picture it on a poster. Just as 'The Jackets' called to mind the denim-clad authenticity of seventies pub rock, Jonzaib's Tactics had a certain edgy angularity that acknowledged we were living in a post-new wave world. Admittedly, their music hadn't changed, but that was just as well. The residents of Overlea Avenue were far likelier to nod their heads to a solid set of canonical rock classics – in this case, 'Virginia Plain', 'Me and Julio Down by the Schoolyard', 'Please Please Me' and 'Stuck in the Middle with You' – than edgy new wave angularity. Our older neighbours sat on chairs at the end of their gardens and clapped politely at the end of each song. I placed myself next to Ged, Emily and Aki on the low wall of the Mays' front garden. With the exception of Aki, who was too cool to raise his voice, we over-cheered to compensate for the sluggish levels of engagement in most of the other front gardens.

By far the most effusive of all the parents was Mrs Hughes, who had never sat through an entire set by the Jackets/Canoe/Kayak/Jonzaib's Tactics. Halfway through 'Me and Julio Down by the Schoolyard', she advanced towards us with a plate of cucumber sandwiches – with the crusts off, of course, as befitted such a momentous day – and exclaimed, 'They're awfully talented, aren't they?' At the end of the final song 'The Jean Genie', Tim leaned into the microphone and told us we'd really been a smashing audience. The silence that remained after the applause subsided was reminiscent of the bathwater after the last of the Matey bubbles have popped. In that moment, you remembered what an unusual thing it is to see people you know burst into song and just keep singing for several minutes while you watch. But it was that silence in particular between stopping and packing up their equipment that made it seem strange. When you see a professional band in concert, they have roadies to clear everything away. That means the musicians can disappear and maintain the illusion of being superhuman. At the Overlea Avenue street party to celebrate the wedding of Lady Di and Prince Charles, this option was not available to Jonzaib's Tactics.

That summer was also memorable because I immersed myself once again in comics. Having scaled new peaks of self-administered terror by reading *The Amityville Horror* and wondering if I might also get up and draw the curtains before bedtime only to see a glowing pair of red pig eyes staring back at me, I fell back on one of the other occasional hobbies that had helped make the school holidays pass more quickly. With no restrictions on the amount of chip paper available to me, I would take eight sheets and fold them in half, pressing as hard as I could down on the fold. Then I'd take a knife from the kitchen drawer and run it along the inside of the fold. Now that eight pieces of paper had become sixteen, I made another fold, and eight pieces of chip paper had become thirty-two empty pages, which I would set about turning into a comic.

In my imagination, '5-Star Fun' was a sort of outsider rival to *Whizzer and Chips*, *Whoopee!* and *Buster*, the three longest-running of the Saturday morning comics published by IPC – groovier johnny-come-lately titles that gave fusty *Beano* and *Dandy* publishers DC Thomson a run for their money. Every hand-drawn issue of '5-Star Fun' I put together was a reaffirmation of my faith in a world where people exclaimed 'Yaroo!' when someone kicked them up the arse; a world where dogs were constantly running off with strings of sausages in their mouths; a world in which you uttered nothing stronger than 'Bah! Foiled! when your plans were frustrated; a world in which people still hadn't learned that it never ends well when you leave a pie to cool on a windowsill.

You didn't need to drill too deep down to guess what inspired some of the 'regular' strips in '5-Star Fun'. Just as *The Beano* had the Bash Street Kids and *Krazy Comic* had the Krazy Gang, '5-Star Fun' had the Brum Bunch, a group of five children, each with a defining character trait, that got up to capers of one sort of another. Ed Case was a conflation of Terry Violett and Suggs from Madness, the madcap de facto gang leader who would do anything for a laugh: applying superglue to his dad's favourite chair; attaching a load of tin cans to the maths teacher's car and writing 'JUST MARRIED' on the back of it. Also in the gang were a punk rocker with green hair called Punky and, in a similar spirit of literalism, Sporty, Brains and a robot called Robot. There was one other member in this gang, but he didn't have a defining trait. He was just a sort of normal everyman sort of a kid, with normal hair, normal trousers and a normal jumper, who seemed sensible and popular and never made a fool of himself and sometimes said funny or wise things that consolidated the respect of the rest of the Brum Bunch. He was called Pete.

In keeping with a long-established convention in other comics ('Strange Hill', 'J.R. – Junior Rotter', 'The Incredible Sulk'), I also had characters whose entire existence hinged on the fact that their name was a pun on another well-known character. This pun determined the defining character trait of the character. So, you had Giggles, who was a pilot a bit like Biggles, but he would get into situations which could invariably only be resolved by having him take to the skies and spell out some sort of vapour trail message or punchline; and the Funz, who was like the Fonz but more fun. And then there was also Boney M who, as well as sharing his name with a well-known pop group, was a cop who also happened to be a skeleton and could therefore dissemble himself in order to get into places that other cops might struggle to enter.

A constant source of inspiration at this time was Denis Gifford's hardback history of British comics, *Happy Days: A Century of British Comics*. Until June, I had renewed it from Acocks Green library for every month that year. Walking down from Overlea Avenue with my little cardboard wallet of blue library cards (each tucked into the other), I left it on a pile of books to be cleared for renewal while I hurried over to the paranormal shelf about twelve feet away to see if any new ghost books had arrived. I didn't even make it over there before the silence was broken by a loud 'Excuse me!' I turned around to see if it was directed at me and saw a cheerful young female librarian waving the sole copy of the most recent '5-Star Fun' in the air. In less than a second, hot burning mortification rushed through me from the legs up and, when it reached my mouth, I stalled.

'Pardon?' I said. I could hear my own voice croaking. There were three or four people in the reading area. They had all looked up to see if it was them.

'This comic. Is it yours?' She held up the Denis Gifford book. 'I found it in here. I thought it might be yours.'

The thing about my comics was that I rarely showed them to anyone. Not Aki or Ged. They were older and they wouldn't understand. Not science-fiction loving William, who I thought would think less of me for doing them. As long as I kept them to myself, I could persist in the fantasy that they were comparable to those you saw in the shops. Besides, I was now twelve. Years previously, I'd come across a trade leaflet for the Fleetway titles in IPC's magazine roster – Fleetway was their comics division – and I had pinned it to my wall., Categorising all my favourite comics together with pictures of each title, it said that these titles were suitable for children aged between six and eleven, so I knew that I was getting a bit old for all this. And this, in that awful little moment, was probably what informed my response to the librarian.

'No. That's not mine.'

'Are you sure?' she asked incredulously.

'Yes,' I shrugged, belatedly attempting to affect a casual air. 'I've never seen it before.'

I hurry-walked out of the library, unable to manage the sense of humiliation – a feeling exacerbated to the point of unbearability by the fact that, even though I had left, the comic was still in that building. They might be looking at it RIGHT NOW. Pointing and laughing at my stupid drawings of the Brum Bunch, Giggles and the Funz. The thought was almost too much to handle. But, of course, I had told them it wasn't mine. What was I going to do? Make it worse by going back and telling them that, actually, it was? That it was the work of my younger brother who is definitely *not* too old to be getting excited about buying *Whizzer and Chips* on a Saturday morning? I couldn't do a thing.

The following Saturday came and went. For the first time, I didn't buy any comics.

And then, a couple of weeks later, when the urge to turn empty chip paper into reading matter overcame me, it was time for the grand launch of a brand-new title.

Aki was now regularly bringing music papers into the house. Sometimes he'd get *NME*, *Sounds* or *Melody Maker*, but never more than one or two of them on any given week. *Record Mirror*, on the other hand, was a regular presence in his school bag on a Thursday. Unlike the other titles, *Record Mirror* had a colour cover and seemed happy to include pop and disco alongside punk and metal in its remit. It had a gossip column written by Paula Yates and colour posters of exciting new pop stars like Kim Wilde and the Human League. If Aki was otherwise engaged, I'd go into the hallway, unzip his bag, and bring the latest *Record Mirror* to our chocolate Dralon corner unit, stopping only to pull out a Banjo bar from the cupboard where we kept the treats. Then I'd sink into the cushions and look for my two favourite sections.

The first was easy enough to locate because it was always in the same place. At the very back of *Record Mirror* was 'Chart File', which featured several weekly charts. They were all interesting to me, but the big one, of course, was the official British singles chart. Other magazines had charts, but only two publications printed the entire Top 75. One was the industry journal *Music Week*. It was sent directly to the record shops, who would pull out the centre spread featuring that week's Top 75 and place it in the countertop slipcase where customers could scan it and tell the assistant what record they were after. Given that you never saw *Music Week* on the shelf of your local newsagent's, *Record Mirror* was my only option when it came to minutely scrutinising the winners and losers over all 75 positions of this week's hit parade.

Once I'd wrung every drop of valuable information out of the charts, the next destination was the singles reviews. I think I figured out pretty quickly that, in any music paper, the review page was as much a showcase for the writer as a guide to what was out this week. The mixture of furrow-browed authority and downright rudeness was mildly intoxicating. It reminded me of the bit in defunct ATV talent show *New Faces* after another aspiring star did their turn and we'd see the judges impassively passing verdict on them. Week after week, I'd see Tony Hatch – writer of Petula Clark's 'Downtown' – and RAK Records supremo Mickie Most casually eviscerate some nervous magician in pastel-blue Terylene flares or a feather-haired David Cassidy lookalike seeking to snag two demographics at once by sitting at an upright piano and thundering through a gorblimey music hall carouse-along.

The job of being a reviewer in *Record Mirror* didn't seem to me so very different to that of Tony Hatch or Mickie Most. Or maybe like that of Mr Garbett when he casually deemed the rise and fall of Ricky Talent worth five marks out of ten. If you worked for *Record Mirror*, you could summarily dismiss the efforts of some hapless punk chancer or the debut solo venture of the bloke from Procol Harum in a manner so offhand that it was like you'd coughed it into a handkerchief. To a twelve-year-old squirt like me, that looked like real power. More than that, it looked like fun – 5-star fun.

Suddenly, I had an idea.

Wouldn't it be *ace* if there were a magazine that took the two best sections of the music papers – the charts and the reviews – and merged them into one unique section? For a few days, I sat on this thought like a chicken sits on an egg. And when it was time for the thought to hatch, out it came.

'POP SCENE'! A music magazine like no other! 'POP SCENE'! The only magazine that features the week's entire Top 75 AND an actual review of every single record in it! Yes! That's right! *Every record!* Counting from 75 down to 1! No one had attempted such a undertaking until now. Who would have been crazy enough to do such a thing? Or daring enough? No one, that's who! At least, not until now!

Roughly two days elapsed between this eureka moment and the execution of it. 'Pop Scene' was launched at around teatime on Saturday, 6 August. Above its hand-drawn logo was the word 'STATISTICS!' written in slightly smaller letters. Because, of course, when you're a twelve-year-old boy writing your own pop magazine on paper taken from your parents' chip shop, there are few more exciting things in the world than STATISTICS! Obviously, it was important to make 'Pop Scene' look as 'proper' as possible. I didn't have access to a printing press or typesetting facilities. I didn't even have transfer lettering. All I had to work with was chip paper, some pens, a ruler, a pair of scissors and some glue with which to stick pictures from other magazines into the pages of my publication.

I noticed that one thing that conferred extra propriety on a publication was the act of having recently swallowed up another title. So just as *Krazy* had been merged into *Whizzer and Chips*, and *Monster Fun* had been merged into *Buster*, I decided that 'Pop Scene' would incorporate (the hitherto nonexistent) 'Chartview'. As far as I know, this is the only time one magazine has joined forces with another from its very first issue.

Below the 'Pop Scene' logo, in my best lettering, were the details of the other things you could expect to find inside.

THE STUFF IN THE CHARTS

THE STARS ON 45 REVIEW

CHART PAGES

TALKING HEADS SENTASUPASPREAD!

NOT-QUITE-MADE-ITS

I surely can't have heard every single record in the Top 75, but looking at the yellowing pages of that first issue of 'Pop Scene' nearly four decades later, it's pretty clear to me that I'd heard a lot of them. Another thing that becomes clear is the degree to which I had attempted to assume the arms-folded, impress-me tone of the writers I'd been reading in *Record Mirror.* I had an idea in my head of what a music journalist should be like. The reviews in 'Pop Scene' would see me assume that persona, but to do so was a job akin to holding your stomach in. You could only do it for so long before having to relax into something more recognisable. The most noticeable casualties of my attempts to sound like a proper music writer were the futurist pace-setters now making frequent incursions into the top 40. I might have been taping Duran Duran, Spandau Ballet and Visage songs from Radio 1's Sunday evening chart rundown, but in my capacity as editor/chief writer of 'Pop Scene', I felt compelled to sound a note of disapproval. My 'Pop Scene' persona seemed to view the charts as a battleground between real and manufactured pop; between the authenticity of guitars and the fakeness of synths and drum machines – and it was pretty clear which side I was on. Writing about Depeche Mode's breakthrough hit 'New Life', I grudgingly conceded, 'It's a good sound but imagine seeing them in concert. It's just as lively as *Crossroads*. All the noises are made by a synthesiser.'

Partly because Antmania had now fully taken hold of Great Britain, making Adam Ant the sole property of schoolgirls, I'd now also cooled off on him and his band. Having entered the chart in May at number 1, 'Stand and Deliver' was now freefalling down the charts. In the privacy of my bedroom, I still played the cassette of *Kings of the Wild Frontier* recorded from Emily May's copy, but in public, I maintained a very different stance. A searing evisceration of his oeuvre continued at some length, but in a little box to the side, the twelve-year-old within could no longer be contained. 'He's bent!' it said.

Such unfortunate aberrations notwithstanding, I mostly managed to maintain the sniffy, supercilious tone I deemed essential to all rock criticism. Pondering Eddy Grant's descent to number 40 with 'I Love You, Yes I Love You', I sounded an ominous note of warning: 'Same ole Eddy and people are getting bored.' After an impressive run of hits such as 'Cool for Cats', 'Up the Junction' and 'Another Nail in My Heart', Squeeze – exponents of the sort of unshowy songcraft I held in high regard – were struggling to penetrate the top 40 with 'Tempted'. 'Squeeze have got two things other groups haven't got – Difford and Tilbrook,' I lamented, before concluding: 'Squeeze deserve more than they're getting.' I could perceive comparable depths to Bob Marley and the Wailers' posthumously released 'No Woman, No Cry', but this merely left me conflicted: 'Brought [sic] in honour of the reggae king's death. It's got feeling, a meaning. But I don't like it.'

With their monophonic synth-prodding, I might have disdained Depeche Mode, but in his own way, the all-conquering Shakin' Stevens seemed no less lazy to me. As Shaky gazed imperiously down from his perch at the apex of that week's Top 75 with 'Green Door', one lone, prepubescent Brummie voice of dissent could be heard: 'I like it, it's good, but it's just not right how he can pick one old song, sing it and sell it. How about some new stuff, Mr Stevens?' The same puritanism extended to pre-eminent medley-makers Starsound, who had the temerity to tackle my beloved ABBA with 'Stars on 45 Vol. 2': 'This ABBA medley is very good but I, being an ABBA fan, hate it. If you like people making money out of other people's songs, buy it.' Meanwhile, five places beneath it, at 14, sat the real ABBA, with their 12-inch-only club hit 'Lay All Your Love on Me': 'The best group the world has ever seen. The only group that can get in the top 10 on 12-inch singles at £1.99 each. Another outstanding ABBA song.'

Of course, I didn't want 'Pop Scene' to be a dictatorship. If you bought *The Beano*, you didn't expect the whole thing to be drawn by the guy who did Dennis the Menace. No, I needed staff. Other views needed to be heard, even if they didn't concur with mine. I started with Aki, giving him dominion over the 'Not-Quite-Made-Its' section. As Aki set about writing his reviews, I detached the blank page on which I wanted Ged to write her section and rang her doorbell.

Bink-bonk.

'Hi Takis! What are you up to?'

'I'm doing a new magazine. It's about music.'

'What happened to your comic?'

'Oh, that's . . . I'm not doing comics any more.'

'That's a shame. What's this one, then?'

'"Pop Scene".'

I held up 'Pop Scene' so she could have a good look at it. 'That's not all of it,' I explained. 'Aki's writing his bit now. But could you write something for it as well?'

'You want me to write something? Yeah. Sure. I'll write something. What do you want me to do?'

'Can you do LP reviews? I've done the singles, but we need some LP reviews.' (Note 'we' – there was no 'we', just me, but it sounded better).

Ged had been raving about the new Joe Jackson album a few days previously, so I wasn't altogether surprised when she told me that was what she wanted to write about. Of course, I was just thrilled that she'd agreed to write anything at all.

'I'll do it now if you like!'

She beckoned me into the house and put the record on the turntable. I remember looking at the sleeve and being impressed that there was a song called 'What's the Use of Getting Sober (When You're Gonna Get Drunk Again)'. That was a funny thing to call a song. By the end of the first track 'Jumpin' with Symphony Sid', Ged handed her article back to me:

'Joe has really changed his image from his attempts at Rock 'n'

Roll. It seems that he recorded this album for sheer pleasure. This appreciation for jazz goes back a long way as he says on the album cover. Jazz was not respectable when his father was young, and so this [is an] attempt at reviving the old favourites of his father.'

For his contribution, Aki wasted no time in testing the limits of his editorial freedom, savaging the new release by one of the editor's favourite bands. Racey were a group to whom I continued to show militant loyalty, in spite of the fact that their hit-making days were fast shrinking in the rear-view mirror and literally everyone I knew found them musically and visually ridiculous. As someone who was also musically and visually ridiculous, this marginalisation merely strengthened the bond between me and Racey. If you slighted Racey, you slighted me. As such, Aki's review of their new single 'Shame' was a bitter pill to swallow: 'I heard this record was used in a geriatric ward to wake the patients,' he wrote. 'No, it's not that bad. It's even worse, but the B-side's good (or so the poxy little wanky ed tells me – not really!! (I mean about the ed)).' Summoning all the maturity available to me, I let it pass. Besides, I knew the chances of getting him to write the page out again, omitting the Racey review, were negligible. So I let it stand, alongside his reviews of Echo & the Bunnymen's 'Crocodiles' ('wonderful'), The Teardrop Explodes' 'When I Dream' ('TRULY WONDERFUL!!!!') and the Ruts' 'West One (Shine on Me)' ('very brill indeed').

I was pretty happy with the inaugural 'Pop Scene'. If I'd accidentally left *this* in the library, I wouldn't have disowned it on the spot. The only problem was that, by the time I'd finished work on it, a new chart was about to appear. The Sisyphean nature of the task I'd set myself suddenly dawned upon me. Actually, that wasn't the only problem. There was also the fact that the Top 75 doesn't change much from week to week. Having reviewed every song in it, I couldn't very well do it all over again. So it became clear to me that if 'Pop

Scene' was to continue, it had to go from weekly to monthly to allow sufficient new songs to enter the chart.

Alas, with the advent of the new school year, I didn't have time to put together a second issue of 'Pop Scene'. When I had last departed the gates of Yardleys School, I was still eleven. But eleven's no age – not really. It's just one more than ten, and ten is a junior-school age. But when you're twelve, you're in your thirteenth year on the planet. You're practically a *teenager*. I needed to reinvent myself a little bit. Well, really, I had already started the process. I'd stopped buying comics and was now allowed to get the bus into town all by myself. Three days before the start of term, I even persuaded my parents to let me go into town *at night*, having redeemed a coupon from the *Evening Mail* which enabled two readers to go and see the flop 1980 remake of *The Jazz Singer* starring Neil Diamond and Laurence Olivier. Finding someone to come with me wasn't easy, but after Ged, Aki and William Osborne all declined, I called Vijay – Vijay who had made me my first chapati five years previously; who recited the Player's cigarettes rhyme for me when I was still mute; Vijay whose family still ran the grocery down the road from our first shop. With both parents working full-time and his cousin Ashok an hour-long ride away in Aston, Vijay had been a confident Midlands-wide bus user since he was seven. And although he had no idea what film I was asking him to see, he clearly had nothing better planned on the final Monday night of August.

And on what basis did I want to go and see *The Jazz Singer*? Barely any, really. My knowledge of the film began and ended with 'Love on the Rocks', which had just scraped into the top 20 a year previously. But the days were long, video recorders had yet to become affordable and there was only so much pogo stick action to sustain you through a summer's evening. So here we were walking out of the fading summer light and onto the balcony of the Birmingham Odeon, our vouchers entitling us to one drink each, along with our ticket. In what might have been the least successful promotional offer in the history of the *Evening Mail*, there were perhaps six or seven other people in the entire cinema – a cinema that, prior to its mid-eighties multiplex overhaul, seated 2,439 people.

Nearly twenty years later, I took my mum to the Odeon in Leicester Square to see *My Big Fat Greek Wedding*. What was intended as a treat for her – a trip into the West End to see a light-hearted comedy about a Greek woman who marries an American guy – took an unexpectedly dark turn in the final twenty minutes of the film. In *My Big Fat Greek Wedding*, the American finally capitulates to the demands of his wife and her family, converts to the Greek Orthodox faith and moves next door to his in-laws. My tearful mum left the cinema comparing this outcome to the real-life one in the equivalent arc of her own children – both of whom settled down with British women, neither of whom felt the need to move next door or change their religion.

In its own way, *The Jazz Singer* also presented me with uncomfortable real-life resonances. Like Neil Diamond's character in the film, I'd been born to immigrants and been pulled away from their culture by the pop music of the country in which I was growing up. Like Neil too, I had also chosen to anglicise my name. To his friends, Yussel Rabinovitch was Jess Robin. The opening five minutes of the film set out the tensions at the heart of Jess's dilemma. They started with Neil/Yussel/Jess in a synagogue and ended showing him with brown face paint and an Afro wig, singing alongside three members of a soul group called the Four Brothers. When a member of the audience realises the singer is a white guy standing in for an absent band member, a riot ends in the arrest of all four musicians and Neil/Yussel/Jess's rabbi father (Sir Laurence Olivier) turning up to bail them out. At this point, we're also treated to the best line in the entire film. As his still blacked-up son walks from the cell towards him, Olivier asks, 'It's not tough enough being a Jew?' Like Neil/

Yussel/Jess, I was also nuts about almost any music other than the stuff my parents listened to. And like Neil/Yussel/Jess, I couldn't envisage any harmonious middle ground between what I wanted and what I knew they wanted for me.

Occasionally, we'd go to Greek-Cypriot weddings and our parents would tell Aki and me about the bride and groom: what villages their parents were from; which chip shop they ran; how they'd met. If the backstories of these Greek-Cypriot romances all tended to follow a similar pattern, that was because the element of happenstance present in most love stories was invariably lacking. Marriage, we were repeatedly told, wasn't typically a union of husband and wife. It was a union of family and family. So it was important that there was a measure of inter-familial compatibility. To which end, this was what usually happened: if there was a family you knew and liked, and they had a daughter who was roughly the same age as your son, you would arrange a get-together, perhaps dinner at one of your houses and, assuming they didn't already know each other, the prospective couple would be introduced. If they were amenable to the idea, they might then go on a date – and things would proceed from there.

'But that's *arranged marriage!*' I exclaimed, a charge which they vehemently denied. As far as they were concerned, it wasn't *at all* like an arranged marriage, because no one was *forcing* you to marry anyone. If you went on a date and it didn't work out, then that was the end of that. The search would merely continue, and they'd see if there were any other families with children who might make a good match.

They were more right than wrong. It wasn't the sort of arranged marriage to which children growing up in Sikh families had to commit. No one was going to force me to marry anyone I didn't want to marry. But in the moments when it wasn't enough to just talk about records and what was on telly, Aki and I spoke about it and struggled to even get our heads around the idea that you could fancy someone who had been pre-approved by your mum and dad.

For Vijay, sitting next to me in the empty Odeon, that had never been an issue. And in a way, I envied him for that. His family was the happiest family I knew. Their approach to their life together was a bit like that of the Dutch football team of the seventies. With the exception of the goalkeeper, Holland played in a perpetually fluid formation, swapping positions as and when their situation demanded it. Sometimes Vijay would be at the till serving a customer. Sometimes he'd be minding a younger sibling. Or, of course, making a chapati. The same applied to all of Vijay's family with the exception of Mr Singh (perhaps then, he was the goalkeeper in this analogy) whose long hours at the bread factory took up most of his days. Their collective identity had solidified in a way that hadn't quite happened with us. Whenever I asked Vijay about arranged marriage, he did so in a manner that clearly indicated that any other sort of matrimony simply didn't interest him. And why would it? His parents adored each other. Why deviate from a proven formula?

When Vijay talked about being a Sikh, he didn't say 'I' – he said 'we'. I noticed that when I talked about being Greek, I didn't say 'we' – I said 'Greeks', as if I didn't quite know whether or not I was one of them. *The Jazz Singer* that Vijay would have watched was probably a very different one to mine. Perhaps he would have felt a benign sort of pity for Neil Diamond's character as he defied his father's wishes, leaving his Jewish wife behind as he did so, in favour of Los Angeles and a shot at becoming a recording artist.

And me? I was just rooting for Jess. When, in the final five minutes of the film, we saw his father rise from his seat and clap along as Jess – yes, Jess, not Yussel – sang 'America' to a packed stadium, it was only the fact that the Birmingham Odeon wasn't totally empty that stopped me from doing the same.

CHAPTER 24

Garry Birtles. No one ever mentions Garry Birtles now. But by the summer of 1981, all of Britain was gripped by the plight of Garry Birtles. In 1977, Nottingham Forest manager Brian Clough had plucked Birtles from obscurity – or, to be precise, Chilwell, where he was employed as a carpet fitter and, following a tip-off, invited him to train with the Forest squad. Birtles went from playing part time for Long Eaton United in Derbyshire to the starting eleven of a team that had just fended off competition from Liverpool and Everton to come top of the English football league. His rise to glory had a dreamlike quality that seemed to defy all reason. In his first full season, he scored fourteen goals – an excellent return from thirty-five games, and another six en route to hitherto unthinkable glory, beating FC Malmo in the European Cup final. The following season, he helped Forest to do it all over again. But, of course, the more surreal the dream, the ruder the awakening. Manchester United smashed their own transfer record – £1.25 million! – to sign Birtles. There had been a Roy of the Rovers quality to Birtles's career up to that point. After that, however, it all went a bit Charlie Brown for him.

With hindsight, there was a certain inevitability about it all. At this point in their history, Manchester United had become something of a Charlie Brown team with a Charlie Brown manager. From the moment he signed the contract, it was as though they'd contaminated poor Garry. Under the management of honest-to-goodness

Dave Sexton, the closest they came to winning anything was the 1979 FA Cup final in which they pulled back from a two-goal deficit in the final five minutes only to concede a soft goal in the dying seconds while some of the team were still celebrating. Birtles was the nearest Sexton had got to a showbiz signing. What could possibly go wrong? He had already scored six goals in nine league games for Forest that season. His debut outing in a United shirt took place in October 1980. But Birtles wasn't an all-rounder. He was a Gary Lineker, a Filippo Inzaghi. His job was to finish off what the rest of the team started. Tap-ins were his forte. Except Garry didn't tap in a single goal for the rest of the season. He'd wandered into a morality tale in which he was the unwitting protagonist. As if his torment couldn't get any worse, the end of Birtles's first season saw Dave Sexton finally given his marching orders. The Birtles disaster somehow symbolised Sexton's luckless reign at Britain's most mythical club.

I couldn't help but empathise a little too much. I also felt like I'd wandered into a parable in which I'd reluctantly become the protagonist. The problem was I didn't yet know what lesson I needed to learn. Manchester United now had a new manager. Brash, tanned, jewellery-wearing Ron Atkinson wasted no time in making a series of key purchases, most notably bringing former Threepennybit regular Bryan Robson with him to Manchester for a record-breaking £1.5 million. Perhaps I needed to be a bit more Ron as well. Before the opening fixture, I also decided I had to make a key purchase.

If you were a boy, your choice of school bag was an essential consideration. Some boys went for canvas, army-regulation rucksacks, on which they would write the names of their favourite bands. If you liked football or considered yourself a sportier sort of person, you would most likely go for a branded holdall. With Nike yet to achieve high street ubiquity, the go-to brand was Adidas, with Pony, Reebok, Puma, Fila and Diadora bringing up the rear. What you really wanted to avoid was having your mum choose your holdall. If you had the misfortune to walk into school with an unbranded bag, you risked having ridicule rain down upon you. A similar whiff of desperation surrounded the Bukta logo, on account of the fact that Bukta were to football strips what labels like Pickwick and Sounds Superb were to proper record companies. Just as those labels specialised in knock-down compilations of hit songs by session musicians pretending to be the original artists, you could find the Bukta logo on football shirts that attempted to get as close as possible to the official designs of popular teams without triggering a lawsuit.

But the worst scenario, brand-wise, was to find yourself walking into school with a logo that, from a distance appeared to be Adidas or Fila, but, on closer inspection, turned out to be Aldida (with four stripes instead of Adidas's three) or Reebak. Only one brand trumped these for awfulness, and that was the 'Sports' brand owned by Arsenal goalkeeper Pat Jennings, which boasted a bubbly lower-case font that would have barely looked contemporary a decade previously.

While not even attempting to understand the minutiae of the bag-brand caste system, my mum seemed to register what was at stake. She had some money set aside in her bedside drawer. It was in a sock ball and she had told me a few months previously that if I ever found myself desperate for some extra cash, I was to go there. Because I'd seen how carefully she budgeted and how rarely she bought new clothes for herself, I couldn't imagine a situation in which I could find myself cracking open the sock ball. But on this occasion, I didn't need to. She went upstairs herself and gave me twenty pound notes rolled up and kept in place with an elastic band. It was hardly an emergency, but I accepted the money anyway, and felt mildly guilty about having done so right up until I walked through the school gates with my new navy-blue Adidas sports bag and briefly registered the approval of almost all the sporty alpha boys.

It was easy to spot which teachers predated Yardleys' transition from grammar school to secondary modern. To start with, there was an age difference. The newer teachers were younger and, by and large, less eccentric. They wore the sort of clothes that you don't have to change for something more casual once you got home. They drove Vauxhall Chevettes and Minis, which they could have conceivably driven straight from the set of *Grange Hill* – the only programme that came close to *Top of the Pops* in terms of playground talk-time. Like the fictional Mr Hopwood and Mr Sutcliffe, our newest teachers were of polytechnic stock. They appeared to have been expecting us. They had no prior experiences against which to measure the challenge of teaching us. When new woodwork teacher (and living proof of nominative determinism) Mr Naylor welcomed us into our first woodwork lesson of the second year, Michael Barrymore was having his first moment of mainstream ubiquity. His 'Awight?' catchphrase had spored across Britain in the space of days. Far from being put out by the sight of fourteen boys all walking into his class cooing 'Awight?' like a flight of cockney pigeons, the bouffant-quiffed, perpetually smiling Mr Naylor merely joined in without missing a beat. 'I'm *awight*! But are you *awight*? How about you though? You don't look *awight*! Oh, you are? Well that's *awight*, then!' And so on and so on. He'd only just arrived at Yardleys, but in the time it takes to stick a pencil over your ear, Mr Naylor had already conferred legendary status upon himself.

By contrast, there was the head of the history department, Mr Newton, my form teacher from September 1981 to July 1982. He didn't even get off his chair the first time we filed into Room 8 – one of ten classrooms that were accessed from the balcony which overlooked the school hall, and the room where he taught all his lessons. Mr Newton's first name was Stanley, which suited him well. He sat, slouched forward onto his desk, surrounded by books, pens, loose pieces of paper and a Thermos flask. Also on the desk was the pipe and tobacco pouch which accompanied him wherever he went.

He looked like Polish Solidarity leader Lech Walesa but with NHS prescription sunglasses.

Like Mr James, who listened to ska and jazz in his classroom rather than join the other teachers in the staff room, Stanley Newton spent most of his lunches running the school chess club from his classroom. The one time I saw him out and about was a shock. He had donned a vest and shorts and gone for a jog up past the massive railway depot at Tyseley, near the municipal tip where I'd attempted to get my dad into the Beatles. My memory has photoshopped a detail into that picture that can't possibly have happened. His vest is blue with a red horizontal hoop and in his left hand is a lit pipe.

Every teacher has favourites and Mr Newton was no exception. Chess club was an attempt to preserve the old grammar school ways for at least a small section of the day. By its nature, it attracted a certain sort of pupil. I tried it for a while, of course, but after a week of self-imposed humiliation I decided to give something else a go. Football was my first sporting love, but I didn't stand a chance of getting into the football team. Rugby was less popular. Mr Nash was always getting people to try out for the rugby team. Perhaps if I attended a couple of after-school practices, that might turn my fortunes around. In the event, it was even easier than that. I turned up for one after-school practice, one of six people to do so. Mr Nash took one look at us, surveyed the rain outside, told us to go home and look for our names when he picked the team to play the next match. The following day, more in trepidation than excitement, I looked on the pinboard in the changing room and saw that I was one of the substitutes for the coming away game against our nearest rivals, Hartfield School, on Saturday morning. The problem was that I hadn't paid attention to the rules. All I knew about rugby was that if you got the ball, you ran forward and passed backwards. You don't forget a rule as totally fucking insane as that in a hurry.

Undeterred, I hauled myself to the school gates at 8 a.m. on

Saturday morning and sat in the back of the school minibus, desperately trying to eke out any morsels of information that might help me in the event of a substitution. I was in it mainly for the camaraderie, although obviously, if any glory came my way and I ended up being carried aloft into the changing rooms by a bunch of muddy, sweaty boys all chanting my name, that would be nice too. After an hour on the touchline spent earnestly doing warm-up exercises (that's what I'd seen substitutes do on TV), Mr Nash told me I'd be coming on for the final ten minutes. Had I spent the previous hour paying attention to the game and not warming up, my hands and feet would have been numb, but at least I would have had a clue what was happening.

Ten minutes isn't a long time to make an impression, but I was, in my own way, sensational. I joined a scrum that already had the required number of people in it and then, minutes later, when the ball appeared to land in my arms, my momentary confusion at seeing it passed backwards prompted me to run with it in the wrong direction. Only when my teammate Geoffrey Hill angrily tackled me did I realise what I'd done. Unable to face the journey back to school in the minibus, I told Mr Nash that my dad was picking me up. Usually a stickler when it came to making everyone shower, Mr Nash made no attempt to stop me as I put on my trousers over my shorts and scurried through Hartfield's silent, unfamiliar playground and out of the gates. That was it for me and rugby.

When it comes to trying to change into something better, twelve might be the worst age. You're attempting to push upwards off an unsteady platform with almost no expertise or real notion of where you're ultimately headed. Sure, you have *ideas*! You're a fountain of *ideas*! But the popular children aren't constantly trying to generate new ways in which they might increase their stock in the playground. At Yardleys, all the popular children needed to do was consolidate their status by simply continuing to be themselves. And now that I think about it, this was what happened. Terry Violett, the exuberant,

wisecracking hard nut; solid, sporty Jez Maher; sharp, parka-wearing
Ant McKenzie – all of them would leave Yardleys pretty much
exactly the same people they were on the day they walked in. The
same went for William Osborne. Having found favour as a *Doctor
Who*-obsessed Numanoid in 1980, there was no reason for him to
be anything else by the time he left in 1985.

You could compare all these boys to bands that had found a formula that worked and felt no need to change it. By contrast, if I wasn't
careful, I might well turn into one of those novelty acts that keep
coming up with ever more wacky and outlandish new gimmicks in
the hope that they might generate some short-term interest. These
acts have no core fan base on which to fall back. With every new
incarnation, they have to start from scratch. Perhaps it was no surprise, then, that I liked the Barron Knights. We had a lot in common.
Indeed, I had started rather fancying that I could gain popularity
by doing something similar to what they had briefly gained chart
success doing. At the end of the first year, en route from Glasbury
(the Welsh youth hostel where Aki had broken his arm), I made up a
song to the tune of a recent New Musik hit, 'Sanctuary' – which, in
keeping with its new subject matter, I renamed 'Glasbury'. In a craven
bid to ingratiate myself with everyone else on the bus, I changed the
words so that they were all about the horrible food we were made to
eat there. Much to the annoyance of Mrs Froggatt, who was driving
the minibus, everyone sang it all the way home.

It was a party piece I attempted to reprise with variable returns.
Only 'I Love Cobs 'n' Rolls' (sung to the tune of Joan Jett & the Black-
hearts' 'I Love Rock 'n' Roll') came close to emulating the success
of 'Glasbury' – and this in itself merely intensified my weird bond
with the Barron Knights. So, as you might imagine, when I saw an
ad in the *Evening Mail* for some Barron Knights shows at a cabaret
club in Solihull called the New Cresta, I lobbied hard. It was a run
of nights in mid-November which included a Sunday. That meant we

could all go as a family. I showed my mum the ad. Other acts booked to play the New Cresta in the coming weeks were future *EastEnders* star Mike Reid and ('Tonight/Tomorrow, the outrageous . . .') Bob Monkhouse. That sort of place.

It wasn't unreasonable to hope that my parents might yield to my overtures. About a year previously, we had started going to the occasional show at another cabaret club called the Kings. In the previous months, we'd seen Karen Kay, mother of Jamiroquai's Jay Kay belting out standards in front of the Kings' house band, and we'd seen Charlie Williams, the first black British comedian to appear on British prime-time television. Every visit to the Kings was a portal into an aspect of British life I had never really seen. So *this* was what you did on a Sunday night if you weren't Greek. You sat four to a table on red velour upholstered seating and you ate hot food from a basket: chicken, fish or scampi, all with chips of course. Spaced equidistantly on either side of the aisles between blocks of tables and chairs were floor lights which served the same purpose as cat's eyes in fog. If the cigarette smoke got too thick, you just followed them back to your table.

Because everyone had to go back to work the following morning, value for money was a paramount consideration, which meant that the Kings was packed within minutes of the doors opening. Opening acts would play to a packed house. Warming up the audience for *Crackerjack* comedian Stu 'I could crush a grape!' Francis, the first thing that singer Rod Allen did was tell the throng that he used to be in a group called the Fortunes who reached number 2 in 1965 with 'You've Got Your Troubles'. It sounded more like a plea than a boast. I'd never heard the song before, but it sounded great. Sad-faced Rod quickly brought the audience onside by opening with his hit. Then, after another four songs, he told us we'd been a smashing audience and closed with it too.

The New Cresta was a lot like the Kings, transplanted to a slightly more well-to-do area. If the Kings audience was eighty per cent dressed-up factory workers and twenty per cent middle management, the New Cresta reversed the ratio. Not just Ansells bitter and Embassy cigarettes but scotch and Hamlet cigars, with Babycham or Britvic for the ladies. As we walked in, I was oscillating at a higher frequency than I had thought possible. Clutched in my sweaty palm was the handle of a carrier bag containing assorted Barron Knights albums and singles. I had attended enough shows at the Kings to know that there'd most likely be some sort of signing afterwards. In the bag there was also their debut hit, 1964's 'Call up the Groups', a medley based around the idea of what might happen to certain groups if national service were reintroduced. This was my secret weapon in the bid to make them see that I wasn't like any other twelve-year-old fans they'd met on tour – my loyalty to the Barron Knights predated even my own existence! I had brought my autograph book too, with its solitary Tony Telfer signature and empty space where outrageous fortune had conspired to keep Linx and a few tipsy West Brom first-teamers from adding their inscriptions. If there was to be a signing, the chances of finally getting some real celebrities to write in my book had to be good.

Unsurprisingly, Aki stayed at home. It was just me and my parents. I felt responsible for their experience here – after all, they wouldn't be here had I not begged them to go – so I dearly wanted them to find it as funny as I was going to find it. And let's be clear about this: I was going to find it side-splittingly funny.

Laughing at a gag you've already heard and are fully expecting to hear again is a totally different sort of laughing to the laughing you do when you hear something funny for the first time. When you're expecting the gag, you laugh in the same way that Queen fans do the double clap after the line 'All we hear is . . .' in 'Radio Ga Ga'. Monty Python fans did it when they turned up to see their heroes do their favourite sketches live, and I found myself doing it when the Barron

Knights, all dressed in suits, performed 'A Taste of Aggro'. It had been nearly three years since I'd heard the line, 'There's a dentist in Birmingham . . .' but that was neither here nor there. Trying to shut out my parents' benign if bewildered glances at my adoring hoots, I laughed as though it were the first time and, to be fair, it helped that this was how they delivered it too. Their professionalism sustained them through a set which took in medleys of other repurposed hits and zeitgeist-seizing moments of pop-portunism such as 'Get Down Shep', 'We Know Who Did It' and their most recent single 'Mr Rubik'.

Before the final song, baby-faced blond co-frontman Pete Langford announced that copies of their new album would be on sale at the back of the venue and they would be on hand to sign them. I turned to my parents. Yes, I could queue up to buy a copy. At the end of the gig, I picked up my carrier bag.

My mum stayed at the table while my dad accompanied me. We paid for the new album. It was called *Twisting the Knights Away* and the sleeve featured a Rubik's Cube with pictures of the individual band members on each panel. As most of the audience filed out, the five members of the Barron Knights scattered themselves across the bar area, drinks in one hand, cigarettes in the other. Most of them were engaged in idle conversation with friends. I couldn't see any of them signing records. There seemed to be no system. I nervously approached the nearest one. I knew he was called Butch Baker because I knew all their names. He was over six feet tall and he had the nose of an ex-boxer. He took one look at my records and without turning to address me directly, briskly signed them one after the other. I held up the 1964 single, 'Call up the Groups', thinking it might impress him. 'I only got this a few weeks ago,' I said, 'I think it's rare.' (It wasn't.) He wordlessly signed that one too and handed it back to me, resuming his prior conversation as he did so. A few feet away were the group's other co-frontman Duke D'Mond and silver-haired drummer Dave Ballinger. By now, I wasn't so much nervous as plain scared, not least because D'Mond's aviator shades and dangly earring gave him an intimidating air. It was too late to rethink my approach, so I tried the same tack as I had with Butch Baker.

'I only got this a few weeks ago,' I repeated, 'I think it's rare.' (It still wasn't.)

It was even worse this time. D'Mond rolled his eyes upwards, presumably at the workload presented by having to sign other Barron Knights records than the one they were promoting. Then, as he signed each record, he handed them over for Dave Ballinger to do the same. They barely paused their conversation. There was no direct exchange this time. In my pocket was the autograph book. Up to this point, I felt that handing this over, along with all the records, might have me ejected from the premises. Never mind. Just give him the records for now. Stay focused. Breathe.

'Look!' I said to my dad, pointing at Pete Langford. With his rosy cheeks and a face that perpetually seemed to be on the brink of outright laughter, it was impossible to imagine him being unpleasant to me. Langford was the furthest away, maybe about twenty feet. The silence between my father and me spoke volumes. For him to address the coldness of the three Barron Knights we had just met would be to acknowledge that a childhood dream that was a bit shit to start with was now being doused with petrol and set alight. No. *Onwards*.

'Excuse me,' I said, 'I thought you were so ace tonight. I'm a really big fan and I've got all these records . . .' – I produced the 1964 single one more time – 'including this really old one here. It's rare. [It really wasn't.] I was wondering . . .'

Suddenly, Pete Langford no longer looked friendly. Not in the least. He looked like the angriest gnome in the garden. He inspected the new album and looked for an empty piece of sleeve to sign.

'I'm called Peter as well,' I added.

He signed the new LP, then he scribbled over a couple more and picked up his drink. I gathered up all the records and momentarily wondered if I really had the heart to complete this. My one remaining missing autograph, the Barron Knights' bass player was seated next to the table where the records were being sold. Like Madonna, Cher and Prince, Barron Anthony didn't have a surname. He had dark, curly hair and he looked older than the others. Every time a member of the Barron Knights had applied their pen to my records, I'd instantly attempted to put their weary indifference out of my mind. I was too invested in my own spectacular expectations of this night to dwell on the ways in which it had fallen short. But I still believed in tonight. I still believed in the Barron Knights. There was time to turn it around.

'I've been waiting for you!'

I looked around to see who Barron Anthony was addressing. There was no one else. I pointed at myself and he nodded.

'I saw you over there. I thought you'd forgotten all about me!!'

I was too shocked to take any meaningful part in this conversation. Thankfully I didn't need to.

'So, what's your name?'

'Peter. I've got some of your records here. Do you think you could—'

'Crumbs!' He turned to my dad. 'Are these all his?'

My dad leaned forward to shake Barron Anthony's hand, as if to establish the fact that he saw him primarily as a fellow adult professional earning a living. 'He loves your group. He has all your records.' (I didn't.)

Barron Anthony picked out the 1964 single and looked across at me. 'Were you even born when this came out?'

'No,' I said, a little too earnestly. 'I wasn't. Is it rare?'

'You know what? I think it might be. [It wasn't and he knew it.] I haven't seen one in a long time!'

He signed every single record, carefully inscribing a message on each one. On the new album, he wrote, 'To Peter. Our biggest fan and an honorary Knight!!'

In a flash, exhilaration and relief ousted everything that had happened in the previous five minutes. Just as a brace of extra-time goals might reverse a result and compel a football journalist to rewrite the entire match report, freighting it with intimations of destiny and approaching triumph, I briefly convinced myself that this had been the greatest evening of my life. Only when I got into the back seat of the car and felt the hard cover of the autograph book pressing into my right bum cheek, did I realise that the shock turnaround of Barron Anthony's conversation with me had erased its existence from my thoughts.

But while it might have been enough to avert disaster, it wasn't quite enough to keep my love of the Barron Knights intact. It wasn't even that they had been rude to me. Prior to that night, I'd never stopped to think about what the life of a comedy group must be like. It had never occurred to me that after you've sung, 'There's a dentist in Birmingham . . .' maybe 150 times in any given year, and had to do so like it's the first time, then a certain nihilistic weariness might set in – one possibly made worse by the sight of a twelve-year-old boy advancing towards you with a pile of your old records.

Suddenly, being a Barron Knight no longer seemed like the best fun you could ever have in a band. It seemed like atonement for the sins of a past life. I played *Twisting the Knights Away* all the way through maybe once. As with the humiliation at Acocks Green library a few months previously, it felt like someone was trying to tell me something.

The daily existential torment that seemed to afflict most of the Barron Knights extended to other people who had chosen to make a living out of hilarity. Half a mile away, in leafy Hall Green, a new shop appeared. 'L Y N E X J O K E S', it said. I couldn't believe my luck. A real joke shop! I'd thought joke shops only existed in the pages of the comics I had reluctantly stopped buying. What were the chances that Birmingham's first ever dedicated joke shop would open a short walk from my house?

With Saturday allowances in our pockets, Terry Violett and I made our way to the new shop sometime during the afternoon when the TV schedules were full of horse racing. Hall Green wasn't our patch, so we didn't know exactly how long Mr Lynex had been open for business. Perhaps no more than a fortnight, but that didn't matter. A fortnight had clearly been long enough for Mr Lynex to lose any remaining appetite he had for dealing with the likes of me. His expression was new to me at the time, but it's one I recognise these days chiefly on the faces of record shop proprietors who have to muster a polite reaction to middle-aged dads who exclaim, 'Vinyl! It's coming back, I see!!!' before holding up a reissue of Fleetwood Mac's *Rumours* and asking if their old copy is worth a fortune. Mr Lynex had exhausted his stock of responses by the end of day one.

A notice on the window said, 'NO MORE THAN TWO CHIL-DREN AT A TIME'. We waited a few minutes before the children already in there finally left. There was a section dedicated to magic tricks, a hanger with fancy-dress outfits and another cabinet full of party paraphernalia, but I had no interest in any of that stuff. I went straight to the glass countertop display of jokes and worked out what I could afford to buy with my limited funds. A set of rectangular sheets of metal, roughly the size of playing cards that were supposed to sound like breaking glass when you dropped them. Pretend Juicy Fruit gum with a spring-loaded mechanism that trapped your finger when you attempted to take a piece. Stink bombs. Several items related to the excrement of more than one animal, including rubber dog turds. At £3, a can of spray-on human poo was a premium item and out of my range. Pointing to a convincing plastic pigeon dropping, I asked Mr Lynex if I could 'please have a closer look at that bird shit'. I felt edgy referring to it as 'bird shit', but: (a) I was trying to impress Terry; and (b) somehow I got it into my head that in this cathedral of irreverence, none of the usual rules applied.

'What did you say?'

The tone of Mr Lynex's voice told me that whatever it was I'd said, it probably wouldn't be a good idea to say it again. But also, Terry Violett was standing next to me and I didn't want to lose face.

'That. There.' I pressed my forefinger on the glass.

Mr Lynex lowered his gaze, so that I could see two of me reflected in his spectacles. 'Listen here, sunshine. If I ever hear you using that sort of language again in my shop, I'll *report* you.'

Report me? But to whom? Mr Lynex didn't know my name. What was he going to do? Perform a citizen's arrest?

None of that mattered. For about ten seconds, I thought I might cry – which, with Terry standing next to me ready to relay the exchange, would have been a fate far worse than anything Mr Lynex could exact upon me. Thankfully, it was Terry himself that relieved me of the joke shop owner's scrutiny by taking the conversation to an unexpectedly philosophical level.

'So it's all right for you to sell it, but it's not all right for us to say it?'

'Look, are you going to buy anything?' blustered Mr Lynex.

'I'll have that,' said Terry, pointing to the can of fake poo.

Terry handed over the £3, and Mr Lynex gave him the poo. Within five minutes of leaving the shop, Terry had squirted its entire contents outside his shop and across the length of the doorstep. This had, by some distance, been the naughtiest and almost certainly the most exhilarating thing I'd been involved in. The following Monday, as Terry told his assembled acolytes what had happened, I figured that joining in only stood to jeopardise the reflected glory of having been with him on the Saturday. I said nothing.

For a few months, it felt as though all of Britain had finally caught up with my belief that there was no greater form of mirth than a well-executed prank. Just a month previously, ITV had launched a new Saturday night show called *Game for a Laugh* – a sixty-minute bonanza of carefully planned hilarity. Some of it was studio-based and involved dunk tanks and pie chairs, which was fine, but of course, we'd seen all that stuff on ITV's anarchic *Swap Shop* rival *Tiswas*. No, the bits of *Game for a Laugh* everyone liked the best were the elaborate practical jokes that involved some poor nobody having to manage some sort of unforeseen calamity involving a DIY disaster – or someone gazing on in horror as a mechanical excavator fills their convertible car with soil. The joke would, of course, end with co-host Jeremy Beadle removing his disguise and telling the victim to wave to the camera. Then we'd cut to the studio where the audience would be invited to agree that the victim had shown themselves to be 'game for a laugh'.

Beadle's self-appointed role as arch prankmeister quickly generated resentment towards him in some circles, usually from adults who saw other adults in the show being publicly made to endure situations that must have put them within touching distance of a coronary. To Beadle-sceptic grown-ups with jobs, children and day-to-day lives that were complicated enough to manage, being applauded by a TV audience for being 'game for a laugh' was scant compensation for being secretly filmed while you vainly protested to the delivery man that you really didn't order a consignment of live alligators. BBC2's *Not the Nine O' Clock News* addressed the ethics of *Game for a Laugh* with a sketch that saw Rowan Atkinson returning home from work to find his wife beheaded, only to have Jeremy Beadle (played by Mel Smith) jump out and tell him he'd been 'game for a laugh'.

It saddened me that even comedians I liked seemed to loathe Beadle. My ongoing list of suitable replacements in the event of 'something happening' to my parents had always been low on men. I didn't wonder what it would be like to have Beadle as a dad because, actually, it was obvious to me what it would be like. Every day would be like April Fool's Day, which, as almost everyone knows, is the funniest day in the British calendar. I say *British* calendar, of course, because Greek parents didn't seem to recognise April Fool's Day alongside Christmas, Easter and New Year's Day as a day of unalloyed cheer. My mum had remained steadfastly unamused on 1 April 1977 when I left a note in the toilet announcing that I'd run away from home and, indeed, she even seemed upset when she found me hiding in the airing cupboard ten minutes later.

I now realise that on the same morning two years later, my mum had forewarned my dad that I had placed a whoopee cushion on his chair as he sat down to have breakfast and that he had to look surprised and amused as otherwise I would be upset. I think I probably rumbled it as I screeched, 'APRIL FOOL!!!' at him, but my staunch faith in hilarity as something that could be manufactured to order by skilled jape practitioners such as myself closed off the neural pathways from the eyes that allow the brain to read the room. And, of course, it's now clear to me that, on 1 April 1981, stealing one of the colouring tablets that we used when soaking the dried marrowfat peas (the first stage of the process of making mushy peas) and dissolving it in my mouth seconds before calling my mum upstairs, complaining that my mouth 'felt funny', wasn't the optimal start to her day.

It was a reversal of the line in the Smiths' 'Shakespeare's Sister' – I can't really laugh about it now, but at the time it was hilarious. But that's who I was at the age of twelve. Sometimes I wonder if the brutality of each adolescence is proportionate to the embarrassment felt at the bit immediately preceding it. The cooler you were before your teens, the less there is to react against; it's cruise control all the way to adulthood.

Two doors away, it was becoming increasingly apparent that this wasn't an option for Emily May. If Adam and the Ants had destabilised the foundations of her childhood worldview, Soft Cell were the earthquake that finished it off. Within four months, the sexually ambiguous duo comprised of former Leeds Polytechnic students Marc Almond and Dave Ball had two huge hits – the first a revelatory synth-pop reading of Gloria Jones's northern soul classic 'Tainted Love', and then 'Bedsitter'. Apropos of God knows what, posters appeared around the school to announce a talent contest in the school hall in a few days' time. Lunchtime would be extended by twenty minutes so that everyone would have a chance to see it. Anyone interested in taking part needed to contact Mr Baxter, the drama teacher. A bunch of girls in my year devised a routine to the Bodysnatchers' 1980 ska hit 'Let's Do Rocksteady'. Four girls in Emily's year swapped their uniforms for rayon and rouge and sang Adam and the Ants' most recent chart topper 'Prince Charming', with choreography copied from the video. A freakishly tall fifth former who had tried to hide his chronic acne with downy facial hair sat at the piano and played Elton John's 'Song for Guy'.

I might not have been there at all, were it not for the fact that Emily had told me she would be dancing to a medley of the two Soft Cell hits. I felt invested in what she was about to do, exceptionally so, because I knew where she came from and where she was trying to get to. At some point, I would probably have to make my own version of this crossing. It wasn't something I liked to think about too much because I still couldn't bear the idea of the hurt I might cause my mum if I rebelled. All of this heightened my fascination. I wasn't there to cheer her on or, indeed, heckle her. I think that, without realising it, I was probably there to find out what would happen. Because in some way, it might shed some light on what might happen to me if I were to try and start growing up.

What the twelve-year-old me saw isn't what the adult me remembers. The twelve-year-old me saw Emily tentatively totter onto a stage more used to enervating assemblies and smile nervously at an

assembled crowd that immediately erupted into laughter. The twelve-
year-old me saw her stand alone on stage, still smiling, waiting a
few unbearably long seconds for Mr Baxter to press 'play' so that
she could start her dance. As she waited, the twelve-year-old me
saw her pull down the hem of her tiny gold sleeveless dress over
her thighs – a dress that she would have nervously stuffed into her
school bag that morning, along with her textbooks and pencil case.
The twelve-year-old me thought it was *hilarious* when Emily raised
both hands towards her left shoulder and shook them like maracas
in time with the synth stabs that take place between 'Sometimes I
feel I've got to . . .' and ' . . . run away'. And then when she pulled
them towards her right shoulder on the next pair of synth stabs, I
laughed even more.

Two minutes later, after a brutal edit into 'Bedsitter', Emily was
dancing out her own fantasy of bedsit life, wagging her finger at an
imaginary mirror as she mimed along with Marc Almond's '. . . kid
myself I'm having fun' line. It was all we could talk about in physics
that afternoon, what an almighty wally that girl in the fourth year
had made of herself. Because Emily and I didn't socialise at school,
I didn't need to let anyone knew that I knew her. I was free to join
in. *What was she thinking of, that Emily May? It wasn't even a dance,
really! Just a bit of hand-shaking and pretending to be Marc Almond!
Had she gone mad?!*

But, like I said, that's not what the adult me remembers. The adult
me can see the entire thing with a clarity that bounced clean off my
young self. The adult me realises that the twelve-year-old me didn't
give Emily a fraction of the credit she deserved for what she did. Did
Emily know that there would be more skilled performers getting
on that stage, and that none of them would feel quite as alone up
there as she would? Of course she knew. Even the piano guy wasn't
totally alone. After all, he had his piano and he didn't have to face
the audience. But Emily wasn't performing to us. Yes, it mattered

that we were there, just as marriages and baptisms require witnesses. But we weren't the designated beneficiaries of Emily's performance. She was honouring a commitment to Marc Almond, just as she might have done if she'd had him tattooed on her arm. The tattoo is there for everyone to see, but it's not *for* them. Emily was doing this for Emily. And really, if the ridicule served any purpose, it merely served to authenticate that commitment. It was a reminder that while cowardice is something we learn, bravery is something we're born with. Alone on that stage, dancing for Marc, dancing for her love of Marc, Emily displayed more bravery in five minutes than I was able to summon in my entire five years at Yardleys.

And here's the paradox. Why can I see that more clearly as an adult, when Emily's motives should have been far clearer to me at that point? After all, wasn't I waiting for a musical epiphany that would turn my world upside down and obliterate my inhibitions just as it had done for Emily, or for Aki with the Bunnymen and The Teardrop Explodes, or for William Osborne and Gary Numan? In fact, my reaction to her performance revealed more about me than it did about Emily. Denial is an act of will and human will is a mental muscle that gets tired when called into constant service, like holding your arms above your head. I think that probably explains why I spent less time thinking about what had happened between me and Henry Bannatyne in the week after it happened than I have in any week over this past decade. Guilt is the interest that racks up when your soul decides to take a payday loan.

No, as 1981 drew to a close, every little initiative undertaken to make myself a little bit more legendary was undertaken with the sort of bluff optimism that is only possible when you have conducted absolutely no research. The transition from child to adolescent is as complex and fraught with perilous long-term ramifications as Britain's decision to leave the European Union. I was about as ready to devolve myself from childhood as Boris Johnson was to lead the

United Kingdom out of Europe. And like Boris Johnson in his conviction that cabinet makers in Uxbridge might single-handedly shore up the British economy after Brexit, I too had some contingency plans that sat at various points in the continuum between insane and suicidal.

No-school-uniform day took place twice a year and presented: (a) children with an opportunity to jettison their dehumanising school uniform and express their unique personalities by granting them total sartorial autonomy; and (b) parents with the opportunity to grasp how much longer and more stressful weekday mornings would be if school uniforms didn't exist. Having said that, it didn't take me very long at all to get my outfit together. I'd decided a couple of days beforehand that I would reaffirm my love for Manchester United in the most public way possible and try and make every single garment on my body a Manchester United one. This meant wearing my Manchester United tracksuit and, underneath it, my Manchester United top and, in lieu of underpants, my Manchester United shorts. On my wrists I wore Manchester United wristbands. Admittedly, there was nothing about my trainers that suggested Manchester United, but I remedied that by attaching Manchester United badges to each of the shoelaces. In an inner-city school in Birmingham, a decision like that is easily enough to invite a barrage of dead arms and dead legs upon your body or, maybe worse still, a mob-handed removal of your outer garments, leaving you helpless as you watch your tracksuit bottom flung onto the nearest bus shelter.

Somehow, none of this occurred to me. In my head, all of these possible outcomes had been supplanted by a fantasy so deranged and detached from anything I had previously experienced that I can only conclude that the neural circuits that flood the brain with dopamine during adolescence had short-circuited my prefrontal cortex, blinding me to reason – indeed blinding me to everything other than the notion that walking into a school playground full of

Aston Villa, Birmingham City and Liverpool fans, while wearing a full Manchester United tracksuit, would make me more legendary.

But it didn't stop there. Surely there was something else I could wear that would finish the job off? Something that would really give people a sight they would never forget? I pulled open one of the drawers in my bedroom. In there was a Manchester United scarf and a Manchester United belt. The obvious thing to do at this point would have been to wear the belt around your waist and the scarf around your neck. Instead I took the red, white and black belt and coiled it around my neck to create a sort of choke. After that, I tied the scarf around my hips, thus contriving what in my head was a sort of edgy 'football punk' look. Then I opened the bedroom door at exactly the same time as Aki opened his door to leave the house. He couldn't have looked more shocked, more instantly nauseous if I'd emerged dressed as Siouxsie Sioux.

Instead of addressing me, he called out to our parents. 'You've got to come upstairs now! Look what he's done!' There was something about Aki's voice that had the power to fling me back down to earth in a blink. 'Look how he's dressed to go to school!' By the time my mum came up the stairs, I'd removed the belt from my neck and the scarf from my waist.

Aki stared at me a bit longer and shook his head. 'Just be careful,' he said, as he brushed past me. 'And if you see me at school, just . . . you know . . . keep away, OK?'

I threw the belt and the scarf onto my bed, but decided to keep faith with the remaining get-up.

If it had happened a couple of months previously, I would have been a dead man. But over the preceding few weeks, Terry Violett and I had become quite close. Even visually, it was an odd pairing: Terry, already approaching six feet, with his green bomber jacket, his drainpipes and his Doc Martens; and the doughy, long-haired sidekick with the St Michael snorkel parka, flares and Clarks slip-ons.

Terry lived just around the corner from me and we had taken to walking to school together in the mornings. So, when I knocked on his door on no-school-uniform day, none of the usual rules applied. He took one look at me and took the piss for a minute before placing his pork-pie hat on his head, positioning his wrap-around 2 Tone shades onto the bridge of his nose and straightening his skinny tie. Walking into the playground at the same time as Terry was just enough to spare me an outright beating.

Not that this was really helping me. If a beating or two might have allowed me to see myself as other people saw me, then it might not have been such a bad thing. But now that Terry and I were walking to school every morning, I had no urgent incentive to do such a thing. One morning while he was upstairs getting ready, his mum confided that he was enjoying our daily journeys to school. Of course, so was I. I got to see a side of Terry that he never revealed to the other boys. He bought records too! Not just the Specials, Madness and Jam records that all boys liked, but less obvious selections. He'd received the Clash's fourth album *Sandinista!* for his twelfth birthday and brought it over so I could listen to it. 'What's this?' asked Aki, when he heard 'Lose This Skin' from his bedroom – and when he clocked that the record belonged to Terry, he nodded his approval. I couldn't remember the last time I'd received one of those approving nods or, indeed, any endorsement of my musical choices.

My unease spidered out into straightforward envy when Aki listened to the other record that Terry had brought with him – a courtesy he would have almost never extended to me. 'Fire' was a new song by an Irish band called U2. It had scraped the top 40 a few months previously, in the process earning the group their *Top of the Pops* debut. I can see why Terry liked it. It sounded like a bored storm looking for somewhere to happen. Somehow, the slightness of its tune accentuated its intended effect. It never quite got going, but what was exciting about it was the sound of the band perpetually

trying to launch itself into action, spoiling for something bigger and
only just getting a sense of how they might achieve it.

'Who's this?' said Aki, by now sitting on the end of my bed.

Terry handed him the sleeve. With 'Fire' being a double 7-inch,
there was still a record in there, which featured '11 O'Clock Tick Tock'.
Aki handed it over to Terry, who placed it on the turntable once 'Fire'
was finished. What even was this? A high, astringent riff set against
the simple melancholy refrain of 'Sad song, sad song'. Over the next
couple of years, you'd barely get to the end of an interview with Echo
& the Bunnymen or The Teardrop Explodes without those groups
heaping ridicule on the gauche, overearnest twit from U2. But at that
moment, on the basis of their existing work, if someone asked you to
list U2, The Teardrop Explodes and Echo & the Bunnymen according
to which band would be most likely to achieve world domination, you
would have placed the Irish band at the bottom. Their melodies were
too weird. And Bono Vox is no sort of a name for a rock star.

'What's your mate's name again?' said Aki, after Terry left. 'That
U2 record's good. I might have to get it myself.'

I felt aggrieved. Aki seemed to think that the least cool thing about
my friends was the fact that they were my friends. It wasn't a view I
shared, especially when it came to music. Having long since accepted
that I could never pull off being a member of a youth tribe, I'd managed to convince myself that I'd transcended the fickle demands of
fashion. It was borderline hurtful to me that no one seemed to like
ABBA anymore. Racey's star had fallen so far that if I wanted to
own their next single, I had to order it in especially from Easy Listening. But that only served to cement my loyalty. One evening, in
what felt like a vision of absolute clarity, I decreed that the practice
of writing your favourite band names on your school bag shouldn't
just be restricted to mods or new romantics. And in that moment, I
felt like I'd alighted on a thought cleverer than any twelve-year-old
boy had ever previously had. And it was this:

Not trying to be cool is actually cooler than being cool.

Delighted with the fresh realisation that I was now the coolest person I knew, I removed the cap from my brand-new metallic silver marker and set about writing the names of all the bands I liked on my Adidas holdall. I started at the bottom, in the gap between the Adidas logo and the piping at the base of the bag. I faithfully copied out the ABBA logo from the sleeve of *Super Trouper*, complete with the backward B. Then came 'Racey', 'The Police', 'Madness' and 'Bee Gees'. On the top right, there was room for a couple more names. Almost certainly to Aki's irritation, I decided that I now liked The Teardrop Explodes sufficiently to claim them for my bag. Above their name, I fashioned a decent facsimile of the Jam's logo, the painted 'graffiti' one you tended to see on patches on the backs of parkas. This was, by some distance, the coolest corner of my holdall.

All that remained was a large space on the top left-hand side. Who had I left out? Only a fortnight or so had elapsed since the Barron Knights debacle, but that was enough to kick them out of contention. In that time, I'd made just one major acquisition – a second-hand copy of Dave Edmunds's *Repeat When Necessary* from Reddington's Rare Records – a densely stocked vinyl grotto located in the subway opposite Moor Street station. I'd bought both of Dave's recent singles – a version of 'Singing the Blues' and a collaboration with the Stray Cats called 'The Race Is On'. But it wasn't just the records I liked. There was something beyond the music that endeared me to Dave Edmunds. On the cover of *Repeat When Necessary* – the album which featured 'Girls Talk' – the black-clad Welsh singer faced down the camera with a granite-jawed air of self-assurance that suggested that it might be even cooler to have him as a dad than Jeremy Beadle. Yes, I decided to award the final space on my holdall to Dave Edmunds. I removed *Repeat When Necessary* from its sleeve and placed it on the turntable.

There are some things you can't cover up with lipstick and powder . . .

Copying the font on the sleeve, I inscribed the outline of a 'D'. Then the 'A', 'V' and 'E'. In my eagerness to fill the space, Dave Edmunds's name ended up three times bigger than every other name on the bag. Just as I applied the finishing touches to the entire thing, Aki wandered by, glanced at the bag, then at me, then once more at the bag.

'Do you know what that looks like?' he said.

'What?'

'It looks like the bag belongs to someone called Dave Edmunds. Someone called Dave Edmunds who's into a load of really *shit* bands.'

CHAPTER 25

We were by no means impoverished, but there were generally fewer *things* than people have nowadays. Fewer things in shops. Fewer things in houses. Less rubbish to throw out. Less of everything. Clutter was rarely used as a noun. And decluttering had yet to become a phenomenon. There were no pound shops stocked to the ceiling with novelties mass-produced in Chinese factories, although when they started to appear, Acocks Green would have one of the first. Crash! Bang! Wollop! [*sic*] did a roaring trade in copper-and-black Durusell [*sic*] batteries that lasted barely any longer than it took to put them in, *Space Invaders* key rings and rulers with lenticular images of lions and zebras that flickered when you moved them. To this day, whenever I see a copy of Gregory Isaacs' *Cool Ruler* album, I think about those lions and zebras.

And because there were fewer things, you tended to hold on to what you had. It was inconceivable that, one day, you might look around you and bemoan the fact that you had too much stuff. Sometimes, the people who ran Easy Listening would put all the empty record sleeves and posters from their last window display into a box by the door that said, 'FREE'. I'd take what there was, even if it didn't bear any relation to any of my likes or interests. One evening, I came home with five identical Van der Graaf Generator sleeves. It would be years before I heard Van Der Graaf Generator, but that didn't matter. The sleeves would come in handy for something. I was sure of it. While I figured out what that might be, I put one of them on my bedroom wall.

On the weekend that the NEC Motor Show took place, I accompanied my dad as he wandered from stall to stall ogling cars that he promised himself he'd buy once he finally moved back to Cyprus. He loved to look at the Jaguars and Bentleys. Rolls-Royces, he said, were for people who wanted to rub their wealth in your face. For sheer class, he contended, you can't beat a top-of-the-range Mercedes. For me though, the Motor Show was a chance to accumulate more stuff. At each concession, skimpily dressed female emissaries of Ford, Land Rover or Volvo would furnish me with key rings, posters and calendars and I'd gratefully gather them all up. In the Saab area, one woman tapped me on the shoulder and handed me an air pressure gauge. It felt like it might be quite valuable. It was metal and heavy for its size, with a retractable component that felt nice to push in and out. It didn't matter that I didn't know what it was. I fiddled with it all the way home, perhaps like someone in this century might do with a fidget spinner. It was stuff.

In the hierarchy of stuff, certain rules applied. With paper stuff, stickers always trumped plain paper. It didn't even matter too much what was on the stickers. So when several boxes of small white square stickers bearing the red logo of HarMo – a local factory that made air filters for cars – were found dumped in various locations near my school, you suddenly couldn't go from one classroom to another without seeing the HarMo brand either on a desk or a wall or, in several cases, on someone's back. I happened upon a few hundred stickers and set about decorating my German exercise book with them, all laid out neatly in rows. It was something to do, and in nothing-to-do Birmingham in nothing-to-do 1981, something was better than nothing, just as stuff was better than no stuff.

According to his police statement, it was a version of that rationale that prompted a boy in my year, Troy Meehan, to wander down to a stretch of wasteland a few streets away from the HarMo factory, locally referred to as 'the old brickworks'. Having heard that thousands of these stickers had been dumped there, he went off in search of them, taking with him an eight-year-old boy who lived on his street, John McLean, who was known as 'Smiler' by the neighbours, on account of his ceaselessly sunny disposition in the face of the learning disabilities with which he was born. I didn't know John McLean, and really, I would have long forgotten Troy Meehan had it not been for what emerged from reports in the *Evening Mail* over the next couple of days. In the first edition of the paper which appeared on 17 September, Troy was named as the last person to see McLean alive before the boy's body was found inside a cable drum in the early hours of the same day, after dozens of neighbours and workers from the nearby Lucas factory had scoured the area. The report said he 'had been strangled and his face battered with a 10lb chunk of concrete by his killer'. It continued that 'a ligature was round his neck. A huge bloodstained chunk of concrete was lying on the boy's face.'

By the time I came home on the day the news broke, subsequent editions of the *Evening Mail* were no longer mentioning Troy Meehan's name. He'd gone from being the last person to see John McLean to being the main suspect. Throughout the day, word about what had happened quickly spread. None of us knew what a boy killer looked like, but if forced to hazard a guess, not a single one of us would have picked out small, slight Troy Meehan with his oversized school uniform and his dark button eyes. The issue of the *Evening Mail* being pushed through our letterboxes was the late-night final. Not only had Troy's name been removed, but so had his quote about looking for the HarMo stickers.

For the teachers who inevitably pooled information in the smoky staff room that lunchtime, it must have been surreal to see the playground so heavily littered by the same stickers that Troy Meehan had gone to search for before committing his unspeakable act. And oddly, when the school's new headmaster Mr Lavery – a cocksure Jeffrey Archer to the J.R. Hartley of his predecessor, Mr Wilford – finally elected to give a special assembly, it wasn't to address the actions of Troy Meehan. It was about the stickers. 'In the last couple of days,' he began, 'the school has been deluged with stickers from the local filter factory. Anyone caught affixing or carrying the stickers on them will be immediately punished.' And that was it. Not a mention of the other thing that had happened that week.

So *this* was how the grown-ups dealt with such crises. I don't think any of us questioned how the school might have better conducted its affairs in the wake of what Troy Meehan did. We had no frame of reference and neither, perhaps, did the school. After a week or so, Troy's older brother returned to school, and no one ever mentioned it again, either to him or to anyone else. I guess we took our leads from the school's reaction. I don't think I read the *Evening Mail* report more than once. I stared at the low-resolution enlargement of the poor victim's grinning visage and attempted to imagine how frightened he must have been. But I couldn't. Not really.

With Peter Sutcliffe's reign of terror still fresh in the collective memory, the truth is that Troy Meehan's appalling actions at the old brickworks and the macabre late-night search party that they prompted seemed consistent with what our favourite records were telling us about the wider world. It was bleak out there. Three years of exposure to the punk and new wave records my brother had brought into the house had solidified an unspoken sense that we were being funnelled into a variety of outcomes that couldn't hope to emulate the freedoms of childhood. At worst, we were all going to instantly perish in a nuclear war, the details of which were graphically outlined by Ian Gillan in his February hit 'Mutually Assured Destruction' ('I can see the mushrooms in the sky / From where I stand / I can watch the bleeding children cry').

At best, well . . . pop was struggling to present many plausible reasons to believe in the future. In the spring of 1981, the Blue Orchids, a Manchester group formed by two ex-Fall musicians, put out a record that took your worst forebodings of adulthood and moulded them into a single demonic drill. One listen on the John Peel show was all it took for Aki to head into town and pick one up from the basement at the old Virgin record shop on Bull Street. The chorus of 'Work' amounted to little more than frontman Martin Bramah shouting 'Work!' over and over again, but its dystopian drag was down to what was happening underneath. Everything Una Baines played on the organ appeared to be coated in a veil of phlegm and soot. It was the sound of sleep and sunlight deprivation compacted into seven inches. It sounded like a love song for an Orwellian nightmare. I couldn't work out whether I loved it or whether it depressed the hell out of me. Sometimes – as in the case of Kate Bush's 'Sat in Your Lap' or Godley & Creme's 'Under Your Thumb' – I'd get as far as buying a record and still not feel like I was any closer to knowing.

I wanted my future to be more like a Nolan Sisters or a Modern Romance song and yet every month, without fail, John Craven would brightly inform us that 'the number of unemployed people' (it was never just 'unemployment') had risen. Next door to us, Ged's mum Joyce had been working part time for Provident Financial, a company founded in the spirit of Victorian philanthropy that existed to provide poor families with affordable credit. Since 1979, Joyce had been going from door to door, seeing families and helping them manage their incomings and outgoings, collecting repayments or issuing Provident cheques which could then be redeemed at certain shops. It wasn't a job you could do without getting to know the families and the circumstances that had prompted them to borrow money in the first place. By 1981, the time it took to cover all the houses in her allotted radius had doubled. Joyce was quick to blame Margaret Thatcher. 'I just had a *feeling* about that woman,' she would say, with increasing frequency, throughout the 1980s.

But Thatcher's premiership formalised an incipient mood that predated her, turning the no-future nihilism of punk into post-punk
fatalism. I couldn't deconstruct it any more than an eleven-year-old
in 1967 might have been able deconstruct the bumper harvest of
optimism that fed popular culture at that time. But did I notice it?
Of course. You didn't even have to watch the news to notice it. *Top
of the Pops* was enough.

Any piece of art that tried to reach out to young people had to
honour that fatalism – a fatalism that was soaked into the storylines
of BBC1's secondary school soap *Grange Hill*, and also in another Phil
Redmond creation, an ITV 'yoof' drama called *Going Out* which,
by virtue of the fact that 'the *Grange Hill* bloke' was behind it, we
stayed up late on Friday night to watch. Common to both *Grange Hill*
and *Going Out* (and, indeed, Redmond's 1983 *Grange Hill* spin-off
Tucker's Luck) was the understanding that a state secondary school
education didn't prepare you for adulthood – it extruded you into
it, as early as sixteen if you chose not to stay on for A levels. Hence,
in the first scene of the first episode of *Going Out*, even before the
opening credits, we saw its three male leads in the final minutes of
their time at school, telling one of their teachers that they were no
longer subject to their petty rules and the threats used to enforce
them. On the other side of the obligatory gobby new wave theme
song, we cut to Sean – blond, handsome, emotionally disengaged,
swigging milk out of the bottle – seated at the family breakfast table,
giving monosyllabic answers to his mother, who wants to know who
else will be going to the end-of-term dance. When his dad walks
in, he asks him, 'What's it like leaving school?' only for his mum to
interject, 'Who said anything about him leaving school? He's got his
name down for the sixth-form college, hasn't he? There's no reason
why he can't go on to do A levels and university!'

'Oh yeah, yeah, yeah – you definitely need a university degree
to fill in the forms down at the social security,' replies Sean's dad,

thus establishing himself as the pragmatic counterbalance to the overbearing mum.

The street scenes in *Going Out* depicted terraces of boarded-up houses and fenced-off areas of scrubland; corrugated iron over windows with 'STOP COUNCIL WRECKERS' spray-painted on. Sean's love interest Cathy lived on a brutalist, breeze-block estate accessed by concrete walkways and looked amazing – like Karen O constructed entirely out of Sunblest and Boots Seventeen. His immediate prospects were personified by another character, Dykey, who had left school twelve months previously and had failed to secure a single job interview.

Paul Weller coined the term 'this modern nightmare' in 'Dreams of Children', but it took post-punk's other pre-eminent band of social commentators the Specials to come up with a song that matched that description. Even at his most bleak, Weller never lacked pugnacity. He was a fighter and a romantic. 'Ghost Town', however, seemed to come from a place far beyond hope, beating UB40's 'One in Ten' to the punch by a month. The song was an accumulation of what the Specials' main songwriter Jerry Dammers had seen travelling from city to city with the Specials over the previous year. Speaking to the *Melody Maker* in 2002, he recalled, 'Margaret Thatcher had apparently gone mad, she was closing down all the industries, throwing millions of people on the dole . . . You could see that frustration and anger in the audience. In Glasgow, there were these little old ladies on the streets selling all their household goods, their cups and saucers. It was unbelievable. It was clear that something was very, very wrong.'

While it's debatable how much of this dereliction could have been blamed directly upon a prime minister who had only been in the job for eighteen months when the song was conceived, certain changes in the political climate – changes that helped create 'Ghost Town' and which, within days of its release, 'Ghost Town' would then soundtrack – were impossible to ignore. At the beginning of April, police in Brixton had introduced a stop and search policy that precipitated rioting in Brixton and civil unrest in Finsbury Park, Forest Gate and Ealing. In the Specials' home town of Coventry, an Asian teenager, Satnam Singh Gill, was murdered in a racist attack. The Specials responded by playing a show in Coventry to promote racial unity. On the same day, the National Front marched through the surrounding streets. Three weeks later, the day before 'Ghost Town' reached number 1, rioting erupted in over twenty towns and cities across England, including Handsworth in Birmingham.

We thought of the Specials as a ska band, but we didn't know what *this* was. It simply couldn't simply be explained with reference to anything else that was happening in pop. Taken in conjunction with the video, which saw the band in a 1962 Vauxhall Cresta barrelling through deserted east London streets, it felt more like a macabre piece of musical theatre. The ascent into the wordless chorus seemed to owe more to the soundtracks of Bernard Herrmann. And then there was the chorus itself, a cartoon banshee choir giving way to the demented music hall flashback interlude of 'Do you remember the good old days before the ghost town?'

If a record as sinister as 'Ghost Town' could get to number 1, it seemed certain to me that The Teardrop Explodes – scaling new heights of accessibility with their latest single – would float to the same position as effortlessly as a lost balloon. It didn't matter that they didn't fit in with the new romantics or the futurists or the mods or the soul boys. It didn't matter that Julian Cope was telling *Smash Hits* journalists that he had changed his name to Kevin Stapleton because that was less of a loser's name than Julian. None of that mattered any more, and the reason for that was 'Passionate Friend'. This was a song that already conformed to one meaning of the word hit – the intense sensory experience that usually takes place after ingesting some sort of stimulant – and soon it would conform to another. There was no way this wasn't going to go all the way to number 1.

Aki bought it on the day of release, confident that anyone who had heard it on the radio would surely do the same. It was that sort of song. A stop-what-you're-doing intro sitting outside of the beat, a bit like the ones you got in the Beatles' 'Here, There and Everywhere' or Dean Martin's 'That's Amore'. These were apt comparisons, for 'Passionate Friend' (apparently written about a brief fling between Cope and Ian McCulloch's sister Julie) felt as much the work of an auteur as those songs had done. That probably had a lot to do with producers Clive Langer and Alan Winstanley whose hit-making streak with Madness showed no sign of abating. The Langer/Winstanley approach seemed to involve building into every section of a song the suggestion that the following section would be sweeter still. In the case of 'Passionate Friend', that involved two tempo shifts, ornate acoustic interludes, soft explosions of ba-ba-bas and doo-doo-doos circling and overlapping each other on an air cushion of exhilarating trumpets. And then, just as you thought it couldn't get any prettier, it happened all over again, but this time with twice the amount of counter-harmonising vocals, hovering up and then finally out of view.

All that needed to happen now was for people to hear the song, and when it climbed from 53 to 33, *Top of the Pops* came calling. It was a performance that Julian Cope recounted in his memoir *Head On*, one rendered memorable on account of the fact that: (a) it was to be a live broadcast; and (b) he and the band's drummer had decided to drop some acid on the afternoon prior to their performance. Cope was to perform the song standing on top of a grand piano in front of the rest of the band. He was wearing leather trousers and a top that he had made from a pillowcase in his hotel room.

I was paranoid as hell. The BBC make-up woman had scared the shit out of me. They had asked me if I'd just come back from the Bahamas and said they loved my tan. Of course, irony is lost on someone who's tripping his brain out, so I figured that I must be turning brown.

They led me reluctantly out to the studio floor. It was total chaos out there. People were running around and freaking out and winding everyone else up. I suddenly felt very becalmed. A group called Bucks Fizz were doing their thing on the other side of the studio. They were a two-boy, two-girl, fun group with cutesy expressions and dance routines. We were to follow them.

I watched fascinated. Then as time moved slowly on I felt sucked into their scene. God, they were brilliant. I wanted to be in Bucks Fizz. I rushed over to Gary and hit him with the idea. The two of us should join. Imagine an acid-soaked dance group with showbiz routines, it would be incredible.

Of course, in the living room of 14 Overlea Avenue, we had no way of knowing what Cope was trying to suppress. We were effectively watching someone attempting to renew their pop star licence only to be duly informed that their application had not been successful. Cope's dilated pupils followed the camera around pleadingly. He mouthed the words too zealously, as if getting the words of his own song right was his only reliable gauge that he wasn't setting fire to his career live on air. It wasn't a disaster, but over the course of the following month 'Passionate Friend' struggled just eight places higher to number 25 – this, in spite of two more *Top of the Pops* appearances. Indeed, given the catchiness of the song, you wondered if the sight of the people responsible for it was actually preventing it from doing better. Whatever the reasons, Cope's lysergic visions weren't misleading him. It was one of Bucks Fizz's best ever *Top of the Pops* appearances.

The full extent of Cope's shrinking relevance in a world that increasingly belonged to the handsome, hard-working Duran Duran and Spandau Ballet was revealed on the B-side of 'Passionate Friend'.

Like David Bowie's 'Ashes to Ashes' exactly a year previously, the main purpose of 'Christ Versus Warhol' seemed to be to beckon you into areas you spend most of your waking hours trying to avoid. With 'Ashes to Ashes', it was death. With 'Christ Versus Warhol', it was its creator's apparent mental disintegration. In both cases, sweet, disarmingly simple melodies lulled you into a true sense of insecurity. The lyrics, insofar as you could discern them, were nonsense – but the sort of ultra-lucid nonsense I'd later encounter in people entering the manic phase of a mental breakdown. The funereal tempo of 'Christ Versus Warhol' underscored the sense that we were laying something to rest, while queasy strings circled over the whole thing, not with the grandeur one normally expects from strings on a pop song, but perhaps more akin to a biplane trying to suck the last dregs of fuel into its engine as it looks for somewhere to land.

I had no frame of reference for what I was hearing. In later years, I might have put 'Christ Versus Warhol' on a compilation tape in between one of the godless hymns on Nico's 1968 album *The Marble Index* and perhaps something from Scott Walker's 1995 album *Tilt*. In the middle of 'Christ Versus Warhol', a dolorous Birmingham accent quizzically uttered the title before Cope replied, 'Cue canned laughter.' What was the joke? Would it help if I knew who or what Warhol was? It wasn't at all clear to me that Warhol might be a person. It certainly didn't sound like a person. It sounded more like a doctrine of some sort. In the context of the song, it was. A song on the recently released album by Liverpool rivals Wah! saw Pete Wylie exclaim 'You've got 15 minutes, I've got 2,000 years.' In his memoir, Cope explained that he wanted both the in-your-own-lifetime zeitgeist-capturing fame defined by Andy Warhol *and* the eternal fame of Jesus Christ.

If this was a joke, then the punchline – that there was nothing remotely as immediate as 'Passionate Friend' left in the pot – wouldn't come until we got to hear The Teardrop Explodes' second album. Given that both that record and ABBA's new albums would be out in December, Aki and I agreed that his Christmas present from me would be The Teardrops' record and Aki would get me the ABBA record. When you know what someone's going to get you for Christmas, it logically follows that there's no room for surprise. In this case, however, it wasn't true. There were plenty of surprises left. When we finally got to hear *Wilder*, it would become immediately apparent that this wasn't the work of championship contenders. They'd made it onto the Christmas Day *Top of the Pops* but the moment would feel strangely unglorious. 'We played "Reward" and I felt as though we were history,' recalled Cope, years later.

Wilder confirmed it. In the post-Christmas dinner, post-*Top of the Pops* lull, my dad padded upstairs, popped a couple of sleeping pills and attempted to sleep away the remainder of the afternoon. Aki and I retreated to the posh room where the music centre was and exchanged glances of recognition after less than a minute of the opening song. We'd heard 'Bent out of Shape' before. They'd recorded it a few months previously for a Richard Skinner session which Aki had taped. This smouldering memorial to an unhappy childhood had sounded like a Walker Brothers song – in particular, a 1966 B-side called 'Archangel', which fanned grandiloquently out over a church organ.

This isn't a retrospective observation. There were two Scott Walker fans in our lives. One of them was a pop star who appeared to be falling apart on our TV screens and on the pages of our music magazines. The other was a forty-six-year-old furniture salesman called Roy, with a seemingly inexhaustible supply of olive-green tank tops. And the beautiful thing was that, without even really realising it, William and Edward Osborne's dad was able to contextualise the heroic folly of Julian, thus allowing us to understand The Teardrop Explodes singer in a way that few people of our age could. Roy used every available opportunity to tell us about Scott's story: about the would-be teen idol years in America that preceded his arrival in Britain with the Walker Brothers. 'He was always so miserable!' enthused Roy, who we *never* saw miserable. 'Every week, you'd open *New Musical Express* and he'd be complaining about all these screaming fans and about all these arty European films he was into! People would write in and accuse him of being ungrateful. But fair play to the bloke! I thought it was great!'

Roy told us about Scott's prime-time TV show and the self-sabotaging succession of solo albums – *Scott*, *Scott 2*, *Scott 3*, *Scott 4* and *'Til the Band Comes In* – full of songs seemingly harvested from the sort of dreams that my limited life experiences couldn't hope to yield. 'The Girls from the Streets' was a case in point:

> *Swallowing the pinwheel clowns*
> *Consuming all the women*
> *Like a giant sponge*
> *Snap! The waiters animate*
> *Luxuriate like planets whirling 'round the sun*
> *Collapsing next to me*

If it wasn't for Roy, I'm not sure we would have really understood that *Wilder* was the ultimate act of hero worship. This was Julian's chance to follow in the footsteps of Scott and drive a stake through his own commercial prospects. Letters had already started to appear in *Smash Hits* from fans who had queued up to meet him backstage only to find him distracted or incoherent. Underneath one, the magazine printed a photograph of a spectrally pale Cope with shades on, his countenance Warhol-like, his hands pressed together next to his face. 'A penitent Cope pleads forgiveness,' read the caption.

Probably by accident, we played side two of *Wilder* first. A swift, silent vertiginous descent from 'Passionate Friend' to the fuzzy-felt breakdown of 'Tiny Children'. This being 1981, when the working classes had yet to embrace lamps and side lighting, it was as bright in here as an operating theatre. We couldn't afford to risk turning the volume dial above two because it was in everyone's interests for my dad to stay asleep for as long as possible. Outside, it had started to snow which, actually, was the perfect weather for the minimalist desolation of what we were hearing. Cope was transmitting from the outermost limits of his vocal and emotional range, over a series of soft keyboard oscillations, rifling through the debris of dreams and formative memories in a vain attempt to comprehend his current predicament.

> *Oh no, I'm not sure about*
> *Those things that I care about*
> *Oh no, I'm not sure, not any more . . .*

What was the appropriate emotional response here? Aki seemed respectful of this act of career immolation, as if it verified Cope's credentials as a proper artist. Although I tried to take my leads from Aki, what I mainly felt was concern, which intensified with the final two songs on *Wilder*: a numb requiem to Cope's disintegrating marriage called '. . . And the Fighting Takes Over', and then, 'The Great Dominions', a 4 a.m. identity crisis peering through an icy mist of anxious synths, occasionally illuminated by slo-mo thunderclaps of percussion. 'Mummy I've been fighting again', sang Cope over and over again as the fug around him slowly cleared.

I'd be lying if I said I expected the ABBA album to be a more uplifting affair. The sleeve art put paid to any such expectations. To put things in perspective, *Arrival* had depicted them all together in matching boiler suits gazing imperiously from a helicopter cockpit; the sleeve of *Voulez-Vous* cast them as futuristic disco overlords, interplanetary groove inspectors, masters of the scene; the cover of *Super Trouper* saw them smiling, having fun, surrounded by circus performers under the spotlight. For *The Visitors*, they were nominally together but worlds apart – photographed in the reception room of a stately home, dwarfed by huge paintings of angels. All four members of the group were bathed in amber light, each of them looking in a different direction. Not a smile anywhere. Frida had also got herself a punky, screw-you, post-divorce haircut. Agnetha looked like a discarded rag doll. In the nuclear winter of separation, it seemed like there was nothing to smile about.

Years later, when I asked Björn about the visual concept, he replied with typical understatement. 'The sleeve designer was a close friend who saw what had happened in our lives.' Maybe he'd heard the songs too. Björn's lament for his children's acceleration into maturity ('Slipping Through My Fingers'); an unflinching post-divorce midlife audit ('When All Is Said and Done'); and a sparse, solipsistic lullaby sculpted out of pure nocturnal terror ('Like an Angel Passing Through My Room'). Emerging from his sleep with the previous day's newspaper in one hand and three or four *keftedes* in the other, my dad saw the ABBA record propped up against the wall and suggested I put it on so we could all hear it. Thirty seconds of deeply uncute electronic noise introduced the first song.

I hear the doorbell ring and suddenly the panic takes me . . .

Anyone applying a Freudian approach to the business of analysing pop songs in which the songwriter assumes a character would say that those characters are manifestations of their creator's personality. The opening song and title track of *The Visitors* is written from the perspective of a Russian dissident who knows his capture is imminent. Soon there'll be a knock on the door and it'll be over for him. There's nowhere to run. It's just a matter of sitting there and waiting. As he does so, he remembers the scenes – both 'the anguish of humiliation' and 'the hope of freedom glow[ing] in shining faces' – to which these walls have borne witness.

Echoes of 'Knowing Me, Knowing You' – with its talk of 'these old familiar rooms [where] children would play', now filled with 'emptiness, nothing to say' – abound on *The Visitors*. But while 'Knowing Me, Knowing You' concerned itself solely with the dissolution of a marriage, something even greater is at stake in *The Visitors*.

> *My whole world is falling, going crazy*
> *There is no escaping now, I'm*
> *Crackin' up*

There's little doubt when you listen to *The Visitors*' title track that this is the last time you'll hear from its protagonist. And in keeping with the severity of the situation, Benny and Björn's arrangement of the song ceded no ground to the expectations of their fans. Even at this late stage, most ABBA fans were people who wanted to hear Agnetha and Frida's interlocking voices fasten onto a hook so huge that you could raise the *Titanic* with it. People who wanted string arrangements and shuffling disco drums and actual pianos. People like my dad, who was so appalled by the glacial synths and Frida's claustrophobic vocal delivery that he simply shook his head and took his *keftedes* to a quieter room.

'I think Boney M have overtaken them now,' he gravely intoned. He'd always had a soft spot for Boney M. I attempted to point out that, actually, Boney M's last top 20 hit had been back in 1979, but he'd already gone.

He was right to leave. There was nothing for him here. It wasn't that I wasn't going to love *The Visitors*. It was an ABBA record! Of course I was going to love it! But these songs – songs forged in the crucible of profound uncertainty – were doing nothing to diminish the increasingly unavoidable sense that some vast, unnameable shadow was extending over us and blocking the last rays of sunlight from the world. If there was one idea that united most of the songs on *The Visitors*, it was something to do with the terrifying fragility of peace. Both the inner and outer sort. Measured out over a mathematically perplexing military rhythm, the nightmarish Nordic prog-folk of 'Soldiers' had Agnetha issuing tense despatches, perhaps from a makeshift hideaway, in anticipation of an invading army. The chorus was one of ABBA's absolute greatest. Multilayered harmonies converged and overlapped on a mesmerising nursery rhyme chorus, Agnetha blankly singing, 'Soldiers write the songs that soldiers sing / The songs that you and I don't sing / They blow their horns and march along / They drum their drums and look so strong . . .' – and this, the clincher – 'You'd think that nothing in the world was wrong.'

I wanted to play the second side, but it was Christmas Day and Aki and I had responsibilities that were specific to this time of year. On 363 days of the year, we were pretty much left to do as we pleased. But over the previous two or three Christmas and Boxing Days, we had become players in a game in which the objective was to distract the homesick Cypriot chip shop proprietor from getting maudlin about having to spend another Christmas away from his extended family. If we failed, an enormous row would erupt and scenes of festive ruination would ensue: the tearful wife asking her husband if he was proud of himself now as their sons sloped off to their rooms by 8 p.m.; the husband marching out of the house and driving off to God knows where, as much out of self-pity as anger. And then, of course, the aftermath – the silent treatment extending into Boxing Day.

I left the record on the deck and wandered off to see where my dad was. He was in the kitchen, staring dolefully into a glass of cognac. I removed one of my presents from my wrist – a Casio calculator watch – and made some numbers appear.

'Turn it upside down!' I said. 'Now read it!'

If you typed 07734 on a calculator and turned it upside down, something resembling the word 'hello' appeared.

'It says "Hello"!' I explained helpfully.

He nodded and smiled. Undaunted, I continued, typing in a 5, followed by a 3, a 1, an 8, two 0s and another 8. 'Look at that! "Boobs!" That's what it says! "Boobs"!'

Aki was leaning against the sink with a copy of the Christmas *TV Times* in one hand and the *Radio Times* in the other. He paused to make sure I caught his look of contempt and then addressed my dad, 'There's something on the TV that you'll like. Come and see.'

We stuck him in front of *Game for a Laugh*, which he'd never seen before, and from there, it was a smooth transition into *It'll Be Alright on the Night 3*. It's perhaps hard to convey to a post-You-Tube, post-DVD extras world, just how much of an event the *It'll Be Alright on the Night* shows were. In America, televised compilations of fluffed lines and on-set mishaps were so commonplace that the clips even had their own category name. Over there, they called them bloopers. That the people in charge of television might release footage of an actor breaking character to swear or giggle when something had gone wrong was just a little bit mind-blowing. Historical even. You see, the only time you normally got to see mistakes or gaffes on television was when they happened live. A case in point was the pissing, shitting baby elephant on a 1969 episode of *Blue Peter*, whose excretions upended their keeper when the elephant tried to bolt, taking him with it. No one seemed to remember it happening the first time around. But, as the finale of *It'll Be Alright on the Night 3*, it imprinted itself upon the national psyche in the same way as the 2017 BBC news interview which saw Professor Robert E. Kelly trying to maintain composure as his children burst into the room, trailed by his mortified wife.

It was 9.30 p.m. when the programme finished. Surely nothing was going to kick off now. I went back into the posh room, plugged in the headphone jack and put on the second side of *The Visitors*. The jewellery-box chime of 'Like an Angel Passing Through My Room' faded, leaving only the ticking clock and, actually, was that . . .? Yes, that *was* the sound of my dad in the next room cursing his incarceration in this shithole country and laying square at my mum's feet the blame for our continuing stay here.

At this precise point in the row, my dad could go one of two ways. He could capitulate and head back into the posh room to stick on a mournful Greek folk record, pouring himself another glass of cognac in the process – but of course, I'd been in there listening to ABBA singing about their own midlife crises. The other option was to aim his fire at the very subject he knew would elicit instant, inchoate rage in her. He could criticise her extended family again, with their fancy Athenian ways and the unearned superiority he perceived in them. And when he saw that they were truly equal – that her anger had finally dissipated into tears and that she finally felt as wretched as he did – he could back away, knowing that his work here was finally done. I put the record back in its sleeve and padded silently up the stairs, hoping that, by freeing up the record player, I might leave the path clear for him to walk away from my mum and drown his sorrows in Martell VSOP and Mikis Theodorakis. But it was too late.

It was hard to see my mum in this state – that would never change – but this time wasn't like it had been in the hospital, when my immediate instinct had been to do something that would put him in hospital too. I was starting to cobble together a grasp of the moods that would make him round on her in this way. It's hard to hate someone when you start to understand them. And once you understand someone, you might even start to feel pity. Pity for the ache of plans gone badly awry. Pity at the knowledge that there would never be a second chance to do this better. Pity at the realisation that, in 1963, a man and a woman made a plan whose ramifications they were far too young to understand. In beginning to grasp their predicament, I learned that recklessness isn't the sole domain of playboys and rock stars. Recklessness can also cloud the judgement of young idealists who believe that you can take love away from the environment in which it began, away from family and home and security, and it will survive longer than an unhatched bird when taken from its nest and placed in a sock drawer. Of course, I would have rather he found a way to resist pushing all the blame onto my mum, but I also knew that I would be there for her the following morning, and that would bring us closer together.

And I knew also that I would redouble my attempts to get them to separate.

'But you don't want to come from a broken home, do you?' she'd protest. 'That would be too upsetting for you, wouldn't it?'

My mum seemed to think that I hadn't thought this through, that their divorce would traumatise me in ways that I simply hadn't foreseen, but I'd planned it all. We could live in a serviced apartment on the outskirts of Birmingham city centre – near a Wimpy, obviously. It would have only side lighting and, what with space being limited, I'd have a bed that pulled out of a wall. We'd be about three floors up and there'd be a little balcony from which I could watch the cars negotiating the rush-hour traffic at dusk. I would have a special tape of city songs that I'd play to accompany this ritual – among them 'Street Life' by the Crusaders, 'Dancing in the City' by Marshall Hain, 'If It Wasn't for the Nights' by ABBA and 'Nights on Broadway' by the Bee Gees.

But my mum's belief in the sanctity of marriage superseded my wishes or, perhaps, hers. I sometimes wondered what sort of man she secretly wished she'd married. As far as I could tell, male singers featured on TV-advertised albums were her type. 'I like him,' she sighed, when presented with an ad for an LP by rugged cowboy crooner Don Williams called *Images*, which featured highlights such as 'She's in Love with a Rodeo Man' and 'Such a Lovely Lady'. That was her Christmas present in 1978. This time around, picking up on similar exclamations of mild excitement at the sight of Julio

Iglesias, Aki and I clubbed together and bought her a compilation featuring on the sleeve a tanned Julio in a suit, seemingly oblivious to the camera, eyes closed, pearlescent teeth beaming with ecstasy.

'I'm glad they only photographed him from the waist up,' said Aki when he saw the photo.

I nodded and laughed. I had no idea what he meant by that, but it sort of sounded like any day now, I probably would.

CHAPTER 26

It was 6 January 1982. How do I know this? I'll come to that.

Ged was at the door. She had a proposition to make.

'All right, Takis! What are you doing?'

I was drinking Nesquik while watching Rolf Harris's *Cartoon Time*. But she didn't need to hear that sort of detail.

'Nothing much,' I said. There was some homework that needed to be done, but there was no need to volunteer that information either, as I was clearly up for doing whatever Ged was about to suggest.

'Me and Emily and Siobhan are going to ride the number 11 all the way round! Do you want to come?'

'All the way around?! Really?'

'We're going in five minutes though. Five minutes, Takis! Do you think you can be ready in five minutes?'

All across Birmingham, similar conversations to this one had been taking place. Two months previously, at the beginning of November, Birmingham's Labour-controlled council decreed that a flat-rate bus fare of 2p would be introduced for under-16s. Perhaps surprisingly, the decision didn't enjoy across-the-board popularity. A low-level moral panic played itself out on the letters page of the *Evening Mail*, with people worried that the 2p flat fare would turn buses into mobile pens for the restless delinquents of Birmingham. A letter to the *Mail* dated 4 November contended that '[young people] have nothing better to do than cause havoc among shoppers and shopkeepers. We are having to pay pounds more to finance the 2p policy that helps them play their game.'

No buses were excluded from the 2p flat fare – not even the number 11, which featured in *The Guinness Book of Records* because it was Europe's longest bus route. It was the West Midlands' own Route 66. Eleven was an apt number given that it was about one-sixth as mythical. No one knew anyone who had done *the entire* outer circle, because it was supposed to take over two and a half hours – twenty-seven miles and 266 stops in total – to make it all the way back to the stop where you boarded. I wouldn't have been allowed to do the entire thing on my own, but that was by the by – I wouldn't have been brave enough either. The furthest I'd been was Stechford swimming baths, about four miles from Acocks Green, scene of several near-death experiences and unplanned nasal enemas with lukewarm chlorinated water.

In sleep, it was a different matter entirely. My dreams kept returning me to places that lay one or two bus stops beyond what was familiar to me, sketching new landscapes in spaces that my eyes had yet to see. In my dreams, I frequently travelled beyond the curve in the road where Stechford ended and the high-rise tower blocks of Bromford stood stoically in the distance. Something different would be waiting for me every time: a fairground floating towards a weir; a committee of Greek relatives welcoming me into the factory where I would have to stir curds with a spoon that was far too small to do the job properly; and record shops with window displays of ABBA records that, even in my dream, I was forlornly willing to be real and not just ABBA records that existed outside of my oneiric imaginings.

So, to all intents and purposes, getting on the number 11 and staying on, beyond Stechford, to locations such as Erdington, Perry Barr, Winson Green, Bearwood and Selly Oak, and being back home in time for *Kelly Monteith* on BBC2, was like going to the dark side

of the moon and back. There was only one stipulation – in all likelihood, the reason I was asked to come along.

'Oh, by the way . . . you know that little cassette player you've got?'

'Yeah?'

'Does it work on batteries?'

'Yeah, but I don't know if I—'

'Great! Don't worry about batteries. My dad's got loads of them.
The only thing is, though, we're leaving from mine in five minutes.
Five minutes, Takis! Do you think you can be ready in five minutes?'

'No sweat!' Nineteen eighty-two was peak 'no sweat'.

'Don't forget the cassette recorder, Takis! We can listen to songs!'

It wasn't difficult to persuade my mum to let me go – Ged was a
safe pair of hands. No, the lion's share of the five minutes was spent
explaining the appeal of sitting on a bus for up to three hours. I
stuffed the cassette player in my holdall, along with my two most
recent compilation tapes and shut the door behind me.

Bink-bonk!

Ged's best friend Siobhan answered the door. As she pulled the
handle with one hand, I could see that she was holding a Mr Kipling
French Fancy with the other. 'Hi Takis. Do you want the last one? It
was my birthday yesterday! I can drive a car!'

'Can you?' I said. 'I thought we were getting the bus.'

'No, silly! I'm seventeen! Yesterday was my seventeenth birthday!
So I'm allowed to drive a car!' It was impossible to feel entirely comfortable talking to Siobhan. For a start, there was her height. By her
sixteenth birthday, Siobhan had reached six feet. On the doorstep of
12 Overlea Avenue, she'd added at least two more inches. But it wasn't
just her height. She was also outrageously beautiful. Her thick blond
hair was cut short and layered into a soft wedge. Her eyes were blue
and the mascara on her lashes accentuated their perpetual look of
surprise. She was very skilled at make-up, but then, the rise of Visage
and Duran Duran had prompted most schoolgirls to get serious about

their cosmetics skills. She was wearing blue jeans pulled up high and tight over her formidable hips, hips that were almost directly in my line of sight. And, far from feeling self-conscious about her height, the pixie boots on her feet merely added to it. Siobhan's abundant confidence also had the effect of magnifying her scale, bringing her into line with pylons, dinosaurs and the Acropolis.

Ged and Emily emerged to join Siobhan. We made the short walk in torrential rain to the bottom of Overlea Avenue and waited for the first bus to come in either direction. The 11C or the 11A – A for anticlockwise and C for clockwise. We went straight to the top deck with the smokers and the rush-hour stragglers. There were at first too many for us to risk causing a disturbance with the cassette machine. By about 7 p.m. though, we had the area to ourselves. I was naive, but even I understood that owning the hardware didn't give me first dibs when it came to the music, not in this company. It didn't really matter anyway. When I was with Ged and her friends, my instinct was to make myself as invisible as possible. They made no attempt to censor the content of their conversations and I didn't want to risk changing that by taking part.

Emily had brought a pouch that was bulging with items of make-up. The three girls passed various lipsticks, mascara pencils and eye shadows among themselves while comparing their latest crushes, some conducted via the pages of *Smash Hits*, others with actual people from their schools. A new group called ABC had scored a modest hit with a song called 'Tears Are Not Enough'. On *Top of the Pops*, their singer Martin Fry had worn a black jacket that sparkled when it caught the lights. He had held the microphone like a crooner. Siobhan liked that a lot, but not as much as she liked the guitarist in the silver suit to his right rattling out a self-replenishing funk riff throughout the entirety of the song, and she didn't like *him* as much as she liked the guy with the geometrically flawless hair beating on a pair of congas and wearing an expression that any handsome young man would wear on *Top of the Pops* knowing that all his old schoolfriends would be watching.

Every member of ABC was classically pleasing to the eye. But Duran Duran catered to a wider range of tastes. Untypically for a lead singer, there was something trustworthy and solid about Simon Le Bon that made him a shoo-in for Ged's affections. Of all the members of Duran Duran, he was the one least likely to forget to feed your cat if you were going on holiday for a week, and those were the sort of guys that Ged seemed to go for. Emily, meanwhile, was always going to fall for the member who was most likely to upset her parents, and that was crimped, peroxided Nick Rhodes, whose mum and dad ran a toy shop just south of Birmingham in the relatively bucolic locale of Hollywood. In Nick Rhodes, Duran had a Brian Eno and an Andy Warhol rolled into one. Like Eno, his keyboard skills were negligible, but his control over the band aesthetic was impeccable. In interviews he'd say that the best thing about being famous was having 'strawberries for breakfast all over the world'. Warhol would have surely approved of the speed with which Nick Rhodes used his new status to foreground his artistic agenda in other disciplines. As well as existing on a diet of fresh strawberries, he started photo-graphing the interference on the TV screen of every hotel he stayed in around the world, for eventual inclusion in a coffee table book which, of course, he called *Interference*.

All of which left the Taylors. Duran Duran had three, none of whom were related. No one fancied diminutive Geordie guitarist Andy. Quite a lot of people – Siobhan being one of them – fancied shy Roger, the drummer who always seemed burdened by his 1950s film-star looks. And, as for John Taylor, well, *everyone* fancied John Taylor. He was the platonic ideal of your best friend's debonair older brother. His hands were beautiful. Even I noticed that. He would rest his thumb on top of his bass and use his long fingers to sinuous effect, negotiating the funkiest route through early singles such as 'Planet Earth' and 'Careless Memories'. And when he wasn't playing, his hands were even more beautiful. He would accentuate every utterance with elegant gestures, making shapes with them that resembled the plumage of exotic birds or suggested that he might be holding an invisible bone china teacup. His lips were pouty and playful. His mullet was the only mullet of the 1980s that never really dated. It was somehow the right shape for his head. Sure, at the end of 1981, there must have been teenage girls that didn't want to discuss John Taylor in considerable detail, but I wasn't on the anticlockwise number 11 bus with any of them. Of course, there was a range of things about John Taylor you might find yourself discussing, but if *Family Fortunes* host Bob Monkhouse were to ask, 'Name one part of John Taylor's body that teenage girls like to talk about,' it was very likely that his hands and lips would score highly.

Ged, Siobhan and Emily ingeniously found a way of discussing John Taylor's hands and lips at the same time.

Siobhan: 'Do you know what I'd think he'd be *really* good at?'

Pause.

Siobhan: 'Eating with chopsticks.'

The excitement generated by this mental image broadened everyone's Birmingham accent by seventy-five per cent.

Ged's eyes lit up! 'Yeaah! He's probably had loads of practice by now. *John Taylor picking up shrimps with chopsticks.* What if you're his interviewer and you're trying to concentrate?! And he's trying to answer your question?!! And he's holding a shrimp with his sticks, right in front of his mouth while he finishes his answer!!! And he's *sta-a-aring* at you!'

Emily and Siobhan squealed with delight. 'And he says, "*Do you want one?!*"'

'What do you think, Takis?' asked Emily. 'Who do *you* think is the best-looking in Duran Duran?'

I knew she was trying to embarrass me, or at least make me feel awkward. For some reason that stuff didn't bother me. Being with older girls felt so easy compared to being with boys of my age. If I was with boys, I'd have to either call them a 'queer' or ask them if they were calling me 'queer'. Indeed, a couple of months later, when Teutonic calypso ensemble Goombay Dance Band reached number 1 with a song called 'Seven Tears', I shamelessly attempted to ingratiate myself with the alpha boys in my class by writing unlovable new lyrics called 'Seven Queers'. I didn't have to be that person when I was around girls.

In the event, I didn't get to answer Emily's question. Gallantly stepping in on my behalf, Ged came as close as she ever did to admonishing Emily. 'You don't have to answer that if you don't want to, Takis.' Then, turning to Emily: 'Come on! He's only twelve!'

'*I* fancied people when I was twelve!' exclaimed Emily.

Ged: 'I don't think Takis fancies anyone. Do you, Takis?!'

All three girls laughed. I laughed too. At quite what, I'm not sure. Anyway, out of all of Duran Duran, I would have said John Taylor too. Sometimes I wondered if it meant anything that a beautiful man was as frequent a distraction to me as a beautiful woman. Would it always be like this? I had no way of knowing and there was no one I felt I could ask.

The top deck had emptied out sufficiently for me to take out the cassette recorder. I pressed 'play' on the tape that Ged handed to me.

'What's that?' I said.

'It's Godley & Creme,' replied Siobhan.

'No, not that. *That!*' I gestured towards the window. A castle with a vast arched entrance, set back from the road. Either side of it were what appeared to be battlements, protruding outwards on either side of the gate, catching the orange glow of the street lights. The wind was pelting fist-sized globules of rain at the bus windows. The pavement was empty. What was *that* doing amid the terraces and corner shops of . . . well, actually, where even were we?

'That's the prison, Takis!' said Ged. 'Winson Green prison! Did you know they used to hang people there? My dad was telling me, the last person they killed was in 1962! Not even twenty years ago! He was accused of robbing a shopkeeper and shooting him dead, but he denied it. And there were witnesses who said that it wasn't him. He was only twenty, Takis! That's just three years older than me! He'd just come over from Jamaica with his mum. She's probably still alive now. *Imagine.*'

I wasn't the only person feeling discombobulated by the clockwork night terrors of 'Under Your Thumb' – a Godley & Creme song whose narrator found himself alone on a stationary train carriage haunted by the ghost of a woman who had thrown herself underneath it to escape an abusive marriage. Siobhan made the unilateral decision to remove the cassette and put her own one in. 'My turn!' she said.

And, given that the tape she wanted to play was the birthday present that Ged had given her, who was going to begrudge her? A brand-new K-tel compilation had appeared in the shops just a few days before Christmas – a bold contemporary foray into genre-specific territory. Even the artwork on *Modern Dance* was a world away from the usual K-tel sleeve art literalism. A world away from the red-hot train tracks of *Hot Tracks* and the TV screen graphics of *Video Stars*, *Modern Dance* featured a robo-punk replicant, her cheekbones accentuated by purple blusher, with asymmetrical, angular peroxide hair and a headband with what appeared to be a diamond-shaped silicon chip stuck to it. Behind her was a white screen through which you could see the silhouettes of pointy-shouldered dancers. I stared at the artwork on Siobhan's cassette box. Yes, this really did seem like a most plausible representation of what dancing in the future would be like. Certainly it looked very different to the most recent Yardleys Christmas disco in the school hall, which peaked when Mr Snabel played Barbara Gaskin and Dave Stewart's version of 'It's My Party' only to see fifty boys bellowing the line, 'Nobody knows where my JOHNNY has gone!!!' right back at him.

'But sir! That's how the song goes! We were just singing along, sir! How is that bad?!'

In pop terms, decades rarely start when they're supposed to. The fifties were already half finished when Elvis Presley and Little Richard hot-wired them into action. Almost a third of the sixties had elapsed before the Beatles scored their first number 1. The seventies instantly disowned the idealism of the sixties, but with the exception of Marc Bolan and Slade in 1971, and David Bowie the following year, had nothing to throw into the vacated space.

It wasn't like that with the eighties. The eighties had taken a good long look at the seventies and decided there were going to be some big changes to the way things were done around here. With a songbook featuring 'I Dream of Wires', 'Praying to the Aliens', 'I Nearly Married a Human' and 'Me, I Disconnect from You', Gary Numan had the right idea, but everyone else had to resubmit their applications. The traditional rock 'n' roll band set-up – vocal, guitar, bass, drums – was no longer the default unit for presenting music. And this was a process that happened almost entirely in 1981. Punk had borrowed the term Year Zero from the Khmer Rouge in Cambodia – using it to will away all music that had come before it, but the Sex Pistols and the Clash were, at their core, still rock 'n' roll bands.

By filtering out all the non-futurist, non-synth-based music that had also been in the top 40 over the past year, *Modern Dance* presented a compelling case that this was the music that the term Year Zero deserved: with 'New Life', Depeche Mode appeared to have harnessed the excited noise you can imagine synthesisers making when they hear their owner's keys in the door; in writing about awful historical events – the bombing of Hiroshima ('Enola Gay') and the death of Joan of Arc ('Maid of Orleans') – with Prophet-10s and home-made drum machines, OMD had effectively reinvented the folk song for the space age. It all sounded incredible on the top deck of an empty bus, but Ged decided that it would sound even better in the deserted green of Bournville, the Quaker village that was famous for its enormous chocolate factory, its art college and the fact that, being a Quaker village, it had no pubs.

Making a brief hunger stop, we all shared two bags of chips from a nearby chip shop and tore holes in the top. The vinegary steam rose out of them and, on the cassette machine, a voice I'd never heard before, simultaneously careworn and naive, allowed itself to be pulled along a tidal current of starlit guitars. The inclusion of the Cure's 'Charlotte Sometimes' on *Modern Dance* sounded accidental, what with the absence of synthetic drums and a keyboard drone that lay statically beneath the bassline. But this was also what made it stand out.

Represented here by two songs, the Human League's status was a given. They were as big at the beginning of 1982 as Adam and the Ants had been twelve months earlier. And, as with Adam Ant's decision to turn the Ants into a sexed-up conflation of boyhood adventure-book fantasies and tribal drumming, Phil Oakey's decision to fire the most accomplished musicians in the Human League and reassemble the group around himself and two schoolgirls he'd seen in a Sheffield disco was an insane idea that surely precluded the only thing that could ever vindicate it – success. And yet, here was 'Don't You Want Me' in its fifth week at number 1 – the biggest of four songs from their album *Dare* to reach the top 20 in the space of seven months.

Also on *Modern Dance* were two songs by Heaven 17, the group formed by Martyn Ware and Ian Craig Marsh after Phil Oakey had thrown them out of the Human League. Punk hadn't rid music journalists of lingering pre-punk habits. The most pernicious of these was the need to feel they were throwing their weight behind substance as well as style, and Heaven 17's new album *Penthouse and Pavement* inflated both the self-importance of its creators and the writers who awarded the group extra points for making a record which addressed social inequality and featured funky guitars.

If the Human League's music had any political content, none of us was aware of it. And yet, they seemed the far more radical proposition. No 'real' instruments! Three keyboards! Two girls who looked like they had just changed out of their school uniforms on the bus! And a singer with a nipple ring and an asymmetrical before-and-after haircut of his own making!

Almost two hours had elapsed before I finally got a chance to play the tape I had brought with me, which was nothing special really – just a mixture of my own records and things I'd taped off the top 40 rundown. Queen and David Bowie's 'Under Pressure' inadvertently portended the post-Band Aid era of privilege singing about poverty. The pavement as viewed from the penthouse – something close to the dichotomy Heaven 17 were addressing on their record. But, of course, the effectiveness of a song isn't contingent on the good (or otherwise) intentions of the people singing it. It was quite simply a song for and about the human fallout of modern life. Not only did it not need to be more specific; if it had been, it wouldn't have been as affecting. The song that immediately followed it was 'It Must Be Love', an old Labi Siffre single that Madness didn't so much cover as grossly exaggerate, adding pizzicato strings and music hall piano. Even when looking you in the eye to tell you how they felt about you, they couldn't quite lose the knockabout schtick. *Smash Hits* wasn't convinced. 'Peculiarly reserved and lop-sided', read the single review. Actually, it was just an attempt to show their sensitivity without collectively breaking character. And in gingerly making themselves vulnerable, Madness became a group that the girls liked almost as much as the boys.

The bus pulled up outside Sarehole Mill in Hall Green, an area of parkland adjacent to Moseley Bog – which Ged's petitioning had helped to protect from developers and which, when it had been called the Dell, lit the touchpaper of Tolkien's imagination. We were all flagging by now, and so was the tape machine, valiantly attempting to suck out the last dregs of power from its batteries. Even when playing at the correct speed, Status Quo's recent hit 'Rock 'n' Roll' sounded like a plaintive plea for mercy from a band running on empty. *Smash Hits* said it was 'dire' and I felt aggrieved on the band's behalf. Quo sounded like they'd been on the road for so long that they no longer had homes to go back to. The more slowly the tape passed along the magnetic head the more threnodic it sounded. And the more threnodic it sounded, the more beautiful it became.

It must have gone ten when we finally got off the bus, because Aki was listening to John Peel. I attempted to go straight upstairs, but my mum called me over. Ged's mum and dad, Joyce and Frank Hughes, were downstairs drinking tea with my mum. From the syrupy, nutty fragments on the plates, I could see that *baklava* had already been served and digested.

'Mrs Hughes has got something to give you!' announced my mum.

Joyce had brought a record over for me. I noticed that people were opening more and more conversations about music with me. That felt good. I wanted to be the sort of person about whom people said, '*He* collects records. Why don't you ask him about that?'

'Do you remember that chat we had about Stéphane Grappelli, Takis?'

It had been on one of Joyce's previous visits, just before Christmas. There had been a Stéphane Grappelli concert on the TV which Joyce was clearly enjoying a lot more than my mum. Knowing that my mum didn't really like any non-Greek music apart from Johnny Logan, Julio Iglesias and Don Williams, I moved quickly to minimise the awkwardness by showing an interest in this old man in a groovy shirt playing a violin. 'That sounds great,' I chirped. 'I'd like to hear more of his stuff!'

It wasn't like I didn't mean it. I wanted to hear all the music ever made. Every note of it. And, as long as conversations like this kept happening, I honestly felt I was in with a chance.

'I thought you might want to borrow this!' she said. 'Ged told me that you take very good care of your records, so I know it's safe in your hands.'

She handed me the record. Stéphane Grappelli was standing in an unfurnished room, smiling. A few feet away from him were the three younger musicians who also played on the record. And on the wall was a framed black-and-white portrait of a handsome man with a pencil moustache, surely a pre-war movie star. The record was called *Young Django*.

'Before Stéphane Grappelli, no one played jazz on violins,' explained Joyce. 'But then he formed the Hot Club of France. Have you heard of that, Takis?'

As was his wont, Frank was a minimal presence in the conversation. His attention had drifted to the corner of the room. On TV was a documentary about a Hot Gossip spin-off troupe called Sponooch.

Joyce continued. 'He formed the Hot Club with Django Reinhardt. And this album is him doing songs that they used to play together.' At this point, she poked an increasingly sleepy Frank in the ribs. 'Frank! Tell Takis about Django Reinhardt!'

'Django Reinhardt? Well . . . he was a guitarist, wasn't he?'

'Yes, but what was unusual about him, Frank?!'

'Oh! His hand! He was in a fire! He shared a caravan with his wife, and it caught fire. They almost died. Django Reinhardt's entire body was burned and two of his fingers were shrivelled and paralysed, so he had to invent a new way of playing guitar. And that became his style.'

'That's why Frank took up guitar!' said Joyce. 'Frank, show Takis your hand!'

Frank obligingly held up his hand, so I could see the stump where his finger used to be. I had never noticed it. I couldn't help but flinch – stumps were still high on my list of things I was scared of – but I'm not sure anyone noticed, certainly not Joyce, who told me that the clarinettist Acker Bilk also had half a finger missing, so Frank might try his hand at that next. I felt a mixture of envy and guilt as I grabbed my school bag and made my way to Aki's room. Envy because Ged's parents were so lovely, both with me and with each other, and guilt, because now that I knew about Frank's stump, I also knew that I'd never be able to look at his left hand again.

'Did you know Mr Hughes has got half a finger missing?!' I asked Aki.

Aki ignored my question and rewound the tape to the beginning of a song that John Peel had just played. He looked pale and bothered. Nothing I could quite put a name to. Just not quite himself.

'Listen to this,' he said. 'It's on 2 Tone. It's the Specials with the singer out of the Bodysnatchers.'

The last time he ordered me to listen to a record had been Echo & the Bunnymen in the garage.

This didn't sound anything like Echo & the Bunnymen. This was queasy hotel lounge exotica, a slinky cross-fertilisation of Latin syncopations and tart Caribbean trumpet intrusions. At least that was how it seemed for the forty seconds before the vocal began and revolved the entire scene 180 degrees into an English high street.

I went out shopping last Saturday
I was getting some gear and this guy offered to pay . . .

I was slow on the uptake. A louche instrumental with a spoken-word suburban vocal. The last time I'd heard one of those was 'Toast' by Streetband, in which future shiny-suited soul geezer Paul Young hymned the versatility of grilled bread. I unconsciously put my facial muscles on standby to hoot uproariously at what was to follow, but they wouldn't be needed. 'The Boiler' by Rhoda with the Special AKA was about as far away from 'Toast' as it was possible to get. With every line, the jauntiness of the music became more and more incongruous. The recurring line in the song related to its protagonist's low self-esteem. The stranger who offers to buy her clothes in the shop offers to take her on a date, but she never stops feeling 'like an old boiler'. They go dancing. Her hair frizzes in the heat, and her mascara runs. 'I must be an old boiler', she repeats. He asks her back to his and she's not sure – after all, 'it's a bit soon, innit?' He storms off and, mortified at the offence she's caused, she follows him. The streets are deserted. He's walking angry and fast; she trips trying to keep up, 'through piss stinking alleyways'.

The song was one of the first written by the Bodysnatchers, but the group split up before they got to record it. The Specials' Jerry Dammers had always wanted to produce a version of it, and now that three members of the Specials had left to form Fun Boy Three, the rest of the band entered the studio with the Bodysnatchers' Rhoda Dakar to record the song. Dammers said it was a song most people would probably struggle to hear more than once. Here was my sixteen-year-old brother, listening to it for a second time. The sound of a woman reliving her own rape: 'There was nothing I could do. All I could do was scream.'

What possessed him to play it to me?

It's what you did when you heard a record that felt important. I'd done the same with him when I heard 'Under Pressure' for the first time. Like I said before, pop was our primary news source. Both for good news and bad.

'Is that a true story?' I said. It had only been a year since they caught the Yorkshire Ripper. I remembered far more about those stories that I cared to. And the screaming. It sounded so . . . *real*.

'I don't know,' he shrugged.

We sat in silence for what seemed like an awfully long time.

'Was it good on the bus?' he asked.

'Yeah, it was brill,' I replied. 'We had chips in Bournville.'

I wanted to hear all the music ever made. Every note of it. Tonight, it felt like I had.

I took the Stéphane Grappelli record to my room and attempted to supplant the memory of what Aki had played me with some non-chalant gypsy jazz. The record was still playing as I fell asleep, just about drowning out the rest of the John Peel show on the night he played 'The Boiler'. Archives show that, on the same night, he also had Steel Pulse in for their fifth Peel session.

And that's how I know it was 6 January 1982.

CHAPTER 27

'I've spunked up!'

Puberty is a bit like the aphids that feed on lime tree sap. All it takes is for them to visit one tree and, before you know it, their sticky excrement has covered everything in its immediate vicinity: the cars, the bins, the walls. One morning in the spring of 1982, Terry Violett bowled into the playground of Yardleys Secondary School and shared his good news with the other boys in our class. It took more than one announcement. First of all, he told his immediate circle: the self-styled 'dossers' who wore their trousers tight and had done their bit to ensure that 'A Town Called Malice' gave the Jam their third number 1 hit. Then he moved down the hierarchy until there was no one left to tell. Other cultures mark the passage out of childhood in formal ways. Jews have bar and bat mitzvahs; Inuit boys go out into the wilderness and weather hostile conditions accompanied by their father and a shaman. Terry didn't need any of that. He just went from one group to another, asking them if they'd spunked up too.

There was no doubt what he expected your answer to be. If Terry had spunked up, it was incumbent upon everyone else to have spunked up too. Now that Terry had declared that his penis was open for business, others swiftly followed. And once you had confirmed that you'd spunked up, you had to tell him how you'd spunked up.

Other boys said they'd been spunking up at the topless women on a new late-night show called *O.T.T.*, which was hosted by a breakaway faction of *Tiswas* presenters. In the diary I kept for the first few weeks of 1982, I eschewed any mention of the topless women or *O.T.T.*'s other headline attraction, a troupe of naked men dancing with balloons in front of their genitals. Apparently, it was someone's impersonation of *That's Life!* presenter Esther Rantzen that had me 'literally crying with laughter'.

It wasn't until morning break that it occurred to Terry that he hadn't asked me if I'd spunked up. The extra hour had allowed me the opportunity to plot my best course of action, and for the first time in my life, I found the tiniest kernel of something that might be called bravery. Except that, actually, I wasn't calling upon it out of principle. I was calling upon it because I was profoundly unclear about the mechanics of 'spunking up'. Was spunking up the same as wanking? Or was it something that just happened by itself? Could you wank and not spunk up? Could you bypass the wanking and go straight to the spunk? What even was spunk, anyway?

'PAPHIDES!'

'Yeah?'

'Have you spunked up?'

I tried as best as possible to affect an air of diffidence.

'No. Not yet.'

'Honest? You haven't spunked up? I don't believe you!'

I shrugged. 'I just haven't.'

Language briefly seemed to abandon Terry at this point. He puffed out a snort of amused incredulity, turned on his heel and paced across the playground like a horny turkey. 'Oi, lads! Paphides hasn't spunked up! He just admitted it!' But there didn't seem to be any appetite for a vendetta, or even mild ridicule.

In time, I started to get a sense of why that might be.

Most of the boys had stopped getting school dinners from the dinner hall. School dinners were very much seen as the 'square' option. Because I was managing to stay on the fringes of Terry's gang, I had to snap into line with this development. Most of us were given around 50p for dinner by our parents. For that, you could buy a Mars and a bag of crisps and still have change for five packs of Panini football stickers. A slightly more extravagant option might be to buy a brand-new snack called Choc Dips, a white plastic tub containing biscuity sticks that you dipped into a separate compartment containing some sort of chocolate goo. On spunk-up day, Darren Cathcart asked me if I could join him for a walk, apart from the rest of the gang. Something about the manner of his question, perhaps a pleading glance, told me I probably ought to join him.

We headed off deliberately in a different direction to the others and sat on a bench near the wasteland where four months previously Troy Meehan had committed his unspeakable act.

'Promise not to tell Terry?'

'I promise.'

'Swear on your mum's life? Like, really swear? No fingers crossed?'

'Swear.'

'You know this morning, when you said you hadn't spunked up? Well, I haven't spunked up either.'

'But . . . but what about Tight Fit? I thought you said—'

'Yeah. I mean, I do fancy Tight Fit. The girls, I mean. But I haven't spunked up to them.'

I suddenly felt a surge of something unfamiliar. It wasn't spunk. It was something much more important than that. It was confidence. I was the marginally more powerful person in this conversation. I moved swiftly to make a virtue of my inexperience.

'Yeah, well . . . we don't all have to be the same. If it makes me weird that I haven't spunked up, then I'm weird.' I pulled out my French exercise book, on which I had written the entire lyrics of XTC's 'Senses Working Overtime', copied out from the back of the 7-inch sleeve.

'Do you like XTC?' I asked him.

'Uh, I think so. I don't know.'

'This song is all about being different to other people,' I told him. With hindsight, I can see it wasn't really a song about that at all. And it certainly wasn't a song about how Andy Partridge had yet to wake up with cum all over his pyjamas. But, at that moment in time, I really wanted it to be about both of those things. To help things along, I started to sing. And at that point, it turned out that, perhaps to his own surprise, Cathcart did know the song in question. Tentatively, he joined in. No one else was around. The sound of buses and lorries whizzing by, along with the wind buffeting the wasteland behind us, all but drowned out our feeble singing voices, appropriating Andy Partridge's paean to the sensory overload in late twentieth-century Britain. Subsequent generations tasked with the job of of navigating their way through adolescence in the age of Instagram and Snapchat would have no doubt gazed on at this impromptu duet and found it, at best, quaint.

But that sort of perspective wasn't available to us. Instead, we pulled off the foil lids of our Choc Dips and started walking back to school. We both knew that it was untenable for us to be this soft at school. There was nothing all that unusual about us. We were just waiting for the aphids to find our sap.

And anyway, until that moment, what even was I? How could I be sure that it was women and not men that I would fancy? How was it working with the other boys? The following Saturday, I descended upon the basement at Debenhams to find two freshly stocked browsers of ex-chart singles on sale at 20p each and there was David Bowie as Baal, a character he played in John Willett's BBC adaptation of Brecht's first play. Baal was a charismatic disrupter and a seductive itinerant, a drinker and a poet who resisted the conventions of bourgeois society and sought to isolate himself from the consequences of his actions. In his book *Rebel Rebel*, Chris O'Leary described Baal as 'a Weimar-era Ziggy, marked by his callousness, charisma and all-consuming need to devour all that he sees, from the women that he tumbles into bed to the clouds that he spies in the forest sky.'

O'Leary's description absolutely accords with what my eyes were reporting back to me whenever I stared at the raffish Bowie on the sleeve of the record. The music wasn't such a huge leap from XTC's 'Senses Working Overtime'. Both seemed to position themselves beyond the reach of pop now. Andy Partridge's vocal was no less potent a piece of musical theatre than the sound of Bowie leading a fifteen-strong band of Berlin musicians – among them a seventy-five-year-old bandoneon player who had played in the original *Threepenny Opera* – helping producer Tony Visconti achieve the sound of a 'German pit orchestra'. But all of this paled in comparison to the main event here, and that was the photo of Bowie: tousled hair, a tan, the beginnings of a beard, a tatty suit jacket, and the four-stringed guitar that he played on the record. It was a scorching look. And, more than that, it was – perhaps not this year, and not the next one or the one after that, but still – achievable. Was it just that I wanted to turn into that, or was this what it felt like to fancy someone? All the information I had amassed outside of pop was messy and vague.

Kraftwerk were the opposite of messy and vague. Their 1981 album *Computer World* was almost certainly a more ambivalent undertaking than any of us realised at the time, addressing as it did the notion that in the future, we'd all be finding romance through the passive interface of a flickering screen. Having listened to Gary Numan almost non-stop for the previous two years, William Osborne was totally on board for the sentiments of that record. But when its title track got a single release, the wider world was slower to climb on board. For Kraftwerk, being ahead of their time could be a curse, but in this case, it turned out to be a blessing too.

That was because the same prescience was a key factor in 'Computer World' being upstaged by its B-side. Though it had appeared on 1978's *The Man Machine*, 'The Model' made more sense in a pop scene that had been reconfigured by a rouge-streaked generation of androgynes who paid as much attention to the mask as to the emotions that it sought to conceal. In the world of Numan, Spandau Ballet, Ultravox, Duran Duran and Visage, some people called themselves futurists and others preferred the term new romantic. In terms of sound and subject, 'The Model' was the exact point where the two intersected. Fifteen years later, teenage boys in denial of the inner terror they felt when pondering the prospect of making themselves attractive to girls would look to American hip-hop and G-funk for templates. For a few weeks in 1982, the impassive narrator of 'The Model' seemed no less aspirational. So much of Kraftwerk's oeuvre is steeped in simultaneous revulsion and adoration for the emptiness of modernity, but we didn't have a clue about that. On his new album *The Garden*, John Foxx had a song called 'Systems of Romance', and that seemed like a pretty good idea to us. If there's one thing we needed as we stood at the foot of a mountain called adolescence, it was systems of romance. Or any sort of manual at all, really.

Not for the first time, it was left to Madness to deliver a song which corresponded so closely to what some of my classmates were going through that it felt more like reportage than pop. The timing of their dispatches was so uncanny that it felt like they existed specifically to comment on the comings and goings of my classmates and their older siblings. Every scenario detailed in their music was locally sourced. If stories had a carbon footprint, no group would have been more ecologically correct than Madness. 'Baggy Trousers' appeared in the week we started at Yardleys and now – just weeks after Terry Violett's big announcement – here they were with 'House of Fun', mining a seam of equivalence between going to the chemist for condoms on your sixteenth birthday and a trip to the joke shop. It didn't matter that some of us weren't even actual teenagers yet. We were gathering information. Looking for clues that, if arranged in the right way, might slide open the bookcase and tempt us into the anteroom of adulthood.

Over on *Grange Hill*, dyslexic bully Gripper Stebson elicited derision from his classmates and unexpected pity from viewers when he was called upon to read from a biology textbook and mistook pubic hair for 'public hair'. At Yardleys School, new biology teacher Mr Chitty went about his business with a blend of exasperation and existential ennui that called to mind a younger Basil Fawlty. One morning, he asked us what we did in the twenty minutes between assembly and our first lesson of the day. 'Sir, it's form period!' I said, cravenly trying to make myself a little bit more edgy to anyone who might be listening. 'We all sit there and have a PERIOD together.' Mr Chitty's response to my utterance was to gently relax his neck muscles so that the desk in front of him bore the full dead weight of his head. Then he lifted it about four inches and allowed his forehead to fall onto it again. He repeated this four or five times, stared into the mid-distance and told us to open our textbooks on page thirty-seven. It was a pure an act of despair as I ever saw from a teacher, and I had been the cause of it. In my peripheral vision, I could see Terry laughing. As long as I occasionally did something like that, my place in the group was safe.

It was easy to impress boys, but I was never going to impress a girl by carrying on like that. The developmental disparity between girls and boys was at its most pronounced at the intersection between puberty and adolescence – and although the boys tried to convince themselves otherwise, there were moments where it was made absolutely clear to us. Since Christmas, Lola Beck, who was in my class, had decided that school was a pointless idea, shaved her hair into a wide Mohawk, soaked it in peroxide and only bothered to attend the lessons that interested her. The most impressive thing about Lola Beck, along with her adoration of the Psychedelic Furs and her resemblance to a supercool punk ferret, was the fact that there was nothing angry about her rebellion against school. Just like the hidden doorway in IKEA that allows you to bypass the showrooms and go straight to the homeware, she quietly wandered into the early stages of adulthood without the bit where you get utterly lost and start to lose hope of ever making it. That she had a seventeen-year-old boyfriend with a proper job seemed shocking to no one. After all, why would someone like that want to spend a minute more than was strictly necessary with a braying gallery of clowns like us?

She wasn't the only one who looked beyond the railings of Yardleys School to sate the desire for boyfriend action. Word had quickly spread that another girl in our class, Erica Weston, had started dating a man in his early twenties. Erica was thirteen. She was one of four or five girls in our class who, within a few weeks of seeing the Human League on *Top of the Pops*, appropriated the look of the group's female backing vocalists Suzanne Sulley and Joanne Catherall. They cut their hair into wedges, ramped up the rouge, tightened their skirts and raised the hems to reveal their knees. In schools across the country the same thing was happening. As much as anything they did on their records, Phil Oakey's decision to recruit Sulley and Catherall into the band was an act of genius. Girls screamed at Oakey because they wanted to get into bed with him. But they screamed at Sulley and Catherall because it could just as easily be them doing that up there.

Erica's boyfriend, it transpired, was a plumber called Paul. One morning, she made the mistake of telling her immediate circle that he'd 'fingered' her in the phone box near the Lucas factory. By lunchtime, the entire year seemed to know about it. A succession of pointed interruptions during one geography lesson gradually gave the teacher Mr Snabel an idea of what was happening, but no single comment was specific enough to prompt him to take action. As her friends attempted to protect her, strenuously exhorting the boys to shut up, Erica finally snapped. And when she did so, it was in response to an interruption from Henry Bannatyne.

'Sir!' he said, raising his hand. 'There's a strange fishy smell in the room. Has anyone else noticed it?'

Did I get it? Not really. And yet, I worked it out pretty quickly. The reaction from the other boys in the class left me in no doubt. No one expected Bannatyne to cross that particular line. Since the incident in the gym back in July, we were no longer on speaking terms, but I was under no illusions. If I'd thought that an interjection like that would make me popular, I wouldn't have hesitated.

And thank God I didn't get involved. Mr Snabel might have felt too awkward to act beyond a cursory 'Be quiet!', but Erica Weston knew exactly what she was going to do. As we shuffled in for morning registration the next day, Lindy Gordon and Jane Fletcher brushed past Bannatyne and told him to expect a visitor at lunchtime. Paul the plumber was going to gallantly come to the school on his lunch break and defend the honour of his thirteen-year-old girlfriend.

Nothing electrifies the atmosphere at school like word of an impending altercation. Even at a relative remove, I could sense the terror beneath Bannatyne's breezy exterior. Like a pack of reporters looking for an exclusive quote, a swarm of boys followed him around during morning break – five or six clustered together and a shifting periphery of others – all with variations on the same questions: 'What are you going to do?' and 'Are you shitting yourself?'

Over in the other corner of the playground, Erica was going through a version of the same thing. A human shield of girls stayed clamped around her. She had had no control over what had happened the previous afternoon in that geography class, so perhaps it felt good to wrest some of that back now. I don't know what was happening in Erica's home life, but maybe this was what love felt like to her.

Having your grown-up boyfriend pledging to turn up at your school and beat up the child who impugned your good name.

Bannatyne went about his business as normally as he could, finishing his lunch in the dinner hall bordering the playing field, then ascending the steps through the school gate. At Yardleys School, there was a front playground and a back one. You accessed the latter by walking through a passage which separated the main building from the toilets and changing rooms. Paul was already there by the time Bannatyne made it back, standing beside the sheltered entrance outside the boys' toilets. Seeing him on the school grounds, a grown man in jeans and a Budgie jacket, was as shocking in its way as finding a fox in your kitchen. I don't know what I'd been expecting, but suddenly we all saw this exactly for what it was. An adult in a children's playground waiting to beat up the child who had insulted his thirteen-year-old girlfriend. In an instant we all went from thinking that, well, *of course* the girls in our class would choose to date a grown-up over one of us lot, to feeling that this was all a bit grubby and dangerous. And there's nothing that makes you more acutely aware of your infantility than proximity to situations that require the intervention of an actual responsible adult.

Mercifully, news of the showdown had made it to the staff room. Cometh the hour, cometh the most unlikely of men. Hugh Saxton had short dark hair, a moustache and a prominent jaw, which meant that, if he ever tired of schoolteaching, he might be able to cut it as the singer in a Queen tribute band. Not that he resembled Freddie Mercury in many other ways. He wore a pinstripe suit with flared trousers pressed so thoroughly that you could cut your fingers on them. His shoes were shiny brogues with dotted patterns like those of Mr Noisy. He rarely smiled. He demanded silence in his maths lessons and he usually got it. On the wooden pelmet that spanned the top of his huge roller board sat a large black-and-white photograph of the Queen. Next to that was a cabinet with a draw-down shutter. Inside it were shelves of Kellogg's Corn Flakes boxes on their sides with the flaps facing outwards. Inside those boxes were photocopied worksheets to cover every lesson he needed to teach. At one point in his life, Mr Saxton had been one of the most promising young table tennis players in Britain and, even now, he took great pride in the stewardship of Yardleys' overachieving table tennis team. His car was a hearse. If any other teacher drove a hearse, it would have seemed weirder, but with Mr Saxton, it somehow seemed to fit in with everything else we knew about him. He only ever relinquished his outward gravitas in the final lesson of term, when he would host one of his famous general knowledge quizzes, dividing the class into three teams, one for each row of double desks. One year, he asked who had recorded the original version of Musical Youth's current hit '007'. When I put my hand up and said 'Desmond Dekker', he let slip an admiring smile which made me feel so good I never ever forgot it.

Mr Saxton's eccentricities merely elevated his status in our eyes. The fuck-you, off-trend width of his trousers alone was enough, in 1981, to inspire an awe that even we didn't quite understand. The hearse merely confirmed it. And so, even if Paul the paedophile didn't utter a tiny gasp as Mr Saxton stepped outside to meet him, it's pretty certain that everyone else would have done.

'All right, mate,' said Mr Saxton, advancing towards him. This alone was dynamite! His deployment of the most un-Saxton-like term 'mate' was fascinating. This wasn't a friendly 'mate'. This wasn't the sort of 'mate' that suggests mutual respect. This was the sort of 'mate' an off-duty policeman might have occasion to use while waiting for backup. Mr Saxton stopped slightly closer to Paul than you might do if you were merely being friendly. Paul's personal space had been breached. 'Can I help you with anything?' continued Mr Saxton.

'No. It's OK,' replied Paul. 'I'm just looking for someone.'

'You need to leave the premises before I call the police. Go on. Hop it, sunshine.'

The trespasser turned to face Bannatyne, shouted, 'You're dead' at him and lurched forward to reach him, but Mr Saxton was ready for him, grabbing his collar and leading him to the school gate. No further resistance was offered. When Mr Saxton walked back towards the heart of the action and into the school, he did so to a deafening ovation that he made no attempt to acknowledge.

As we neared the end of our second year at Yardleys, it became increasingly apparent to me that if I found a way to be impressive to girls, then that would automatically make me impressive to boys too. Plus, if I could get girls to talk to me, perhaps the mere act of doing so would give me a push start into puberty. Did it matter who I impressed? Well, setting aside the fact that there wasn't a single aspect of this plan that wasn't a ludicrous fantasy, yes it did. Obviously, I had to try and impress a girl who all the other boys found attractive. With her punky insouciance and her seventeen-year-old boyfriend, Lola Beck didn't even come into it. Nicky Tyrell's older brother was a boxer, so maybe not her either. That left Allison Ward, whose family had moved to Birmingham from South Africa two years previously, and who I had bumped into a couple of times in Easy Listening. Allison's favourite singer was Toyah, who just happened to be playing at Birmingham Odeon three weeks before the end of the school year.

Suddenly, I needed to convince my parents that attending that Toyah show was a matter of medical urgency. But who to go with? Allison herself? I couldn't risk the ridicule that would follow if she turned down my invitation. It wasn't even a question of being out of my depth. I wasn't even in the same pool. Besides, my parents were keen for someone older to keep an eye on me. They approached Aki, of course, but he swiftly made his feelings clear. If I was having some sort of moment to punk's very own Violet-Elizabeth Bott, he wanted no part in it. The normally ever-patient, protective Ged declared herself out of this one. With the exception of Allison Ward, I didn't know anyone who liked Toyah. Indeed, the bitter olive stone of truth I'd made myself swallow was the fact that I didn't like her either. But that was in the past – a past in which I simply hadn't given Toyah a fair chance. With my next pocket money, I ventured into town and bought her most recent album *Anthem*, whose sleeve illustration depicted its winged creator gazing imperiously out from the rocky outpost of an alien landscape. With titles like 'Masai Boy' and 'Jungles of Jupiter', it sounded more prog than punk. But I was invested now.

Finally and humiliatingly, my mum called me from the shop to tell me that she'd found someone willing to accompany me to 'the concert'. Elaine Valk was two years above me at Yardleys School and she worked behind the counter at our shop on Fridays. Apparently she liked Toyah and she'd be happy to accompany me to the show. Her only stipulation was that she didn't have to pay for the ticket.

Well, actually, there was one other condition. One further indignity. Elaine's sister Carol was in my class and, on the morning after Elaine had agreed to accompany me to the Toyah concert, Carol was waiting for me at the school gate.

'Elaine says she'll only go to see Toyah with you if you promise not to tell anyone that you're going together. Do you promise?'

I could feel my face burning: 'I promise.'

Carol proceeded on towards the classroom as the bell rang. The proximity of Carol Valk and Allison Ward in the alphabetically ordered seating plan meant that they sat one in front of the other during registration. Carol gazed up at me with enough of a smirk to suggest she had intuited the exact reason I had bought tickets to see Toyah.

A couple of days later, my paranoia was further stoked when Allison approached me at the bus stop and told me she'd heard I was going to the concert. 'I didn't know you liked Toyah,' she said.

'Yeah, I've got all her records.' This was a lie, and probably not even a particularly necessary one. After all, it wasn't as if Allison owned a copy of Toyah's 1980 album *Sheep Farming in Barnet* either.

'Cool,' she said. If she wasn't trying to keep a straight face, she was about to sneeze. And given that she didn't sneeze before the bus arrived, I had to conclude it was the former.

I don't remember a concert so much as a surreal punishment lasting around four hours. I met Elaine outside the Dolcis shoe shop opposite the Odeon. She had a fringe and a plastic hairband that pulled the rest of her hennaed hair behind her ears. She wore a tight white pencil skirt which stopped just above her knees, with low matching stilettos. It was hard to tell exactly how embarrassed she was to be with me because she was wearing quite a lot of blusher anyway. She was about a foot taller than me and, looking back, I didn't make things easier for either of us by wearing a brown and yellow campus jacket, slightly flared blue jeans and Dunlop Green Flash shoes. I gave her a ticket and, as we walked through the door, offered to buy her popcorn from the money my mum had given me. She told me she'd prefer Coca-Cola with ice. I got one for each of us and a big bag of Toffo, which I ended up eating myself. As the stage was prepared for Toyah, Elaine managed to avoid talking to me by reading my tour programme. And what about Toyah? What was she like? You couldn't fault the commitment she put into her uniformly terrible songs. But no amount of denial, no amount of willing this to be a special evening could erase the reality of what I'd put myself through and why I had put myself through it.

Not a single aspect of this plan had made any sense. Not a bit of it. It was as if a caterpillar desperate to turn into a butterfly comes to the conclusion that its best bet of doing so is to let it be known that it has access to a rare leaf, and when news of this leaf spreads to the other butterflies, the interest they show him will somehow turn him into a butterfly too. All I had to show for my experiment was the most awkward evening of my life and a record I never played again.

CHAPTER 28

With hindsight, it was obvious that Aki had found himself a girlfriend. If he was ever at home, I might have noticed the change in
him, but of course, his sudden withdrawal from the once sacrosanct
routines of our shared world was enough of a clue. He wasn't there
for *Top of the Pops* or the repeats of *A Kick up the Eighties*, the BBC2
sketch show that had introduced Rik Mayall's investigative reporter
alter ego Kevin Turvey to the world. Even worse, he absented himself from watching that year's FA Cup final. I really hadn't seen that
one coming. We'd watched every cup final together since the 1978
game that saw a single goal by John Wark snatch victory for Bobby
Robson's Ipswich Town over Arsenal. Some years, the match was
thrilling; others were forgotten almost as soon as they ended, but that
didn't matter because the best thing was the build-up. With ITV *and*
the BBC allowed to televise the game, it was incumbent upon both
channels to lure the biggest audience from the outset by commencing
their coverage from 10 a.m. We got to see them in their hotels the
night before, eating steak and chips; we were treated to footage of
the squads in recording studios atonally bellowing their cup final
singles; there was a special edition of *A Question of Sport* featuring
players from the opposing teams; and, of course, the coaches en route
to Wembley had cameras on board poised to capture self-conscious
banter between two players who would probably much rather be left
in peace to continue their card game.

In the 1981 final, our eyeballs practically collided with each other at the sight of Spurs' leonine attacking midfielder Ricardo Villa dancing around two Manchester City defenders (one of them twice) before despatching the ball through the legs of their keeper Joe Corrigan. The following year, Spurs made it to the final again, but Ricky Villa decided to stay away as a result of the Falklands War (British forces had landed on the islands the day before the game). It was shit without him (a tedious 1–1 draw, which necessitated an equally tedious 1–0 victory against Queens Park Rangers a few days later) and, actually, it was shit without Aki.

Of course, I didn't tell him that, but he would have been able to deduce it with minimal effort. In the first six months of 1982, my standard greeting to anyone entering the room was 'Katanga!' or, occasionally, 'Katanga my friend!' – this being the greeting-cum-catch-phrase of Lenny Henry's latest character, African comedian Joshua Yarlog. On this particular evening, I soberly withheld my Katanga.

'What was the match like?' he asked me in the kitchen when he finally returned.

'It was pretty good actually,' I lied. 'Spurs won again. Where have you been?' I asked him, trying to affect mild curiosity rather than hurt.

'Oh, just out. A mate's house. You don't know him.'

'But I know all your mates,' I said.

'It's just someone I play football with,' he replied. A slight top note of irritation was now detectable. Finally, he closed the fridge door and turned to face me. In his left hand was a slice of bread; in his right a tube of Primula with tiny pieces of dried prawns inside it. He started from the middle of the slice, squeezed out a spiral of the cheese spread onto the bread, folded it over and pressed down on it. Having avoided eye contact prior to this point, he now allowed his eyes to linger on me for one second longer than was strictly comfortable.

What I was about to receive was pity, but I put that to the back of my mind, because if I admitted to myself that it was pity, I would have refused it and ended up with nothing.

'Do you want to set up the table? Best of three?'

Now that Aki and I no longer shared a room, the space vacated by his bed allowed for the installation of a 6 foot by 3 foot snooker table. For the first two months of 1982, we had settled into an early evening routine. We never used it to play snooker. It was always pool. One of us would be reds and the other would be colours. It never needed to be best of three because he always won, but if he was enjoying himself, we'd extend it to best of five and, on the rarest of occasions, first to ten. We'd start by flipping a coin to see who had dominion of the turntable for the first game. After that, control of the tunes defaulted to the winner of the last game. So basically my only chance to have my records on while we played was dependent on a coin toss.

It was almost always 7-inch singles if I won the toss. If I was confident enough that Aki's desire to beat me at pool exceeded his hatred of my most intolerable music – 'Arthur's Theme' by Christopher Cross; Meat Loaf and Cher's 'Dead Ringer for Love'; 'Wired for Sound' by Cliff Richard – my selections didn't have to take his tastes into account. And yet, the overlapping area in the Venn diagram of mine and Aki's tastes was starting to increase. The Stranglers' 'Golden Brown' was a song whose hypnotic harpsichord hook and unfathomable time signature reawakened memories of Lasry and Baschet's 'Manège' – or, as we all knew it, the theme to *Picture Box*. 'You do know it's about heroin, don't you?' Aki told me, idly tying to see if this new information would dent my puritanical disapproval of mind-altering substances or my love of 'Golden Brown' – but, in this case, 'Golden Brown' won. Knowing what the song was really about merely added an easy, transgressive frisson to the experience of listening to it.

Malcolm McLaren finally found a way of converting the cleverness of his Burundi pop blueprint into something that might finally make him some money when Bow Wow Wow scored their first proper hit with 'Go Wild in the Country'. For the record sleeve, he persuaded the newly Mohawked Annabella Lwin – still only fifteen at this point – to appear topless in a recreation of Manet's *Déjeuner sur l'herbe*. The fallout prompted the singer and her mother to stop speaking to each other. You would exchange this information as though you were gossiping about someone from your school who had gone completely off the rails, especially so in this case, as Lwin would have been in the year below Aki had she stayed at school.

But still, the record was thrilling. Inevitably, McLaren's name was on the credits, but then this wasn't a Svengali corkage charge. When *Smash Hits* printed the lyrics to 'Go Wild in the Country', it read like the work of an older, smarter brain than any of the erstwhile Ants enticed into backing McLaren's teenage muse. And even though interviews with Lwin revealed her to be the liveliest mind in the group, there was surely only one person who could have cooked up a slogan like, 'Where snakes in the grass / Are absolutely free'. It was as if the National Trust had thrown over their marketing budget to a situationist collective. Not that I knew what a situationist was, of course. But we instinctively knew – as indeed, we did with that first airing of *The Great Rock 'n' Roll Swindle* soundtrack – that we were privy to some manner of arty mischief.

I think we also sensed, at a deeper, intuitive level, that if we heard enough records that took you by the hand into uncharted territory, we might never find the way back. For Aki, there was no downside to that realisation. He wore our parents' expectations lightly, discarding them every time he left the house. It wasn't like that for me. As a twelve-year-old boy who wanted desperately to change into some-thing – anything – other than what I was now, but also felt terrified by the risk and ridicule that that might involve, the surfeit of freaks colonising the chart in 1982 was a source of increasing fascination. How did they cross the ravine from childhood to become what they were now? More to the point, what did their mums have to say about it? Probably, you suspected, the same as what they said when, ten years previously, the cathode ray had beamed David Bowie into their front room and set their errant children on the path to starring in their own 'Starman' moment.

And, of all those freaks and outliers, none of them in the first few months of 1982 made an impact like the Associates did with 'Party Fears Two'. Yet for all of the flamingo-pink plumes of dry ice billowing out around the band, Billy McKenzie's performance was anything but that of a slick operator. On their *Top of the Pops* debuts Bowie, Kate Bush and Adam Ant never lost sight of the red light. They were virtually climbing out of your television to get you.

By contrast, the Associates' debut outing on the show had McKenzie intermittently gazing up at himself on the monitor, fascinated by the sight of his own face on a TV screen. Or perhaps he was just convinced that someone in the gallery would take one look at these interlopers and cut to something else. The conviction that this was all part of some colossal oversight and that, any minute now, the Associates would be swiftly dispatched back to what McKenzie called 'the scuzzy scheme in fuckin' Dundee' where he had grown up, characterised everything the Associates did in 1982. When their record label gave them a £60,000 advance to record their debut album *Sulk*, McKenzie and his sidekick Alan Rankine block-booked three rooms at the Holiday Inn in Swiss Cottage – the third was for McKenzie's beloved whippets which he fed room-service smoked salmon. Nothing about who they were, where they came from or what they stood for suggested to them that they'd be given a chance to make another album. Hence the deranged opulence that characterised both *Sulk* and the circumstances in which it was made. If McKenzie and Rankine made sure they spent every penny, then they couldn't very well give it all back.

I couldn't infer any of that from merely listening to 'Party Fears Two', yet by the same token, it was utterly apparent that a mind which decided to start a song with the lines, 'I'll have a shower and then phone my brother up / Within the hour I'll smash another cup' was transmitting from a rapidly altering reality. Lots of bands wrote about how different the world seemed once you'd taken drugs, but 'Party Fears Two' simulated the journey from one state to the other with almost unparalleled acuity. The actor David Suchet once pointed out that the secret to acting drunk was that you're not trying to act drunk; you're acting like someone who is trying to come across as sober. There was something of that in 'Party Fears Two' – that sense of keeping yourself busy while you wait to come up and, then, before you know it, the increasingly bizarre things you're doing to distract yourself *become* the trip. In 'Party Fears Two', that sense that there may not be enough fuel for the journey back was centred around Billy McKenzie's operatic ascent through the end of the first verse and back into the mighty piano hook that kicked off the song.

View it from here, from closer to near
AWAKE ME!

As it happens, there was another record released within days of 'Party Fears Two' which achieved the same trick, albeit by different means. During one of our nightly pool matches, Aki placed his newest acquisition on the turntable. The 12-inch of The Teardrop Explodes' 'Tiny Children' featured a live version of 'Sleeping Gas' recorded at Liverpool's Club Zoo on New Year's Eve. At ten minutes, it was just long enough to monitor the journey of whatever Julian Cope had taken as it dispersed inside him. We listened to it, partly in admiration at Cope's fearlessness, but more, if truth be told, in the same way we might have laughed at the exhibitionist antics of the class clown. With Cope, you sensed an awareness that, far from

being mutually exclusive, class clown and rock god were comple-
mentary roles. A huge Doors fan, Cope had taken to calling Jim
Morrison 'Bozo Dionysus' and lauded his ability to tread the fine line
'between untouchable sex god and total asshole'. Two minutes into
'Sleeping Gas', you could hear Cope declaim, 'You're going to be the
first audience ever to be savaged by the lead singer of a group' while
the band established a sonic holding pattern, no doubt learned from
listening to live Doors recordings where Morrison's lysergic flights
of fancy demanded the same from the other members of the band.

I've no reason to imagine that Aki didn't enjoy our evenings gently
bonding over the baize. But as the nights started to get shorter, there
was more fun to be had in town than trouncing your little brother
at pool. It was to be found in Birmingham 'nitespots' like Boogies
and Snobs, where sweet alcoholic drinks were yours for the price of
loose change as long as you arrived before 8.30 p.m., and no one had
ID because no one ever needed to show it.

Ged's friend Juliet Finer must have noticed Aki mooching nearby
on one of her visits to Overlea Avenue. Ged made no attempt to
conceal her surprise when Juliet (top stream, self-assured, looked
like Cathy from *Going Out*) began to ask questions about Aki (second-from-bottom stream, aloof around girls, but looked like Ian
McCulloch if you were in a badly lit room). Ged had made several
attempts to befriend Aki, but she hadn't got much in return. During
one afternoon we spent at her house, he contrived to get into her
bedroom and steal her diary. By the time she discovered what he'd
done, he'd already read several pages which revealed she'd started
seeing a trainee policeman called Graham and, although she didn't
really fancy him, she didn't want to lag behind Siobhan, Emily and
Kleppy, all of whom had made incursions into the world of dating
and boys. It was, of course, a shitty thing to do. But even as he handed
back her diary, Aki didn't seem remorseful.

In fact, now that I thought of it, Aki didn't seem to like any girls all that much. He seemed to regard the whole lot of them as frivolous imbeciles perpetually engaged in an endless conversation that he regarded with mild contempt. Unlike me, he would not be at all flattered to be included in a discussion with a bunch of girls seeking to list the things that John Taylor might be best at doing with his hands. Ged had noticed this too. Not only had she noticed it, but she made it the basis of a case study in her psychology A level project which centred on the long-term effects of parental separation at a formative age.

'There's this psychiatrist called Lawson Lowry, Takis. She looked at people who had spent long periods in hospital when they were little. And a lot of them went on to have problems settling down in life. You should read it!'

I glossed over her offer, but nonetheless, it stayed with me. What if Ged was right? Aki perpetually seemed tetchy around my mum. That had been the case for as long as I could remember. Even five years previously, when Aki had stepped in to take over on the evening our mum broke down over my refusal to talk, it hadn't felt so much like he was helping her as proving to himself, and perhaps to her, that he could succeed where she had failed.

Whatever Ged said to Juliet Finer only served to further arouse her interest. Aki was lost to us in the spring of 1982. If I hadn't been so busy wondering when my sexual alarm clock was going to go off, it might have occurred to me to notice. It wasn't so much to do with what had changed. It was more a question of what had disappeared. Even when Aki was at home, The Teardrop Explodes appeared to have been indefinitely banished from his turntable. Replacing them was a brand-new noise. It sounded like spring. It sounded like oxygen. It sounded silly. It sounded a lot like innocence and a bit like its opposite. It sounded like one enormous joke but also something you would die defending.

Woah-woah!
Woah-woah!
Woah-woaaaah!!!

This was the song to which Aki kept coming back. Almost every night at 10.15 p.m., I'd hear his key scraping in the lock, and three minutes later, it would begin.

1. The three shakiest woah-woahs known to man.
2. A get-set, GO!-GO!-*GO!*-sounding bell simulated on a rickety piano.
3. And then, well, it was all thrillingly downhill from there.

If Bryan Ferry looked like he was perpetually on the verge of sneezing when he sang, Orange Juice singer Edwyn Collins actually sounded like that. Not that it mattered. None of that mattered because nothing about Orange Juice was quite as it should have been. Their songs were stuck together with the glue of gusto. When they took flight, they did so in the same way bumblebees do, in a manner that would confound comparative zoological physiologists for decades. Now, almost forty years later, we know how bees fly, but the mysteries of Orange Juice's 'Felicity' endure. It's no clearer what guitarist and author of the song in question James Kirk meant by the opening lines, 'I objected / When they took it / Away from here'. His singer recalled asking him after he first played him the song, and Kirk merely answered 'Concrete'.

But the devil had long escaped the detail. The vertiginous rush of infatuation appeared to be the sole energy source of 'Felicity', not least on its chorus which merely consisted of Collins repeating the line 'I guess so, Felicity'. Every section of the song seemed to outdo the previous one. Collins made no attempt to hide his own delight at the preposterous sound of his voice commanding his band to

'Take me to the bridge now!' before euphorically repeating the word 'Happiness!' over and over again. I didn't know that a bridge could be something other than a structure designed to take people between two otherwise hard-to-access points. Nor did I know that instructing your band to take you to the bridge was something that you only got to do if you were James Brown. And if you'd told me, I would have merely asked you who James Brown was.

So *this* was Orange Juice. I'd heard of Orange Juice because pretty much every *Smash Hits* and *Record Mirror* review of Haircut One Hundred had mentioned their influence on the latter group. Haircut One Hundred studied the run of singles Orange Juice had released on the independent Postcard imprint throughout 1980 and 1981 and effectively set about answering their own question: 'What would these songs sound like if they were played by proper musicians with pin-up looks?' Orange Juice must have been quietly enraged as they saw Haircut One Hundred ease into their lane at the end of 1981 with the kinetic Milky Bar funk of 'Favourite Shirts (Boy Meets Girl)'. And even though Orange Juice would get their turn on the cover of *Smash Hits*, the girls in my class would never fall for Edwyn Collins the way they fell for his C&A doppelgänger Nick Heyward.

How I wished I'd heard Orange Juice before Aki had. More than any other band he'd brought into the house, I wanted to be able to say they were mine. Indeed, it seemed needlessly selfish of him to have effectively bagsied them. He didn't *need* a band who sought to make a virtue out of their weediness. After all, he had a girlfriend. Meanwhile, I was buying tickets to see singers I didn't even like in order to try and impress girls who, even if they did turn out to be impressed, I was in no position to date, because at this moment in time, I couldn't even be entirely sure that my feelings for girls were different to those for Spurs' absent hero Ricardo Villa.

*

'Do you want to set up the table? Best of three?'

I had just taken receipt of some pity, but I put that to the back of my mind, because if I admitted to myself that it was pity, I would have refused it and ended up with nothing. And pity was better than nothing.

Over a month had passed since our last game, but in the interim I hadn't stopped playing. On winning the coin toss, Aki scuttled to his room and returned with an Orange Juice record. Not 'Felicity' this time, but an entire album. By the time he removed the record from its sleeve, I was already streaking ahead. Four consecutive reds – just two to go and then the black. His surprise manifested itself in a sort of high-pitched giggle which ascended as I got closer to the black ball. Attempting to slow the game down, he tried to snooker me. The temptation was to let him because the longer this game lasted, the more of this record I'd get to hear. But I'd been practising the whole time and I really wanted him to see the results of that.

I gently sent the cue ball diagonally across the table towards the cushion where it slowly ricocheted towards a red ball that had been nestled behind the pink and the black. I wanted to humiliate him a little bit, but something else was happening, and it involved the fervid, acidulous thrashing of Edwyn Collins and his co-guitarist James Kirk, added to the sound of Collins trying to get his words out before the last molecules of air left his lungs.

> *I'm falling, falling and laughing*
> *Because I want to take the pleasure with the pain pain pain*
> *Pain pain pain pain pain pain pain pain pain*

By the end of the song, I'd potted the black.

'All right, then. Your turn to choose,' said Aki, retrieving the balls from the pockets.

'It's OK. Leave it on.'

In a pre-punk era, Edwyn Collins's tart cocktail of self-deprecation and self-assurance combined with the gambolling amateurism of his band would have been perceived as some sort of outsider art curio. But in the final days of the seventies, the jumble-sale wonderland of Glasgow provided a level playing field for shambling teenage dilettantes like Collins to hook up with like-minded outsiders and form bands who didn't quite know what they were. It was no surprise that when Derry's Undertones set eyes on Orange Juice they immediately recognised them as one of their own. Most post-punk bands weren't shocking. They were too awkward, too self-conscious to wear clothes that upset their mums and dads. Those, like Edwyn Collins, who dressed up, went about it like seagulls at the seaside, picking through the scrag-ends of whatever most people had left behind. For Aki, who now had his sights set on art school and had started cutting his own hair, this was a game he could also play without giving my parents a stroke.

After an hour spent trying to reclaim his supremacy on the baize, Aki decided to restrict the conversation to the album we'd just heard.

'Do you like it, then?'

Of course I liked it. Every evening he spent with Juliet Finer, I'd been secretly taking it from his room, practising my game while listening to it and returning it before he came home.

No one in *Smash Hits* sounded like they were having as much fun being in a band as Orange Juice. I assumed that they were maybe no more than a year or two older than Aki because it seemed implausible that you could reach your teens and still sound so amused by your own ineptitude. Listening to these songs was thrilling in the same way as driving home in a car that's only held together by the weight of its passengers might be thrilling.

The best thing about this record though, was that it appeared to be about love. On the sleeve was an idealised picture-book illustration of two dolphins leaping into a cloudless sky. Its title, *You Can't Hide*

Your Love Forever, was something you'd be more likely to see on the front of a Mills & Boon novel. For a band to do that in a post-punk era didn't just stand out. It seemed brave. And, in doing so, it allowed me to believe that my sappy, sentimental outlook on love was also brave or, at any rate, not entirely stupid.

After all, what was there to be ashamed of when you had the lead singer of Orange Juice singing about his feelings in such unabashed terms, declaring, 'We'll run away / And I'll always believe until / My dying day / My dying day' – his band's shambolic battle charge merely adding an extra dimension of gonzoid underdog heroism to the entire enterprise. Only years later would I read the lyrics and discover that the song appeared to be a rebuttal to a lover who lacks commitment. By then, it didn't matter. I'd soaked up their version of Al Green's 'L-O-V-E (Love)' and also 'Tender Object' with its exhortation to head for the arcade 'so we can laugh at our reflections in the window'. I didn't think I'd ever hear two songs that go together as well as 'Three Cheers for Our Side' and 'Consolation Prize'. The former sounded like a fireside lament for friends bonded, yet not beaten, by adversity. 'Consolation Prize' was a gender-reversed 'Take a Chance on Me' which danced from preposterousness to pathos in the space of a few lines, beginning with what I assumed was an in-jokey reference to an old schoolfriend.

> *I wore my fringe like Roger McGuinn*
> *I was hoping to impress*
> *So frightfully camp, it made you laugh*
> *Tomorrow I'll buy myself a dress.*
>
> *I don't mean to pry but didn't that guy*
> *Crumple up your face a thousand times?*
> *He made you cry*

And then . . .

> *I'll be your consolation prize*
> *Although I know . . .*

Spontaneous laughter. The band picks up the beat and reassembles behind an irresistible circular riff . . .

> *I'll never be man enough for you*
> *I'll never be man enough for you*
> *I'll never be man enough for you*

Orange Juice believed in love and – God knows why – so did I. The sort of monogamous, lifelong love that can weather the seasonal shifts of crush, infatuation, marriage, parenthood and old age. And this in spite of the fact that neither Chris and Victoria Paphides (my parents) nor ABBA (my pop parents) had meaningfully managed to stay the course.

In the absence of other skills, perhaps this was something I might not actually screw up. I mean, if you were up for it, if you had love inside you and you felt you could decant it into somebody on a daily basis, how could you screw it up? My parents and ABBA had just bitten off more than they could chew. But I'd be different. I had, after all, witnessed my dad's mistakes at close quarters. His inability to be tactile. His serial forgetting of birthday presents. The fact that he never bought my mum flowers. Or took her out to dinner. Or suggested going on holiday to any place other than Cyprus or Greece.

I couldn't rescue my mum from my dad's shortcomings, but I could implement my observations when the time came for me to fall in love with someone.

I could totally avoid all these basic errors.

People fell in love and they had sex and that was fine because the love made the sex clean – but then you could also have sex and not be in love and that's the bit that confused me. The irreconcilability of love in all its beauty with sex in all its turpitude confused me. It confused me, of course, because I was still a child. And all my favourite love songs – 'If I Had You' by the Korgis; 'Duke of Earl' by Darts; 'There It Is' by Shalamar; 'It Must Be Love' by Madness; Racey's recent flop single 'Rest of My Life' and, just a few weeks away, 'Zoom' by Fat Larry's Band – were fairy tales that perpetuated and reinforced my prepubescent puritanism.

Like John Lennon in 'A Hard Day's Night', I was fine with the idea of working all day to get my sweetheart money to buy her things. I didn't imagine for a second that the pudgy, slack-jawed, adenoidal oddity in the mirror would be, on the basis of looks alone, enough to keep someone close to me. In the posh room of our house, the 1958 photo studio picture of my dad with his gleaming new Elvis pompadour gazed down at the rarely used dinner table and reminded me that you could only attract nice girls and then not put in the leg-work if you were as good looking as that. That option would never be available to me – and neither, in fairness, did I want it to be. In matters of love, I believed in the fairy tale.

Piously holding on to that sort of romantic idealism when penises appeared to be exploding all around me wasn't always easy. On a Monday morning school trip to Sparkhill swimming pool, David Mills found a discarded porn mag on the top deck of the bus. The two staples that kept the pages of *How To* monthly together didn't stand a chance against 2A's insatiable hard core of self-pleasers. In a flash, they converged upon the back seat where Mills had held his discovery aloft and, within a minute or two, we all knew why the back of the top deck was the only seat to have a smooth, hard, easy-to-wipe surface. It was easy for me to maintain a supercilious remove from such vulgarity with a hibernating, possibly stillborn, dormouse in my trousers.

But on the screen of the Warwick Bowl, where I'd also seen Danny Zuko and Sandra Dee fly their roller-coaster car into the sunset, backup arrived in the form of an unlikely new romantic role model. Like me and the bloke out of Orange Juice, the eponymous star of *Gregory's Girl* seemed to believe in love as a beautiful idea that superseded the tawdry requirements of the body. Like me, Gregory was an unremarkable slow-developer in a testosterone-charged secondary school environment. Like me, Gregory loved football but lacked the coordination and quick wittedness to hold down a place in the first team. Like me, Gregory was happy to let his mum buy his clothes for him. Like me, Gregory had no idea what he was going to do with his life. And like me, Gregory believed that all this stuff might magically sort itself out if a girl decided to send shockwaves through the school's alpha-male community and decide that she liked him rather than them.

In the film, the sudden object of Gregory's affections is Dorothy (Dee Hepburn), who overcomes resistance from the school football coach Phil Menzies in order to earn herself a place in the team, the first girl ever to do so. So smitten is Gregory (John Gordon Sinclair) that he doesn't even mind that it's his place in the team that she has taken. Demoted to goalkeeper, he allows himself to become distracted by his friend Andy, who is stood behind the goal fulminating against the practice of having a girl in the team ('their tits get in the way!'). Caught off guard, love-smitten Gregory concedes a goal, retrieves the ball and runs out to the halfway line, wiping the mud off it as he goes, before presenting it to an incredulous Dorothy. The only differences between me and Gregory were that: (a) I didn't have a Madeline – a smarter younger sister to furnish me with worldly advice; and (b) Gregory really did have feelings for Dorothy. My attempts to impress Allison Ward by taking another girl to a Toyah concert had been the actions of a confused fantasist.

Everything about Bill Forsyth's second full-length feature was so impeccably, tenderly observed that I didn't want to leave the cinema, because leaving the cinema would entail leaving the improbably beautiful springtime new-town sunsets of Cumbernauld, and its young inhabitants whose behaviour never seemed to teeter into nastiness or belligerence; where the girls find the boys as ridiculous as they do intriguing and the way to a headmaster's heart is almost always a cupcake backhander. *Gregory's Girl* had music in it too, a wistful saxophone-heavy soundtrack that gently shepherded you to the film's core emotional truth: that you will forever look back upon these years in order to try and better understand what you became.

Be that as it may, it was a soundtrack that, within days, became supplanted by something else entirely. In my head, two Scottish masterpieces merged together. *Gregory's Girl* and *You Can't Hide Your Love Forever* somehow became one and the same thing. 'Consolation Prize' seemed tailor-made for the 'dancing' scene at the end of the film featuring Gregory and Susan (Clare Grogan from Altered Images!); 'L-O-V-E (Love)', 'Dying Day' and 'Tender Object' all worked in comparable ways. I was so invested in the world that *Gregory's Girl* presented to me that I returned to the Warwick Bowl to see it one last time after school on the Thursday before *Conan the Barbarian* had its turn.

When I got home in time to see a stylish-looking John Gordon Sinclair on *Top of the Pops*, fronting the Scotland football team's official World Cup song, 'We Have a Dream', I realised that the actor who loaned out his body to Gregory wasn't also a gauche freak whose arms seemed to work independently of his body. And although Scotland's song was twenty times better than England's dolorously apologetic 'This Time (We'll Get It Right)', I couldn't help feeling let down by the realisation that Gregory was no more real a creation than Charlie Brown.

I lay in bed, stuck my hand down my pyjama bottom and attempted to illuminate a slide show of amorous thoughts using my hand as a dynamo: the topless women that routinely wandered across the set of *O.T.T.*; Kim Wilde; shiny-haired Sally Ann Triplett from Britain's 1982 Eurovision hopes Bardo; new wave Bridget from the record counter in Woolworths.

Nothing stirred.

Then, just to make sure, I allowed my thoughts to turn to Ricardo Villa.

Still nothing.

In six weeks, I'd be thirteen. Maybe I'd have another go then.

CHAPTER 29

I couldn't say for sure exactly when it was, but by the summer of 1982, something in my dad had snapped. In the middle of each afternoon, when the shop shut and he got to spend about one and a half hours at home, his mood would plunge and his entire posture would change as if to warn us away. His shoulders would fall forward and his walk would shift into a tormented prowl. He'd get home at around 2.20 p.m., have some lunch and then attempt to sleep for a bit, re-emerging at around 3.30 p.m. Far from leaving him recharged, the afternoon nap seemed to compound his resentment at the prospect of spending the next seven hours behind the fryer of the Kingfisher. During term time, I learned that it was better to delay our return from school by half an hour, thus avoiding his increasingly splenetic soliloquies about this shitty country and what it was doing to him.

He clearly needed a holiday, but at some point between 1979 and the present moment, he had made the decision that: (a) the only country he was interested in visiting was Cyprus; and (b) it was just too painful to go there only to have to come back to Birmingham, and therefore it was best not to go at all. I can't speak for Aki, but the effect of all this on me was to instil a sort of embarrassment at being part of the circumstances that were keeping him here. Sometimes I'd clock a fleeting look of incomprehension directed at us, perhaps something akin to opening a parcel and realising the contents weren't what you had ordered.

His occasional bewilderment at having strayed so far away from his youthful plans could be inflamed by the oddest situations. One Sunday evening, I remember accompanying him to a wedding reception at the Westley Arms, the real-life Crossroads Motel at the bottom of our road. Both newlyweds were regular customers at the Kingfisher. It was a provincial Saturday night disco just like thousands of Saturday night discos happening across the country. I think he just intended to drop off the present and leave at the first opportunity.

A DJ was cueing records in a booth embedded with flashing lights. Music journalists might have been willing disco to die, but the hits just kept on coming: cheesy British offerings mixed in with state-of-the-art dance floor manna from seasoned American artists: 'It's a Love Thing' by Whispers; 'Dance Yourself Dizzy' by Liquid Gold; 'Let's Groove' by Earth, Wind & Fire; 'Feels Like I'm in Love' by Kelly Marie. The main reason I remember this wedding reception was registering my dad's reaction when the DJ played the Gap Band's 1980 hit 'Oops Up Side Your Head' and everyone on or near the dance floor got down, organised themselves in rowing formation and proceeded to do the dance popularised by that song. I momentarily glanced across at him to see if we were going to follow suit, but of course, I hadn't even been able to persuade him to play Twister three Christmases previously. He shifted his weight from one foot to the other, finished the last of his scotch and said, 'Shall we go now?' The last time I'd seen him look this out of place was when he used cutlery to eat the chicken at the Osbornes' house.

In moments such as these, he seemed to realise anew what a strange place he had ended up in. During the daytime, my parents kept the shop radio tuned into Radio 1, so I guess my dad would have heard Talking Heads' 'Once in a Lifetime'. But being a Western pop song that wasn't by ABBA or Boney M, he wouldn't have listened closely enough to realise that David Byrne was describing a version of his predicament. As Byrne himself told NPR Radio in 2000, 'We operate half-awake or on autopilot and end up, whatever, with a house and family and job and everything else, and we haven't really stopped to ask ourselves, "How did I get here?"'

Most of the time it was fine. But on days when an exchange of sincere sentiments was expected, I think we both felt a strange pressure. The process of choosing appropriate birthday and Father's Day cards for him felt onerous and unachievable. It felt as though there wasn't a card design in the whole of Britain that could have minimised the awkwardness I felt when I stood there and waited for him to open the envelope. But that didn't stop me looking. Illustrations of dads reclining in favourite armchairs with a pint and a pipe were too British – he didn't have a favourite armchair or a pipe, and he never poured himself a pint. Neither could I give him a card that depicted father and son bonding over a shared activity, perhaps flying a model airplane, because it would merely draw attention to all the things we didn't do together. There were cards that said, 'World's Best Dad', and although I was acutely aware of the sacrifices he made on a daily basis merely by honouring mine and Aki's wish to stay here, I simply wouldn't have known what to do with my face when I handed it over, any more than he would have known what do to with his face if he gave me a 'World's Best Son' card.

That year, after what seemed like a tiny eternity standing before the Father's Day card rack in Preedy's, I finally decided to try a humorous card. Lift the mood a bit. Maybe even elicit a laugh. On a good day, my dad could single-handedly change the atmosphere of a room. He was a confident, charismatic piss-taker and, if he sensed it was possible to get away with it, he delighted in saying the unsayable, especially around my friends, who had never heard anyone's dad swear in their presence. One afternoon, when Terry Violett came over to the house, he asked my dad what his name was in Greek. '*Malakas*', responded my dad, and made me promise not to tell him the real meaning of '*Malakas*' until he left the room.

'Terry, do you know what you've been saying?' I asked him when the time came. 'You've been calling yourself a wanker for the past ten minutes.'

Terry exploded with delight. By the end of Monday, *malakas* was the new playground buzzword. And I had the coolest dad in the school.

So, yes, all things considered, a humorous card was probably my best bet. My eyes alighted upon one cartoon which depicted a middle-aged man looking sadly down in the direction of his pendulous belly. I can't remember the joke, but the gist of it concerned the fact that the man on the card hadn't seen his feet for a long time. After breakfast, I handed the card to my dad. He took one look at it and, without opening it up to read the message, ripped it into tiny pieces. He addressed my mum instead of me as if to lay the blame for this arrant disrespect directly at her feet. *Was this how she'd taught me to see him?* Aki and I retreated swiftly from the kitchen, fast but not fast enough to miss the volcanic fury of my mum's response. He had thought the joke centred around the suggestion that the man in the drawing couldn't see his own cock.

Almost certainly embarrassed, he left the house and failed to return that night. While he was gone, my mum had got down on the kitchen floor, picked up every single piece of the ripped-up card and stuck it back together so that, years later, she could use it to remind him just how much of a cunt he could be. Maybe twenty years elapsed before I found out that she'd done this. Sometime in the 2000s, she produced it from a hessian folder in which she kept birth certificates and passports, and there it was, laminated by all the Sellotape she'd used to stick it back together.

After my dad's meltdown, two days went by before I saw him again. He was at the breakfast table and I was getting ready for school. There was no apology and neither did I want one. Not because I hadn't forgiven him, but because there had been enough awkwardness already. I knew that, in spite of the fact that he would never quite reconcile himself to just how British I seemed, he loved me. Whenever he sliced open a watermelon, he'd take a sliver from the centre and come and find me, wherever I happened to be in the house. Then he'd hand it over to me and say, 'Here you are, that's the sweetest bit.' I'd figured that he'd have no reason to do that if he didn't love me. Years later, I'd do the same with my daughters whenever I sliced open a watermelon. So I could forgive any ways in which his behaviour towards me fell short. I just wanted him to be a bit kinder to his wife.

If anyone in my family had any cause to take umbrage at my birthday offerings, it would have been my mum, two months previously, on the occasion of her fortieth birthday. I bought her Audrey Eyton's *The F-Plan Diet*, the pioneering book which espoused a high-fibre diet for effective weight loss. It wasn't meant to be a pointed gesture. TV programmes and newspapers and their accompanying supplements had been trailing the miraculous effects of Eyton's diet for weeks beforehand. Implementing my elementary observations of what women did and what men did at a certain time of life, I figured that this book contained information for which my mum would be grateful. And, of course, what breaks my heart now is the memory of her unwrapping it in front of me, taking one look at it and, without so much as a blink, leaning forward to hug me. But it must have hurt. Her tummy had been left looking permanently bloated by the hysterectomy and – according to doctors – by her reluctance to rest before going back to work. But, of course, I wouldn't find that out until years later.

In the diary I kept for the first few weeks of 1982, the entry for 2 January records that my own diet – clearly a New Year resolution – had lasted one day before I 'postponed' it. I'd yet to reschedule it by the end of April, which was just as well, because following a period of scarcely bearable civic anticipation, Birmingham's first branch of

McDonald's opened for business. It must surely have been mentioned in the local news, and yet no footage of the historic event appears to have survived. However, if you want a flavour of how it felt, I can direct you to 1990 news footage from Moscow which captured Russians queuing around the block to eat at the first McDonald's to open in the Soviet Union. Not even the price of a Russian Big Mac – the equivalent of a month's wages – could dampen their ardour. In unemployment-free Russia, 35,000 people applied to work beneath the golden arches.

But, of course, they were just participants in a process that I was no less thrilled to experience eight years previously. When you live outside London and a major chain opens in your town, you feel flattered. You're proud that your town has finally been deemed worthy of a McDonald's. And because you have been deemed ready to receive this honour, you're keen to step up and prove yourself worthy of it. So, really, on the morning of 24 April, I wasn't just electing to spend most of that week's pocket money on a Big Mac, fries and vanilla milkshake for me. I was doing it for *Birmingham*. I was doing it to show that we were just as capable of enjoying a Big Mac as Noel Edmonds, the Emanuels, Spandau Ballet, Ian Ogilvy, Tracey Ullman and all the other comparably glamorous London people who could no doubt be found sitting in the Trafalgar Square branch of McDonald's at any given time.

There wasn't much discussion about who would come with me. William Osborne was just as excited about the new McDonald's as I was. Wimpy had seen me through some key moments in my life, but even Mr Wimpy had to admit that his staid Beefeater get-up was no match for the thrilling red-and-yellow branding of his American usurpers. It wasn't even midday by the time we got there, but the queues already extended out of the shop and onto the ramp on Stephenson Street leading towards New Street station. There was no debate about what we would order. We were going to have a Big

Mac because that was the famous one. And surely the famous one must be the best one.

We didn't mind the wait because the waiting merely confirmed the importance of the occasion. William and I had a history of waiting for important things. We'd waited outside Preedy's three years earlier when Tom Baker came to Acocks Green to sign copies of the first ever *Doctor Who Weekly*. We'd waited years before our respective parents capitulated to our requests for Soda Streams. Half an hour for a meal that effectively put Birmingham on the map was a mere blink.

We took our plastic trays upstairs and proceeded in the baselessly optimistic belief that somehow there would be a table waiting for us. Our food was lukewarm by the time we found a space. You couldn't really call it a table. It was a formica-topped quarter-circle on a chest-high, steel-plated stem, flanked by a sloping cushion fixed to a partition. The idea was that you stayed standing while leaning your bum onto the sloping cushion. It was just comfortable enough to facilitate the consumption of a Big Mac but not enough to make you want to stay a minute longer. And like everything else in McDonald's, we loved it. We loved our Big Macs too. We even loved the horrible bits, like the floppy gherkin. And we loved the bits we didn't really understand, such as the circular bit of bread between the two patties. We loved it quite simply because it was here and it was new. We loved it in the way that people love concerts by big-ticket mainstream acts at arenas that charge you £30 to park your car and £3 for a tiny bottle of water. We loved it because we'd invested too much money and faith in the experience not to love it.

The summer holidays presented a welcome opportunity for my parents to spend a few weeks apart from each other. It was good for my mum to get away, and it might also do Aki some good too. A week before the end of the school year, we left for a five-week stay in Athens. And in the hours leading up to our departure, Ged took me to one side and told me that not only had Aki been seeing her friend Juliet Finer, but that Juliet had decided to finish with him the day before. Given that he never told me he'd been dating her in the first place, there was little I could do to console Aki. After barely a word exchanged for the duration of the flight, we boarded a bus from Athens airport and returned to my mum's childhood home, the same house where Aki had spent eighteen happy months as a toddler with the same aunt who lived there now. We were to share a room. I was perpendicular to Aki's bed, which gave me the opportunity to scrutinise him for long periods without him realising I was doing so. I was looking for outward signs of heartbreak – all the better to spot them in myself if the time ever came – but the only possible sign was his continuing silence. Emotionally, he didn't appear to be on the verge of tears. He wasn't writing long, intense diary entries. He woke up at a reasonable time of the morning. He appeared to be handling this break-up the same way he handled all adversity: like a hostage determined not to be worn down by his tormentors.

One thing that slowly became apparent to me though, was that if I asked nicely, he might give me his Orange Juice album when we returned to Birmingham. His post-heartbreak internal landscape would require a different sort of soundtrack. Echo & the Bunnymen could now call themselves bona fide pop stars thanks to their new single 'The Back of Love', which smashed their previous chart high of 37 by eighteen places, vaulting them onto *Top of the Pops* in the process. Part of the thrill of seeing them perform the song on the show was the knowledge that, with his own band in disarray, Julian Cope would also be watching, basting in his own envy. The Teardrop Explodes had to submit their catchiest songs to full-on pop productions in order to scale the hit parade. These terms and conditions didn't apply to Echo & the Bunnymen. The thing about the Bunnymen was that the more they appeared to try and undermine each other, the better they sounded. Far below Sergeant's stuttering, suffocating sonar signal and the febrile ticker-tape dispatches of McCulloch's OCD ('I'm on the chopping block chopping off my stopping thoughts'), bassist Les Pattinson played the same four notes repeatedly, only rising alongside Sergeant's pyrotechnics to meet him on the coda to the chorus: 'We're taking advantage of / Breaking the back of love'.

I didn't know exactly what it all meant and neither, I suppose, did Aki but, of course, a record could act like a set of emotions you could express by proxy if you craved the release but also wanted to keep inquisitors at bay. That was probably the case with the Bunnymen's most bellicose display yet and I think it was also the case with its flipside. 'Fuel' was their strangest song yet: a forlorn, disembodied lament in which electronic textures paid host to a glockenspiel loop that flickered and faded into view like a malfunctioning VDU display.

Given the frequency with which Julian Cope and Ian McCulloch referenced them, it was inevitable that Aki would fall hard for the Doors. He brought a compilation called 13 which began with 'Light My Fire'. Aki told me that the song was banned from American radio stations because of the line, 'Girl we couldn't get much higher'. The group had been asked to play the song on some huge American chat show (*The Ed Sullivan Show*) but only on the proviso that Jim Morrison replaced 'higher' with another word. Morrison agreed, only to go ahead and sing the offending word as the show aired live across America.

When I needed a break from the soundtrack of Aki's inaugural heartbreak, I wandered out onto the porch and pondered the strangeness of being here when there was still a week left before we broke up for the summer holidays. If it hadn't quite been the year I'd planned that's because I hadn't let go of the idea that I could get myself high up on the leader board of total legends. In reality, however, the only thing that even put me in contention was Terry Violett's continuing affection for me. Really, I was in with the alpha gang for as long as Terry tolerated me. But I wasn't one of them. If I were, I wouldn't be sitting in a porch in Athens wondering if my place in the cool gang was secure. That simply wasn't the sort of thing that legends did.

Just as middling football teams write off the season just gone and start assembling a brand-new dream for the upcoming one, I set about doing what I had done the previous summer and would do for the remaining summers of my time at Yardleys. I wondered what I could do to increase my social share price on the stock exchange of legendariness. That was when the light-bulb moment happened. There was still a week to go before the school term finished! Ever since I crashed out of his chess club, Mr Newton appeared to have it in for me. Nothing appeared to be off limits when it came to singling me out for attention. Some days it was my excessive nose-wiping. Other days, it was the perpetually slack-jawed expression with which I stared out of the classroom window. Most of the time though, it was the length of my hair. And the more he mentioned it, the greater was my reluctance to draw further attention to myself by doing anything about it. But now I was 3,400 kilometres away, I was never going to have to hear him call my name on the register again and there were six days remaining before the last day of term.

With this foremost in my thoughts I made the short walk to the news kiosk in Nea Kifisia and bought a postcard. Minutes later, I was killing two birds with one stone: exacting revenge and making myself a little more legendary in the process. 'Dear Mr Newton . . .' It only took me five minutes. I read it back and felt like, in my own small way, I'd done something as outrageous and unforgettable as Jim Morrison had done by singing the world 'higher' on The Ed Sullivan Show.

I wrote that this postcard was to be read in front of the class. I made a series of what I considered to be risqué comments about his age. I asked him if he enjoyed teaching us about the layout of medieval churches because he had been alive long enough to remember them. I told him that Michael Foot – then-leader of the Labour Party and figure of ridicule in *The Sun* for wearing a donkey jacket at the Cenotaph Remembrance Day commemoration – wanted his glasses back. And I also pointed out that when I'd seen him out jogging on his lunch break a few months previously, the gleam of his (usually concealed) bald patch had almost blinded me.

So delighted was I by the thought of him reading it out to the rest of the class (and by the status this would confer upon me) that I barely waited for the stamp to even dry.

I interrupted Aki's lovelorn bed-in, told him what I'd just done and then waited for him to see me in a new light.

'You did what?'

'I just told him what I thought of him. He can't get me now.' I relayed the contents of the card to Aki, watching the incredulity spread across his face as I did so.

'But what if he doesn't think it's funny? What if he decides not to read it out? What if you have him for history next year?'

'He'll think it's funny,' I said. As the reply left my mouth, I realised it sounded more like a question than a statement.

'I don't know. It doesn't sound that funny to me. Taking the piss out of his bald patch. And anyway, how many days are there left before the end of term?'

'Six. Seven including today.'

'Well, it won't get there in time, will it? He'll get the card when he comes back in September. And, by then, it won't be funny. What if he passes it on to the head of year? Have you *really* sent it?'

'Erm, yes.'

'You *div.*'

Oh God. It hadn't occurred to me for a second that the postcard might not get there in time. Nothing else had occurred to me other than an imaginary camera swinging around to reveal me walking through the school gates on the first day of the new school term greeted by an ovation of cheers by the rest of my class. *Yes, things were going to be pretty different for me in 3A.*

'What am I going to do?' I asked Aki.

'I dunno,' he shrugged. 'Change schools? Kill yourself?'

The worry consumed me more with each passing day. I felt that as long as the card somehow arrived in time for the end of term, it might be all right. But that now seemed unlikely. I didn't have the number of anyone I could call to check. I just had to find a way to keep my mind off it. In between visiting relatives and whatever day trips our mum was able to plan for us – the ruins of Delphi; long bus rides to the beach – that wasn't always easy. Acutely aware that this was our mum's one chance in the year to have a proper rest, I tried to keep the boredom to myself, but she wasn't insensitive to what was happening. Halfway through the holiday, at the posh uptown apartment where her cousin Marina lived, she asked Marina if she knew of any record shops nearby where Aki and I might be able to while away an hour.

My dad despised Marina, but my dad wasn't here. He was avoiding Cyprus for emotional reasons and the reason he was steering clear of Greece was people like Marina. There were certain relatives of my mum who he would always mention when embarking on his frequent eviscerations of the bourgeois Athenian mindset with all its unearned airs and graces. Even at thirteen, I could see what it was about my Greek relatives, particularly Marina, that stoked the fury of the Cypriot socialist contrarian in him. He thought that Athenians, with their sophisticated locution, were condescending around him. He couldn't spend more than an hour in a room with them and shake the conviction that they were judging him. But what he thought about her wasn't what I thought about her. I didn't care that her politics veered to the right or that she bolted the suffix '-*aki*' onto every other noun as a matter of course – a standard metropolitan colloquialism, akin to using the word 'darling' at the end of sentences. I saw her as a Greek Gabrielle Drake, an Athenian Anne Bancroft, a vision of cheekbones and mascara in impeccably tailored pencil skirts, with bony, manicured fingers which perpetually had a cigarette on the go, protruding at all times from the end of a hand-carved cedar cigarette holder.

The apartment she shared with her husband and daughter was an angular exhibition space of glass-topped surfaces and Miró prints, with a balcony that always contained the right number of chairs and a low coffee table with a tray of upscale Greek pastries.

Shortly after we arrived there, Marina turned to my mother and gestured towards me. 'Is he old enough for Greek coffee?'

Like Istanbul and Constantinople, Turkish coffee and Greek coffee were the same thing –a hot, sweet, tarry version of coffee served in an espresso-sized cup, in which the ground beans weren't separated from the rest of the drink. However, since the escalation of tensions between Greece and Turkey, there had been a patriotic drive to rename it 'Greek coffee'. After the Turkish invasion of Cyprus in 1974, a Greek coffee company, Bravo, even built an advertising campaign around the name change. '*Emeis to leme Elliniko*,' said the adverts – 'We call it Greek.'

'Takis? He's never tried it before, but maybe he'll have some. Takis? Do you want Aunt Marina to make you some Greek coffee?'

'Yes please,' I said. In aspirational, uptown Athens, it felt remiss not to try and do some aspiring too.

I sipped it slowly, remembering not to breathe through my nose every time I did so.

'So you like records, do you?'

'Yes, I collect them.'

'And Savvakis?' she said, formally addressing him by his full name. 'Do you like English music too? John Byers?'

'What sort of music does he play?' asked Aki.

'It's "she", not "he". What sort of music does *she* play? *Joan Baez.*

She came to Athens in the sixties. Everyone loved her. She looked like one of our own.' Realising that we had nothing to offer back, Marina uncrossed her legs, pulled her skirt tight over her knees, and leaned forward. 'There's a record shop just around the corner from here, and do you know who owns it? *Ourania Xylouris!*'

Having failed to get a response with Joan Baez, Marina wisely elected not to wait before telling us who Ourania Xylouris was. She was the widow of Nikos Xylouris, the singer and folk hero whose death in 1980 had thrown Greece into mourning two years previously. Since her husband's death, Ourania had opened a record shop. In Greece, where sales of counterfeited cassettes vastly eclipsed those of vinyl albums, Ourania Xylouris's shop was a clever way to preserve his legacy and ensure that people came to buy records from whose sales she might receive some revenue. But Ourania's shop didn't just sell records by her husband. Non-Greek music comprised about a third of what was on sale. If Nikos Xylouris was to my parents' generation of Greeks what John Lennon was to British post-war children, then this was like going to Yoko Ono's record shop. 'Here you are,' said Marina, pressing two pairs of 1,000-drachma notes into our hands, roughly £15, which was easily enough to buy three albums each.

Records (no one called it vinyl in 1982) were the preferred format by far. You could tape an LP but you couldn't LP a tape. Anything you could theoretically make at home could never be as good or, let's face it, magical as something that just arrived fully formed in a shop. But we were stuck here for another two weeks in a house that didn't have a record player, so the usual considerations no longer applied. I placed two cassettes – *Dare* by the Human League and ABC's *The Lexicon of Love* – and a Greek vinyl pressing of Madness's *Complete Madness* on the counter and handed my money over to Ourania Xylouris. Aki chose an LP whose sleeve featured an illustration of a ripe banana on a plain white background. In the bottom right-hand corner, it said 'Andy Warhol'. I remembered wondering who or what 'Warhol' was after hearing The Teardrop Explodes' 'Christ Versus Warhol'. And now I knew.

'I didn't know Andy Warhol was a singer,' I said to Aki on the bus back to Nea Kifisia.

'He isn't,' said Aki. 'He's an artist. We've been doing him in art. He's brilliant.'

'Why has he brought out a record?'

'This isn't him. It says "Andy Warhol" on it because he did the banana. The album is by the Velvet Underground. He discovered them and told them what to do.'

I had more questions, but for now that was enough. Even though I had nothing on which to play the Madness LP, it came with liner notes, mostly made up of various members of the band recalling how they came up with the songs. They talked about consuming 'tea and dunkies' while writing lyrics, and about the changes that songs go through before being immortalised on record. They named the tracks without which certain Madness songs wouldn't exist. There'd be no 'My Girl' had it not been for Elvis Costello's 'Watching the Detectives', while 'Grey Day' had originally sounded like Roxy Music's 'The Bogus Man'. I didn't need to write these references down. They lodged themselves into my brain tissue like bullets in clay. If I ever happened to see a discounted copy of the record being mentioned, all I needed to do was rotate the Rolodex of my memory and there it was.

And so to *Dare* and *The Lexicon of Love*. Two albums, two Sheffield bands; both formed in the aftermath of punk, both of whom had made a conscious decision to embrace pop. Both records responded to the same challenge in entirely different ways. Punk had unseated the old order and rendered a whole generation of rockers obsolete, but most critics and serious music fans still looked in the same places for signifiers of authenticity and sincere intent. You still garnered more respect if you wrote your own songs and played your own instruments. The only difference with punk was its inbuilt suspicion of virtuosity.

Personally, I didn't have a problem with virtuosity or the precision-tooled production that came as standard on records by the Bee Gees and ELO. ABC's debut album was a polished, proficient match for anything their browser rack neighbours ABBA had released over the previous years. But ABC were greeted as edgy and exciting while ABBA made 'safe' music. The irony here was that ABBA's most recent album featured moments far more austere and challenging than 'Poison Arrow', 'The Look of Love' or anything else on the ABC record. To make matters more confusing, the Human League's Phil Oakey made no secret of the fact that he saw ABBA as his main competition. 'This new pride that I'm always talking about in pop music,' he explained, '– *that* was destroyed by punk, the garage band ideal.' In a 1981 issue of *Look-In* magazine he further enthused about ABBA, and years later, he confessed that the main digitised bassline of 'Don't You Want Me' was heavily inspired by the intro hook of ABBA's 'Eagle'.

I was becoming dimly aware of complicated aesthetic battle lines that decreed it was OK to like some sorts of pop music but not others. I didn't really understand why I shouldn't be moved by the impassioned, soulful pleas of Bernie Nolan on the Nolan Sisters' 'Don't Make Waves', but suddenly think she was cool because the blokes from Heaven 17 had got her to sing 'You Keep Me Hanging On' (featured on *Music of Quality & Distinction* – the 1982 album of updated covers they released as British Electric Foundation). In all honesty, it was hard to keep up with some of the more rarefied pop discourse taking place on the pages on Aki's favoured music paper *NME*. One of their writers, Paul Morley, invented the term New Pop, and in doing so designated a space in which clever musicians who wanted to enter the pop mainstream could do so without appearing to have sold out whatever ideals compelled them to pick

up an instrument or enter a studio in the first place. It was a space
into which a Marxist punk iconoclast like Green Gartside of Scritti
Politti – having finally admitted to himself that he wanted to make
records like Shalamar's 'There It Is' – could move without totally
renouncing his identity. But it was also a space into which you could
move from the opposite direction.

Boy-girl pop duo Dollar had been going for just over three years
before the Buggles' Trevor Horn was given the chance to produce
them. In doing so, he used them as a Trojan horse for his own state-
of-the-art pop blueprint. I was still twelve when 'Give Me Back My
Heart' came out. Synthesisers had featured heavily on their early
singles such as the deliciously desolate 'Who Were You With in the
Moonlight', but you still felt as though the voices singing the songs
were attached to bodies which occupied the same physical space
as session musicians and producers. On 'Give Me Back My Heart',
David Van Day and Thereza Bazaar's voices appeared to have had
liquid nitrogen poured over them. I would have bought it, irrespective of whether or not the *NME* thought it was cool to do so. But,
as the music journalist and author Simon Reynolds noted, Horn's
involvement saw 'the duo's fabricated fakeness [take] on an almost
conceptual extremity, as if they were a work of Pop Art'. It was the
first time I'd heard someone take the idea of a group and proceed on
the basis that once the idea is nailed down, the group barely needs to
even be there. Twenty-five years later, a bunch of Swedish and American producer-writers used the same principle to construct Britney
Spears's phenomenal *Blackout* album, using vocals that she literally
appeared to have phoned in half the time. As for Trevor Horn, it
was no accident that two years later, he'd preside over Frankie Goes
to Hollywood's first two singles and – using a similar conceptual
approach to the one he first tested on Dollar – construct two of the
biggest-selling singles of all time.

The Dollar records were also what prompted ABC to contact

Trevor Horn and ask him to work with them. ABC told Horn that they wanted to make 'superhuman' records. He duly obliged by taking their song 'Poison Arrow' – a smart inversion of the Cupid myth – and creating an opulent soundstage for the real-life heart-break that prompted that song and, indeed, most of his lyrics on the album. It was an easy record to love. Whenever I pressed 'play' on it, Aki never put up a protest. Perhaps 'The Lexicon of Love' reminded him of his own situation. Perhaps it even glamorised it. Wasn't that the conceit of the record? Calling it 'The Lexicon of Love' gave it an almost instructional quality. They could just as easily have borrowed the title of Jimmy Ruffin's 'What Becomes of the Brokenhearted?' and simply left off the question mark. The genius of the protagonist Fry created for his real-life anguish was his lack of self-pity. And the reason for that lack of self-pity was the record itself. There he was under the proscenium of his own theatre, presenting his broken heart from behind a gold lamé lapel . . .

> *If you gave me a pound for all the moments I missed*
> *And I got dancing lessons for all the lips I shoulda kissed*
> *I'd be a millionaire*
> *I'd be a Fred Astaire*

. . . dispensing sharp innuendos that I wasn't quite old enough to spot . . .

> *No rhythm in disco*
> *No tempo in drums*
> *It's love on arrival*
> *She comes when she comes*

Being dumped had never sounded so aspirational, not to mention fun. On 'The Look of Love', Trevor Horn even suggested that Fry persuade his ex-girlfriend to come back for a vocal cameo. That was her saying 'Goodbye' following the line, 'When the girl has left you out on the table'.

For a few days, *The Lexicon of Love* and *Dare* had dominion of our little cassette player. *Dare* sounded the more radical of the two albums. It was only hindsight that allowed me to see that both records were equally bold and clever in different ways. But, by the end of 1982, Phil Oakey was less sure. He'd heard ABC and started to wonder if his own group had taken their experiment as far as it could go. 'We've got to compete in the areas of great string sections [and] great horn sounds – like they're doing.'

The strange thing about that quote is that it was given when the Human League were sitting on top of the chart with 'Don't You Want Me' and less than a month from doing the same with *Dare* – a record which eschewed guitars and drums entirely. We don't have to wonder whether Andy Warhol would have seen fossilised traces of his own aesthetic scattered throughout both albums. When ABC played their first New York show, Warhol turned up and invited Martin Fry back to his Factory studio at the north end of Union Square. With a sleeve that was designed to look like an issue of *Vogue*, *Dare* was a visual concept that could have emerged straight from Warhol's Factory. And because ubiquity is as important a component of being iconic as cultural significance, it was no exaggeration to say that *Dare* achieved iconic status on the week of its release.

By contrast, *The Velvet Underground & Nico* album perched on the shelf next to Aki's bed took longer to get there. Even though fifteen years had passed since its release, most music fans hadn't heard a note by this group. In this regard, Aki was barely any different. His art teacher Mr James had recently introduced Andy Warhol to the class and played them a recording of a song called 'Venus in Furs'. Aki had started bringing home his own Warhol-ised depictions of Diana Dors, Ian Curtis and Margaret Thatcher. Because there was no record player where we were staying in Greece, my mother arranged for us to visit the house across the road, the same one that had been occupied by German soldiers during the war. The Christodolous had moved back in there once the war had ended and had stayed ever since – as had ensuing generations of the family.

A female voice answered the intercom and warned us that there were two turkeys loose in the grounds. If they gave chase, we were simply to run. We proceeded gingerly, me with my Madness album, Aki with the first Velvet Underground album, ready to sprint in case one of the Christodolous' guard turkeys caught sight of us.

We reached the door where a girl roughly Aki's age called Sophia greeted us and led us into a sunlit lounge annexe which had its own mini-fridge stocked with bottles of Sprite and Coca-Cola. Exciting! It quickly became apparent that she: (a) saw it as her duty to stay with us throughout the listening session; and (b) out of me and Aki, I was palpably less welcome here. But I had nowhere else to go and nothing else to do and, besides, I wanted to hear my Madness album. Sophia had an earnest bearing, dark shoulder-length hair, square steel-rimmed spectacles and tight blue jeans. When she spoke to Aki, she leaned forward and looked into his eyes, and when he replied, she held her gaze there respectfully, fascinated by what he was saying.

She told him he was so lucky to live in England. All the bands she loved were from England. Had he heard of Nazareth or UFO? Aki shifted uneasily. No, not really. The fact that we lived in the West Midlands – birthplace of the Moody Blues, Judas Priest, Robert Plant, Black Sabbath and Electric Light Orchestra – was deeply impressive to her. Duran Duran were conspicuous by their absence in the roll call. Her serious rock leanings were also evidenced by the fact that she only referred to Electric Light Orchestra by the full unabbreviated version of their name, as if this were the only version of ELO a serious music fan need bother with. After all, why listen to recent confections such as 'Hold on Tight' and 'Don't Bring Me Down' when you could immerse yourself in quasi-symphonic early works such as 'Kuiama' – a twelve-minute opus about a soldier who encounters an orphan girl and has to tell her that it was he who killed her parents – or their English Civil War saga, 'The Battle of Marston Moor'?

She picked up the Velvet Underground record and turned it around, looking for clues as to what the hell it was she was holding. 'Ah, Lou Reed!' she nodded. 'He was in this group?'

Aki regurgitated what he remembered his art teacher telling him about the record. About Andy Warhol's Exploding Plastic Inevitable events in New York; about his discovery of the Velvet Underground and about how Warhol persuaded a German model and occasional film actor called Nico to join the band. Sophia asked him what the group sounded like and Aki, trying to remember that one song he'd heard in a school classroom, talked about noise and drugs and experimentation. A photograph on the back cover showed these subversives in wraparound shades on a stage bathed in amber light. I prepared myself for something important, extreme and so arty that I probably wouldn't understand it.

But, of course, the opening song on *The Velvet Underground & Nico* was none of these things. Asked by Andy Warhol to write some lyrics about paranoia, Lou Reed had obliged with 'Sunday Morning', a compositionally perfect song (verse, chorus, verse, chorus, eight-bar instrumental break, coda, fade) whose chorus exhorted, 'Watch out, the world's behind you / There's always someone around you who will call / It's nothing at all'. But with a picture-box-pretty celeste hook from John Cale and an unsurpassably tender delivery from Reed, 'Sunday Morning' sounded like a song you'd play to keep your paranoia at bay.

Only the autumnally pensive strings hovering almost motion-lessly throughout the record suggested that there might be more to 'Sunday Morning' than first meets the ear. But you'd have to be . . . well, paranoid to think that this – a song that seemed far better suited to, say, Dusty Springfield or a young Petula Clark – could be a song about paranoia. I wasn't expecting pop songs, but for all of its left-field diversions, *The Velvet Underground & Nico* felt – as did the ABC and Human League albums – like the work of musicians whose intelligence extended to understanding and celebrating the fact that pop was just as good a place to harvest ideas as other more esoteric branches of music. John Cale may have previously played with La Monte Young and John Cage, but he was no less receptive to working with Lou Reed on 'There She Goes Again', a song that plagiarised its intro from Marvin Gaye's 1962 single 'Hitch Hike'.

It was the second song on the album that more closely corresponded to my expectations. Here was the same guy talking us through his narcotic itinerary in such detail that you felt he was trying a bit too hard to shock you. 'I'm Waiting for the Man' sounded like a demo of a song destined to feature in a gritty musical about drug addiction. Its creator even seemed to have included a part for the dealer: 'Hey white boy / What you doing uptown?' It sounded like the sort of thing someone might write to appal their super-straight censorious parents – and, actually, in the case of Lou Reed, whose parents were concerned enough about his rebellious behaviour to make him undergo electroconvulsive therapy, this might not have been so far from the truth. Four songs separated 'I'm Waiting for the Man' from 'Heroin', but on subsequent plays they sounded to me like two halves of the same suite. Here was Reed now getting down to the mechanics of his habit: the 'spike into my vein' and the ensuing feeling of invincibility, all stretched out over the accelerating pulse of Moe Tucker's drums and the exotic fumes of Cale's viola. If you were road-testing potential adverts for the Heroin Marketing Board, this would have come a safe second to the Stranglers' 'Golden Brown', a song that left you longing to do whatever it took to feel whatever its protagonist was describing.

The Velvet Underground & Nico was the sound of disparate ideas being workshopped to fruition by a bunch of musicians who, once you got a really good look at them, you couldn't imagine being in anyone else's band. Nico's intermittent presence on the album further accentuated the sense that we were privy to a countercultural piece of musical theatre. And in this production, Nico appeared to be playing an ancient soul incarcerated in the body of a much younger woman. She sounded regal yet bereft, riding the opium drag of Reed's guitar on 'All Tomorrow's Parties', as if reluctantly recalling the rituals of her own youth with all its attendant hopes and dreams.

But, of course, the centrepiece was 'Venus in Furs'. Sitting with your brother and a girl you've never met before in the sun lounge of a house in Athens guarded by two giant turkeys isn't the optimal setting in which to experience your first listen of a modal dirge inspired by a nineteenth-century novel centred around female dominance and sadomasochism, but here we were. Moe Tucker's brace of beats on the floor tom drum at the turn of each bar conspired with John Cale's viola and Reed's detuned guitar to make you feel like you had no control of what was about to happen to you. It was strange and exotic, but it wasn't entirely alien. I'd yet to trace my own path back through the earliest folk songs my parents listened to and further still, before the sanitised version of *rebetika* sanctioned by Ioannis Metaxas's fascist government, right the way back to the music of the hash dens that lined the Greek port of Piraeus. But I'd grown up listening to music that descended from it. I didn't know what 'Venus in Furs' called itself. Was this a sort of pop music? Perhaps so, but 'Venus in Furs' was sonically closer to Markos Vamvakaris's hypnotic hybrid of Hellenic and Ottoman blues than, say, the record sitting on top of the British chart at that moment.

Having said that, let there be no doubt that the record sitting on top of the British chart at that moment was *totally brilliant*.

You ain't seen the best of me yet
Give me time
I'll make you forget the rest

Aki saw a poster for an open-air cinema in a park in nearby Kifisia. Most of the films were Greek, but not all of them. About a week before our return to Birmingham, he and I boarded a bus for an evening screening of Alan Parker's *Fame*. The film had been made a couple of years previously, but a spin-off TV series had launched in America and was poised to air in Britain. Irene Cara's reissued theme – to both the film and the TV show – was topping the charts across Europe in anticipation of its arrival. It's easy to miss the emotional small print of the song, more so when it's booming from a speaker stack in a Greek park. And I definitely missed it that night. Why on earth would I have perceived any ambivalence in a chorus that went, 'Fame! I'm gonna live forever / I'm going to learn how to fly (high) / I feel it coming together / People will see me and cry'?

The thing about 'Fame' though, is that if you listen to Michael Gore's lyrics for the song *once you've seen the film*, only then do you start to notice that it's really a song about pursuing a preposterously unlikely outcome to the detriment of your relationships and your personal well-being and with no backup plan. It's a song that comes from a place of desperation and the attendant knowledge of what it means to run that risk. By the final section of the film, when we see Coco Hernandez – the same Coco whose hopes are captured in the amber of Cara's theme song – weeping in the squalid apartment of the 'auteur' who asks her to take her top off, we finally see what that risk amounts to.

Fame interwove the stories of six young applicants who are offered a place at the New York School of Performing Arts. It was fiction, but Parker's decision to shoot *Fame* like a fly-on-the-wall documentary meant that you couldn't quite disbelieve what you were seeing.

There was almost no incidental music, which meant that when people spoke, you could hear their voices reverberate in low-lit classrooms and corridors. In fact, there was very little music in it at all. One of the major exceptions was Linda Clifford's 'Red Light', which is the song playing in one of the film's funniest *and* most sexually charged scenes – the moment where Leroy Johnson accompanies his friend to the dance auditions and upstages her with a routine that culminates in him quite simply standing there and running his hand over his crotch while fixing his gaze upon the two female teachers running the admissions process. The song hasn't finished and he hasn't even filled in his papers, but he knows he's done enough to earn a place.

Like *Gregory's Girl*, it was a coming-of-age movie. And when anyone who has yet to come of age watches a coming-of-age movie, they immediately try and work out: (a) who they most want to be; and (b) who they're actually closest to being. Aki most closely identified with Leroy, who never appeared to try and rarely allowed the expectations of others to get under his skin; Leroy, who, asked why he was even attending a class to which he was paying no attention, merely exclaimed, 'Cuz I'm young and single and I *loves* to mingle.' Once heard, never forgotten – Aki repeated that line endlessly. It seemed to crystallise an attitude to authority that, to him, was utterly laudable.

The disparity in how we saw ourselves was summed up by the *Fame* characters we wanted to be. While Aki was obsessing upon Leroy, I nurtured a mini crush on Bruno Martelli, the perpetually unperturbed piano prodigy with the cascading curls and piercing blue eyes, whose bond with his keyboards seemed to preclude any pressing need for human companionship. His dad drove a New York cab and, an hour into the film, you got to see him screech to a halt by the kerb outside the NYPA and pipe out his son's latest recording through a speaker he's fixed onto his roof rack. It's the song 'Fame'. Students flood out of the building and start to dance, bringing the traffic to a standstill. Swept along with the human tide is a shocked

Bruno who thinks his dad has lost his mind. 'Those tapes aren't ready! They're not supposed to be played . . .'

'But Bruno, look at the people!' his father pleads, 'They don't know it's not ready! Bruno, look at it! They like it!' How cool, I thought. To be so secure in yourself, to have such a fixed internal quality meter that not even the sight of your work wreaking pandemonium upon the whole of the Upper West Side can disturb it.

Yep, it sure would be great to be Bruno. And yet, the uncomfortable feeling scratching away on the underside of my subconscious was that my situation was closer to that of Doris Finsecker – 'as flamboyant as a bagel', and unclear about how to proceed with the business of making herself happy in a way that wasn't going to upset her mother. Sometimes it didn't seem that such an outcome was at all possible. Mostly, I tried not to think about it.

Aki and I were back at the open-air cinema a few days later, this time to watch *An American Werewolf in London*. The fact that it had been given an X certificate (an 18 in old money) didn't stop us from being waved straight through. The action in the film centred around American hitchhikers David and Jack who are savaged by a werewolf on the moonlit Yorkshire moors. Jack dies from his injuries, but after David wakes up in a hospital in London, he commences a passionate affair with one of the nurses, Alex (Jenny Agutter), who agrees to let him stay at her flat in London. On the day of his arrival at Alex's flat, they can no longer contain themselves. As she gives David the room-by-room tour, their feelings for each other get the better of them. To the sound of Van Morrison's 'Moondance' – a song I'd never heard before – they take their clothes off, roll into the shower together and end up having sex.

If any film was going to light the touchpaper of my adolescence, surely it would have to be one in which I got to follow the statuesque lines of Jenny Agutter's silhouette from her face to her collarbone and further down in a steamy shower scene. Well, actually, no. I can't speak for what was happening inside Aki's trousers, but for me, the most exciting thing about David's living arrangement with Nurse Alex was the scene where he finds himself locked out of her ground-floor flat and simply slides up the sash window to let himself in. The action of the heavy window was so smooth and his entry so effortless that it instantly became the most attractive representation of grown-up life that I'd ever seen. None of the houses in Birmingham had these huge, pleasing windows whose name I didn't know. In Birmingham, all the houses had small windows that you had to open by pulling a handle upwards. Once you'd seen an American werewolf sliding open Jenny Agutter's window amid the bustling backdrop of rush-hour London, there was no going back.

But it wasn't just Jenny Agutter's sash window that sent my mind scurrying to places far beyond Athens' municipal greenery. There was the incredible scene in which David transforms into a werewolf before our very eyes, his torso and hands elongating as bones crack into new positions and hairs sprout on previously hairless parts of his body, all of which played out to the cathartic rattle of Creedence Clearwater Revival's 'Bad Moon Rising'. The moment scorched itself into my mind, not just because I needed to know who had recorded that song, but also because of what it represented: imminent, inevitable change with unknowable consequences. Sudden change was what terrified me more than anything else. And every encounter I had that reminded me of that – from the conversation three years previously with the newly conscripted Notis to the prospect of shaving for the first time – charged that song with an urgency that was almost unbearable to me.

Pre-global warming, you'd return home in late August and the air was fresh with the first intimations of autumn. The drop in temperature would instantly make you feel more alert and impatient to do things. Every time we went away, it made me realise that my life was in Britain. And as long as I wasn't in the place where my life was, I had no life to get on with. But, of course, that was how my dad felt about Cyprus. That's why he could no longer countenance the idea of even taking a holiday there. Because the heartache of leaving wasn't worth the transient joy of arriving. On the penultimate Sunday before September, we walked through the arrivals gate and there he was. He looked pale and slightly disengaged. He'd cut his hair shorter and got rid of his sideburns. It gave him a more serious demeanour. Perhaps to circumvent the awkwardness of the absence of physical affection, he relieved my mum of the trolley she was pushing and we all walked towards the car park.

When we got home, all the beds were unmade. Like a cross between Goldilocks and the three bears, my dad had slept in one bed for a week and simply gone on to another one when he longed for the sensation of clean sheets. My mum set about stripping all the beds and putting a series of washes on so that we all had fresh bed linen that evening. In the fridge were the remains of a tray of moussaka that Mrs Hughes next door had made for my dad. While we'd been away, every Sunday after breakfast, she had once again set about doing on a weekly basis what she had done when my mum was in hospital, looking through her cookbooks and bringing to life a recipe for a classic Greek dish. Stuffed peppers and onions one week. *Stifado* on the second week. *Kleftiko* on the third. And *pastitsio* (baked macaroni and minced pork with béchamel) on the fourth. As before, wary of inadvertently wounding his pride, she would wait until his car had left the drive, and leave the tray of still-warm food on the doorstep alongside a cheerful handwritten note.

But on 22 August 1982, I didn't care about any of that. I was good for Mrs Hughes's moussaka. I didn't care about the cleanliness of the sheets I slept in that night. I needed to find out if my postcard had reached Mr Newton before the last day of term. I needed to know if it had been the most awful mistake I'd ever made or if it had, somehow, against all earthly odds, finally confirmed me as some kind of maverick prankster outlier. I put on my trainers and ran around the corner to Terry's house. I couldn't wait a second longer.

Terry thundered downstairs and practically pushed his mum out the way so that he and I were face to face on his doorstep. Skipping merrily on the spot, he raised his left hand to point at me and started making an indistinct noise which finally came into focus around the words, 'Oh man! Oh man!'

'What? WHAT?' I replied.

"WOOHOOHOO-OOOHOOO! WOOOHUHUHUHUHOOO! YOUR POSTCARD! OH GOD!! YOUR POSTCARD! FUCKING HELL!!"

Ah, so it had arrived.

'Am I in trouble?'

'It was wicked! He read it out to the class. Everyone was killing themselves. Even Mr Newton thought it was funny. I can't believe you mentioned his bald patch. Oh man! OH MAN!'

'And he read it all out, did he?'

'Yeah, on the last day of term. I tell you . . . oh man!'

I didn't understand it. Though this was clearly the result for which I'd hoped, there was also a part of me that didn't understand it. If Mr Newton had disliked me as much as I thought he did, why was he so happy to read out my postcard to the rest of the class? Why allow himself to be the butt of the joke? I think about it now and I think about a bored teacher on the last day of term, happy to make the day go by a bit more quickly. You imagine as a child that it must constitute some sort of ego trip for a teacher to be up there and have thirty children all staring at them. But they might not see it that way. For some teachers, it might be the opposite of an ego trip, especially for those who didn't envisage that they would be spending their late forties trying to make children care about all the different bits of medieval churches. And, for those teachers, any deviation from the business of a normal schoolday is probably quite welcome. Maybe that's why he was so willing to make himself the butt of the joke and grant me the satisfaction of a moment in which I had an entire classroom laughing at me for the right reason, albeit one which I would only experience vicariously.

Whatever it was, it seemed to have an immediate impact. Terry's excitement at returning to school was compounded by the news that an old friend of his from primary school, Kevin Flynn, would be transferring to Yardleys from a rival school for the beginning of the new school year, taking the place vacated by Troy Meehan after his murder conviction.

'Ooooh! You don't wanna get on Flynn's bad side, I tell you. Flynn was the cock of Hartfield. I mean, most of the time, he's sound as a pound, like, really funny, but if you get him angry, he goes fucking bonkers. Always did. Can't help it. His whole family's the same. They live in this tiny house with his twin brothers and three Alsatians.' Each sentence of Terry's description had the effect of making Flynn seem somehow more terrifying than the previous one: the incident with the air rifle that saw one of Flynn's brothers partially blinding the other; the time he stole three tins of Evo-Stik from the metalwork room, which were found emptied into a bag inside his desk and led to his expulsion.

But perhaps the most terrifying of all was the bit when Terry let me know that he'd told Flynn all about me: my postcard to Mr Newton; the story about the time we got thrown out of the joke shop; about my hilarious swearing dad and the fact that if you went to his chippy with me, you got given chips and free goes on the *Space Invaders* machine. I can see now that he was trying to sell Flynn the idea of me being co-opted into a group of old friends that would also include me. And these atypical instances of my crazy behaviour were designed to help seal the deal. It was strange to see Terry happily relinquish his alpha status to a newcomer who had yet to even start at the school. It also had the effect of making me anxious in a variety of ways. Even setting aside the fact that he was taking the place of a pupil who had actually *murdered* someone, Flynn sounded like a psychopath. I didn't want to be friends with a psychopath, no matter how far back his friendship with Terry extended. And yet, it didn't seem like I had much choice over that.

It was a worry, but for now, it was a worry that could wait. The top 40 had changed five times since I left Birmingham. Without access to newspapers or magazines, I had no idea what the chart looked like. 'So you don't know about Dexys?' said Terry.

'What about Dexys?'

'It's number 1! Haven't you heard it? "Come On Eileen"?'

Dexys Midnight Runners at number 1? But how? How on earth could a band that was over at the beginning of the summer holidays suddenly be back at number 1? A year had elapsed since their last hit. Of course, in twenty-first-century pop terms, a year is the space between breakfast and lunch. But in 1982, a year was one-thirteenth of our lives. And in that period, Dexys had continued releasing singles that consistently fell short of the top 40. There was nothing to suggest they had anything in reserve that might prompt posterity to remember them as anything more than the band that did 'Geno'.

'What's it like?'

'Paphides, are you taking the piss?'

'I've been away, haven't I?'

Terry couldn't find the words to describe it, so he moved on to their new look, a gypsy sort of thing, apparently: torn denim dungarees, messy hair and a new-found suspicion of footwear.

I left Terry's house and went straight to my room so I could listen to the top 40 rundown presented by Tommy Vance on Radio 1. The combination of my insatiable curiosity coupled with the fact that, being number 1, 'Come On Eileen' would be the final song, ramped up the suspense. Even without seeing what they looked like, it seemed immediately shocking to me that, in 1982, you could have a hit as big as that with a record that sounded like that, with violins and mandolins at its centre. But then, how could it have been anything other than a hit? Everything on 'Come On Eileen' was a hook. It was like a medley of best bits from standards that had somehow eluded our ears prior to this point. Even the intro gave you twice as much as you were expecting, with one hook, played mostly on violins, in the first twenty seconds, giving way to a second more urgent earworm which introduced the piano and mandolins.

Consciously or not, 'Come On Eileen' pulled off the same trick that, two years previously, Madness had become increasingly adept at deploying on their records – instilling in us a sense of yearning for something that was still ongoing; making us nostalgic for the present. 'Come On Eileen' described what was happening in our interior world: the desperate quest for some sort of encounter that might circumvent the awkwardness of courtship. The need to stop being a person that hadn't done it and to start being someone who had. The Eileen immortalised in Kevin Rowland's lyrics was a teenage crush idealised by the passage of time. To listen to the song now is to be put in mind of Jonathan Richman and the Modern Lovers' 1984 single 'That Summer Feeling' – in which Richman poignantly attempts to disentangle the things that happen to us as teenagers from our unconscious emotional editorialising of those memories.

> *And you boys long for some little girl that you dated*
> *Do you long for her or for the way you were?*
> *That summer feeling's gonna haunt you the rest of your life*

In the case of 'Come On Eileen', there was something extra at work that forged a deeper connection for me. It really didn't sound all that different in parts to some of the Greek music I grew up with. The mandolins sounded just like bouzoukis and, on the verses, they locked into a rhythm that sounded like it was constantly being thwarted by itself. It wasn't a new invention, this rhythm. It was on dozens of hits that came before it, from Unit 4 + 2's 'Concrete and Clay' to Tom Jones's 'It's Not Unusual'. But the clincher in 'Come On Eileen' was the sweet release of a chorus that blows that rhythm apart in order to finally lay its *raison d'être* on the line.

> *Come on Eileen*
> *I swear (well he means)*
> *At this moment*
> *You mean everything*

From then on, almost every schoolday throughout September, I'd sling my bag in the hallway and run upstairs to play it. It was so perfect that, for the time being, it didn't occur to me that I might want to get its parent album *Too-Rye-Ay* to see if there was more where that came from. Not least because it seemed inconceivable that there could be anything on there that would come close to it. For the time being, everything I could possibly need from Dexys Midnight Runners could be found in the four minutes and twelve seconds of 'Come On Eileen'.

CHAPTER 30

'Here he comes! Ey! EY! *Here he comes!* Oi! Flynn!'

Terry Violett looked back at his classmates in the playground to signal that his old buddy was here, then back at Flynn.

'Watch out! Here he comes!'

I couldn't see anyone who fitted the bill. Nothing. Except for . . . oh wait. Hang on. *That's* Flynn?

I'd expected an ogre, but Kevin Flynn was short and skinny. Bomber jackets are supposed to be tight, but this one was loose on him. From a distance, his thin blond hair merged into the translucent pallor of his skin. Beyond a quick play-fight with Terry, he made no attempt to ingratiate himself with the rest of the group. But this didn't look like shyness. It looked like the total opposite of shyness. The core of his coldness was his blue eyes, which never seemed to blink or narrow. This, combined with his slightness and the fact that he was filling a space made vacant by an actual killer, had the effect of making him seem even more sinister.

It didn't matter whether or not I wanted to be his friend. That had already been decided for me. We were quickly augmented by a fourth member of what now appeared to be a gang. Dean Tookey also went way back to primary school with Terry and Flynn. Putting his constant disruption of lessons down to the fact that he was under-stimulated, the school decided to move him up a class so that he and Terry and I were now classmates. His first meaningful gesture as a pupil in my class was to wait for the quietest moment of our first maths lesson and, mid-exercise, place a pencil case on his head and then continue as though nothing had happened. He had a catchphrase which, actually, wasn't his catchphrase at all. All he had to do to reduce everyone around him to shoulder-shaking convulsions was deliver it.

'What'chu talkin' 'bout, Willis?'

It was from *Diff'rent Strokes*, the American sitcom shown here on Friday teatimes, in which a widowed Manhattan businessman adopts two black children from Harlem. Arnold, the younger of the two boys, had a catchphrase which he directed at his brother. There was a sort of genius about Tookey's unaltered, out-of-context use of it. And, to his credit, he never overdid it. Perhaps once every two days if you were lucky. And if you were really lucky, he might even use it on a teacher. Nothing was funnier than seeing Mr Bruce, the physics teacher, trying not to laugh as he told Tookey not to address him like that. Dean Tookey was effortlessly funny and he enjoyed all the power it gave him. Unlike Flynn, who I continued to regard with caution, I wanted to impress Tookey. Actually, I just wanted to be near enough to be able to laugh at whatever he did next. I even went home and attempted to use 'What'chu talkin' 'bout, Willis?' on Aki as if I'd invented it, but he just glared at me in bewilderment. And then, two weeks later, when I brought Tookey home and he used the same catchphrase on Aki, the game was up.

'So that's where you got it from,' he said in front of Tookey, as I felt my face burning. Tookey noticed it too, but didn't say anything. It was credit in the bank if he needed it.

Now that I was legendary, I needed to make sure that, once in a while, I did things that replenished my legend stocks. On the first day of the half-term holidays, I outdid myself. We cycled from Acocks Green to Solihull. If you pedalled hard it was just fifteen minutes, but felt much further than that. Semi-detached mock Tudor houses with names as well as numbers loomed over driveways on which sat Land Rovers that were assembled in the nearby factory. And when the women that lived in these houses went shopping, they'd head for Mell Square, Solihull's geometrically pleasing shopping area. They might buy themselves a nice top at Beatties department store, buy a storybook for their children at Midland Educational and take tea at Drucker's Viennese patisserie. And if the weather was nice, they might sit on the low wall of the municipal fountain.

Solihull also serviced the needs of people from outlying villages such as Hockley Heath and Tanworth-in-Arden. In the early sixties, it was where Nick and Gabrielle Drake's mother Molly would sometimes take her children on a Saturday afternoon. If she had ventured into town a couple of decades later, she wouldn't have been able to miss the commotion being generated by four teenagers lowering their bikes into the water and attempting to cycle from one end of the fountain to the other, noisily splashing each other as they did so. Nearby, mothers with small children gazed on at us, mostly with contempt but also with a little bit of fear.

In my mind, two competing thoughts fought for supremacy. The first went something along the lines of, 'I'M IN A GANG! LOOK! I'M IN A GANG!' I'd say that thought took up about eighty per cent of the available space. But, in the other twenty per cent, struggling to be heard, was a very different thought. A list of all the people who I didn't want to see me like this. Ged, Aki, Vijay Singh, William Osborne, Henry Bannatyne. Anyone who might tell my parents.

But, like I said, these were like the cries for help you attempt in sleep. The ones that never manage to burst through the vacuum of unconsciousness. No, the main thing going on here, the presiding emotion, was the profound sense of well-being that comes of peer acceptance. And because that was what was being rewarded, it felt important to find ways to feed that feeling.

'Do you dare me to cycle all the way back from Solihull on the wrong side of the road?'

'Are you mad? You'll *die*!!'

I didn't feel like I was going to die. In fact, I'd never felt less like I was going to die.

'What will you give me if I do it?'

The other three boys pledged 50p each. My net worth in the middle of October 1982 was £1.50. Still soaked from the fountain, we hared out of Mell Square, past the roundabout where Warwick Road heads in a straight line back to Acocks Green. I waited for a gap in the traffic and moved over to the right-hand side, pedalling harder as I did so. To my left, in the correct lane, were the others, cheering me along. Every time an oncoming car sounded its horn at me, they cheered. From two hundred yards away, where the road widens by Olton station, a lorry sounded a low, long warning, like a foghorn. It scared the shit out of me, but fear and excitement really aren't so different from each other, and so I kept going, sometimes weaving from left to right, negotiating a perilous path through dozens of vehicles, some moving, some swerving, some braking suddenly.

In a pre-electric windows era, not many drivers managed to manually wind their windows down in time to tell me I needed my head examined. And if they did, what would I have done? A 'wanker' sign? I hadn't perfected the requisite wrist action for a good 'wanker' sign. Every time I tried, I'd move my entire forearm, as though lubing an invisible broom handle. Would I have shown them the middle finger? This being Britain in the early eighties, it would have most likely been a curt two fingers. But not, I hasten to add, at the poor woman in a Morris Minor who pulled out of a side road, failed to see me in time (well, why would she?) and applied her brakes at the same time as I squeezed mine. No near miss this time. My pedal scraped against her chassis. I lost my balance and fell onto the kerb. From across the road, all I could hear were the chortles of the other boys.

The woman was about sixty. She had huge Deirdre Barlow glasses and a strawberry-blond perm. She looked like she might be about to cry, but that wasn't the worst thing. The worst thing was that she instinctively apologised *when she had nothing to apologise for.* She got out to make sure I was OK. I pointed at the damage to her car, but she just wanted to know if I was OK.

'Yes, I'm fine, thank you,' I said, just desperate to get away.

I got back on my bike and reconvened with the others a couple of hundred yards away outside the newly built Safeway supermarket. We threw our bikes down and I waited for a tide of admiration, respect and praise to wash my way. Seeking to help it along, I asked the others to hand over their 50p pieces. Flynn and Tookey looked at each other but said nothing. Finally, Flynn muttered something about the incident with the car invalidating the bet. Terry and I waited outside while the other two went in to get themselves drinks. Minutes later, Flynn unzipped his jacket and out fell four cans of Coke. A looming sense of dread started to gather around me. Almost as if to remind myself who I really was, I cycled to William's house. I'd hardly seen him over the summer and, right now, I really needed to know that we were still friends.

Every bonfire night, the Osbornes would host a party. In terms of anticipation, the build-up to it was comparable to Christmas or a birthday. Our first one had been in 1976. Prior to that, the only firework action we'd ever seen had been the previous year when, under pressure to provide something, anything, to mark the date, my dad unfastened his overall and went to Elsie's grocery two doors away and came back with a Roman candle, two packs of sparklers and a box of matches. He went through the games room of the old shop and out of the back door, past his waiting children, lit the firework and told us to stand well back. We stood there watching a geyser of sparks shooting into the air, and by the time it was done, my dad was back behind the counter serving customers. It might sound to you like the rubbishest bonfire night that any child has had since little Tommy Fawkes asked his mum when daddy would be home from work – but it really wasn't. It was thrilling. Aki lit his sparkler and instructed me to touch it with the end of mine. We repeated the action again and again, and then when there were no more left, Aki created an extra firework by setting fire to the rest of the matches in the box.

A year later, we got to see how it's really done. Aki and I walked from the Osbornes' hallway through their lean-to kitchen and out into their back garden. We handed over our contribution, a box of fireworks, and William's mum emerged into the garden holding a dish of shiny silver boulders. As she unwrapped one for me, I grabbed a plate and she placed it on there. A second later, she prised open the cross-shaped incision at the top of the potato and eased a lump of butter into it. What sorcery was this? A potato with the skin on? *You can eat the skin?* This was news. We'd never had jacket potatoes at home. Did my parents know you could eat the skin of a potato? If so, why did they go to the daily trouble of emptying sacks of potatoes into the potato peeler? I watched William to see what he was going to do with his potato and, on seeing him mash the butter into its flesh with the back of a fork, I did the same. We walked towards the source of the heat – the bonfire Roy Osborne was tending while talking to his best friend Malcolm.

To the left of the fire was a wheelbarrow on which sat the effigy of Guy Fawkes the Osbornes had made some days previously. Roy hammered a Catherine wheel to the garden fence. The walk towards the firework always seemed to command a silence that was pitched between anticipation and respect. Adults never seemed more adult than when they were extending a lit match towards the fuse of a firework. The hissing neon spiral blur of the Catherine wheel would kick off the fireworks section of the Osbornes' bonfire nights every year, and it would never look anything less than breathtaking.

There was no question of the Osbornes' bonfire night not happening this year. But William and I were no longer as close as we had been in that final year of primary school. And suddenly the idea that we might have drifted apart to the extent that I might not be given the chance to spend the fifth of November at this house seemed unbearable to me.

If William was surprised to see me standing there, he hid it well. 'I've got something to show you. Come and look at this.'

I followed him into the front room and towards the corner where the TV was.

'Look!' he said. 'A video recorder!'

I don't remember saying much at all that afternoon. I just sat there agog as William showed me what you could do with his new Ferguson VHS machine. To have a video recorder in your house was to be able to control television. To watch one thing while recording another. To replay something again and again, and not have to reawaken the visceral thrill of your favourite band's *Top of the Pops* performance with nothing other than memory. He pressed down one of six buttons that extended out from the front panel like manicured robot fingers and the empty cassette compartment rose up from the top. William took a nearby cassette from a shelf and placed it into the machine. It made a pleasing, heavy click as it did so. William pushed down another button and a haze of interference dispersed to reveal Bauhaus on the previous week's *Top of the Pops*, performing their version of David Bowie's 'Ziggy Stardust'. Pete Murphy negotiated the song's dramatic peaks with a poise that suggested he had been rehearsing for this moment ever since he had first heard the song ten years previously.

As Murphy sang that final 'Ziggy played . . . guii-tarr!!' to the clang of a concluding power chord, a crude edit bumped us forward two days to a clip of Japan on *The Old Grey Whistle Test* performing 'The Art of Parties' and then to selected excerpts from *The Paul Daniels Magic Show*. William's family barely lived within their means, but the fact that they were the first in our world to get a video recorder was entirely in character. Roy proceeded through life on the basis that the only bank that matters is the one where you place memories. And the money that some people squirrel away in the former is far better used on the latter. Roy's memory bank was filled with fireworks, Scott Walker and old episodes of *The Tony Hancock Show*, which he knew verbatim, thanks to their availability on LP.

So, given how little money came into the house, how could they afford the must-have consumer durable of 1982? Well, they couldn't. They rented it. This future-facing hardware of endlessly repeatable joy cost the Osbornes £15 a month from the Rediffusion TV rental shop in Acocks Green. A snip!

I tried not to outstay my welcome. After all, this was an impromptu visit and, besides, even though my clothes had dried, the fountain had left a faint stink. I stayed long enough for William to demonstrate a few other key features of the video recorder. This being the first generation of vaguely affordable VCRs, its manufacturers weren't sure exactly how people would want to use such a machine. This was evidenced by the 'audio dub' button, which was afforded equal prominence to that of core buttons, such as 'play' and 'stop'. Ferguson and Sony clearly imagined that this was a country full of consumers impatient to start recording their own audio content onto this week's *Play Your Cards Right* and *That's Life!*

In truth, they weren't entirely wrong. William's keenness to squeeze every drop of value from the new VCR had prompted him to record a string of profane interjections onto the previous night's *Songs of Praise*, in the process creating brand-new hymns, 'Praise My Soul the King of Wanking' and 'The Lord's My Bum Chum'. I thought it was hilarious, and perhaps it was through flattery at this that William asked me if I'd be coming to his fireworks party in a couple of weeks' time.

'Yeah . . . that'd be brill,' I said, trying to strike a balance between aloofness and gratitude.

I zoomed home on my bike as if I'd become a firework too, burning up relief and euphoria.

CHAPTER 31

After the business with the Father's Day card, I remained circumspect around my dad, continuing to avoid him in the explosive half-hour before he had to go and open the shop. His escalating resentment at what he frequently likened to a prison sentence prompted him to propose a revised division of labour. With immediate effect, he was to have a weekday evening off. Every Thursday, my mum would be in charge of the shop from 4 p.m. until 11 p.m. closing time. There was no debate of which we were aware. Of course I felt for my mum, especially during those final long hours edging towards midnight. When it came to getting us to perform household chores, she'd always been soft. We never had to do anything. But on the nights she worked at the shop, I made sure the kitchen was spotless for her return.

Somehow the washing-up got to be an unlikely area of tension. Once my dad noticed me doing that, he'd sometimes try and wash up before me. It was no hardship for me to do it – after all, it wasn't like I had that much else to do. But I guess this was more about his residual guilt at the fact that he was at home and my mum would be standing behind the counter at the Kingfisher until the end of the night, dealing with the drunks who rolled out of the Lincoln Poacher across the road at chucking-out time. The problem with him washing the dishes was that when my mum came home she could always tell when he'd done it. If the glasses didn't shine and the plates had grease marks left on them, she'd do the whole lot again and he would then take umbrage at what he considered an act of passive aggression. However, I couldn't *rewash* the plates when he was there in case that also caused offence. So my only option was to wait until he left the house at 11.15 p.m. to pick her up and do it then.

It felt good to do it. My life was a tangle of long-term goals whose successful execution totally eluded me. Washing dishes was something I could do well. And those glasses, well, I could really make them shine. It was a knack. You had to hold them firmly by the base and hold each one of them up to the light before putting them back in the cupboard. And always bottom up. That was another signifier that my dad had done the washing up. He always placed them in the cupboard bottom side down.

Nearly five years had elapsed since he had been a presence at home on a weeknight. First it was just Thursdays, and then later, when Thursdays weren't enough to stave off his darkening moods, he started to take Wednesday evenings off too. I didn't begrudge his clamour for more downtime – I'd long drawn up a mental list of more menial jobs I'd much rather do in adulthood than run a fish and chip shop. What I did begrudge though was his insistence that my mum be there when he wasn't. His worry was that if we employed someone outside of our family to run the shop, they might not be trusted to put all of the takings in the till.

His paranoia about petty theft made me feel judgemental of him – after all, it was adding to my mum's already heavy workload. But by now, my parents' savings had become something more than money. They functioned as a sort of sacrifice index; something they could point at in lieu of the years they would do completely differently were they to go back and do it all over again. Their money was the measure of the gratification they were delaying until, well . . . until when? Until Aki and I were old enough to take over the shop; or perhaps until we finally relented and assented to a new life in Cyprus.

But if money had come to represent something other than a

means by which to make the present more fun (which was what the Osbornes used it for), the chip shop had started to represent something just as knotty to me. What was once a source of recreation, with pinball machines, a pool table and free chips mere footsteps away, had now become a threat. Aki had long since been told he had to pull his weight in the shop during school holidays and weekends. Any week now, it was going to be my turn. Drawing on the self-interest so naturally abundant in thirteen-year-old boys, the realisation of what was coming merely ramped up my urgent desire to procure that video recorder, so that all the TV shows I missed could be waiting for me when I got home. After seeing the Osbornes' video machine, I told Aki, and he agreed that we needed to mobilise all our efforts into getting our parents to follow suit. In a couple of weeks, on BBC2, a new comedy called *The Young Ones* was due to air. They must have trailed it weeks in advance because not only did we know about it, we anticipated it with breathless excitement, having clocked the involvement of Rik Mayall, the guy who played Kevin Turvey in *A Kick up the Eighties*. But that in itself wasn't going to be enough to force my dad's hand. There needed to be something else.

You could tell a lot about my parents by the sitcoms they liked to watch. On Monday nights, my mum would make sure the TV was switched to BBC1 in time for *Butterflies*, and set up the ironing board in front of the telly so she could watch it as she ironed. *Butterflies* was funny, but I'm not sure that was reason enough for my mum to remember it from week to week. In depicting the interior world of a woman attempting to reconcile what she has ended up with to what she had once hoped for, its creator Carla Lane gave a platform to a form of existential anxiety that had almost never been dramatised or turned into comedy prior to this point: the anxiety of a mother and wife. Wendy Craig's character Ria wasn't in exactly the same situation as my mum; we didn't employ a cleaner and there was no lonely single businessman called Leonard with designs on her, ordering his chauffeur to pull up alongside her outside Safeway.

Unlike Ria, my mum was a capable cook. But like Ria, her culinary creations weren't always appreciated. They were bolted down by two children who rarely stopped to consider the effort that went into making them, and a husband who, as ever, was never slow to tell her that some Cypriot dish she'd made for him wasn't quite as tasty as the version his sister or his mum used to make. But clearly there were enough similarities to resonate. Ria was as smart as her husband, an emotionally incontinent dentist (played with saturnine acuity by Geoffrey Palmer). Somewhere along the line though, she had turned into a drudge and she didn't quite understand how and when it had happened.

While my mum saw glimmers of her own situation in *Butterflies*, my dad revelled in a version of his situation that looked like an absolute blast by comparison. Writing about *Only Fools and Horses* for the *New Statesman* in 2017, Jason Murugesu reflected, 'I don't think there has been a show with which the British Asian community has identified more . . . Del Boy's circle of friends looked like my dad's. They were electricians, shop owners, and street cleaners. People who weren't always comfortable, but they were doing all right.' It wasn't just British Asians. Murugesu could have just as easily been talking about my dad. Sometimes on Sunday, if he didn't fancy going to church, he'd head off to the main shopping thoroughfare of Small Heath which was now mostly populated by Indian and Pakistani immigrants. This was where his friend Abdul ran a small electrical shop. Abdul's shop wasn't the sort of place you'd go to order a cassette player or a TV that you'd seen advertised on TV. He had what he had – a combination of reconditioned goods, a mixture of authentic and counterfeit branded watches and, really, whatever else had come his way.

My dad remained suspicious of High Street chains for his entire life. Those places were for mugs. Markets were a better fit for the streetwise self-image he'd felt no need to update since his teenage years. He didn't trust places where haggling was discouraged. At Abdul's shop, market rules applied. You told him what you were after and he'd see what he could get you. That was how we got our first microwave oven, a lime-green cube that weighed as much as a safe and remained forgotten for decades until the faintly nauseating colour scheme of Duncan Jones's sci-fi movie *Moon* brought it back.

And it was to Abdul's shop that our dad drove after Aki and I finally succeeded in getting him to agree to get a video recorder for the house. The clincher had come when we had left the TV on after *Top of the Pops* finished and the opening titles of *Only Fools and Horses* had started to roll. It depicted a world he recognised. All we needed to do was let him enjoy it over the course of two or three weeks and then tell him about this magical machine that would allow him to watch the show again and again. Not only that, but on the nights he was working at the shop, we could record the news and have it waiting on a videocassette for him when he got home.

In spite of all that, his resistance to the idea wasn't unexpected.

'How much do they cost?' he asked.

At Currys and Dixons, they were going for upwards of £400.

He pointed out that £400 was a lot of money, and in 1982, it really was. But we weren't quite done. We mentioned that the Osbornes had one.

'How much did the Osbornes pay for theirs?' he asked. We told him that they rented theirs, and that if we couldn't afford to buy one outright, perhaps we could rent one too?

Affronted by the insinuation of poverty, that was enough to spur him into action. Abdul explained to him on the phone that he was trying his best to work through a long list of orders for video recorders. Everyone wanted one in time for Christmas. But, of course, this not being Dixons or Currys, everything was subject to negotiation.

'Abdul, you know I like to look after my friends. What do Muslims do for Christmas? I'll get you anything you like from the wholesale market! Half a lamb. I'll take care of you.'

Abdul told him that his family liked to do what other British people did at Christmas. Turkey with all the trimmings. Halal, of course.

'I'll get you a king-size turkey if you can get me a video recorder this weekend. You will feed HALF OF PAKISTAN with it, never mind your family! And fish and chips for everyone next time you come and see me at the Kingfisher. Yes?'

I could hear Abdul laughing on the other end of the line. There may have been some umming and aah-ing, a bit of I'm-not-sure-about-that, a garnish of you-drive-a-hard-bargain, but essentially, the promise of chips and a giant turkey had fast-tracked us to the top of Abdul's list. Del Boy would have been proud.

The other good thing about getting your electrical goods from Abdul's shop was that Abdul was open every day. And so, the following Sunday, I accompanied my dad to Small Heath so I could bear witness to the historic moment and, well . . . actually, to make sure he didn't fuck it up by getting the wrong machine. It was a rare moment of prescience on my part. With my dad insisting that he didn't want to go over £300, Abdul readied two machines for him, both of which used dying videocassette formats: Betamax (£300) and U-matic (£200). The U-matic machine was too huge for Abdul to place on the glass counter where he kept his fake Seikos. But . . . but . . . £200!! I didn't have to be Uri Geller to read my dad's mind. As Abdul waited for us to choose, I quickly remonstrated with my dad, aware that his tolerance was close to breaking point. 'I can get you VHS by the end of the week for £350! Good price for VHS!' said Abdul.

I told my dad that in two years' time, you probably wouldn't be able to get videotapes for those machines, but he seemed unsure. I had one card remaining now and, in desperation, I threw it on the table. 'I'll pay the extra £50! I'll come and help in the shop! I'll do jobs in exchange for it.' He turned around to Abdul and told him we'd take it. Three days later, Abdul came to the Kingfisher to redeem his fish and chips token and deliver a reconditioned Ferguson Videostar machine. It was waiting for me when I came down for breakfast the following morning. As my Frosties turned to sweet, milky mush, I hooked it up to the TV. There was no instruction manual, but through a tortuous string of deductions, I set the clock and worked out how to record BBC lunchtime magazine show *Pebble Mill at One* with the timer. It had been years since I'd shown this sort of initiative in any of my actual lessons at school, but this sudden surge of brain activity meant that, if I'd done it properly, I'd have hitherto unim-aginable technological wonders awaiting me when I came home.

This being a Thursday, my dad was there to watch this scene of simpleton enchantment playing out before him. Terry had also come straight from school to share this historic moment with me. As we watched Essex power poppers the Pinkees play their sole hit 'Danger Games' to the elderly Pebble Mill audience, my dad made a quick sortie to the shop to get our dinner. As he left, he asked Terry what he wanted to eat. Terry had already eaten, but hey, in 1982, if your mate's dad offered you free food from their chippy, there could only be one answer. 'Saveloy and chips, Mr Paphides!' He returned with our order halfway through *Top of the Pops* – a *Top of the Pops* which was rendered more exciting to me than any other by virtue of the fact that I knew I could watch the good bits over and over again later, scrutinising them with a thorough, analytical eye that would have propelled me to the top of my year if I could only have been this fas-cinated by Roman roads, quadratic equations and the periodic table.

And because I was now an archivist, storing and cataloguing

these moments for grateful future generations, I needed to be vigilant – sitting by the VCR, fingers poised to press 'pause' or 'play' and 'record' at a moment's notice. If I hadn't recorded most of the other songs that week, the memory of one performance would have almost certainly swallowed everything else on that episode. 'Starman' moments were now happening on an almost monthly basis, but next to Culture Club's performance of 'Do You Really Want to Hurt Me?', Bowie's actual 'Starman' moment was a vision of quaint home-made glamour soaked with the botanical funk of Aqua Manda, Rothmans and bitter. Sure, people who were there at the time maintain there was real confusion regarding the gender of Bowie's guitarist Mick Ronson, a confusion heightened by the fact that Bowie draped his arm around Ronson in an apparently homoerotic way. But no matter how many times this version of events was repeated, when I eventually saw the footage, nothing could make Ronson seem like anything other than what my eyes were faithfully reporting back to my brain – I was looking at a hod-carrier in drag.

All of which is worth dwelling on because what my eyes reported back to my brain on seeing Boy George couldn't have been more different. And it wasn't just me. The following day's newspaper headlines bore that out with *The Sun* asking if 'it' was 'a Boy or a Girl?' Whatever it was, it looked stunning. Tied into George's dreads were torn-off cotton ribbons, matching the brilliant white of his top which had some sort of Urdu slogan sprayed onto it. His blue eyes radiated a vulnerability that was echoed by the song, a rocksteady companion piece to Ken Boothe's 'Everything I Own' (a song that would propel Boy George back to number 1 when he launched his solo career with it).

Over two years had elapsed since 'Ashes to Ashes'. Pop's centre ground would never again be this androgynous. That meant that even to someone as laddish as Terry, it wasn't a good look to shout 'queer' at the TV screen when Boy George appeared on it. If you took against Boy George on the basis of his androgyny, then you had to take against his music and alienate yourself from the girls at school who thought he was dreamy, the same girls who you might be hoping to go out with one day.

For my dad though, none of these considerations applied. 'That's a boy??!!' he spluttered. To Terry's delight, a torrent of swear words surged out of his mouth, a résumé of every homophobic term he'd heard in his two decades here. The more appalled he became, the more Terry tried to egg him on.

'What would you do if one of your children looked like that, Mr Paphides?' asked Terry.

'I would kill him and then I would kill MYSELF,' he declared. I could tell he was enjoying the attention, but what I couldn't quite tell was whether he actually meant what he was saying, or indeed what exactly it was that would make him react in that way. We didn't know if Boy George was gay, straight or bisexual. The word most commonly used at school to describe any behaviour outside heterosexual norms was 'queer' – and 'queer' could connote anything from effeminate behaviour to actual homosexuality. It was used as a pejorative term ('you fucking queer') but sometimes in a less loaded context.

Back in 1982, it didn't occur to me that gayness didn't have to be something you manifested outwardly. In fact, such was our naivety around sexual orientation that even when gay men made no great attempt to conceal it, we remained oblivious to the clues. Our form teacher that year was also our music teacher: Mr Simpson, whose cropped hair, bushy moustache and Cuban heels all conspired to set him apart from the other teachers. He called himself a 'bachelor' and it took us years to realise that to do even that was a risqué admission for a secondary schoolteacher. He used to spend every summer indulging his obsession with extreme roller coasters. He once sent me to the newsagent's next to the school to buy a box of pencils and pronounced the brand 'Staedtler' in such a comically proper German accent that it sounded like he had dislodged a tablespoon of phlegm in the process.

We liked Mr Simpson because of what he didn't care about and what he made us care about. He didn't care what we thought of his camp demeanour. And he made us care about Dmitri Shostakovich. By any metric, that was an astounding achievement, one that required him to teach us about life under Stalin's totalitarian rule, so that we could then learn how Shostakovich, the sometime avant-garde prodigy of Russian classical music, had to find ever more subtle ways to insert 'covert musical symbols of dissent' into his work. He played us a snatch of Shostakovich's Fifth Symphony and told us about the envy it instilled in the poet and novelist Boris Pasternak, who wrote, '[Shostakovich] went and said everything, and no one did anything to him for it.' Aware of the job that lay ahead of him, Mr Simpson had come prepared. He announced that at some point during his talk on Shostakovich, he would be working in the names of three of the seven dwarves, and whoever wrote down all three correctly was in with a chance of winning a giant Cadbury's Fruit & Nut bar. I didn't get the Fruit & Nut bar, but I *really* wanted it. That's why, thirty-five years later, my recall of Shostakovich's story is still pretty good.*

By somehow winding up in a peer group to which I was utterly unsuited, my life at school was starting to feel stressful. But at home, no one really bothered me. I'd go through the *Radio Times* and *TV Times* with a fluorescent Stabilo Boss highlighter, looking for any programmes that might feature musical content, setting the video for whatever I couldn't record in person. An E180 videocassette would

---

* Mr Simpson stayed at Yardleys School until February 1999, when he was found strangled in his room at the Spring Street Rodeway Inn in San Diego. He was on holiday in America, pursuing his hobby of riding the world's most spectacular roller coasters. 'He was in a position of having taught all 900 pupils and he knew all of them by their name,' head teacher Heather Jones told BBC News, 'He was a real Mr Chips. He was revered and respected.'

typically cost around £7. If I'd hoped that my promise to work off some of the cost of the VCR would soon be forgotten, the need to keep buying cassettes made that prospect an inevitability. The price of videotapes was instantly wiping out my weekly pocket money and, to make things worse, we seemed to be entering a period of unprecedented significance in TV history.

Two weeks after we bought the video recorder, an entire new channel – a self-styled 'alternative' to BBC1, BBC2 and ITV – was being launched. One of Channel 4's flagship programmes was *The Tube*, a live music show lasting almost two hours. My parents told me I'd be needing to put in a few hours in the shop during the week's busiest period, Friday teatimes, which happened to directly coincide with *The Tube*. I was working to pay for the videotapes I needed to record *The Tube* while I was working. Given how few other errands I was made to run, it was a soft introduction to the world of work. My old friend Vijay had been helping out in his parents' shop ever since he was six, and it wasn't as if he was being paid for it. Most immigrant shop owners kept these things in the family. My dad was no different – either he or my mum always had to be on hand to make sure every penny taken went into the till.

My duties were made clear to me on the first day. I had to carry buckets of chips from the storeroom to the front of the shop and remove the corks from the bottom of the barrels of chipped potatoes early enough for them to drain properly before it was time for them to enter the fryer. I also had to ladle curry sauce and mushy peas into polystyrene cups and bring them to the counter whenever they were needed. My inability to undertake these tasks with any sense of urgency was exasperating to my parents, and in particular my dad. Drawing on reserves of tolerance he didn't even know he had, he asked me if I could, as a favour to him, *really* try and ensure that there was more curry sauce inside the cup than spilled all around the sides of it. You try and see yourself in your children, but what could he possibly recognise in himself when he gazed down at me? He had clearly been a very different sort of teenager to me. By the time he'd got to my age, he'd already held down his first job, hunting and killing rabid dogs in his village for extra cash. He was just three years older than me when he was conscripted. I wasn't even ready to serve chips, let alone serve in the army. There was nothing in his upbringing or psychological make-up that equipped him to understand the listless insularity that was reaching almost pandemic proportions among wan, pubescent misfits like me. And this was an entire twelve months before the Smiths came along to enable our high-handed self-absorption and allow us to pass it off as an aesthetic.

In truth, never more than half of my brain was focused on the job I was there to do. Every Friday, between 5.45 and 7 p.m., Radio 1's weekly singles review show *Roundtable* was on. With the shop radio permanently tuned into the station, I was constantly trying to keep tabs on whatever current record was playing and what that week's panel had to say about it. One week saw John Peel and Sheena Easton dispensing their verdicts on the new releases. Once in a while throughout his career, the avowedly alternative Peel would declare a perverse adoration for a mainstream pop star, and that year, he had been vocal in his love of Easton, the cheesy proto-reality show success story. Clearly flattered by his approval, she immediately bonded with Peel in the Radio 1 studio. Among that week's featured songs was 'It's Raining Again', the long-awaited return by Swindon prog-poppers Supertramp which, insofar as I could discern between the demands of the teatime rush, negotiated a gorgeous equidistant point between yearning and jauntiness. Whatever people liked about their biggest hit 'Breakfast in America' seemed to me abundant in a song which gently exhorted its subject to believe that a life after love is still worth living. But then I wasn't on the *Roundtable* panel that week. The song ended with some schoolchildren singing an interpolation of the nursery rhyme 'It's Raining, It's Pouring' over the chord sequence of the Supertramp song.

I felt that even John Peel would have to grudgingly concede that this was pretty irresistible. But, of course, he did nothing of the sort. He found the entire thing woeful, singling out for special attention the words of the middle eight which saw Roger Hodgson sing, 'Come on you little fighter / No need to get uptighter'. His tone of weary indignation was so total – and Sheena's agreement with him so emphatic – that I convinced myself that, over the noise of the customers and the till ringing and the oil sizzling, I must have accidentally heard a better song than the one playing on the radio. It is one of my first clear memories of simply telling myself that I must have got it wrong. And, of course, this is what you start to do in your teens. You start to lie to yourself because a John Peel – who plays edgy records about rape on his late-night show; the only *Top of the Pops* presenter who's allowed to be a bit sarcastic about the records he doesn't like; the man who introduced your brother to Joy Division – must know something you don't. And when you get around to learning it, you too will think that Supertramp are worse than Joy Division.

CHAPTER 32

I'd always craved the approval of adults, but suddenly I was in a gang that went out of their way to repel it. Every lunchtime Terry, Tookey, Flynn and myself would head in the opposite direction to the mass of pupils running across the road to the dinner hall next to the playing fields. Instead, we'd slope through the back gate towards Medina Road, a residential street with one single corner shop on it. Mr Bansal, the owner, had the enterprising idea of selling single cigarettes passed through the hole of a Polo mint. You sucked the mint after smoking the fag in order to avoid detection by teachers or parents. Flynn and Tookey would buy one each, which they'd occasionally try and pass around to Terry and myself. Terry almost always declined, something for which I was grateful because it alleviated from me the pressure to have a drag. From here, we'd go on to an off-licence on Reddings Lane that had recently started doing hot lunch options for nearby factory workers. You could buy a Pot Noodle into which the brassy, bleach-blonde mum who ran the shop would pour the hot water and give you a plastic fork to go with it. On a blackboard outside was a list of other options including 'BAKED POTATOS'. One lunchtime, I ordered my Pot Noodle and pointed out to her that she'd spelled 'potatoes' incorrectly.

'You put the "e" in when it's a plural,' I told her.

'When it's a what?' she spluttered.

'When it's a plural. When there's more than one potato, you put an "e" in "potatoes".'

'But it's just one potato!' she replied. 'It's 50p for one potato.'

'I know, but you've written P.O.T.A.T.O.S. There's an "e" between the "o" and the "s". Potatoes.'

As her face reddened, I could hear Terry sniggering behind me.

'Thanks for the lecture, sunshine. Now, I tell you what, here's your Pot Noodle. Give us your money and fuck off out of my shop. And if I ever see you in here again, I will make a *complaint* to your school. How dare you talk to me like that. How DARE you. Go on. Piss off! The lorra you. Piss off.'

If I wasn't going to smoke Mr Bansal's cigarettes, then getting myself thrown out of the off-licence took the heat off me for a week or two. But it didn't change the fact that I was in a bind. Tookey had started calling for me at home on weekends and several evenings. On Saturday mornings, I was usually alone. He'd repeatedly ring the doorbell until I finally came to the door. With his dad long disappeared, his mother had to work evenings and weekends to support her two children. Tookey's sister Lottie, an academic high achiever, had assumed the role of a second adult, helping around the house, a dynamic which inevitably left Tookey feeling ostracised. And that ostracism instilled in him a barely suppressed anger which even his jokes never quite managed to conceal. He was constantly daring you to see what happened if you rejected him. The boundaries observed by most people in friendships, even children, were not set in stone for Dean Tookey. And the more I realised this, the less comfortable I became with our friendship. Sometimes, for want of anything better to do with him, I'd suggest we made the twenty-minute walk to my parents' shop. Typically, my mum or dad would ask us what we wanted. I might ask for a spring roll (a new and exotic addition to our menu) or a few chips. Increasingly, Tookey seemed to be going there for his dinner. One morning I came down for breakfast only to be told by my mum that, the night before, Tookey had turned up at the shop on his own, asking for a steak and kidney pie and chips. When my mum gave it to him, he thanked them and went on his way without handing over any money.

A shiver of panic. Did they call him back and ask him to pay?

No, said my mum. She didn't want to embarrass the boy. But with the silence she allowed to hang in the air as we sat at the table, something was communicated. My mother was anything but tight when it came to giving out free food. Pensioners would often come in and ask for 'a few chips' with their fish, meaning that it wasn't worth giving them a full portion because they wouldn't finish it. My mum never charged for the chips. After a while, word got around among the senior citizens of Olton and Acocks Green. Those who came on other days switched to Thursdays, when my mum was there on her own. On those teatimes you could see them slowly advancing up Pierce Avenue – the long sloping road which stretched out towards the Kingfisher – like turtles on a moonlit beach. 'Just fish, please,' they'd say, knowing full well that my mum would throw in the extra chips. She knew that one customer, Sam, was struggling to pay off some debts carried by his wife who had recently died, so she gave him the fish for nothing too. When he died, his son came into the shop to let her know that he had left my mum the entire contents of his house in his will. She told him to donate it all to charity. Dean Tookey, on the other hand, wasn't a pensioner and my parents couldn't very well start feeding him for free on a daily basis. But something was telling me that if he pushed me or my family to a point where we humiliated him, things would quickly get worse for me.

I'd never had to learn how to stand up to other children. Ever since the day William and I had been pushed towards each other by our brothers, I'd never minded assuming the non-dominant role in a friendship if it meant that I was allowed to roll along without attracting scrutiny. Tookey needed to find solutions to problems that were his and not mine. Either he wasn't getting pocket money or what he did have was being spent on cigarettes. When I told him that I was struggling to buy videocassettes fast enough for all the programmes I wanted to record, he suggested we place a card in the newsagent's window, offering to do 'odd jobs'. We listed examples of the sort of things we could do: washing up, polishing cars, mowing lawns, cleaning windows. I asked Tookey if we could write down his phone number instead of mine. My parents would have been mortified to discover, by way of a call from a stranger, exactly what I'd let myself in for. In the event, they barely needed to worry. On the first Sunday of December, Tookey called to say that we needed to be at a house later that day for a two-hour job.

'Do you know what it is?' I asked.

'They didn't say,' he replied.

'But what if we can't do it?'

'Don't sweat, Paphides. How hard is it gonna be?'

'What did they say?'

'I told you, didn't I?' The sudden chippiness took me aback slightly. 'They just said come over at four o'clock. You've got to do it. I said it would be both of us.'

It was already dark by the time we got to the place. The woman who greeted us was about thirty with long blond hair, jeans and a loose-fitting overcoat (she needed it because it was as cold inside the house as it was outside). She didn't seem surprised when she saw two thirteen-year-olds standing in front of her.

She beckoned us up to a narrow carpeted staircase which led to a landing with three or four closed doors. On each one was a different number. She took a key from her jeans pocket and opened the door to reveal a mostly empty flat. In a space which, by virtue of having a sink but not a toilet, we'll call the kitchen, there were about two dozen bags filled with bits of skirting board, plaster and similar debris. Once we'd carried all of them down to the front garden, she would tell us what our next job was. We tried to manage the bags on our own, but when one of them split and spilled rubbish all down the stairs, we carried them together. It took half an hour just to do the bags. My trousers were filthy. I had no idea how I was going to explain the state of them to my mum.

As we disposed of the final bag and returned upstairs, a much older guy emerged and attempted some small talk. Where did we live? Did our parents know where we were? He was dressed in a suit but had taken his tie off at some point. His hair was brushed back and held in place with some sort of product. He looked Italian or maybe Cypriot. About a year later, when the South African snooker player Silvino Francisco crawled up the world rankings and onto televised snooker tournaments, I half convinced myself that he was the same person. He produced a box of tools and told us that he'd pay us once we'd scraped the wallpaper off a fireplace wall and pulled up and disposed of the carpet in the same room. 'If you've got any questions, she'll be next door.' I didn't know if he meant the flat or the house next door, but that didn't occur to me until later.

I think we both felt out of our depth and maybe a little scared of what we'd got ourselves into. Tookey seemed to deal with it by being defensive and telling me to stop complaining. By six o'clock, our supposed finish time, we were still on our hands and knees using chisels to try and lever up the carpet. Every time we peeled it back, the foam underlay – much of it reduced to grey dust – stayed stuck to the floorboards. I'd done less manual labour in my entire life than I ended up doing on this afternoon. The soft area between my wrists and the base of my thumbs was sore. The kitchen radio was tuned into that week's top 40 rundown and, while that made a pretty bad situation a lot better, it did start to feel as though every other song was coming out of the speaker with the specific intention of taunting me.

The video to Ultravox's 'Hymn' was fresh in my mind from *Top of the Pops* two days previously. It had depicted the four members of Ultravox struggling in lowly occupations only to be presented with a sinister contract by a shadowy figure whose true identity was given away by his glowing red eyes. We saw the group's bassist Chris Cross engaged in menial ancillary work, pushing a tea trolley into an important-looking wood-panelled boardroom. After he accidentally knocked over a bowl of sugar lumps, the Devil appeared before him with said contract and, before you could say 'Faustian pact', Cross's lowly trolley operative had become CEO of the entire company. Had the devil appeared in the doorway with the offer of forty-eight blank videotapes in exchange for my soul, you wouldn't have seen me for carpet dust. But of course, no one was going to come and rescue me, not least because, I'd already made my Faustian pact. Or, at least, that's how it increasingly felt to me.

'This is bollocks,' said Tookey. 'They're taking the piss.'

I looked at my watch. Not that I needed to. The chart rundown finished at 7 p.m., and we'd reached number 6 – Lionel Richie's enervating love dirge, 'Truly'. We'd long passed the agreed two hours, and we hadn't even asked them how much they were planning to pay us. Also, wasn't someone supposed to have turned up by now? After another half-hour, Tookey put down his scraper and told me he was going next door to get our money. A minute later, he re-emerged.

'Cunts. They've locked us in.'

'What do you mean?'

'They've locked the door from the outside. We can't get out.'

The difference between me and Tookey was embodied by our reactions. Tookey's upbringing, or perhaps the lack of it, had toughened him. If there was anything to destroy at that point, he would have set about it in an instant. As he entered fight mode, I started to panic. I'd read too many tabloid reports about abducted children to keep calm. I could feel myself about to cry, but I also knew that if we ever got out of here, I'd never hear the end of it. Perhaps it was better to actually be abducted than to cry in front of your hard mates.

Tookey started banging on the wall, asking for his 'fucking money', but as eight o'clock approached, the rising imperative was just to escape. We opened a window. There was no way I was going to jump from the first floor. Tookey, who was smaller and lighter than me, managed to stretch a leg out onto a flat roof next door while I passed a stepladder through to him. As he lowered the ladder down from the flat roof, I followed him out and we gingerly made our way down to the back garden. However, we were still trapped. Our only means of escape was to climb over two garden walls and over the roof of a garage that sat between two houses. By the time we made it onto the street, I just wanted to get home and screw the money.

I didn't want to see the woman in the overcoat and 'Silvino' again. But Tookey had other ideas. He picked up a brick and lobbed it at the window of the room where we'd spent the last three-and-a-bit hours. He didn't stop to see if it hit its target. As the brick bounced off the wall next to the window, Tookey released a second brick, and this time its arc peaked exactly as it shattered the glass and landed on the newly exposed floorboards. Not that we waited to hear the bump. We sprinted away, and when we got to the end of the road, we took different directions, Tookey haring off towards the leafy boulevards of Hall Green and me towards home, terrified that somehow, the overcoat woman and Silvino were in pursuit. I ran straight to my room, took off my clothes and placed them under my bed. They'd stay there until the next time the house was empty and I could hand-wash them without attracting suspicion.

My intensifying dread of school was starting to manifest itself in new ways. It suddenly became very important to not tread on any cracks in the pavement between the bus stop and my house. Once this ritual bedded in, I merged other rituals into it. I had to kick a small stone all the way home, and it needed to be the same stone. If

I accidentally kicked it into the road, I had to go into the road and kick it back onto the pavement, all the time not stepping on any cracks. Needless to say, it was taking me longer and longer to get home. One evening, Ged, who had been walking behind me and caught up with me, asked me what I was doing. The only answer I could think of was the truth.

'I used to do that too,' she said. 'Do you wish you didn't have to do it?'

'I don't know,' I replied. 'Maybe.'

'Don't worry about it. You won't be doing it when you're thirty. And married! With kids!'

Ged made no secret of her amusement at the image of me being thirty. And married! With kids! She slowed down her walk in order to accommodate my ongoing attempts to guide the stone back to Overlea Avenue where all the previous weeks' stones were waiting to welcome it. It was a relief that she could imagine it because I certainly couldn't. I had no idea what kind of an adult I could be; how I could become the sort of person you'd want to go out with. I didn't know what fancying someone would really feel like or how you would go about letting them know without risking humiliation so great that you'd never be able to leave the house again. There didn't seem to be anything I could turn into that wouldn't be the cause of profound embarrassment for my parents. I mean, of course, there was the shop. There was always the shop. But the shop was what had made my parents miserable. And I knew with absolute certainty that, unless I replaced my entire personality with a different one – perhaps a Greek one – it would make me unhappy too.

Outside of school, I maintained absolute fidelity to my pop-cultural lodestones. ABBA were back with a new album. *The Singles (The First Ten Years)* was the first time they'd gathered all of their hits onto one record. Unlike their last album, *The Visitors*, the mood of the photograph on the sleeve was celebratory. They looked imperious before a mottled caramel backdrop, dressed as if poised to receive some sort of lifetime achievement prize. The sleeve was designed to remind you that they'd notched up more chart-topping hits than anyone since the Beatles, and the subtext of that title – *The First Ten Years* – was no less clear: namely, that Benny and Björn's pop masterpieces would continue to colonise the airwaves for another decade. But not everything was quite as it seemed. The release was a stopgap. Sessions for their tenth studio album had stalled, and when it became clear that the record wouldn't be ready in time for Christmas, two new songs were chosen to augment the track listing of what was effectively an act of brand consolidation.

Even if my fanatical thirteen-year-old brain wasn't quite ready to see ABBA's new album for what it was, I could soon see that something was up. I'd grown up with ABBA, so whatever intuition allowed me to detect whether my parents had had a row seemed to twitch in a similar way when ABBA were in my sights. The group had set aside a day of promotion in Britain. Now with the means to record their TV appearances, I went about my duties with scholarly care.

On *Saturday Superstore*, presenter Mike Read hosted a phone-in with a bored-looking Agnetha and Benny. Wearing an Arsenal top, Benny talked about 'changing direction a little' and about 'an eagerness to do something else'. While Agnetha zoned out and smiled at the watching children, Benny explained that he and Björn had met with Andrew Lloyd-Webber's lyricist sidekick Tim Rice in order to explore the idea of writing a 'pop opera'.

Later that same day, all four of ABBA joined Noel Edmonds on his new teatime vehicle *The Late, Late Breakfast Show*, for the video premiere of their new single 'The Day Before You Came'. If they had seemed bored at lunchtime, they were, by now, growing feral. The song ended and we cut back to the studio audience clapping and whooping as all light entertainment audiences are instructed to do. But, of course, left to their own devices, no audience would ever respond in that way to a song like 'The Day Before You Came'. It was as senseless as seeing an audience cheering dementedly as the closing credits to *The Seventh Seal* start to roll. The ABBA of 'The Day Before You Came' were a fever dream version of themselves that, as with all fever dreams, would somehow lurk in your thoughts long after it was over.

The trademark harmonies were wholly absent. In fact, Frida didn't seem to be on the song at all. The genius of Björn's lyrics lay as much with what they didn't tell you as what they did, all of it imparted by Agnetha with a voice that she'd never used before. No projection. No power.

> *I must have left my house at eight because I always do*
> *My train I'm certain left the station just when it was due*
> *I must have read the morning papers going into town*
> *And having gotten through the editorial no doubt I must have*
> *frowned*

It was almost as if she wasn't aware that she was singing; just itemising the details of the last ordinary day she would ever experience before . . . before . . . well, before *what*, exactly?

'You've spotted it, haven't you?' said Björn when I asked him about it twenty-eight years later. 'The music is hinting at it!' I spotted it, but not straight away. Any song with a title like 'The Day Before You Came' has to be a love song, doesn't it? And, on the basis that it was a love song, I didn't know why 'The Day Before You Came' felt so creepy to me. But, of course, the song only tells us what happened with mechanical regularity on every single day before he walked into her life. The 'you' in the title of the song could be an assailant or an abusive partner. The mystery of what 'you' did in the song is up there with Carly Simon's 'You're So Vain'.

The other thing to remember about 'The Day Before You Came'

is that it was almost six minutes long. Six light-entertainment show minutes of bleak Nordic pop noir don't adhere to the usual rules of horology. To the twelve million people watching at home, the day that Agnetha was singing about must have felt like it was unfolding in real time. Perhaps it felt like that to ABBA as well, because when the camera swung around to show Noel Edmonds welcoming them onto the empty sofa next to him, their expressions suggested this wasn't an interview so much as an ongoing hostage situation.

If Benny and Björn's answers at the time intimated that they'd quite simply had enough, hindsight confirms it. When asked by Noel if they thought they would know when it was time to call it a day, Björn's answer, given in hypothetical terms, described what had *actually* been happening in the studio over the preceding months. 'It would be more of a feeling, I think, because when we were recording an album, we would feel that it's not fun any more. We haven't got anything more to give and that would be the time to split, you know?'

'We should have done that a long time ago,' replied Benny.

'I know!' said Björn, easing into a recklessly offhand tone that he maintained throughout the remainder of the interview. While he and his ex-wife Agnetha sat on opposite ends of the sofa, the more recently separated Benny and Frida were nestled side by side in the middle. Frida's post-divorce fuck-you haircut had evolved into something truly extraordinary. Her spiky metallic grey mullet with pink streaks was light years ahead of anything most of us could meaningfully appraise. Frida relayed her amusement at certain sections of the British press that accused her of 'alarmingly ageing'. Turning to the audience, she asked, 'Am I really?' In the response that followed, the yeses quite audibly drowned out the noes – in doing so, further perpetuating the feeling that this was more like a weird dream than anything that belonged to the waking world.

In this section of the interview, the four members of ABBA were supposed to take it in turns to name their favourite of all their hits, explain why they had chosen it over all the others, and then we'd see a clip of it. When it was time for her to choose, Frida exclaimed, 'It's difficult because Benny and Björn has [sic] written so many good songs.'

'Thank you,' interjected Benny flatly, his arms folded.

'Well, you should know that by now,' chided Frida.

'Well, you never said that [before],' shot back Benny.

Usually the more abrasive of the two ABBA men, Benny's answers to Noel remained courteous. In this instance, Björn seemed the more volatile of the two. Every answer carried a slight subtext of 'fuck this' with the merest hint of 'I'm done here'.

Finally, Noel asked him to select his favourite ABBA hit. Casually dismantling the very conceit of this section of the interview, he explained, 'I'll pick "The Winner Takes It All" partly because I was *told* this was to be my choice.' With a concluding fuck-you flourish, he leaned back on the sofa and impishly hymned his own wonderful lyrics as the song faded up.

My love of ABBA was so thoroughly soaked and dried into me that it felt like traces of it could be found in my bones and tissue. I rewound the tape and watched the interview all over again, gradually coming to the realisation that this was the end. I knew what grown-ups looked like when they were done with civility. I knew what people did with their eyes when they'd checked out. ABBA had been out of focus when they first entered my life. 'Waterloo' was something like the sound of a distant pop landslide or perhaps the abstract thrill of artillery fire in the next town. With 'Mamma Mia' the picture became a bit clearer. The genius of the rapid C to G chord change on 'Why, why . . .' and the decision to withhold the drums from the first chorus of the song. I'm sure it wasn't my first experience of delayed gratification, but if asked to try and remember an earlier instance, I'm not sure I'd be able to summon anything I'd experienced prior to the thrill of hearing the full band come in on the final chorus at two and a half minutes.

Almost everything I'd seen in my parents' relationship seemed to have its equivalent in the story of ABBA, from the harsh economic truths of 'Money, Money, Money' to the knackered mid-life audit of 'Happy New Year'. Even in ostensibly happy songs like 'Take a Chance on Me', it wasn't hard for me to unconsciously find a parallel between my mum and the song's neglected protagonist. On the flipside of 'The Day Before You Came' was a new song called 'Cassandra'. From a brace of aborted Greek mythology lessons my mum had attempted to give us, I knew that they were singing about the eponymous prophetess of the Trojan War. And actually, if you played the songs on *The First Ten Years*, it was hard to escape the sense that ABBA had been unwitting Cassandras to their own Trojan War. Björn and Agnetha were still married when they released 'Knowing Me, Knowing You' and 'SOS', but these were the songs that previewed the emotional winter of a world where love's liquid has drained away to reveal the *duty* and the *maintenance* and the *work* that it once used to render weightless.

It was a season of farewells. Like ABBA, The Teardrop Explodes couldn't bring themselves to complete their final album before deciding to call it a day. Julian Cope's slow self-sabotage couldn't have been more different to that of Paul Weller who announced that he would be disbanding the Jam while they were still at their commercial and artistic peak. Within days of Weller's admission, David Sylvian gave an interview to *Smash Hits* in which he explained his reasons for calling time on Japan. He described a messy break-up, laying much of the blame at the feet of his bassist Mick Karn, who he accused of having 'an ego that won't let anyone supervise his work'.

I didn't really know what I should think about either the Jam or Japan splitting up but, not for the first time, I found myself in Ged's house listening intently as she and her friends unpacked it all. Maybe their thoughts could be mine too. Siobhan had brought her newly acquired 12-inch of Japan's farewell release 'Nightporter'. It seemed to soften the blow that David Sylvian's physical radiance was in no way contingent on who he chose to appear with on stage or in a recording studio. Sad as Japan's demise was, Ged admitted that she'd be more upset with David had he decided to separate from his hair rather than his band. Siobhan parlayed the feasibility of getting her hair cut in the same way.

'Do you think it would look as good on a girl?' she asked no one in particular.

'Yeah, I do,' said Ged. 'You've got lovely thick blond hair, so it would definitely suit you. Are you gonna do it?'

Siobhan leaned up close to the mirror above Ged's fireplace, applying rouge onto her cheeks, and wondered aloud whether her fringe was long enough to be swept across her forehead and sprayed into position like the Sylvian do. 'Apparently Rimski's in Selly Oak will cut your hair exactly like David if you bring a picture.'

Three teenage girls and me, listening to the parched nocturnal ruminations of Japan's tormented frontman, softened into song by Richard Barbieri's piano accompaniment. We'd never heard anything like it, but when Ged called her dad into the room so that Siobhan could complete her transformation by borrowing Frank Hughes's glasses, Frank took a sudden and unlikely interest in Japan's new single.

'Who's this?'

'It's Japan,' said Ged.

'Japan? Like the country? Sounds like one bloke.'

'No dad, it's a pop group. Do you like it?'

'It's nice. It sounds like Erik Satie. It sounds *just like* Erik Satie. But with singing. Are you finished with my glasses now?'

Siobhan handed Frank's glasses back to him. David's were a rounded shape. Frank's were square like Eric Morecambe's spectacles. 'Maybe I should get my eyes tested,' she said hopefully.

For the first time, almost all of my favourite bands were past entities. It bothered me that bands split up, but then all change bothered me. How do people change and not mind the scrutiny that comes with it? How can they leave the house and ride out the risk of ridicule or failure? In the case of ABBA, Japan and The Teardrop Explodes, there hadn't really been a choice. These groups simply couldn't continue. But with the Jam, it was different. I'd never seen anyone control the narrative like Paul Weller did. It seemed almost incomprehensible to me that you might sacrifice perhaps three or four more years of success in order to ensure that when the time came to end it, you ended it when your stock was at its highest. And not only that, but when you did, you did so by explaining your reasons in the words of your farewell single.

All the things that I care about (are packed into one punch)
All the things that I'm not sure about (are sorted out at once)

In keeping with this emphatic gesture of self-determination, the *Top of the Pops* performance of 'Beat Surrender' saw Weller even go to the trouble of reconfiguring the way his group presented themselves. With more than a nod to the set-up of sixties pop shows such as *Ready Steady Go!*, Weller dispensed with his guitar and stood on a platform at the back of the stage. Beside him was the first signing to his new label Respond, wedge-haired seventeen-year-old schoolgirl Tracie, whose vocal was as high in the mix as his own. In front of him, slightly lower down, were his bassist Bruce Foxton and drummer Rick Buckler. Foxton had made no secret of the fact that Weller's decision to break up the band had left him in shock. Look at the footage now and it's heartbreaking to see Foxton, his loyal lieutenant, savouring the dying days of a period of his life he must have known he wouldn't better.

And as it was in the beginning, so shall it be in the end
That bullshit is bullshit, it just goes by different names

I didn't see much of myself in Weller – that was what was so awe-inspiring about him. I saw far too much of myself in Foxton. If I'd been in the Jam, I would have been the one begging him to give it just a couple more years. I would have been the one confiding my sorrows to the *Smash Hits* journalist. In 1993, when Foxton was interviewed by *Select* magazine, he lamented the fact that Weller had stopped returning his Christmas cards. A few years after that, he formed his own Jam tribute band, From the Jam. You could somehow extrapolate from that first *Top of the Pops* of December 1982 that this would be what fate had in store for everyone involved. Between Weller's serene, half-smiling delivery and Foxton's frantically committed performance the script appeared to have already been written.

The thing to remember about *Top of the Pops* was that it wasn't a slick production. There was very little directorial instruction from the people who make the show. The impression you made on *Top of the Pops* was down to how much you prepared for it. Given that you were being piped straight into over ten million homes, it was crazy that most bands didn't give this a second thought.

But there was another group who had prepared their performance as meticulously as the Jam. However, this wasn't a grand farewell gesture. It was the very opposite. In his memoir, *Black Vinyl White Powder*, Simon Napier-Bell – who later went on to manage Wham! – recalled seeing George Michael and Andrew Ridgeley's prime-time TV debut: 'When Wham! came on to do "Young Guns", they completely changed the way the programme looked. It was as if they'd rehearsed with the TV crew for days.'

It was also the first time my dad had taken an interest in *Top of the Pops* and, indeed, any pop music since his unpleasant encounter with ABBA's *The Visitors*.

'You should record *Top of the Pops* so your mother can see it,' he declared gnomically.

'Why would my mum want to see *Top of the Pops*?' I replied.

'They've got a Cypriot singer on there tonight. Yiorgos.'

Yiorgos?! There was no Yiorgos in the chart. I knew every record in the top 40, and there was no way I would have forgotten a Yiorgos. I patronisingly informed my dad that his information was poor. Or perhaps someone had played a joke on him.

But he wasn't having any of it. His friend Stratis, who owned a chip shop in Tottenham, knew Yiorgos's dad personally. The way my dad was carrying on, you'd have thought he'd known Yiorgos's dad personally too. 'His father is from Patriki,' he told me, as if this might mean anything to me.

'Whose father?'

'Yiorgos,' he said.

'Yiorgos, the singer?'

'That's right. Patriki in Famagusta. Yiorgos's father moved over here and opened a restaurant in Watford.'

'So Yiorgos's father is a friend of yours?'

'Kyriacos?'

'Is that what he's called?'

'Yes. Kyriacos Panayiotou. Of Patriki.'

'You know him?'

'Well, I'll almost certainly know some of his family.'

'Right. Well, anyway, I think you've made a mistake. There's no Yiorgos on *Top of the Pops*.' I showed him that day's *Evening Mail* with a full list of the artists performing on that night's show. 'See? Where does it say Yiorgos?'

My dad took the paper into the hallway where the phone lived and started dialling Stratis's shop in Tottenham. What was already becoming a tortuous and seemingly pointless process became even more protracted when someone who wasn't Stratis answered the phone. Stratis had gone home, presumably to watch Yiorgos the son of Kyriacos from Patriki on TV, leaving someone who was: (a) British; and (b) unaware of the Yiorgos thing to run the shop and answer the phone.

All I could hear from the living room was my dad's voice booming, 'It's Chris! Tell him it's Chris from Birmingham! He's . . . pardon me? Oh. Yes. Yes, please. Do I want Stratis to call me back? Yes. Tell him it's an emergency!'

Tomorrow's World was coming to an end. *Top of the Pops* was maybe two minutes away, and all we knew for sure about Yiorgos the singer was that he was the son of Kyriacos from Patriki. It was still far from clear whether Yiorgos the singer would be on tonight's *Top of the Pops* and, if so, in what capacity. However, as instructed, I pressed 'play' and 'record'. As I did so, the phone rang. It was Stratis – Stratis who was friends with Yiorgos's father, Kyriacos from Patriki. The call lasted half a minute at the most. There was no time to spare now. 'TAKI, IT'S JUAN! IT'S GEORGE MICHAEL AND JUAN!'

I was sure that George Michael and Juan were no more a presence in the top 40 than Yiorgos, the son of Kyriacos from Patriki. But, as it turns out, I was wrong and my dad was right.

'Oh, Wham! *Wham!*'

So, Yiorgos was George Michael and George Michael was one of our lot.

Simon Napier-Bell had been right. These guys had left nothing to chance. They cared far more about wowing you with their crisp dance moves than pretending to play their instruments. The gene pool from which George Michael had grown would have been enough to make my dad take proprietorial pride in the success of Wham! But the look sealed it for him. With the slicked back quiff, it was as though George had taken a picture of the young Chris Paphides to the hairdresser. And the combo of leather waistcoat and jeans merely completed the comfortable familiarity of George's look. As the performance finished, the on-screen graphics flashed up to tell you what you'd just seen. My dad instinctively ignored them. In his mind, there was no Wham! – only Yiorgos, the son of Kyriacos from Patriki.

George's Greekness had the immediate effect of getting my back up. He looked like the Greek I knew I could never be. Thin. Handsome. Confident. Masculine. Outgoing. Normal. Successful. Attractive to girls. It took me years to realise that we had more in common than I could have ever imagined. The erstwhile Yiorgos Panayiotou, son of a Greek-Cypriot restaurateur, had been a pudgy teenager with unmanageable curly hair, stuck in the suburbs, using pop music to try and establish for himself the cultural identity that his parents could never truly give him.

But if pop music was what gave George Michael his cultural identity, he needed to look elsewhere when it came to establishing a pop star identity. Over time, we all came to realise that the persona he invented for himself in Wham! was that of the *other* guy in Wham! – Andrew Ridgeley. But George had gone about the process so thoroughly that it seems he even fooled himself. How could it be that his entire adolescence came and went without activating the realisation that he might prefer men over women? I couldn't speak for George, but I can remember, as 1983 approached, feeling such a disconnection between my emotions and my body that I didn't have a clue what needed to change for me to truly know what I was.

While George Michael had yet to articulate that disconnection either to himself or to anyone else, I'd just discovered a song that managed to distil it perfectly. The irony was that the same song – Queen's 'Somebody to Love' – had once made such an impression on George himself that, at Wembley in 1992, he delivered a fearlessly perfect rendition of it, locating pockets of melody in it that had even eluded its creator.

All these years later, it isn't difficult to see what the young George Michael might have seen in Freddie Mercury. Even if George had yet to untangle his own sexuality, he would have seen in Freddie plenty to help him map his own route to pop stardom. Here was a singer in a band who had so totally detached his identity from his background that even most Queen fans didn't seem to know or care that their favourite rock star was a homosexual Parsi Indian whose birth certificate had him down as Farrokh Bulsara. By the force of his personality and his songs, Freddie Mercury seemed to suspend all speculation concerning his background and sexuality. You could be forgiven for failing to spot the signs if you just listened to the records, but the videos made it clearer.

Pre-recorded videotapes were far too expensive to buy, but we had the Video Man, a guy with an upholstered blue nylon anorak and a wiry Gene Wilder comb-over who had posted six stapled-together sheets of A4 paper with the titles that we could 'book' for the following weekend. Newly released feature films were £2 to rent, but on the final page there was a selection of music titles which you could rent for £1. For a month, I repeatedly selected Queen's *Greatest Flix* – the VHS complement to their massively successful *Greatest Hits* LP. Every Sunday morning, while Aki and my parents were still in bed, I enjoyed the music in a way that wasn't possible with just the album. With music alone, it's hard to work out who your favourite member is or to get a handle on the interpersonal dynamic of the band. That was what television and magazines were for. But Queen didn't seem to figure much in the magazines that Aki and I used to buy. In my head, they were a logo sewn onto a denim jacket next to Status Quo and Saxon. I had needed to file Queen somewhere, and so I had filed them under heavy rock, subconsciously viewing 'Another One Bites the Dust', 'Crazy Little Thing Called Love' and 'Under Pressure' as mere aberrations.

But you couldn't watch all of Queen's videos back-to-back and continue to hold that view. They were at least as much pop as rock. Their use of multitracked harmonies was outrageous. On 'Bohemian

Rhapsody', 'Somebody to Love' and 'You're My Best Friend', there was absolutely no attempt to create something that could be replicated live. Even choirs didn't sound like this, because a hundred individual voices *couldn't* sound like this. By multiplying the same three- or four-part harmonies dozens of times over, the effect was to create a noise of such density that it felt like it might break apart in mid-flight. Hearing the rest of Queen swoop in to fill the space around their singer was an early form of augmented reality, as startling in its way as seeing cartoon birds fly out of a tree or waking up to see two animated feet poking out of the duvet. The studio-based videos of 'Somebody to Love' and 'You're My Best Friend' seemed to authenticate the sentiments of songs that hymned the glories of tenderness and companionship. Here were four grown men being soft around each other, close-huddling around overhead mics, separated only by the cotton of their shirts. Their hair was long, their body language bordering on effete. This was a vision of male adult friendship I had never seen before; a version of manliness in which, alone in my front room on a Sunday morning, I had become a vicarious participant.

Even the rock songs seemed to draw from a different well than those written by other rockers. Queen's camp theatricality wasn't a smokescreen; it wasn't an ironic device to keep you at a distance. It was quite the reverse. It was as if, while you were asleep, someone had installed an emotional subwoofer inside you. 'Save Me' amplified the sadness of separation to near-apocalyptic proportions and, of course, the results were breathtaking. There's a chunk of a boy's psyche that corresponds closely to the way Queen records work. 'We Are the Champions' was a supersized version of the playground chant – *nyer-nyer-nyer-nerrr-nerrr!* – deployed by boys when taunting other boys. Because Queen found it impossible to scale down, 'Save Me' was an emotional inversion of 'We Are the Champions'. The ingredients were the same, but the result was not. It was as though the vast sonic soufflé of the latter had collapsed under its own weight.

To be able to watch Freddie Mercury as I listened to him was, at times, a source of mild torment. How do you get to be like that? How do you become so unafraid of the reactions of those around you that you can write and inhabit a song like 'Don't Stop Me Now'? How do you get that brave? How do you stop caring? When he sang, 'I'm a rocket ship on my way to Mars on a collision course', he sounded excited about the fact. Stuck with a bunch of friends who seemed to think I was something other than what I was; guilty about growing up British in a Greek family; terrified of change; terrified of its opposite; terrified of scrutiny; bewildered by my own body; avoiding the cracks in the pavement because that was the only thing left to control. I was also a rocket ship on my way to Mars on a collision course. And it frightened me.

CHAPTER 33

I was back in Acocks Green police station, but this time I wasn't looking over the balcony at the black water below. This time I was inside it with Dean Tookey. Tearfully remonstrating, pleading for my life, while a policeman gazed down at me from above. Tookey seemed indifferent to his fate. He was treading water beside me, staring up defiantly. Any second now, the shark would smell my fear and it would all be over. No one would ever find me.

'Just say it. If you admit it, we'll let you out.'

'But I didn't do it. *Please.* I'm begging you. I wasn't even there. I didn't do it.'

In the dream, it wasn't Troy Meehan that had been accused of murdering the eight-year-old boy. It was me and Tookey. All we needed to do was confess to the crime and we'd be allowed to get out and face trial. As my whimpering escalated, it wasn't the policeman I saw gazing down at me. It was my mum, calling my name over and over again. She crouched down and asked me if I was OK. I didn't know the Greek word for 'nightmare' – I'd never had occasion to use it – so I told her that I'd had an *oneiro*. She didn't ask me what had happened in the dream and, in any case, I didn't want to tell her.

Tookey had continued to turn up at the shop expecting free food and, for the time being, I had assurances from my parents that they wouldn't do anything that risked humiliating him. Since our attempt to establish a sideline as casual labourers had ended as soon as it started, a sort of aggressive neediness characterised his dealings with me. Into this was built an implied threat that if we didn't stay friends I would feel the sharp end of the resulting betrayal. One Saturday morning he turned up at our front door. He was out of breath. In his arms was a giant box of Walkers prawn cocktail crisps. On the side of the box, the perforated circle had been removed, so that shop customers could reach into the box and pull out however many bags they wanted to take to the counter.

'I got you this!' he exclaimed.

'You nicked it?'

'Fucking hell, Paphides.'

'Where did you get it from?'

'Are you scared?'

'No! It's just—'

'You said it was your favourite flavour.'

'Where did you get it from?'

'Fucking hell, man. That's the last time I do anything for you.'

He turned on his heel and threw the box down. Afraid of who might see – for all I knew, the owner of the shop where he'd taken the crisps might come haring around the corner and catch me handling the stolen goods – I grabbed the crisps and rushed up to my bedroom. I didn't invite Tookey in, but he followed behind anyway. There was only one place to hide a giant box of crisps without arousing my parents' suspicion. I pulled out the 7-inch singles from the shelf beneath the record player and laid the crisps in rows directly behind them. Having heard the commotion, Aki walked in, took one look at Tookey lying on my bed, and asked me what I'd been doing.

'Give us a bag, then,' said Tookey. I reached back into the alcove and threw one over to him. He glanced over at Aki, then back to me. 'Aren't you gonna give him one?'

'D'you want some crisps?' I asked Aki, painfully aware that it must have looked to him like Tookey was controlling my actions.

He shook his head and walked out, only to return after Tookey had finally left the house. 'Where did you get those crisps from?' he asked me. I told Aki what had happened, perhaps in the hope that he might be able to aid my predicament with Tookey, but I was out of luck. Aki sided with the owners of the shop, pointing out that they were most probably just like our mum and dad – ordinary people standing behind a shop counter, just trying to make a living. He was right, although in all likelihood, Tookey's actions were almost certainly an attempt to 'pay' for some of the free food my parents had given him over the previous weeks. Any hesitation in accepting his offering was just another weight on the *Buckaroo!* donkey of his pride.

But just as I couldn't help him, neither could anyone help me. All the different fears I felt about my life – both about growing up and about my peer group quandary – had merged into a tinnitus pulse of anxiety that only abated with sleep. When my unconscious mind wasn't trying to scare the hell out of me, it was trying to offer solutions. In another dream, I'd skipped school and boarded a Birmingham bus – blue at the bottom and a condensed milk off-white at the top – with an unfamiliar number at the front of it. This one was going all the way to London. Contained in my holdall were my schoolbooks, a map and a copy of that week's *Record Mirror*, folded back onto Susanne Garrett's advice column. Printed on top of the page, next to her byline picture, was the address and phone number to be dialled by readers in need of advice. I'd been reading Susanne's page, clocking her face ever since Aki started bringing *Record Mirror* into the house in 1980. Her calm gaze suggested that she really cared, but her strong jawline and the absence of a smile implied that if necessary, she wouldn't pull her punches. Her halo of wavy, shoulder-length hair was brushed away from her face, establishing an intermediate point between prettiness and practicality.

All of which explained why, in my dream, I was alighting the bus beneath the neon billboards of Piccadilly Circus, map in hand, looking for the offices of *Record Mirror*. When I finally got to see Susanne and told her what was happening in my life, she would surely find a way to make it all better. What happened after this point sits in my memory more as a collection of stills than a flowing narrative. In my dream, the *Record Mirror* building was fully visible from the outside: a glass-fronted ground-floor office full of groovy grown-ups sitting beneath fluorescent strip lights, with typewriters and record players with piles of records around them. It looked like the most exciting place in the world, perhaps the only place where I stood a chance of fitting in if I ever made it beyond Yardleys Secondary School. I was across the road, keeping vigil, waiting for Susanne to emerge for her lunch break. When the moment came, I'd catch her up and introduce myself.

'*Susanne! Susanne! Excuse me, Susanne. I'm sorry to bother you. My name is Peter Paphides and I was wondering . . .*'

The next scene lodged in my memory after half a lifetime is that of Susanne finally emerging from the offices of *Record Mirror*. She's wearing a leather jacket, elasticated at the waist. She's wearing dark-blue jeans and she's smoking a cigarette. She's with two or three other *Record Mirror* writers – not ideal, but I have to take my chance. I run in pursuit, but every time I step on a crack in the pavement, I have to go back to my starting position and do it all over again.

At some point in this inescapable loop, my alarm went off. It was Friday morning. I couldn't just bunk off school and go to London, but I could call the number in *Record Mirror*. Perhaps *that* was an option. Who knows? Perhaps she might even pick up. What if she picked up? What if she liked me? What if she asked me about records? What if she invited me down to the offices of *Record Mirror* and offered me a job? *What if I became the youngest person ever to write reviews for a music magazine?*

Because I had no real idea who I was or what my value was, it was easy for me to veer between, at one end, the conviction that I had irreversibly screwed everything up for everyone, and, at the other, the hope that someone from beyond my immediate world would swoop down and fly me off to a place where being myself had some sort of currency; *a place where the grown-ups got me.* But, of course, in order to help me out of my situation, my rescuer needed to know I existed. To borrow from pop's kindly supply teacher Sting, if I didn't send my SOS to the world, how were those hundred million bottles ever going to wash up on my shore? Taking the dream as a sign, I put that week's *Record Mirror* into my school bag with the germ of a plan that I'd action when the bell rang at 3.45 p.m.

I slipped out of the back gate, careful not to be seen by Terry Violett, who sometimes wanted me to walk home with him. I ran about a half a mile, as fast as the cracks in the pavement would allow, to the foot of the Lucas factory on Shaftmoor Lane. Illuminated in the darkness were stripes of yellow light, one for each of the floors where Yardleys school leavers were expected to spend most of their weekdays attending to assembly lines of field coils and starter motors.

I stopped at the phone box outside, pulled out the *Record Mirror* in my bag and dialled the number, wondering if Susanne would pick up. Surely it couldn't be as simple as that? I could feel my pulse racing. With my thumb I slid forward the first of six or seven 10p coins in my hand, ready to push it into the hole. The phone at the other end rang perhaps two times. When someone appeared to pick up, I pushed in the coin only to forget entirely why I was calling. In a panic, I slammed the phone down and leaned forward onto the small ledge, underneath which the residential directory and the Yellow Pages were clamped into place by their spines. In my mind, I nervously ran through the main reason I was calling. I pulled out my rough book, wrote down the main bullet points – Tookey; the cracks in the pavement; the fear of change; the fear of things never changing – and, satisfied that I'd covered everything, I dialled the number again. It went straight into an answerphone message, asking me to leave my name and number. But, of course, there was no way I could leave my home number. *Quick. Think of something.* I looked at the number printed in the centre of the rotary dial and began to speak.

'Hello? My name is Peter. If you get this message straight away, would you mind calling me on 021 706 3013? Thank you.'

I replaced the handset and stared at it for a bit. I was supposed to be helping out at the shop, but what if someone called back? I couldn't leave yet. *What to do? Quick. Think of something.* Suddenly I heard a knock behind me.

Shouting to be heard through the glass, a woman about my mum's age asked, 'Are you using the phone?!'

'Sorry! Yes! I'm . . . just five minutes!'

I picked up the receiver and dialled while subtly leaning my right forearm onto the handset cradle to ensure outside calls could still come through. Then, I pretended to have a conversation with William about meeting up the next day. A second knock from the woman, five minutes later, called time on the entire exercise. I was really late now. I couldn't stop shaking. I didn't know why then, and I'm not sure I do now. But the adrenalin seemed to be surging around my body like cars on a Scalextric track – round and round and round with no apparent end in sight.

I ran into the centre of Acocks Green as though someone were giving chase. I felt like if I stopped running, I might burst into tears, and so I just kept on running, past the stop where I'd normally get the bus to the Kingfisher, all the way to the shop. For the first time in weeks, I forgot about the cracks in the pavement, but slowing down about half a mile from the shop, by the stretch of road where my bike had collided with the woman in the car, I remembered again. I knew I was late so I avoided eye contact with my parents, headed straight for the peg where my apron was hanging, picking up an empty bucket along the way, and filled it with chipped potatoes from the backroom. I checked the levels of curry sauce and peas, pulled down the tray of rice flour from its shelf and coated a dozen or so pieces of cod so they were ready to be battered. I barely paused for breath. Perhaps this really was all I was good for. If I just accepted that my destiny was to fry fish for the hardworking people of Acocks Green and Olton, then everything else would recede into irrelevance. O levels wouldn't matter. School wouldn't matter. And records, well, records would always be there.

And yet, that never seemed to be how it worked. I thought about Nick, my parents' friends' son, who was being groomed to take over their chippy; about the disco 12-inches he gave me because there was no time for that stuff any more. Did it really have to be that way?

Perhaps it did. If you spend most of your time in a chip shop, then things that once seemed to define you as a teenager would disappear in the rear-view mirror of time. And what might seem like tiny niggles to an outside observer might become intolerable bugbears. You do things that might seem petty to the outside world, but they're the things that help you to get through the day. It bothered my dad that we sold more cod than haddock or plaice at the Kingfisher. To him, the popularity of cod symbolised the conservatism of the British palate. When a customer came in and ordered haddock or plaice he was visibly nicer to them. At around 8 p.m. on a Friday, we always had a customer, Mr Rhys, who would park his Daimler on the double yellow line directly outside the shop and, as he joined the back of the queue, would grandly roar the same order to my dad, irrespective of whether he was in mid-conversation with one of the other customers (it was always my dad and never my mum): 'Chris! I'd like you to sort me out with your *very* best piece of fish.' Short of tapping his cane on the counter, he couldn't have been more annoying. My dad always had set aside a reheated piece of fish that had remained unsold from that lunchtime for him. He'd pull it out with the tongs and place it onto the mound of chips my mum had ready on the counter. 'Here you are, Mr Rhys. Only the best for you.'

Mr Rhys's arrival in the shop, by virtue of it being 8 o'clock, was usually the trigger for me and my mum to go home. While my mum went upstairs to run a bath, I'd check the video machine that I'd set to record *The Tube*. Then I'd wind back the tape and watch it while eating the dinner I'd brought back with me. That suited me fine. Increasingly, I felt more comfortable alone with the TV and something I'd recorded on video than with other people – the companionship provided by performing musicians filled the void while bringing with it none of the attendant anxieties that attached themselves to real-life relationships. Among the attractions featured on tonight's episode of *The Tube* were newly unearthed footage of the Beatles and, live in the studio, Dexys Midnight Runners.

I hadn't explored the Beatles beyond the 1966 compilation I'd taped from Ged, but a twentieth-anniversary re-release of 'Love Me Do' had just charted. The Beatles' reissued debut single stuck out a mile alongside Kid Creole and the Coconuts, Culture Club and Blancmange in the chart. It didn't sound like pop to me. It sounded like something that slightly predated pop. It sounded like a test transmission. It sounded like levels being checked. It sounded like a spectacle in a theatre whose doors had yet to open. It sounded like the screaming had yet to start. John Lennon's harmonica sounded to me like the bracing stink of Mersey mud. And yet, I'd never been to Liverpool. How was that even possible?

The previously unseen film had belonged to Dezo Hoffman, a Slovak photographer who frequently shot the Beatles in the early years of their ascent. He also filmed Super 8 footage of them, fre-quently handing over his camera to the group. There was no sound on the moving footage, so we got to hear Hoffman reminiscing about the fraternal bond between John, Paul, George and Ringo; their willingness to don Victorian bathing costumes and horse around with each other on the beach, simultaneously playing to the camera and yet never being anything other than themselves. 'Good Day Sunshine' faded up in the bits when he wasn't talking. The lilting nostalgia in Hoffman's voice was somehow accentuated by his Eastern European accent. If you didn't understand the words, you might have guessed you were listening to a Jewish tailor recalling the period between the wars.

As with the Queen video, the sight of four men being tender and at ease with each other, creators and occupants of their shared world, constituted something of a safe space for me. I was watching a surrogate family with a collective goal. But then, of course I was – because this is what all groups have to be in the years after childhood, but before marriage and parenthood come along to supplant that dynamic. The shared lifetime of every group is an unrepeatable golden age. But, according to Hoffman, the shared lifetime of the Beatles was a golden age among golden ages. To younger viewers, the deflating subtext of his words seemed to be 'Take your fun wherever you might find it, but you missed the main event. Nothing this exciting could ever happen again.'

As if to underscore his point, we got to see the film the group made for 'Penny Lane' in 1967, just fifteen years previously. It was the first time I'd heard 'Penny Lane', but it didn't feel like a beginning. It felt like a memento of something that had died. Had I simply heard the song on its own, I might have mistaken its outward jauntiness for something insubstantial. But with the film, that wasn't possible. Strolling through their home town in their psychedelic proto-Pepper threads (it was shot in London, but I didn't know that at the time), they didn't just look like pop stars. They looked like dandy older brothers from a gentler age, privy to a host of in-jokes that would somehow be rendered even funnier for the fact that you didn't always understand them.

'Penny Lane' was pathos squared. A song that paused the videotape of memory on a moment to which its author knows it can never return. The passing of time had turned it into a memory of a memory. In 'Penny Lane', I wanted so badly to be the Beatles' friend, but in the film that followed swiftly afterwards, 'Strawberry Fields Forever', I was slightly scared. It wasn't the sight of them walking backwards through a field at dusk that did it. Neither was it the bit where they attach tuning keys to the branch of a tree and tie strings to it which rise up from the back of a piano over which they've emptied out dozens of pots of different-coloured paints. It was the succession of individual head shots in which the four Beatles stared into the lens with expressions I'd never seen before, certainly not from a Beatle. It was as though they were trying to impart some unsayable truth with their eyes. It was as though, to quote John Lennon talking about the Maharishi, they might 'slip me the answer'. And that if I stared into the TV screen just as intently, I might finally get it too. For now though, it was enough to know that somehow the Beatles were there to help me. It was enough to hear John Lennon sing, 'It's getting hard to be someone / But it all works out' and hope that when I finally worked out who I was going to be, it would all work out for me too. The previous weekend, Aki had come home from town and reported that he'd seen Kevin Rowland and Dexys' violinist Helen O'Hara descending the escalator at the Bull Ring shopping centre. The escalator in question led from an overhead walkway, lined with shops, down to ground level from an atrium area. The thing about it was that you were totally exposed. Anyone could look up and see you. And Kevin and Helen, far from trying to blend in, were dressed in their *Too-Rye-Ay* gear – the ripped denim dungarees and tousled hair they sported in the 'Come on Eileen' video. It was like seeing Martin Fry walking out of the C&A toilet in his gold sequinned suit or Adam Ant alighting the 37 bus dressed as a dandy highwayman.

The image stayed lodged in my memory from the moment he relayed it. At this moment, there was a vacancy in my life for someone who meant it. Who dealt in cast-iron certainties. Who walked the talk without heed for the consequences. I had no reason to believe it was going to be Dexys. But then, the field didn't seem overly crowded right now. From Aki's room, John Peel mainstays New Order, the Fall and Wah! were snapping at the heels of reigning champions Echo & the Bunnymen. But they belonged to him, not me.

And Kevin Rowland? Who did Kevin Rowland belong to? No one in the past eighteen months had written 'Dexys' on the back of a parka. Some of the boys had grown out their skinheads into wedges or artfully sculpted Sylvian dos. A handful of boys wanted to be Suggs. But Kevin Rowland? Dexys were selling more records than ever. And yet, either in spite or because of that, Kevin Rowland didn't really belong to anyone any more.

Straight in from the ad break, Dexys commenced the new single, a catchy slice of rustic soul called 'Let's Get This Straight (From the Start)', which pleaded for unambiguous communication in a world of prevarication and equivocation. Like so many Dexys songs – 'Let's Make This Precious' and 'Soon', to name two – it was about trying to anchor yourself in worthwhile certainties. Certainties that might sustain you through the bad times and the good. It was about working out what you stand for so that others might be better able to work out whether they're for you or against you. Maybe at some level it was about Kevin's lapsed Catholicism, or at the very least, the space left open by it.

In a sense, that's also where the next song was coming from. 'Celtic Soul Brothers' upped the tempo and, seemingly, gave the musicians around Kevin a chance to forget that they were playing to millions of people. On the instrumental break, you got to see Kevin drop to one knee and strum his guitar while gazing up at O'Hara as if he were proposing. Not that anyone knew it at the time, but they were an item during this period. She was in love with him, but actually, looking at this performance, it's clear that she wasn't the only one.

With every passing verse, something was collectively stirring. They stopped looking at each other because they no longer needed to. The song appeared to accelerate slightly. They had collectively taken leave of their surroundings. They were a single entity. You can see it. Even now. If you watch, you'll see it.

Finally, he spoke to the crowd.

'So, let me tell you this. This, ah, well it used to go like that. But then one day something happened, as it so often does, and now it goes like this.'

A single note repeated on a bass string – a noise which somehow instantly commands your attention – and then, 'Ro . . . Ro . . . Ro . . . ROBIN!'

Two years previously, 'There, There, My Dear' sailed into the top 10 in the slipstream of 'Geno'. In its original incarnation, the song was an amphetamine-burning evisceration of Kevin's greatest bête noire – the left-leaning protest singer whose cold correctness arouses suspicion in a frontman struggling to locate the passion that corresponds to *his* reasons for stepping into the spotlight. By December 1982 though, it was no longer possible – at least not after what I was about to hear – to think about the song purely in those terms. 'There, There, My Dear' was no longer about the person addressed in the line 'I don't believe / You really liked Sinatra'. Once you've written a song, you're free to do what you want with it. You can remove one set of emotions from it and replace them with another. The words might stay the same, but it's your song and you can use it however you see fit.

Because *one day something happened as it so often does.*

In the seconds that followed the Sinatra line, you could begin to apprehend the measure of Dexys' commitment. A tidal rush of horns and a thermal upswell of Hammond filled the available space before the second verse. A camera positioned at the back of the room caught Kevin, eyes closed, arms wide apart, head shaking, seemingly

attempting to absorb the energy of the noise around him, energy he'd
need to take him through the next part of the song.

> *Rrrrrobin! You're always so happy*
> *How the hell?*
> *Just a dumbed-down patriot . . .*
> *. . . And you're supposed to be angry*
> *Well, let's fight.*

No one appeared to be engaged in conscious thought now. No one
was looking at the camera. Not even Kevin. Especially not Kevin. And
that made it even better. It was more like peering through the window
of a gospel tabernacle church. It made it feel like he'd be doing this
anyway, irrespective of whether we were here. It took it away from
show business to some place closer to ritual. And because it made
him seem the opposite of needy, it increased his power. He could
barely string a few chords together on a guitar, and yet the devotion
he inspired in skilled musicians was total. Helen had jettisoned a
promising career as a classical violinist to join Dexys, and at a time
when it looked as though they might never have another hit. And
what about the backing singers? Was it the mere promise of work that
would have persuaded former Ike Turner sideman Jimmy Thomas
to swap his sharp suits for a pair of dungarees? The answer properly
revealed itself after about three and a half minutes. Everything but
the rhythm section dropped out and Kevin sank to his knees. Now I
was starting to feel things I didn't entirely understand.

The next four minutes would effectively place him within touching
distance of Sam & Dave, Otis Redding and Van Morrison – the
singers who shaped his earliest notions of what it was to be a great
frontman. But perhaps more than any of those, the figure who sprang
most readily to mind was a singer I'd only seen and heard for the
first time fifteen minutes previously. On the same programme, we

had been shown some archive footage of James Brown in 1964, a human firestorm of priapic and spiritual yearning, throwing his head back with a scream, lifting his microphone off the floor only to find himself repeatedly falling to the ground, physically overwhelmed by the sound he had inspired his band to make.

Now here was Kevin channelling the same mystic energy:

'Robin . . . Robin . . . Robin . . . I've been searching . . . Two years and three months ago, I began my quest . . . [It had been just a bit longer than two years and three months since *Searching for the Young Soul Rebels* had been released and on it was the original version of 'There, There, My Dear', with the line, 'I'm just searching for the young soul rebels, and I can't find them anywhere'.] The point is, Robin . . . I'm starting to get concerned that . . . it occurs to me for the first time that you're not listening. I'm saying Robin, do you hear me . . . Robin, are you listening? Can you hear me?'

The band responded with a rising torrent of yeses, as if keen to let Kevin know that someone could hear him, that all this wasn't in vain. And finally, when he was satisfied that he had the attention of everyone in the room, when he had the numbers, only then did he issue the command: 'Let's go, let's go, let's go!' As he did so, his saxophonists stepped forward, one foot each on the monitors, as Kevin sang:

Cos the only way to change [things]
Is shoot those who arrange [things]
Robin, let me explain
But you'd never see
In a million years . . .

What even was this now? What was rehearsed and what was improvised? Was this something they did night after night? Or was I gazing on at some spontaneous, unrepeatable spectacle taking place at the psychodramatic intersection of folk, soul, theatre and revelation? At almost six minutes, he released a scream and, on his knees once again, let his torso fold forward so he was facing the floor. 'Witness! Witness!' he called. The band were playing out of their collective skin. Those who weren't blowing into something were calling out 'STOP!' and 'GO!' alternately on every bar. I was on my knees too, as oblivious to his next utterance as his own band. And then . . .

'At this point, I do some press-ups.'

What?!

I think that was the moment I fell in love with him. Watching him merge the ridiculous with the sublime in one surreal action, stretching out his 6-foot 2-inch frame across the stage, this seemed to me an act of outright heroism. En masse, the string and horn sections rushed to the front of the stage again. The noise was transcendent. In a song that defied its subject to forget his inhibitions and *commit*, his performance demanded the same of you. Aged thirteen, self-conscious in all sorts of ways, I sat stock-still watching Kevin Rowland cradling an imaginary baby, seemingly in a dream state, insisting, 'I didn't mean the things I said.' Behind him, the band seemed unable to hold anything back now. If he didn't call time on the song, you felt like they might start to drop one by one. Finally, just shy of nine minutes, came the signal that told his band they could finally ease up. In alternating motions, his arms pushed down towards the floor and the song was over.

A trip switch had been thrown. I dug out the single version of what I'd just heard, and listened to those lines anew.

> Cos the only way to change things
> Is shoot those who arrange things

Lines delivered by the right voice at the right time could radicalise a young man. Maybe parents are right to worry about this stuff. Popular culture can have an irreversibly corrupting influence on the young. But if it can do that, then it can also save lives. It can educate them. It can parent them when parents have no parenting left in them. And it doesn't have to be a pile of records. It doesn't have to be a shelf full of books. It doesn't have to be a stack of films. If the right song/film/book/play/TV show comes along at the right time, nothing else is needed. Just that one thing.

I rewound the tape and watched the whole show as if it were the unbroken narrative of a film. It all merged into a single arc. It was the greatest story ever told. When all hope was lost, when the world could end at any minute and nothing would ever be as good as the Beatles, along came Dexys Midnight Runners. They'd been there all along, but this time they had come for me. The old man talking about the Beatles was wrong. Epiphanies were still possible.

CHAPTER 34

First day of the Christmas holidays. I was back with the gang in Mell Square for the first time since we'd colonised the municipal fountain and laid on a spontaneous exhibition of synchronised cycling for the shoppers of Solihull. Only a few weeks had elapsed since that episode, but a lot had changed. Back in October, I'd been excited about my induction into a group of boys that got up to daring adventures. For a brief period, I thought that this might be the person I was waiting to turn into. In the interim, it had become apparent to me that I'd never stood a chance.

For the time being though, they were still my friends, and this was what we were going to be doing today. It was never presented to me as an option. At some point during the final few days, going to Solihull for a day of 'dossing about' became the plan. Tookey was now routinely eyeing me with suspicion, the way a gang member eyes up a potential informant. My life was morphing into a cross between *The Godfather* and *Grange Hill*. A week previously, my dad had told Tookey he could no longer keep giving him free food. As I'd expected, Tookey took his humiliation out on me, sometimes asking me to empty my pockets at lunchtime before deciding how much he would ask me to lend him, other times asking me why I kept using long words that no one understood.

'Paphides! What was that word you said in English yesterday? Mega-what?'

The word had been 'metaphorical'. Our teacher Mr Garbett had asked the class what it had meant. Stupidly, I had put my hand up.

'"Metaphorical",' I told Tookey, trying to maintain a tone that suggested I thought it was a poncey word too.

'Do you think you're clever when you use long words?'

'I didn't use it. I just told Garbett the answer.'

'Do you think I'm thick?'

'No.'

'What was that word you said?'

'Metaphorical.'

'What does it mean?'

'It doesn't matter.'

'You think I'm too thick?'

'No!'

'Tell me what it means, Paphides.'

'It's like a coded way of saying something. Like, if you're an "early bird", you get up really early in the morning. That kind of thing.'

'You're a *cunt*. Is that a metaphor?'

Either side of me and Tookey, Terry Violett and Kevin Flynn made no attempt to conceal their delight at this exchange. And then, an odd thing happened. Terry perceived a tipping of the scales. Suddenly, my discomfort outweighed his amusement. He snatched Tookey's scarf and ran off with it. Tookey gave chase and caught him up, but not before Terry managed to throw Tookey's scarf onto the overhanging concrete shelf that protruded out of WH Smith. As Terry and Tookey started rolling around on the nearby pavement, Flynn barely uttered a word. Although he was smaller than any of us, the combination of his silence and his reputation gave him a seniority that no one questioned. Finally though, on registering a hubbub from the other side of the fountain, he piped up.

'Fuck! It's ... It's ... Look! It's wossisname! "Save Your Love"! It's that *twat*!'

Singing waiter Renato Pagliari and his co-vocalist Renée were, if only for that week, the most successful pop stars in Britain. They'd fended off competition from Boy George, Shaky, the Jam and Madness to secure themselves the Christmas number 1 with 'Save Your Love'. Most days Renato could be found unleashing his tenor while decanting Chianti for the diners of nearby Sutton Coldfield, but that was definitely him in front of us, singing Christmas carols for charity, flanked by a handful of adults with collection buckets. Terry scuttled over, beckoning the rest of us as he did so.

'Oi Renée! RENÉE!' He pronounced Renée like you'd pronounce Rennie indigestion tablets. For a second, I started to tell him that the bloke whose attention he was trying to catch was actually Renato. But after the 'metaphor' business, I thought better of it. For his part, Renato was mercifully oblivious. There was a crescent of about thirty people protecting him from us, most of them singing along with his operatic rendition of 'Silent Night'. Stirring as it was, his Italian accent also had the effect of making it sound like he was exhorting us to 'slip in heavenly piss'. We joined in, singing twice as loudly as anyone else. The song ended to cheers and applause. Renato wasn't going to leave without singing the song that had propelled him to sudden stardom.

'I've lost Renée!' he exclaimed to the throng. ''As anyone-a-seen my Renée?! Oh well, who issa gonna sing "Save Your Love" with me?'

Terry pushed Tookey forward and, pointing to the top of Tookey's head, shouted, 'RENÉE! HE'LL DO IT! PICK HIM! PICK HIM!'

Whoever Renato picked in the end, it wasn't Tookey. In that moment, an enormous splash momentarily averted everyone's attention from Renato and to the bin that Flynn had dislodged from a nearby lamppost and thrown into the fountain, splashing the back of Renato's tuxedo. As its contents floated out onto the surface, the four of us legged it down one of the roads that branched off from the square, finally coming to a stop on the second floor of Beatties department store.

'Fucking hell, Flynn! What'd you do that for?' asked Terry, more in nervous admiration than anything.

Flynn shrugged. One long word I didn't know was 'nihilist', but looking back, I think Flynn was one of those. Or he might just have been a sociopath. On the basis of the 300 words we exchanged over four months, I couldn't say for sure.

Somewhere along the line, it had been decided – by whom, I'm not quite sure – what we were going to do next. But it was a conversation I hadn't been in on. We were going to jump on the number 37 bus and head off to Mr Elverston's, the old man who ran the barber shop beside the school. Once we got there, we were going to get all our hair cut off. Terry had done it once before in the second year. He had come back from his lunch break with a skinhead haircut. With his Crombie and Docs, it was like Chas Smash had just walked into Mr Snabel's geography class. Not all barbers did skinheads without a parent being there, but Mr Elverston was one of the few who did.

In that moment, I felt a wave of absolute sickness flood my insides. My hair was as long as I could get away with having it. It rested around my shoulders. I liked having it there. I couldn't imagine not having it. If I had any sort of identity at all, it was in my hair. I couldn't imagine what my parents would say. I wondered if this was a test or a trick or a ritual. Or was it all three?

'Oh, man!' said Terry. 'Are you gonna do it?'

I shrugged a shrug of compliance, something to take the heat off me. 'Yeah, it's just hair. I'm not bothered. Are *you* gonna do it?' I said, trying to deflect some of the attention. I could hear my heart hammering against my ribcage.

'Yeah, man! I love getting my hair cut!'

'I'm parched,' I said, pointing across to the cafeteria where the blue-rinsed senior citizens of Solihull sipped lukewarm tea from shallow cups and attempted to spread rock-hard rectangles of Kerrygold onto helpless teacakes.

'Fuckin' 'ell, Paphides. Hurry up,' said Terry. I took a beaker from the stack next to the squash machine and pressed it against the lever which released blackcurrant squash from the see-through tank. As I did so, I could see Flynn and Tookey – now prolific shoplifters – conferring by the display of confectionery and dried fruit adjacent to the café. Terry went off to see what they were up to. I had maybe a three-second window to make my run. I put my drink down, backtracked from the checkout where I was waiting to pay and darted across the other side of the display, through the toy section and out through the rear door which led directly onto the top of the multistorey car park.

I didn't dare look back. Instead, I ran towards the ramps that connected the levels to each other, a spiralling sprint to the bottom which continued until I found myself at the train station half a mile away. I leaned into the ticket window and, momentarily sensing that they might come and look for me at home, asked the man on the other side of the glass for a ticket to Birmingham city centre. I needed to disappear for the rest of that day. The relief of being on a train leaving Solihull merged with the smell of the iron-sprung upholstery in the Pullman carriage, a nostalgic yearning for afternoon sorties into town with my mum and a Mr Men book. Nothing else in the world smells like a Pullman carriage. This is a fact.

I had more money on me than usual. Irene and Jack had paid their annual Christmas visit the evening before, and now that I was talking, I was happy to accept their generosity – a Christmas card containing £10. The £10 note was still inside the folded card in my coat pocket. I pulled it out to check it was still there and, for a few hours, allowed myself to think that whatever Terry, Tookey and Flynn thought about my disappearance, I would find a way to explain it later.

I hit every record shop in town and every record section of every department store. I crossed the underpass opposite Moor Street station and walked into Reddington's Rare Records, set back alongside one of the ramps coming out of the subway. I bagged myself tatty but playable copies of Black Slate's reggae hit 'Amigo' and Raw Silk's 'Do It to the Music'. The bearded guy at the till, who bore a striking similarity to Rick Wakeman, took them off me and told me I could have three for £1. I picked up 'Living Eyes', the pensive 1981 single by the Bee Gees, whose stock had gone into freefall, seemingly never to recover.

Via Boots and WH Smiths, I popped into HMV on New Street to check the price of *Too-Rye-Ay*. However much money I spent, I needed to ensure that I had enough left to go home with the Dexys record. I took a right turn along Corporation Street towards Lewis's record shop and the Virgin shop on Bull Street, where I found a 12-inch of 'Red Light', the Linda Clifford song on the *Fame* soundtrack, rendered unforgettable by Leroy's suggestive dance. Just 50p. I swung back in the direction from where I'd come, cutting alongside the back of Rackhams through the illuminations of Cathedral Square and out onto the far end of New Street where the huge Woolworths was located. I looked through the countertop box of reduced singles and pulled out 'Mirror Man', the debut release by a group called Talk Talk, who had opened for Duran Duran on their recent tour, and a copy of 'King's Call' by Phil Lynott. I'd taken a chance on the Talk Talk record – I'd never heard it – but when I finally did, it would sound incredible to me. An urgent, ambivalent synth-pop paean to the tyranny of fashion – 'And she laughs cos we look the same / Follow all of the rules' – whose rising, anguished strings portended the increasingly astounding deviations of their future releases. The Phil Lynott song was a brooding account of what he did on the day that Elvis Presley died. Because it was produced by Mark Knopfler and also featured him on backing vocal and guitar, it sounded more like a Dire Straits song than anything by Lynott's band Thin Lizzy.

Thin Lizzy and Dire Straits were both present on my next purchase. In the basement of Littlewoods department store, the clearance rack in the tiny music section yielded a K-tel compilation with a 99p sticker on it called *The Summit*, which featured 'The Boys Are Back in Town' and 'Sultans of Swing', alongside Cliff's 'Devil Woman', Elton John's 'Sorry Seems to Be the Hardest Word', ELO's 'Shine a Little Love', Gerry Rafferty's 'Baker Street' and Eric Clapton's 'Let It Grow'. With the exception of ELO and Thin Lizzy, everyone on that record sounded worn down, worried or knackered. Years later, I'd realise that Eric's plea for love to grow naturally between two people probably owed more to heroin for its sweet, soporific ambience than any other factors.

With my total outgoings amounting to £3.49, I returned to Woolworths and bought two more singles: a discounted copy of the Pretenders' 'Back on the Chain Gang' and a full-price 'Our House' by Madness. Madness had given us nostalgic reminiscences of school and puberty. 'Our House' turned its attention to the red-brick, two-up two-down upbringing of Chas Smash and Chris Foreman, who wrote the song together. I didn't resent my family at all. I'd been raised to understand their predicament – and even though I knew that Aki and I were the only thing keeping them here, I knew no one was really to blame. But the family in 'Our House' – well . . . in a family like that, everyone seemed to be just getting on with their life, free of expectations. Father wearing his Sunday best, getting ready for church; brother with a date to keep; the sister sighing in her sleep. Also – and this was my guiltiest secret – they were British. I knew what to do in a *British* family. I knew the beats. I knew the jokes. I knew the cultural references. I'd be good at that. I could talk Tony Hancock with William and his dad: 'A *pint*? Have you gone raving mad? . . . Why, that's very nearly an armful!!' I could talk to Ged and her parents about the Beatles and Django Reinhardt. But Greek? I was the worst Greek I knew. I didn't know what to do in church. I couldn't get through a sentence without replacing a Greek word I didn't know with its English equivalent. And the music on my dad's records was now synonymous with the homesickness it engendered in him – homesickness which I efficiently processed into guilt. Set against all of that, 'Our House' was a fantasy of a life that suited me better, to be filed alongside the contemporaneously released 'Come Dancing' – the first song I ever heard by the Kinks. But the final record I bought was the one that I hoped might get me through this actual set of circumstances. I brought Dexys Midnight Runners' *Too-Rye-Ay* to the counter and handed over my cash, certain that, come the moment, whatever was on this record would somehow tell me what to do with my life. It had to work. Who else was there to turn to?

The Bull Ring market was festooned with Christmas lights. I'd spent almost all of my money, but it didn't feel safe to go home, so I weaved through the stalls and, with the rest of my loose change, bought a do-it-yourself paper chain kit and a tinsel lantern. I don't know if it was the desire to bring a bit of 'Our House' into our house, but I figured our usual decorative concession to Christmas – a silver tree beside the TV – could do with a bit of help. With nowhere left to go, I began the five-mile walk home from town, past the '*Céad Míle Fáilte*' banner of the Irish Centre; past the 'Lesbians Are Everywhere' graffiti I'd first clocked after 'Roxanne' prompted me to look out of my parents' car for signs of prostitute activity; past the Sari shops and Indian restaurants of Sparkhill; left onto Warwick Road, past Yardleys School and Mr Elverston's shop, now closed for the day; past the panoramic expanse of Tyseley Railway Depot, and all the way home through the residential streets of Tyseley where I twisted off several branches from a holly bush in someone's garden to go with the paper chains.

It was 7 o'clock when I finally arrived. My parents were at work but Aki was there. I hadn't eaten since breakfast.

'Did anyone call round?' I said, as I spooned some jam onto a slice of white bread.

'Like who?' he replied.

'Oh, just anyone.'

'No. You've still got no mates.'

He grabbed the bags to see what I'd bought, pronouncing his verdict on every record he held up. 'Shit. Shit. Good. Shit. OK. Good. Probably shit.'

I got to work on the paper chains, taking each individual piece, licking the gummed bit and looping it around the previous one.

'What are you doing?'

'What does it look like I'm doing?'

'Who said you could do that?'

'Everyone else's Christmas decorations are better than ours. It's embarrassing. So I bought these paper chains.'

'And how are you going to get them up there?'

'I dunno. With a ladder.'

'It's going to take you all night.'

'So?'

'I'm not helping you.'

'I didn't ask you to help me.'

I got the ladder from the garage, softened a splodge of Blu Tack between my thumb and forefinger and pushed one end of the paper chain into the corner where the walls met the ceiling. Then I did the same at the other corner. While I'd been getting the ladder, Aki had gone up to his bedroom and put on a record I'd never heard before. Wah!'s 'The Story of the Blues' seemed to be coming from a space far bigger than a bedroom in Birmingham. The group's mainstay Pete Wylie had, until this point, been the most underachieving member of mythical Mersey supergroup the Crucial Three. But while Julian Cope and Ian McCulloch had been slugging it out for supremacy, Wylie set his sights on penning the sort of everyman anthem that, if executed properly, would leapfrog both of them. 'The Story of the Blues' was the perfect vehicle for his motivational bellowing – a post-punk 'You'll Never Walk Alone' inspired by *Boys from the Blackstuff*, Alan Bleasdale's drama series about the effects of unemployment in Liverpool.

Aki was playing it at such volume that the paper chains were shaking in time with the beat. He played it once and then he put it on again. Halfway through the second time though, I could hear the needle being abruptly lifted from the grooves. Seconds later, he thundered downstairs.

'All right, then. Give me some of those.'

I handed him a pile of long gummed rectangles and we got to work on the second chain, adjourning occasionally for more jam sandwiches and tea.

The day ended pretty much the way it ended almost every day in December 1982. I took the videotape off the shelf, pushed it into the machine, pressed 'rewind' and counted to seventeen seconds – the exact amount of time it took to get back to the start of 'There, There My Dear'.

'So, let me tell you this. This, ah, well it used to go like that. But then one day something happened, as it so often does, and now it goes like this.'

'Aren't you gonna put the record on, then?' said Aki.

'Which one?' I said.

'The one you just bought? The Dexys album. Let's hear it, then.'

'Nah, it's OK. I'm sleepy. I'll probably go to bed.'

I gathered my bags and padded upstairs to my room. I didn't want to share *Too-Rye-Ay* with anyone else. I didn't want Aki to approve of it. I'd never felt like that about a record before. The only person in the world who could help me right now was the man depicted on the sleeve of the record I was holding. Sitting on the ground with his back to a fence and his knees drawn up to his chest, pressing a stick down into the dirt.

On the face of it, *Too-Rye-Ay* was only an album by default: a mishmash of singles that had failed to chart ('Plan B', 'Liars A to E', 'Celtic Soul Brothers'), repurposed B-sides ('Soon') and covers ('Jackie Wilson Said (I'm in Heaven When You Smile)'). *Too-Rye-Ay* was recorded at the apex of Kevin's obsession with Van Morrison's 1974 live album *It's Too Late to Stop Now*, which captured Van and his Caledonia Soul Orchestra at their absolute peak. But, like the random aggregation of misfits that comprised the present Dexys line-up, *Too-Rye-Ay* exceeded both its influences and its constituent parts. Kevin's evangelical zeal was matched at every step by the melodic maximalism of his producers. Langer and Winstanley had piloted Madness's hit-making run, helping establish them as the seven-headed Greek chorus to the unfolding story of post-punk Britain. On the Dexys album, they made backing vocalists sound like choirs and cleared space for the strings to whizz, dip and rise around Kevin's exhortations like dolphins to a trawler. *Too-Rye-Ay* met the one non-negotiable requirement of pop – that it should require no effort from the listener. But, as important as pop was, it felt more significant than that. It was a spiritual recruitment drive.

It felt like all the hope that was left in the world could now only be found in the grooves of *Too-Rye-Ay*. This was a version of Dexys I could claim for myself a little bit without feeling like a phoney. I couldn't quite do that with the 'Geno' version, with their woolly hats and Crombie jackets; I couldn't do it with the group that rocked the boxing club cottons of their last pre-'Come On Eileen' hit, 'Show Me'. But this was different. This looked like an abdication from fashion, a retreat from contemporary discourse. This was akin to running *away* from the circus.

It didn't matter what Kevin Rowland said. Ever since that *Tube* performance, it was my duty to agree with him. And if I held an opposing opinion before he said it, then I relinquished it the moment I heard what he had to say about it. He ran Dexys like a cult leader, demanding absolute commitment not just from his band but from his fans. It was fine to repudiate the expectations of the adult world. 'Your experience will teach me no more lessons', he sang on 'All in All (This One Last Wild Waltz)', 'From lower down you just seemed so much better'. The tone wasn't angry here. It was one of bittersweet acceptance. A sense that this was a safe place from which to regroup and, if necessary, never resurface. After all, how many friends did I even have left to lose at this point?

Each song seemed to bring my situation more sharply into focus. 'You've always been searching for something', began 'Plan B', 'But everything seems so-so'. Like Bill Murray in *Groundhog Day* checking that all of Andie MacDowell's criteria for a suitable husband apply to him – 'Me. Me. Me. Me also . . .' – every successive line in 'Plan B' seemed to apply directly to my situation: 'Plan B / They're testing you – but don't worry / This week I'm strong enough for two'. On the middle eight, a female voice appeared, seemingly to warn of what might await me when I went back to school: 'It starts off just joking / And then they stop talking to you / And that's the worst thing of all'. I didn't realise, prior to this moment, how totally the sensation of companionship had receded from my life. I loved my parents, but your parents can't tell you who you're going to turn into. Whatever it takes to thrive in a school environment had totally eluded me.

But the strange, comforting sensation that these songs released in me came from a sense of companionship. That perhaps I wasn't such a bad person, and with a bit of guidance, I might even become better. 'I'll Show You' snapped into action right off the back of 'Plan B'. This was a spoken-word monologue measured out over a bright soul canter, in which Kevin exhorted us to find our own humanity by imagining the adult casualties of modern life as they once were.

> *It's so hard to picture dirty tramps as young boys,*
> *But if you see a man crying, hold his hand, he's my friend*

If those lines stopped me in my tracks, it was partly because I was starting to believe that I might turn into one of those tramps. Adrift of my parents' expectations. Academically unexceptional. Seemingly unable to maintain friendships. Both socially and physically ill-equipped to last longer than a week at the Lucas factory. Terrible at football. Unable to access my sexuality. What exactly *did* happen to people like me?

CHAPTER 35

Ten years had elapsed since the incident which had seen me remove the ornamental antelope from the shelf and hurl it at my dad. Now, albeit in a less dramatic way, I was about to elicit comparable surprise. It was New Year's Eve and a friend of my parents called to say he'd booked a large table for dinner at the restaurant where Renato worked. Finally, after the Tony Telfer let-down; after the West Bromwich Albion chip shop no-show; after the Barron Knights disaster, I would finally be afforded the chance to actually have a real celebrity sign my autograph book. 'Put your best clothes on!' instructed my dad. 'We're leaving in an hour.'

I knew in an instant that I couldn't go. What if Renato remembered me from the incident in Solihull Shopping Centre the previous week? With hindsight, I realise the odds of that happening were almost zero. But it was a chance I couldn't take. I pictured the singing waiter serenading the tables – left hand gesticulating sincerely, right hand carrying a tray of spaghetti Bolognese – only to stop dead when he recognised a member of the gang that had shouted 'Renée!' at him before splashing him with a bin. I couldn't risk having Renato frogmarch me out of his restaurant while my bewildered family gazed on.

'It's . . . it's OK. I don't think I can go.'

My dad looked me up and down and told me not to be so silly.

'Come on. It's New Year's Eve. Get ready.'

'Really. I'll stay here. You can go.'

My mum was upstairs, already getting dressed. 'Victoria!' called my dad. 'Taki says he doesn't want to go.'

She came down to check on me. 'Why not? Are you OK?'

'I don't feel too well. It's fine though. You go.'

She looked at my dad. 'If he's not well . . . I shouldn't go either.'

'No. I mean, I'm OK. I feel better than I did. It was worse this morning. Really. I want you to go.'

My dad made it clear to my mum that we'd already committed and he could hardly turn up alone. On the other side of the room, Aki was monitoring the conversation. If I wasn't going, he didn't see any reason to go either. 'I tell you what!' he said. 'If you two go, I'll stay and keep an eye on him.'

'You're not ill,' he said flatly after my parents left the house.

'You won't tell them, will you?' I replied.

'It's all right. I didn't want to go either.'

I didn't know what was going to happen when I got back to school in four days' time. My friendship with William had intensified since that bonfire night. He had his peer group, and I continued to envy that, but he clearly regarded our friendship as something separate and strong – something for which I was more grateful than ever. We both loved *The Young Ones* and we repeatedly got together to watch William's video of the Monty Python sketch film *And Now for Something Completely Different*. Certain sketches seemed to get sillier every time we rewound them. We were rendered helpless by anything involving repressed sexual deviance: from the sketch in which Michael Palin reports a theft to a policeman and, halfway through the exchange, they slope off somewhere, presumably to have sex; similarly, the unexpected detour of 'The Lumberjack Song' into cross-dressing was a source of gut-aching delight. The sight of adults behaving more like children than any of the children we knew acted as a release valve for the tensions and uncertainties of our young teenage lives.

The feeling I had with William was that if he could welcome me into his friendship group, he would. But he didn't have that power – and, besides, we were in different classes. I hadn't necessarily expected to hear anything from Dean Tookey or Kevin Flynn over the holidays, but Terry and I had a closeness that wasn't contingent on being part of a wider group. Over time, Terry had several chances to push me away forever, but as with William, there was something else going on in our friendship. I was the only boy in my class who bought more records than he did. And he knew that if he'd just heard something that excited him then no one was more likely to know it than me: 'Listen' by Stiff Little Fingers; 'Jimmy Jimmy' by the Undertones; 'Turning Japanese' by the Vapors; 'Rock the Casbah' by the Clash. Even now, I associate all these songs with the sight of Terry on my doorstep. But Terry hadn't appeared on my doorstep since before Christmas. In that one week, so much had changed – and *Too-Rye-Ay* had been the agent of that change.

It had been eight years since the Rubettes' 'Sugar Baby Love' somehow piggybacked onto my inarticulate mortification at what I was putting my parents through. That was just one song though. Here was an entire album that somehow seemed to bear witness to the crisis I appeared to have contrived for myself. I don't suppose there was anything new about any of my feelings for these songs. If I'd been ten years older, it might have been David Bowie pledging to ease the pain of the knives that 'seem to lacerate your brain' on 'Rock 'n' Roll Suicide' from *Ziggy Stardust*. Ten years later, it might have been the secular consolation hymns of REM's *Automatic for the People*. But at the end of 1982, *Too-Rye-Ay* rode into my interior world like the cavalry. It was the agony aunt on the other end of the line in the phone box at night. It was the ghost of Christmas future dropping in to tell me that it wasn't going to be easy, but it would be OK.

I wanted to tell Terry about it, just like he'd told me about 'Come on Eileen' back in August. I wanted to show him this mattered more than anything we could ever get up to on a Saturday afternoon in a rainy shopping centre. I wanted to play him the confession-booth soul of 'Soon' and the rallying reassurances of 'Plan B'. I wanted him to see that if you were going to be in a gang, why not make it a gang like Dexys Midnight Runners? Why on earth wouldn't you want to make *this* the focal point of everything you did?

The chance came sooner than I expected. Five minutes after my parents left, there was a knock at the door. It was a shock to see Terry's shorn head illuminated by the light from our hallway. There was no small talk. No asking me what I got for Christmas. Terry was quite simply there to tell me that I owed him a massive thank you.

'Thank you? What for?'

'If it wasn't for me, you would have already had the shit beaten out of you. Tookey and Flynn wanted to come back here and wait for you. Fucking running away.'

'I didn't run away,' I lied, 'I lost you. After I went to pay for my drink, I came back to find you, but you'd gone. I looked everywhere.'

'Liar. You were too chicken come with us. Tookey wants to kill you. But I told him I'd come here and see what you had to say.'

It was important to get Terry onside. If I didn't get Terry onside, I didn't want to imagine what Tookey and Flynn might do to me when we went back to school three days later.

'Tookey's always on my back,' I said. 'It's not on. It's like he's always pissed off with me, like he wants to start on me.'

'He's not that bad,' protested Terry. But I was just getting going. The frustrations of the preceding weeks percolated to the surface and I told him about the incident with the crisps; about Tookey's repeated visits to my parents' shop. About the fact that most of his jibes amounted, as far as I could see, to bullying. 'Sometimes I just feel like I can't be in a gang with him. He won't stop picking on me. And I've done nothing wrong.'

Terry looked deep in thought. Finally he spoke. 'You should have him.'

In my kitchen in Overlea Avenue, just me and Terry; in this hypothetical conversation about my tormentor, it felt good to briefly entertain the idea that I could put Tookey in his place. It felt like a safe place to put my anger. Terry left a few minutes later, placated by my protestations about trying to find them in Beatties.

'Are you walking to school on Wednesday?' I asked him.

'Yeah.'

'I'll call for you on the way.'

'All right. See ya.'

It was barely light when I knocked on Terry's door. And when someone came to the door, it was Terry's mum, somewhat surprised that her son had left without me. 'Sorry, Peter. He left early this morning. I thought he was with you.'

I'd woken up imagining all sorts of scenarios about today, but the one reassuring thing I had to hold on to was the fact that the day would start with me and Terry walking to school together. We had made that arrangement, so surely that suggested I could rely on his continuing friendship as protection against whatever else might happen. But none of that applied any more.

It was the first time I'd done this walk without Terry. Usually about ten minutes into the journey, we would pass a corner where a girl about three years younger than us, dressed in the blazer, pleated skirt and hat of some private school, would wait for her dad – who was presumably separated from her mother – to stop and pick her up. We'd been walking past her for weeks and then suddenly, out of the blue, she held up one hand and asked us, 'Can you do this?' She then proceeded to do the tricksy hand gesture perfected by Ted Rogers, host of ITV game show 3-2-1: three fingers, then turn your hand 180 degrees while going down to two fingers, then repeat to show just one. And I think both Terry and I found it cute that this girl had randomly issued us with this challenge. So every day since then, we'd do the gesture at each other, almost in a sort of shoot-out fashion. Without Terry next to me, even an exchange like that felt awkward. I realised in that moment that one of the things I liked best of all about Terry was that I could use him to camouflage my awkwardness.

With mounting trepidation, I walked through the school gates, past the teachers' parked cars, past the science annexe, towards the bike shed that hadn't seen a bike for years – a default hangout on account of the fact that the bike shed was about the same width as a goalpost. As I turned the corner, Dean Tookey saw me and allowed his gaze to linger for longer than felt comfortable. Terry and Flynn were already there. Tookey said something to them and the other two laughed. I couldn't work out whether backing away and going elsewhere would make things better or worse. I put my bag down and bought myself some time by pretending to look for something in there.

Finally Tookey directed something at me. 'All right, Paphides.' He looked like a vengeful alien. 'Have you got something you wanna say to my face?'

'What do you mean?' I asked him.

I looked across at Terry, who shifted from one foot to the other, staring straight at the tarmac beneath his Doc Martens. Tookey turned around and the conversation continued. I decided to keep walking, past the scene of Mr Saxton's confrontation with Erica Weston's adult boyfriend, through the school hall and up to the relative sanctuary of Mr Simpson's classroom for registration. I was first there, and by the time everyone else had filed in, all eyes were suddenly on me. Tookey brushed past my seat, carrying his holdall over his shoulder, making sure my head was in the way of it – an action that elicited a ripple of mirth from the surrounding desks. Finally, as we filed back down for assembly, Darren Cathcart let me know what I'd got myself into. 'Is it true that you've challenged Tookey to a scrap?'

Now I knew why Terry hadn't been there this morning. That also explained the conspiratorial giggling by the bike shed that morning. Nothing supercharges the atmosphere at school like the promise of a fight. The boys froth over possible outcomes; the girls view the whole thing from a superior remove. As morning turned to lunchtime, a steady procession of pupils asked me: (i) when it was happening; (ii) why it was happening; and (iii) whether I was shitting myself. I didn't know the answer to (i) and I sort of knew the answer to (ii). As for (iii), yes, I absolutely was. And whatever spin I decided to put on it, it was obvious that I was. The worst thing of all, however, was that I was believed to have issued the challenge. No one understood what had possessed me to do so – why would anyone challenge any of those three to a fight?

Vijay could see how scared I was. Although we moved in different circles, he was still my friend. Outside the physics lab, he took me to one side. If I wanted, he could secretly tell a teacher and they could intervene before Tookey laid a finger on me. That was the measure of Vijay. If he had a lucky sailor in his pocket at that moment, he would have pressed it into my palm. I told him it was fine. I somehow reasoned that if it happened on the school premises, then someone might stop it before it got really bad, but if it happened elsewhere, there was every chance it might be a lot worse.

And so, actually, by the final break period of the afternoon, I was willing Tookey to just get it done. One option might have been to approach him myself and issue the standard 'Come on, then!' that began all playground fisticuffs. But I just couldn't bring that upon myself, no matter what the alternatives were. And besides, if I just avoided Tookey indefinitely, perhaps there would be no fight.

In the few minutes after the final bell rang, that was the hope I allowed myself. I shuffled out of the classroom, expecting a swarm of excited spectators to follow me. There were a few, but it turns out that Tookey – or perhaps Terry or Flynn – had told everyone to wait by the gate next to where Mr Saxton's hearse was parked. Tookey had walked ahead of me and had already removed his blazer and jumper. The only way of getting to the pavement was to get past Tookey. And the only way to get past Tookey (and the rapidly expanding crowd gathering around us) was to fight him.

I'd only felt anything close to this once before. On that occasion, however, the stakes were lower. All I'd needed to do was open my mouth and tell the children of Cottesbrooke Infant School that the best bit about being a fireman was sliding down the pole. But there was no benevolent adult to get me out of this spot.

'Come on, then!' said Tookey, pushing me hard. I didn't know how to punch. I thought I did. I mean, how hard can it be to throw a punch? I went for his stomach, but he went for my face, landing a single punch on my nose and then several more on my mouth. In schools in the West Midlands, a fight was always greeted with the same noise. A massed chant of 'OOH! OOH! OOH! OOH!' that accelerates and intensifies until a teacher comes along to break it up or a winner has been declared.

I'd never been punched like this before. I'd never felt pain like this before. It felt like my lips were being pumped at speed with boiling water. 'OOH! OOH! OOH! OOH!' I feebly attempted to fight back, but the mere act of doing so unlocked a jackhammer fury of blows from both of Tookey's fists, all directed at my face. Now, it was a matter of trying to cover my head until he stopped.

I fell to the ground. My mouth tasted like raw meat. Mixed with the warm, salty taste of my own blood was the grit of three, maybe four fragments of teeth. The surging heat in my lips had now spread to my face. But Tookey's rage showed no sign of dissipating. I attempted to pull myself two or three feet into the alcove beneath the steps leading up to one of the prefabricated classrooms. Tookey had now taken to kicking me as I did so. All I could do was stay still, curled up into a ball until the accumulated anger of thirteen years began to fade.

Finally someone stepped in. To my surprise, it wasn't a teacher, a bunch of older girls or a passer-by. It was Terry.

'Fucking hell,' he interjected. 'That's enough. THAT'S. ENOUGH.'

I looked out into the light. As Terry crouched down and dragged him away, Tookey's fists and legs continued to flail. Tookey released a single marble of phlegm into my hair as Terry fastened his hands around Tookey's torso. For a second, Terry's eyes met mine. The horror on his face was unlike anything I'd seen there before. But why had he told Tookey what I'd said about him? Did he just want to see a punch-up? Did he think I deserved to be punished? Was it his way of trying to free me from an otherwise impossible situation?

I don't know how much time elapsed between Terry's intervention and the crowd dispersing. A throng of girls from the year above stayed behind. As they crouched down to see if I was OK, one of them handed me some paper – the non-absorbent single sheets that used to come as standard in secondary school toilets. The blood from my nose and mouth glistened back at me on the paper. My lips felt huge. I could barely see out of one eye. I tried to stand up and my legs immediately gave way. But it was only when one of the girls started to cry that I realised that whatever Tookey had done, it must really look pretty bad.

'I'm gonna get a teacher,' said one.

'NO! PLEASE! YOU CAN'T.'

'Are you mad? Why not?'

'Because if he thinks I grassed him up, he'll do it again. Only this time it won't be just him.' These were the age-old codes that all schoolchildren had to live by. Nothing that had happened in the past five minutes was going to change that.

When I was finally able to stay upright, I saw a familiar face waiting by the gate.

'William . . .'

'Do you want me to call my dad? He'll be just leaving work. I can get him to drive us home. Like, if you can't get to the bus stop . . .'

'Um, no it's OK. I think . . .' The place was deserted now. Mr Saxton drove his hearse out of the gate, right past us, but it was dark now. If he noticed the state of my face through his windscreen, he didn't stop to say anything.

William and I got on the bus. His house was two stops away and a short walk up Stockfield Road, but when it was time to ring the bell, he stayed on, an act of friendship somehow compounded by the fact that neither of us acknowledged it. My longing to be home was tempered by apprehension at what my mum and dad might say when they saw me. But suddenly, it was too late to worry about that. The sound of a car horn alerted me to the sight of my parents skidding to a halt outside the Warwick Bowl. As I pulled up my zip to hide the bloodstains on my shirt, my mum opened the car door and hurried towards me.

'Your face. Your eye. What happened to you?'

'I fell,' I told her. There was no question of telling her the truth. If they took it up with the school, my life wouldn't be worth living.

'Don't lie to me,' she said. 'Who did this to you?'

I allowed my voice to rise. I needed to sound angry in order to shut down this line of enquiry. In the future, this would be what people would call 'tough love'. I replied in English, so that William could understand. 'Bloody hell. Why don't you believe me? I was running for the bus and I tripped and fell onto a bollard.'

Across the road, my dad was still in the car, waiting for my mum to get back in. To an impartial observer, *his* might have seemed like the less humane response, but at this moment, I much preferred it.

He pressed the flat of his hand on the klaxon and allowed it to stay there for a few seconds.

'You'd better go,' I told my mum, pointing at my watch. 'Shop's opening in fifteen minutes.'

She turned to face my dad in the car, loudly addressing him in Greek as she did so: 'The shop can go to hell!' With that, he put the car into first gear and sped off. None of us were quite expecting that. I looked at my mum and, with my one good eye, tried to will her to leave me alone with William. Then, when that didn't work, I reverted to Greek, so that William wouldn't hear me.

I'd long since lost count of the domestic showdowns between her and my dad, in which I thought I might be able to make the difference and formally approve her pursuit of an alternative future to the one for which she was presently on course. But right now, she couldn't help me any more than I had been able to help her on any of those occasions. I told her what she already knew. That my dad couldn't open the shop on his own. In the life they had chosen to share, need and love were sealed into the amber of duty. He needed her. And it was her duty to meet that need. That's how it worked. That's how it had always worked. It had just taken me a while to work it out.

And, really, I was fine. More than fine, I instinctively knew what I had to do next. I told William to wait there a minute. Then I linked her arm tightly, just like I had always done when helping her with the shopping every Saturday, and walked her to the stop where William and I had alighted the number 44 – the same bus that went all the way to the Kingfisher. I asked her to bring me and William back some chips when the teatime rush was over, not because I wanted chips, but because I knew that my making the request would increase the likelihood of her getting on the bus.

As William and I turned back and finally advanced towards the house, I almost bumped into Ged and Siobhan who were walking in the other direction.

'Oh my God. Takis. Your face. Your *shirt*.' I looked down at my shirt, ripped at the arm, with its giant Rorschach blob of bloody snot and snotty blood.

'What happened?' asked Siobhan, looking more like the new romantic twin sister of the Cadbury's Caramel bunny than ever.

I told them everything, but only as long as they promised not to tell my parents. Outside 14 Overlea Avenue, I could see the tiny orange light of Aki's cigarette being hastily extinguished (not that much of a surprise – I'd been able to smell it on him since we came back from Greece that summer). Now, I could keep his secret as long as he kept mine. Next to him was William's brother Edward – quite the welcoming committee, really.

Stopping in the hallway, I phoned my dad to tell him my mum was on her way. Then the six of us walked up the stairs to my room. Behind my 7-inch singles were the remains of the crisps that Tookey had stolen. Perhaps a dozen bags. Aki grabbed the lot and threw them onto the bed. Ged and Siobhan disappeared into the bathroom and returned with a wet flannel, which one of them told me to place over my black eye.

'Siobhan and I are registered first-aiders, aren't we?' said Ged.

Siobhan nodded, explaining that you got to miss PE if you did the first aid course.

Ged handed me a cup of orange squash and two aspirin, then told me to remove my shirt, promising to wash it and iron it by the end of the evening. 'Your mum's going to spaz out if she sees it.' I felt like a ghost at my own wake.

William and I bunched up on the floor. I attempted a single crisp, but the saltiness made it impossible. On the turntable was a new record. Five years since Edward had knocked on the door of our old house with the *Grease* soundtrack, he and Aki had kept with the same tradition of going to each other's houses with their newest acquisitions. The hypermobile funk of Orange Juice's 'Rip It Up' squelched outwards with disruptive flamboyance. It sounded like the town dandy goading the locals into having a go. If you walked in time to it, along a crowded street on a Saturday afternoon, you might be beaten up for your trouble.

Not a day had gone by in which I hadn't wondered who I was going to turn into. But for the first time, a whole host of options had been eliminated. Perhaps *that's* how growing up works. You start with a full list and move in reverse. Eliminating all the things that, in your heart of hearts, you know you can never be. Then, one day, what you are is what you're left with once everything else has been crossed out.

My new heroes were daring the world to have a pop at them. They were travelling down escalators in crowded shopping centres in gypsy dungarees, singing 'pretend I'm Bill [Withers] / And lean on me'. My new heroes were going to be lank-haired fops with fringed suede jackets and bootlace ties. They would be slight, sensitive gay men singing in plaintive falsettos about fleeing their home towns and starting anew. Teen-mag casualties staring ruefully into the lens with nothing but a tortoise shell on their back. Wan Americans with long hair and paisley shirts, mumbling indecipherable lyrics. Ethereal women with eyes like marbles channelling some unknowable trauma over gauzy guitars and glacial machine beats in words that corresponded to no known language. Sexually ambiguous men in oversized women's blouses with daffodils in their back pockets. Androgynous funk agitators in purple satin exhorting us to dance into Armageddon. The voice coming out of the speakers exhorted me to rip it up and start again. And to my surprise, I noticed that I wasn't scared.

ACKNOWLEDGEMENTS

Most of this book was written in a variety of cafés across north London. I'm especially indebted to Aida, Efe, Suna and everyone at the Palace Café in London N8 for allowing me to sit there for several hours at a time and bringing me frothy coffee without me even having to ask. As soon as I finished one mug, another would magically appear in front of me.

I spent a long time trying to get the details right. That wouldn't have been possible were it not for the time and generosity of Ged Hughes, Joyce Hughes, Chris Waters (formerly Miss Haylor) and my own parents, Chris and Victoria Paphides. My brother Aki has been invaluable throughout this time. I hope this book allows him to see himself as I have seen him my whole life.

A number of people suggested I write a book. I wish I'd written all their names down at the time. But among the ones I can remember are Chris Salmon and Alexia Loundras, Harvey Williams, Gail O'Hara, Linda Thompson, Lauren and Graeme, John Niven, Lauren Bufferd, Kieron Moyles and Jamie McKelvie. Thank you all.

And once I got started, it was Bob Stanley who set aside the time to read every single chapter as soon as I could bear the thought of sending them to him. There are thirty-five chapters, so that must have happened thirty-five times. Bob's encouragement was the difference between me thinking that the book was a colossal folly and electing to keep going. I can't imagine a better friend.

Thank you also to Daniel Scott, John Simm, Grace Maxwell, Edwyn Collins, Julian Cope, Luca Balbo, Susie Ember, Paul Weller, Kevin Rowland, Helen O'Hara, Fiona Stewart, Mike Batt, John O'Connell, Stephen Duffy, Nick Duffy, Angeline Morrison, Alison Owen, James Yorkston, Pascal Blua, Pete and Claire Everest, Steve Carr, David Morrissey, Danny Finkelstein, Robert Forster, Nina Stibbe, Debbie Sanders, Sali and Dan, Nadia Shireen and Neil Barker at Kingbee. I will also forever be grateful to John Saddler for his early encouragement at a time when I wasn't able to reciprocate his good faith.

Thank you to my magnificent agent Jo Unwin and to Milly, Donna and Rachel at JULA. Jo was the first agent to return my email. First agent I saw. Last agent I saw. I couldn't imagine anyone better. Jo asked me what sort of an agent I needed her to be, and then offered me a list of possible options. I was simply shocked that she wanted to be any sort of agent to me. Jo, I'm so grateful to have you alongside me.

I only showed this book to one publisher: Katy Follain at Quercus, who first got in touch with me back in 2002 and then intermittently after that until finally I started work on Broken Greek early in 2017. I always wanted Katy to be the first editor who saw the book. I couldn't have wished for anyone more supportive, empathetic and intuitive in that role. Incalculable thanks go out to Katy and to all of the team at Quercus: Ana, Elizabeth, Laura, Jon, Alison and Andrew. I'm so lucky our paths crossed all those years ago. Thanks also to my copy-editor Seán Costello for his phenomenal care and attention to detail. Thank you to Anna Doble from Reviewed & Cleared for the miraculous feat of making the legal issues surrounding the writing of this book a pleasure to address.

When your wife also happens to be your favourite writer on the planet, the question 'Are you actually going to let me read what you've been doing at some point?' becomes a pretty terrifying one. Thank you, Cate, for your for your fathomless encouragement and also for stopping me from throwing away the only existing copy of 'Pop Scene' when I found it in my parents' loft twenty years ago. Thanks also to Dora and Eavie for instructing me not to sound embarrassed when I uttered the words 'my book'.

Finally, thank you to the hundreds of singers, musicians and songwriters mentioned in the preceding pages. Their records not only soundtracked the story; they effectively translated it into a language I could understand.

Lots of love,

Pete Paphides